AF449180

Thomas Chimes
Adventures in 'Pataphysics

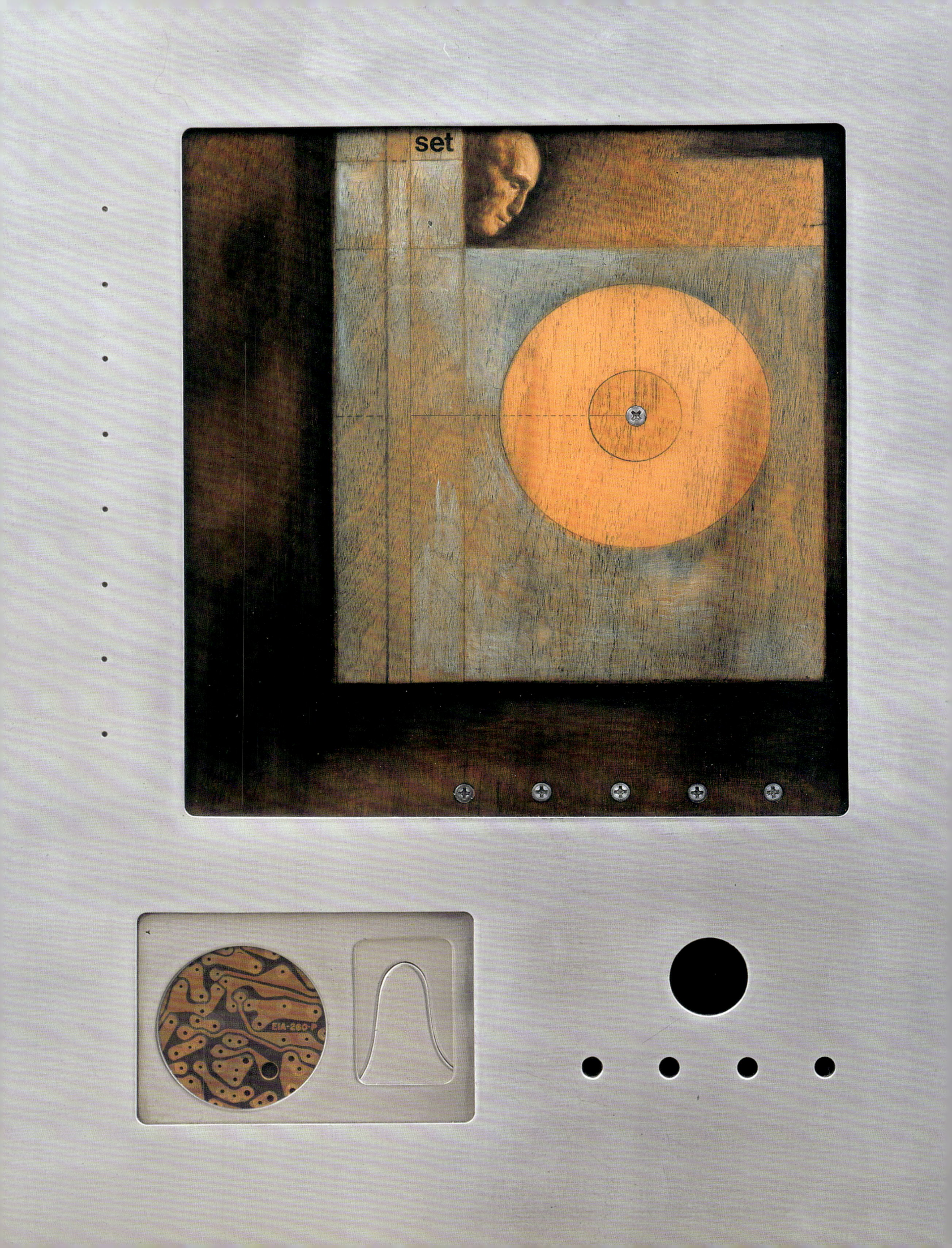

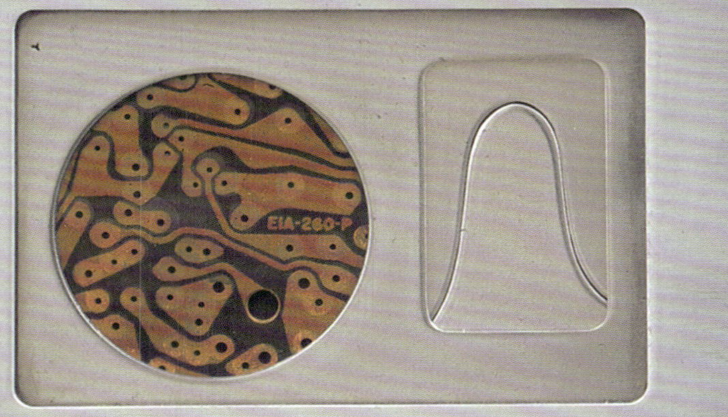
EIA-260-P

Thomas Chimes
Adventures in 'Pataphysics

Michael R. Taylor

Philadelphia Museum of Art

This book is published on the occasion of the exhibition
Thomas Chimes: Adventures in 'Pataphysics
Philadelphia Museum of Art
February 27 to May 6, 2007

This exhibition was made possible by the Philadelphia Exhibitions Initiative, a program of the Philadelphia Center for Arts and Heritage, funded by The Pew Charitable Trusts, and administered by The University of the Arts. Additional support was provided by The Locks Foundation, the J. F. Costopoulos Foundation, The Robert Montgomery Scott Fund for Exhibitions, Jill and Sheldon Bonovitz and The Robert H. and Janet S. Fleisher Foundation, the Areté Foundation / Betsy and Ed Cohen, Susan and Washburn S. Oberwager, Linda and Paul Richardson, and other members of The 'Pataphysical Society, a group of generous donors.

Jacket/cover front: Thomas Chimes, *Watcher of the Night* (detail), 1989 (plate 87)

Jacket/cover back: Thomas Chimes, 1999. Photograph by Sid Sachs

Page ii: Thomas Chimes, *Set (The Descent)* (detail), 1972 (plate 39)

Page xii: Thomas Chimes, *Faustroll/Air* (detail), 1989. Oil on canvas, 40 x 64 inches (101.6 x 162.6 cm). Collection of Duane Morris LLP, Philadelphia

Pages 16–17: Thomas Chimes, *Mural* (detail), 1963–65 (plate 13)

Pages 56–57: Thomas Chimes, *Master and Own* (detail), 1966 (plate 22)

Pages 104–5: Thomas Chimes, *André Breton (Glove)* (detail), 1977 (plate 69)

Pages 176–77: Thomas Chimes, *Nous constaterons plus loins que de passé est par de la future vu de la machine* (detail), 1996 (plate 90)

Produced by the Publishing Department
Philadelphia Museum of Art
Sherry Babbitt, Director of Publishing
2525 Pennsylvania Avenue
Philadelphia, PA 19130
USA
www.philamuseum.org

Edited by David Updike
Production by Richard Bonk
Designed by Katy Homans
Color separations by Oceanic Graphic Printing, Hong Kong
Printed in China by C&C Offset Printing Co., Ltd.

Text and compilation © 2007
Philadelphia Museum of Art

Works by Thomas Chimes © the artist; works by Alan Davie © the artist; works by Marcel Duchamp © Artists Rights Society (ARS), New York / ADAGP, Paris / Succession Marcel Duchamp; works by Max Ernst, André Masson, and Nicolas de Staël © ARS, New York / ADAGP, Paris; works by Jess © ARS, New York / Beeldrecht, Amsterdam; works by Jasper Johns © the artist / Licensed by VAGA, New York; work by Ellsworth Kelly © the artist; works by Man Ray © Man Ray Trust / ARS, New York / ADAGP, Paris; works by Henri Matisse © Succession H. Matisse, Paris / ARS, New York; work by Robert Morris © the artist / ARS, New York; works by Pablo Picasso © Estate of Pablo Picasso / ARS, New York; work by Jackson Pollock © The Pollock-Krasner Foundation / ARS, New York; work by Ad Reinhardt © Estate of Ad Reinhardt / ARS, New York; works by Robert Smithson © Estate of Robert Smithson / Licensed by VAGA, New York; work by Tom Wesselmann © Estate of Tom Wesselmann / Licensed by VAGA, New York. Every effort has been made to contact the copyright holders for works reproduced herein. Any omissions are unintentional.

All rights reserved. No part of this publication may be reproduced or transmitted in any form or by any means, electronic or mechanical, including photocopying, recording, or any other information storage or retrieval system, without permission in writing from the publisher.

Library of Congress Cataloging-in-Publication Data

Taylor, Michael, 1966–
    Thomas Chimes : adventures in 'pataphysics / Michael R. Taylor.
        p. cm.
    Published on the occasion of an exhibition at the Philadelphia Museum of Art, Feb. 27–May 6, 2007.
    Includes bibliographical references and index.
    ISBN 978-0-87633-252-8 (PMA : cloth) — ISBN 978-0-87633-253-5 (PMA : paper) — ISBN 978-0-300-12217-6 (Yale : cloth)
    1. Chimes, Thomas, 1921– —Criticism and interpretation. 2. Chimes, Thomas, 1921– —Exhibitions. I. Chimes, Thomas, 1921– II. Philadelphia Museum of Art. III. Title.
    N6537.C4915T39 2007
    759.13—dc22   2006034951

Contents

Thomas Chimes: Adventures in 'Pataphysics

MICHAEL R. TAYLOR

CLAIRE HOWARD

Lenders to the Exhibition

Dr. and Mrs. George Amrom, Philadelphia

The Buckingham Family Collection, Larchmont, New York

Mr. J. Frederick Cain and Mr. Lars Cain, Fort Myers, Florida

Dawn Chimes, Venice, Florida

Dmitri and Sheila Chimes, Philadelphia

Thomas Chimes, Philadelphia

Corcoran Gallery of Art, Washington, DC

Delaware Art Museum, Wilmington

Anne d'Harnoncourt and Joseph J. Rishel, Philadelphia

Daniel W. Dietrich II, Philadelphia

Robert Edwards, Swarthmore, Pennsylvania

Janet Fleisher, Philadelphia

The Forbes Collection, New York

The Gårder Family Collection, Bangor, Maine

Smokie Kittner and Harry Anderson, Philadelphia

Marguerite and Gerry Lenfest, Huntingdon Valley, Pennsylvania

Mr. and Mrs. Robert P. Levy, Bryn Mawr, Pennsylvania

Locks Gallery, Philadelphia

Lowe Art Museum, University of Miami, Coral Gables, Florida

Dr. and Mrs. Elliott Mancall, Miquon, Pennsylvania

Robert F. Matticks, Philadelphia

Mr. and Mrs. Martin and Margy Meyerson, Philadelphia

Phillip Mitsis and Sophia Kalantzakos, New York

The Museum of Modern Art, New York

The Pennsylvania Convention Center Authority, Philadelphia

The Phoenix Art Museum

Dr. and Mrs. Paul Richardson, Philadelphia

The John and Mable Ringling Museum of Art, Sarasota, Florida

Mr. and Mrs. Mark E. Rubenstein, Philadelphia

Rodney Sharp, Greenville, Delaware

Peter and Mari Shaw, Philadelphia

Mrs. Burton S. Singer, Villanova, Pennsylvania

Smithsonian American Art Museum, Washington, DC

Frances and Bayard Storey, Philadelphia

Wadsworth Atheneum Museum of Art, Hartford, Connecticut

Three anonymous private collections

Preface

I first had the pleasure of exploring Thomas Chimes's mysterious work and its tangled roots in the history of art, turn-of-the-twentieth-century French literature, and esoteric philosophy thirty years ago as the Museum prepared its Bicentennial exhibition devoted to three hundred years of art in Philadelphia. He was at the time preoccupied with the series of small, carefully wrought portraits of long-gone poets, playwrights, novelists, and philosophers who came uncannily alive under his brush. Discovering his brilliantly colored early paintings, also compelling in their intensity, I was fascinated by the artistic journey so thoughtfully described in this book. Had anyone asked me then what Chimes would be doing now, I no more could have answered than the man in the moon—yet, moonlight might be the ethereal stuff of which his recent paintings are made. Tom is a magician. It is not the aim of this retrospective exhibition, nor of its devoted and indefatigable curator, Michael Taylor, to reveal all the secrets—but rather to draw our viewers and our readers into the artist's charmed circle.

It is no surprise that Chimes has chosen to make Philadelphia, his birthplace, the locus of his life and work, despite the far-flung sources of his inspiration. The city's history as a center for the visual arts extends back to the eighteenth-century when the young painter Benjamin West and the future *pater familias* of painters, exhibitions, and museums, Charles Willson Peale, set ambitious artistic agendas for themselves, and as far forward as the imagination and dreams of the youngest of the students in the city's remarkable number of art schools can carry them. This Museum, together with our sister institutions in the city displaying distinguished collections of art, rejoice in the plethora of artists who make Philadelphia their home and our galleries their frequent haunt. It is the electric encounter between living artists and the art of the past that engenders the great continuum that we all too inadequately describe as art history. This encounter also lies at the heart of the subtle and complex art of Thomas Chimes. For visitors to this exhibition, his work now takes its place in that continuum, revealing, among many other things, the artist's abiding fascination with two stars of the Museum's collections—Thomas Eakins and Marcel Duchamp—which he absorbs into his own highly individual, not to say idiosyncratic, vision, which will in turn affect future generations of artists.

The exhibition and its handsome catalogue are made possible by the generosity of a wonderful array of funders and individual donors: The Philadelphia Exhibitions Initiative and its director, Paula Marincola, who have done so much to raise the sights of exhibitions in Philadelphia over the years; The Locks Foundation; the J. F. Costopoulos Foundation; The Robert Montgomery Scott Fund for Exhibitions; Linda and Paul Richardson, Jill and Sheldon Bonovitz and The Robert H. and Janet S. Fleisher Foundation, Betsy and Ed Cohen, Susan and Washburn S. Oberwager, and other members of The 'Pataphysical Society, a group of generous donors.

Without the commitment and enthusiasm of the lenders, the range and depth of Chimes's art could not have been made manifest. We are especially grateful to the Ringling Museum of Art in Sarasota, Florida, for the loan of Chimes's spectacular eighteen-foot-long *Mural* of 1963–65. Sueyun Locks and the Locks Gallery in Philadelphia have been extraordinarily supportive at every step along the way, and the film commissioned from Michael Blackwood illuminates Chimes's remarkable odyssey in his own words. It is a pleasure to put this book, elegantly designed by Katy Homans and thoughtfully edited by David Updike in the Museum's Publishing Department, into the hands of lovers of art and literature, and to anticipate the adventures they will find herein as they accompany Thomas Chimes on his journey of discovery.

ANNE D'HARNONCOURT
The George D. Widener Director and Chief Executive Officer
Philadelphia Museum of Art

Acknowledgments

Thomas Chimes: Adventures in 'Pataphysics began with a public conversation between the artist and myself in the Graduate School of Fine Arts at the University of Pennsylvania on October 15, 2001. I surprised Tom at this event by showing him slides of early works that he had not seen in several decades. Moved by his emotional response to these paintings and metal boxes, as well as his eloquent descriptions of their subject matter and meaning, I decided to pursue a full-scale retrospective at the Philadelphia Museum of Art that would help to introduce Chimes's work and ideas to new generations of visitors. With the generous support of the Locks Gallery, and especially its director, Sueyun Locks, who has dedicated herself to preserving the artist's work and legacy through important exhibitions and catalogues, the retrospective began to take shape in early 2002. Since then, the artist has been exceedingly generous with his time and attention, granting me unprecedented access to paintings, metal boxes, drawings, photographs, and letters. He and his family, including his former wife Dawn, his son Dmitri, and his daughter-in-law Sheila, have been gracious hosts, as well as becoming good friends. Tom and I have held weekly meetings, either in his studio overlooking Washington Square or at his favorite delicatessen, Zeke's on Fifth and Delancey, where our free-flowing conversations have often lasted for several hours. The most a curator can hope for in working with a living artist is the opportunity to see art and the world through another set of eyes and to have his or her own world enriched in the process. I am extremely grateful to Thomas Chimes for providing me with just such an opportunity.

I am deeply thankful to many people throughout the Museum for their encouragement and thoughtful contributions to this exhibition and catalogue. First and foremost, I wish to express my undying gratitude to the artist's treasured friend and champion, Anne d'Harnoncourt, whose early enthusiasm and steadfast support have made this project possible. Suzanne Wells in Special Exhibitions, aided by her assistant, Zoe Kahr, provided invaluable encouragement and advice in the conception and organization of the exhibition. The Conservation staff, headed by Andrew Lins, has also played a crucial role in this endeavor; special thanks go to Adam Jenkins for his treatment of the metal boxes, and to Suzanne Penn, who worked on some of the more fragile paintings in the exhibition, including the monumental *Mural*. Nancy Ash and Scott Homolka also assisted in the presentation of the artist's prints and drawings. In the Department of Prints, Drawings, and Photographs, Innis Howe Shoemaker, John Ittmann, Shelley Langdale, and Gary Hiatt provided generous assistance with the artist's works on paper.

The Publishing Department at the Philadelphia Museum of Art worked with untiring devotion in seeing this book through to publication. I would especially like to thank Sherry Babbitt, Director of Publishing, for her attentive readings and helpful suggestions regarding my manuscript in its early stages. Likewise, David Updike has worked with care, enthusiasm, and dedication in the editing of this publication. The exhibition catalogue was sensitively designed by Katy Homans, to whom I express my sincere thanks for her superb artistry and innovation. This publication has also been significantly enhanced by the thoughtful and creative photography of Graydon Wood and Andrea Simon, who have captured the beauty and mystery of Chimes's paintings, metal box constructions, and works on paper with great skill and devotion. These images have been lavishly reproduced through the technical expertise of Production Manager Richard Bonk. Warm thanks also go to Conna Clark, Sahar Coston, and Amanda Jaffe in the Department of Rights and Reproductions for their help with permissions and photography requests, and to Corinne Filipek for processing image rights requests with the utmost efficiency.

Marla Shoemaker and her staff in the Department of Education, especially Adam Johnson, created a dynamic series of lectures, films, and events to accompany the show. Kaki Gladstone and Annabelle Pelta in the Volunteer Services Department organized an enthusiastic group of Museum guides, who did a wonderful job of introducing the artist's complex work and ideas to the general public. Charles Croce, Norman Keyes, and Frank Luzi in the Department of Marketing and Public Relations, and M. E. Bissert in the Membership and Visitor Services Office helped to get out the word about the exhibition with great dedication. Ruth Abrahams, Heather DeRonck, Jenny Profy, and Maia Wind in the Department of Editorial and Graphic Design conceived the printed materials and graphics for the Philadelphia presentation, while Bill Ristine and Jaime Bramble designed an innovative and informative web page for the exhibition. Finally, I am immensely grateful to Ann Kessler and her colleagues Jack Schlechter and Andrew Slavinskas in the Department of Installation Design, and Stephen Keever, Manager of Audio-Visual Production, for their remarkable work in designing an exhibition space inspired by the spiral motif that adorns the belly of Alfred Jarry's King Ubu, which proved to be of enormous importance in our effort to present the artist's work in a new light.

Betty J. Marmon, Kelly O'Brien, Molly Dixon, Kirstin Mattson, and Peter Dunn in the Development Department, along with William Valerio in the Executive Offices, worked tirelessly to obtain funding for the exhibition. In the Library and Archives, Lilah Mittelstaedt assisted with innumerable interlibrary loan requests, while Susan Anderson provided access to important letters in the Museum's Archives. Senior Registrar Irene Taurins, Assistant Registrar Nancy Baxter, and Associate Registrars Mary Grace Wahl, Linda Yun, and Elie-Ann Chevrier dealt gracefully and patiently with the intricacies of the exhibition loans. Martha Masiello, Michael MacFeat, and their teams in Packing and Installations handled and installed Chimes's work with the utmost care. Lastly, this publication and exhibition would not have been possible without the supreme dedication and indefatigable energy of the staff in the Modern and Contemporary Art Department. My most heartfelt thanks go to Carlos Basualdo, Emily Hage, Ashley Carey, and Lauren Bergman, who embraced this project with tireless professionalism and boundless good spirits.

Beyond the Museum's walls, I am deeply grateful to the lenders, both public and private, who have temporarily parted with their important and beautiful works of art to share them with the viewers of this exhibition. I am also extremely thankful for the support of the exhibition's funders, especially the Philadelphia Exhibitions Initiative and its visionary director, Paula Marincola, whose overwhelming generosity made possible an exhibition and a catalogue worthy of their subject. Special thanks go to The Locks Foundation, the J. F. Costopoulos Foundation,

The Robert Montgomery Scott Fund for Exhibitions, Linda and Paul Richardson, Jill and Sheldon Bonovitz and The Robert H. and Janet S. Fleisher Foundation, Betsy and Ed Cohen, Susan and Washburn S. Oberwager, and other members of The 'Pataphysical Society, without whose generosity this project would have been impossible.

The staff at the Locks Gallery, in particular Doug Schaller, Philip Mott, Reneé Shortell, John Caperton, and Joseph Hu, were extremely generous with their time during my extended visits to select the works to be included in the retrospective. Many people who have known Chimes over the years have shared with me their memories and impressions of the man and his work, most notably Harry Anderson, Edna Andrade, J. Frederick Cain, Daniel W. Dietrich II, Helen Drutt English, Per Gårder, Rodger LaPelle, Cissie Levy, Martin and Margy Meyerson, Patrick Murphy, Phillip Mitsis and Sophia Kalantzakos, Eileen Neff, Edith Newhall, Washburn Oberwager, Sid Sachs, Peter and Mari Shaw, Doris Singer, and Richard Torchia. I also wish to express my profound appreciation to Penny Balkin Bach and Laura Griffith for granting me access to the archives of the Fairmount Park Art Association. My understanding of the artist's role in the *Sleeping Woman* was considerably enhanced through several highly enjoyable conversations with Steve Berg, Chimes's close friend and collaborator on this important public art project in Philadelphia.

Finally, I would like to mention two people without whom this project would not have come to fruition. I was extremely fortunate to work alongside Claire Howard, whose energy and creativity, as well as her sound advice and intellectual input, are evident in every part of this exhibition and publication. A formidable research assistant, Claire enthusiastically handled the myriad organizational details of this retrospective, which ranged from loan agreements to photography requests. She has also done superb research in compiling the exhibition history, bibliography, and chronology of the artist's life that appear in this volume, which built upon earlier research by Jacky Hayward. Claire has been a true collaborator, in the fullest and most enriching sense, and her contribution has been in every way critical to the success of the exhibition and its accompanying catalogue. Last, and by no means least, thanks are due to Sarah Powers, who provided patience, humor, and support though each phase of this project, graciously allowing me to embark with Tom on this 'Pataphysical journey to the inner world.

Thomas Chimes
Adventures in 'Pataphysics

MICHAEL R. TAYLOR

INTRODUCTION

Where do we go from here? The great artist of tomorrow will go underground.
—MARCEL DUCHAMP, 1961[1]

In the future everybody will be world famous for fifteen minutes.
—ANDY WARHOL, 1968[2]

NOTES FROM UNDERGROUND

The Philadelphia-born artist Thomas Chimes has spent most of his career exploring the space between the two famous statements quoted above. In the 1960s the artist experienced a flickering moment of fame, akin to the egalitarian aspirations of Andy Warhol's prediction, when Alfred H. Barr, Jr., acquired two paintings and a drawing for the collection of the Museum of Modern Art in New York, as well as a small painting for himself.[3] Chimes's reputation as a promising young painter was further enhanced through two highly successful one-person shows at the Bodley Gallery, New York, in 1963 and 1965, followed by a critically acclaimed mid-career retrospective exhibition in 1968 at the John and Mable Ringling Museum of Art in Sarasota, Florida. By the end of that decade, however, Chimes had embraced Marcel Duchamp's advice to younger artists that they avoid the endemic venality of the New York gallery scene and "go underground, don't let anyone know that you are working."[4]

Warhol and Duchamp represent two important and at times competing strains in Chimes's work. The example of the former encouraged him to engage with images and techniques derived from mass media and popular culture, while the intellectual approach of the latter paved the way for the artist's own investigations of esoteric subject matter, often derived from the work of nineteenth-century poets and other literary and philosophical forebears. The two artists were also associated with the city of Philadelphia, since the Philadelphia Museum of Art houses the world's largest collection of Duchamp's work, through the bequest of his patrons, Louise and Walter Arensberg, in 1954. Similarly, Warhol's name has been indelibly linked with the city since 1965, when the Institute of Contemporary Art (ICA) at the University of Pennsylvania gave the artist his first museum survey exhibition.

Chimes was one of some four thousand people who attended the now-legendary public opening of the Warhol exhibition at the ICA on October 8, 1965 (figs. 1–3), and the impact of the Pop artist's use of non-art materials and commercial art techniques, as well as his ideas about fame and celebrity culture, were keenly felt in Chimes's subsequent work. This thematic presentation of Warhol's work reinforced the artist's groundbreaking engagement with popular culture, as seen in the rooms devoted to silkscreened paintings of Elvis Presley and Liz Taylor.

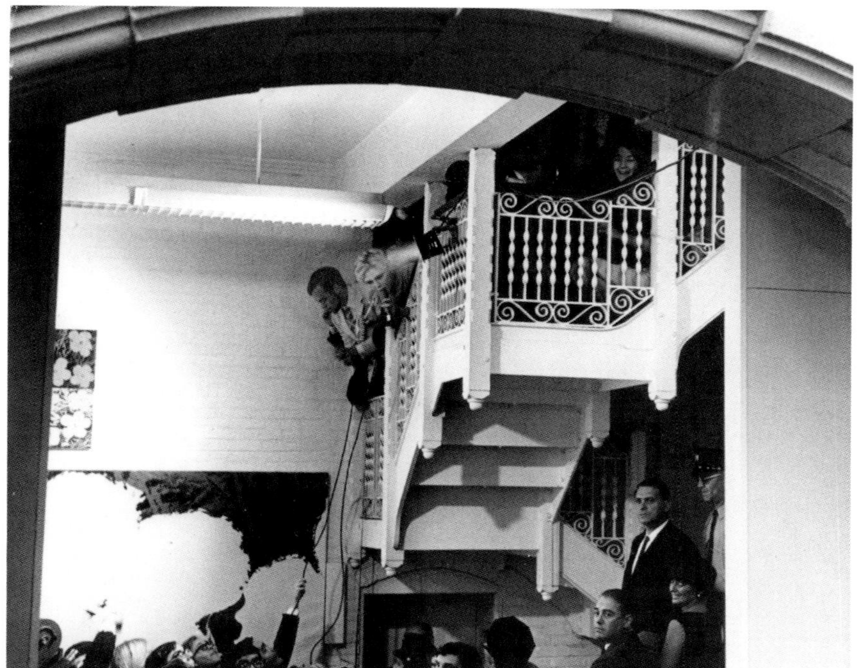

Fig. 1
Edie Sedgwick on a stair-
case at the opening of the
Andy Warhol exhibition,
Institute of Contemporary
Art, Philadelphia, October
8, 1965. Courtesy of Sam
Green

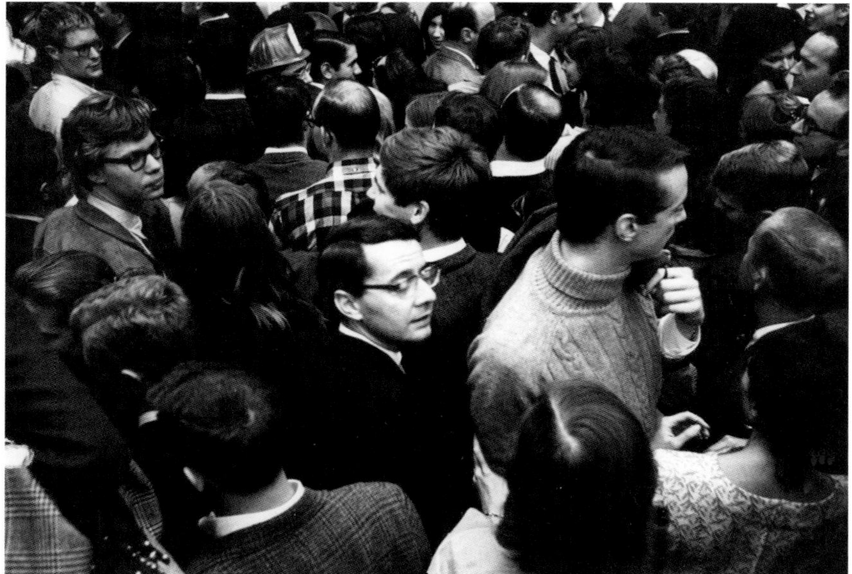

Fig. 2
Opening of the *Andy
Warhol* exhibition, Institute
of Contemporary Art,
Philadelphia, October 8,
1965. Courtesy of Sam
Green

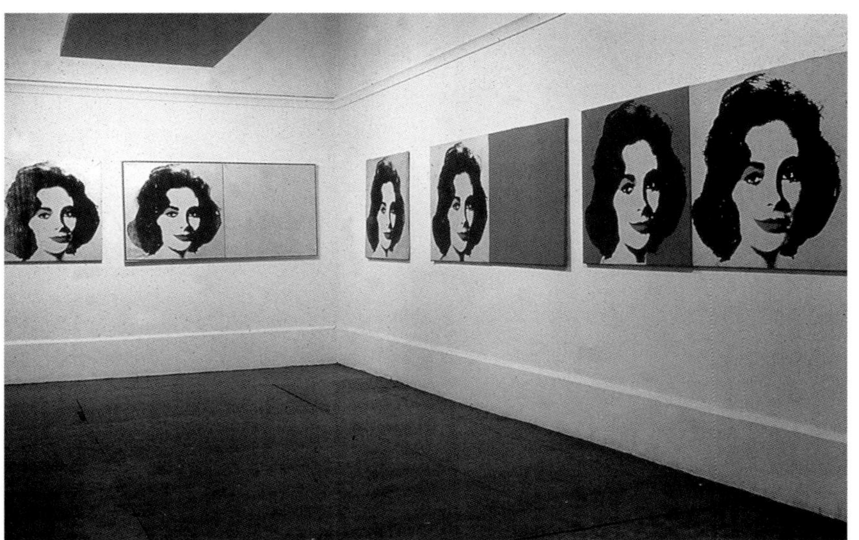

Fig. 3
Installation view, *Andy
Warhol* exhibition, Institute
of Contemporary Art,
Philadelphia, October–
November 1965.
Courtesy of the Institute of
Contemporary Art,
Philadelphia

The impact of seeing these Pop paintings, which were derived from newspaper photographs and film stills, would encourage Chimes to paint from photographs in the 1970s, when he began his series of panel portraits based on images of Alfred Jarry and his circle. Beyond the work itself, the artist also vividly remembers the excitement of the opening, with Warhol's entourage arriving in white T-shirts and black-leather motorcycle jackets, a cool, tough-guy look they borrowed from Marlon Brando, and pushing their way through the crowds that were jam-packed into the Frank Furness building on Thirty-fourth Street, between Spruce and Walnut streets, which then housed the ICA. Warhol and his close circle of friends, including Gerard Malanga, Baby Jane Holzer, Taylor Mead, and Edie Sedgwick, then began dancing wildly to the music, only to be moved to the second floor by security guards as the unruly crush of the excited crowd threatened their safety. Chimes has never forgotten the image of Warhol's "super-stars" being escorted up an old iron staircase that led to a ceiling landing, where Sedgwick, in a floor-length, shocking pink Rudi Gernreich sheath, continued to tease and incite the throngs below by dangling her long sleeves over the crowd and pulling them up again, while dancing and ad-libbing into a microphone (fig. 1).[5] By this time, Sam Green, the youthful director of the ICA who organized and installed the show, had been forced to remove many of the paintings on view, especially after one of Warhol's *Tuna Fish Disaster* paintings was damaged by a television lampstand.[6]

The glamour and excitement of Warhol's landmark exhibition marked a key turning point in the Philadelphia art scene, which was no longer viewed as a provincial outpost, but rather a cutting-edge alternative to the New York gallery system. Duchamp's iconoclastic example also resonated with many artists of Chimes's generation, and it is often forgotten that he made his famous statement about the great artists of the future going "underground" during an artists' panel discussion at the Philadelphia Museum College of Art on March 20, 1961. "Where Do We Go from Here?' was moderated by the Chicago art critic Katherine Kuh and featured Duchamp, Louise Nevelson, Larry Day, and Theodoros Stamos. Duchamp delighted the audience with a verbal assault on the rampant commercialism of the art market, which had turned art into "a commodity like soap or securities."[7] According to Duchamp, "Material speculation leads art to a massive dilution, a lowering of taste into the mist of mediocrity," with the only hope being an "ascetic revolution" (a delightful pun on aesthetics), in which the artist works outside of the gallery system in a kind of hermitlike seclusion.[8]

Although Chimes did not attend the artists' panel discussion, he learned of it afterward through his neighbor Rodger LaPelle, a Philadelphia gallery owner and photographer, whom he met in 1965. Duchamp's famous "underground" pronouncement struck a chord with Chimes, whose interest in the writings of Antonin Artaud and Alfred Jarry had encouraged him to explore the margins of mainstream art and literature. By the end of the decade, Chimes had deliberately begun to withdraw into a monklike, hermetic position akin to Duchamp's highly individualistic stance against the pressures of the art market. As a consequence of this withdrawal from the contemporary art scene, Chimes began to investigate issues such as esotericism and mystification in metal boxes and paintings whose irrational and often willfully obscure imagery reveals his affinities with Surrealism. This methodical effort to delve into his unconscious in order to portray a level of reality beyond surface appearances can be compared to Arthur Rimbaud's notorious claim that the poet or artist "makes himself into a visionary by means of a long, immense, and calculated derangement of the senses."[9] However, for Chimes this flight from reality was achieved, not through abuse of drink or drugs, but through a prolonged engagement with literary and artistic subcultures, whose radical nature deeply enriched his artistic practice. The result was that Chimes disappeared from the New York art scene at the end of the 1960s and entered a reclusive, almost monastic phase that has now lasted nearly four decades.

In tracing the stylistic evolution of Chimes's idiosyncratic art, this essay and exhibition seek to provide a comprehensive—and long overdue—examination of the artist's remarkable career. The diverse body of work that Chimes has produced since the late 1950s—which ranges from the early crucifixion paintings to the metal boxes, the celebrated panel portrait series, and the more recent white paintings—reveals his remarkable ability to reinvent himself periodically, while also underscoring the conceptual nature of his artistic practice. In recent years, the artist has come to view the progression of his work in relation to the four stages of alchemy. This revelation followed his reading an essay on Jackson Pollock that related the four colors of alchemical evolution to the blazing palette and melting forms of the latter's 1947 drip painting *Alchemy* (fig. 4).[10] Chimes

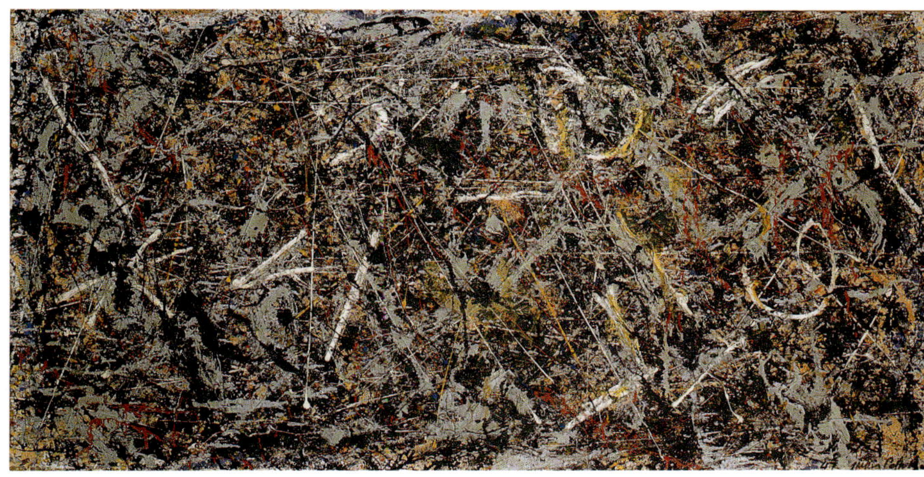

Fig. 4
Jackson Pollock
(American, 1912–1956),
Alchemy, 1947. Oil,
aluminum (and enamel?)
paint, and string on
canvas; 45⅛ x 87⅛ inches
(114.6 x 221.3 cm).
The Solomon R.
Guggenheim Foundation,
New York. Peggy
Guggenheim Collection,
Venice, 1976, 76.2553.150

was intrigued by the fact that in the medieval science of alchemy, the colors of the four stages—black, white, red, and yellow—that symbolized the transmutation of base substances into pure matter through burning corresponded with those found in his own work. However, he was forced to change the order of the original colors to match the chronology of his own artistic development, which moved from yellow to white. Thus, *xanthosis* (yellowing or gold) corresponds with Chimes's van Gogh–inspired landscapes and crucifixion paintings of the late 1950s and early 1960s; *iosis* (reddening) represents the metal boxes of the late 1960s, with their heated eroticism; *melanosis* or *nigredo* (blackening or putrefaction) relates to the panel portraits of the 1970s; and *leukosis* or *albedo* (whitening or quicksilver) symbolizes the glowing light of the subsequent white paintings.[11]

In this essay, these four distinct periods of the artist's career will be used to frame an extended discussion of the works themselves, which will be placed within the context of the literary, artistic, and philosophical ideas that informed them. A key theme that emerges from this critical overview is Chimes's interest in the discourse of madness and delirium. What links his own efforts to express inner emotional states with those of Edgar Allan Poe, the Marquis de Sade, Antonin Artaud, and Alfred Jarry, all of whom Chimes has identified with at some point, is the notion of the artist as a prophet or seer who through his sensitivity and extreme clairvoyance is able to teach us about the void. These writers all embarked on what the Scottish psychiatrist R. D. Laing described, in the final chapter of his 1967 study *The Politics of Experience*, as "the inner voyage," in which the artist moves away from the external world toward the self.[12]

This voyage into inner space and time is extremely hazardous, and many of Chimes's
literary heroes lived short, miserable, and tormented lives, often marred by extreme poverty
and critical neglect. Shunned by a hostile and intolerant world that could not appreciate the
seriousness of their endeavors, many of these *poets maudits* were driven to drug abuse, alco-
holism, and other forms of self-destructive behavior. In the case of the nineteenth-century
Scottish poet and novelist Robert Louis Stevenson, for example, a lifetime of mental and physical illness, compounded by overwork and a peripatetic lifestyle, led to his death at age forty-
four, while living on the Samoan island of Upolu. Chimes's 1976 panel portrait of Stevenson
captures the heroic spirit of the writer, who resisted depression and ill health to live out the
dreams of travel and adventure he presented in novels such as *Treasure Island* and *Kidnapped*,
as well as his fragile, trouble-worn features, which hint at his early demise. As Laing points out,
asylums have been filled with voyagers like Stevenson who become shipwrecked on the reefs,
but the rewards of this voyage into the inner world are infinite, since the exceptional, hallucinatory visions that these doomed figures bring back with them have redefined art and literature in
the modern age.

During the past five decades Chimes has found inspiration for his evocative imagery in
the work of these literary and artistic predecessors, and others who have followed in their wake,
such as James Joyce and Marcel Duchamp. But, above all, he has felt the deepest empathy with
the nineteenth-century French poet and playwright Alfred Jarry (1873–1907), whose visionary
writings have informed and nourished the artist's work, primarily as a vehicle for imaginative
re-creation of the self. As I will argue, this word-and-image component of his paintings links
Chimes's work with that of his contemporaries, including William Anastasi, Cy Twombly,
Richard Hamilton, Nancy Spero, and, above all, Jess, the late California collage and assemblage
artist with whom he shares an interest in hermetic symbolism and an obsessive attention to
detail and craftsmanship. Chimes's artistic practice also resonates with that of other artists, such
as Gerhard Richter's use and manipulation of photography and Robert Smithson's interest in
religious symbolism and entropy. Although Chimes is rarely discussed within the context of
contemporary art, such comparisons illuminate important aspects of his work and ideas and,
in doing so, reveal his hitherto overlooked contribution to the art of his time.

BEGINNINGS

Thomas Chimes was born in Philadelphia in 1921. The eldest son of the Greek immigrants
Demetrius (James) and Aglaia (Agnes) Chimes, the artist grew up in West Philadelphia, where
his father owned a restaurant. From an early age he showed an aptitude for art that was nurtured
and encouraged by his uncle, Thomas Pope, as well as his teachers at the Mastbaum School of
Art at Broad Street and Columbia Avenue, where he made sculptures in clay when he was in
the fifth grade. Chimes's interest in art intensified when he attended West Philadelphia High
School, where he won a drawing prize, but his father dismissed his dream of becoming an artist
as a romantic fantasy that would not come to anything.[13] The elder Chimes's hopes that his
son would pursue a career in the military were dashed when Tom was assaulted by a customer
while working at a newspaper stand, near the subway station at Thirteenth and Market streets,
and received $500 in compensation. Determined to prove his father wrong, Chimes used the

money to enroll at the Pennsylvania Academy of the Fine Arts, on September 29, 1939, writing a heartfelt statement in support of his application that outlined his serious approach to art, as well as his lofty ambition to follow in the footsteps of the masters:

> It has only been within the last two years that my love for art has developed to such an extent that I think I would be very unhappy at any other field. My aim is to receive a warming satisfaction from my work, and to give to others the same pleasure. However, the one thing that most true artists strive for is fame and not fortune. A painter adores being pointed out as the master who did that great work while he barely exists in the traditional attic. Someday, I would like to be a renowned oil painter and etcher, and only God knows whether I shall. There must be more Leonardo da Vincis, Rembrandts and Sargents, so why not I.[14]

On October 2, 1939, Chimes began his studies at the Academy, where he took classes with Daniel Garber, Henry McCarter, and Francis Speight, but his studies were quickly interrupted by lack of funds, compounded by pressure from his family. Things came to a head on November 20, when he had a falling out with McCarter, whom he felt had unfairly criticized one of his still-life paintings. Chimes impetuously threw the work in the trash and promptly resigned from the Academy, answering a call from his father to help out in the Post Exchange Restaurant in Fort McClellan, Alabama, where James Chimes had moved to take a job as manager and chef.[15] Remaining committed to a career as a painter, Chimes returned to his studies at the earliest available opportunity, enrolling at the Art Students League in New York in the fall of 1941 in order to study with Frank Vincent DuMond, who had earlier taught Georgia O'Keeffe and John Marin. Once again, however, his studies were interrupted, this time when the Japanese bombed Pearl Harbor on December 7, 1941, thus forcing the United States to enter World War II.

In the spring of 1942, Chimes enrolled at the Palmetto School of Aeronautics in Columbia, South Carolina, where he obtained a license to become an aircraft mechanic. During his five months of training, Chimes learned to make cables, repair tires, and weld aluminum, a skill that would come in useful in the mid-1960s when he began to construct metal boxes. After graduating at the top of his class, he enlisted in the U.S. Army Air Forces shortly thereafter, where he served as a radio gunner on B-17 aircraft, while always dreaming of returning to art school and resuming his studies. The artist was demobilized in June 1945, following the death of his father earlier that year. Chimes agreed to help run the family business until his brothers returned from their war service in the fall of 1945, at which point he was free to pursue his career as an artist. Chimes attempted to enroll again at the Pennsylvania Academy of the Fine Arts, only to be informed no places were open due to the huge influx of former servicemen under the G.I. Bill. Chimes caught the next train to New York and enrolled again at the Art Students League, as well as at Columbia University, where he studied philosophy with Joseph Margolis. Chimes took classes in painting, sculpture, and printmaking at the Art Students League from February 1, 1946, through February 28, 1949; his teachers included Reginald Marsh, Will Barnet, Julian Levi, Robert Beverly Hale, Harry Sternberg, Václav Vytlačil, and John Hovannes, as well as George Grosz, whose classes he periodically sat in on. Located on West Fifty-seventh Street between Seventh Avenue and Broadway, the Art Students League then

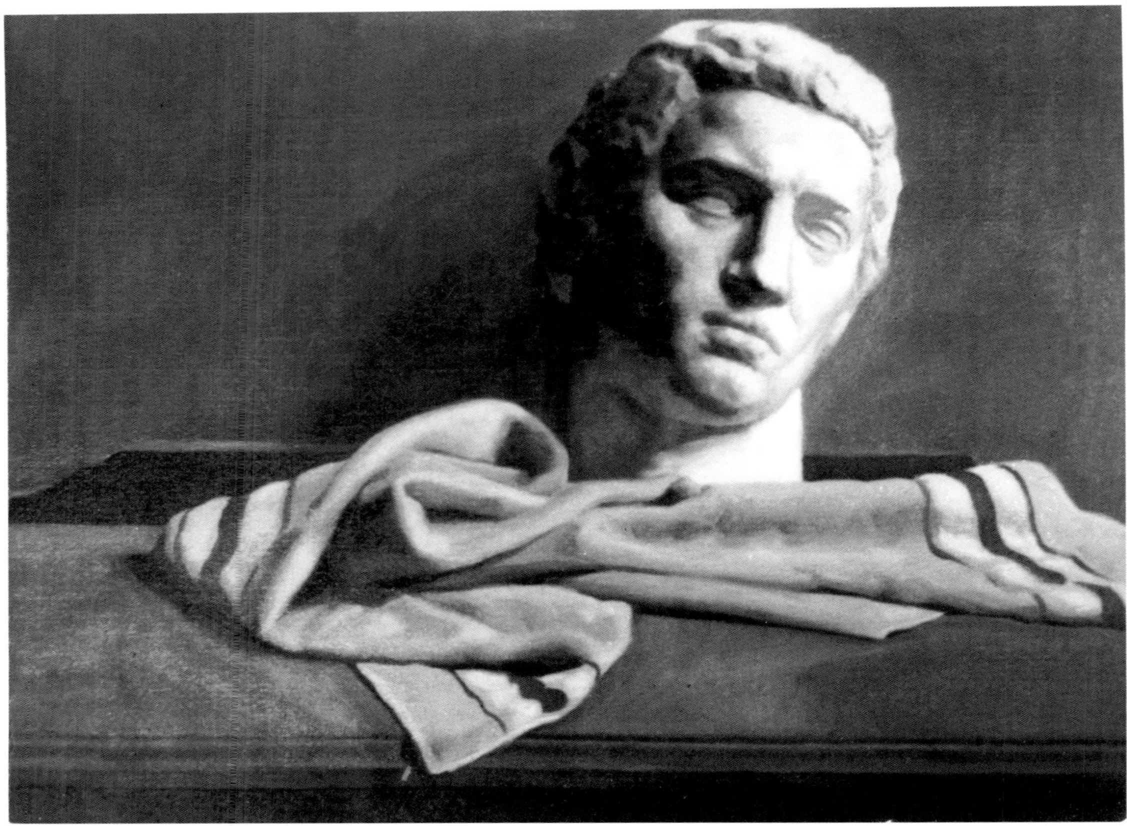

enjoyed a reputation as a germinative force for avant-garde painting, thanks to its impressive list of recent students such as Mark Rothko, Adolph Gottlieb, and Barnett Newman.

During his studies at the Art Students League, Chimes focused almost exclusively on the human head in painting and sculpture. His earliest recorded works, made in the spring of 1946, consist of conventional still-life compositions, which Chimes set up in a studio at the Sixty-third Street YMCA, using drapery and a plaster cast of Michelangelo's bust of Brutus (fig. 5). The resulting paintings reveal the artist's skillful use of chiaroscuro and modeling, as he rearranged the bust to show it from different viewpoints. Although clearly the work of a student learning his craft, they anticipate Chimes's later fascination with the human head in the panel portraits of the 1970s. This is particularly true of an accomplished portrait of the artist's younger brother George (see fig. 148) that he made soon after his return to the Art Students League, as well as a self-portrait (fig. 6) in which Chimes is shown in three-quarter profile, wearing a blue shirt whose collar has been turned up, which confers on him a certain nobility. The artist's stern expression in this youthful, academic portrait, which makes him look much older than his years, reveals his fierce determination to succeed as a painter in the tradition of Rembrandt.

A crucial turning point in Chimes's career was the classical head of a male that the artist made in the spring of 1946 in Hovannes's sculpture class (fig. 7). This plaster head preoccupied the artist for most of the spring term as he sought to re-create the perfection of surface and proportion found in the classical Greek statuary that he saw on frequent visits to the Metropolitan Museum of Art. In the end the project failed, as Chimes readily admitted to his Greek-American teacher; the stylized features and attenuated neck of the plaster head gave it an unmistakably modern look, like a neoclassical sculpture by the modern artist Elie Nadelman,

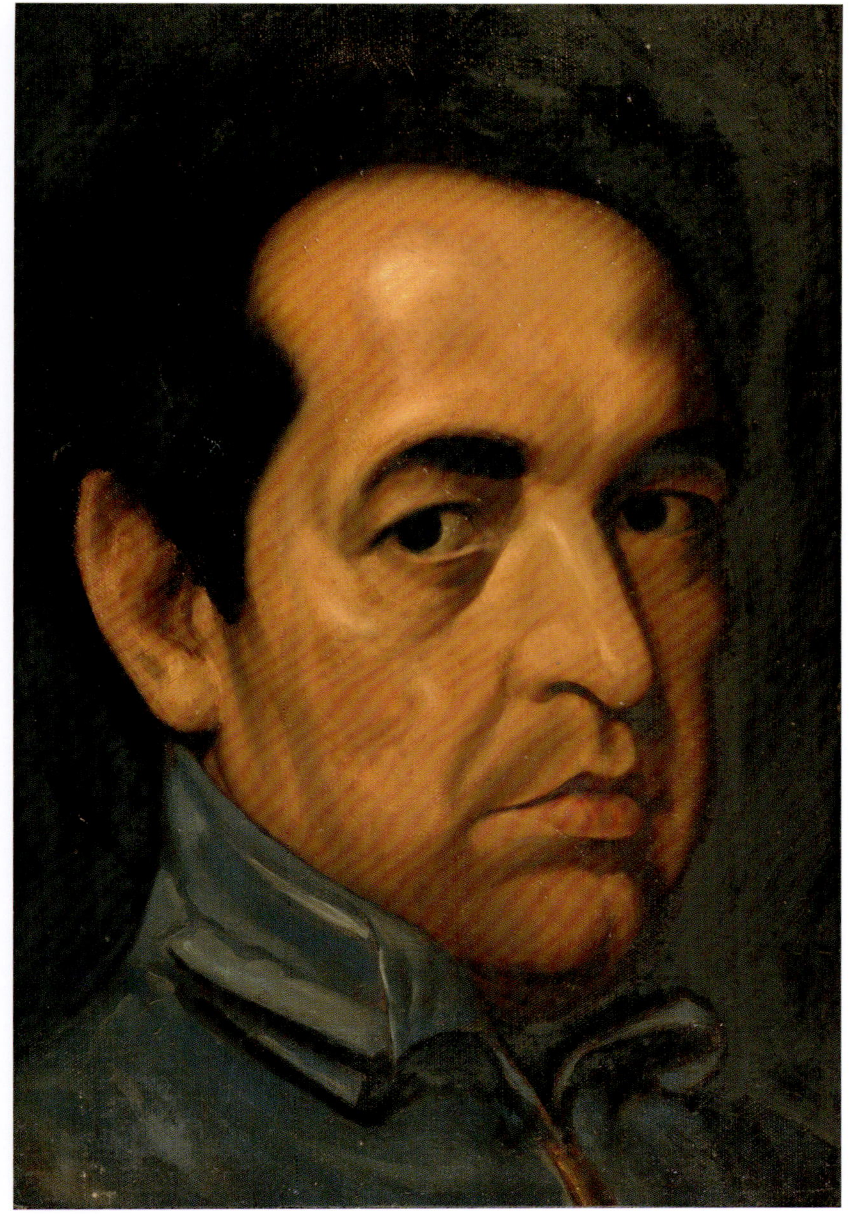

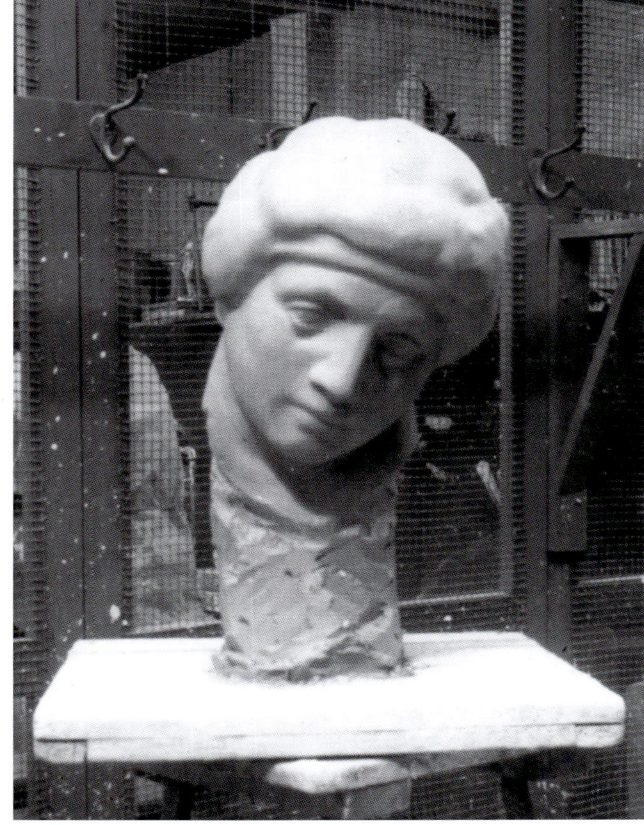

rather than a work by Phidias or Praxiteles. The artist thus learned a valuable lesson, namely, that he could not make works of art outside of his own time. From then on, Chimes embraced modernism and began to frequent the Museum of Modern Art, where his encounter with Pablo Picasso's *Guernica*, of 1937 (fig. 8), would challenge everything he had been taught up until this point.

Picasso's monumental painting addressed the Spanish Civil War that began on July 17, 1936, when General Francisco Franco led a military coup against the democratically elected Popular Front government of the Second Spanish Republic. Picasso, who had publicly sided with the Republican forces in their attempt to resist the Nationalist's armed insurrection, sought to convey the horrific carnage inflicted upon the Basque town of Guernica on April 28, 1937, when it was bombarded by German warplanes in support of Franco. When Chimes first saw the painting at the Museum of Modern Art, probably during the late spring or summer of 1946, he was resistant to its aggressive modernity, singling out the work's monochrome palette, which has been reduced to shades of black, white, and gray, as well as its flattening of forms and lack

Fig. 6
Thomas Chimes,
Self-Portrait, 1946. Oil on canvas, 17 x 11⁷⁄₁₆ inches (43.2 x 29 cm).
Collection of Dawn Chimes, Venice, Florida

Fig. 7
Thomas Chimes,
Classical Head, 1946.
Plaster. Destroyed.
Photograph courtesy of the artist

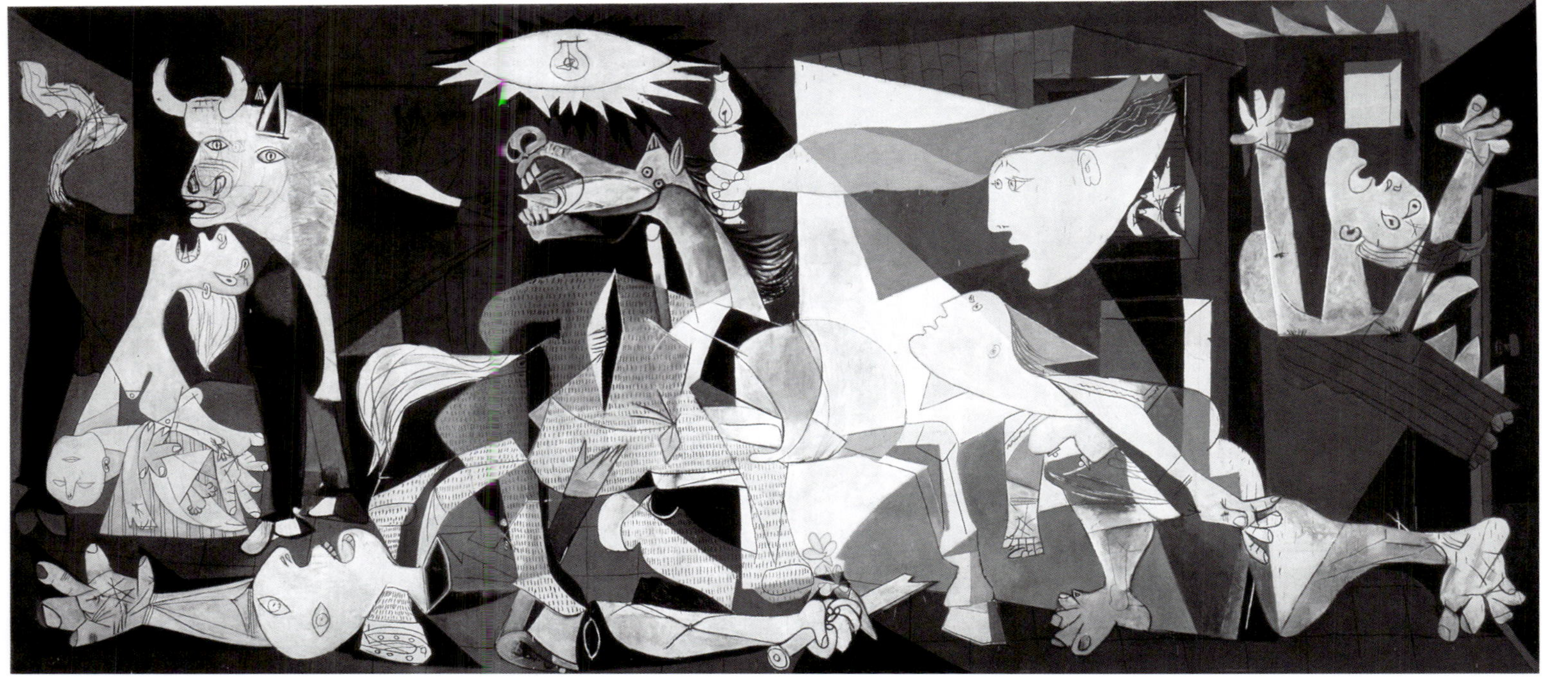

of modeling, which he considered to be flaws in its design and execution. However, the raw emotional content of the work made a powerful impression on the young artist, who repeatedly returned to study it. Chimes eventually changed his attitude toward the painting, admiring the way Picasso used compressed forms and newspaper-like colors to convey the tragic events. The lesson that Chimes learned from *Guernica* was that Picasso had created a universal icon decrying human hatred and destruction without resorting to traditional means of expression.

From this point on, the young artist became increasingly interested in modern art and sought out other artists who shared his predilection for Picasso's work and its legacy, including Jackson Pollock and the other Abstract Expressionists whose work Chimes had seen at the Betty Parsons Gallery, located a few blocks from the Art Students League. He began attending, in an unofficial capacity, Hans Hofmann's school at 52 West Eighth Street, where he listened intently to the German-born artist's theories of "push and pull," used to describe the simultaneous operation of flatness and depth in painting on a two-dimensional surface. Another important formative experience was a conversation he had with David Smith at the opening of the noted American sculptor's exhibition at the Willard Gallery, New York, in April 1947, during which Smith discussed his own work and encouraged Chimes's burgeoning interest in modern art.

During his time at the Art Students League, Chimes also became acquainted with such contemporaries as Tony Smith, Barnett Newman, William Baziotes, George Constant, Aristodimos Kaldis, and Theodoros Stamos. He was introduced to these avant-garde artists, many of them also Greek-American, by the sculptor and poet Michael Lekakis, who had been a camouflage instructor at the overseas replacement depot at Greensboro, North Carolina, where Chimes was briefly stationed during the war. An older, more established artist who regularly exhibited at the Bertha Schaefer Gallery in New York and was on first-name terms with many of the Abstract Expressionists, Lekakis became an important mentor to Chimes during his years as a student in New York, and a lifelong friend in the decades that followed. Chimes's own works from the 1940s and early 1950s reveal a strong debt to the artistic trends dominant in

New York at that time, especially the gestural paintings associated with Abstract Expressionism. However, the artist has also recalled the tremendous pressure placed on painters in New York in the late 1940s and early 1950s, from gallery owners, museum curators, other artists, and, above all, the influential formalist art critics of the time, to emulate the work of these powerful fore-runners. Chimes resisted this pressure to conform, which he viewed as an intrusion into his privacy, recalling in a 1978 interview that "your studio wasn't even safe."[16]

In 1953 Chimes made a conscious decision to return to Philadelphia, much to the bewilderment of many of his friends and colleagues in New York, and he has lived in the city of his birth ever since.[17] It was in Philadelphia that Chimes would find inspiration from the many artists and writers whose names have become associated with the city, most notably Thomas Eakins and Edgar Allan Poe, and formulate his intensely personal and highly original iconography, which often draws upon childhood memories, dreams, and associations. Freed from the constraints of the New York art world, where artists often felt pressured into joining groups and adhering to the styles being promoted at that time by powerful critics such as Clement Greenberg and Harold Rosenberg, Chimes reveled in the peace and solitude of Philadelphia, where he could work in relative isolation and develop his own visual vocabulary.

The return to Philadelphia was precipitated by a seven-month trip to Europe that the artist made in 1952, accompanied by his wife, Dawn DeWeese, whom he had met in Reginald Marsh's evening class at the Art Students League and married in 1947. Chimes had been suffering from a debilitating depression, during which he had no interest in making paintings or even getting out of bed. Concerned for her husband's well-being, Dawn suggested that they embark on a trip that would take the artist to Greece, the land of his forefathers, as well as Paris, where he had always dreamed of living and working. The trip began in Greece, during the hottest part of the summer, when Chimes, his wife, and their two-year-old son Dmitri stayed in Athens and visited the Parthenon, accompanied by Chimes's younger brother George and his French wife, followed by excursions to Delphi and Crete. The two families then sailed to Venice, where they stayed for a week, before driving in George Chimes's Hillman Imp across northern Italy into southern France. They spent the month of August sightseeing and sunbathing in Nice, Cagnes-sur-Mer, and Vence, before arriving in Paris in September 1952.

The experience of living and working in Paris was not as exhilarating as Chimes had hoped and expected. Postwar Paris was no longer the center of the international art world, but appeared to him as a bombed-out, cultural backwater compared to the vibrant energy and excitement of New York. Chimes was extremely disappointed with the quality of the work he saw by the younger abstract painters of the postwar School of Paris, such as Jean Bazaine, Roger Bissière, Antonio Corpora, André Lanskoy, Alfred Manessier, Georges Mathieu, Serge Poliakoff, Jean-Paul Riopelle, and Marie-Hélène Vieira da Silva. Shortly after arriving in the French capital, he had purchased the July 1952 issue of *Cahiers d'Art*, which contained important illustrated articles on Bram van Velde and Hans Hartung, but once again the work of these painters failed to impress him.[18] Of all the artists whose paintings Chimes saw in Paris, only Nicolas de Staël appeared to offer an alternative to the American Abstract Expressionists, whose work he felt was far superior to that of their French counterparts.

Chimes rented a studio opposite the Luxembourg Gardens, where André Derain had worked in the 1920s. However, he failed to make any inroads in his painting during his two months there due to outside distractions. The artist preferred to walk the streets and experience the romantic atmosphere of Paris and its inhabitants. Indeed, his favorite memory of this time is a visit to Alberto Giacometti's famous, dust-filled studio at 46, rue Hippolyte-Maindron in Montparnasse, in the company of his friend Michael Lekakis, who had secured a letter of introduction from the Greek publisher Stratis Eleftheriades, better known as Teriade, whose Verve publishing house had collaborated with many famous artists, including Giacometti, to produce high-quality art books.[19] The two Greek-American artists were met at the door by Giacometti's

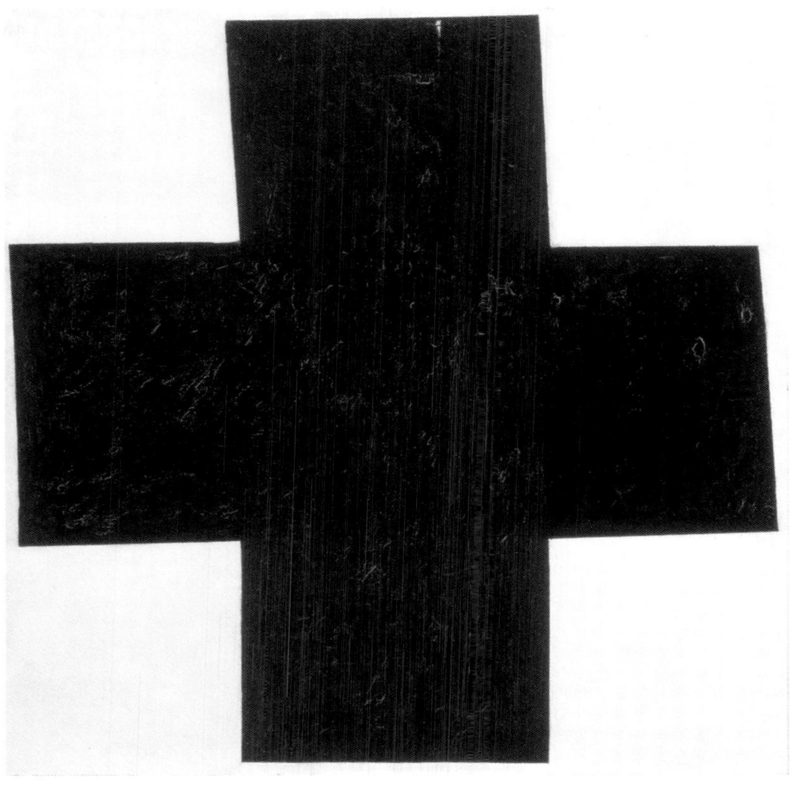

beautiful and enigmatic companion, Annette Arm, who brought them through an atriumlike space to the sculptor's cramped, dilapidated studio, before retiring, never to reappear.

With the help of a French translator, the young artists learned about Giacometti's latest works, such as *The Chariot*, of 1950, while older works like a bronze version of *The Invisible Object (Hands Holding the Void)*, cast in 1935, stood around the studio in which the artist had worked since 1927. Chimes remembers that Giacometti smoked and fidgeted a lot as he answered their questions for nearly two hours, politely nodding in approval when the younger artist spoke of his admiration for Matisse's chapel at Vence, which he had just experienced. What impressed Chimes most, however, was the cluttered, ramshackle studio itself, in which an intense atmosphere of creativity was enhanced by the accumulation of dust, plaster, and spattered paint that coated everything in gray. For Chimes it provided the perfect setting for the sculptor's standing bronze figures, in which the human form is reduced to its essence, at times threatening to disappear altogether as Giacometti's existential crisis forced him to keep working on his slender, elongated female bodies until "they were nothing but sticks, but powerful like ancient goddesses."[20]

The at times disappointing experience of living and working in Paris strengthened Chimes's resolve to return to the United States and work on new paintings. It was at this point, in early 1953, that he decided to move permanently to Philadelphia, setting up a makeshift studio in the house in which he and Dawn lived on Forty-fourth Street in West Philadelphia, and supporting the family by making architectural models and renderings for Raoul Ibarguen, a Cuban-born architect and industrial designer.[21] The trip to Europe had successfully alleviated his depression, and the artist was excited to get back to the studio. Chimes stretched a rectangular canvas and prepared to get to work, only to experience a terrifying existential crisis akin to writer's block that prevented him from painting. Staring at the blank canvas day after day, as if waiting for divine inspiration, Chimes could not find a way "in" to his painting. He had reached a dead end. The impasse was eventually broken when, after another day of prolonged examination of every

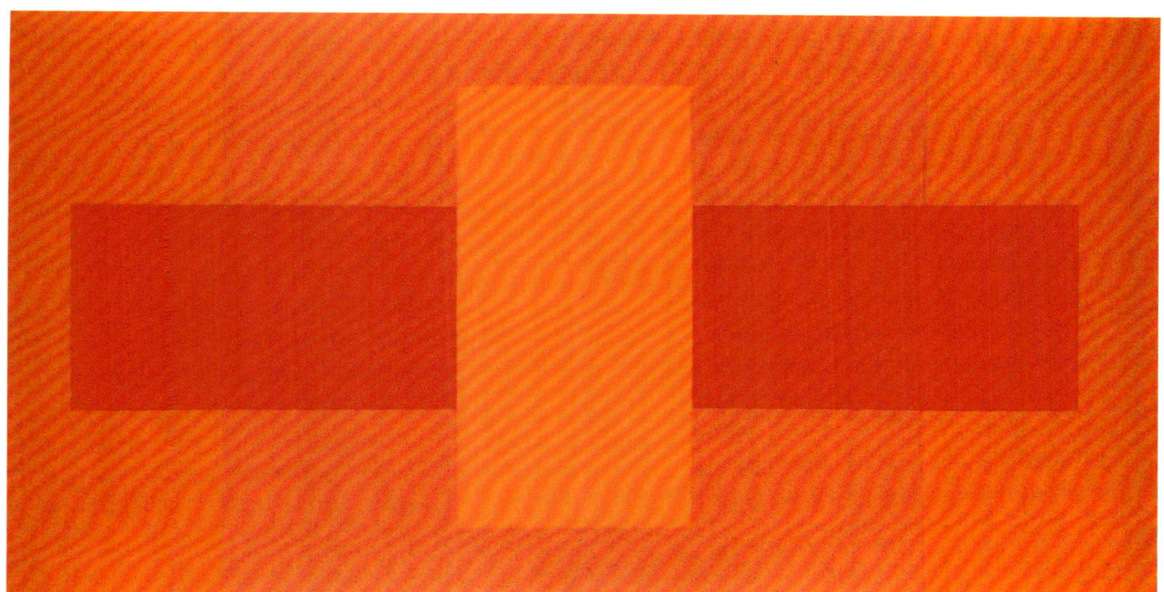

inch of the bare canvas and support, he began to discern the underlying geometric configuration of the stretcher bars beneath its pristine surface. He started to see invisible lines, such as the diagonals that connected the four corners of the empty canvas, and began to put down shapes in close values of gray, blue, and green that echoed the rectangular format of the canvas.

Much to Chimes's surprise, "a cross appeared in the space between the rectangles, a purely mathematical consideration having nothing to do with religion."[22] This discovery would later inform his landscape and crucifixion paintings of the late 1950s and early 1960s, but at this point he was primarily concerned with exploring formal and structural relationships in his work, which he associated with earlier systematic efforts by modern artists to reduce painting to its basic components. With this in mind, Chimes began to examine the early plus-and-minus paintings of Piet Mondrian and the pared-down austerity of Kazimir Malevich's *Black Cross*, of 1915 (fig. 9), as well as more recent exponents of abstraction like Ad Reinhardt, whose work Chimes admired, especially the shimmering canvases such as *Red Painting*, of 1952 (fig. 10), in which overlapping rectangular shapes coalesce into a central cross after extended viewing.

It was from this serious interrogation of the canvas surface that Chimes began to make the abstract paintings that would preoccupy him throughout the rest of the 1950s. Conscious of his debt to the New York School, and fearful that he had nothing new to add to their legacy of gestural abstract painting, Chimes began to produce boldly painted abstract canvases whose thickly scumbled impasto surfaces owed a profound debt to the French Tachist painter Nicolas de Staël. This Russian-born artist was one of the few painters whose work had impressed Chimes during his stay in Paris, and he emulated de Staël's signature style of building landscapes, figures, and bouquets of flowers through rectangular or square slabs of heavy pigment smeared on the canvas with a palette knife, trowel, or spatula. What the younger artist admired about de Staël was that his paintings never lost touch with reality, as opposed to the nonobjective work of Mondrian, Malevich, and Reinhardt, which Chimes had been studying closely since his return from Paris but had finally rejected as too emotionally detached and self-referential for his own temperament. As he later explained, "An artist like Mondrian lets the unknown slip through his net by being too rational."[23]

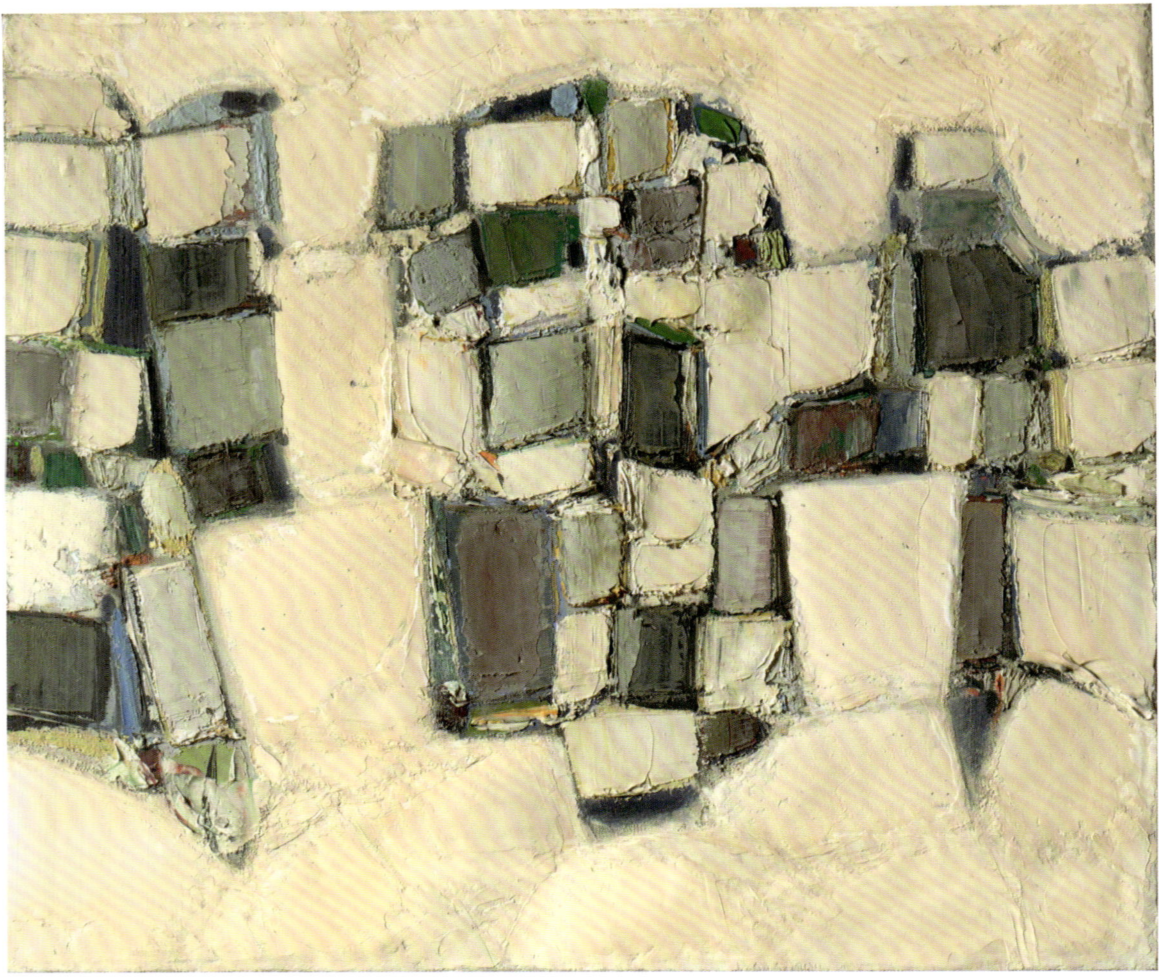

By the mid-1950s, Chimes had successfully adapted de Staël's method of gradually simplifying a composition until, with four or five broad patches of color, he could evoke the constituent elements of a landscape, such as sky, hills, buildings, and a road, while retaining the appearance of radical abstraction. Chimes was also drawn to the tragic nature of de Staël's life, which ended prematurely on March 16, 1955, when the artist committed suicide by throwing himself from the terrace of his studio in Antibes in southern France. The numerous obituaries and memorial exhibitions that followed de Staël's suicide, including a traveling retrospective organized by the American Federation of Arts, may have intensified Chimes's interest in the older artist's work. Chimes's *Untitled* (fig. 11), of about 1954, for example, bears the memory trace of de Staël's paintings of the early 1950s, such as *Fugue*, of 1951–52 (fig. 12), which had recently been acquired by the Washington collector Duncan Phillips, a great admirer and supporter of the French artist. Indeed, the Phillips Gallery, as it was then known, held two important exhibitions of de Staël's work, in 1953 and 1956, which helped introduce his work to younger American artists.[24]

In 1958, Chimes exhibited a group of de Staël–inspired paintings in his first one-person show, at the Avant-Garde Gallery at 166 Lexington Avenue in New York, which was run by the prominent Philadelphia collector Bernard Davis, whom Chimes had met through Lekakis. The paintings on view, small in scale and heavily encrusted with brickworklike patches of oil paint laid on with a palette knife, did not sell, and Chimes ended up agreeing with Dore Ashton's

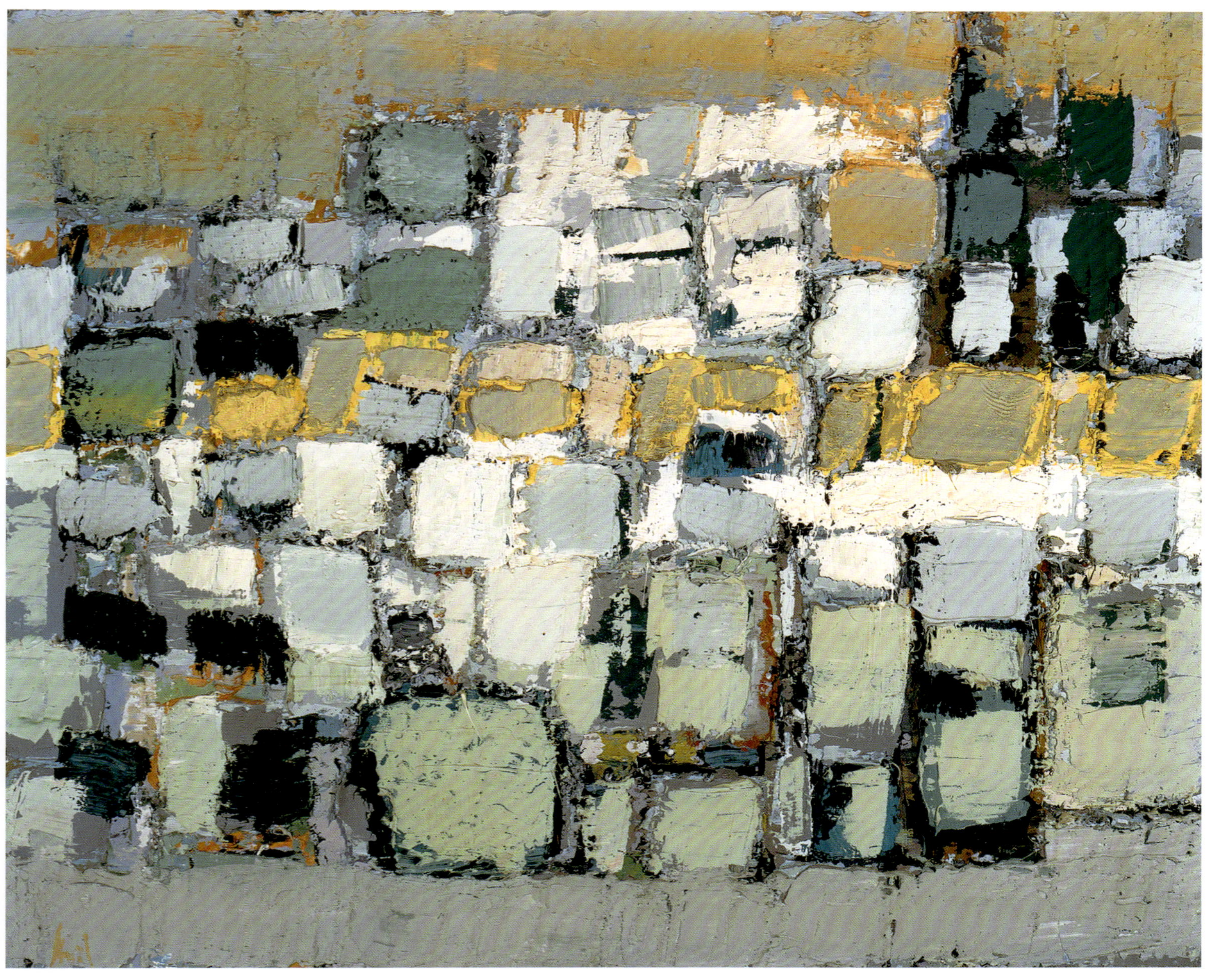

Fig. 12
Nicolas de Staël
(French, born Russia,
1914–1955), *Fugue*,
1951–52. Oil on canvas,
31¾ x 39½ inches
(80.6 x 100.3 cm). The
Phillips Collection,
Washington, DC

review of his work in the *New York Times*, even though she mistakenly credited Bradley Walker Tomlin, rather than de Staël, as his primary source of inspiration: "In the small gallery of the Avant-Garde, a young painter, Thomas Chimes, shows a group of small oils, some inspired apparently by late work of Tomlin, others more cubist in derivation. Chimes paints well, particularly when he keeps to a gentle tonal range, but he has yet to give expression to the emotions peculiarly his own."[25] Emboldened by Ashton's astute observation, Chimes returned to the studio determined to find his own authentic artistic path.

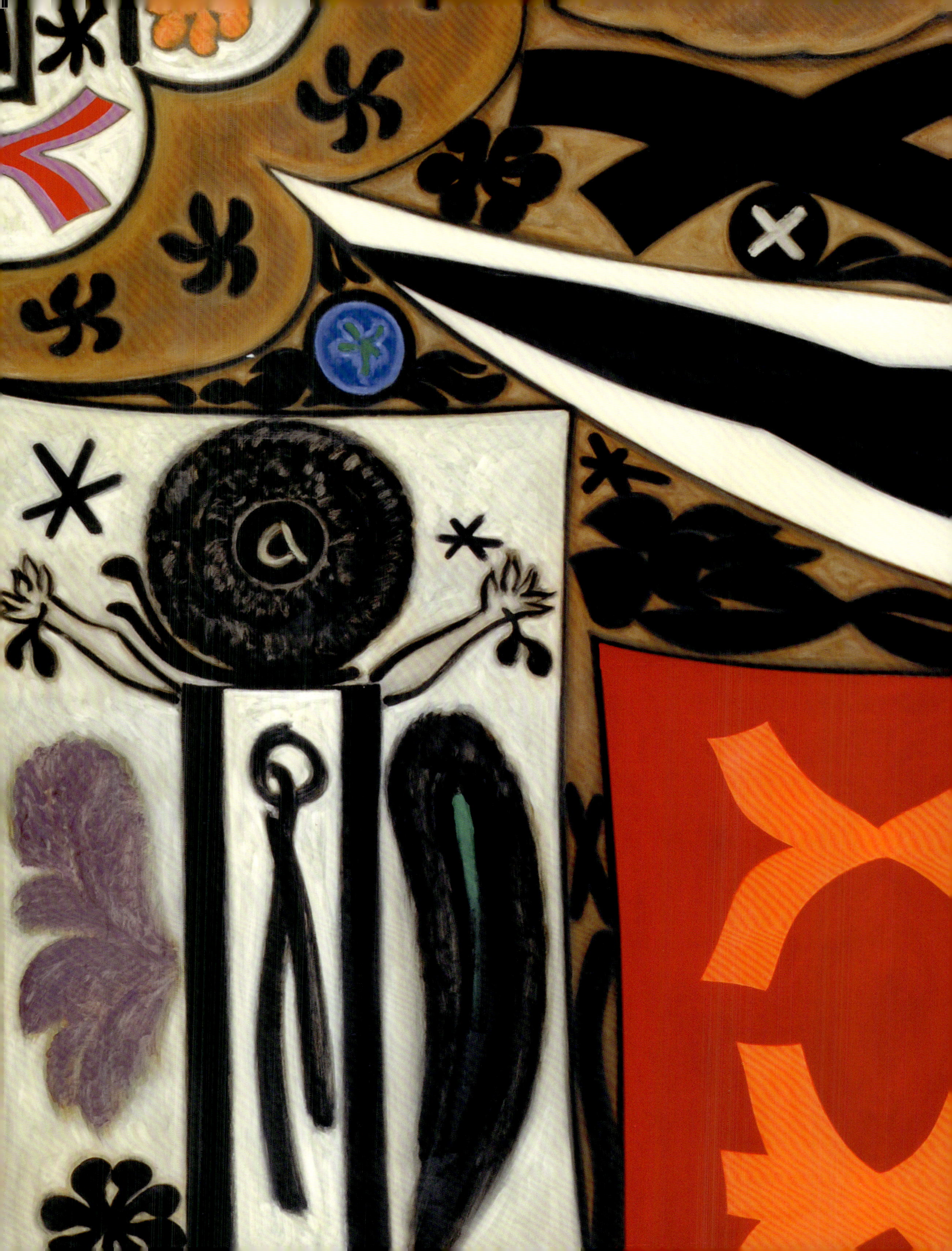

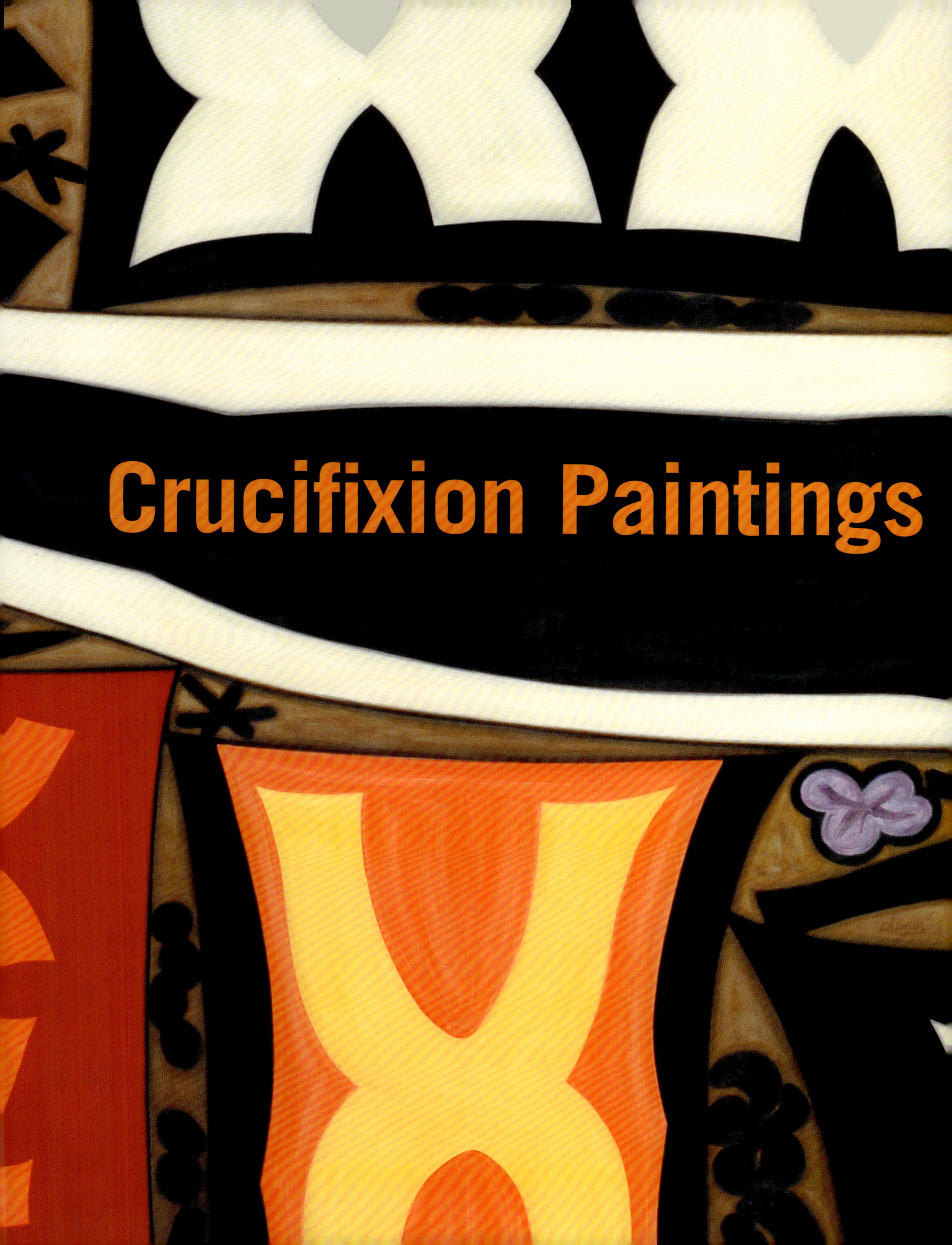
Crucifixion Paintings

By the late 1950s, Chimes had moved on to a new series of landscape paintings that were directly inspired by Vincent van Gogh's anguished subject matter and vivid yellow hues. A strong revival of interest in van Gogh's life and work had occurred in the 1940s and 1950s, culminating in Kirk Douglas's romantic portrayal of the Dutch painter as the archetypal tortured artistic genius in the 1956 Hollywood movie *Lust for Life*. Like many artists of his generation, Chimes regarded van Gogh's ability to transform emotion through expressive color and agitated brushwork as an important precursor to the artists of his own time, as seen in the gestural abstract paintings of Willem de Kooning, Franz Kline, James Brooks, and Jack Tworkov.

The artist's interest in van Gogh predated his exposure to the New York School. In December 1944, during stopover in New Orleans while en route to Columbia Air Base in South Carolina, Chimes had the great fortune of seeing a room of van Gogh paintings in the exhibition *Art Treasure from Holland* at the Isaac Delgado Museum of Art. These paintings, with their high horizons and expressive use of color, hit him with the force of a revelation. Talking about van Gogh's paintings more than sixty years after this first in-depth encounter, Chimes remains awestruck by the Dutch artist's contribution to modern painting. The intense colors, energetic brushwork, and exaggerated distortion of perspective and anatomy, which for Chimes often verges on caricature in van Gogh's portraits, convinced him that the Dutch painter was a "possessed" artist whose work was almost miraculous in its execution, as if an external force or power from above had guided his hand when painting. It was the assurance of those unexpected color combinations and rapidly executed brushstrokes that seemed unfathomable to Chimes, who could only understand these paintings as the product of an artist working in a trancelike state:

> The yellows and greens of van Gogh's paintings are intense and have great impact, and they impinge on my feelings, ecstatically provoking in me a similar kind of feeling, a kind of ecstasy. Then the rapid brushstrokes, to me, are absolutely amazing, and what struck me from the very first time I saw his paintings was how he was able to put down those strokes, making no adjustments. When they were put down, they stayed down, as if there was something directing the strokes rather than van Gogh himself. In fact, he was in a kind of trance. So part of what I feel is a kind of astonishment at the terrific virtuosity that I see in van Gogh's paintings, which went hand in hand with his compassion for humanity and understanding of suffering.[26]

In Chimes's view, the "possessed" van Gogh was thus able to take risks with his color choices and formal distortions, while at the same time utilizing his unique insights into the human condition. A key source for Chimes's understanding of van Gogh's life and work was Antonin Artaud's essay "Van Gogh, le suicidé de la societé" (Van Gogh, the Man Suicided by Society), which won the coveted Sainte-Beuve literary prize in 1947.[27] This beautiful and highly perceptive essay may have forced Chimes to reconsider his own art in relation to van Gogh's chronic physical and psychological struggle, since the Dutch painter's terrifying bouts of mental illness, which led to his hospitalization in the clinic of Saint-Paul-de-Mausolée near Arles in southern France, paralleled Chimes's own periods of deep depression. Artaud's seminal text was prompted by a review of the 1947 retrospective exhibition of van Gogh's paintings at the Musée de l'Orangerie in Paris by a psychiatrist, Dr. Joachim Beer, who dismissed his art as the work of a "degenerate" in the weekly magazine *Arts*.[28] Artaud's explosive and heartfelt response, which questioned the accepted definitions of both madness and sanity, was an early but seminal influence on Chimes, who would later find inspiration for an important series of metal box constructions in the astonishing poetry that Artaud wrote at the end of his life, having spent the previous decade incarcerated in a French asylum.

In his essay on van Gogh, Artaud claims that like him, the Dutch artist was the victim of a cruel society unable to cope with creativity: "Medical science, by asserting van Gogh's madness, resembles a stale and useless corpse. In comparison with the lucidity of van Gogh, which is a dynamic force, psychiatry is no better than a den of gorillas who are themselves obsessed and persecuted and who have only a ridiculous terminology to alleviate the most appalling states of anguish and human suffocation."[29] Artaud goes on to argue that through the institution of the asylum, society has managed to silence those unconventional, compassionate, and often artistic individuals who refuse to conform, and that the "lunatic" is actually the man whom the dominant society has prevented from "uttering certain intolerable truths."[30] Artaud thus concludes that van Gogh was driven to suicide by society's cruel indifference and unjustly sacrificed by the malicious actions of psychiatrists who were threatened by the unique imagination of a creative genius.

Such an argument would have been music to the ears of Chimes, given his own susceptibility to bouts of depression, as well as his belief in the role of the artist as a clairvoyant prophet or visionary who strives to interpret human experience. The artist may also have been drawn back to van Gogh's painting as a way of answering Ashton's insightful observation in 1958 that he had thus far failed to give expression to his own emotions in his work. Indeed, the psychologically charged landscapes that he produced in the late 1950s can be seen as the artist's first mature works after almost two decades of false starts and failed experiments, which included a poorly executed rendition of a Jackson Pollock drip painting that Chimes destroyed almost as soon as the skeins of poured oil paint had dried.

From 1958 to 1960 Chimes taught evening drawing classes in the School of Architecture at the Drexel Institute of Technology in West Philadelphia, which allowed him to spend more time in the studio during the day. It was at this point that the underlying cruciform structure of his paintings again began to reassert itself, just as it had in 1953 when the slabs of color he had applied to create a visual rhyme with the rectangular shape of his canvas coalesced to form a cross shape. To his amazement, he began to glimpse the shape of a crucifix in the thrusting diagonals and in the crossed vertical and horizontal lines of the landscapes that he had been painting since the close of the Avant-Garde Gallery exhibition. This form brought to mind the compositions of several van Gogh landscapes that feature a steep white path upon which two figures are framed by an opening in a wall at the high horizon, where the path and the wall meet to form a "T" shape, which Chimes likened to the shape of a crucifix (figs. 13, 14).

The artist's memory of van Gogh's landscape paintings was so strong that he returned to their basic, crosslike compositions in paintings such as *Van Gogh's Landscape* (pl. 1) and *Yellow with Cross* (fig. 15), both of 1958. However, Chimes updated van Gogh's landscape by utilizing the palette-knife technique he had learned from the work of de Staël. A photograph of the artist, seated alongside his wife, Dawn, and his children, Dmitri and Eva, taken around 1959, reveals

Fig. 13
Vincent van Gogh
(Dutch, 1853–1890),
*Langlois Bridge at Arles
with Road Alongside the
Canal*, 1888. Oil on
canvas, 23⁷⁄₁₆ x 29⅛
inches (59.5 x 74 cm).
Van Gogh Museum,
Amsterdam

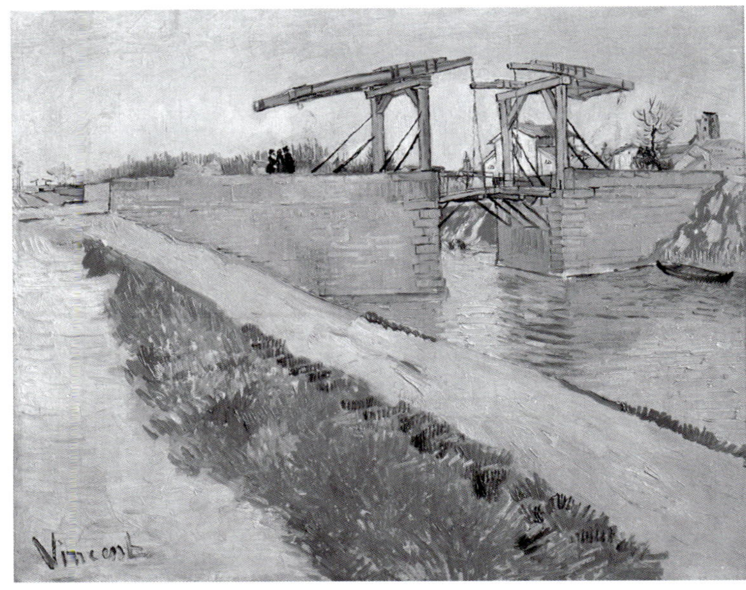

Fig. 14
Vincent van Gogh,
Autumn Garden, 1888.
Oil on canvas, 28⁹⁄₁₆ x
36¼ inches (72 x 92 cm).
Nationalgalerie, Museum
Berggruen, Staatliche
Museen zu Berlin

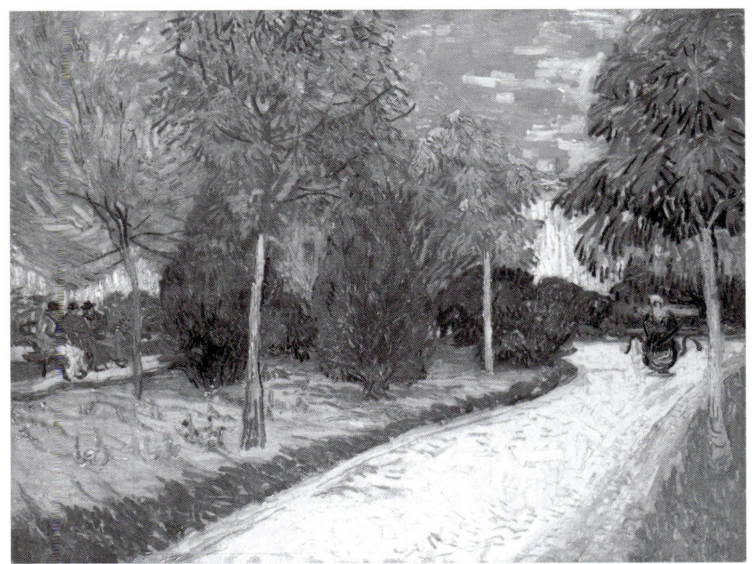

Fig. 15
Thomas Chimes, *Yellow
with Cross*, 1958. Oil on
canvas, 12 x 14 inches
(30.5 x 35.6 cm). Private
collection

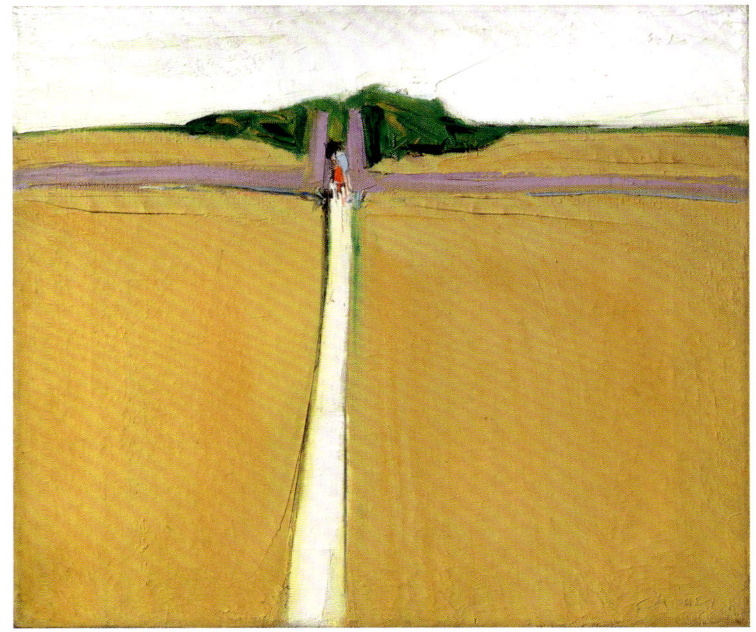

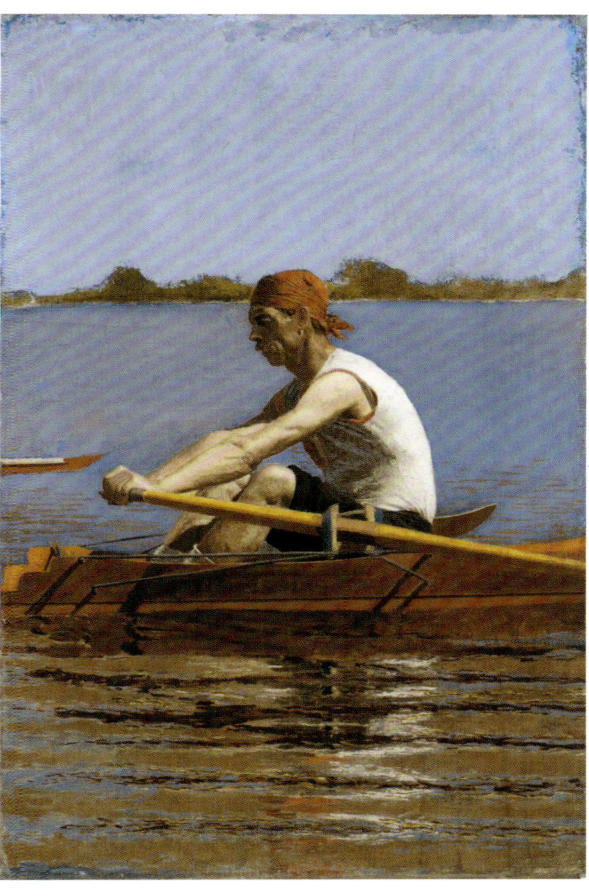

that Chimes had on at least one occasion painted a monumental version of this theme (see fig. 37). Another important feature was the horizontal stretch of blue water and green hillside in the background of these paintings, which was derived from Thomas Eakins's *John Biglin in a Single Scull*, of 1873–74 (fig. 16), and thus situated Chimes's landscapes and subsequent crucifixion paintings on the banks of the Schuylkill River in Philadelphia. There can be no doubt that the artist had melded this imagery borrowed from van Gogh and Eakins with his own personal vision, which was now focused on his life as a highly ambitious, yet struggling artist in Philadelphia, with bills to pay and a family to feed.

MATISSE'S CHAPEL AT VENCE

By the early 1960s Chimes had moved on to paintings and watercolors that combined landscape references with specific symbols such as stars, ladders, rosettes, medallions, letters, dice, and crucifixes (figs. 17, 18). The crucifixion motif relates directly to the artist's upbringing in the Greek Orthodox Church, as well as to Henri Matisse's Chapel of the Rosary of the Dominican Nuns at Vence, near Nice in southern France, which Chimes visited several times during his trip to Europe in 1952 (figs. 19, 20). The artist had been alerted to the existence of the Dominican chapel through Alfred H. Barr, Jr.'s landmark study *Matisse: His Art and His Public*, published to accompany the important Matisse retrospective that opened at the Museum of Modern Art in November 1951 (a section devoted to the Vence chapel was installed after the rest of the exhibition opened) Chimes read Barr's chapter on Matisse's audacious designs for the decoration of the chapel with great interest and was determined to visit Vence as soon as possible.

When he finally saw the chapel in person in August 1952, he was overwhelmed by the emotional force of Matisse's late masterpiece, which the French artist himself viewed as his artistic legacy, "the culmination of a life of work, and the coming into flower of an enormous, sincere and difficult effort."[31]

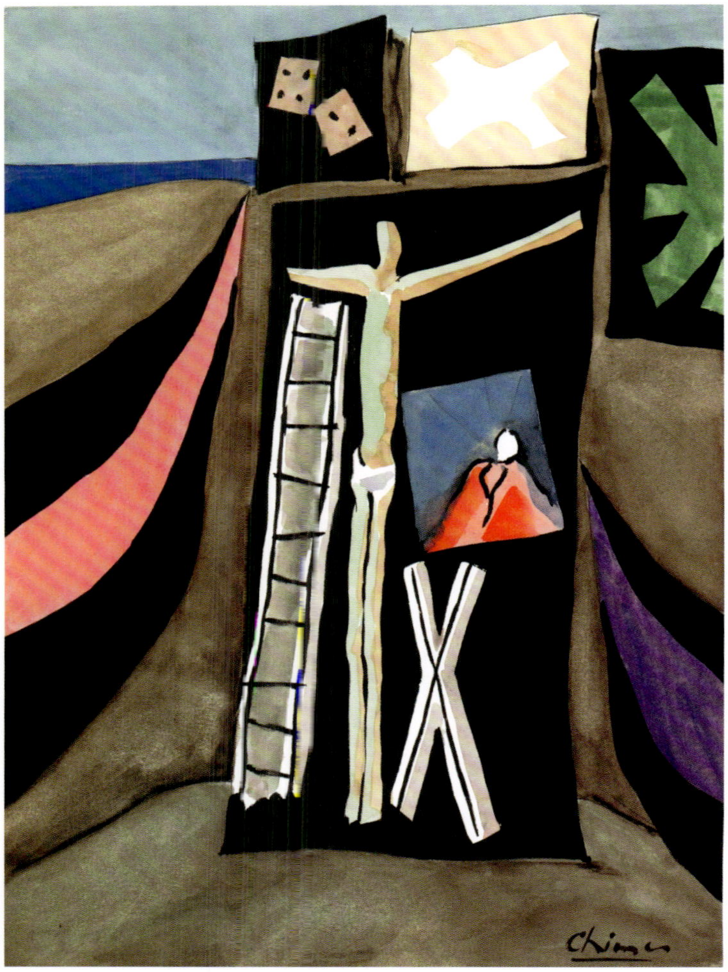

Chimes was profoundly moved by the older artist's radical decoration of this small chapel, which measures just fifteen by nine meters (about fifty by thirty feet), yet has all the spatial complexity and epic grandeur of a Gothic cathedral. Matisse worked on the chapel between 1948 and 1952, and the project carries special significance as the French artist's first religious commission, as well as being a triumphant demonstration of his formidable creative energy at the end of his long life. The radiant efflorescence of the large stained-glass windows featuring stylized palms, cacti, and other plant forms floods the interior space with bright light and intense color, which is balanced by the coolness of the white-washed walls opposite, embellished with glazed ceramic tiled murals, and the floors of crystalline Carrara marble. The gleaming white surfaces of the earthenware tiles are adorned with linear drawings in lustrous black of *The Stations of the Cross, Saint Dominic,* and *Virgin and Child,* thus creating a visual rhyme with the black-and-white habits of the Dominican nuns, who "complete" Matisse's design whenever they enter the chapel. Matisse's desire to unify the materials and color of each component of the chapel extended to his choices for the vestment fabrics and liturgical accoutrements, the exterior spire and ceramic roof, the gilded metal crucifix and candelabra on the altar, and the tabernacle door, all of which combine to create a harmonious environment in which architecture, stained-glass windows, and large mural drawings on tiles are fused together to form a perfect unity.

Chimes saw Matisse's chapel just over a year after it had been consecrated, and he still remembers the euphoric feeling of standing inside the building as the strong sunlight streamed through the colored glass and bathed everything in sapphire blues, lemon yellows, and emerald greens.[32] He was one of the first American artists to respond to Matisse's resplendent orchestra of iridescent color and light, although the full impact of the chapel was not felt in his work until the early 1960s, when he returned to the French artist's late masterpiece out of a desire to intensify the color range of his paintings. In the fall of 1961 Chimes visited an exhibition of Matisse's late cut-and-pasted gouache compositions at the Museum of Modern Art, which reawakened his memories of seeing the artist's powerful religious statement at Vence and led him to envision his own architectural setting for his paintings, based upon the ruins of a Byzantine church in Delphi (fig. 21).

Fig. 17
Thomas Chimes, *Study for Crucifix,* c. 1961. Gouache on paper, 11 ¹³⁄₁₆ x 8½ inches (30 x 21.6 cm). Collection of the artist

opposite:
Fig. 18
Thomas Chimes, *Untitled,* 1961. Oil on canvas, 18½ x 20½ inches (47 x 52.1 cm). Private collection, courtesy of Locks Gallery, Philadelphia

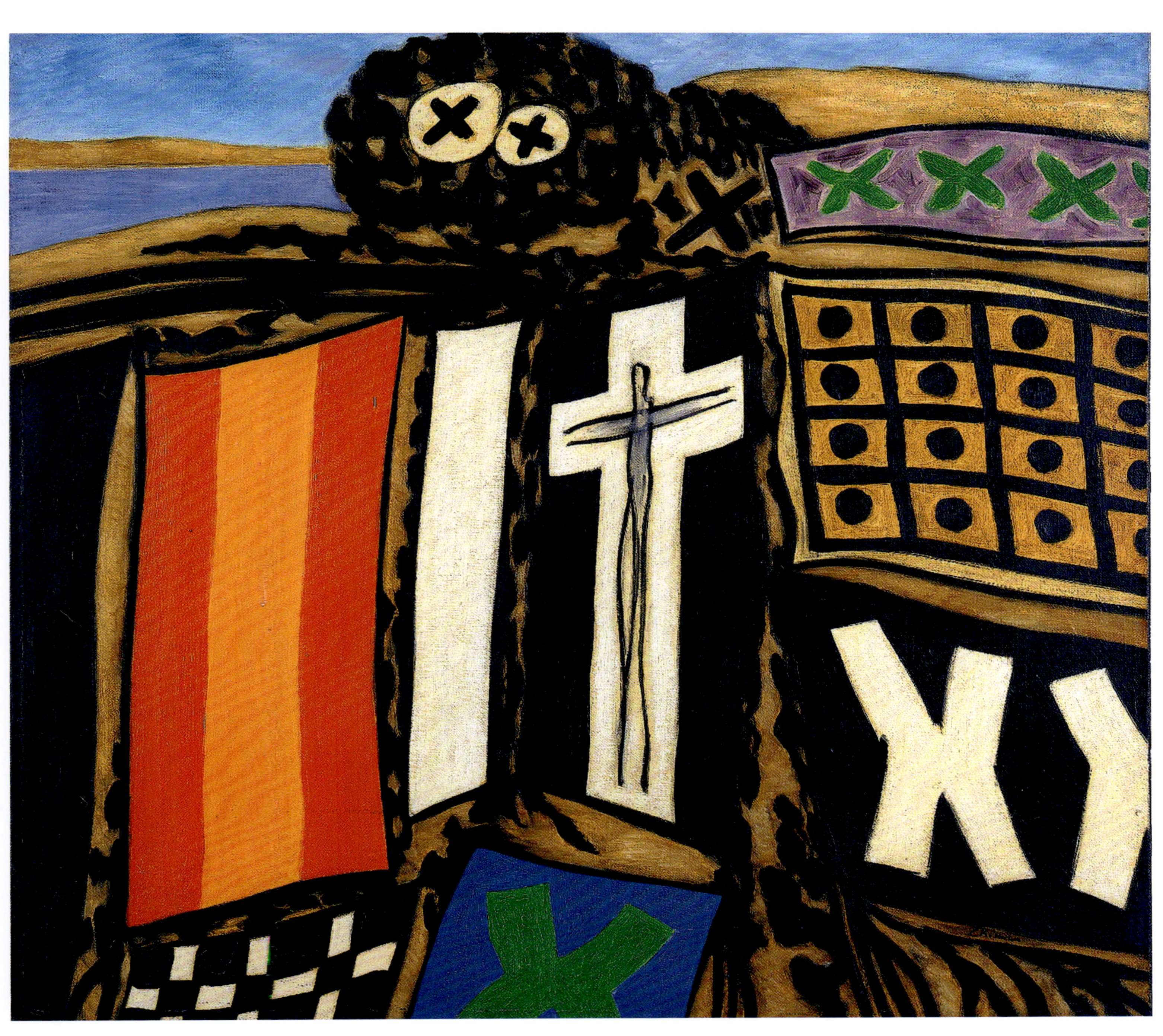

Fig. 19
Henri Matisse (French, 1869–1954), The altar with crucifix and candlesticks, ceramic-tile mural of *Saint Dominic*, and *The Tree of Life* (stained-glass window), 1950–51. Chapel of the Rosary of the Dominican Nuns, Vence, France

Fig. 20
Henri Matisse, *Virgin and Child*, door of the confessional, and *Stations of the Cross*, 1950. Ceramic-tile mural. Chapel of the Rosary of the Dominican Nuns, Vence, France

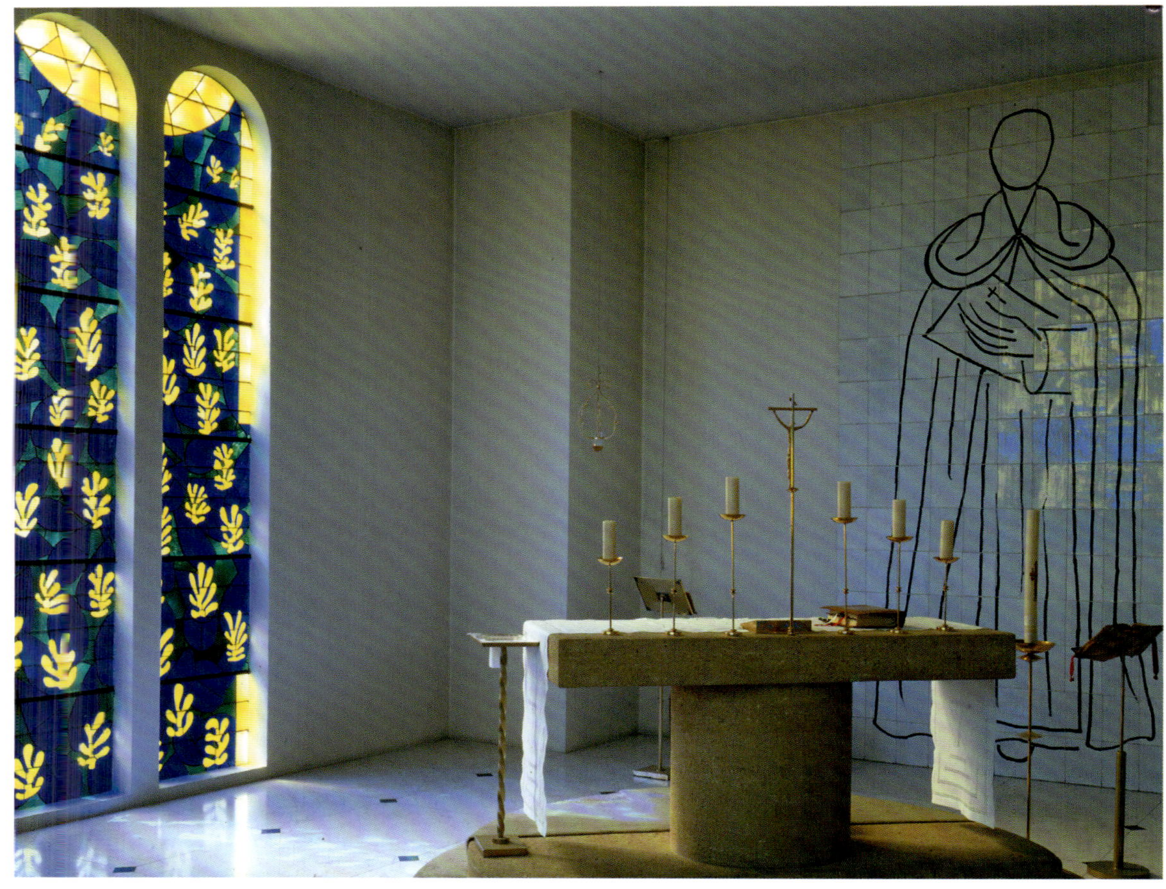

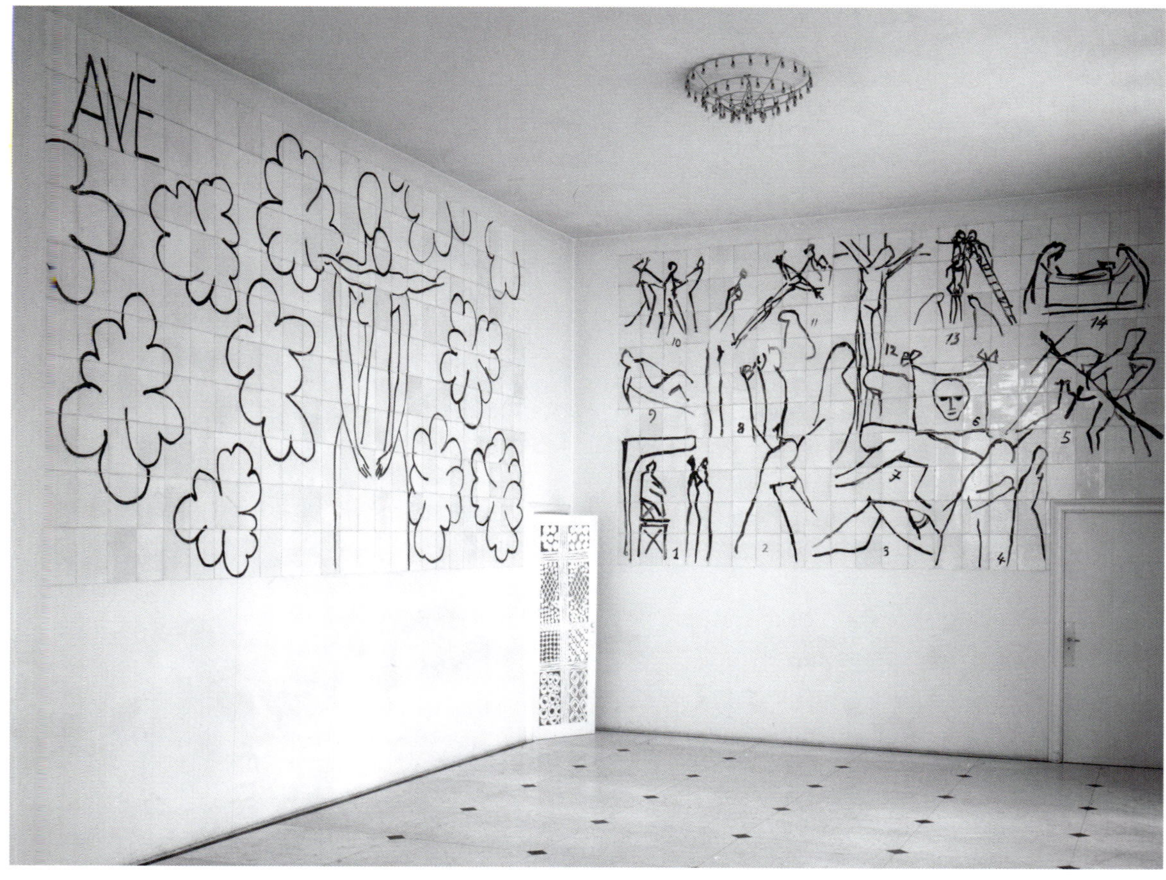

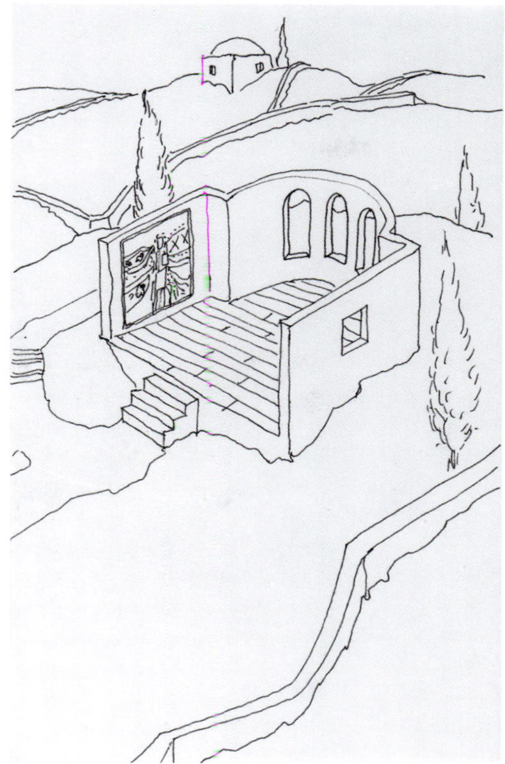

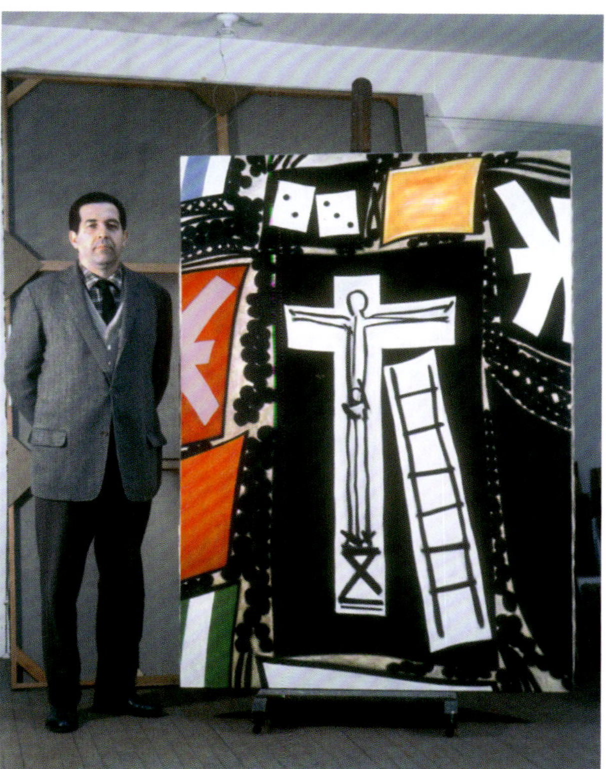

It was around this time that Chimes began to assimilate the French artist's lexicon of floral and tropical motifs in the stained-glass windows at Vence, as well as in the *The Stations of the Cross* (see fig. 20) that Matisse painted in thick black lines on the white-glazed ceramic tiles. Matisse's moving account of Christ's Passion, which Barr had considered "shocking in its terse austerity," informed Chimes's own images of the crucifixion, such as *Crucifix*, of 1961 (fig. 22), which combines the schematic image of the crucified Christ with related motifs, such as the ladder from Matisse's *Descent from the Cross* and the circular, grapelike clusters from the tabernacle door at Vence.[33] In doing so, Chimes achieves his own radical synthesis of Matisse's chapel, which has been condensed into an episodic composition that references the chapel's luminous stained-glass windows, the *Stations* drawn in black paint on the shiny white tiles, the tabernacle door, and even the slender, attenuated metal crucifix on the altarpiece.

Other works by Chimes, such as *Bread*, of 1961–62 (fig. 23), also looked back to the slashed diagonals of the dust jacket that Matisse designed for Barr's 1951 monograph, as well as his gouached-paper cutouts, such as *Chinese Fish*, of 1951 (fig. 24). However, Chimes always transformed his frequent borrowings from the French artist's vocabulary of vibrant "X" forms and schematized animal, fish, and vegetal motifs to create his own style of dynamic compositions. *Bread*, a large-scale painting measuring ten feet wide and nearly six feet tall, still holds onto the landscape format of Chimes's earlier, van Gogh–inspired works of the late 1950s, yet updates this imagery through the use of Matisse-like bold, flat colors and rows of "X" shapes that unfurl over the composition like flags or banners.

In an interview published in the *Philadelphia Evening Bulletin* on January 14, 1962, Chimes explained how his recent paintings were "variations on the same theme—man's search for ultimate truth."[34] This article was accompanied by an image of Chimes standing next to *Bread*, which at that time was called *To the East*, in his studio on the second floor of the rambling

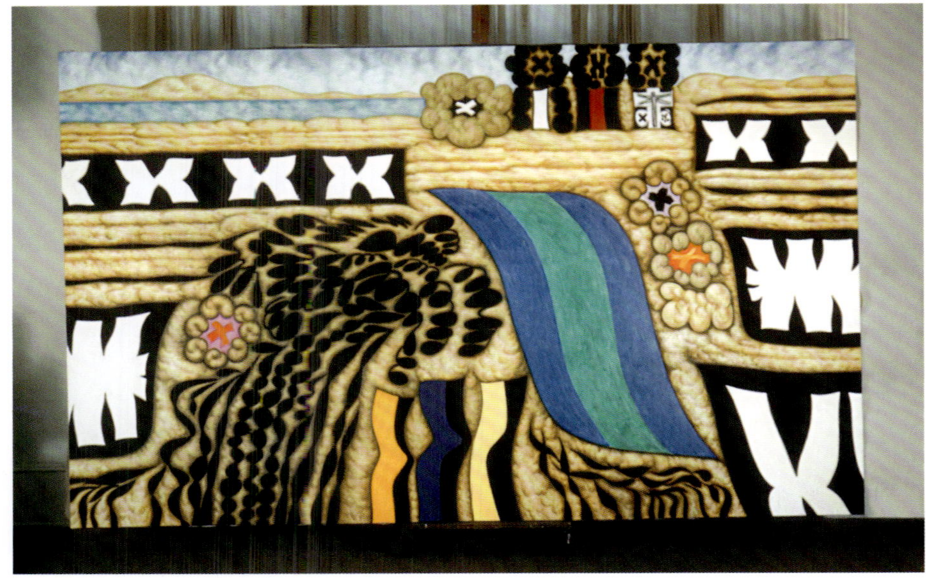

Middle City Building at 34 South Seventeenth Street, where he had been working since 1960. The interview with *Bulletin* staff reporter John F. Morrison had been prompted by the Museum of Modern Art's acquisition of *Study for "The Inner World"* (pl. 6) in 1961, as well as Barr's own purchase of a small painting for his personal collection. Bolstered by these important sales, a clearly ecstatic Chimes announced, "I've got places to go and things to do."[35] This feeling of optimism and elation had a direct impact on his subsequent work, which he said came out of a compulsion to communicate his particular vision of the universal sensation that "there is a truth and beauty beyond the realities of everyday life."[36] When challenged by his interviewer to say whether he saw any end in sight to this pursuit of new possibilities in painting, Chimes replied enigmatically, "In the end . . . we come to God."[37]

The artist repeated this quasimystical pronouncement in his response to a request from the Museum of Modern Art in 1961 to answer questions about *"Study for The Inner World."* Chimes's statement about his work tells us a great deal about his approach to art at the time:

> The questions "what is art?" and "what good is art?" are, to me, the same question. My experience teaches me that art, in itself, has no especial value or importance. Properly, it is a language, a means of communication, it is imitation, in short, a means to an end other than itself. Therein, lies its only value. Beauty is not an end, but an attribute of means. It has the power to glorify. This is true of emotion, expression, thought, idea, abstraction, realism, and so on, each having its own power. Therefore, the end of art is something other than its means. Truth is an attribute of mind, and mind is a means, and consequently, truth is a means. In the end, we come to God.[38]

THE LAST TEMPTATION OF CHRIST

Another crucial source for Chimes's crucifixion paintings and related works was Nikos Kazantzakis's *The Last Temptation of Christ*, which he read with great enthusiasm in 1961, in an English translation (fig. 25).[39] The artist was fascinated by this highly controversial book, in which the Greek writer constructed a poignant modern novel out of Christ's suffering, and much of Chimes's crucifixion imagery of the 1960s was stimulated by the dreamlike imagery found in the final chapter as filtered through Matisse's luminous environment at Vence. Just as Matisse, a resolute nonbeliever, repeatedly emphasized that the Chapel of the Rosary of the Dominican Nuns represented a spiritual space, so Kazantzakis, a non-Christian, attempted to explore the spiritual transformation of Christ through the medium of the modern novel. The Greek author challenged traditional Christian dogma by presenting Jesus as a fusion of God and man, rather than a purely divine being. Kazantzakis achieved this synthesis by vividly portraying an alternative life for Christ, who resists God's will by rejecting martyrdom in favor of a natural human existence on earth in which he works, marries, has children, and grows old. More human than divine, Christ is thus susceptible to the hopes, desires, doubts, fears, passions, and temptations that we all face. However, at the end of the novel Christ realizes that this alternative life has been a cruelly deceptive dream conjured by Satan, in the form of a boy-angel, who has taken advantage of his excruciating pain and self-doubt to offer a life without suffering in the hope that he will lose faith in the path laid out for him by God. Waking from this spellbinding vision of earthly contentment, Jesus finds himself still on the cross, in sheer agony, but ready now to openly embrace his fate as redeemer of mankind:

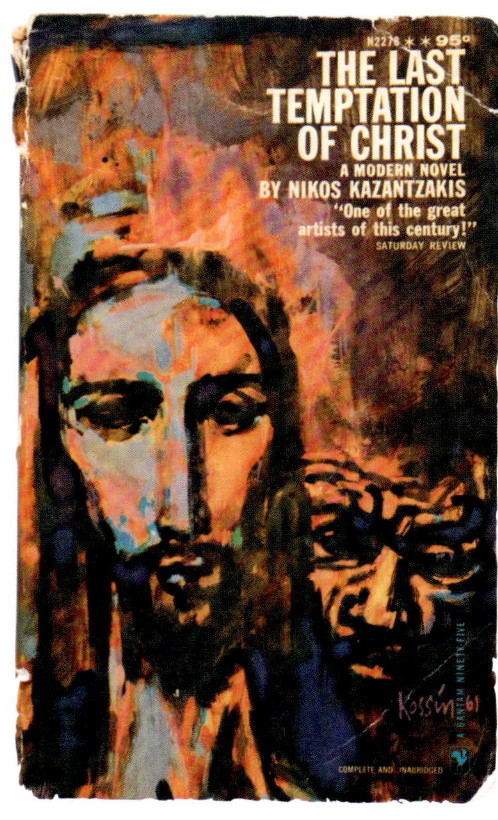

Fig. 25
Cover of Nikos Kazantzakis's *The Last Temptation of Christ* (New York: Bantam, 1961)

> A wild, indomitable joy took possession of him. No, no, he was not a coward, a deserter, a traitor. No, he was nailed to the cross. He had stood his ground honorably to the very end; he had kept his word. The moment he cried ELI ELI and fainted, Temptation had captured him for a split second and led him astray. The joys, marriages and children were lies; the decrepit, degraded old men who shouted coward, deserter, traitor at him were lies. All—all were illusions sent by the Devil. His disciples were alive and thriving. They had gone over sea and land and were proclaiming the Good News. Everything had turned out as it should, glory be to God!
>
> He uttered a triumphant cry: IT IS ACCOMPLISHED!
>
> And it was as though he had said: Everything has begun.[40]

Chimes vividly recalls reading this final passage and identifying with the figure of Christ as a man who is torn between his heroic mission in life and the beguiling allure of domestic bliss. As Darren Middleton has argued, Jesus in *The Last Temptation of Christ* is "someone who confronts life with heroic pessimism, who gives voice to the Cry bellowing within him, and who consequently saves God through his own spiritual entropy."[41]

Chimes, in turn, found inspiration in the psychological realism of Kazantzakis's fictional exploration of Jesus's messianic evolution, which reaches its climax in the hallucinatory dream sequence on the cross, in which Satan in the form of a guardian angel momentarily confuses Christ as to which world is real and which is a dream. The visionary nature of the final chapter, where Jesus succumbs for a split second to Satan's temptation to enter into an unconscious netherworld where his crucifixion never took place, appealed to Chimes, whose passion for Surrealist painting and writing had fostered in him an appreciation for dream imagery and the unconscious. The artist also connected the climax of Kazantzakis's novel with a remarkable dream that he had when he was fifteen years old: "I am walking on the street where my family was living at the time. Crossing an intersection, I suddenly hear a deafening clap of thunder. I turn and look up. In the sky, I see the head of Christ, in agony, with blood dripping from his mouth and falling on the city. I stagger back and fall against the porch railing of a row house, as if being crucified on the cross."[42] This terrifying dream reveals that Chimes had identified with the suffering figure of Christ from an early age, prefiguring his interest in Kazantzakis's conception of Jesus as a flawed human being, akin to the modern artist who suffers in order to create, rather than an omnipotent and infallible deity.

In Kazantzakis's novel, Christ's final struggle, the last temptation, takes place within a microsecond and yet appears to last for a lifetime. Thus, as Randolph Jordan has cogently suggested, "Kazantzakis's Christ illustrates a key symptom associated with schizophrenia: a breakdown in the mind's ability to manage time in a linear fashion, giving way to memory or hallucination being as central an experience as the lived present."[43] Given his earlier interest in van Gogh's emotional and physical suffering as a metaphor for the creative struggle of the "possessed" artist-seer who sacrifices everything to art, Chimes was naturally drawn to the novel's final passage, in which Christ accepts his role as humanity's savior, thus ending his long and bitter struggle on earth. The artist welcomed the radical humanity of Kazantzakis's warts-and-all portrayal of Christ as a guilt-ridden mortal, adrift in a sea of existential doubt and despair that leaves him weak and fearful, rather than omnipotent and serene. Jesus for Kazantzakis was a tormented soul who exteriorized his torment in order to communicate to others his agonizing pain and suffering.[44]

Finally, like Chimes, Kazantzakis was in continual conflict with his powerful and overbearing father, who steadfastly objected to his chosen career as a writer. The influence of this paternal conflict is found throughout *The Last Temptation of Christ*, which provides the paradigmatic exemplification of the heroic individual who overcomes patriarchal authority and finds redemption on his own terms, achieving for humanity the promised renewal after dissolution. Jesus's spiritual transformation in the novel, combined with Kazantzakis's own emancipation from familial and societal strictures, must have struck a chord with Chimes, given his personal liberation from the influence of his domineering father, who did not support his renegade son's decision to become an artist. This self-recognition, along with the notion of Christ as a man

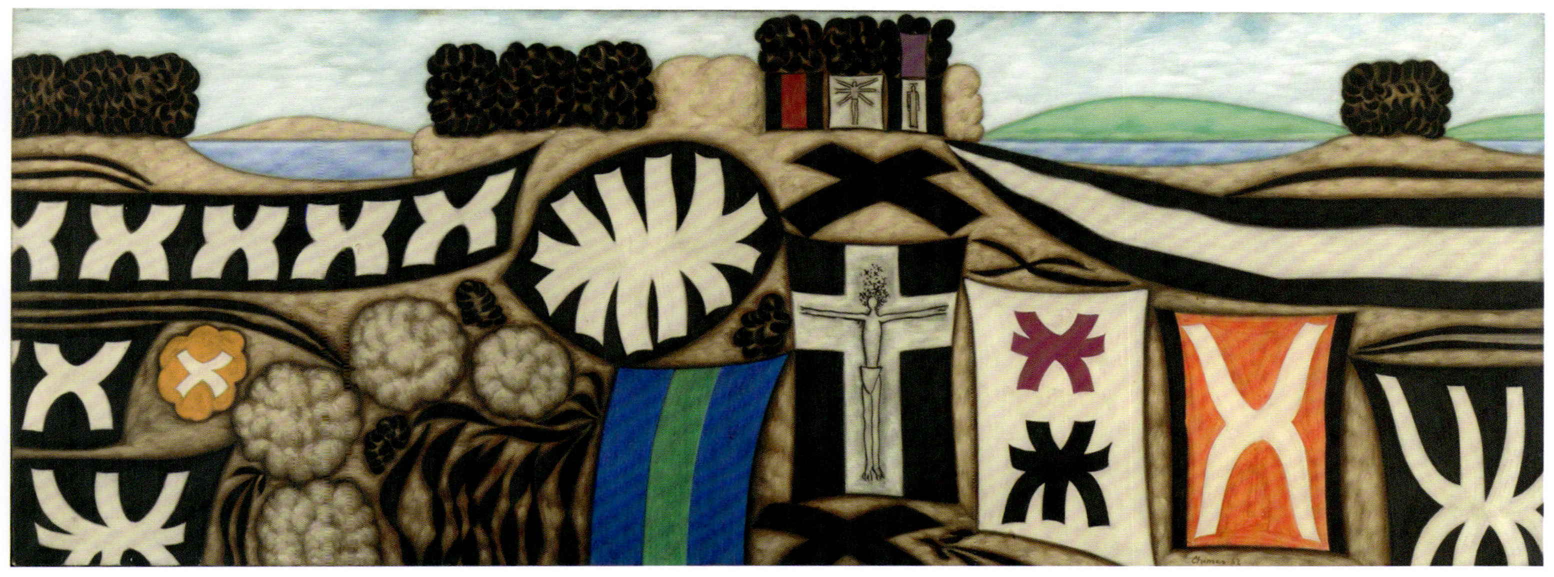

capable of succumbing to temptation, inspired Chimes to use the imagery and message of *The Last Temptation of Christ* in his subsequent paintings.

The 1962 *Philadelphia Evening Bulletin* article had mentioned an enormous blank canvas, over seven feet high and eighteen feet wide, that crowded one wall of Chimes's Middle City Building studio. The artist began making studies for this painting that year, but he would not finish work on the canvas until 1965, due to its complicated subject matter and dramatic scale, which brings to mind his earlier interest in Picasso's monumental *Guernica*. Chimes had originally titled his painting *Man in Exile in the Universe*, but later shortened it to *Man* and then finally to *Mural* to reflect its wall-size scale. The work remains by far the largest and most ambitious painting he has made.

The subject matter of *Mural* (pl. 15) reflects Chimes's continued interest in the suffering and plight of Christ as analogous with the struggle of the artist in modern society. Reading *The Last Temptation of Christ* had reinforced these ideas and provided new imagery based upon Kazantzakis's vivid description of Christ as the supreme model of a man in torment. Tempted by the devil and scorned by his people, Christ finally eschews conventional happiness and triumphs through his own free will. The original title of *Man in Exile in the Universe* correlates with Chimes's understanding of the meaning of Kazantzakis's novelistic re-creation of Jesus's life as a struggle between conventional family life and the self-sacrifice required of an artist or visionary. In the *Evening Bulletin* article, Chimes was asked how he supported his family — which by then included Dawn and their two children, eleven-year-old Dmitri and six-year-old Eva — to which he replied that he had sold several paintings to private collectors and had also managed to save some money from his teaching position at the Drexel Institute of Technology and his work making architectural models for Raoul Ibarguen.[45] However, Chimes went on to lament that if it wasn't for his family he would work much longer, thus highlighting the struggle between his love for his wife and children and his desire to spend more time in the studio.[46]

Chimes made two painted studies for *Mural* in 1962, as he worked out these ideas on canvas. In his first study for the mural (fig. 26), we see three religious figures isolated within a landscape environment that contains familiar Matisse-like symbols of flora and fauna. While two of these figures clearly denote the crucified Christ, the third has been identified by the artist as Saint

Francis of Assisi, the patron saint of animals, who is often shown surrounded by birds. This standing figure was added to the composition following an incident in which a sparrow alighted on the head of the artist's son, Dmitri, much to the young boy's delight. Chimes viewed this chance encounter with the bird, which seemed to rest on Dmitri's head for an inordinate amount of time, as if unafraid, as having deep significance for the painting he was working on. The addition of the figure of Dmitri in the guise of Saint Francis, whose famous sermon to the birds led Chimes to identify him with his son, no doubt reflects the impact of *The Last Temptation of Christ*, since the artist is clearly struggling here between family life, parenthood, and domesticity, on the one hand, and the solitude, loneliness, and freedom required of an artist on the other.

Kazantzakis's ideas are also prevalent in the second study for the mural (pl. 7), which is much closer in design to the finished mural-scale painting. The three figures are now reduced to two, with a large crucified Christ in the center of the composition and a second image of Christ on the cross floating above in a cloudlike quatrefoil. This dreamlike vision corresponds with the final section of *The Last Temptation of Christ*, in which Jesus is no longer able to distinguish between reality and dream—a state of confusion that Kazantzakis memorably describes as "the hoar frost of the mind."[47] Chimes gave this painting, which he considers one of the most successful of his early crucifixion period, to his wife shortly after it was completed. In 1963, Barr tried to purchase the work for the Museum of Modern Art, only to find out that Dawn Chimes would not part with it, arguing that she did not know when her husband would give her another painting. In the end, Barr acquired *Crucifix*, of 1961 (pl. 4), from the Bodley Gallery, and Dawn Chimes has lived with the mural study ever since.

FORGING THE LILYSTICK

In February 1963, the artist opened his second one-person show in New York, this time at the prestigious Bodley Gallery at 223 East Sixtieth Street. The Bodley Gallery was at that time the leading venue for Surrealist painting outside of Europe, where works by Max Ernst, Yves Tanguy, Joan Miró, René Magritte, Victor Brauner, and Matta were shown alongside those by younger artists such as William N. Copley and Eugenio Granell. Chimes's work had come a long way in the five years since his unsuccessful debut at the Avant-Garde Gallery, where his thickly encrusted, abstract canvases, derivative of postwar French painting, had failed to impress the critics.

Given the Bodley Gallery's reputation for promoting the work and ideas of Surrealism, it might seem a strange venue to display the artist's new crucifixion imagery. Chimes had in fact been forced to defend his work the year before, in the face of criticism from Alexander Iolas, a prominent gallery owner and dealer in Surrealist art, who had accused him of being a "subversive Catholic."[48] Iolas had visited his studio in Philadelphia in 1962, accompanied by the Greek artist Chryssa, with a view to giving him a show at his gallery in New York. A former ballet dancer and choreographer, Iolas (born Iolas Coutsoudis in Greece) was a powerful figure in the New York art world in the 1960s, whose opinion could often make or break an artist's career. Chimes was thus horrified to see Iolas's negative reaction to the plethora of Greek and Saint Andrew's crosses in his latest paintings, which the dealer argued were antithetical to the anticlerical stance of the Surrealist movement.

Chimes countered Iolas's allegation that he was a "subversive Catholic" by calmly explaining that it was Christ's suffering, which he related to the emotional struggle and loneliness of being an artist, that interested him, rather than any sentimental religious overtones. The artist also recounted how the cross motif had emerged in his work in the early 1950s, when he began to put down shapes echoing the rectangular format of his canvas. The cross shape appeared in the space between these rectangles, thus confirming that the crucifix paintings that followed had their origins in purely formal and mathematical considerations, rather than any religious impulse. The artist later downplayed the religious connotations of his paintings in a written statement sent to the Museum of Modern Art in 1963, after Barr had acquired *Crucifix*, arguing in formal terms that "the Crucifix symbol is only one symbol among many in my work. The interaction between symbols comes much closer to the intent of the painting than any single symbol. The whole painting is cruciform."[49] Iolas was so impressed by Chimes's arguments, which were clearly derived from his close reading of Kazantzakis's *Last Temptation of Christ*, that he became an important early supporter of the artist's work, and soon thereafter persuaded his former employee David Mann, now director of the Bodley Gallery, to give Chimes an exhibition. Mann, along with his business partner, Georgie Duffee, became a powerful advocate for Chimes, believing him to be one of only a handful of artists who were capable of extending the Surrealist legacy in painting.

Iolas never showed Chimes's work at his own gallery, perhaps due to his continued belief that the artist's crucifixion imagery could be construed as supporting organized religion. On one memorable occasion, in October 1962, Iolas invited Chimes to see a new painting by the French Nouveau Réaliste artist Niki de Sainte Phalle at his gallery. According to Chimes, the thickly painted, five-foot-tall canvas depicted the façade of a cathedral, reminiscent of Claude Monet's paintings of Rouen cathedral under changing light conditions. However, the towering cathedral had been crossed out by the artist with two diagonal red lines, smeared into the paint to form an "X," in a manner that an overjoyed Iolas proclaimed to be "utterly blasphemous."[50] Chimes believed that Iolas had shown him Sainte Phalle's painting as a way of letting him know that if he ever wanted to show with his gallery, his work would need to incorporate a similarly unambiguous condemnation of religion.

Chimes's interest in crucifixion imagery was unusual but not unique in avant-garde painting in the 1960s. Robert Smithson, whose openness to mystical and transcendental ideas shares much common ground with Chimes, was making turbulent, expressionistic paintings on religious themes early in the decade. Smithson's paintings and poetry of the time reflect a similar desire to explore forbidden areas of reference, as in *Creeping Jesus*, of 1961 (fig. 27), which reconfigures the standard iconography of Christ on the cross by permeating the scene with collaged elements of consumer products drawn from a magazine advertisement.[51] Another important, though often overlooked, figure during this time was the Scottish painter Alan Davie, who used a visual language, derived from Pollock's totemic forms, in which archetypal imagery merges with calligraphic and gestural mark-making. Davie's paintings, which Smithson acknowledged as an important precursor to his own religious works, were frequently exhibited in New York during this period, including solo exhibitions at the Catherine Viviano Gallery in 1957 and the Martha Jackson Gallery in 1961. In works such as *Entrance for a Red Temple No. 1*, of 1960 (fig. 28), Davie uses totemic imagery, rendered with characteristically unbridled brushwork, to

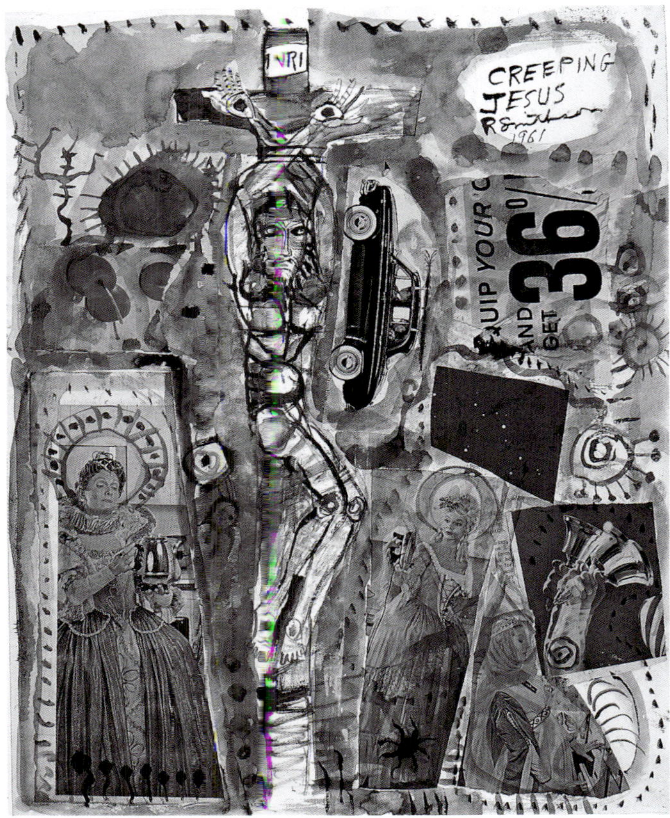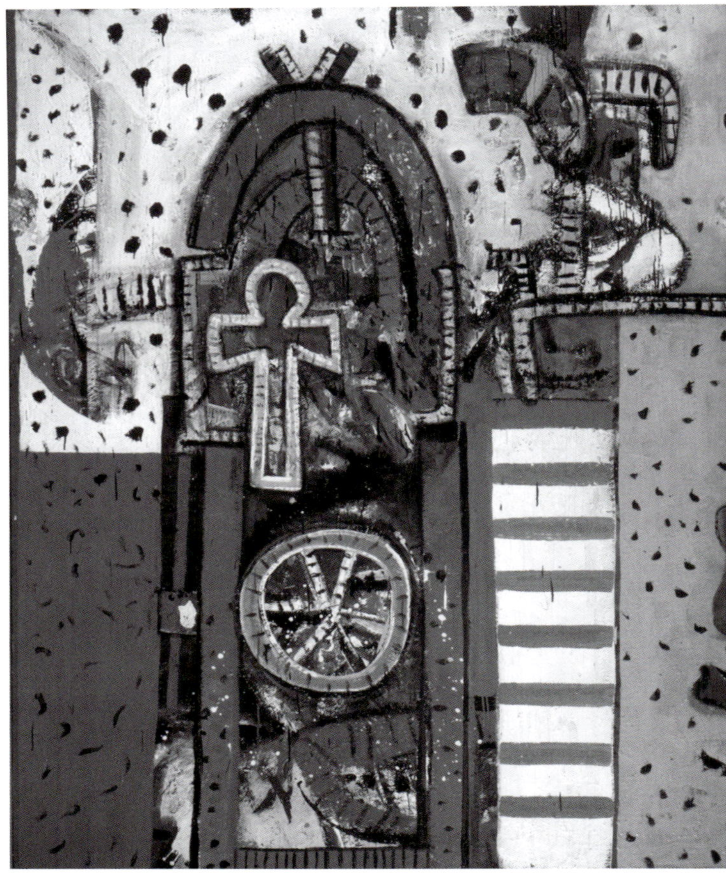

Fig. 27
Robert Smithson
(American, 1938–1973),
Untitled (Creeping Jesus), 1961. Oil on
paper, 14 x 12 inches
(35.6 x 30.5 cm). Private
collection, courtesy of
the James Cohan
Gallery, New York

Fig. 28
Alan Davie (Scottish,
born 1920), *Entrance for
a Red Temple No. 1*,
1960. Oil on canvas,
84 x 68 inches (213.4 x
172.7 cm). Tate Modern,
London

explore mythological and religious archetypes, especially those related to Zen Buddhism and other non-Western belief systems.[52] Although Chimes may not have been aware of their work at the time, his crucifixion paintings share Davie's and Smithson's overriding interest in mysticism, conveyed through symbolic imagery and highly energized color, as a way out of the formalist cul-de-sac of Abstract Expressionism.

Many of the works on view in Chimes's 1963 Bodley Gallery exhibition referenced his Greek origins, such as the print he made for the opening invitation poster, in which a centaur and a sphinx flank the central image of a crucifix (fig. 29). Chimes made the print at the Falcon Press in Philadelphia in January 1963, with the aid of their master printmaker, Eugene Feldman, who worked from the artist's pen-and-ink drawing. Although Feldman disliked Chimes's mythological imagery, he enjoyed the challenge of reproducing the artist's large expanses of deep, unrelieved blacks, which he was able to achieve only after running the sheet through the press three times.[53] The poster also featured a beautiful, hand-lettered poem by Chimes, written in a style vaguely reminiscent of Edgar Allan Poe, whose poetry had obsessed him since high school. These verses represent a fragment of a much longer poem that Chimes wrote in the early 1960s, which provided the titles for several of his early paintings, including *Bread* and the subsequently destroyed *Inner World* (fig. 30): "Here is the bread of my inner world, / the hunger, the lust / caught between my eyes. / Eat, love, eat / while I choke on my tears / and my body becomes / a blackened olive tree."[54] The bleak imagery of this poem speaks to the artist's morbid state of mind and sheds new light on the tortured visions of his contemporaneous paintings, where the crucified Christ takes the form of the impaled artist as revealed to him in his boyhood dream.

The artist's close friend Michael Lekakis was a published poet who also drew upon his

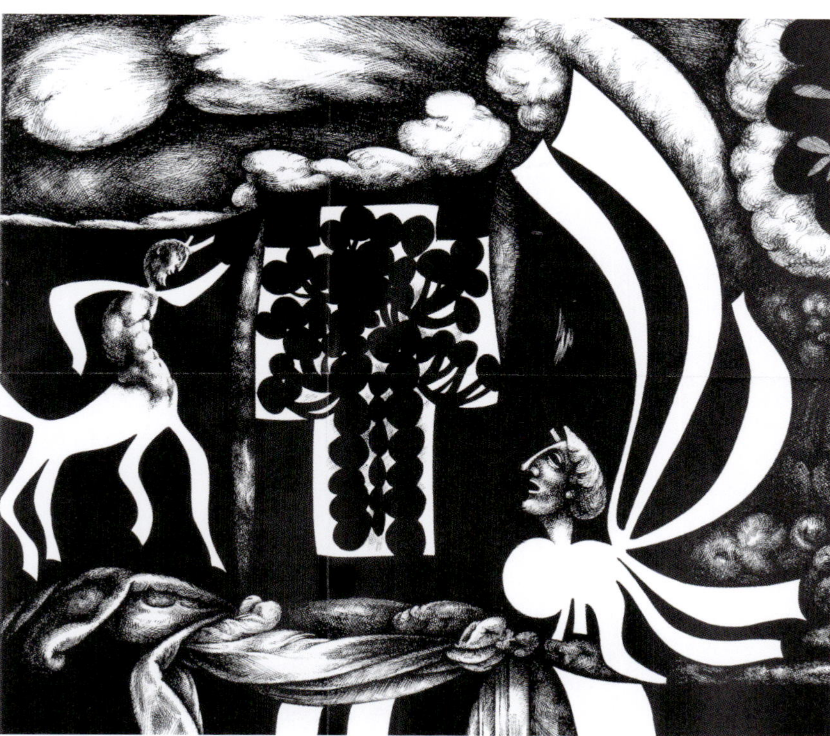

Fig. 29
Thomas Chimes, *Bodley Gallery Opening Invitation*, 1963. Lithograph after a pen-and-ink drawing, 15¹⁵⁄₁₆ x 24½ inches (40.5 x 62.2 cm). Made in conjunction with Falcon Press, Philadelphia. Collection of Dawn Chimes, Venice, Florida

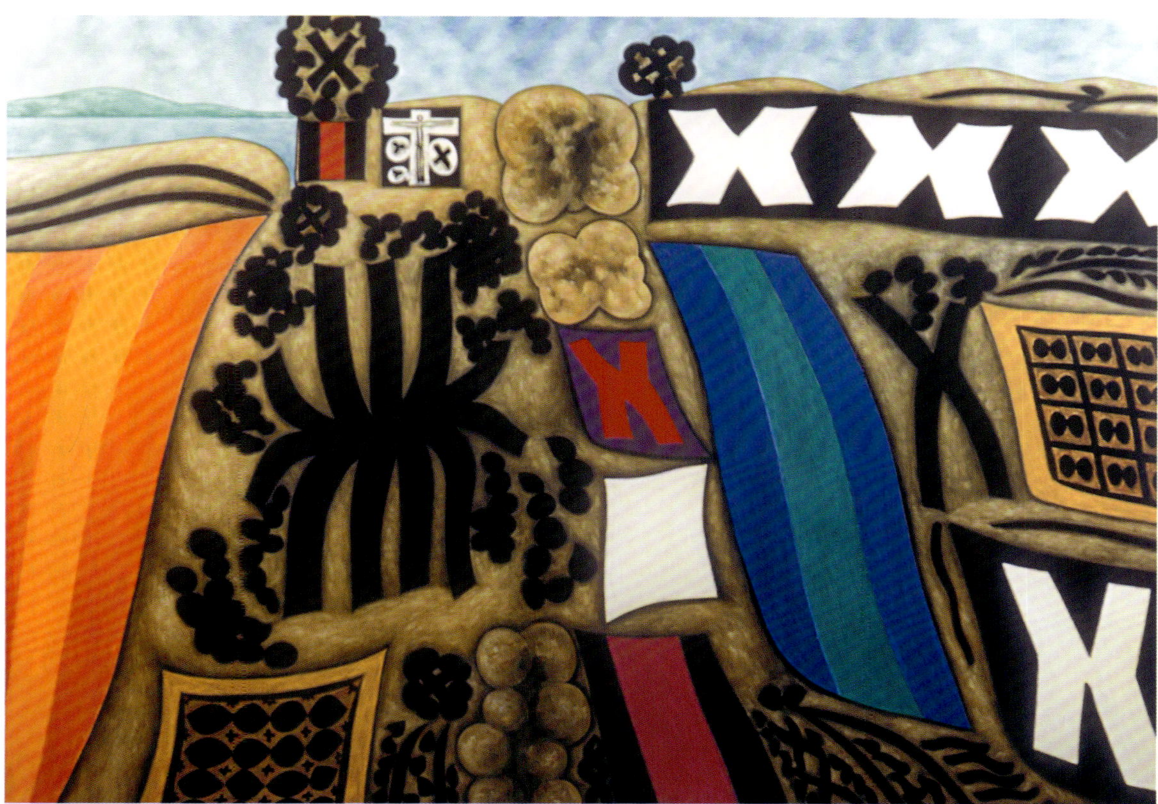

Fig. 30
Thomas Chimes, *The Inner World*, 1961. Oil on canvas. Destroyed. Photograph courtesy of the artist

Greek heritage in poems such as "The Sphinx Garden" of 1947, whose symbolism of "ancient flowers" blooming in a perfumed garden strongly resonates with Chimes's poetry of the early 1960s.[55] Lekakis knew many modern poets, including William Carlos Williams, e.e. cummings, and Ezra Pound, and no doubt encouraged Chimes to use poetry as a means of exploring mythological and archetypal imagery that could subsequently be explored in his paintings, and vice versa, thus producing an endless interweaving of visual and verbal meaning that deeply enriched his work. The two men even visited Pound and his wife, Dorothy, in the mid-1950s, a meeting that took place on the grounds of the notorious St. Elizabeth's Hospital in Washington, DC, an institution that housed hundreds of criminally insane patients, as well as the aged poet, who was incarcerated there as a political prisoner charged with treason for the pro-fascist statements he made during World War II. Lekakis recited Homer in Greek, before reading his own poems in English, which Pound declared to be the best he had heard or read by an artist since coming across Henri Gaudier-Brzeska's poetry in the 1910s. Chimes, however, was disturbed by the mental state of the poet, whose nervous twitches and agitated demeanor were clearly exacerbated by the hospital's appalling, bedlamlike living conditions.

The melancholic symbolism of Chimes's poem for the invitation poster, in which "lilysticks" are forged from the purest gold and lilacs are beaten to the ground, can be related to the palette and imagery of many of the paintings on view in the exhibition, as well as the centaur and sphinx on the poster itself, whose faces resemble the tragicomic masks of ancient Greek theater. References to Greek mythology abound in the artist's *oeuvre*, such as the Pegasus figure, whose calligraphic wings evoke the variegated, flamelike forms of Matisse's cut-and-pasted gouaches. Chimes has even coined the phrase "the Classical imperative" to describe his lifelong attraction to the Greco-Roman tradition, which links his work to that of contemporaries like Cy Twombly, who recasts works of classical literature, such as Homer's *The Iliad*, through a sensual visual language full of scrawling marks, clumps of paint straight from the tube, drips, erasures, and legible numbers and letters (fig. 31).

The Bodley Gallery exhibition resulted in a number of sales to prominent collectors, including Larry Aldrich, Walter Bareiss, G. David Thompson, and Muriel Bultman Francis. However, the most important sale was Barr's acquisition of *Crucifix* for the Museum of Modern Art, which represented the third work by Chimes that Barr had brought into the collection, following the purchase of *Study for "The Inner World"* in 1961 and a related drawing in pen, brush, and ink that he donated in 1962 (pl. 5). Chimes had given Barr the drawing, which directly relates to the composition of *Study for "The Inner World,"* in February 1962, in gratitude for the acquisition of this painting. In a letter dated May 9, 1962, Barr thanked Chimes for "the very

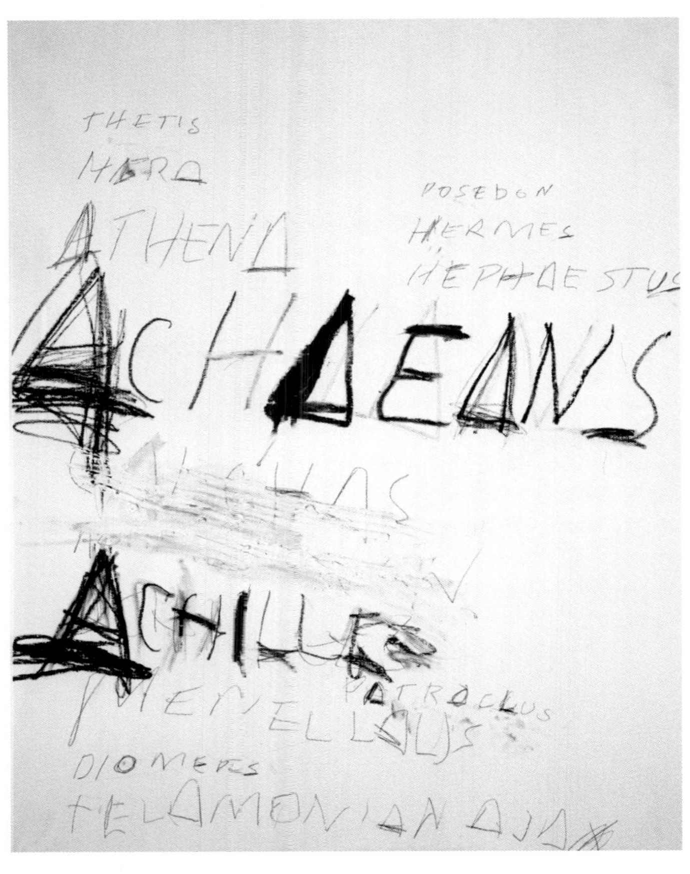

Fig. 31
Cy Twombly (American, born 1928), *Fifty Days at Iliam: Heroes of the Achaeans*, 1978. Second of ten parts. Oil, oil crayon, and graphite on canvas; 75½ x 59 inches (191.8 x 149.9 cm). Philadelphia Museum of Art. Gift (by exchange) of Samuel S. White 3rd and Vera White, 1989-90-2

handsome drawing which you gave me" before asking his permission to offer it to the museum, which Chimes duly approved.[56] Barr was no doubt drawn to Chimes's work due to its overt references to Matisse's Vence chapel, which he had discussed at length in his 1952 monograph on the French artist. With the possible exception of Robert Motherwell in paintings such as *Mural Fragment,* of 1950 (fig. 32), Chimes was the only American artist to respond in a profound way to the spatial implications, luminous color, and symbolism of Matisse's late work. The two studies for *Mural* share with Motherwell's painting an attempt to energize the canvas through a large, colorful, episodic composition, which gives the impression that a number of separate paintings have been cut up and sewn together to form an endless frieze. Barr must have appreciated these qualities in Chimes's work, which, like Motherwell's paintings of the previous decade, can be seen as a poetic reiteration of the French artist's form and content.

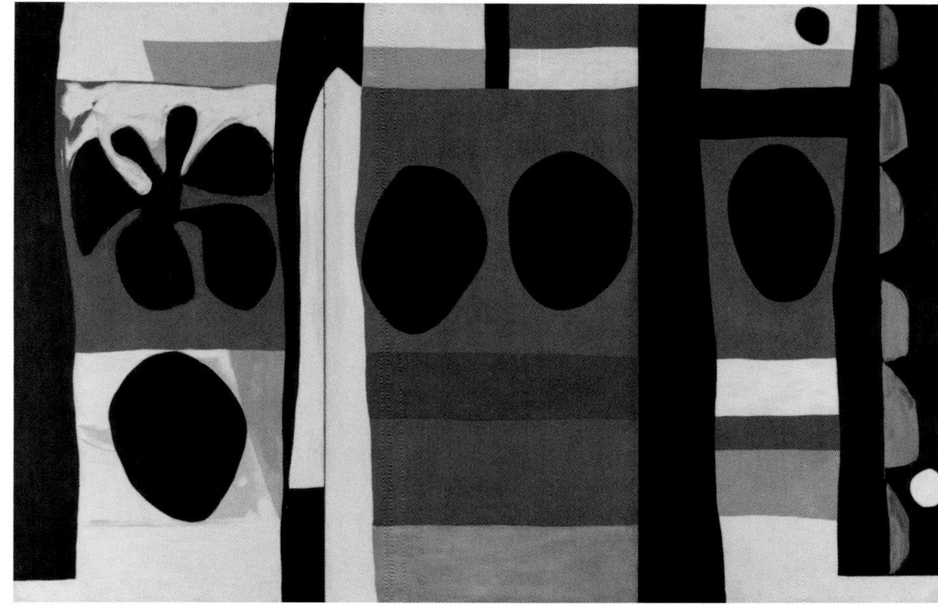

Fig. 32
Robert Motherwell
(American, 1915–1991),
Mural Fragment, 1950.
Oil on composition
board, 96 x 144 inches
(243.8 x 365.8 cm).
Frederick R. Weisman
Art Museum at the
University of Minnesota,
Minneapolis. Gift of
Katherine Ordway

The success of the 1963 exhibition resulted in a second one-person show at the Bodley Gallery's new headquarters at 787 Madison Avenue in January 1965, for which the artist produced an enormous body of work. During the interim, the Matisse-inspired crucifixions had given way to a new series of paintings featuring highly abstracted symbols mixed with recognizable imagery, such as letters, dice, mathematical equations, and X-rays. In *Crucifix* 3 (pl. 13), for example, the cartoonlike figure of Christ on the cross has a balloon-shaped head containing a geometrical configuration, while his torso resembles an open flower, and his arms and legs are reduced to linear X-rays revealing the underlying bone structure. In works such as this one, the artist did not want to know what all the symbols meant, preferring his work to remain mysterious, even to himself.

Elsewhere in his works of this period, such as *Untitled* (pl. 17) and *Shells for Breakfast* (fig. 33), both painted in 1964, Chimes turned his attention to Max Ernst's highly decorative paintings in the late 1920s of sea anemones, snow flowers, and shells, including *Seashell,* of 1928 (fig. 34). Ernst's dense, scumbled surfaces inspired Chimes to create his own works featuring undulating, fanlike passages of paint put on with a palette knife or with individual brushstrokes that have a staccato rhythm to their application. The artist had been exposed to the technical innovations of Ernst's work, from collage and frottage to grattage and decalcomania, when he and Ernst were shown together in a group exhibition at the Bodley Gallery in January 1964, entitled *Six Surrealist Painters,* which also included works by Matta, Magritte, Brauner, and Granell. The heavily textured, abstract imagery, redolent of seashells, signaled Chimes's move away from the crucifixion iconography that had dominated his *oeuvre* since the late 1950s

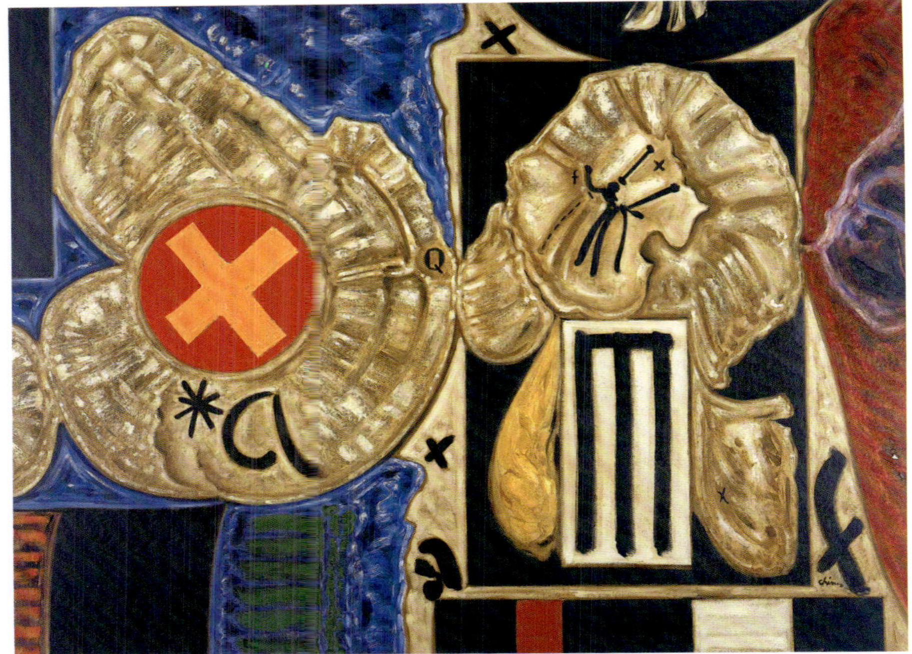

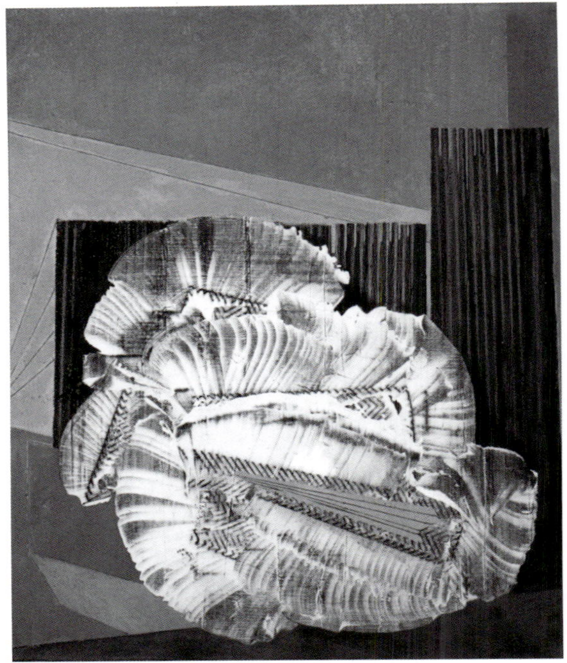

Fig. 33
Thomas Chimes, *Shells for Breakfast*, 1964. Oil on canvas, 36 x 48 inches (91.4 x 121.9 cm). Private collection, courtesy of Locks Gallery, Philadelphia

Fig. 34
Max Ernst (American, born Germany, 1891–1976), *Seashell*, 1928. Oil on canvas, 25½ x 21¼ inches (64.8 x 54 cm). Philadelphia Museum of Art. The Louise and Walter Arensberg Collection, 1950-134-86

toward greater experimentation and risk, inspired by the radical examples of Ernst and, slightly later, Artaud.

In a review of Chimes's 1965 Bodley Gallery exhibition, Charlotte Lichtblau, art critic for the *Philadelphia Inquirer*, claimed that with these breakthrough paintings Chimes

> may well emerge as one of the major new talents of contemporary painting. His luminous symbolic abstractions, both visually gratifying and meaningful, have already found favor with some top collectors and museums, but the unusual quality of his work will probably bring even greater acclaim and success. The 43-year-old artist has evolved an imagery, unquestionably his own, which incorporates highly abstracted symbols of his Greek background as well as some pictorial concepts of Miró and Matisse. His works might make splendid stained glass designs, tapestries or murals for public buildings, but are equally arresting as paintings.[57]

Lichtblau's enthusiastic response confirmed the general consensus among artists and critics that Chimes had arrived as an artist of merit. Having mined a rich vein of personal iconography that was now unquestionably his, the artist had answered the earlier criticism of Dore Ashton and come into his own.

THE RINGLING MURAL

The series of crucifixion paintings would culminate in the monumental *Mural* (pl. 15), measuring almost eighteen feet wide and seven feet tall, that the artist completed between 1963 and 1965. However, the glowing colors surpass in intensity the saturated Matisse-like reds, greens, and blacks seen in the first Bodley Gallery show in 1963, reflecting the impact of the younger generation of artists associated with Pop and Op Art, such as Victor Vasarely, Andy Warhol, and Robert Indiana, whose work Chimes had encountered during the intervening period. The artist was, for example, greatly impressed by *The Responsive Eye*, an exhibition of Op Art that opened

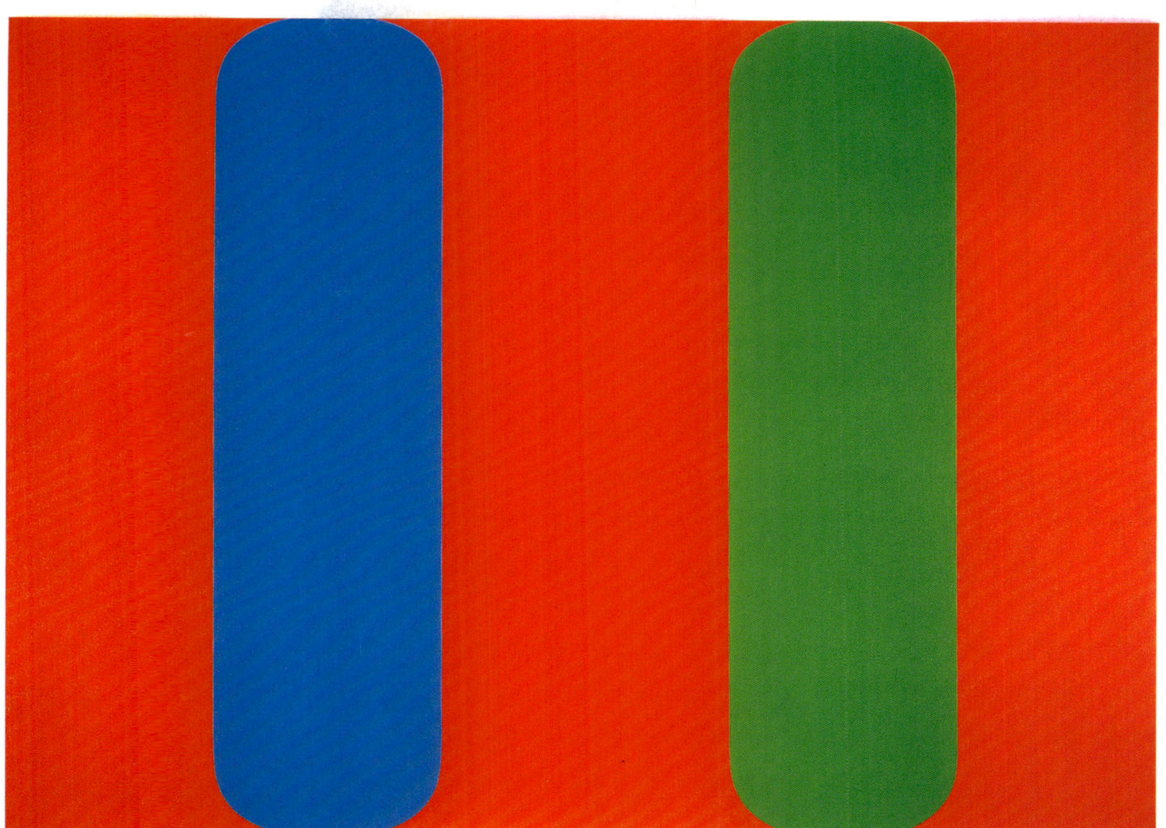

at the Museum of Modern Art in February 1965, and the striking combinations of complimentary colors used by Ellsworth Kelly in a large painting in that show (fig. 35) can be felt in Chimes's own color choices in *Mural*, which also utilize strong color contrasts such as green and red. The psychedelic, Day-Glo colors, deployed in a way that gives the sensation of advancement or recession, have a hypnotic, vibratory effect in the painting, where flat, hieratic shapes appear to pulsate in an orgy of riotous color.

The deep perspective and ordered landscape of blue water and green hills in the two painted studies for *Mural* were eliminated as the painting evolved into a flat, wall-like expanse of interlocking shapes redolent of lush vegetation. In 1968, Alfred Scheinberg praised the painting's panoramic sequence of almost pure abstractions, in which "Chimes's vision assumes a comprehensiveness and emotive strength unparalleled by any of his earlier works."[58] The organic imagery of curvilinear forms, again borrowed from Matisse's repertory of stylized crosses, open leaf forms, palm-cum-flame images, small spiky stars, and X-shaped sprays of leaves, surround the central figure of the crucified Christ. No longer the suffering messiah-artist inspired by Kazantzakis's *The Last Temptation of Christ*, this Christ on the Cross has been abstracted to the point where the figure resembles a watering can or gasoline pump, which probably explains why the artist dropped the original title *Man Alone in the Universe*. As Chimes later explained, "The gesture of the crucifixion was there, but the form of the figure was radically changed. I felt something was emerging, something was coming from beneath, below, reaching up, something almost ominous and that feeling was caught by the canvas for me."[59]

In May 1968, the John and Mable Ringling Museum of Art in Sarasota, Florida, acquired *Mural*, and later that year the same venue presented the artist's first retrospective exhibition. Selected by Chimes's friend James Harithas, then director of the Corcoran Gallery of Art in

Washington, DC, this mid-career survey consisted of seventy-two paintings and eight mixed-media metal box constructions. Karl Nickel, the assistant curator who acquired the mural and also co-organized the retrospective, praised the immense painting, which he argued was "a symbolic picture with the forms suggesting a number of things such as blossoms, leaves and the general texture of vegetation. It has the lushness of color of a flower garden and, in passages, seems almost harsh and violent in its sharp, abrasive forms. The painting makes an enormously powerful emotional impact, growing out of its purely formal qualities while at the same time hinting at a cryptic meaning for the symbols it employs."[60]

As Chimes explained in a newspaper interview conducted in 1968, shortly after the Ringling Museum purchased *Mural*, the symbols in his work had gone through several mutations in keeping with his definition of the creative act, which states that "the artist's subconscious is the reservoir of all his experiences whether or not the experiences are consciously felt. The creative process involves dipping into this reservoir, filtering and adjusting what is found there to be useful as the artist transfers it into a visual art."[61] As a direct consequence of retrieving images from his subconscious, the crucifix symbol "can take on decidedly unconventional forms, as Chimes seeks to take the religious measure of himself (and mankind)."[62] This interest in the subconscious reflects his growing awareness of the legacy of Surrealism in painting—probably as a result of his involvement with the Bodley Gallery—which effectively ended his interest in the crucifixion motif after the completion of the Ringling *Mural*.

A key turning point in Chimes's career was his inclusion in the *Twelfth Exhibition of Contemporary American Painting and Sculpture* at the Krannert Art Museum at the University of Illinois at Urbana-Champaign, from March 7 through April 11, 1965. Chimes was represented by *Baroque* of 1963–64 (pl. 16), arguably his strongest painting from the second Bodley Gallery exhibition. This work takes its title from the complexity of the composition and its palette of vivid colors, which glow like crushed jewels. The exhibition placed Chimes's work within the context of other recent developments in American painting, such as Pop and Op Art, as represented in works by Roy Lichtenstein, Wayne Thiebaud, Tony DeLap, Robert Indiana, and Leroy Lamis. Although Chimes was already cognizant of Lichtenstein and Thiebaud, whose work he had seen in New York galleries, the box constructions in Plexiglas, wood, and steel by artists such as DeLap and Lamis that were included in the Krannert exhibition do appear to have had a lasting impact on his subsequent work, and especially on the metal boxes that he began making later that year. DeLap's statement in the exhibi-

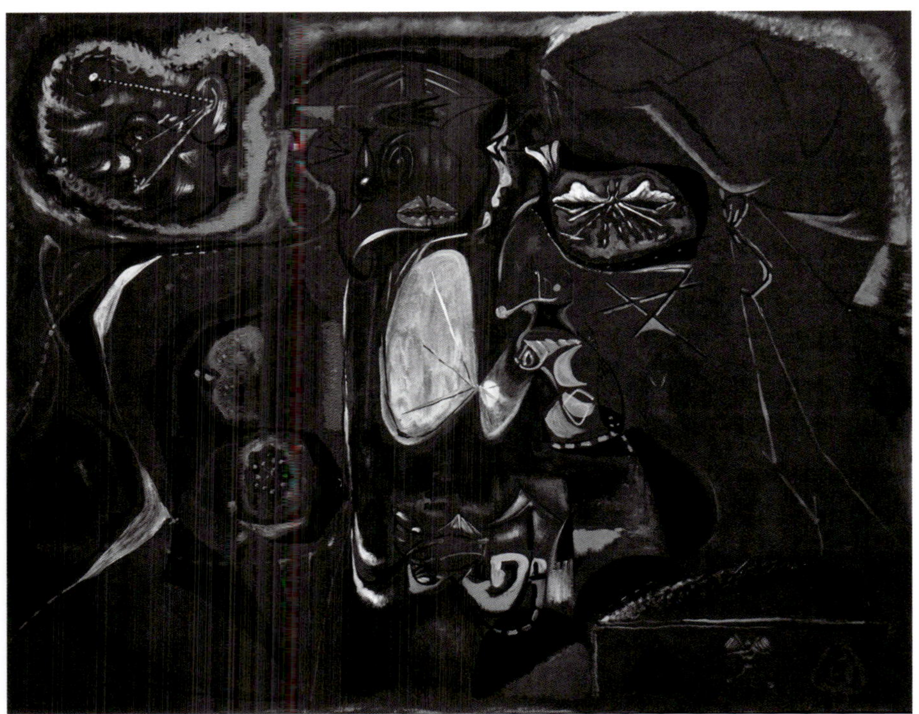

tion catalogue, in which he compared his work with "sputniks, computers, and Maseratis," would resonate with Chimes's desire, later that year, to engage with the tools and industrial materials of his own time.[63]

Another important event in the artist's career was his inclusion in the 1966 group exhibition *Surrealism: A State of Mind* at the Art Gallery of the University of California at Santa Barbara. Selected and organized by Ala Story in conjunction with Julien Levy, the legendary dealer in Surrealist art, who wrote the catalogue essay, this exhibition sought to redefine Surrealist painting and sculpture in the era of Pop Art and "Happenings." Significantly, younger American artists like Chimes, Granell, Barbara Rice Poe, and William N. Copley were singled out—through their inclusion alongside older, established artists of the Surrealist movement, such as Brauner, Ernst, Magritte, André Masson, Matta, Miró, and Tanguy—as continuing the "mythic progress" begun by their famous forebears. According to Levy, "Exploring the unconscious, not for the ill, but for the better, has only just begun, and may continue so long as man has even one dream left with which he may feed his computer."[64] Chimes was again represented by *Baroque*, and it is fascinating to compare its variegated surface and compartmentalized composition with the works by Copley, Granell, and especially with Masson's *Leonardo da Vinci and Isabela d'Este*, of 1942 (fig. 36), which were all on view in the Santa Barbara exhibition. By the time of this 1966 Surrealism show, however, Chimes had moved away from the thinly disguised crucifixion imagery of *Baroque* toward new avenues of expression in which oil painting was temporarily replaced by metal box constructions.

In *Hieropornophany*, made around 1965 (pl. 18), Chimes impulsively glued a piece of aluminum on an earlier crucifixion painting featuring a flying mythological creature. This idea of using a collage piece of aluminum as a color encouraged the artist to transform the painting completely by housing it in an elaborate frame made from riveted plates of aluminum, thus anticipating the metal boxes that immediately followed. Simultaneously, the artist had become fascinated by the tumultuous writings and drawings of Antonin Artaud, whose impact would also be felt in subsequent drawings and aluminum box constructions.

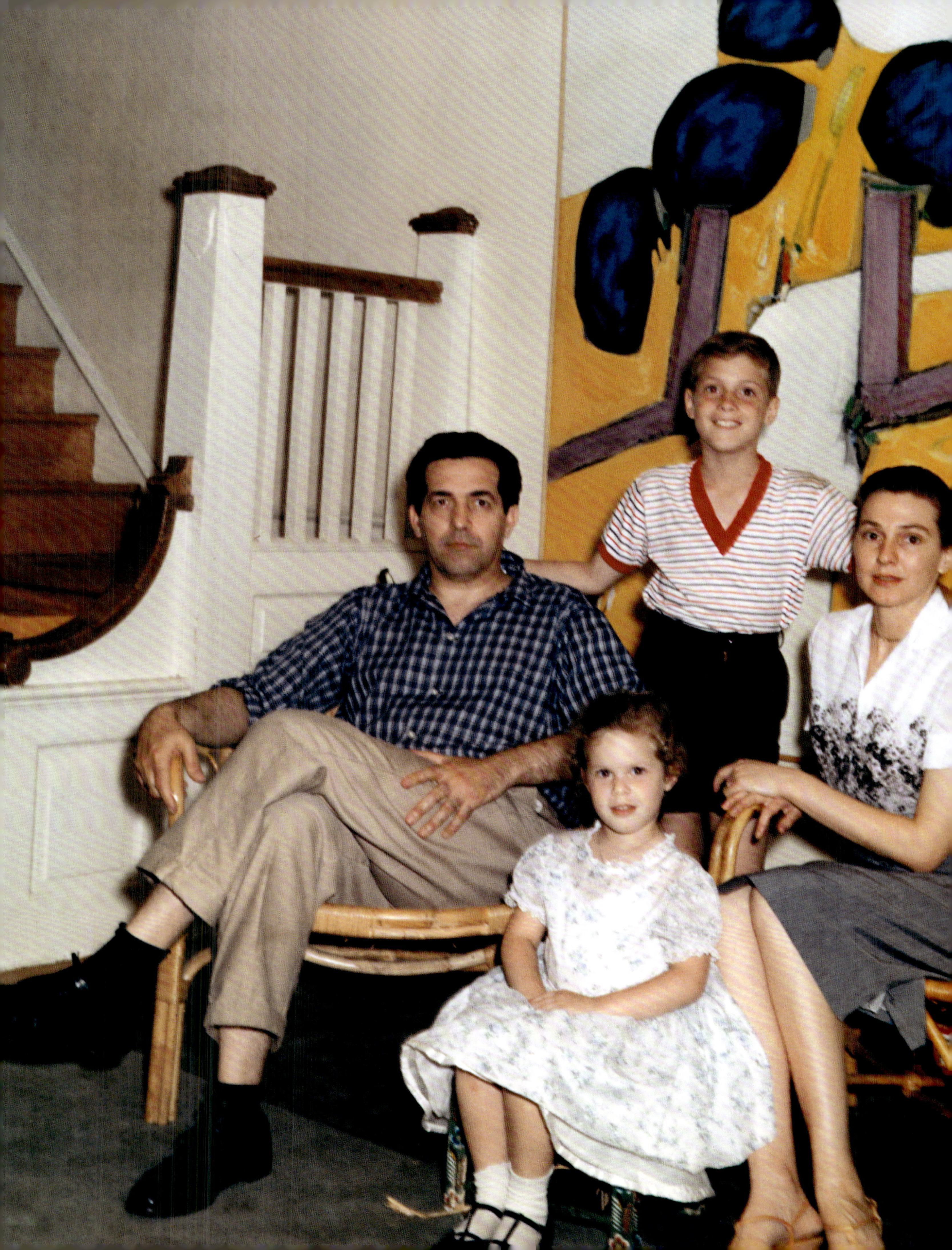

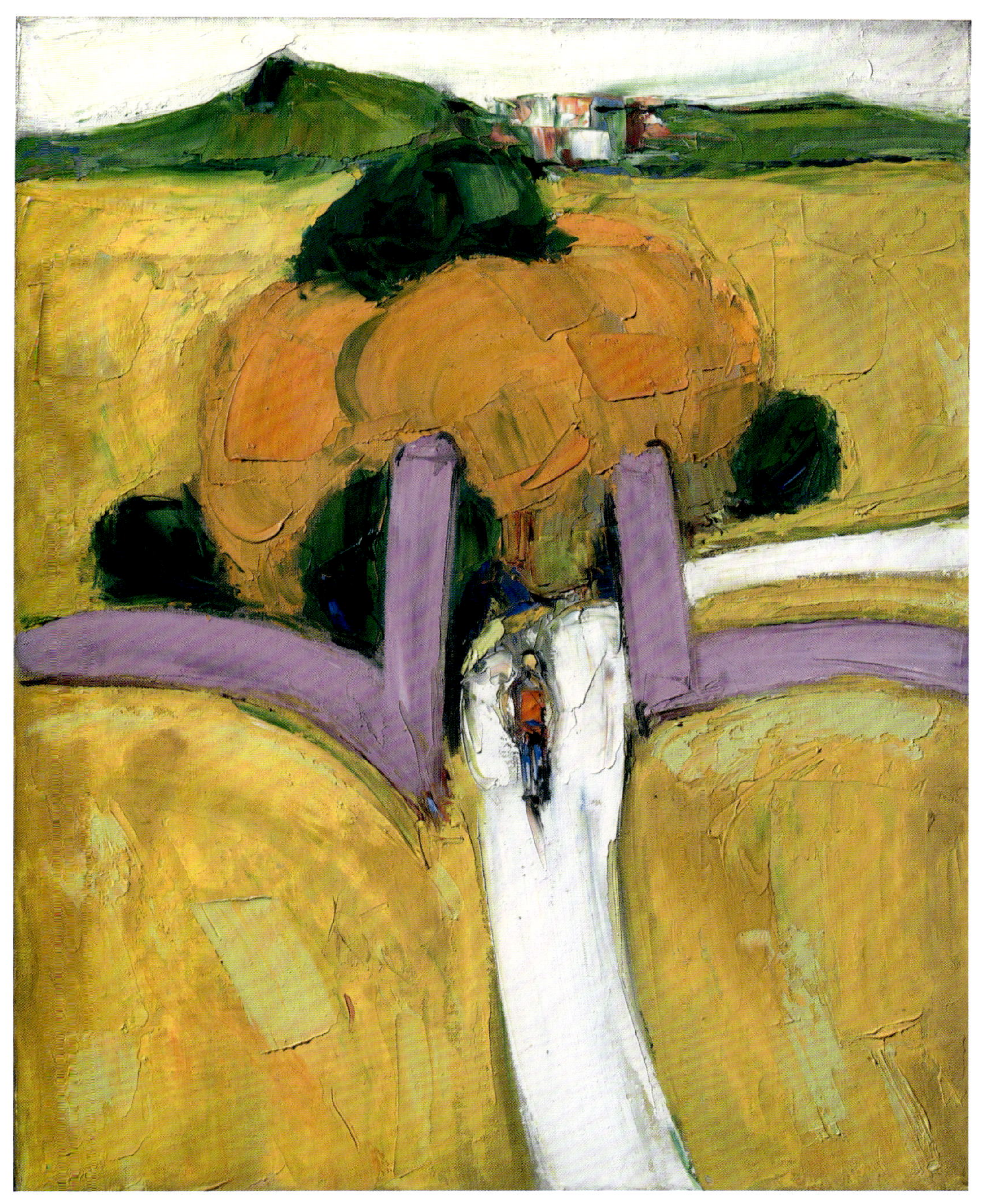

PLATE 1

Van Gogh's Landscape, 1958

OIL ON CANVAS

20⅛ x 16 INCHES (51.1 x 40.6 CM)

PRIVATE COLLECTION

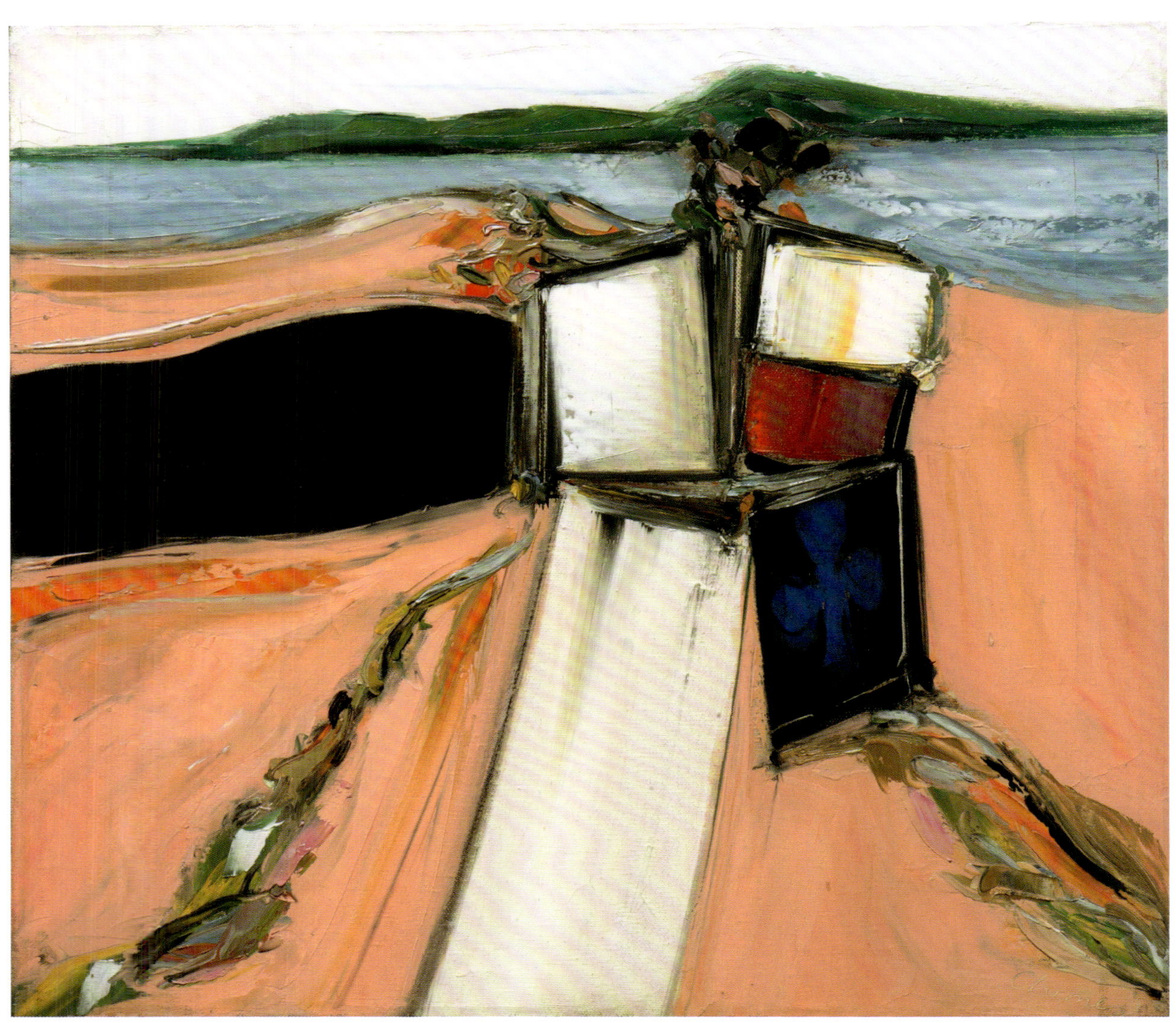

PLATE 2

Untitled, 1959

OIL ON CANVAS

16 X 18 INCHES (40.6 X 45.7 CM)

COURTESY OF LOCKS GALLERY, PHILADELPHIA

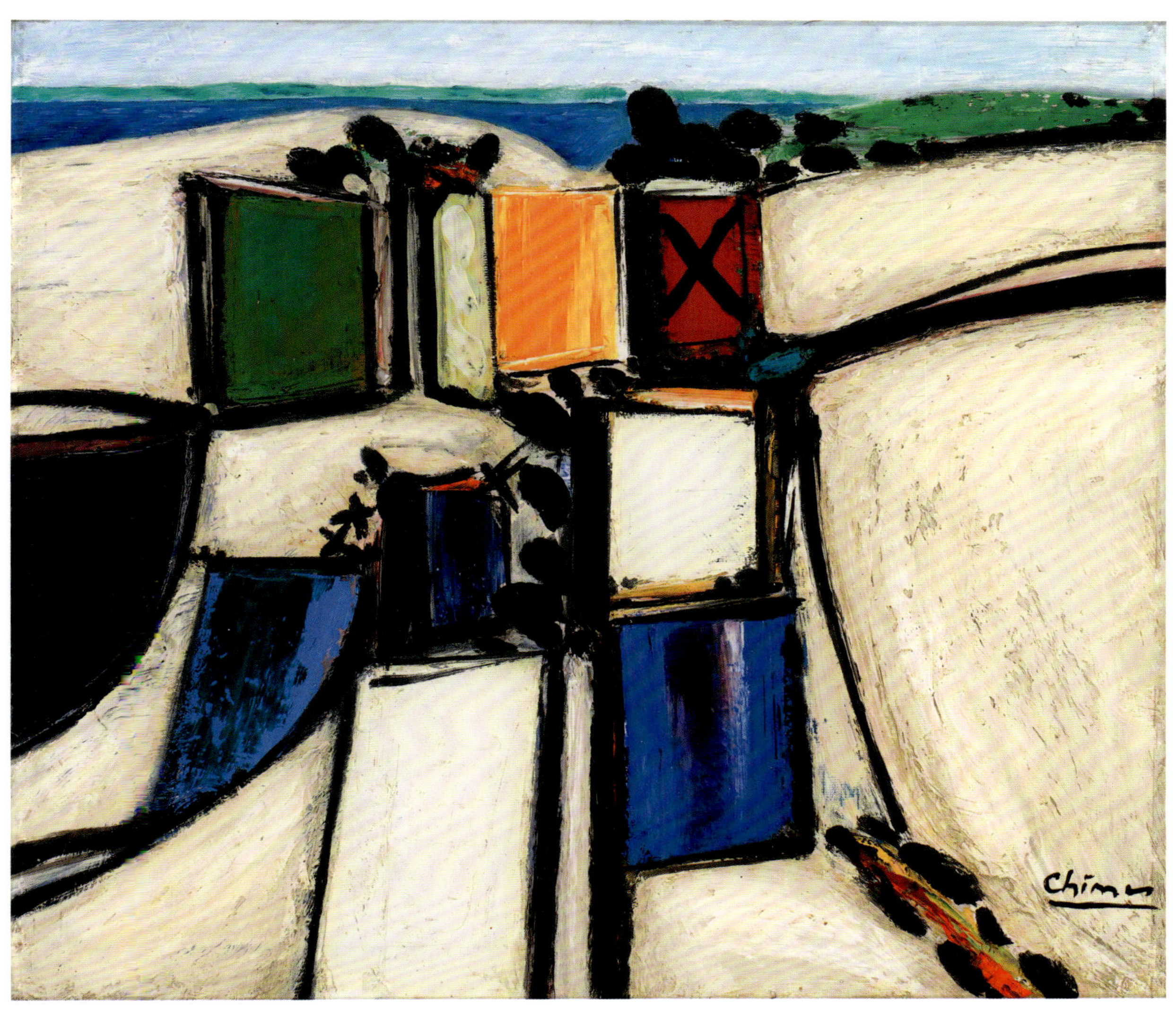

PLATE 3

Untitled, 1962

OIL ON CANVAS

14 X 16 INCHES (35.6 X 40.6 CM)

SMITHSONIAN AMERICAN ART MUSEUM, WASHINGTON, DC. GIFT OF THE WOODWARD FOUNDATION, 1976.108.27

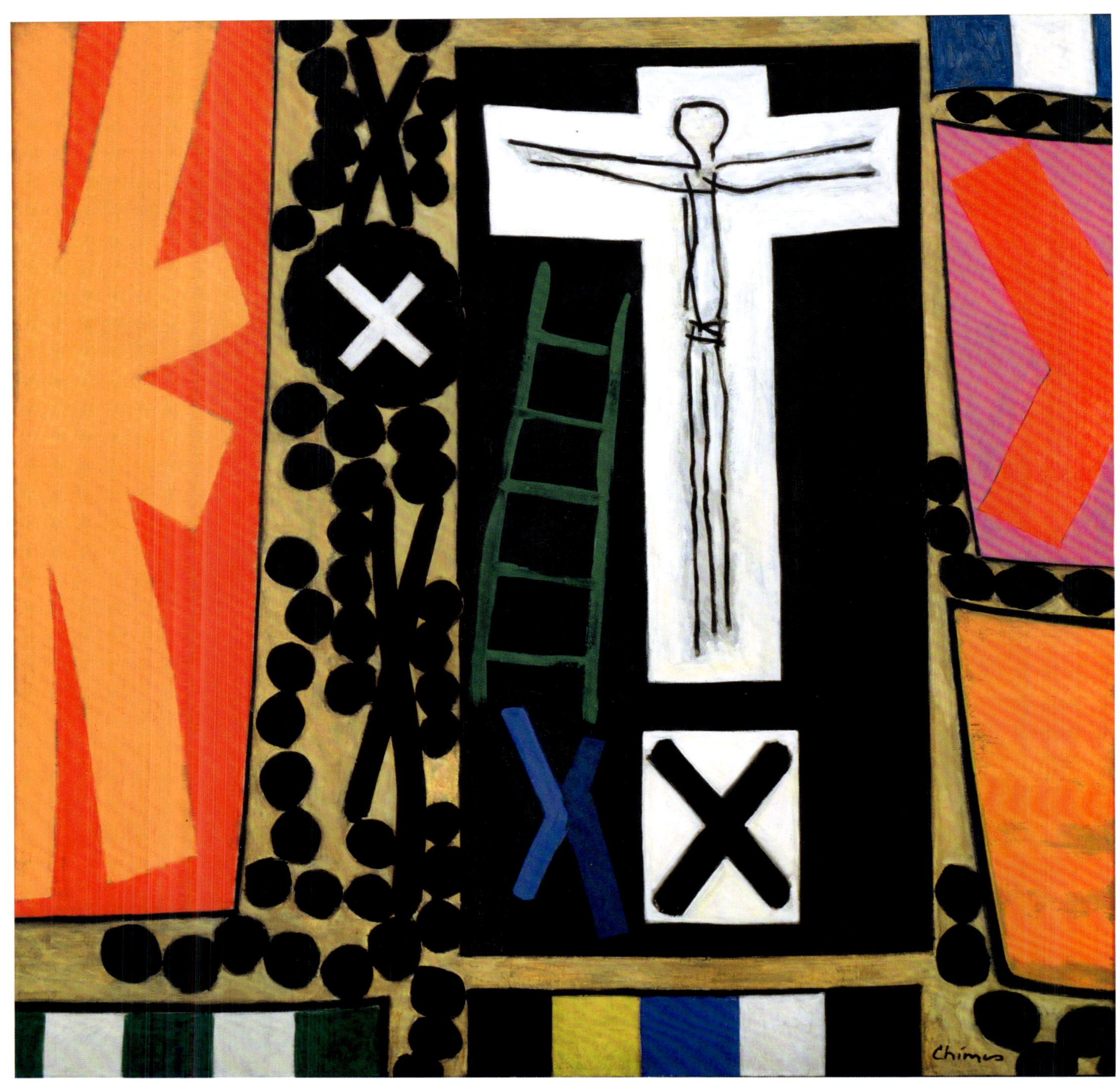

PLATE 4

Crucifix, 1961

OIL ON CANVAS

36 x 36 INCHES (91.4 x 91.4 CM)

THE MUSEUM OF MODERN ART, NEW YORK. LARRY ALDRICH FOUNDATION FUND, 198.1963

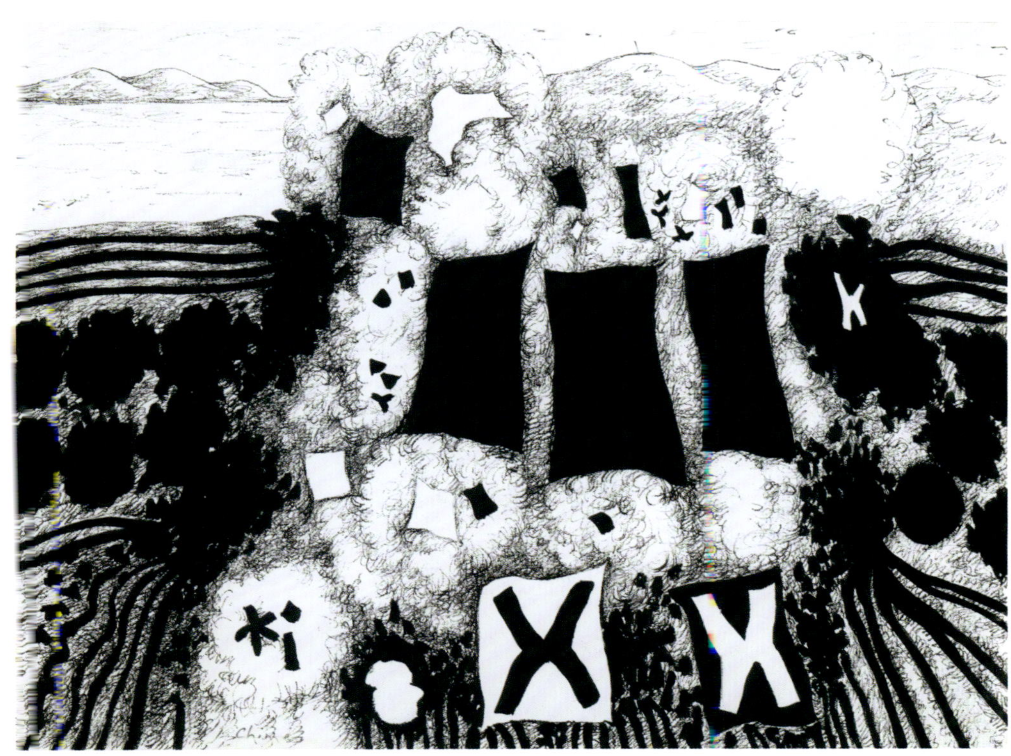

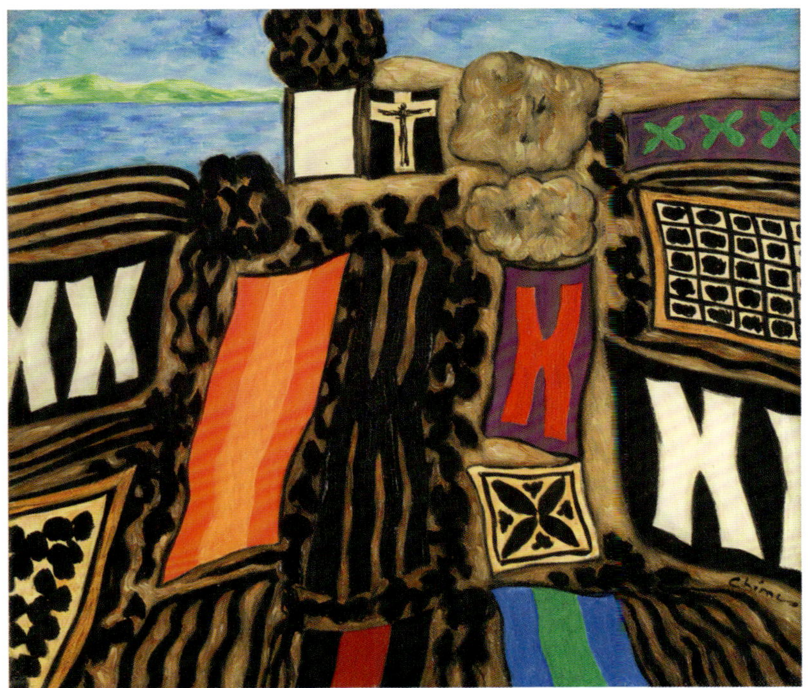

PLATE 5

Untitled (Study for "The Inner World"), 1961

PLATE 6

Study for "The Inner World," 1961

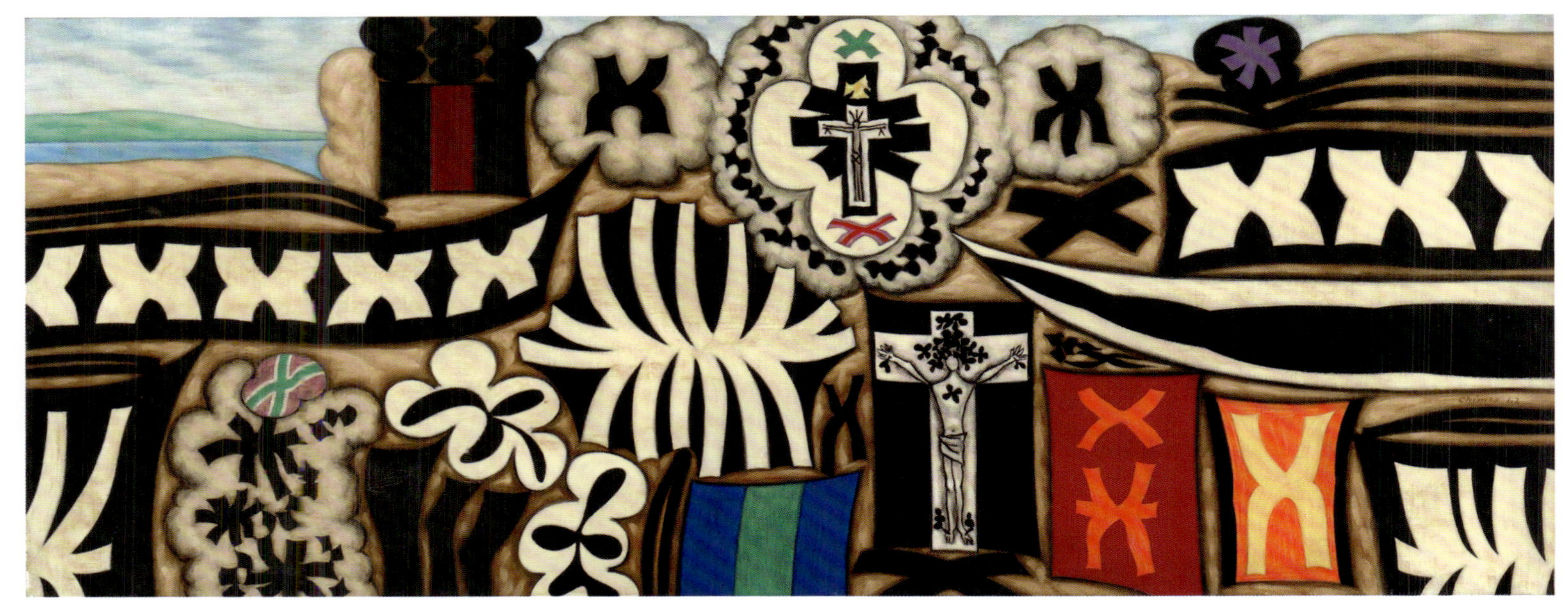

PLATE 7

Untitled (Study for Ringling Mural), 1962

OIL ON CANVAS

14 X 36 INCHES (35.6 X 91.4 CM)

COLLECTION OF DAWN CHIMES, VENICE, FLORIDA

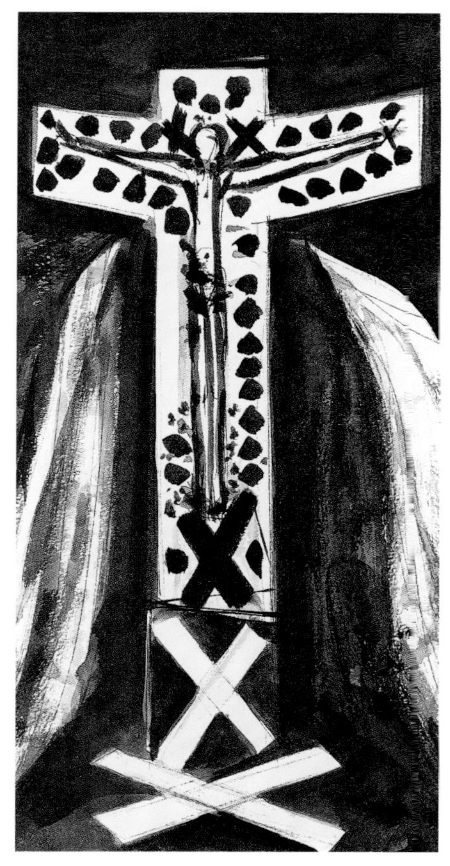

Untitled (Study for Mural), 1963–65

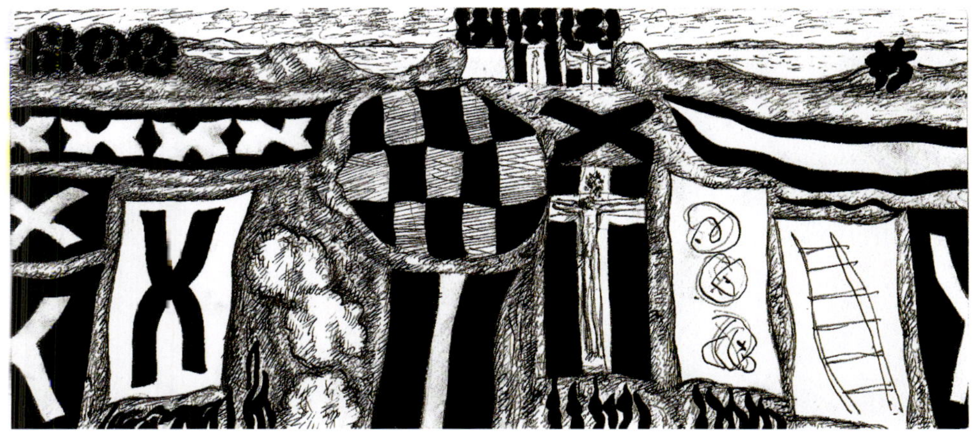

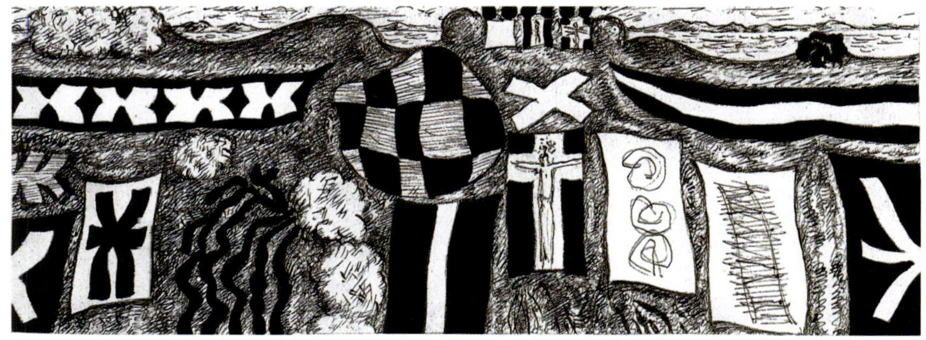

PLATE 9

Untitled (Study for Mural), 1963–65

PEN AND INDIA INK ON PAPER

4¼ x 9⅝ INCHES (10.8 X 24.4 CM)

JOHN AND MABLE RINGLING MUSEUM OF ART, SARASOTA, FLORIDA.

GIFT OF THE ARTIST

PLATE 10

Untitled (Study for Mural), 1963–65

PEN AND INDIA INK ON PAPER

3⅜ x 8½ INCHES (8.6 X 21.6 CM)

JOHN AND MABLE RINGLING MUSEUM OF ART, SARASOTA, FLORIDA.

GIFT OF THE ARTIST

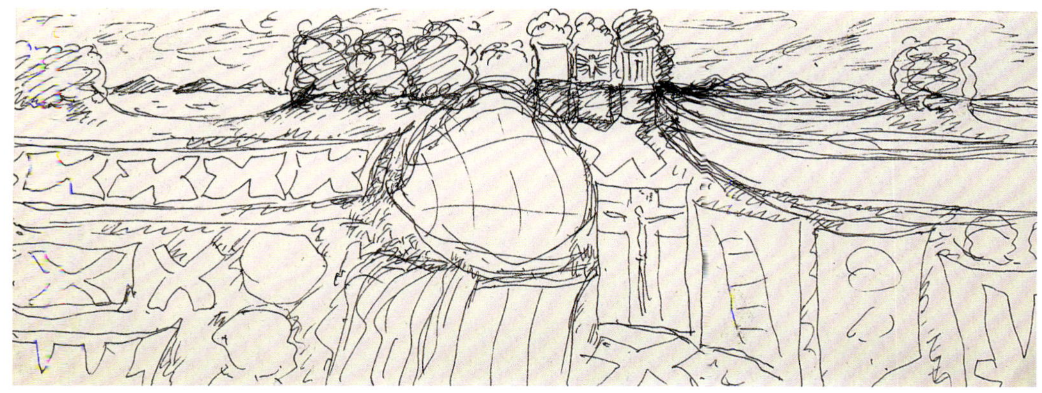

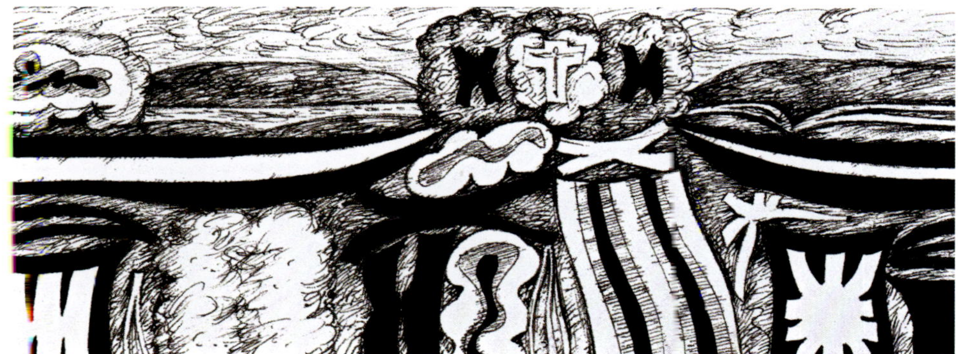

Untitled (Study for Mural), 1963–65

PEN AND INDIA INK ON PAPER

3½ x 9¼ INCHES (8.9 x 23.5 CM)

JOHN AND MABLE RINGLING MUSEUM OF ART, SARASOTA, FLORIDA.

GIFT OF THE ARTIST

Untitled (Study for Mural), 1963–65

PEN AND INDIA INK ON PAPER

3½ x 9½ INCHES (8.9 x 24.1 CM)

JOHN AND MABLE RINGLING MUSEUM OF ART, SARASOTA, FLORIDA.

GIFT OF THE ARTIST

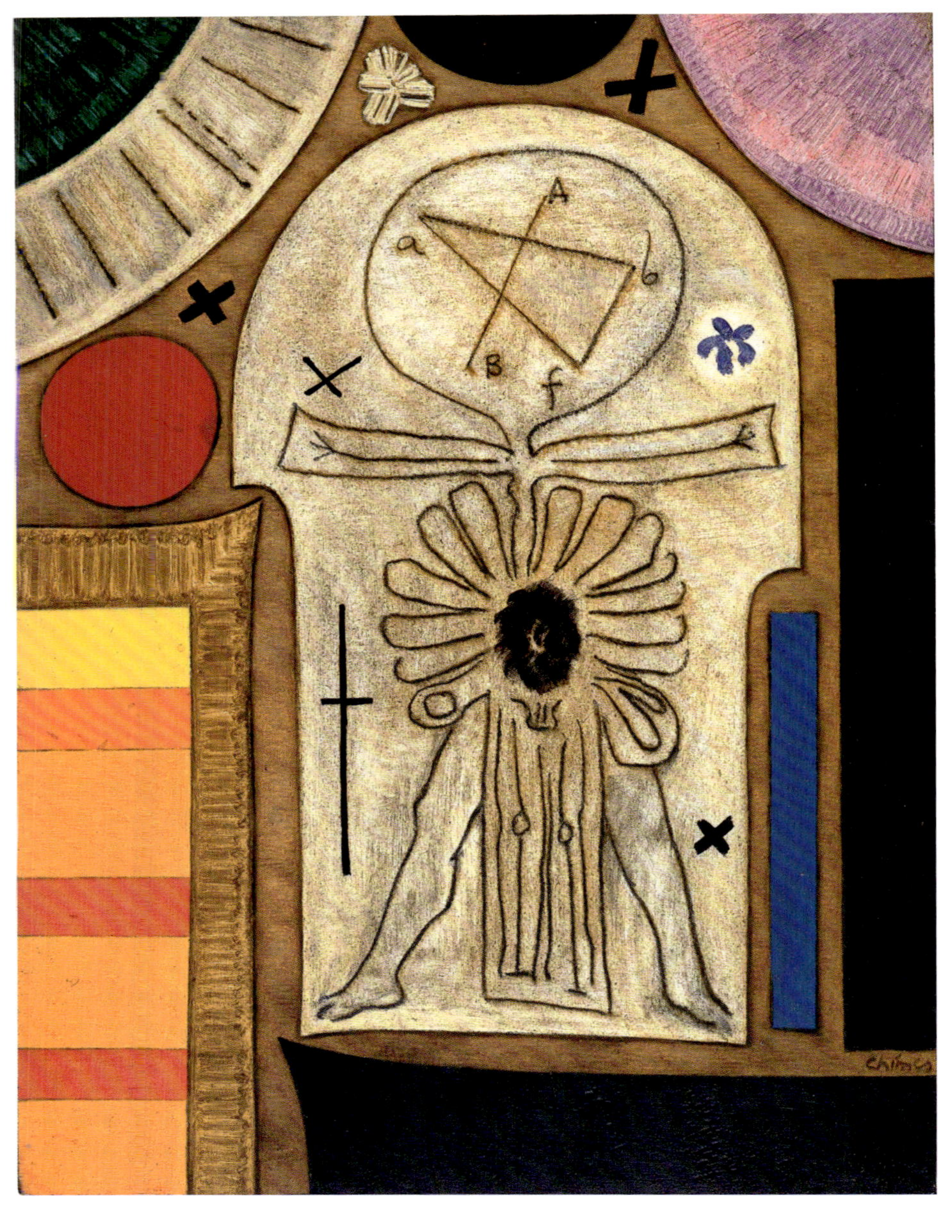

PLATE 13

Untitled (Crucifix 3), 1964

OIL ON LINEN

10¼ x 7⅝ INCHES (26 x 19.4 CM)

COLLECTION OF MR. AND MRS. ROBERT P. LEVY, BRYN MAWR, PENNSYLVANIA

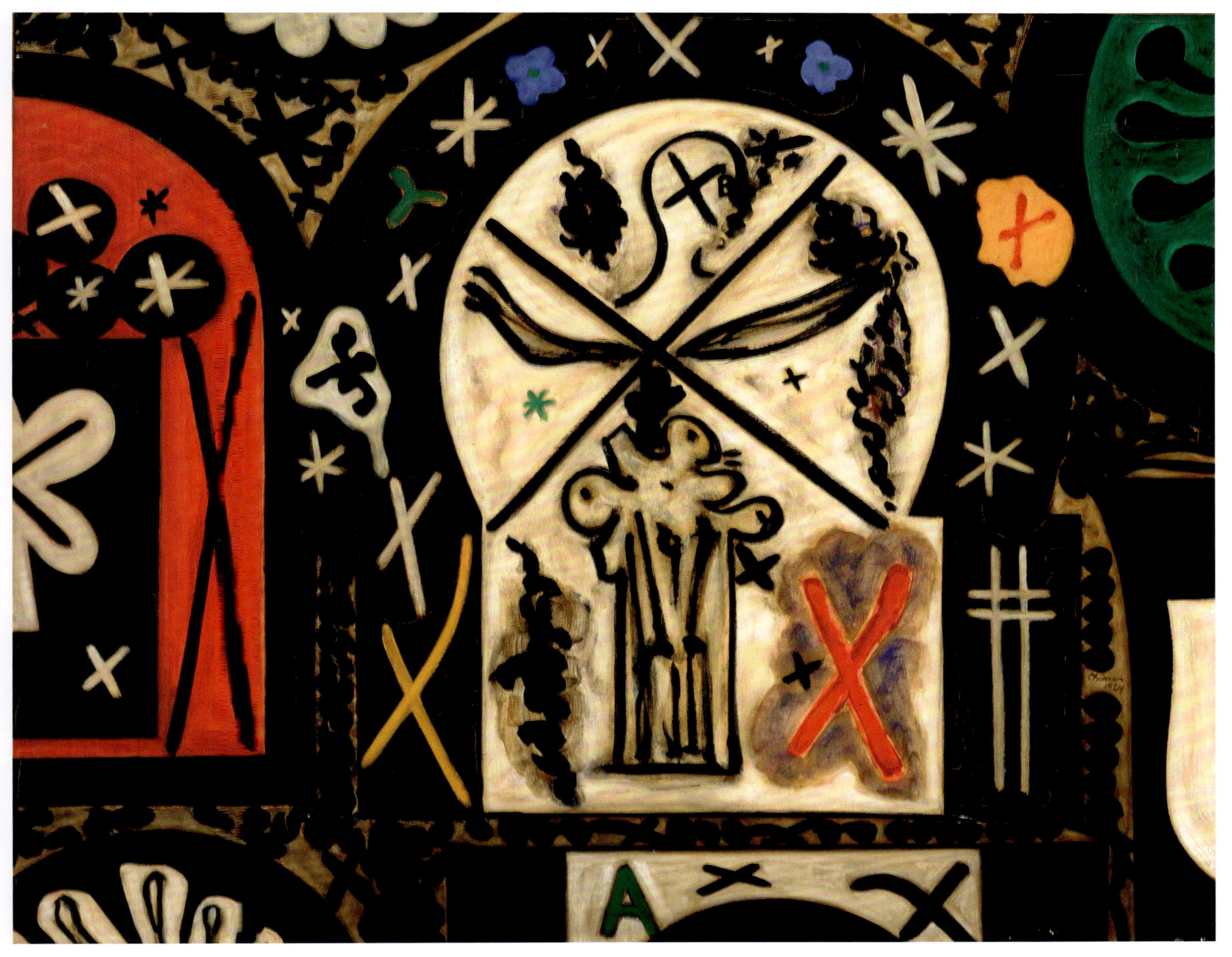

Plate 14

Abstraction #86, 1964

OIL ON CANVAS

23⅛ x 29 INCHES (58.7 x 73.7 CM)

LOWE ART MUSEUM, UNIVERSITY OF MIAMI, CORAL GABLES, FLORIDA. MUSEUM PURCHASE THROUGH FUNDS FROM THE BODLEY GALLERY,

NEW YORK, 65.036.000

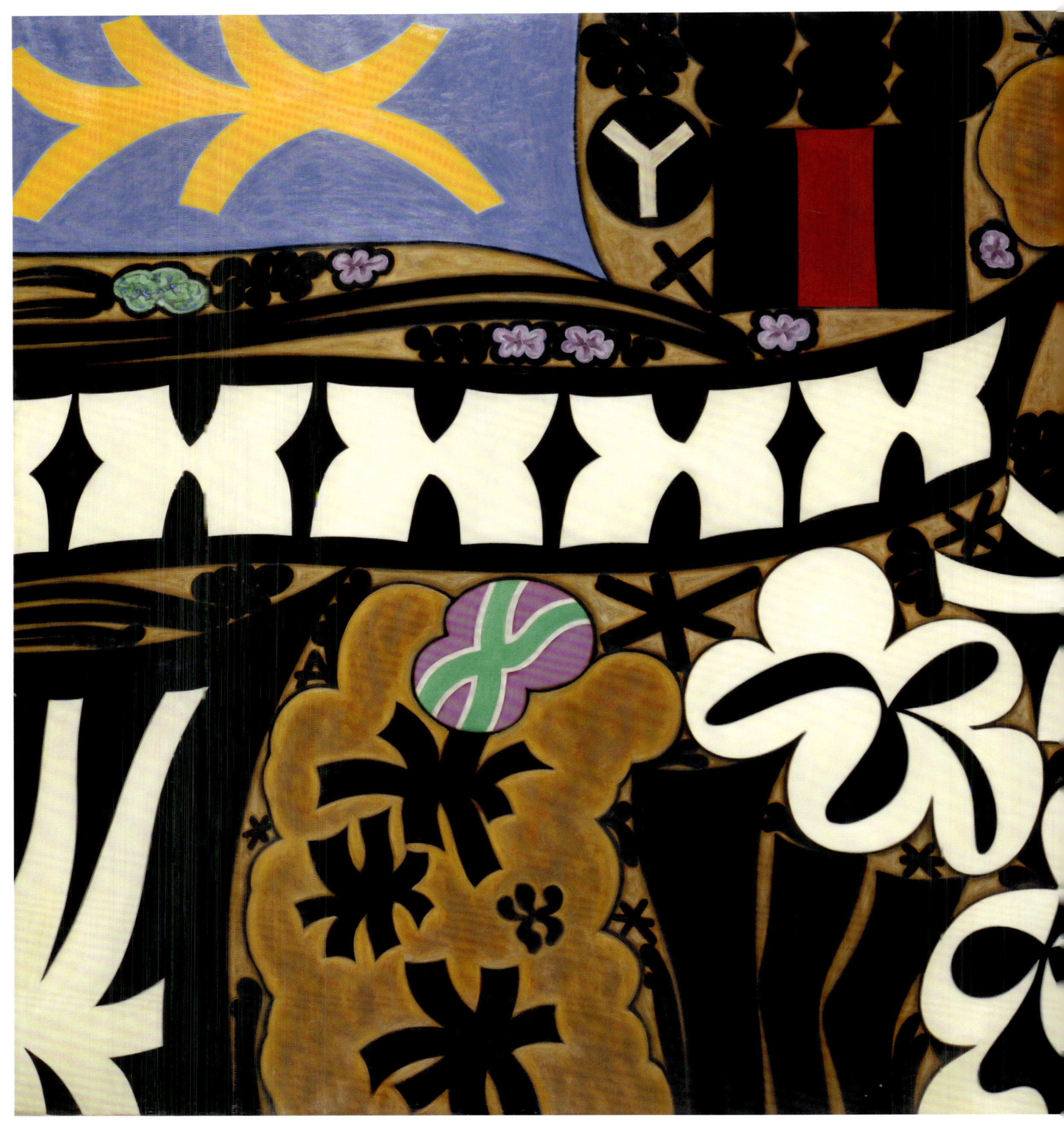

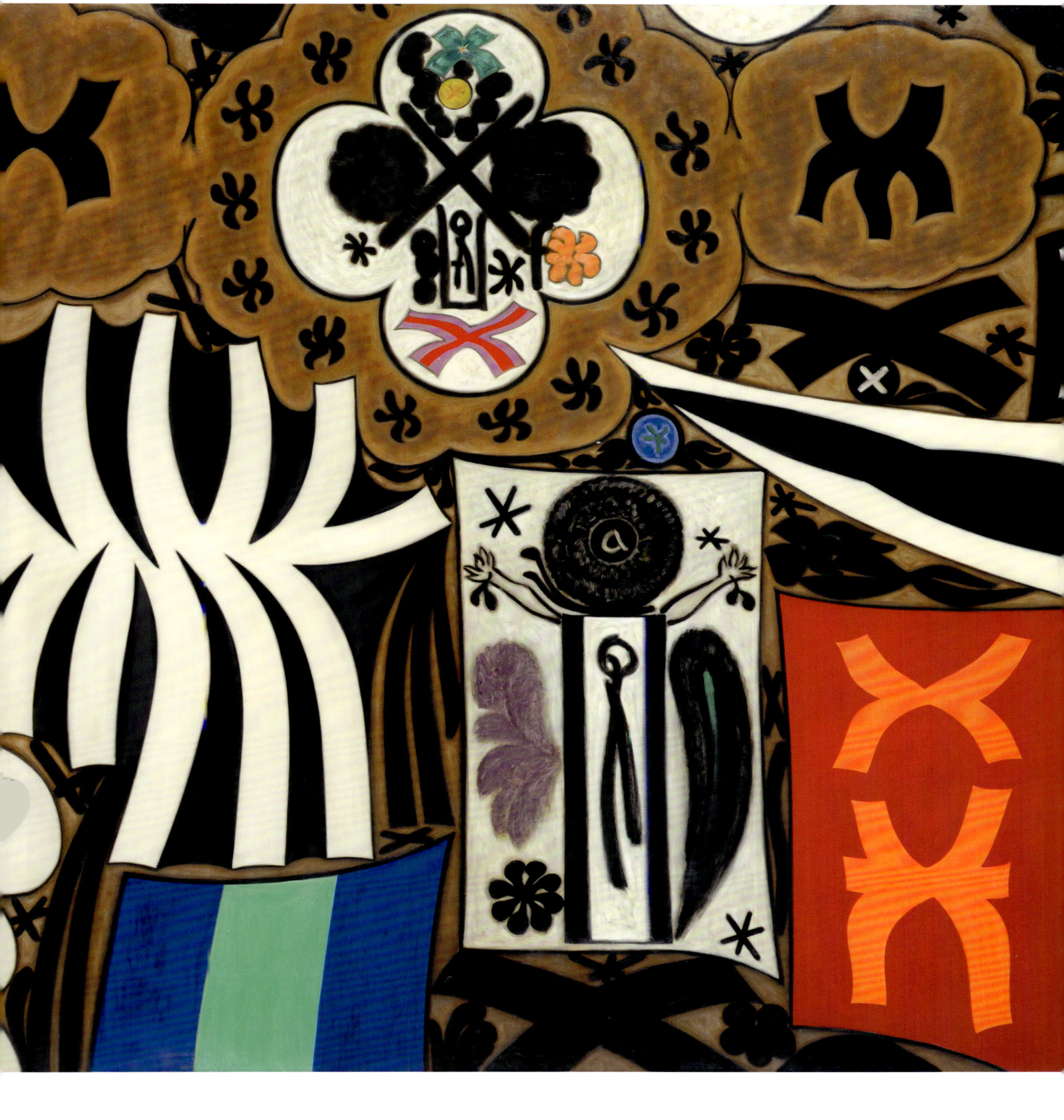

Mural, 1963–65

OIL ON CANVAS

83 x 213¼ INCHES (210.8 x 516.3 CM)

JOHN AND MABLE RINGLING MUSEUM OF ART, SARASOTA, FLORIDA. GIFT OF THE FRIENDS OF THE RINGLING MUSEUM

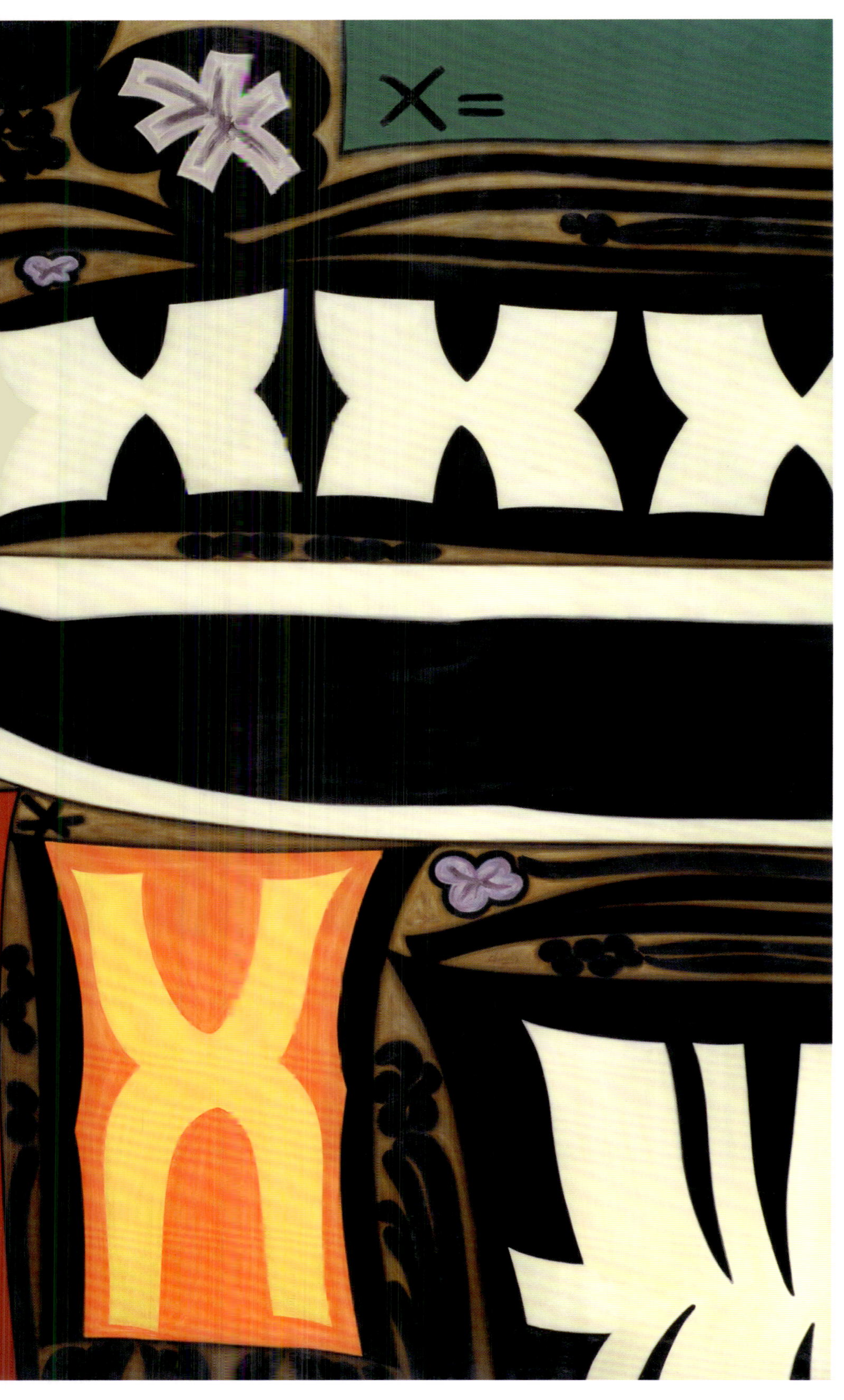

X=

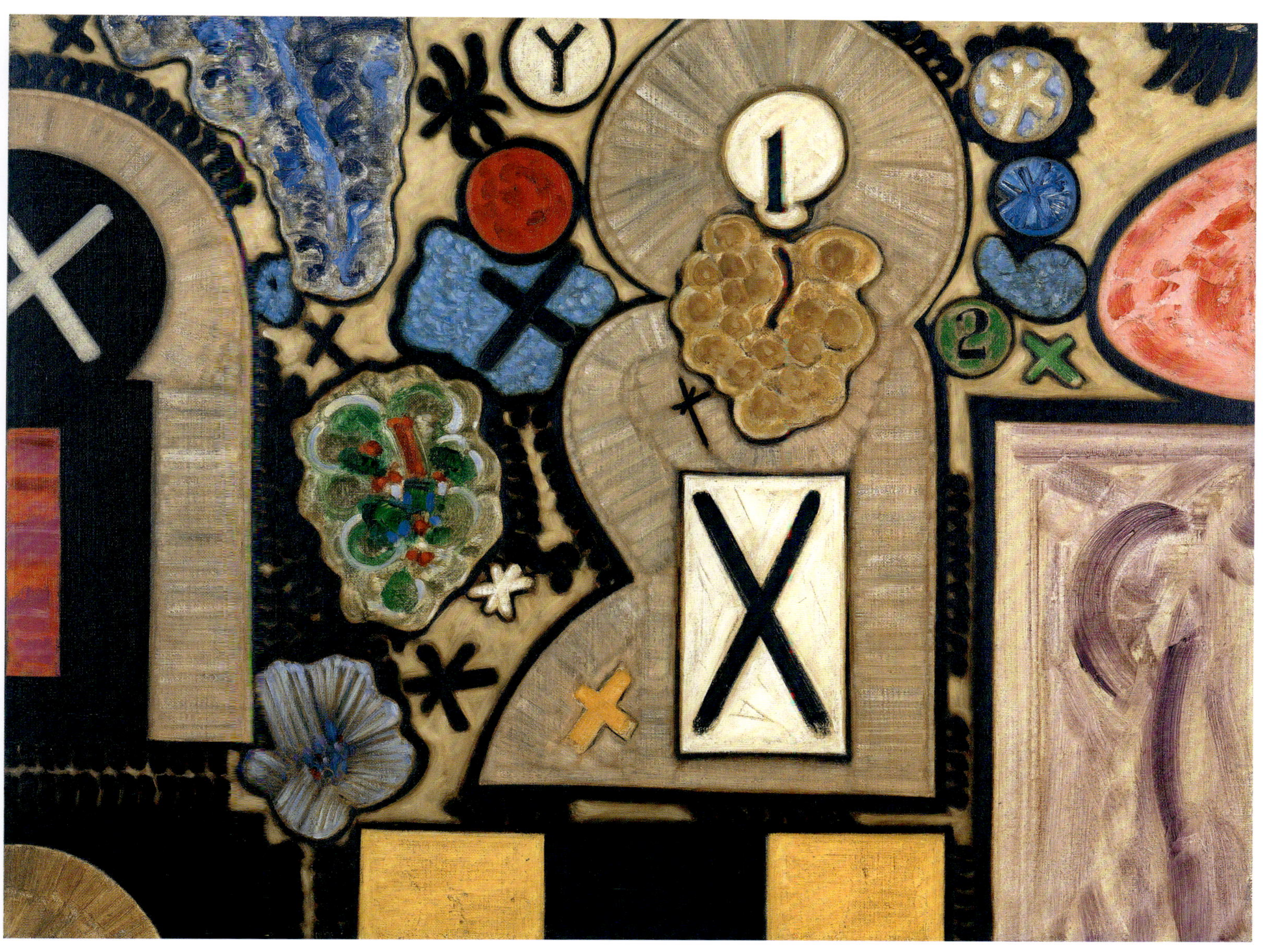

PLATE 17

Untitled, 1964

OIL ON LINEN

25⅛ X 33⅛ INCHES (63.8 X 84.1 CM)

PRIVATE COLLECTION

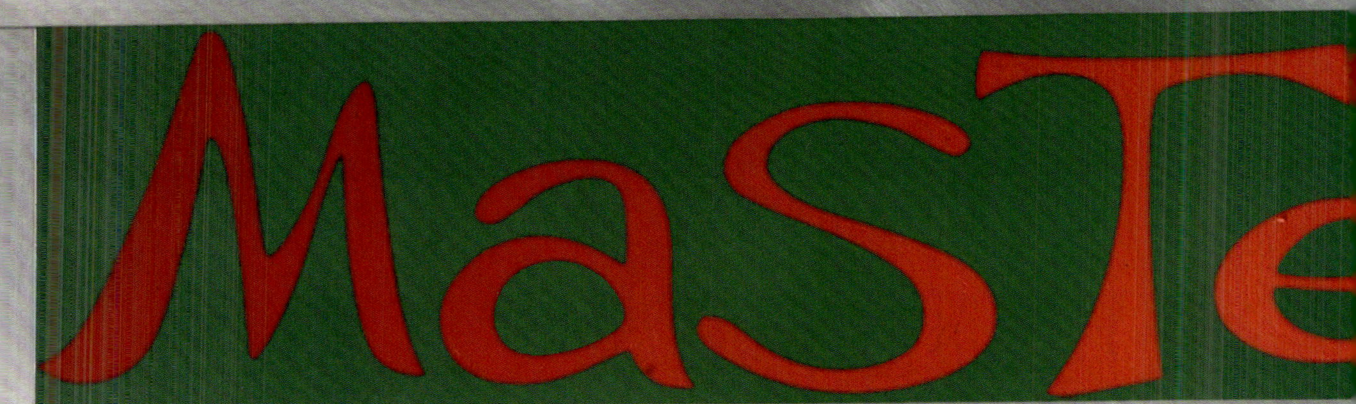
MaSTe
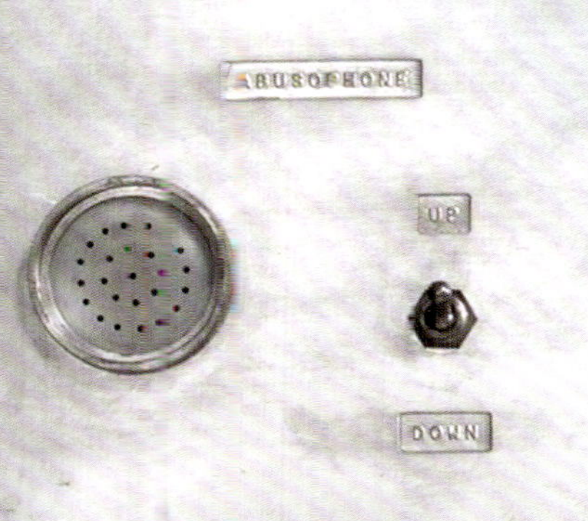
ABUSOPHONE
UP
DOWN
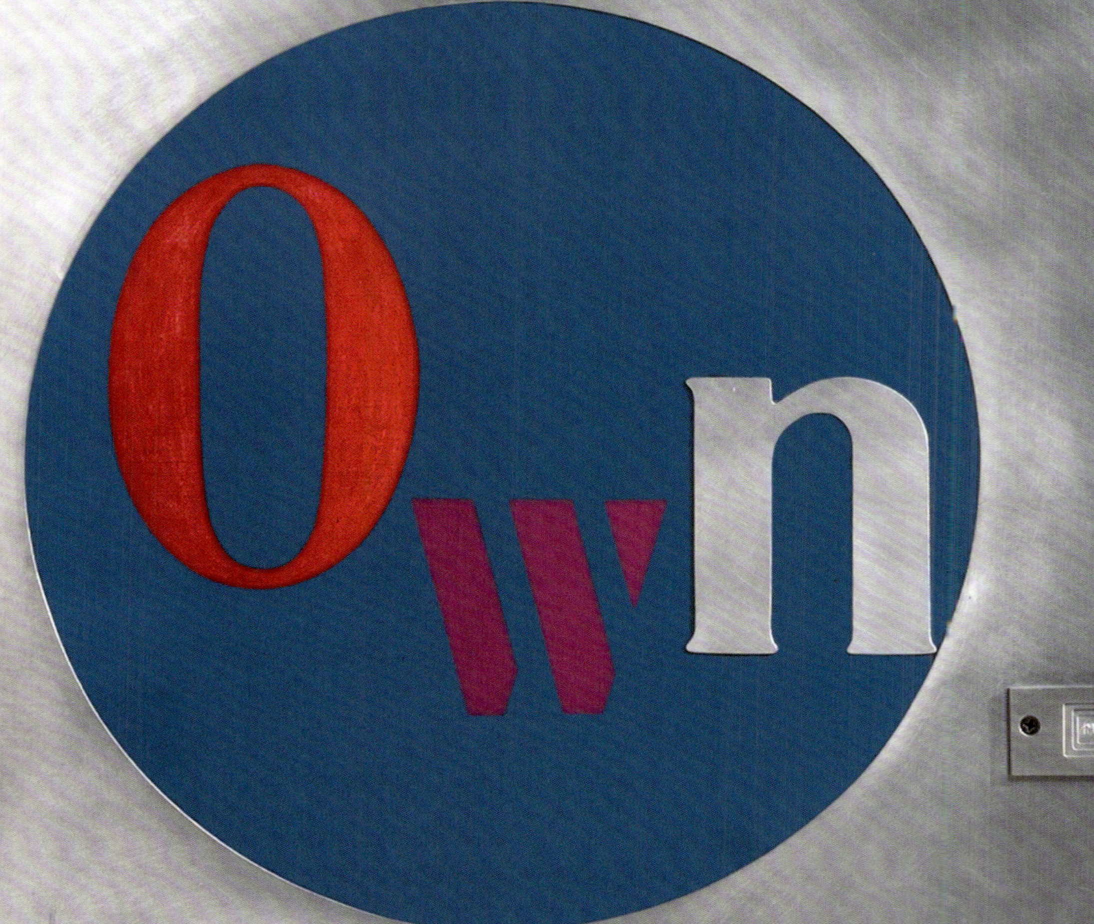
Own

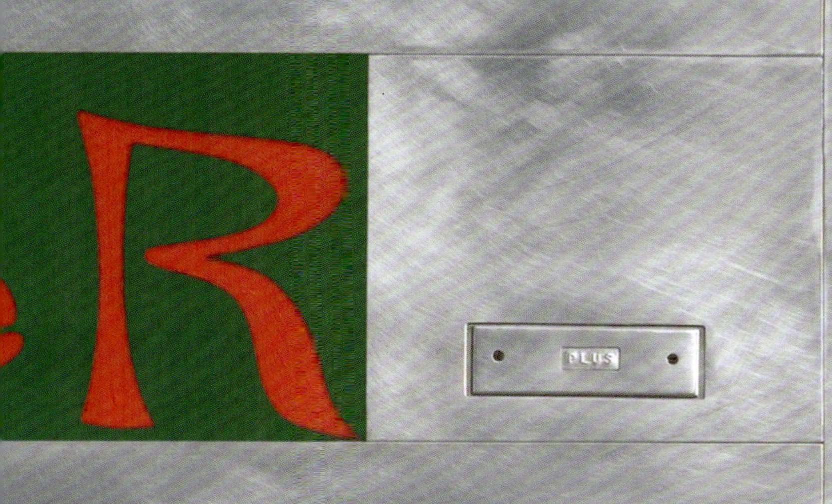

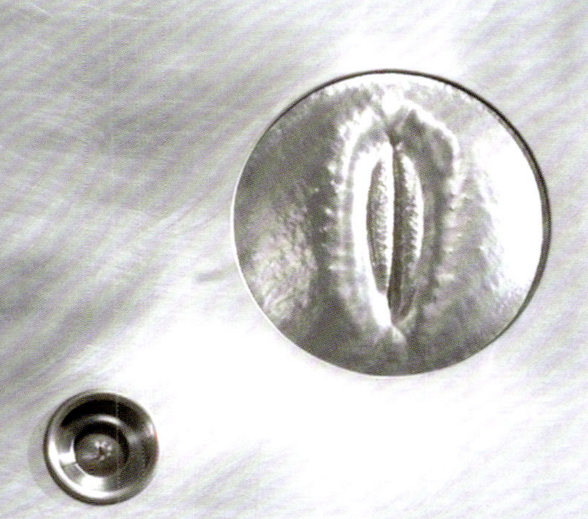

AND

METAL BOXES

In 1965 Chimes's work took a new and exciting direction when he was commissioned to illustrate the dust jackets for two books by Bettina L. Knapp, an assistant professor of French at Hunter College. Chimes met the author through his younger brother, George, who lived in the apartment above Knapp's in New York, and with whom she had spent many hours discussing Artaud's Greek heritage and literary and philosophical sources. In her introduction to *Antonin Artaud: Man of Vision*, her study of the French writer's intellectual, philosophical, and psychological development, which was eventually published in 1969, Knapp thanks George Chimes for his "conversance with philosophical and religious concepts" that helped her "through the all too hazardous *ways* of mystic teachings."[65] Excited by Knapp's notion that Artaud was a visionary writer who lived ahead of his time, George introduced her to his older brother and the two hit it off immediately, due to their shared passion for French Symbolist literature.

Chimes's first jacket illustration was for Knapp's lively modern translation of Bonaventure des Périers's *Cymbalum Mundi* (fig. 38), an enigmatic satirical work that has puzzled scholars since its publication in Paris in February 1538.[66] The hermetic nature of the *Cymbalum Mundi*, which contains numerous references to Greek mythology, alchemy, and the philosopher's stone, would have appealed to Chimes given his lifelong interest in mysticism. Indeed, the figure of Mercury (known as Hermes in Greek mythology), the messenger god of the alchemists, that Chimes incorporated in his white Hermes-cycle paintings of the 1990s perhaps bears the memory trace of the *Cymbalum Mundi*, in which the god is described as smashing the philosopher's stone into a powdery substance that can be likened to the luminous surface of the artist's more recent works.

Chimes illustrated the cover with an ink-wash drawing that contained many of the symbols, such as arrows and letters, with which he had embellished his earlier crucifixion paintings. Other motifs, such as the heart and spade, reinforce the perception of the image as a playing card, a trope that would appear increasingly in his subsequent work. The word *oui* in the bottom right corner acknowledges that the text was written by a French author, while the central motif of an encircled bird's head surrounded by four arrows suggests that Chimes had carefully studied Knapp's translation of the original text, which, as its subtitle suggests, takes the form of "Four Very Ancient Joyous and Facetious Poetic Dialogues" that were suppressed in Bonaventure's time for their pernicious and possibly blasphemous nature.[67] The artist almost certainly found inspiration for his cover illustration in the third dialogue of this slim volume, which contains a memorable passage in which we are told of a parrot "who can sing Homer's entire *Iliad*," a raven "who can jabber away on all subjects," and a magpie "who knows all philosophy's precepts."[68]

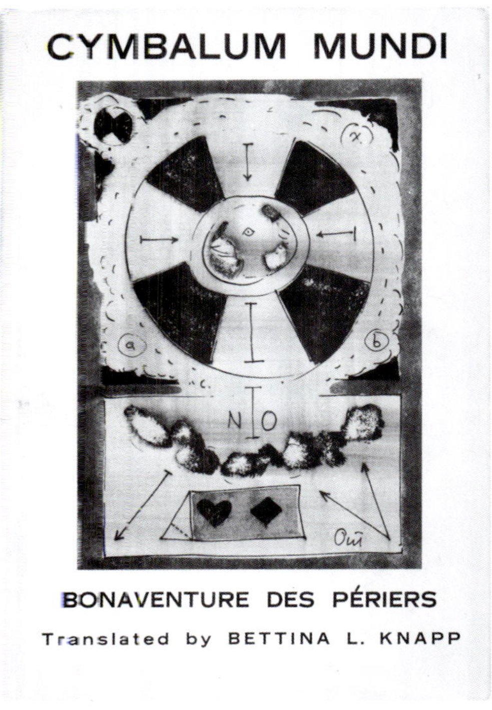

Fig. 38
Thomas Chimes, front cover illustration for Bonaventure des Périers, *Cymbalum Mundi*, trans. Bettina L. Knapp (New York: Bookman Associates, 1965). Collection of the artist.

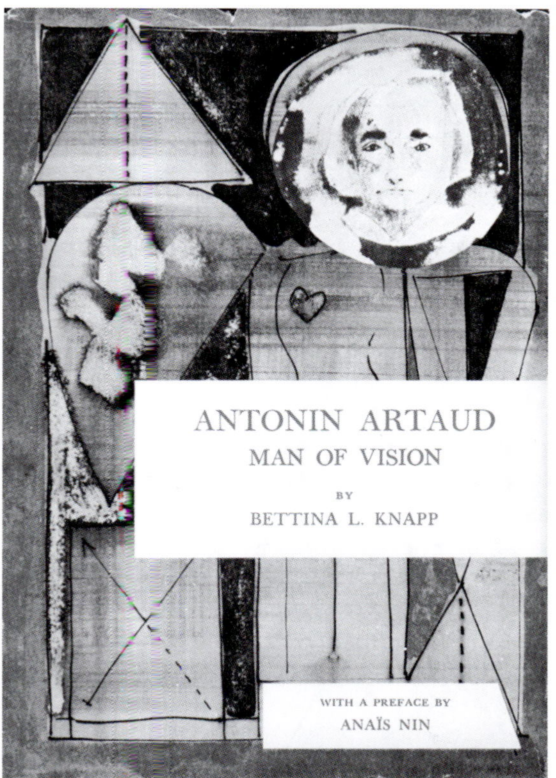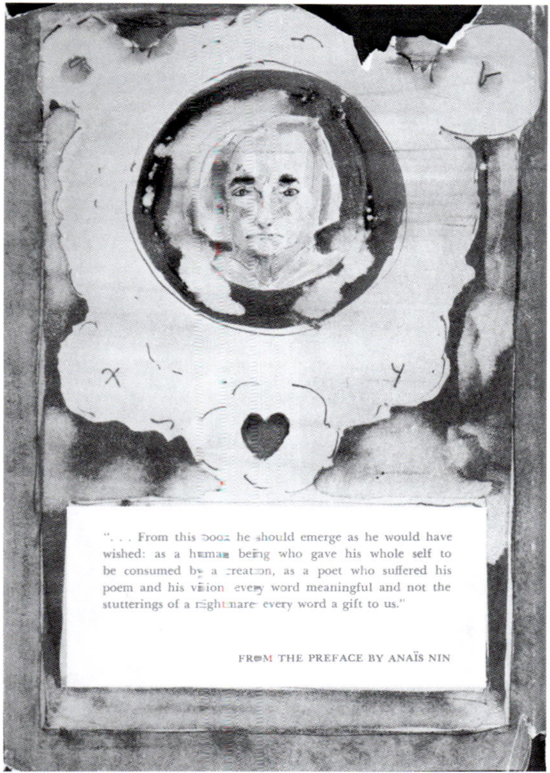

Fig. 39
Thomas Chimes, front cover illustration for Bettina L. Knapp, *Antonin Artaud: Man of Vision* (New York: David Lewis, 1969). Collection of the artist

Fig. 40
Thomas Chimes, back cover illustration for *Antonin Artaud: Man of Vision*. Collection of the artist

The success of this jacket led to a second commission from Knapp, this time for her ground-breaking critical study of Artaud's writings. Published in 1969, with a preface by Anaïs Nin, Knapp's *Antonin Artaud: Man of Vision* (fig. 39) represents an important landmark in the reception in the United States of the French writer's revolutionary ideas on art, music, film, and theater, and would exert an enormous influence on subsequent artists and performers, including Nancy Spero, Patti Smith, Kiki Smith, and Julian Schnabel. Chimes illustrated the front and back covers with two separate portraits of Artaud, each placed inside a circle and surrounded by familiar symbols such as hearts, arrows, and letters of the alphabet (fig. 40). These ink-wash drawings date from 1965, thus suggesting that Knapp had asked Chimes to design the jacket before she had completed her book, and are part of a large series of works on paper inspired by Artaud's writings that the artist would complete that year as he worked feverishly on this commission.

The artist had been aware of Artaud since 1951, when he attended a screening of *The Passion of Joan of Arc* at the Museum of Modern Art in New York (fig. 41). This 1928 film provided Artaud with a rare opportunity to display his unique acting style on the big screen, under the sensitive direction of the Danish filmmaker Carl Theodor Dreyer. Artaud played Jean Massieu, the monk who accompanied Joan of Arc to the stake, in a performance that has been described by his biographer, Stephen Barber, as oscillating "between paroxysmal seizure and emotional grandeur."[69] Chimes was sufficiently impressed by Artaud's performance and extraordinary appearance—the actor had a tonsure for the role, in which he became the living embodiment of Massieu—to want to find out more about his life and work through research in libraries and bookshops.

This research led to the discovery that Artaud had played an important role in the continuation of Alfred Jarry's subversive legacy in the French theater. Chimes had already come into contact with the legendary French playwright through the May–June 1960 issue of the

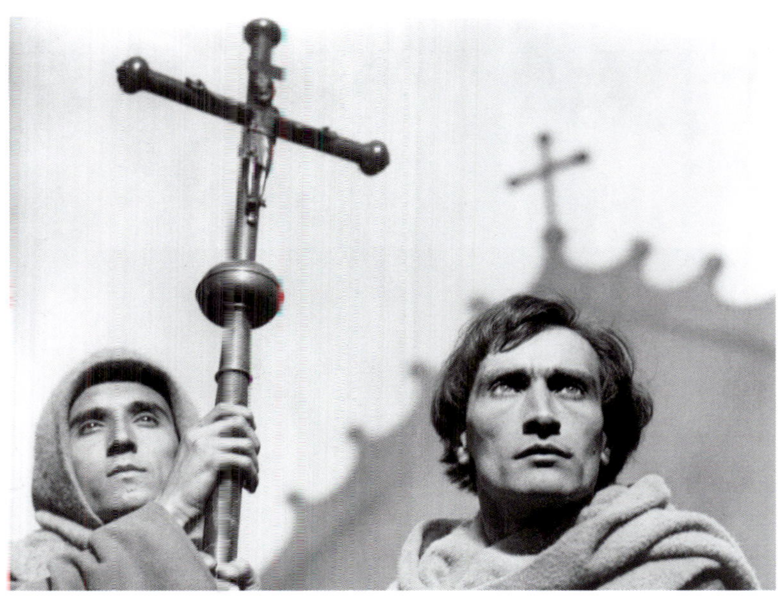

Evergreen Review devoted to Jarry, which was given to him by his brother-in-law, Herb Nelson, in 1964. As his obsession with Jarry's life and work began to take hold, Chimes embarked on a systematic exploration of the playwrights, poets, and artists who followed in his footsteps, such as Guillaume Apollinaire, Marcel Duchamp, and Artaud. The latter, along with his colleagues Robert Aron and Roger Vitrac, had in 1926 cofounded the Théâtre Alfred Jarry in Paris, where they revived the extreme tactics and shocking iconoclasm of the *Ubu* plays.[70] However, Knapp's scholarly reappraisal of Artaud, which relied heavily on the tragic details of his life to present him as a man possessed and pursued by inner demons, deepened the artist's understanding of the French writer, with whom he felt a strong empathy, both in terms of his artistic struggle and his tortured life and visions.

Chimes also felt a strong personal connection to Artaud through their shared Greek heritage and the fact that they were both the first sons of powerful women. The artist remains haunted by an astonishing photograph of Artaud's mother, Euphrasie Nalpas, a Levantine Greek from Smyrna who was married to her cousin, Antoine Artaud, a shipbuilder. This formidable woman, the mother of nine children, although only three survived infancy, reminded the Philadelphia artist of his own mother, who came from Sparta and had all the strength, courage, and self-discipline associated with the legendary warrior-state of ancient Greece. To this day, Chimes beats his chest when he mentions that his mother came from Sparta, and she, like Artaud's mother, appears to have raised him with a mixture of strict discipline and maternal tenderness.

The ink-wash drawings that Chimes made in 1965, as he began work on the second dustjacket commission, reveal his excitement at reading Knapp's book, to which he must have had access in its earliest development (fig. 42). The publication that year of the *Antonin Artaud Anthology*, edited by Jack Hirschman, by City Lights Books in San Francisco also provided Chimes with invaluable source material for his jacket design, since it included several poems and essays that were previously unavailable in English.[71] Twelve drawings from this campaign are known, but many more were made and may resurface. Of the known drawings, the strongest are those that deal with the figure of "le Mômo," Artaud's alter ego, whom Chimes portrays as a monstrous creature, half fish and half bird, with a streamlined head. The profiled features of Chimes's Mômo (pls. 19–21) were clearly derived from the parrotlike bird that graced his cover design for *Cymbalum Mundi*, as well as Artaud's own distinctive features, such as his sunken cheeks, beaklike nose, and crest of swept-back hair, which were often compared to those of eagles and other birds of prey.[72]

The features of Chimes's Mômo were also indebted to a traumatic event in the artist's life. In 1965, while vacationing with his wife and children at Southampton, Long Island, Chimes became deeply disturbed by the antics of a drunken man who had gone for a swim. He has never forgotten the terrifying sight of this enormous, beer-bellied figure emerging from the

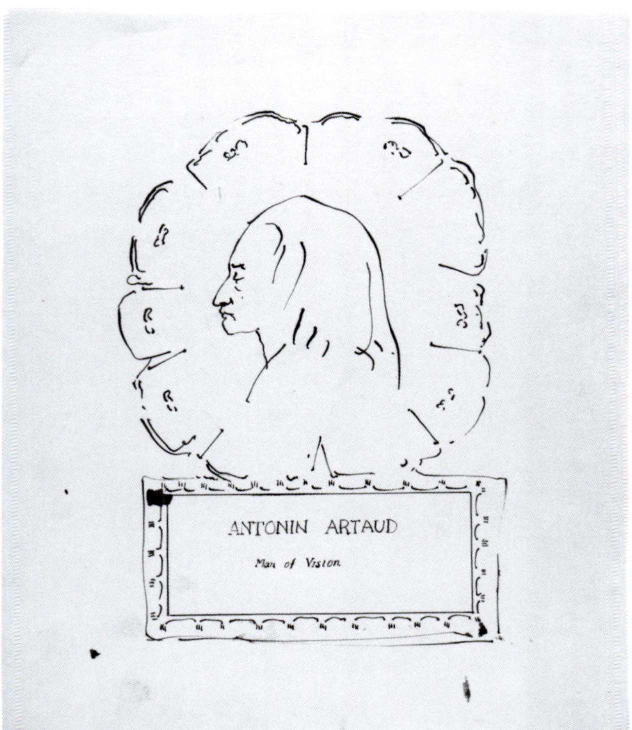

Fig. 42
Thomas Chimes, study for *Antonin Artaud: Man of Vision*, c. 1965. Pen and ink on paper, 12½ x 10½ inches (31.8 x 26.7 cm). Collection of the artist

waves like a creature from the primordial depths, with seawater clinging to his head and hair like a helmet or cocoon. Although fearful for his family's safety, Chimes was also profoundly disturbed by the image of this bloated, almost inhuman figure, which, according to Dawn Chimes, would assume a mythological status in his mind, like the Minotaur from the legend of Theseus and Ariadne.[73]

For Artaud, "le Mômo" was the phoenixlike figure that rose from the ashes of his own "death" during the fifty-one unanaesthetized electroshock treatments he received at the Rodez Asylum between June 1943 and December 1944.[74] The violence of the shock treatments caused him to lose all of his teeth, fractured one of his vertebrae, and often led to heart failure that required him to be resuscitated. Following his release from Rodez on May 26, 1946, after nine years of therapy and with undiagnosed cancer that had left him painfully thin, his face ravaged, and his cheeks sunken, Artaud reinvented himself as "le Mômo," a name he derived from a slang word commonly used in his hometown of Marseilles to describe a simpleton or buffoon. But as the American poet and editor Clayton Eshleman has argued, "One must also take into consideration this word's relation to the Greek god of mockery and raillery, Momus, said by Hesiod to be the son of Sleep and Night, the nocturnal voice of Hermes."[75] Thus, "le Mômo" is a complex literary creation—a new, transformed self who is part ghost, part village idiot—and Chimes's decision to base his portrayal of the French writer on the frightening vision of the drunken man in the waves suggests that he was fully aware of the multivalent connotations of Artaud's alter ego.

Between July and December 1946, Artaud wrote what has come to be viewed as his most important and polished poem, "Artaud le Mômo," which was published in book form the following year.[76] Described by the American poet John Ashbery as "less a poem than a shriek, a horrible, crippled attacking thing, the breath of reality," "Artaud le Mômo" focuses on his cancer-ridden body and its attendant ills, but also deals with the author's recurring bouts of mental illness and the incandescent rage he felt about the electroshock treatment he received at the Rodez Asylum.[77] Replete with obscenities, blasphemy, violence, eroticism, and an obsession with bodily functions, this extremely bitter, declamatory poem can be seen as a unique transformation of the horror and terror of his past experiences. Like his earlier identification with van Gogh's struggle, which Artaud also commemorated in his own writings, Chimes's reading of Artaud's poem in 1965 must have been revelatory, given that he had also suffered from bouts of severe depression throughout his adult life.

Transcending his own schizophrenic psychosis, Artaud fashions a new, imaginative self-identity in "Artaud le Mômo," one that allows him, under the guise of a village idiot, to address in an uncompromisingly honest and direct way the brutal realities of his treatment at Rodez. The constant cursing and harsh language in the poem can be seen as a rebellious assault on bourgeois standards of good taste, as well as those in authority who would tolerate and sanitize the abuse that his mind and body suffered under the "care" of doctors and psychiatrists like Dr. Gaston Ferdière, who treated his acute schizophrenia with a combination of insulin and electroshock therapy. In the section of the poem entitled "Alienation and Black Magic," for example, Artaud condemned the therapeutic electroshock techniques utilized at Rodez as a form of black magic that had resulted in his "death": "Those who live, live off the dead. And it is likewise necessary that death live; and there is nothing like an insane asylum for gently incubating death and for keeping the dead in incubators. It began 4000 years before Jesus Christ this therapy of slow death, and modern medicine, an accomplice in this of the most sinister and crapulous magic, subjects its dead to electroshock or to insulin therapy so as daily to thoroughly empty its stud farms of men of their egos, and to expose them thus empty, thus fantastically available and empty."[78] As John C. Stout has observed, in this poem Artaud writes of himself "as if from beyond the grave, declaring that the old Artaud is dead and has been replaced by a ghostly double, the 'Mômo,' who is the product of incarceration and electroshock."[79] It is through the persona of this Frankenstein's monster that the reborn Artaud, assassinated in his previous life, could fully exteriorize his thoughts and emotions.

Artaud first read his new poem in public at Jacques Copeau's Théâtre du Vieux-Colombier in Paris, on January 13, 1947. "Histoire vécu par A-Mômo" (The Story Lived by Artaud-Mômo), announced the handbills. Around seven hundred people packed the tiny theater to see the return to public life of this now-legendary poet and playwright. The audience was a who's who of the Parisian artistic and literary avant-garde, including André Breton, André Gide, Roger Blin, Jean Paulhan, Henri Michaux, Albert Camus, and Arthur Adamov. Although only fifty years old at the time, Artaud looked twenty years older; this once handsome actor was now toothless, wrinkled, and emaciated from years of malnourishment, drug abuse, cancer, and electroshock treatment. The frail and disheveled Artaud took the stage and unleashed a blistering assault on his audience's senses as he read his cathartic poems, among them "Artaud le Mômo," with passion and fury, interrupted now and then by sobbing and stammering, before collapsing through nervous exhaustion at the evening's end.[80]

The shocked audience remained transfixed in their seats, not knowing how to respond except in stunned silence and disbelief. The writer and critic Maurice Saillet, in a detailed account of the evening's events, described the horrendous and almost intolerable experience of sitting through Artaud's reading:

When he came onto the stage with his worn, emaciated face, looking like Edgar Allan
Poe and Baudelaire at the same time; when his impetuous hands fluttered like a pair
of birds round his face; when his raucous voice, broken by sobs and stumbling tragi-
cally, began to declaim his splendid—but practically inaudible—poems, it was as if we
were being drawn into the danger zone, sucked up by that black sun, consumed by
that "overall combustion" of a body that was itself a victim of the flames of the spirit.[81]

The evening ended when Artaud, sensing that his audience was skeptical of his bitter
denunciation of electroshock therapy as a form of black magic, appealed for "at least someone"
to share his beliefs. According to some reports Artaud panicked and fled the stage in terror,
while others claimed that he began improvising after dropping his notes, before losing his train
of thought and continuing to rant and hurl abuse for more than two hours until his voice gave
out. The silence that ensued was not broken until André Gide climbed onstage and embraced
him. Five days later, in a letter to André Breton, Artaud recounted the events of that fateful
night before ruefully admitting that he "had not taken account of the fact that the only language I could use with a public was to take bombs out of my pocket and throw them in its face
with a characteristic gesture of aggression. And that blows are the only language I feel capable
of speaking."[82]

Saillet's account of that unforgettable night was reprinted in the May–June 1960 issue of
the *Evergreen Review* devoted to Alfred Jarry (which by this time had assumed talismanic importance to Chimes), and it clearly made a deep impression on the artist. His ink-wash drawings
for Knapp's forthcoming book on Artaud, as well as his subsequent metal boxes featuring the
character of "le Mômo," thus combined references to Artaud's tragic life, his incantatory poems,
and the 1947 reading of "Artaud le Mômo" at the Vieux-Colombier, to create an image of
"Artaud–the Mômo—the mummified living child," as Saillet described him.[83] Chimes may also
have been aware that Artaud had originally requested that Picasso illustrate the poem for publication before deciding that he would use his own notebook drawings, since "Picasso would
never be able to understand me as I understand myself."[84]

Chimes's Mômo drawings often take the vertical form of playing cards, with hearts, spades,
and diamonds (fig. 43), or even Tarot cards, as in the work entitled *Artaud the Magician* (fig. 44),
which refers to the writer's interest in black magic and the occult. Artaud's habit of casting
spells began during a trip to Ireland in 1937 when, in a state of destitution, he started sending
imprecations, scrawled along with magic signs on fragments of colored paper that were then
burned with cigarette ends, to former friends in Paris, as well as authority figures such as doctors, and even to Adolf Hitler, whose despicable treatment of the mentally ill was just becoming
known at that time. According to Stephen Barber, these "spells" were designed "literally to
embody his sense of fury and isolation, and to exact retribution on their recipients, who, he felt,
had abandoned him."[85]

When seen together, Chimes's drawings reveal his profound admiration for Artaud's writings. This in turn inspired the artist to break with his earlier crucifixion paintings and start
making metal box constructions in 1965, many of which contain overt references to Artaud
through the birdlike emblem of "le Mômo," his new, transformed self as seen in works such as
Yes (fig. 45) and *Le Momo* (pl. 21), as well as the extraordinarily detailed drawing *Registered in*

Fig. 43
Thomas Chimes, *Artaud le Momo*, 1965. Pen and ink on paper, 8½ x 5⅝ inches (21.6 x 14.3 cm). Collection of the artist

Fig. 44
Thomas Chimes, *Artaud the Magician*, 1965. Pen and ink on paper, 8¾ x 5¹³⁄₁₆ inches (22.2 x 14.7 cm). Collection of the artist

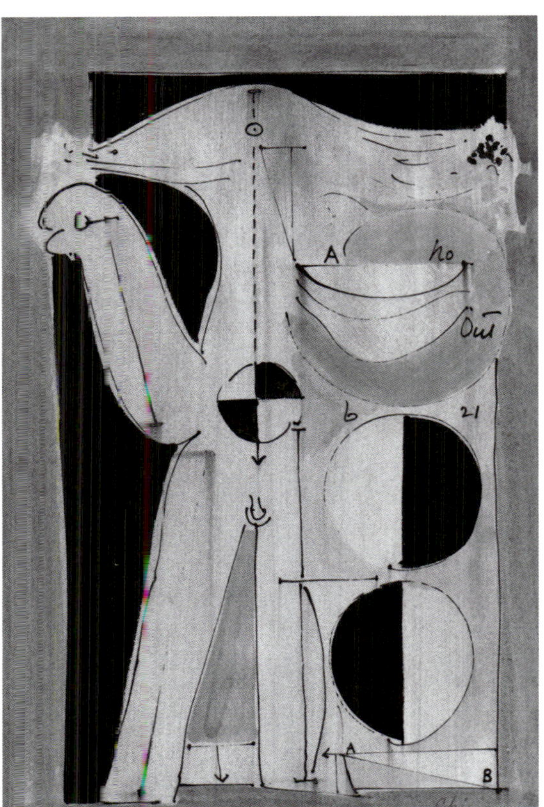

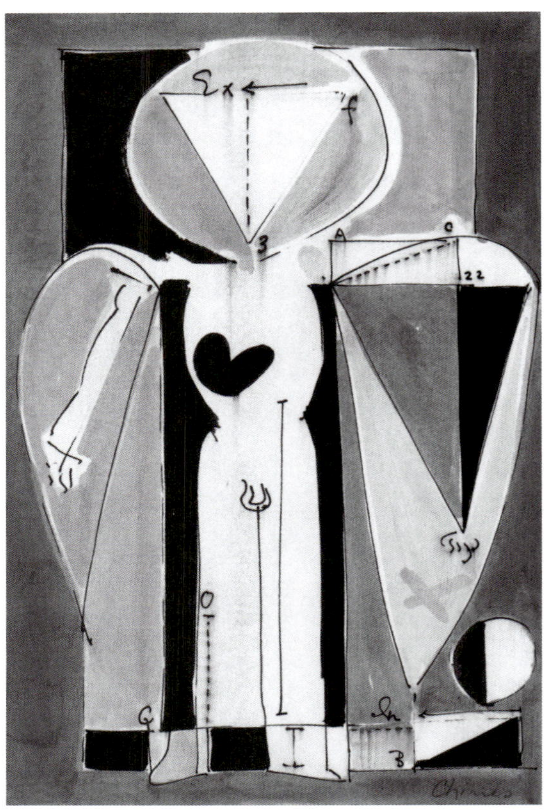

Fig. 45
Thomas Chimes, *Yes*, 1965. Mixed-media metal box, 13⅝ x 16 inches (34.6 x 40.6 cm). Collection of the artist

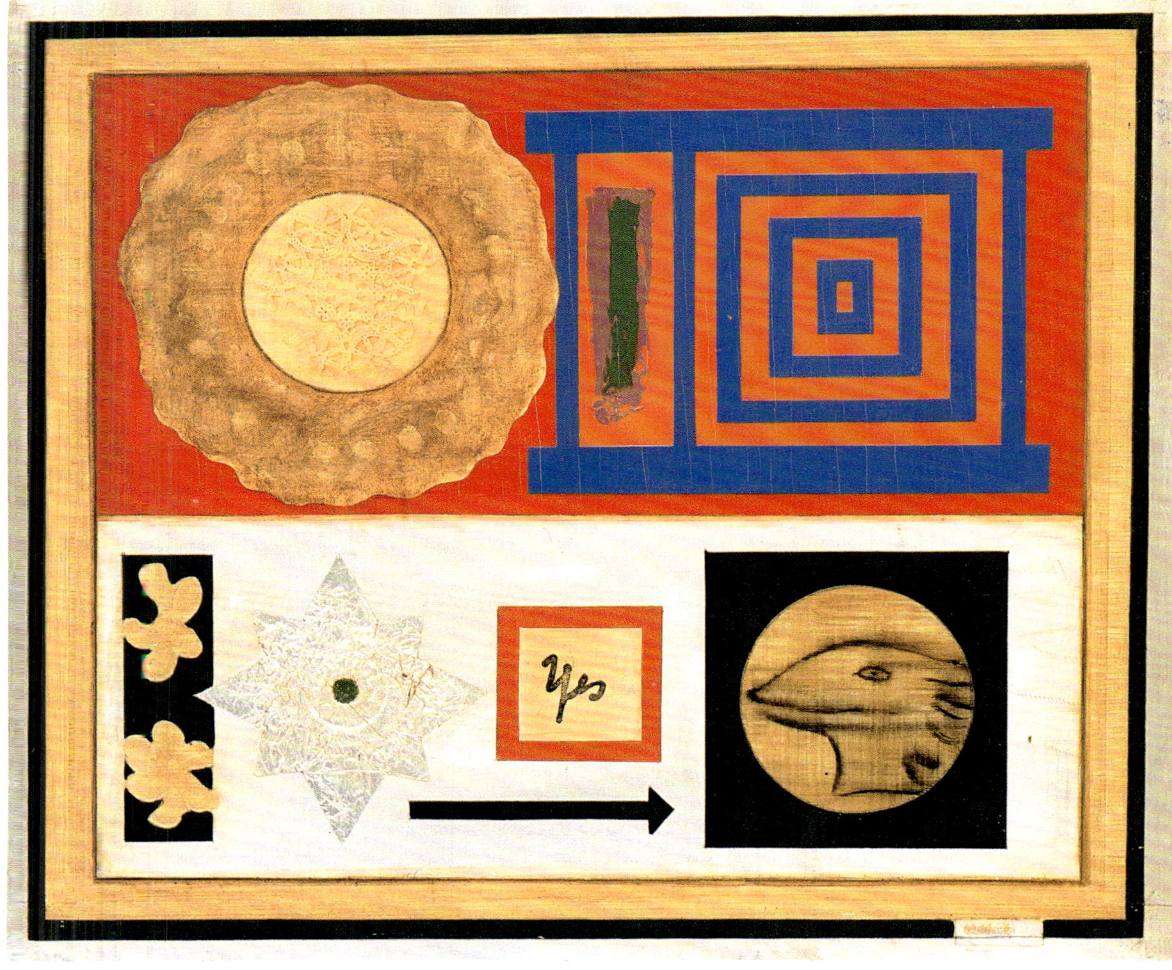

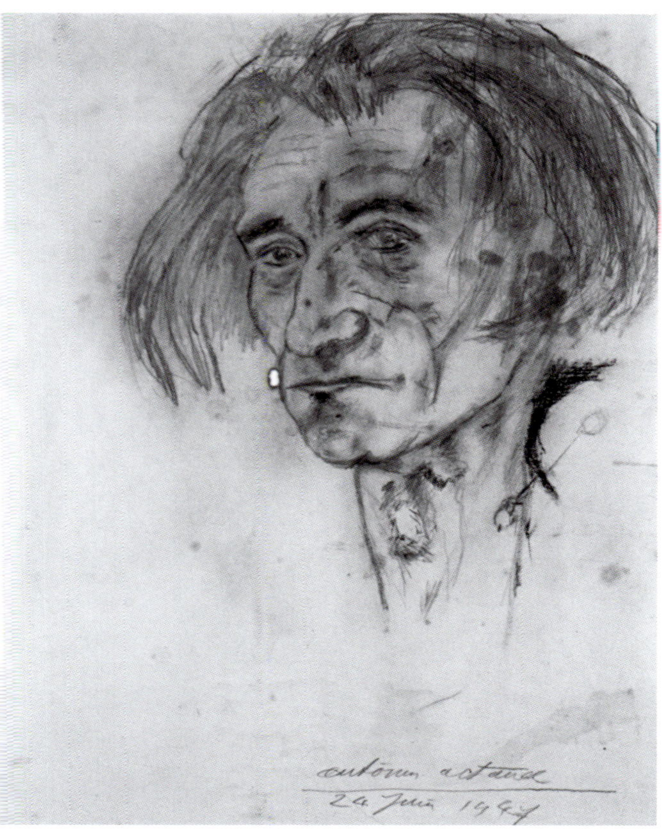

Fig. 46
Antonin Artaud (French,
1896–1948), *Self-Portrait*,
1947. Pencil and chalk on
paper, 21⅝ x 16⅞ inches
(55 x 43 cm). Private
collection

the Bureau of Tempo Catastrophe (pl. 20), in which the Mômo figure faces an unidentified man in a Renaissance-like setting. Other works from this period reveal the impact of Artaud's own drawings, which are often filled with pictograms, hieroglyphics, X-rays, and other fractured and disjunctive images, many of them derived from his shattered psyche and martyred body following his institutional confinement.[86] The raw, gestural power of drawings such as Artaud's 1947 *Self-Portrait* (fig. 46), which can be viewed as an uncensored document of his inner condition, also pushed Chimes toward greater freedom and experimentation in his own subsequent work. As he recently acknowledged:

> Artaud taught me to trust my intuition. His poem about Mômo, whom I connect with the Greek god of mockery, was all about being a clown, making a fool of yourself, being a jerk, and putting yourself down. But this mocking has an ominous cast as well. That is to say, he was rebelling against authority, being an outsider, an outcast, and showing them that he wasn't going to take it anymore. There's a seething rage underneath it all that I remember responding to at the time.[87]

Another artist who responded to Artaud's writings, albeit slightly later, was Nancy Spero. Between 1969 and 1971, Spero made an extended sequence of works on paper, the earliest of which are known as the "Artaud Paintings" (fig. 47), which were inspired by the French writer's subversive challenge to a society that had failed to silence him. As a feminist, Spero recognized Artaud as a kindred spirit whose work addressed issues, such as censorship and exclusion, that she could relate to her own struggle with patriarchal authority: "Artaud screaming and yelling, hysterical about the silencing, the castration of the tongue. And I said, That's me, you know? That's myself the artist, a woman artist. I didn't quite zero in on it, but I knew it was about

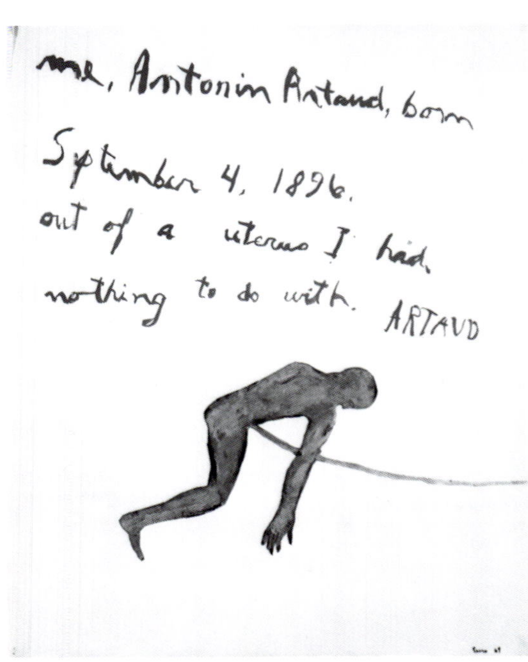

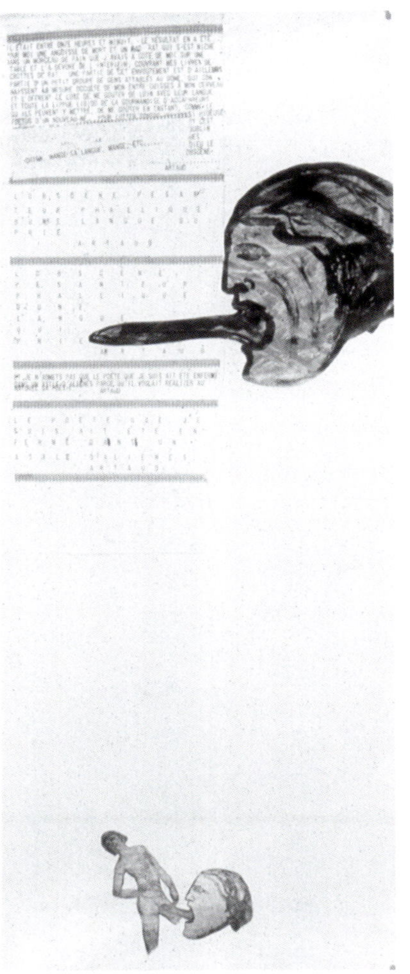

being a woman artist."[88] In the works that followed, especially those found in the highly visceral *Codex Artaud* (fig. 48), Spero incorporated typewritten fragments of Artaud's inflammatory prose alongside her own equally obscene images of disembodied, scattered heads with long, stiff phallic tongues sticking out of their gaping mouths.[89] This deliberately disturbing and violent imagery, which references torture and lynching, but also copulation and birth, allowed Spero to exorcize her own demons and stick "my own tongue out at the world—women silenced, victimized and brutalized, hysterical, 'talking in tongues.'"[90]

Like Spero, Chimes was liberated by Artaud's radical dislocation of language and meaning. He immediately followed his cover designs for *Antonin Artaud: Man of Vision* with a series of metal box constructions that represent an abrupt break with his previous work. One of the first of these boxes, *Momo Talk*, of 1965 (fig. 49), contains a drawing of the now-familiar emblem of Artaud's alter ego, which has been reduced to a blur, as if shown at high speed. The image is placed within a stark composition of sheet aluminum panels, whose rectangular configurations might resemble a Mondrian-like series of grids were it not for the two adjacent panels depicting male and female genitalia, and the push buttons labeled "MOMO" and "TALK." This connection between genitalia and communication can be viewed as Chimes's response to "Artaud le Mômo," since references to sexual organs and bodily functions are frequently embedded in those lines that attempt to radically recast language and its relationship to the repressed body—a body that has been violated, tortured, confined, maimed, and, in Artaud's mind, ultimately extinguished, only to return as "le Mômo."

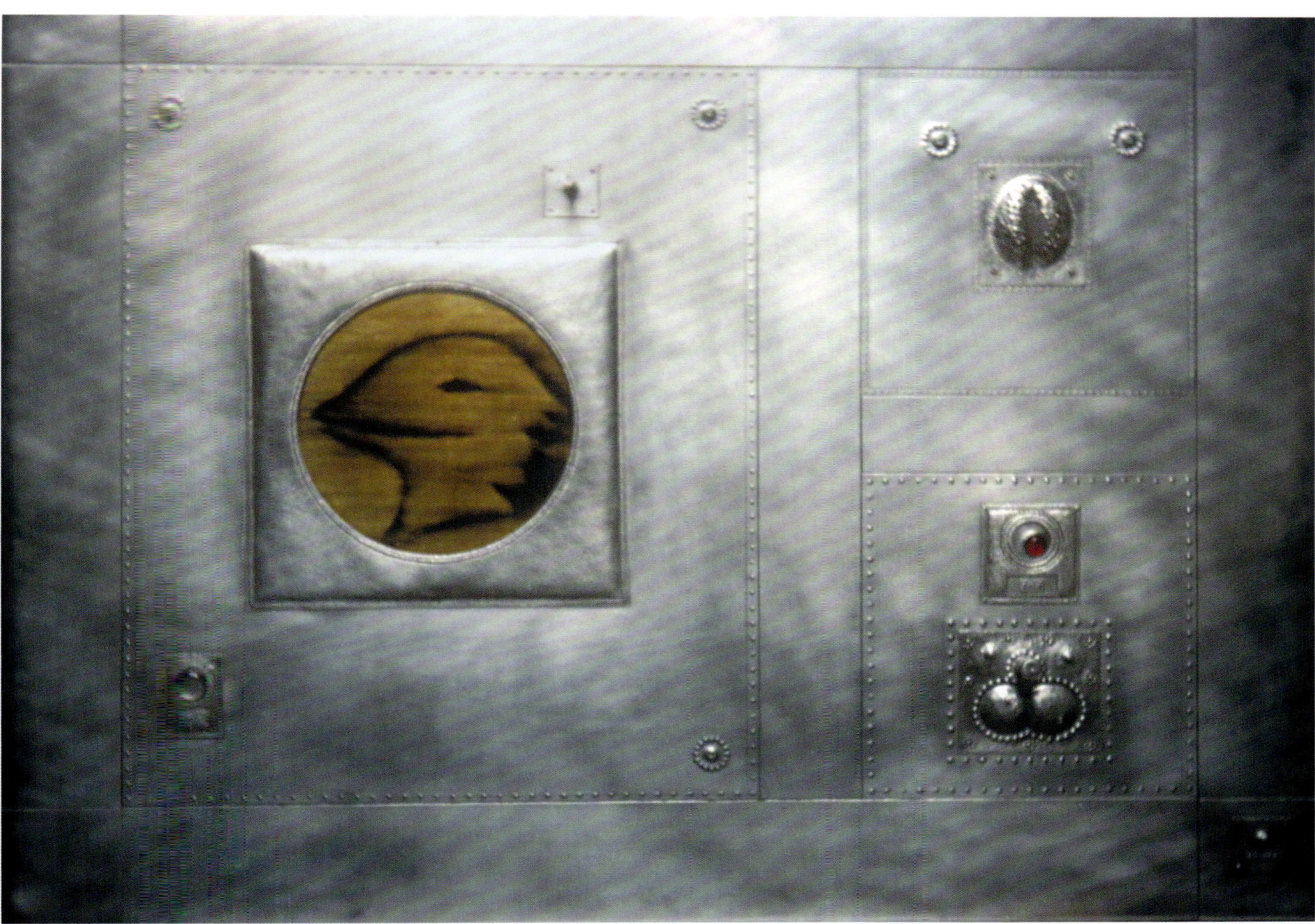

Chimes's self-identification with Artaud/Mômo liberated the artist to explore the erotic dimension in his work, which also reflected the atmosphere of sexual freedom and experimentation in the 1960s. The French writer's utter revulsion for conformity and his resistance to the social and political order he abhorred mirrored the disillusionment that the postwar generation felt about conventional forms of society, as they, like Artaud, sought to escape reality through hallucinatory drugs and challenge moral strictures through sexual freedom. This would help to explain why Chimes would incorporate such a frank depiction of sexual organs, which in the case of the vagina included bristling pubic hair made of steel wires that extend into the air like antennae, and then have the courage to enter *Momo Talk* in the 1965 Chautauqua Exhibition of American Art, an annual juried show held at the Chautauqua Art Association near Lake Chautauqua in southwestern New York State.[91]

Chimes's bold decision was vindicated when Peter Selz, curator of painting and sculpture at the Museum of Modern Art, awarded *Momo Talk* the five-hundred-dollar first prize, which the artist's extremely proud son, Dmitri, accepted on his behalf at the awards ceremony (see fig. 150). The following year, Selz praised "the originality of the concept and the extremely fine craftsmanship of the work." He added: "In fact, I found it to be one of the most interesting works by a younger artist, especially because of the many different suggestions it evokes."[92] Such was its success that Chimes later ritualistically destroyed *Momo Talk* when he moved on to the panel portraits in the early 1970s, believing that he needed to do so in order to make a new beginning. While taking a chainsaw to the aluminum construction made a clean break with his past, this destructive act also acknowledged that the illusions and enthusiasms of the metal box era, and by association the artist's own utopian dreams of the 1960s, were over.

In *Master and Own*, of 1966 (pl. 22), Chimes continued to explore the erotic potential of machine forms, a dimension he found lacking in Minimalist sculpture. Arguably the most important of the metal box constructions in terms of scale and ambition, this work again incorporates male and female sexual organs in an aluminum box environment whose pristine surface references Minimalist sculpture's attempts to replicate the impersonal look of industrial fabrication. The title might be taken as a reference to the dominant "master" of sadomasochism, were it not for the knowledge that concealed beneath the adjacent aluminum panel, labeled "plus," is the additional word "baiting" (fig. 50). Viewed together, "Master" and "baiting" turn into "masturbating," suggesting that "Own" could become "onanism," although there is in fact no substitute word underneath the "minus" plate. The "up" and "down" electric switch and intercom-like speakerphone, labeled the "abusophone," continue the idea of self-abuse, while the raised inscription beneath the Momo drawing, which reads "ethocybernetorgastia," followed by a serial number, conjures up an image of sexual pleasure and orgasmic release via electronic stimulation.

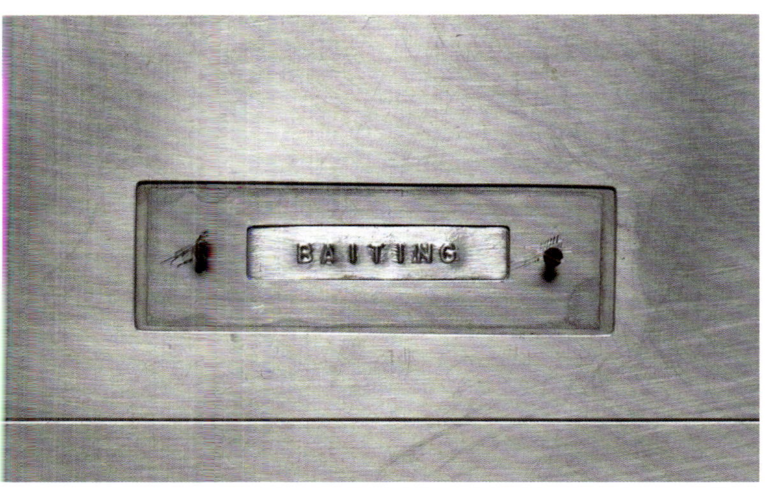

Fig. 50
Thomas Chimes, detail of
Master and Own (pl. 22)

The humorous touch of concealing the word "baiting" beneath a metal plate can be understood as a reference to Jasper Johns's enigmatic *Target with Plaster Casts*, of 1955 (fig. 51), with its set of closable wooden panels containing casts of body parts, including a green painted penis (third from the right). Chimes greatly admired the cerebral nature of the artist's iconic target paintings, to the point of painting his own version in 1964, which he subsequently destroyed by cutting the work into four separate quadrants. Like Chimes, Johns was interested in creating a complex interplay between the perceptual (the exposed target below) and the conceptual (the concealed body parts above) as a way of extending Duchamp's legacy into painting. This dual nature of the work requires the viewer to take an interactive role in the piece, which is only "completed" when the hinged wooden slats are lifted to reveal the painted plaster casts.

The sexual imagery of *Target with Plaster Casts* and later works such as *Painting with Two Balls*, of 1960 (fig. 52), made a profound impression on Chimes, who felt a deep kinship with Johns's work and ideas. Both artists had looked to Duchamp's example as a way of moving beyond the slavish imitation of Abstract Expressionist painting, and *Master and Own* also reflects Chimes's newfound appreciation of the erotic apparatuses at work in *The Bride Stripped Bare by Her Bachelors, Even (The Large Glass)*, of 1915–23 (fig. 53), which is filled with references to masturbation, such as the revolving drums of the chocolate grinder in the bachelors' domain. Inspired by the steam-powered chocolate machine in a well-known confectioner's window in Rouen, where Duchamp went to school, the chocolate grinder became connected in his mind with the childhood memory of the aroma of hot chocolate wafting enticingly down the rue des Carmes, which he associated with his burgeoning sexual awakening. The masturbatory symbolism of the rotating machinery is explained in a note Duchamp published in *The Green*

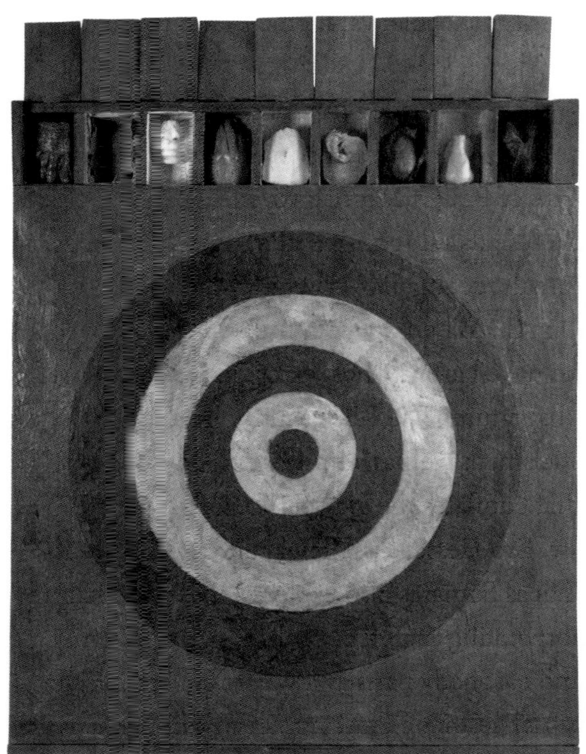

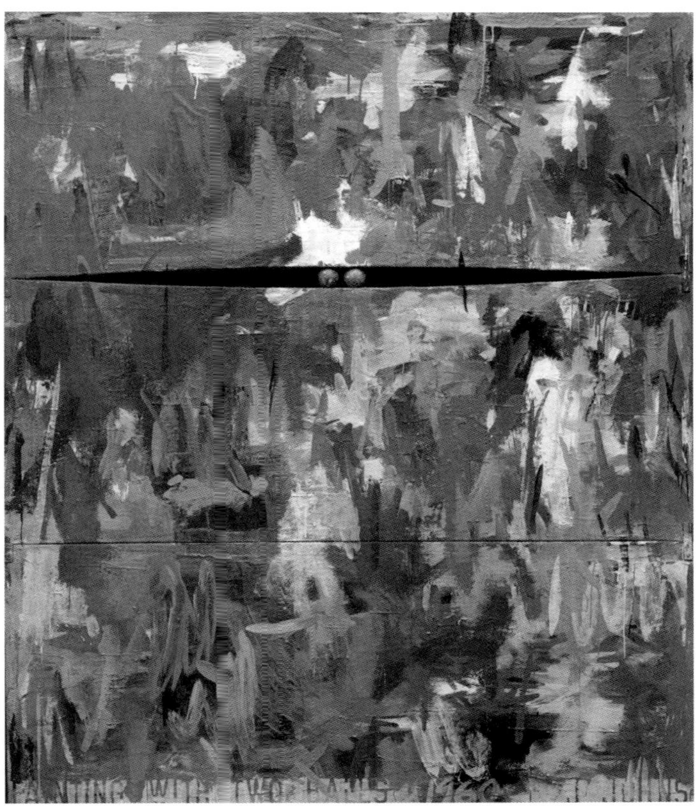

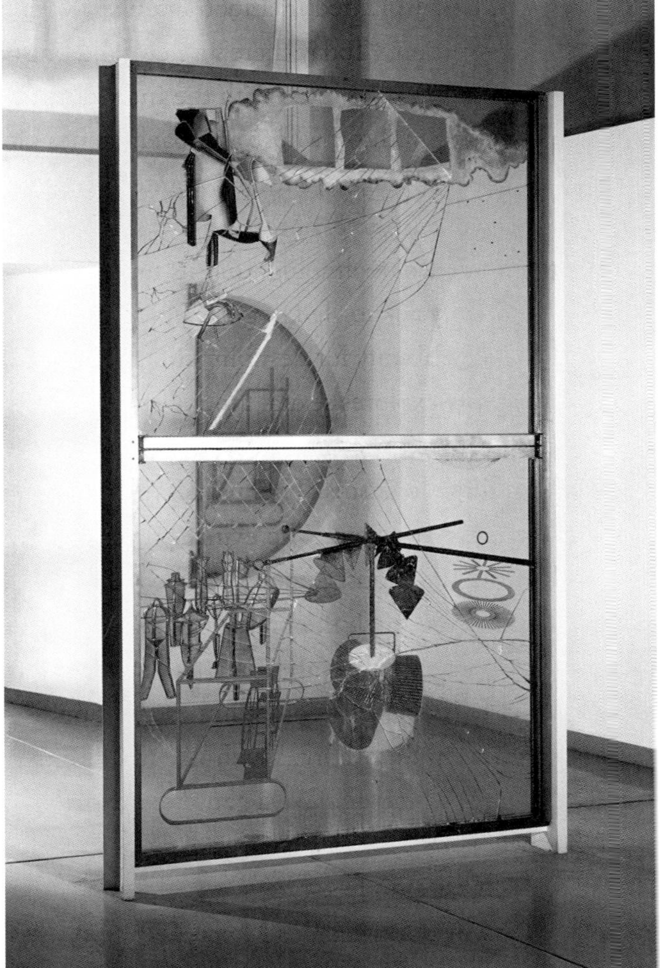

Fig. 51
Jasper Johns (American, born 1930), *Target with Plaster Casts*, 1955. Encaustic and collage on canvas with objects, 51 x 44 inches (129.5 x 111.8 cm). Collection of David Geffen, Los Angeles

Fig. 52
Jasper Johns, *Painting with Two Balls*, 1960. Encaustic and collage on canvas with objects, 66 x 54 inches (167.6 x 137.2 cm). Collection of the artist, on long-term loan to the Philadelphia Museum of Art

Fig. 53
Marcel Duchamp (American, born France, 1887–1968), *The Bride Stripped Bare by Her Bachelors, Even (The Large Glass)*, 1915–23. Oil, varnish, lead foil, lead wire, and dust on two glass panels; 109¼ x 69¼ inches (277.5 x 175.9 cm). Philadelphia Museum of Art. Bequest of Katherine S. Dreier, 1952-98-1

Box that links the action of the chocolate grinder with the bachelors' onanistic activity, thus equating chocolate with semen: "Le célibataire broie son chocolat lui-même" (The bachelor grinds his chocolate himself).[93]

Chimes was not alone in his quest to inject some much-needed humor and eroticism into what he perceived to be the overly formal and austere painting and sculpture of the 1960s. He was no doubt aware of Robert Morris's voyeuristic *I-Box*, of 1962 (fig. 54), which updated Johns's earlier peek-a-boo target boxes through a small rectangular structure with a door shaped as the letter "I." When opened, the door gave way to a photograph of the naked artist, whose dangling penis rhymes with the I-shaped aperture. The *I-Box* thus fuses the act of looking with eroticism, as well as with the ego, as the work turns on a pun that conflates the viewer's looking eye with the artist's identity. Eva Hesse, Paul Thek, and fellow Greek-American artist Lucas Samaras also explored the erotic nature of sculpture, incorporating materials such as mirrors, hair, fur, wax, resin, and cast body parts as a way of subverting the impersonal industrial aesthetic of Minimalism through a refiguring of the Surrealist practice of displaying found objects for their fetishistic or sexually charged qualities. As Thek explained in a 1966 interview with the art critic Gene Swenson, "Today there's a new kind of Surrealism around. . . . Maybe it has to do with the individual gone underground."[94]

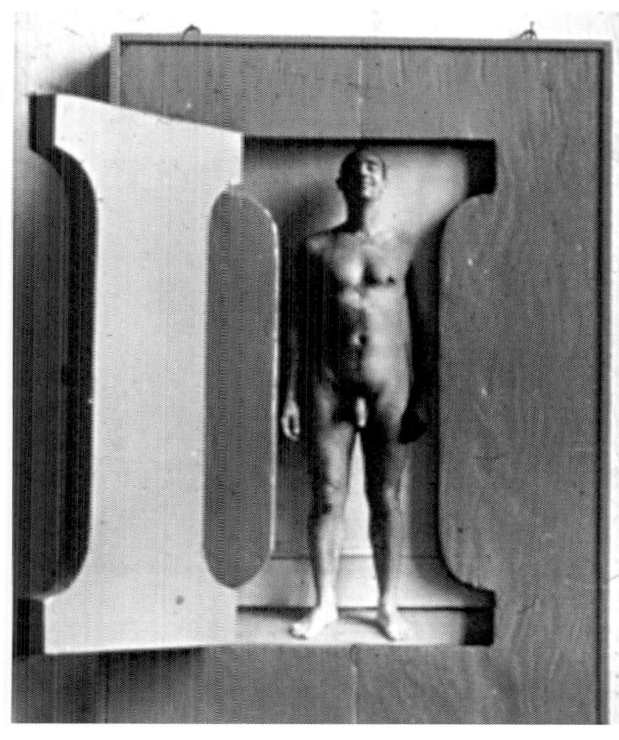

Once again, however, it is Robert Smithson whose approach comes closest to Chimes's artistic practice in the mid-1960s. As Caroline A. Jones has pointed out, Smithson's writings and works of this time, such as *Honeymoon Machine*, of 1964 (fig. 55), reveal that he had come "to understand the psychological dimension of technology and its function within the matrix of human desire. By implicitly or explicitly acknowledging the libido that drives the technological sublime, Smithson's works open that sublimity for desublimation."[95] Like Chimes's *Master and Own*, Smithson's *Honeymoon Machine* explores sexual arousal through electronic stimulation. In this case, the recumbent bride's nipples are wired to an elaborate turbine-like motor that presumably enables her to achieve multiple orgasms. The insatiable bride's electrified pleasure is contrasted in the work with the impassive groom, who evinces no signs of reciprocal arousal.[96] Smithson's device, like Chimes's metal box constructions, can be seen as a response to Duchamp's mechanical bride in *The Large Glass*, although the bride's domain is no longer the ethereal clouds and vaporous gases of the upper section of the glass, but the sleek, modern technological environment of the pinball machine or jukebox. Both Chimes and Smithson conflate sexual pleasure with mechanical apparatuses in their work, much like the desiring machines described by Gilles Deleuze and Félix Guattari, which achieve a genuine consummation that can be seen as "the nuptial celebration of a new alliance, a new birth, a radiant ecstasy, as though the eroticism of the machine liberated under other forces."[97]

The eroticized technology seen in works such as *Momo Talk* and *Master and Own* is also present in a large number of drawings on sexual themes that the artist made around 1966, which combine his interest in Artaud as a liberating force with new sources of inspiration, such as the deliciously perverse writings of the Marquis de Sade and the fin-de-siècle decadence of Aubrey Beardsley's Illustrations for Oscar Wilde's notorious play *Salomé*, of 1894, whose stylish blend of erotica and caricature would have a lasting impact on Chimes's work. Chimes appears to have based several self-portraits of the mid-1960s on the sinister, welcoming figure, half showman and half dramaturge, in the lower right corner of *Enter Herodias* (fig. 56), which Kenneth Clark once described as "the most evil of all Beardsley's drawings."[98] Appropriately enough, this master of ceremonies, who draws our attention like a circus barker to the dramatic entrance of the towering, omnipotent figure of Herodias, with her over-ripe breasts, is a caricature of Wilde, wearing the owl cap of a sage magician or sorcerer, who cradles the text of his play in the crook of his left arm, along with a caduceus. This symbolic scepter with two intertwined snakes is associated with the Greek herald-god Hermes, a figure of enormous importance for Chimes, which may explain why he was drawn to Beardsley's image of the arch-dandy Wilde. The Irish writer is depicted with Beardsley's trademark swarms of phosphorescent dots and masterly control of pure outline—features that Chimes emulated in his own pen-and-ink drawings of the mid- to late 1960s such as *Untitled (Costumed Figure in Profile)* (fig. 57) and *Portrait of Guillaume Apollinaire* (fig. 58).

Chimes's exquisitely rendered drawings of this period also reflect his awareness of the changing conditions of Surrealism after World War II, when group members embraced Tarot cards, black magic, pagan rituals, arcane imagery, and, above all, a new conception of Eros, as Alyce Mahon has persuasively argued in her recent book on the Surrealist movement between 1938 and 1968.[99]

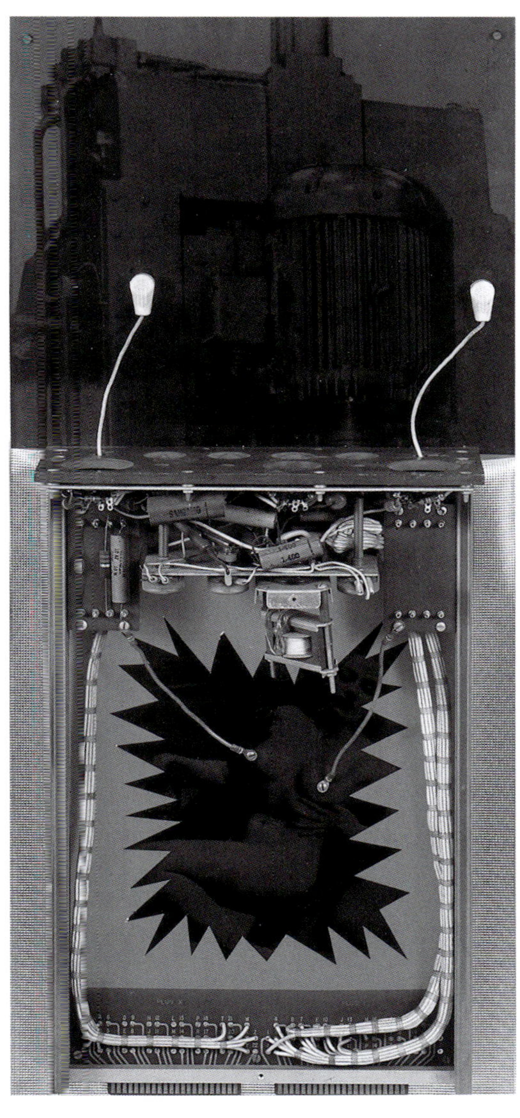

Chimes was clearly looking back to the work of Man Ray, Joseph Cornell, and Marcel Duchamp in these drawings and related mixed-media constructions, which often incorporate small symbolic drawings or objects such as soap or hair. These often humorous and erotic works were also a commentary on the formal austerity of Minimalism, which had begun to dominate the artistic climate of the mid- to late 1960s.

As Surrealists in the postwar era began to regard the sexual act as one of the last expressions of absolute freedom in a world dominated by brutal dictatorships, a key figure in their thinking was Donatien Alphonse François, the Marquis de Sade (1740–1814), whose deviant behavior and subversive ideas led to twenty-seven years of imprisonment, under three different regimes and in eleven prisons, before his death in 1814 in the asylum at Charenton-Saint-Maurice on the outskirts of Paris. A debauched, impious libertine who refused to submit to authority, Sade was yet another "possessed" historical figure with whom Chimes identified to the point of making a pen-and-ink drawing in 1966 titled *Hieropornometric Fix of a Drawing of and by the Master of the Charenton Iconographies* (pl. 23). The title, with its reference to the Charenton asylum

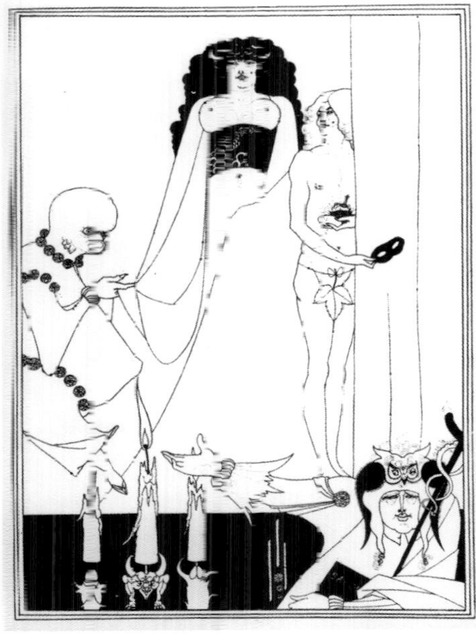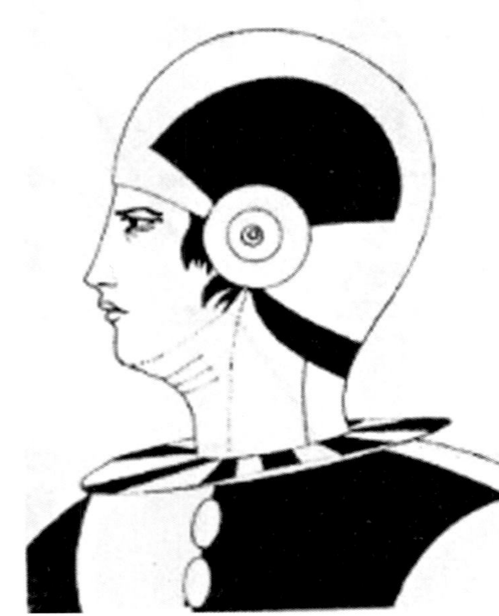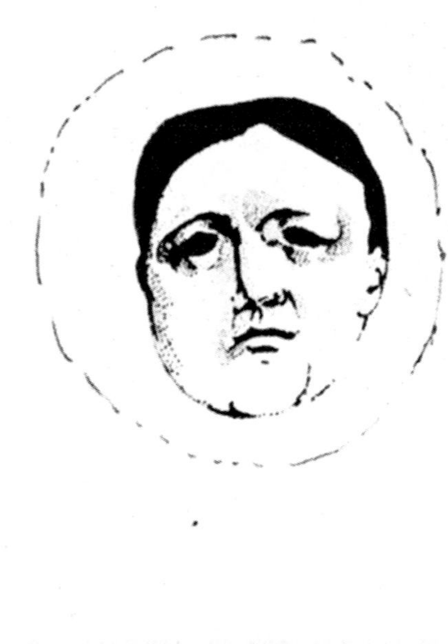

where Sade spent the last years of his life, reveals the work to be a coded self-portrait of the artist as the irascible, dissolute Marquis with his exhaustive "iconographies" of sexual aberrations.

The excessive cruelty, violence, and sexual depravity of Sade's writings, as laid out in pornographic novels such as *The 120 Days of Sodom* and *Juliette*, reflect his long years of captivity, which, far from dulling his imagination, instead spurred him on to conjure ever more elaborate scenarios for his insatiable heroes to carry out their perverse sexual practices. Vilified and repressed by "respectable" French society, which failed to comprehend his libertine fantasies and moral philosophy, Sade was revered by the Surrealists, as seen in Man Ray's *Imaginary Portrait of D. A. F. de Sade*, of 1938 (fig. 59), in which the writer witnesses the burning of the Bastille, symbolizing his temporary freedom from institutional bondage. However, Man Ray symbolically "built" his monument to Sade out of bricks and mortar to underline the fact that prison defined the Marquis; he could never be rehabilitated and would spend the rest of his life in the Charenton asylum. Sade's incarceration at Charenton connected him in Chimes's mind with Artaud, who also spent a major part of his adult life behind bars. Like Artaud, Sade was a nonconformist and at times a dangerous extremist, a revolutionary in art and life, who threatened to throw open the floodgates of delirium and the imagination and sweep aside the oppressive moral restraints of church and state in a raging torrent of unfettered libidinous desires.

Sade's complete freedom from taste, morality, and convention inspired Chimes to make a number of important drawings in the mid-1960s, some of which were intended to be included in metal boxes, while others were made for private delectation. In their Sadean impulse these works on paper can be compared to the erotic drawings of Hans Bellmer, André Masson, and Matta. On occasion, it could lead to extraordinary results, as in *Priapus*, of 1966 (pl. 27), in which the Greek god of male generative power is represented appropriately as a giant, erect phallus with eyes and a mouth, possibly derived from Beardsley's use of oversized male genitalia in his illustrations for *The Lysistrata of Aristophanes*. Chimes continued this "dickhead" imagery in a number of works, including a self-portrait with a large, columnlike penis growing out of his head and breasts made out of spherical testicles. This drawing may have been inspired by passages in

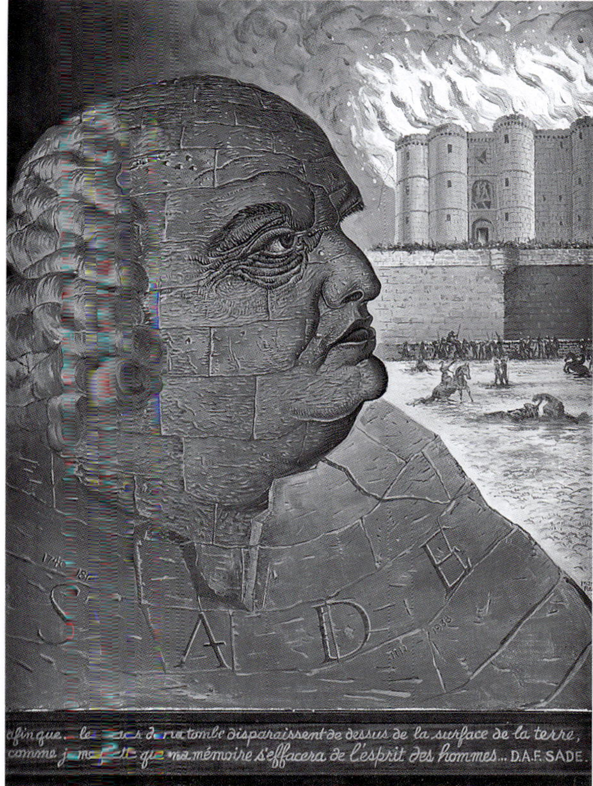

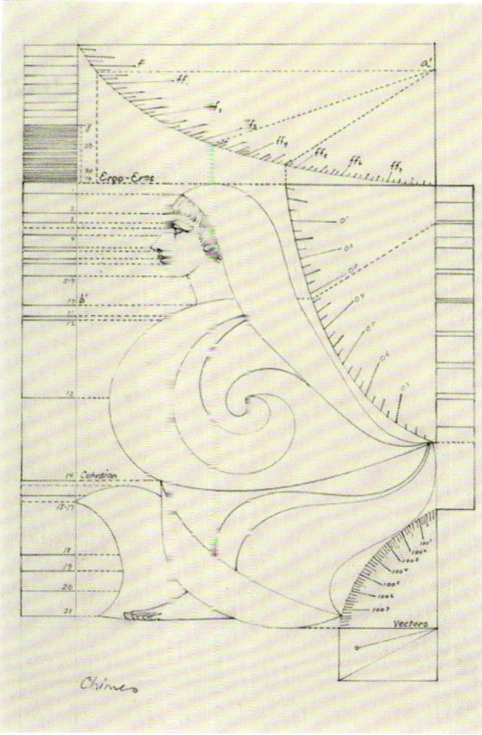

Fig. 59
Man Ray (American, 1890–1976), *Imaginary Portrait of D. A. F. de Sade*, 1938. Oil on canvas, 21⅝ x 17¾ inches (54.9 x 45.1 cm). The Menil Collection, Houston

Fig. 60
Thomas Chimes, *Ergo-Eros*, 1966. Pencil on paper, 8½ x 5½ inches (21.6 x 14 cm). Private collection

Sade's writings, which often describe columns, tables, armchairs, chandeliers, and other furnishings composed exclusively of the naked bodies of young men and women artistically arranged.

Other pencil drawings from this time, such as *Vectors* (pl. 28) and *Ergo-Eros* (fig. 60), both made in 1966, present women as sphinxlike, ambivalent beings, rendered in a mysteriously diagrammatic side view that relates to the artist's preoccupation with equating the sexual act with mathematical equations and geometry. In *Vectors*, the complex accoutrements worn by the mysterious woman in profile take on the appearance of armor. Concealed within their hermetic environments, these armor-plated women can be compared to the corseted prostitutes and gauntleted chorus girls of Richard Lindner, the German-born American artist whose lascivious erotic fantasies were widely shown and reproduced during the 1960s, when critics and art historians rightfully recognized their importance as a powerful precursor to the work of the Pop artist.

THE MESSAGE OF MARSHALL McLUHAN

On April 28, 1966, Tom Chimes and his wife attended a lecture at the University of Pennsylvania that would prove to be the decisive turning point in his move from oil painting to metal box constructions. The lecture, part of a symposium on Pop Art and popular culture,[100] was given by Professor Herbert Marshall McLuhan of the University of Toronto, who was billed as "a controversial authority on communications."[101] McLuhan was a Canadian philosopher and cultural theorist, famous for gnomic utterances such as "the medium is the message," who articulated the impact and application of new technology, especially the electronic revolution of television and computers, in a postindustrial society that was increasingly shaped by a rapidly advancing consumer and entertainment culture (fig. 61).

Chimes may have been attracted by the provocative title of McLuhan's talk, "From Gutenberg to Batman," but he was probably already aware of the Canadian author's writings, such as his Duchamp-inspired *The Mechanical Bride: Folklore and Industrial Man* (1951) and the better-known *Understanding Media* (1964). Given his earlier interest in Edgar Allan Poe's writings, Chimes may also have been drawn to McLuhan's reference, in *The Mechanical Bride*, to the short story "A Descent into the Maelström," in which a Norwegian sailor saves himself from drowning in a stormy sea by studying and cooperating with the action of the prodigious whirlpool that is sucking him under.[102] Poe's account of the mariner's rational detachment amidst the apparent chaos and crisis of the sea's foamy vortex provided the perfect metaphor for McLuhan's method of analyzing the societal and cultural impact of new technologies such as radio, television, movies, and advertising.

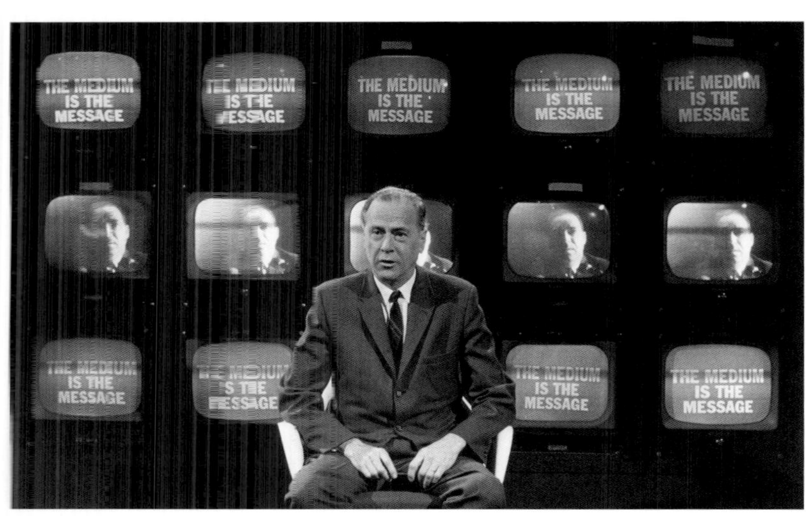

Fig. 61
Marshall McLuhan during an interview on the Canadian Broadcasting Corporation's *Other Voices*, June 22, 1965. Courtesy of the CBC Archives, Toronto

In 1962, in *The Gutenberg Galaxy*, McLuhan coined the term that would make him famous when he wrote, "The new electronic interdependence recreates the world in the image of a global village."[103] By 1966, when Chimes heard McLuhan speak at Penn, the philosopher had become an international celebrity, not just through his books, but also thanks to the many television appearances, book reviews, and attempts to interpret his controversial theories. McLuhan's work focused on the implications of the post–World War II cultural shift from hardware to software, as the centuries-old technology of moveable type introduced by the Gutenberg printing press was challenged by the instant speed of electric information via satellite telecommunication and its byproducts, such as television, which he viewed as a "technological extension of our central nervous system."[104]

McLuhan's lecture at the University of Pennsylvania reinforced many of Chimes's own ideas about the role of the artist in an age of rapid technological advancement that had led to an enormous speedup of information services. Beginning with the notion that "the future of the future is the present," McLuhan went on to proclaim that only the artist "has the courage or the sensory training to look directly into the present."[105] The central idea of McLuhan's lecture was that this new world of electronic all-at-onceness had created, on the one hand, a condition of nonperception and confusion about the present, and on the other, a clear image of the preceding era of Gutenberg type. As a seer or prophet, it is the role of the artist (and here McLuhan quoted Wyndham Lewis) to write "a detailed history of the future because he alone is capable of seeing the present."[106]

These ideas were perhaps best expressed by the Pop artists, whose work was not the product of "a new environment of electric information," McLuhan argued, but rather "the old mechanical environment suddenly observable as an art form." In other words, new technology renders the existing technology obsolete and thus ripe for artistic appropriation. In the case of Pop Art one can think of the world of Hollywood movies, comic books, and commercial advertising that artists such as Andy Warhol, James Rosenquist, and Roy Lichtenstein mined for imagery in the

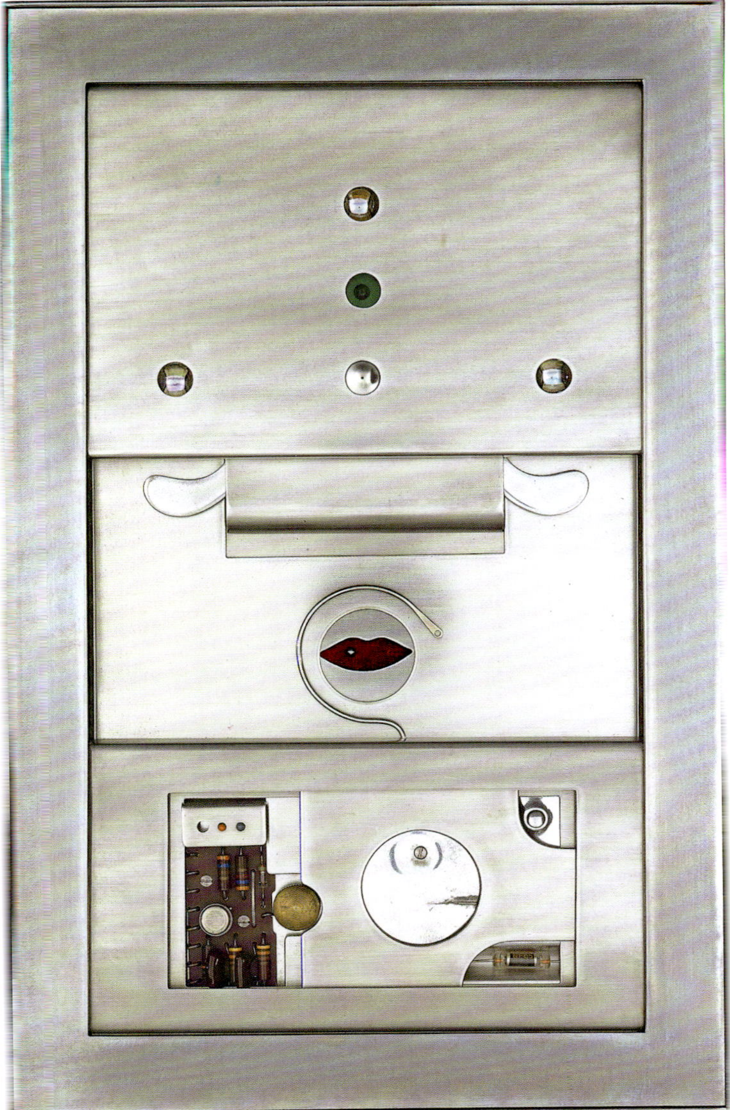

Fig. 62
Thomas Chimes, *Untitled
(Pearl)*, 1968. Mixed-
media metal box,
12½ x 7½ inches
(31.8 x 19.1 cm). Private
collection

early 1960s. "Pop Art," McLuhan observed, "is an indication that as the whole planet goes inside a new satellite-and-information environment made by man, we can no longer afford to deal with the human habitat as something given to us by Nature. We now have to accept the fact and responsibility that the entire human environment is an artifact, an art form, something that can be staged and manipulated like show biz."[107] Pop Art had thus managed with pinpoint accuracy to reflect the shallow surface of Hollywood glamour and the manipulative tactics of the advertising industry.

McLuhan went on to explain to his audience that they were about to witness "a large change-over in our entertainment industry. Like many large changes, much has been hidden from view until the last minute. The American public is about to enter the entertainment industry as participant. While attention remains riveted on the rear-view mirror of audience ratings and packaged programs, the audience, in fact, has moved ever closer to an active role."[108] According to McLuhan's prophecy, electronic technology would transform the nature of the audience from passive viewer to active participant. This in turn would have a domino effect, ensuring that business would now resemble show business, and we would move from a world of continuity and gradualness to one of abrupt interface and rapid encounters, where no meaningful connections are possible. The key point here, and one that was not lost on Chimes, was the

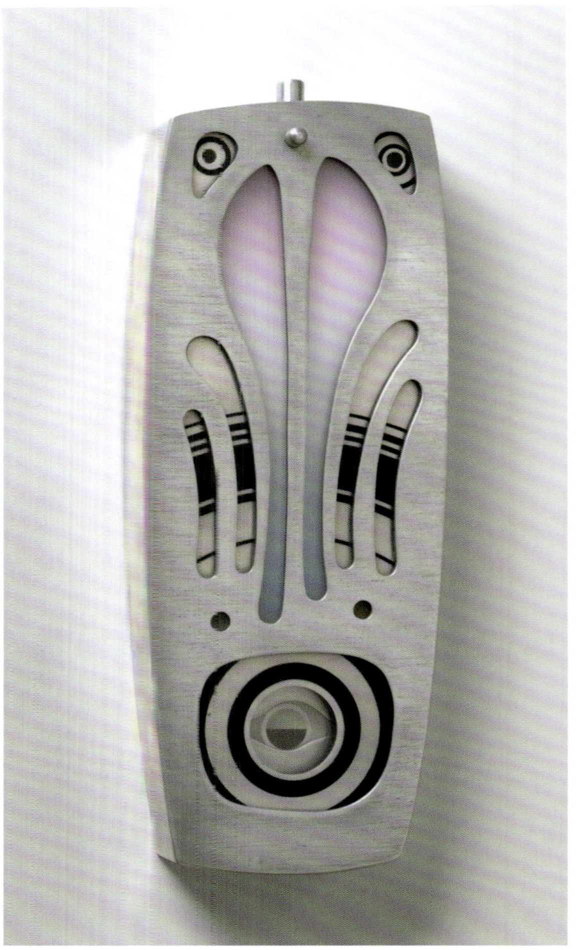

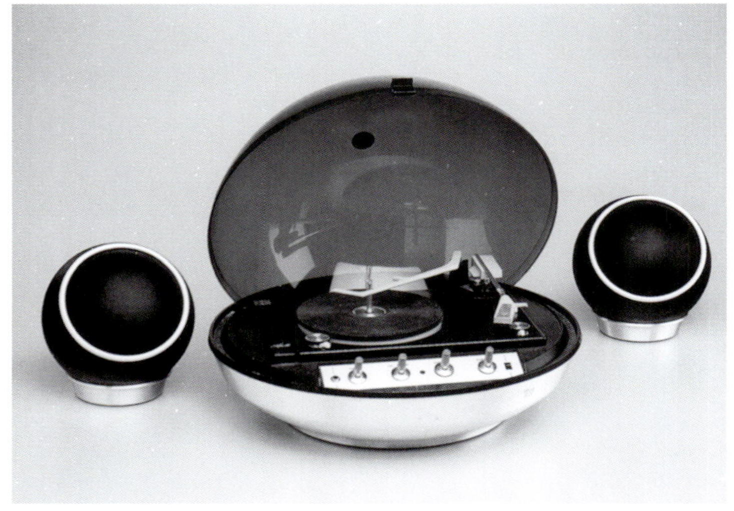

role of the artist in this new world of interface and encounter. McLuhan viewed the artist as a kind of seer or prophet, whose radarlike ability to predict and anticipate the future allows us to cope with technological and social change when it finally arrives. This is why McLuhan concluded his lecture by countering this one-way flow of speeded-up information with praise for the artist as someone who sharpens our perceptions, since by their very nature poets and painters are "antisocial types who refuse to go along with the main currents and trends."[109]

The impact of McLuhan's lecture is keenly felt in the metal boxes that followed, such as *Untitled (Metal Box)* of 1966 (pl. 25), and *Untitled (Pearl)*, of 1968 (fig. 62), which display an increasing concern for systems and process over symbols and images. The finely crafted metal constructions are embellished with electronic circuitry and references to computers, radios, walkie-talkies (fig. 63), record players, speakers, and other forms of new electronic media. These works reveal Chimes to be optimistically open to new technology as a revolutionary and McLuhanesque extension of life, although at times he reverts to the sinuous lines and sensuous exteriors of the Art Nouveau movement, as in *Untitled (Radio)*, of about 1967 (pl. 26). The first metal box, created in 1965, was designed to hang around the artist's neck, like a medallion.[110] Chimes was clearly playing with the idea of inner versus outer vision in this work, which he inscribed "proto invisigraph," and whose rectangular structure, assembled from embossed metal plates over a wooden core, closely resembles a camera. However, the subsequent metal boxes went further in their exploration of electronic media, often displaying the inner workings of machines, such as circuit boards and inverters, as well as their sleek exteriors. A comparison between Chimes's metal boxes and the brushed aluminum and smoked Plexiglas of the curvaceous Apollo 861 record player, of 1966 (fig. 64), for example, reveals that the artist was paying close attention to the industrial design of the consumer products of his time, whose erotic allure he enhances in his own work through body parts and electric switches. In these works, Chimes can be seen as imagining the future in the present, since according to McLuhan, the electronic environment will eventually be replaced by new technology that will turn the old gadgets into works of art. The metal box constructions thus anticipate the planned obsolescence of new technology. They are art works before their time, strange artifacts from an imaginary future that replaced the electronic age with technology born of a new situation.

Some works, such as the *IBM Box* (pl. 24), relate specifically to McLuhan's writings. In his famous essay "The Medium Is the Message," published in 1964, the philosopher praised IBM, which had put the first fully transistorized computer on the market in the United States in 1959, as one of the few industrial companies that had "become aware of the various kinds of business in which they are engaged. When IBM discovered that it was not in the business of making office equipment or business machines, but that it was in the business of processing information, then it began to navigate with clear vision."[111] Chimes's metal box can be understood as a response to McLuhan's ideas, since it is a work of art that could easily be mistaken for an electronic device, while it also displays an awareness of the personal and social consequences of its medium. This may explain the artist's decision to place a surrogate self-portrait within a circular aperture of the *IBM Box*. This drawing appears to hover between a Leonardo da Vinci–like embrace of new technology, given its allusions to science and geometry, and an apprehension about the inherent dangers of the new information age, as suggested by the threatening arrows that impinge on the portrait like daggers.

Metal boxes such as *Geometry Love*, of 1966–69 (pl. 29), and *Construction #403*, of 1967 (pl. 30), similarly fuse a McLuhanesque interest in new forms of technology and communication with the heated eroticism that came out of Chimes's admiration for the debauched writings of the Marquis de Sade. In a 1968 interview in *Playboy* magazine, McLuhan predicted that technological advancements would lead to the development of a "love machine" that would take care of all our sexual needs: "Projecting current trends, the love machine would appear a natural development in the near future—not just the current computerized datefinder, but a machine whereby ultimate orgasm is achieved by direct mechanical stimulation of the pleasure circuits of the brain."[112] This notion of a love machine stimulating our senses through electronic circuitry found popular expression in Jane Fonda's explosive, mechanically induced orgasm in the 1968 erotic sci-fi movie *Barbarella: Queen of the Galaxy* (fig. 65), as well as Woody Allen's hilariously kinky "Orgasmatron" in the 1973 film *Sleeper*, which accidentally traps Allen inside, leading to a

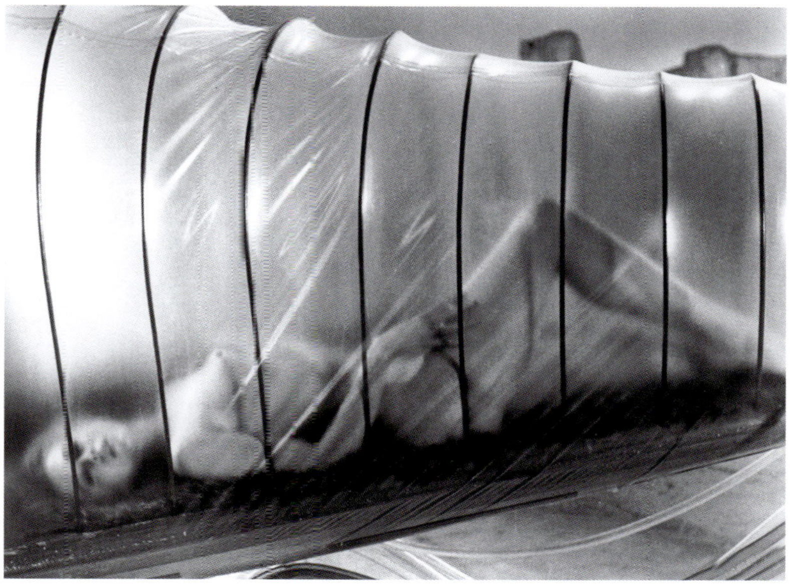

Fig. 65
Jane Fonda in *Barbarella: Queen of the Galaxy*, directed by Roger Vadim, Paramount Pictures, 1968. Photograph © Motion Picture & Television Photo Archive

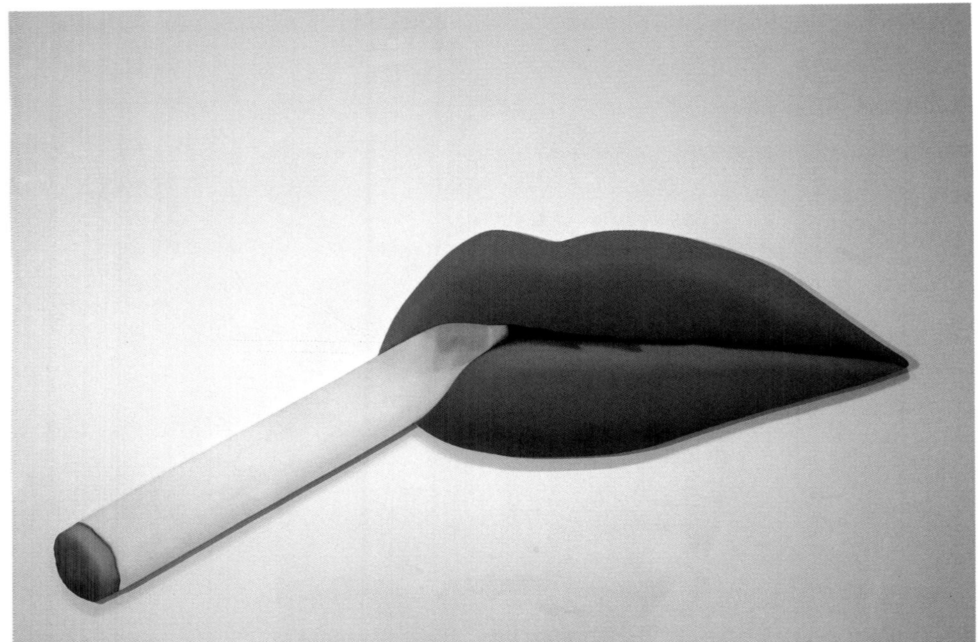

Fig. 66
Tom Wesselmann
(American, 1931–2004),
Mouth #11, 1967. Oil on
canvas, 68 x 152 inches
(172.7 x 386.1 cm). Dallas
Museum of Art.
Foundation for the Arts
Collection, Mr. and Mrs.
Edward S. Marcus Fund,
1968.7.FA

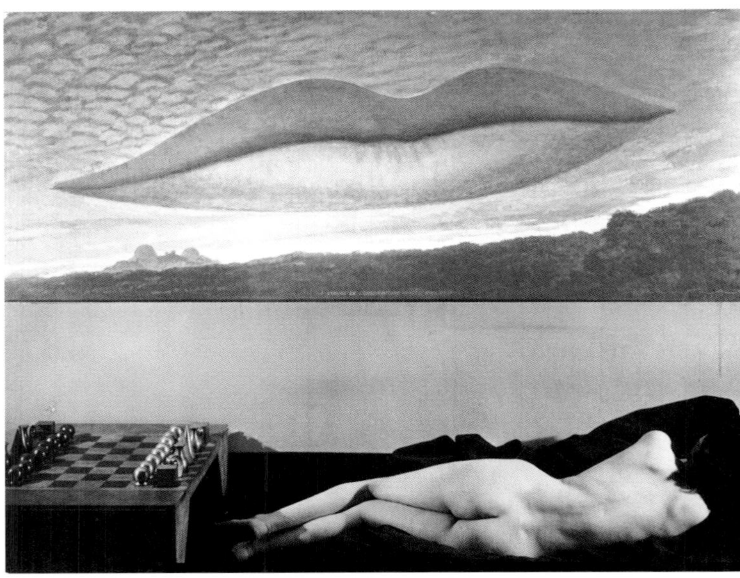

Fig. 67
Man Ray, *Observatory
Time— The Lovers*, 1934.
Collage. Musée National
d'Art Moderne, Centre
Georges Pompidou, Paris

sensory overload! McLuhan's idea of a futuristic love machine resonates in many of Chimes's metal box constructions of the late 1960s, which project the idea of oral and genital stimulation through the connection of electric switches and circuitry with body parts and lips. The frequent incorporation of images of open mouths and parted lips may relate to the work of American Pop artists such as James Rosenquist and Tom Wesselmann (fig. 66), although Chimes has also referenced Man Ray's floating, disembodied lips in *Observatory Time— The Lovers*, of 1934 (fig. 67). However, the resulting metal boxes, despite their formal elegance, transcend their origin in Surrealist and Pop imagery to produce a startling iconography of sadomasochistic pleasure and pain in the age of McLuhan. In the case of *Construction #403*, the artist has equated the pleasure or pain inflicted on the erect phallus, to which electric wires have been ominously connected, with the suffering of Jesus Christ by incorporating a tiny fragment featuring a head of Christ that was once part of a larger crucifixion painting that he later cut down. The body of

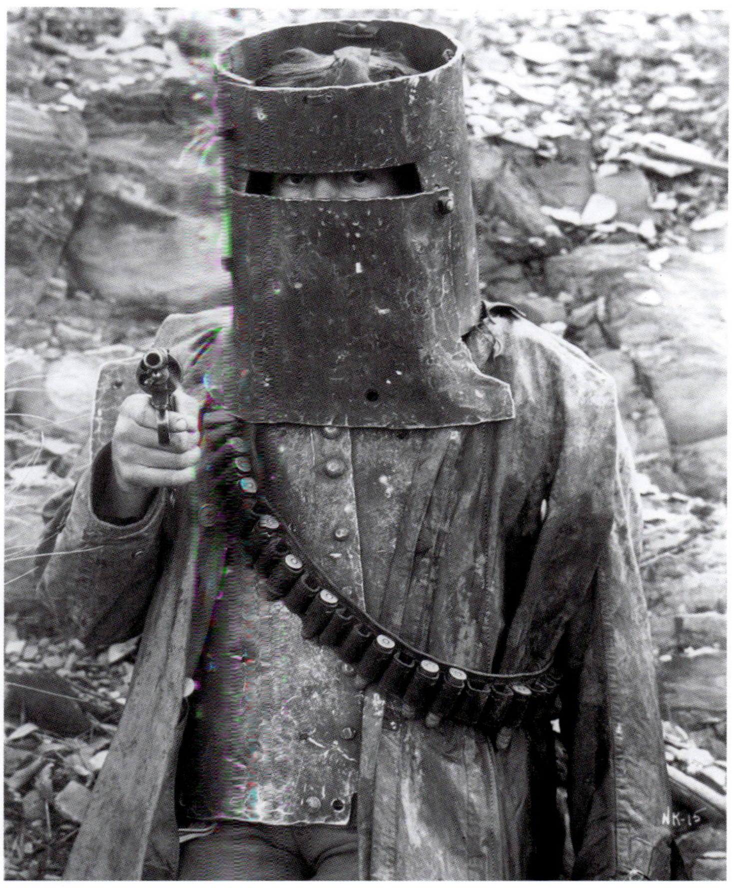

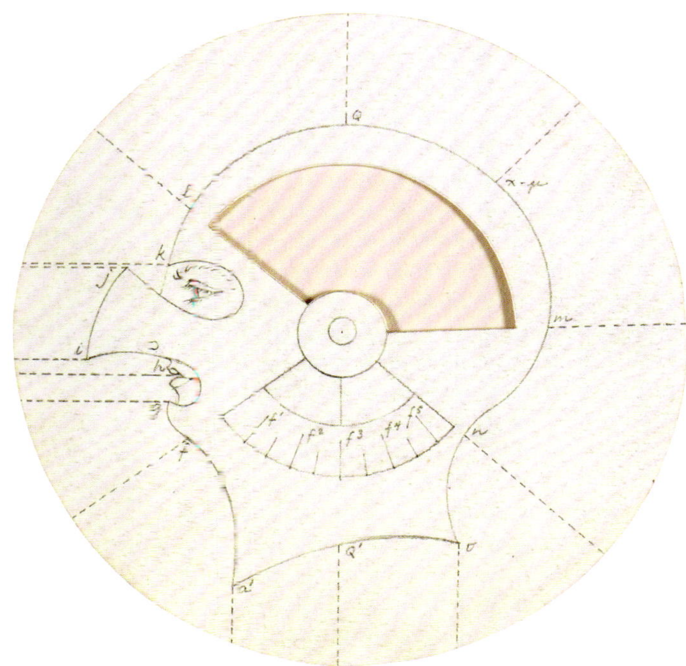

Christ from this earlier work appears in another metal box of the same year, where it was presented as an erect phallus.

By the early 1970s the metal box constructions increasingly incorporated portraits of celebrities and icons of popular culture, such as Mick Jagger and John Lennon, albeit disguised through helmets and beards. In *Top Hat*, of 1970 (pl. 35), we can identify the figure underneath the strange helmet as Mick Jagger in his title role in the film *Ned Kelly*, directed by Tony Richardson which was made in the same year (fig. 68). Jagger played the legendary Australian outlaw who was famous for wearing a cast-iron bucket on his head for protection against police bullets, and whose armed gang robbed two banks and killed three policemen in a crime spree that began in April 1878.[113] The Kelly gang successfully evaded capture by the authorities until their last stand at Glenrowan Station in the Australian outback in 1880, when their failed attempt to ambush a police special train ended with three gang members killed and Ned captured and badly wounded. The twenty-five-year-old Kelly was quickly taken to Melbourne, where he was hanged on November 11, thus passing into Australian legend as a Robin Hood–like bandit who paid a heavy price for resisting authority. Chimes admired Jagger's charismatic performance in the film and made *Top Hat* from memory. He was naturally drawn to the bushranger's trademark bulletproof helmet due to his earlier interest in armor, as seen in works like *Green Box*, of 1966–68 (pl. 33), and the two related drawings (figs. 57, 69). Chimes was interested in the way that helmets conceal one's identity while at the same time allowing an outlaw like Kelly to attain the mythic status of a medieval knight by wearing an iron bucket on his head.

The three-dimensional metal box constructions came to an end around 1972, when Chimes sensed that he had exhausted the format and wanted to return to painting on a flat

Fig. 68
Mick Jagger in *Ned Kelly*, directed by Tony Richardson, 1970. Courtesy of Photofest, New York

Fig. 69
Thomas Chimes, *Armor Head*, c. 1968. Pencil on paper, diameter 3¾ inches (9.5 cm). Private collection, courtesy of Locks Gallery, Philadelphia

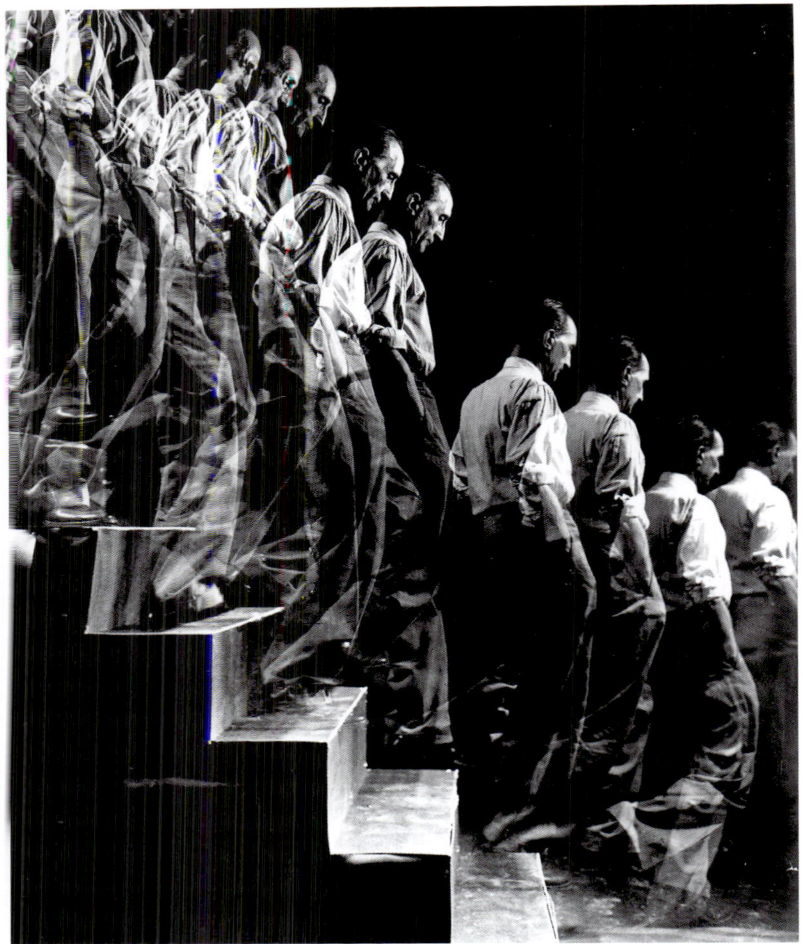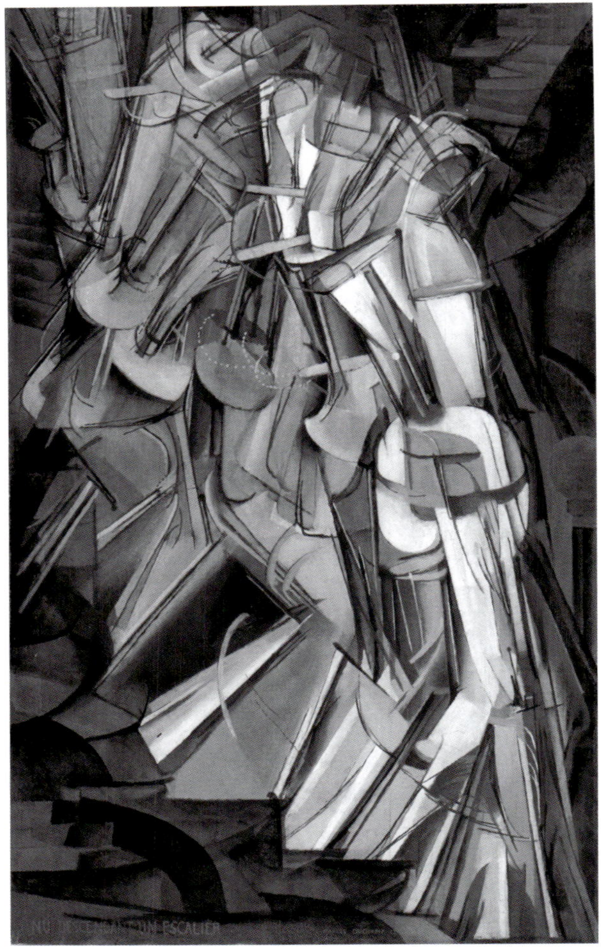

surface. A key work in this transition is *Set*, of 1972 (pl. 39), which features the disguised profile of Marcel Duchamp based on a 1952 *Life* magazine photograph (fig. 70). The source image, taken by Eliot Elisofon, was used to illustrate an article by Winthrop Sargeant entitled "Dada's Daddy,"[114] for which Duchamp agreed to walk down a set of stairs in imitation of his infamous 1912 painting *Nude Descending a Staircase (No. 2)* (fig. 71), which had made him an international celebrity after it was shown at the 1913 Armory Show in New York. Elisofon's repetitive flash photograph of the fully clothed artist nonchalantly descending the stairs with his hand in his pocket paid homage to Duchamp's landmark painting, as well as to the chronophotographs of Etienne Jules Marey and Eadweard Muybridge that inspired it.

Chimes took as his source material one of the sequential images of Duchamp's head in Elisofon's photograph, even retaining the dazzling white reflection of the flashbulb on his bowed head, but then flattened the nose like a boxer's so that the famous artist would not be instantly recognizable. The curved snout is also a reference to the Egyptian god Set, for whom the work is titled. Set was the god of chaos, thought to resemble an aardvark, who seized the souls of ordinary Egyptians on their journey through the underworld, perhaps linking him in Chimes's mind with Duchamp's descent in the photograph, as well as his famous notion that in the future artists would go underground. The Philadelphia artist's reverence for Duchamp's detached, ironic mind, his absolute individualism, and his disdain for the commodification of the art world can be traced back to Sargeant's *Life* magazine article, which recounted in great detail the artist's role in the international Dada movement of the 1910s and early 1920s. The article ended with a description of Duchamp's tiny, garretlike studio on the top floor of the building at 210 West Fourteenth Street in New York, where he had removed the telephone in order to avoid people who might disturb him with trivial phone calls. Sargeant was clearly moved by the sixty-four-year-old artist's spartan existence and his lack of ambition, both in chess and art, which might threaten his individuality by entangling him in competitive activity.

"It seems a strange place for a high-brow to live," Sargeant wrote, "but that is probably the very reason Duchamp has chosen it—to outwit anyone who might expect him to compromise his individuality by doing the obvious thing. . . . His rent is $40 a month, fitting into an extremely economical budget by means of which he succeeds in outwitting the whole competitive commercial rat race of New York."[115] Duchamp's living arrangements like Alfred Jarry's "reduced" quarters at 7, rue Cassette (the so-called *Grande Chasublerie*),[116] resonated strongly with Chimes's own sense of himself as a reclusive visionary in the mystical tradition of William Blake and Albert Pinkham Ryder. Duchamp was thus an important role model for Chimes in the 1960s and early 1970s, at a time when the younger artist's work was becoming increasingly hermetic and antithetical to the current interests of the New York avant-garde to which he had previously belonged.

Taking Duchamp's advice that the great artist of tomorrow will go underground, Chimes began to cultivate a hermitlike existence that suited his fierce intelligence and voracious reading habits. The artist had supported himself and his family since the mid-1960s through teaching positions at the Philadelphia College of Art, where he taught painting classes from 1966 to 1967, and Moore College of Art, where he joined the faculty in 1971 and by 1972 was chairman of the sculpture department. Teaching provided financial support but also drained him, both physically and intellectually, and his work suffered as a result, especially during the early 1970s when he began experimenting with gridlike compositions made up of vertical or horizontal strips of Plexiglas plastic. These works are among the artist's least successful, perhaps because their highly formal relationships displaced, at least temporarily, Chimes's natural inclination toward hermetic imagery and enigmatic subject matter.

Chimes's increasingly reclusive behavior may therefore reflect a desire to conserve his energy for the studio, rather than waste it frivolously. The result of the artist's underground activity was the startling revelation that his previous work had an internal coherence. What brought together this seemingly random and eclectic group of landscapes, crucifixion paintings, metal boxes, and portraits was an overriding interest in the tradition of inward-looking writers and artists from Poe to Duchamp, whose radical work and nonconformist behavior transgressed social norms. Chimes has described a kind of "guild secrecy" that links the work of van Gogh, Artaud, Jarry, and Duchamp in his mind, and it was this discovery that led him to embark on his series of panel portraits that immediately followed the completion of *Set*.

The use of a photograph as source material for the image of Duchamp in *Set* prefigures Chimes's working practice in the haunting series of forty-eight panel portraits he would make between 1973 and 1978. The artist also enjoyed the challenge of painting a portrait or likeness on wood panel, with a heavy grain that resisted the brush. These two things came together in his extended series of panel portraits of French Symbolist poets, philosophers and other nineteenth- and early-twentieth-century literary and art-historical figures, all of which were painted from photographic sources with a loving attention to detail.

overleaf:
Fig. 72
Thomas Chimes with
metal box self-portrait,
c. 1968. Courtesy of
Rodger LaPelle

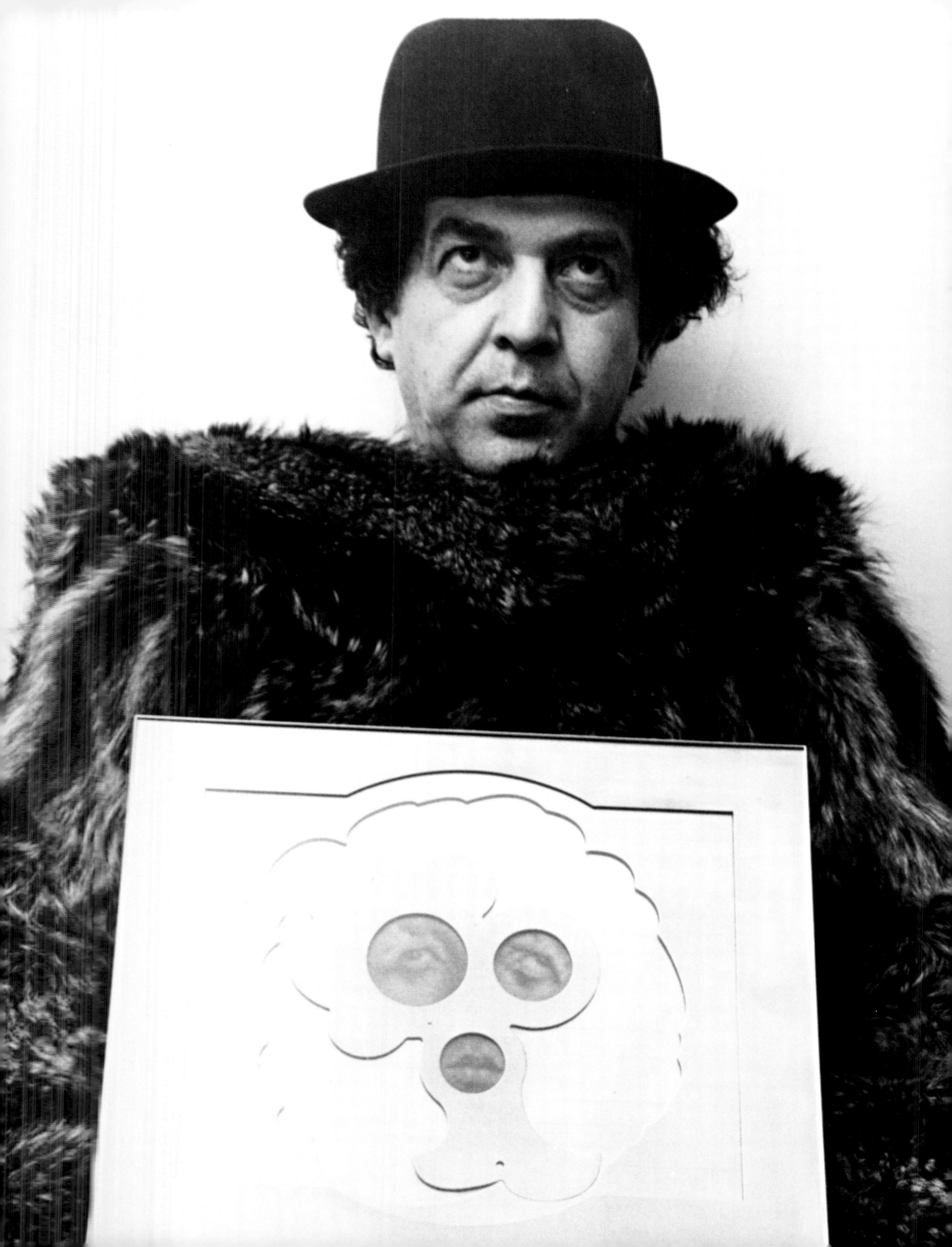

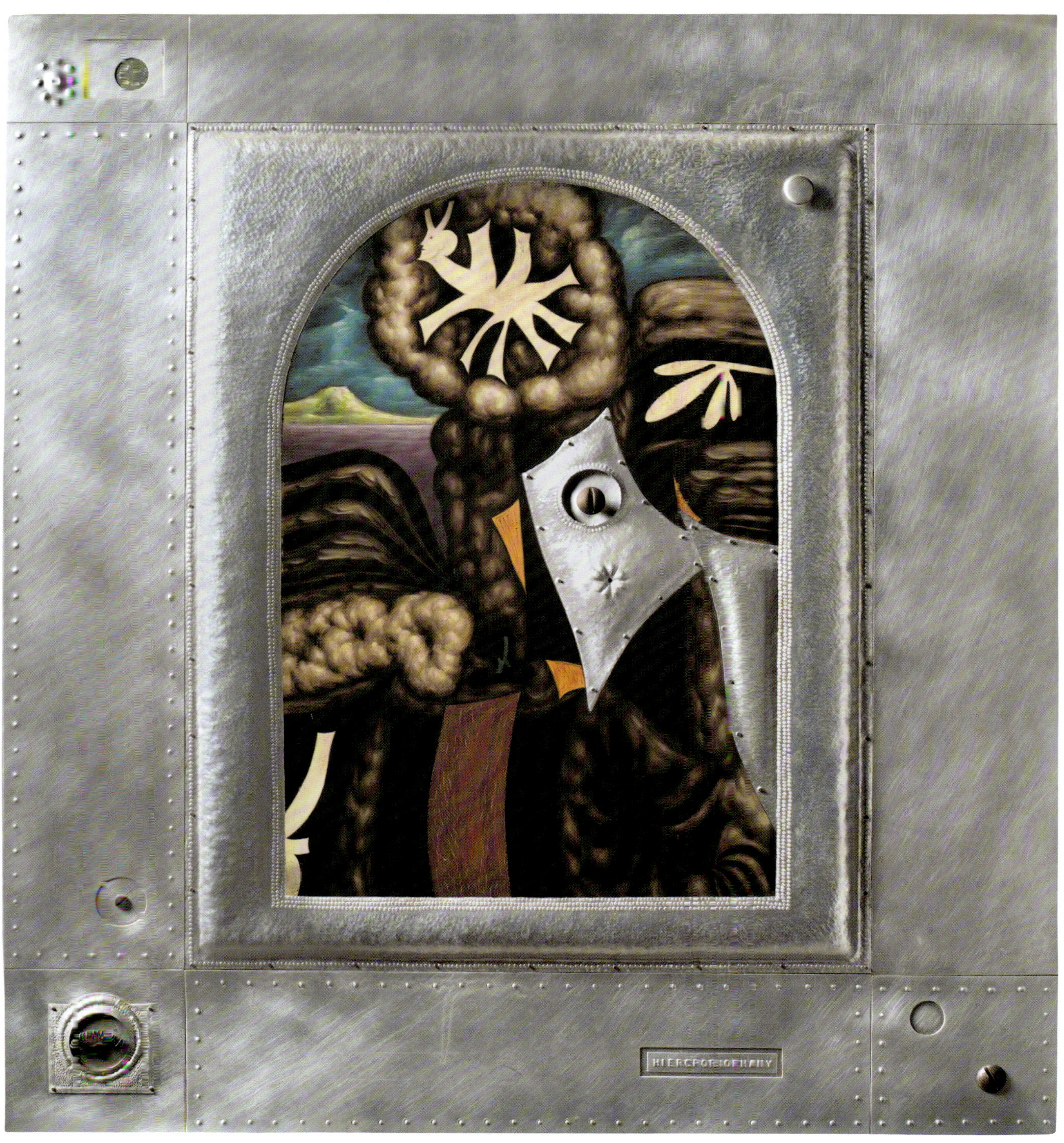

PLATE 18

Hieropornophany, c. 1965

OIL ON PANEL IN ALUMINUM FRAME

22 x 20 INCHES (55.9 x 50.8 CM)

PRIVATE COLLECTION

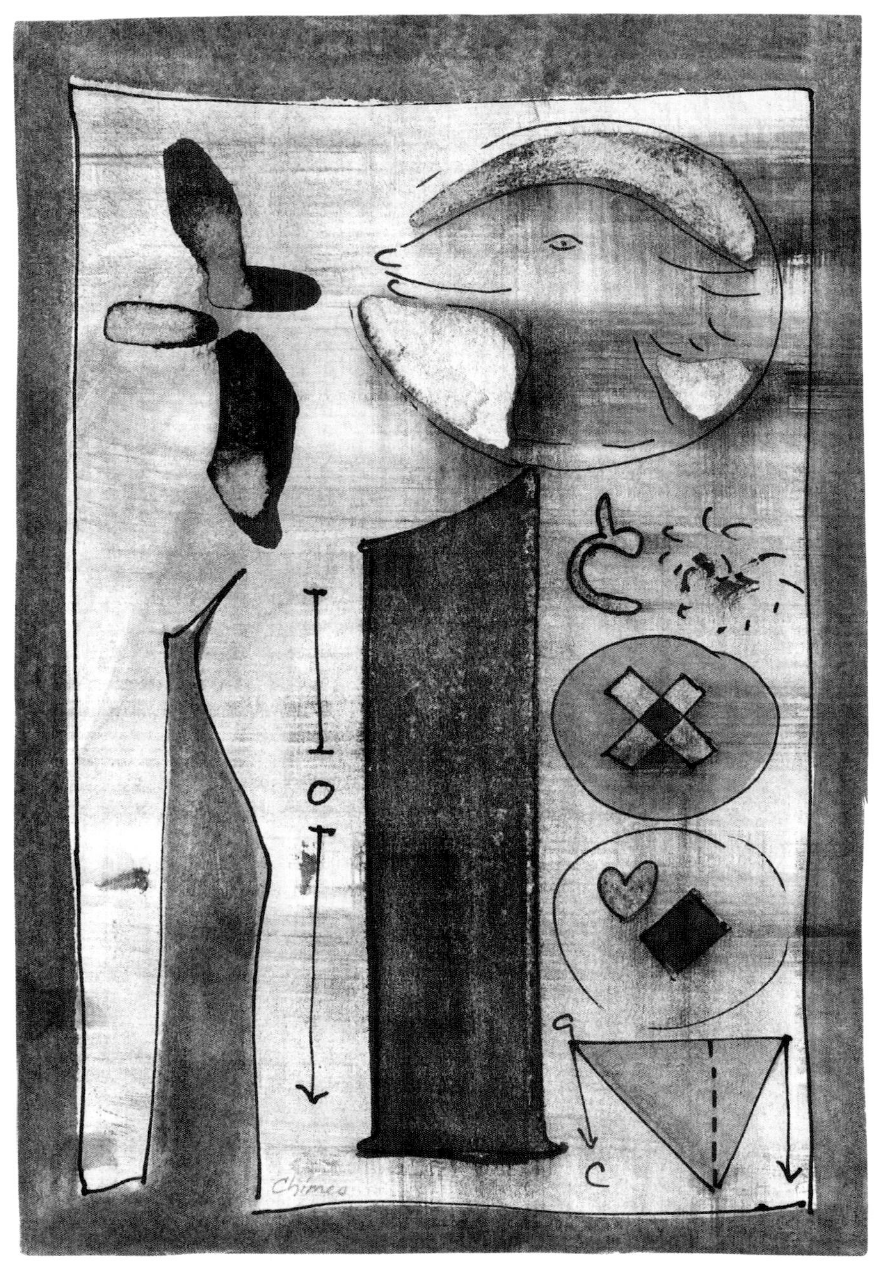

PLATE 19

Momo, 1965

INK AND WASH ON WOVE PAPER

8½ x 5⅝ INCHES (21.6 x 14.3 CM)

PHILADELPHIA MUSEUM OF ART. JULIUS BLOCH FUND PURCHASE, 2001-75-1

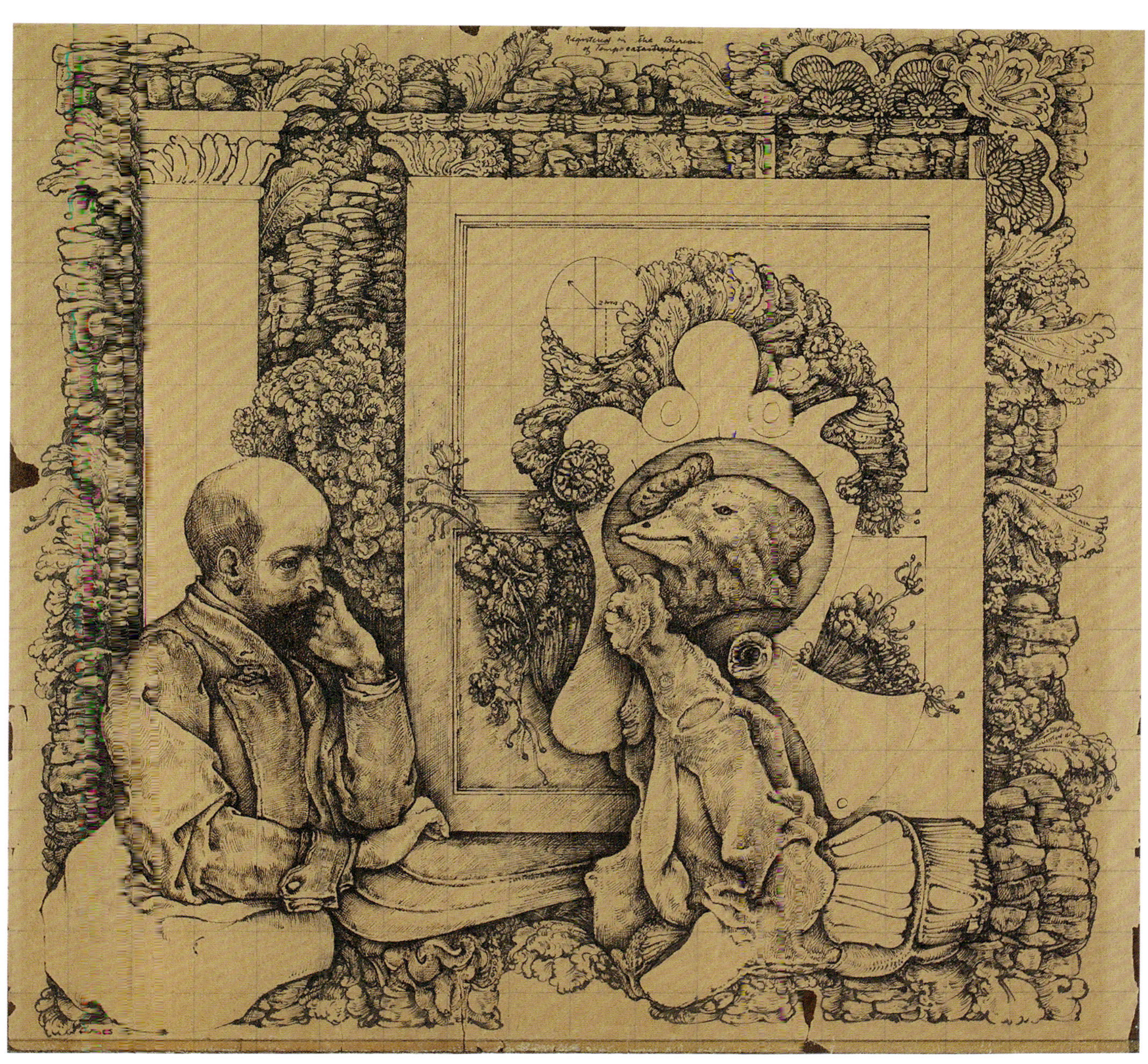

PLATE 20

Registered in the Bureau of Tempo Catastrophe, c. 1966

INK ON PAPER MOUNTED ON MASONITE

17¼ x 19½ INCHES (43.8 x 49.5 CM)

COLLECTION OF DAWN CHIMES, VENICE, FLORIDA

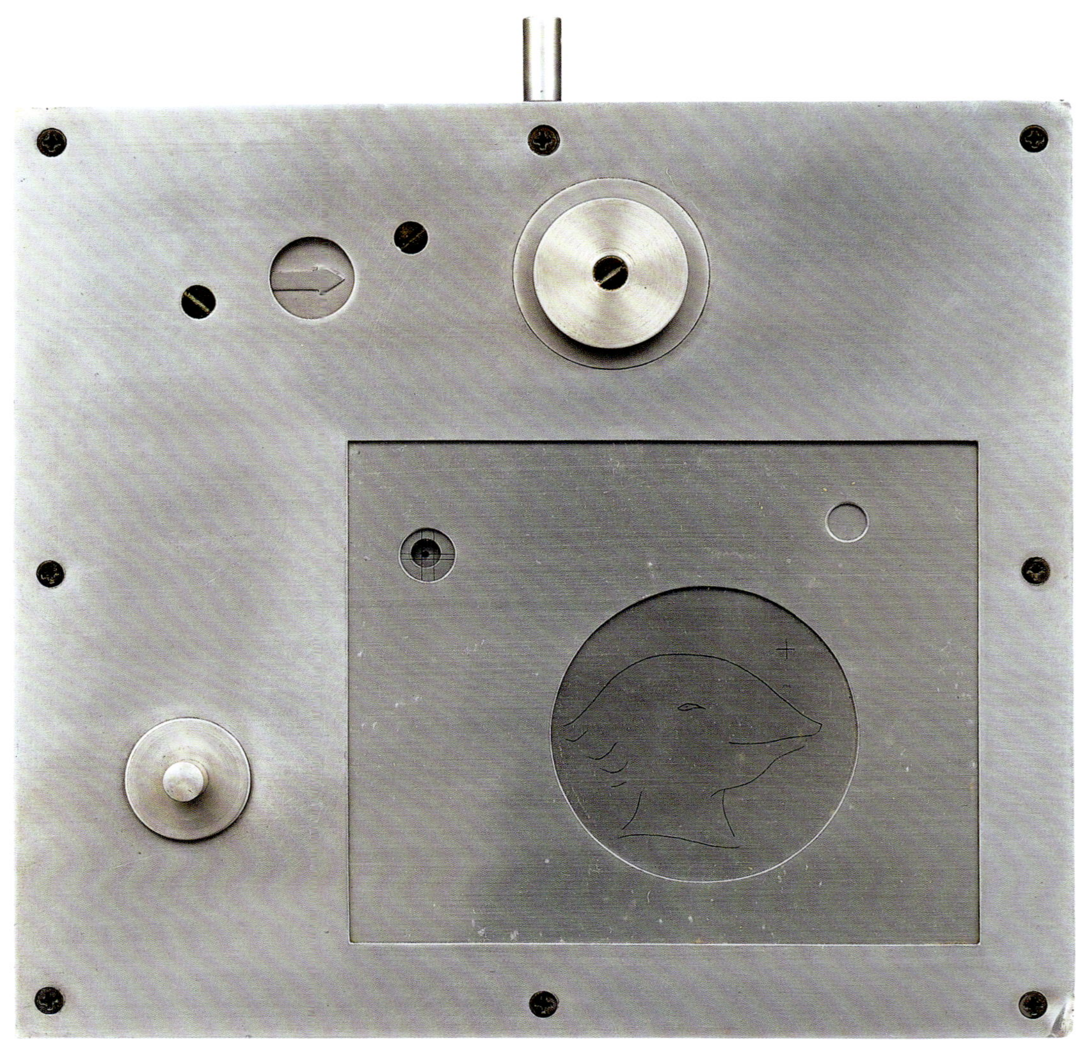

Le Momo, 1965

MIXED-MEDIA METAL BOX

9⅛ x 10 INCHES (23.2 x 25.4 CM)

PRIVATE COLLECTION, COURTESY OF LOCKS GALLERY, PHILADELPHIA

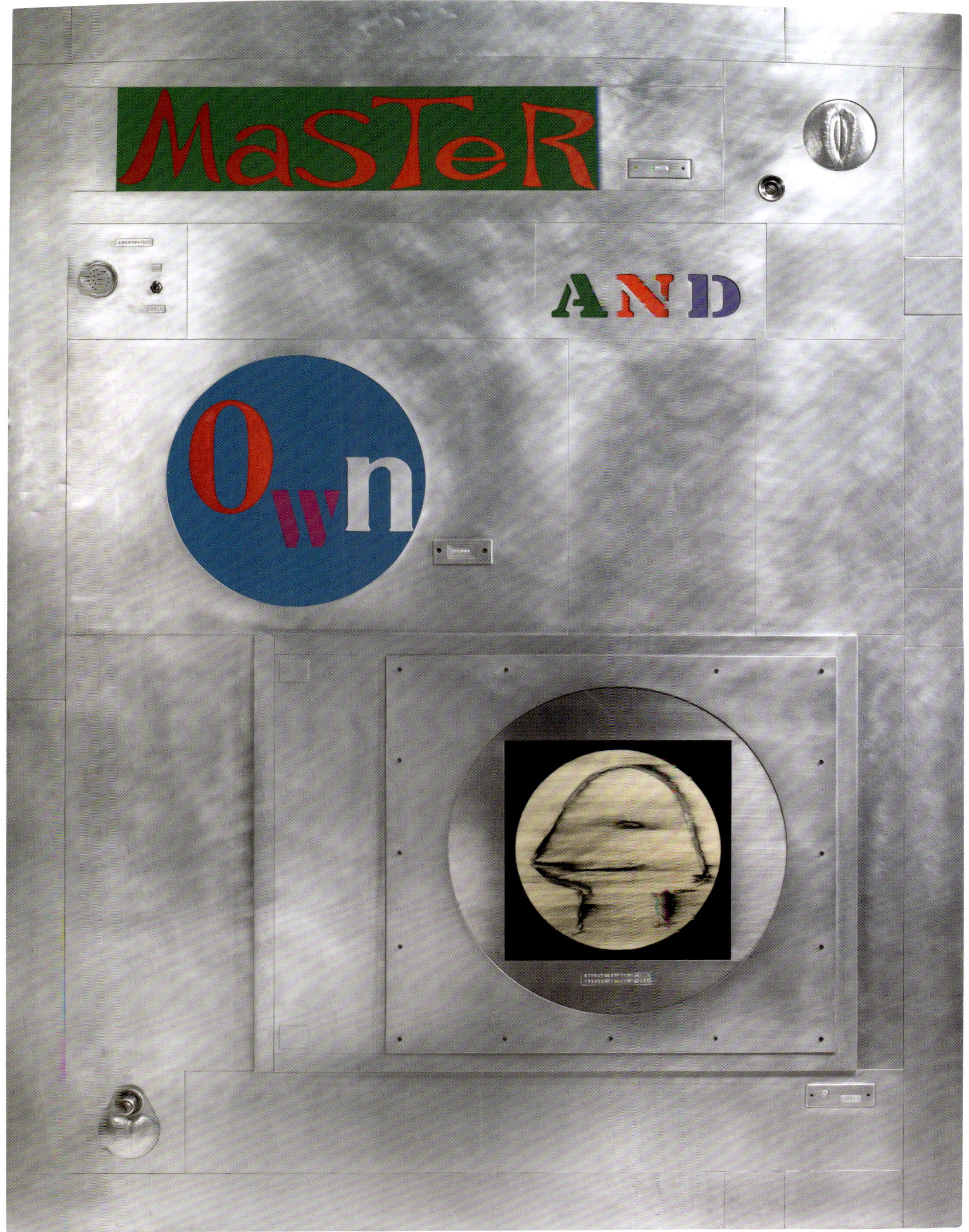

PLATE 22

Master and Own, 1966

MIXED-MEDIA METAL BOX

64 x 48 INCHES (162.6 x 121.9 CM)

PRIVATE COLLECTION, COURTESY OF LOCKS GALLERY, PHILADELPHIA

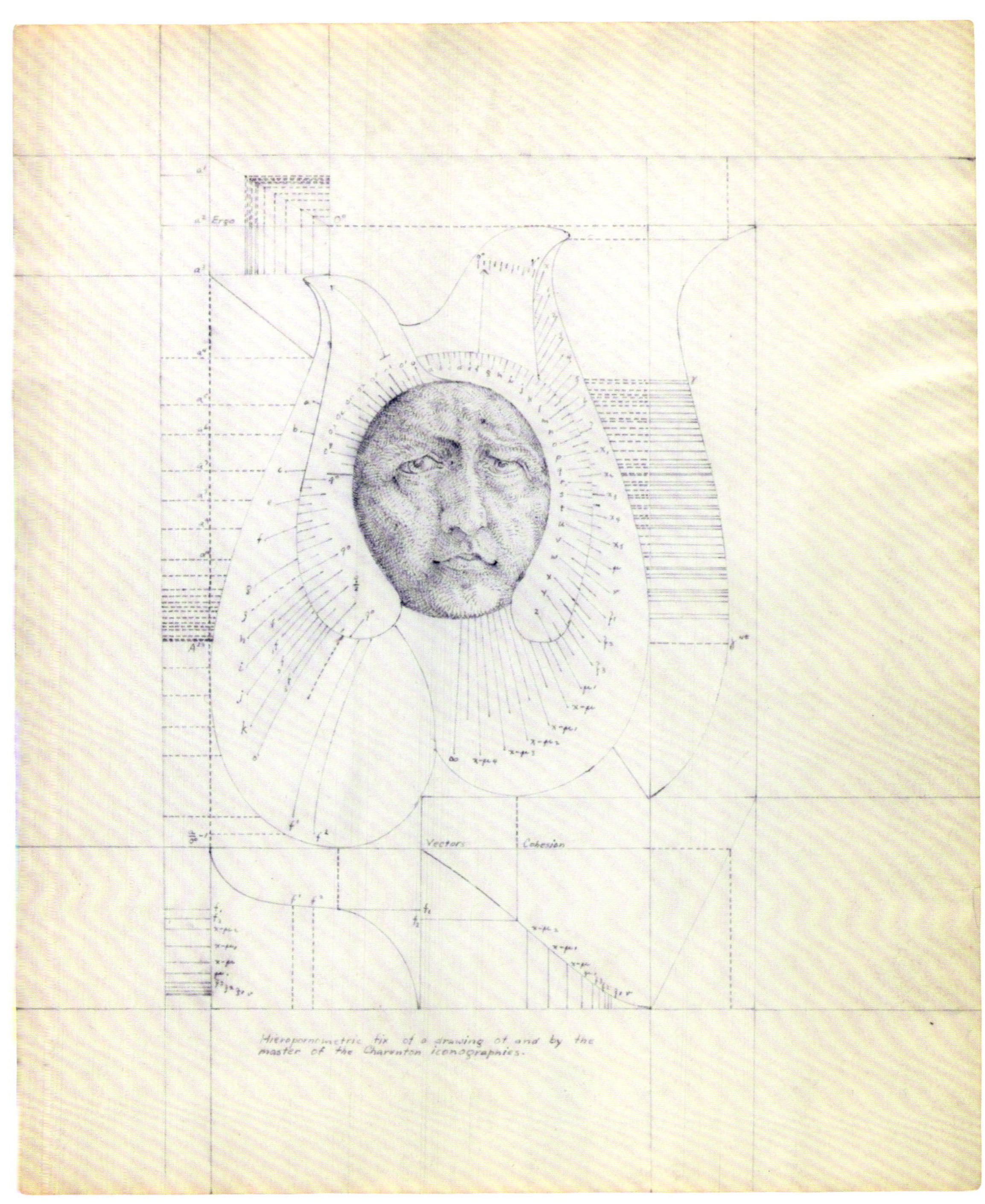

Hieropornometric Fix of a Drawing of and by the Master of the Charenton Iconographies, 1966

PEN AND INK ON PAPER

13¾ x 11 INCHES (34.9 x 27.9 CM)

COLLECTION OF THE ARTIST

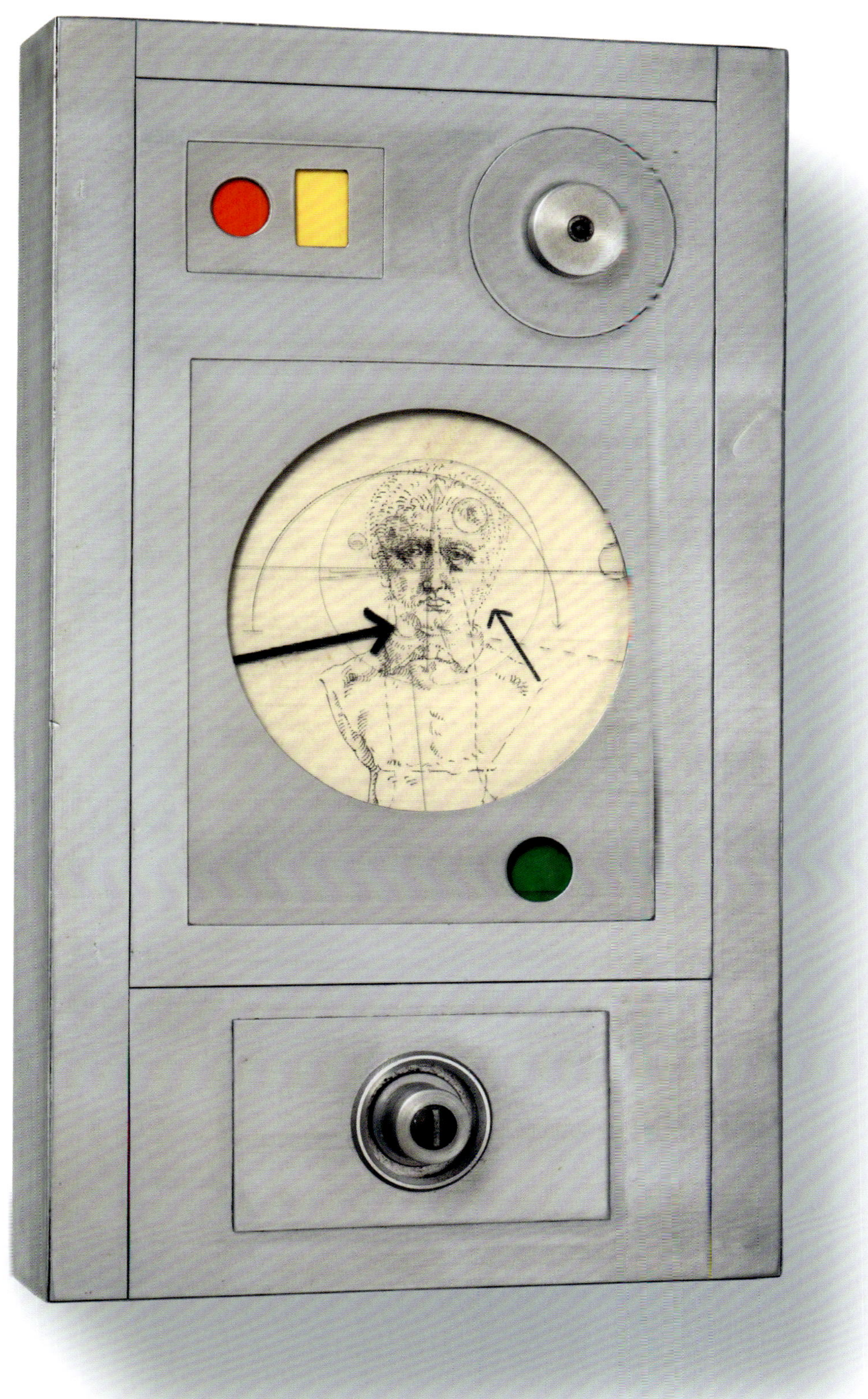

Plate 24

IBM Box, 1965

Mixed-media metal box

Metal box 13½ x 8 inches (34.3 x 20.3 cm); aluminum and wood box 12¾ x 7½ inches (32.4 x 19.1 cm)

Collection of Rodney Sharp, Greenville, Delaware

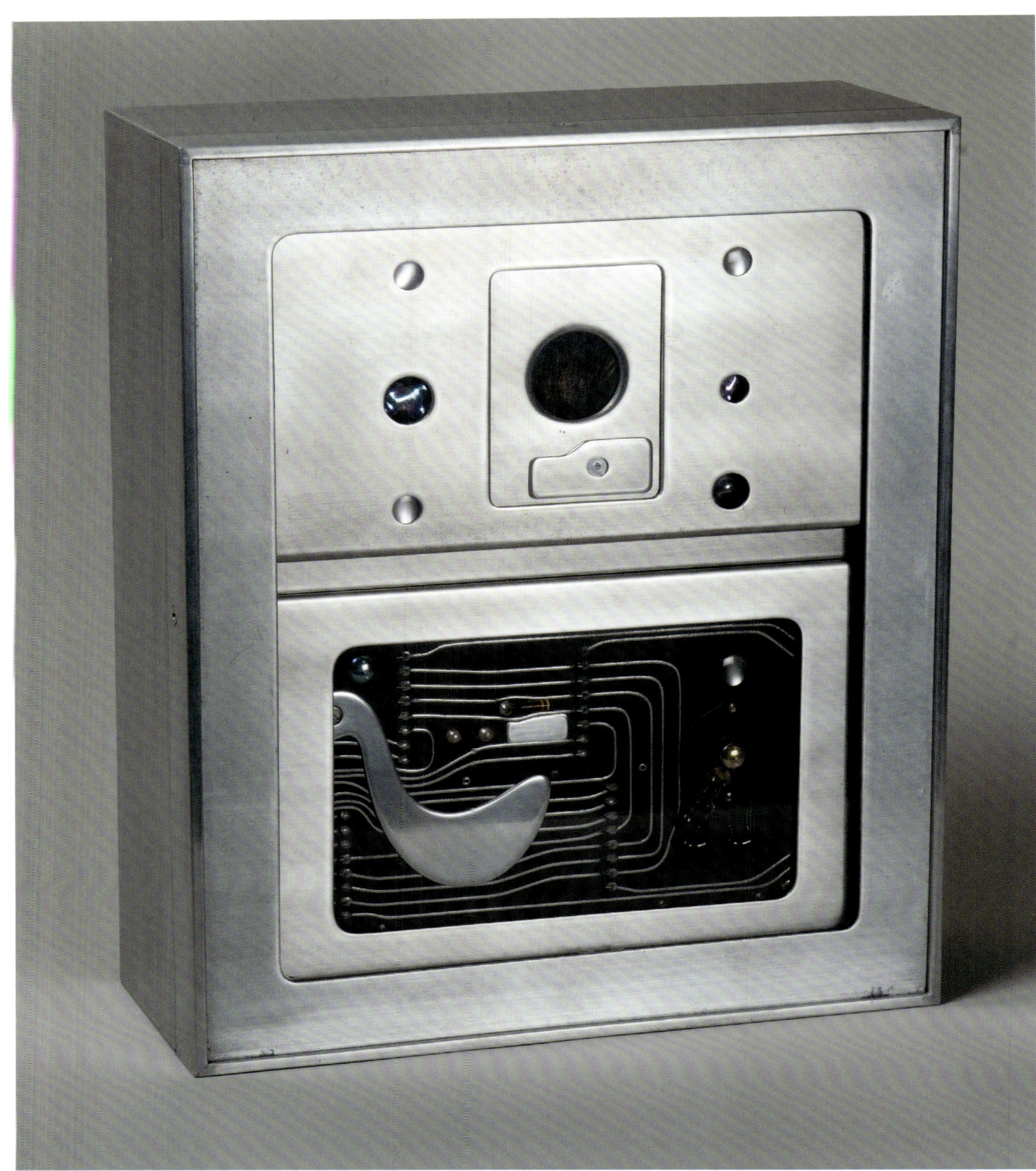

PLATE 25

Untitled (Metal Box), 1966

MIXED-MEDIA METAL BOX

12¼ x 10¼ INCHES (31.1 x 26 CM)

WADSWORTH ATHENEUM MUSEUM OF ART, HARTFORD, CONNECTICUT. GIFT OF MR. HERRICK JACKSON, 1976.102

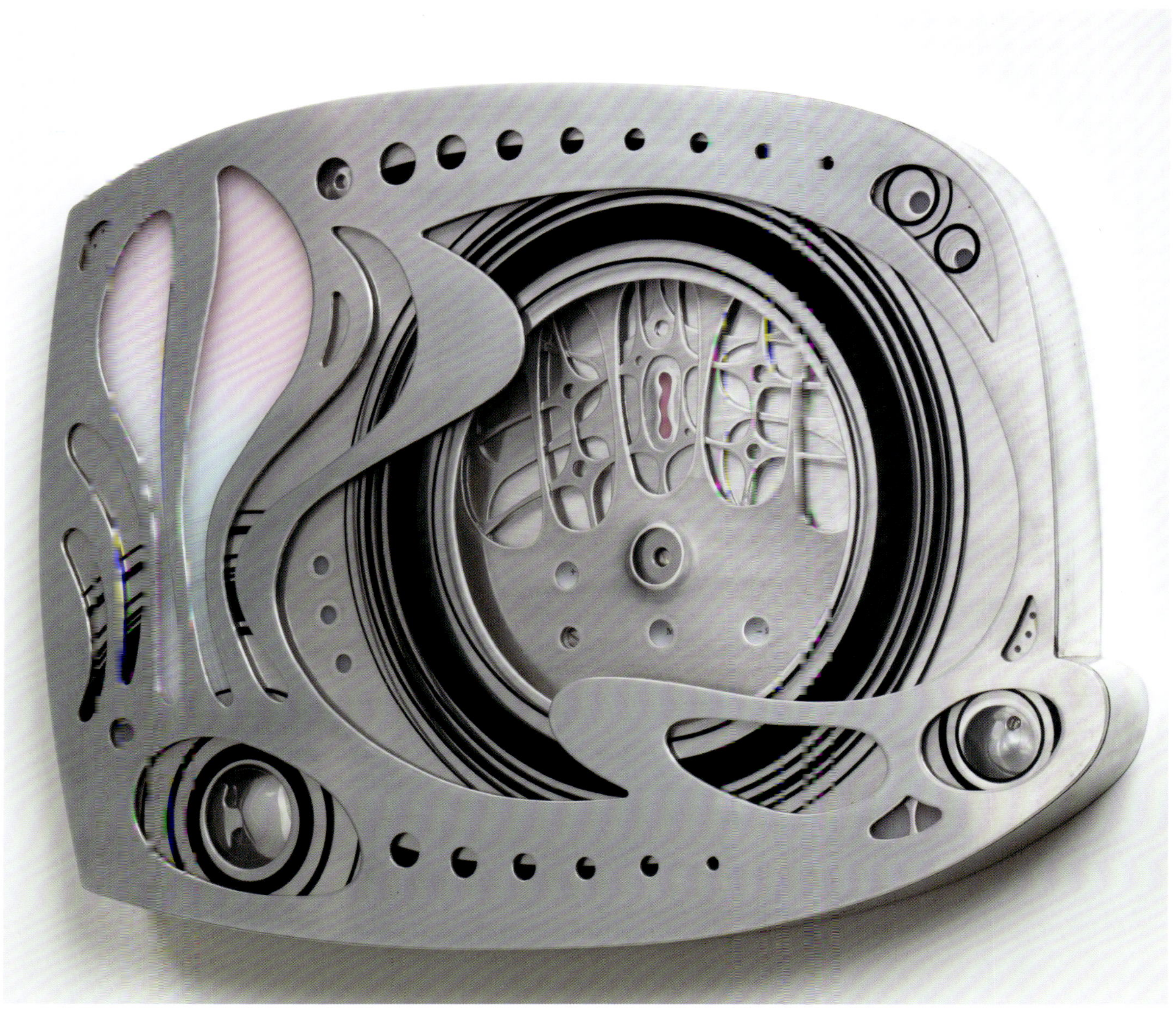

Untitled (Radio), c. 1967

Mixed-media metal box

12½ x 17½ inches (31.8 x 44.5 cm)

Collection of Mrs. Burton S. Singer, Villanova, Pennsylvania

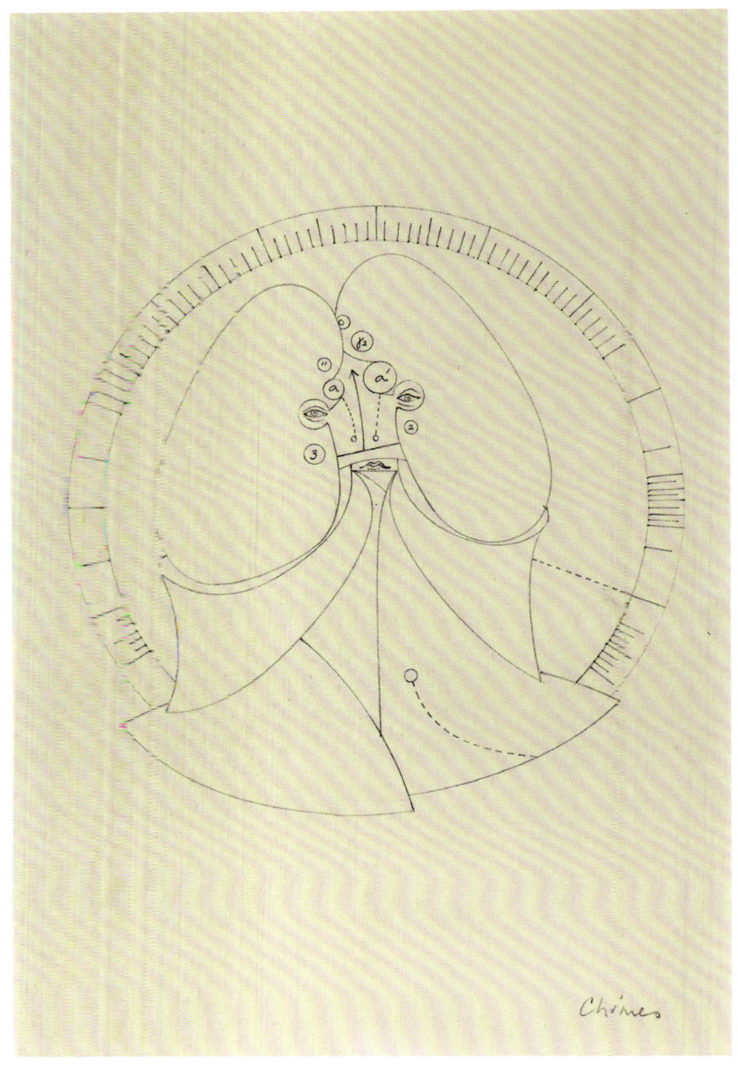

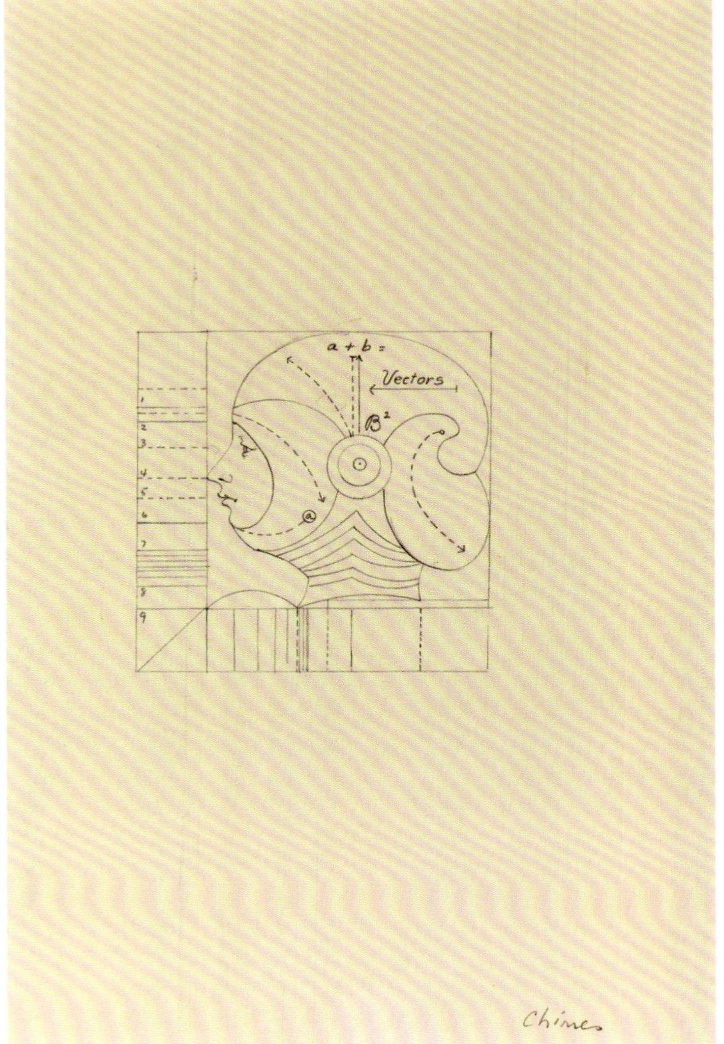

PLATE 27

Priapus, 1966

PENCIL ON PAPER

8½ x 5½ INCHES (21.6 x 14 CM)

COURTESY OF LOCKS GALLERY, PHILADELPHIA

PLATE 28

Vectors, 1966

PENCIL ON PAPER

8½ x 5½ INCHES (21.6 x 14 CM)

COLLECTION OF PETER AND MARI SHAW, PHILADELPHIA

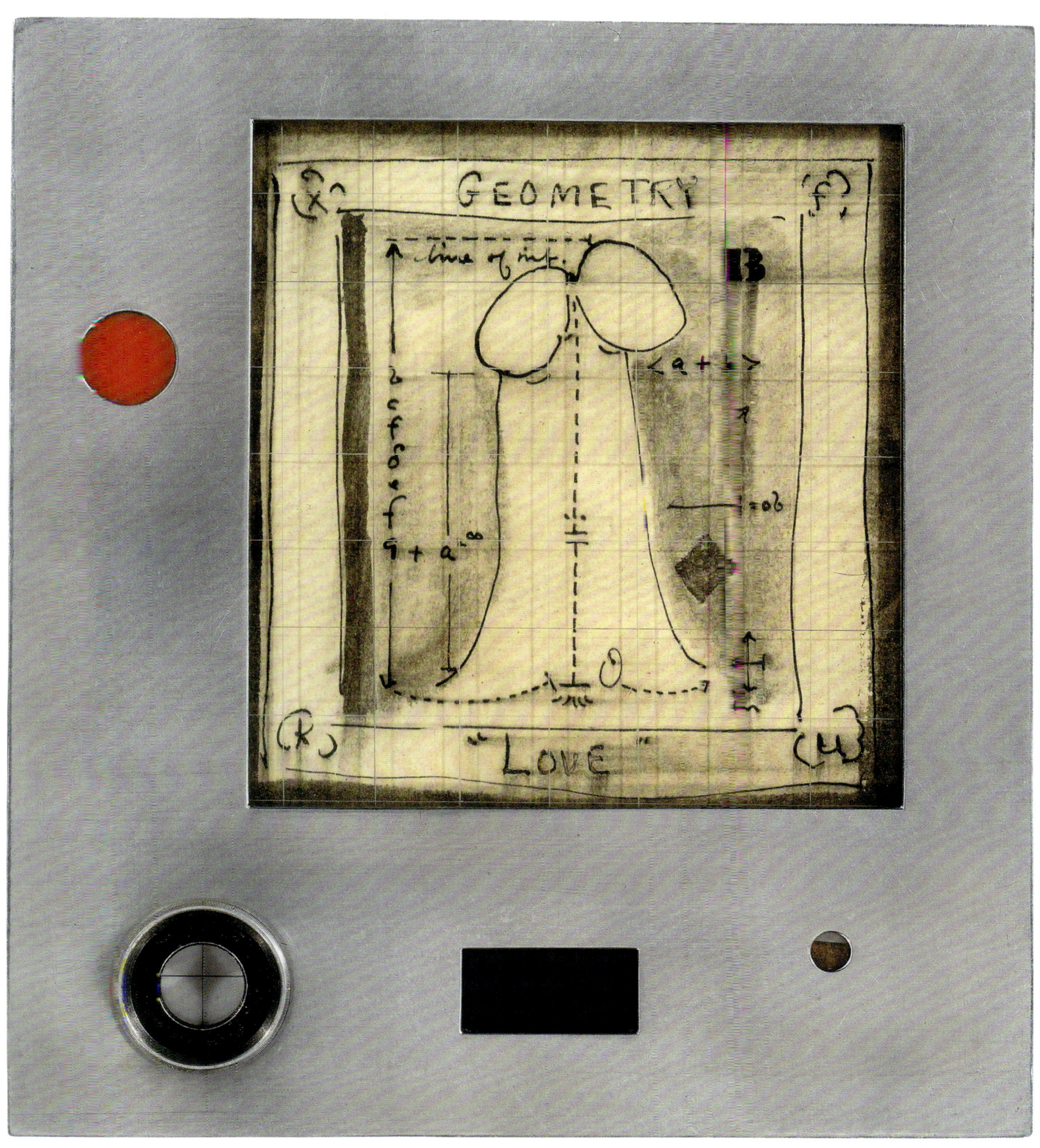

Geometry Love, 1966–69

MIXED-MEDIA METAL BOX

9¼ x 8¼ INCHES (23.5 x 21 CM)

PRIVATE COLLECTION, COURTESY OF LOCKS GALLERY, PHILADELPHIA

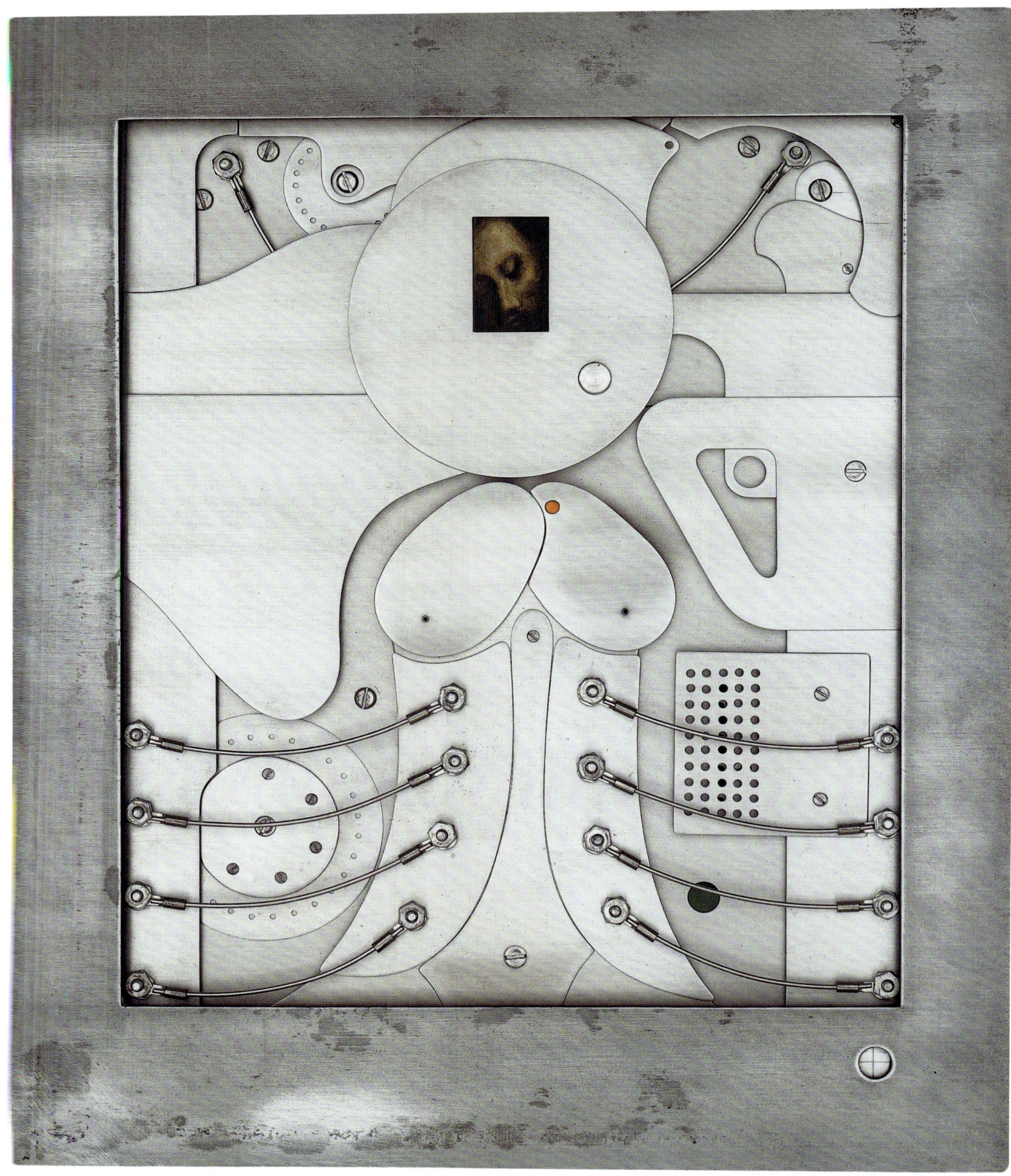

Construction #403, 1967

MIXED-MEDIA METAL BOX

14 x 11 INCHES (35.6 x 27.9 CM)

THE BUCKINGHAM FAMILY COLLECTION, LARCHMONT, NEW YORK

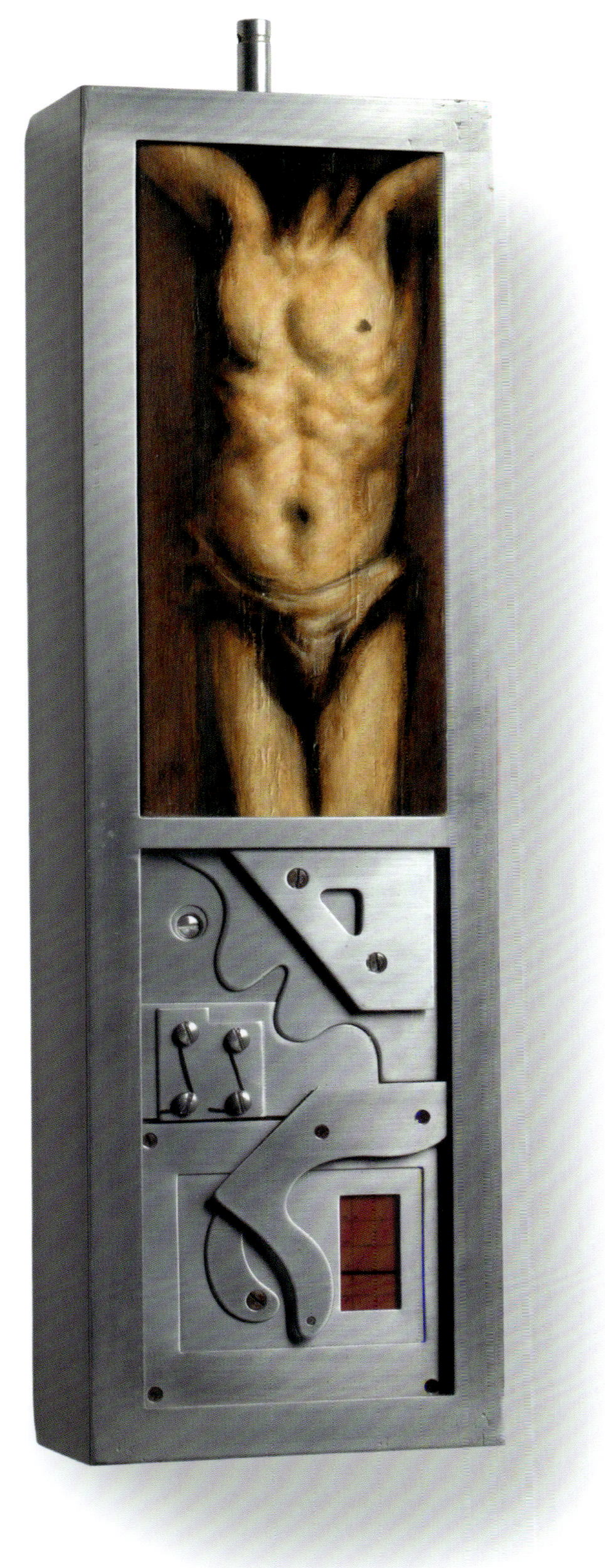

PLATE 31

Untitled (Crucifix), 1967

MIXED-MEDIA METAL BOX

15½ x 4¾ INCHES (39.4 x 12.1 CM)

COLLECTION OF DAWN CHIMES, VENICE, FLORIDA

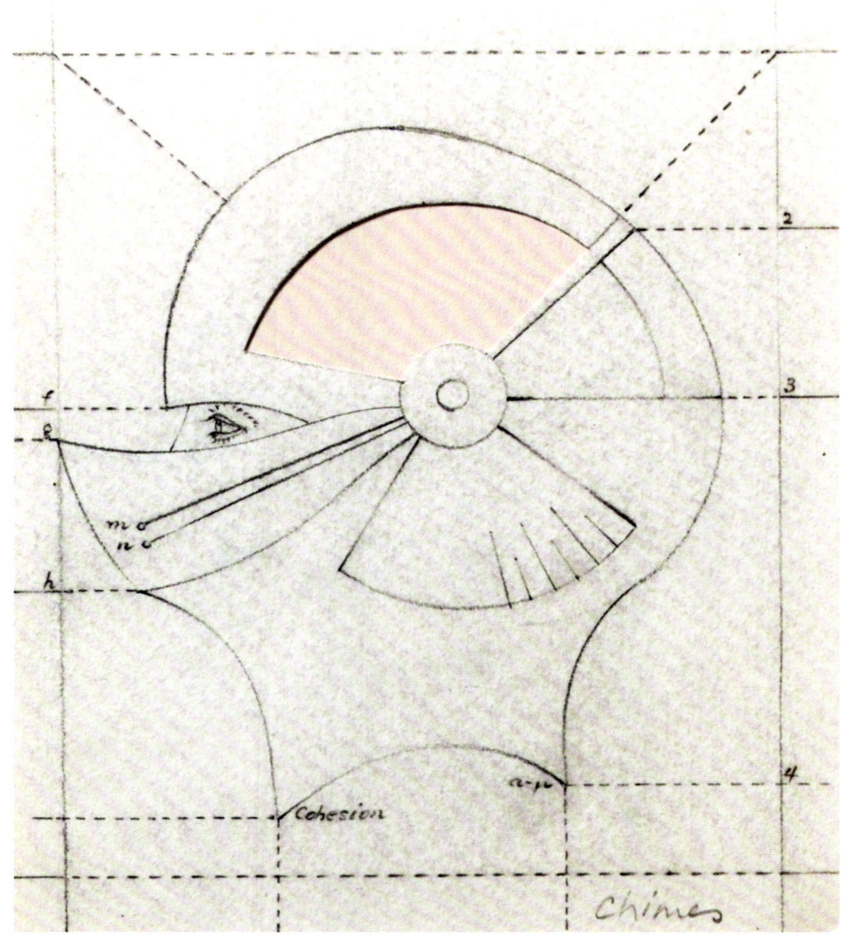

PLATE 32

Armor Head, 1967

PENCIL ON PAPER

4½ x 4 INCHES (11.4 x 10.2 CM)

COLLECTION OF MR. AND MRS. MARTIN AND MARGY MEYERSON, PHILADELPHIA

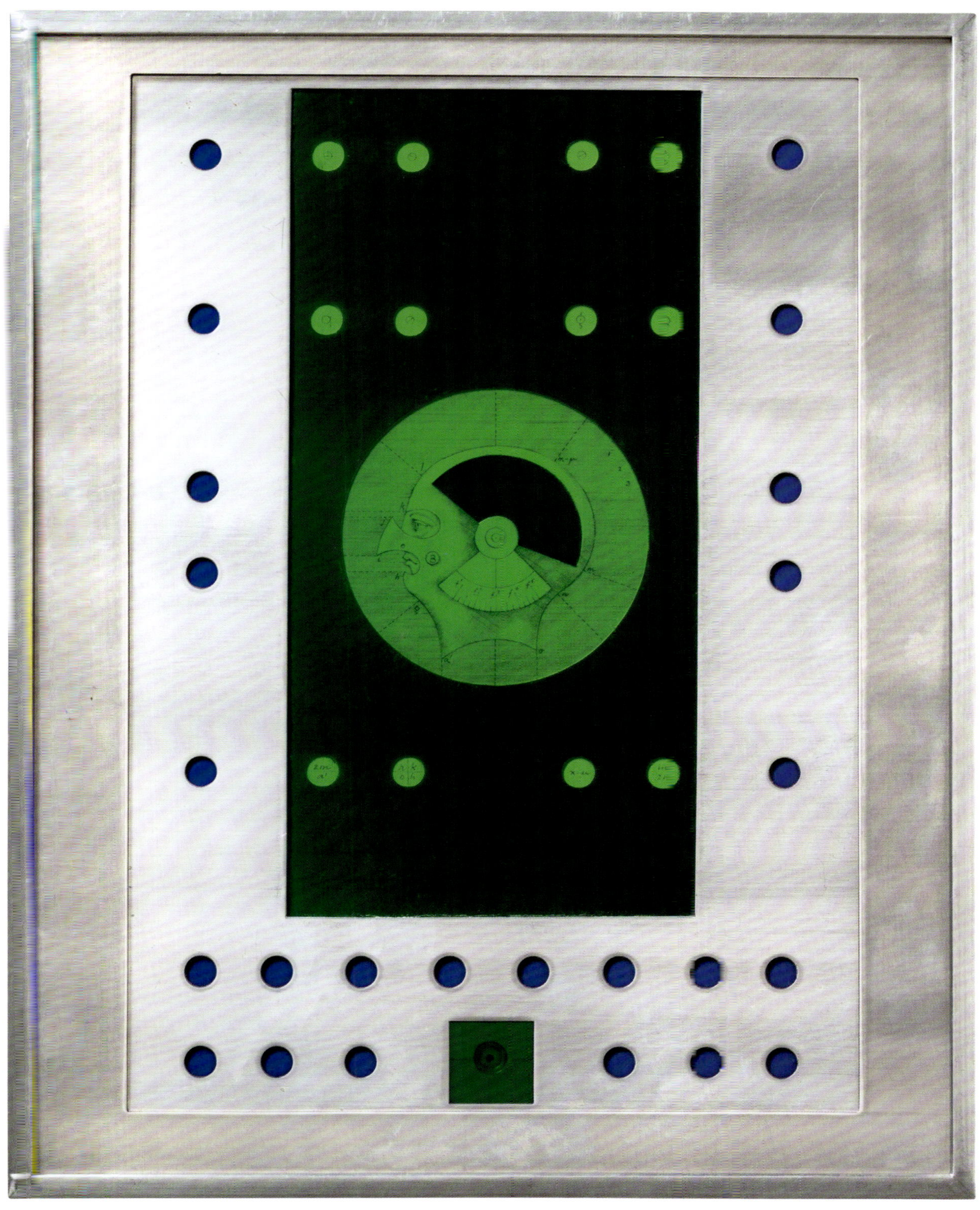

PLATE 33

Green Box, 1966–68

MIXED-MEDIA METAL BOX

14¼ x 11¼ INCHES (36.2 x 28.6 CM)

COLLECTION OF JANET FLEISHER, PHILADELPHIA

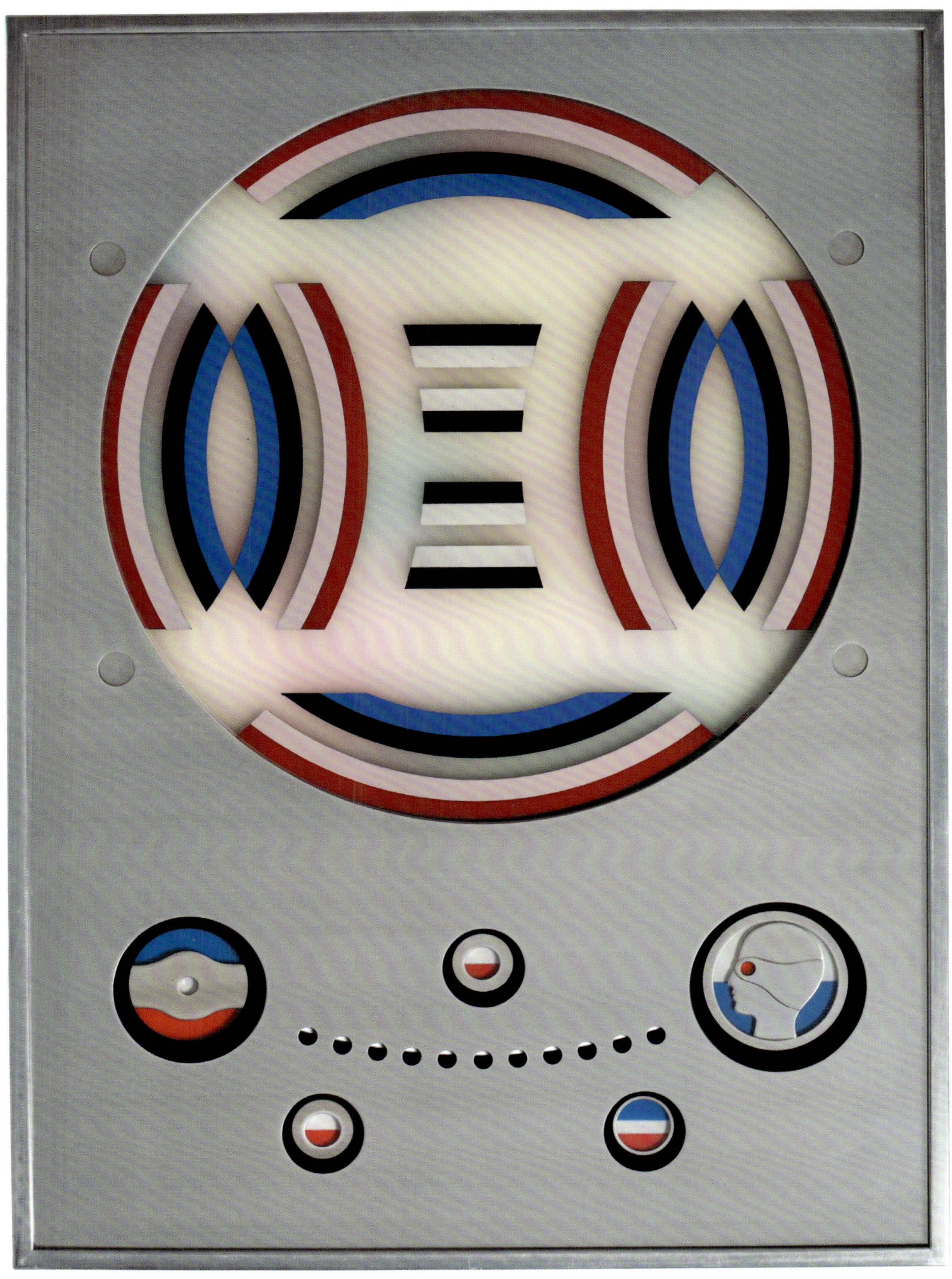

PLATE 34

Pinball Racer, 1969

MIXED-MEDIA METAL BOX

18½ x 13⅜ INCHES (47 X 34 CM)

COLLECTION OF PHILLIP MITSIS AND SOPHIA KALANTZAKOS, NEW YORK

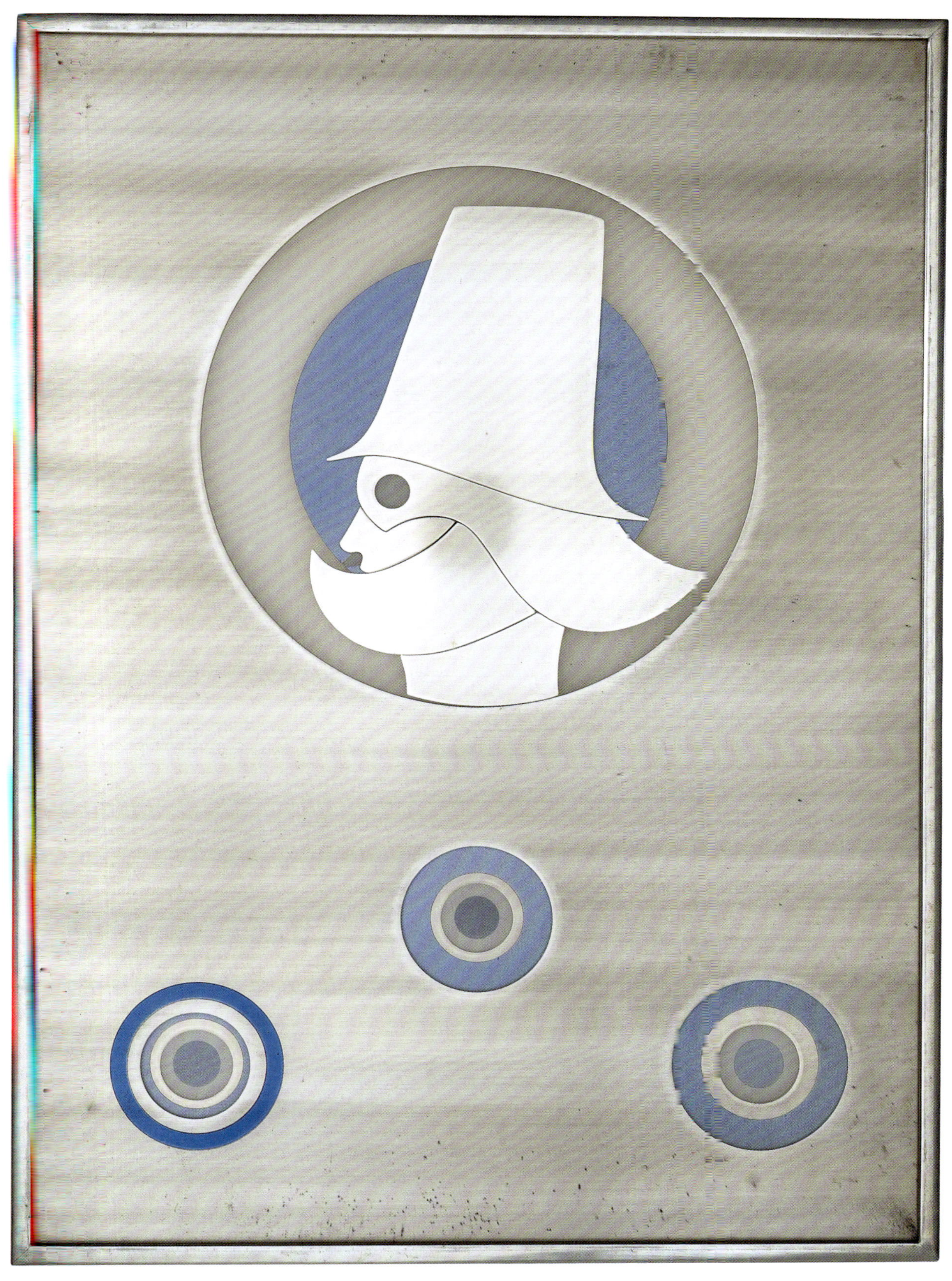

Top Hat, 1970
MIXED-MEDIA METAL BOX
18½ x 13 INCHES (47 x 33 CM)
PRIVATE COLLECTION

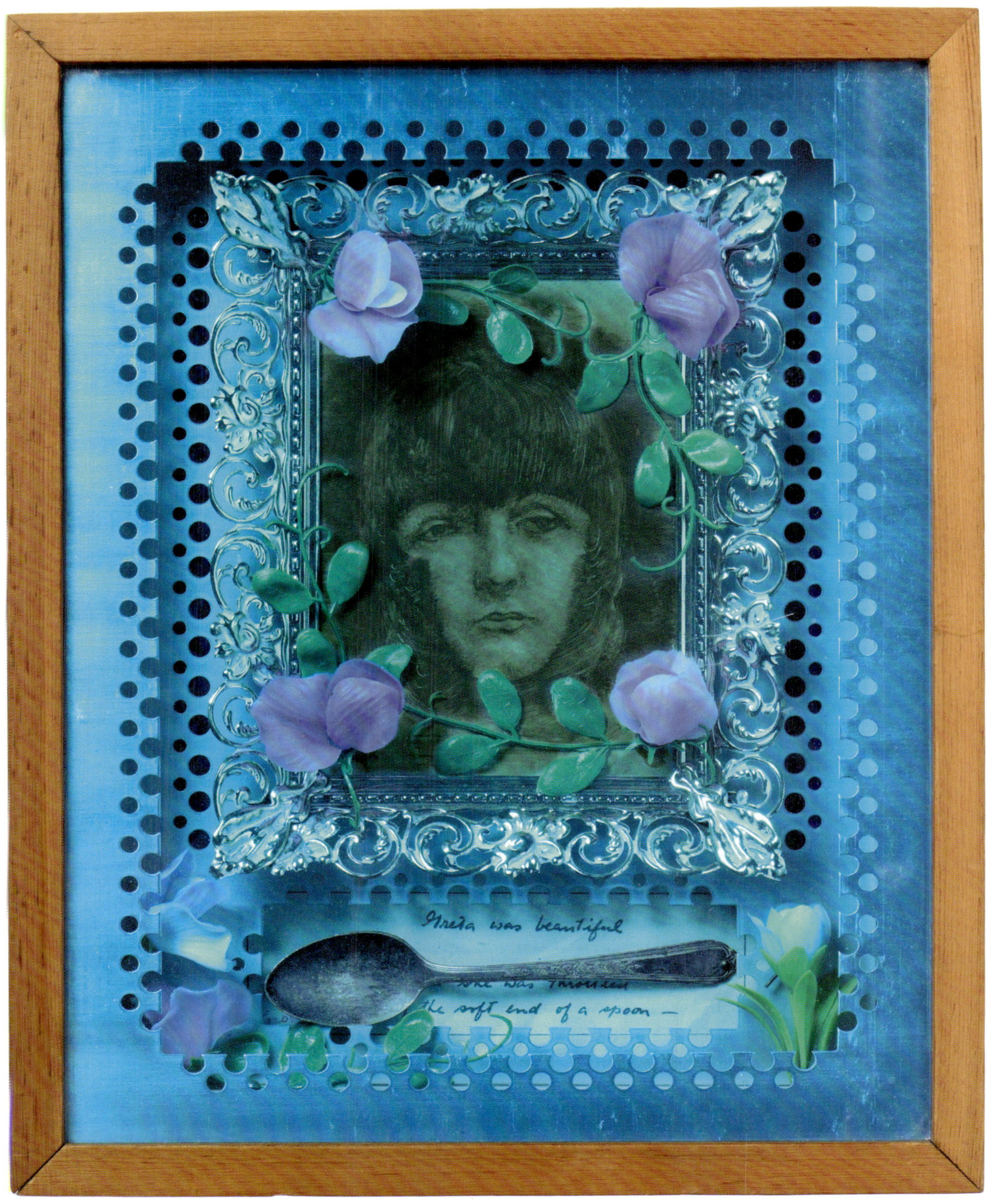

PLATE 36

Untitled (Greta Garbo), c. 1967

MIXED-MEDIA METAL BOX

15 x 12 INCHES (38.1 x 30.5 CM)

COLLECTION OF DMITRI AND SHEILA CHIMES, PHILADELPHIA

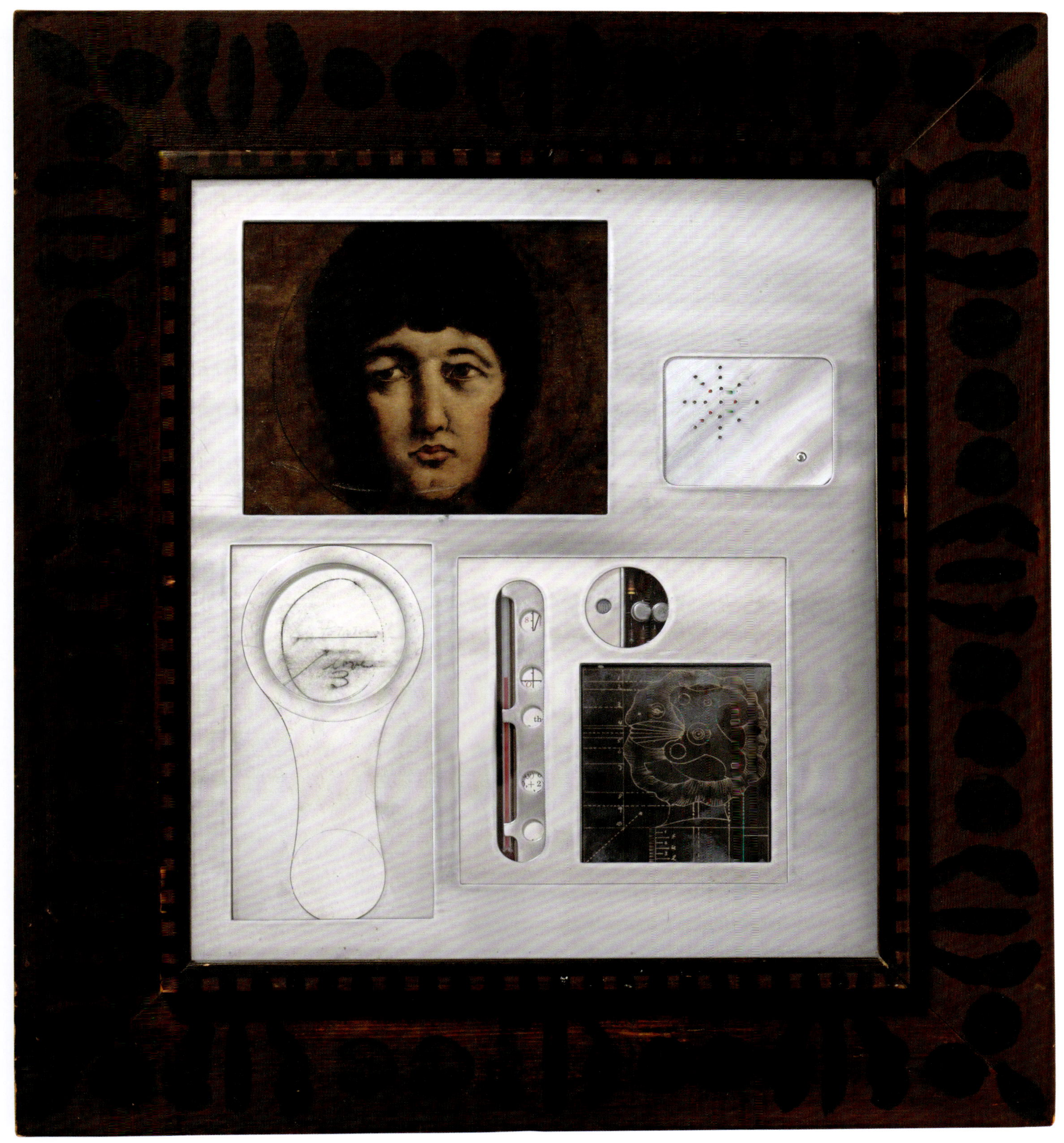

PLATE 37

Untitled (John Lennon), c. 1969

MIXED-MEDIA METAL BOX

20 x 18 INCHES (50.8 x 45.7 CM)

COLLECTION OF ROBERT F. MATTICKS, PHILADE_PHIA

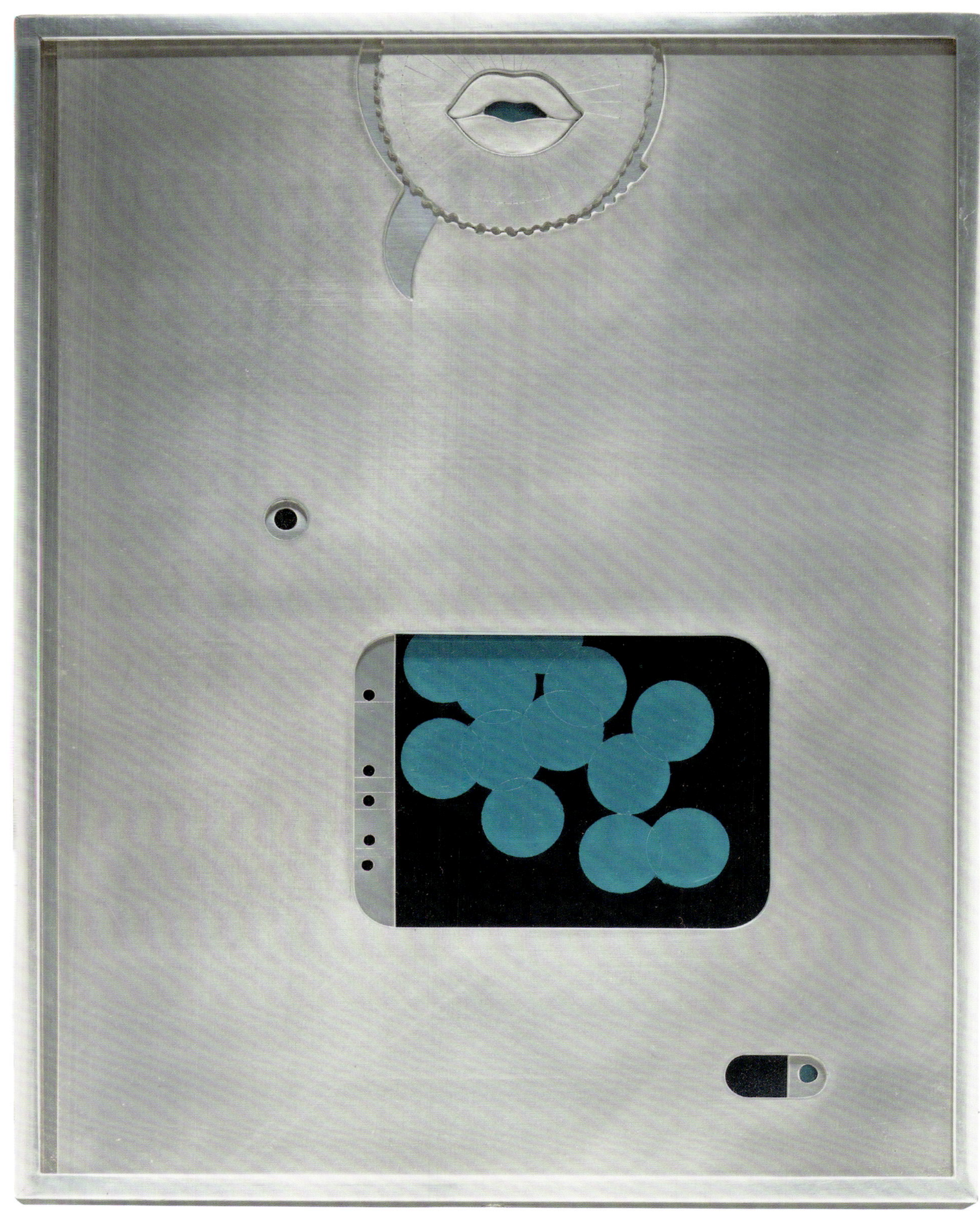

OF METAL BONES

PLATE 38

Untitled, 1969–70

MIXED-MEDIA METAL BOX

14⅜ x 11⅜ INCHES (36.5 x 28.9 CM)

PHOENIX ART MUSEUM. GIFT OF DR. AND MRS. LORENZ ANDERMAN

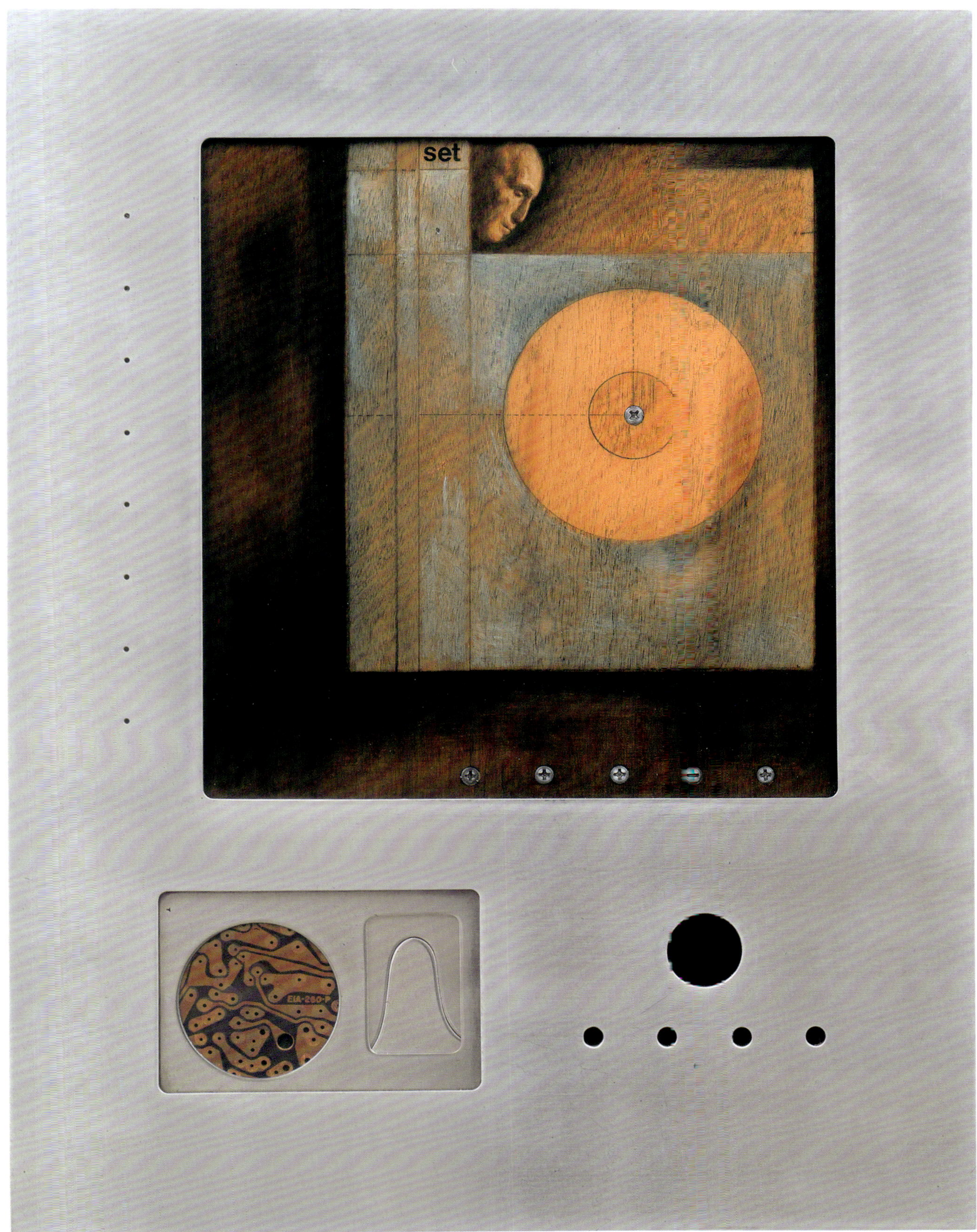

PLATE 39

Set (The Descent), 1972

MIXED-MEDIA METAL BOX

17⅟₁₆ X 13⅛ INCHES (43.3 x 33.3 CM)

PRIVATE COLLECTION, COURTESY OF LOCKS GALLERY, PHILADELPHIA

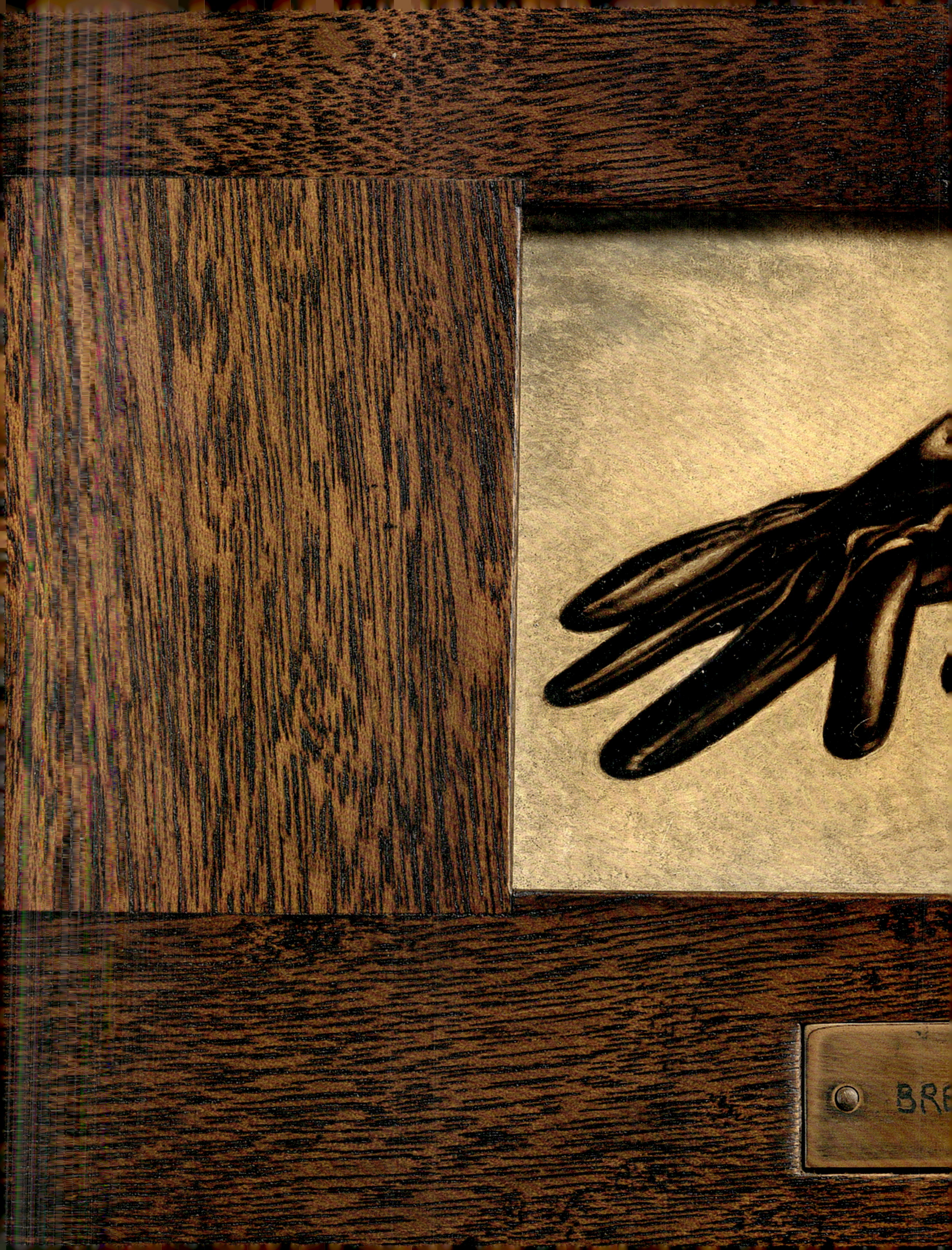
BRE

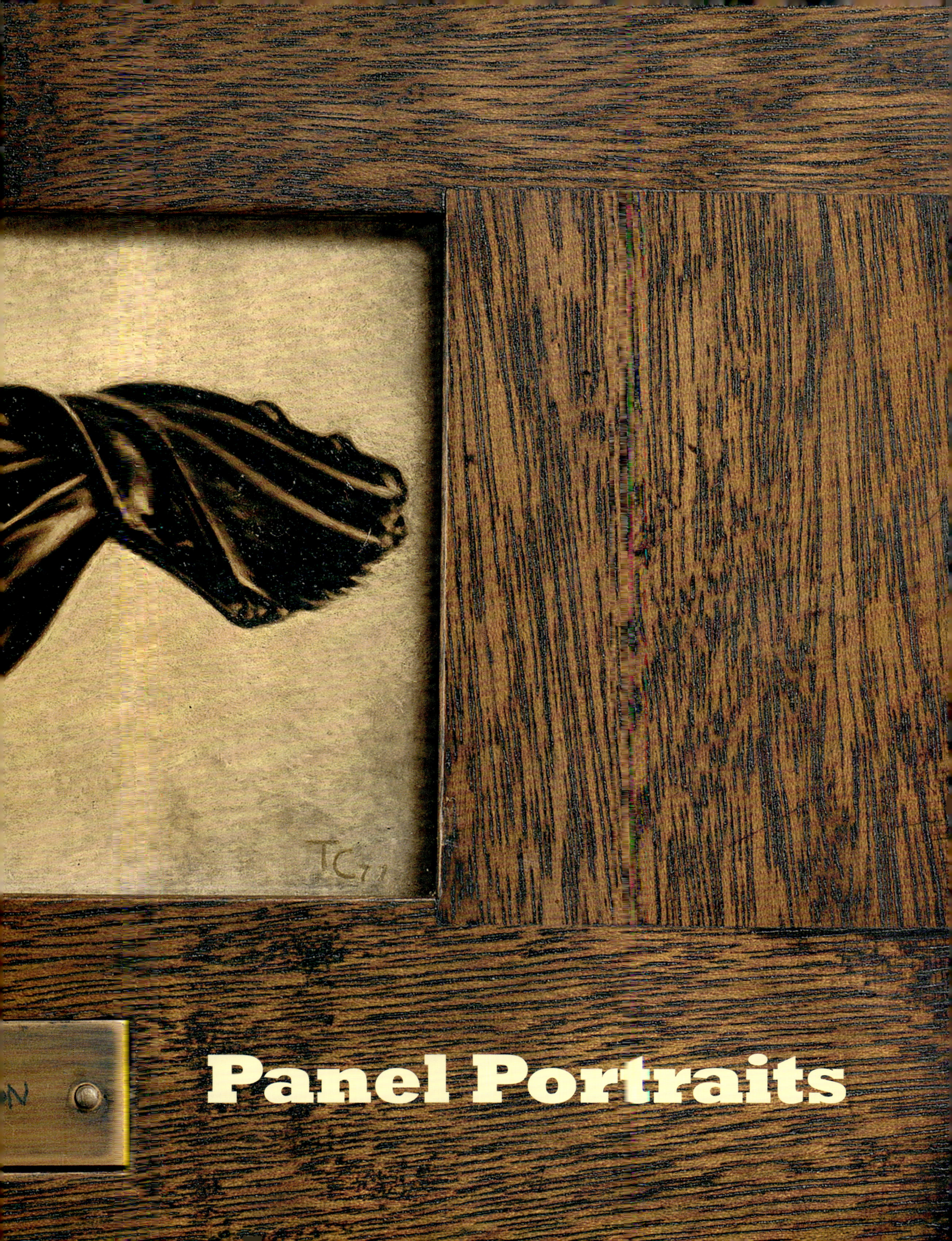
Panel Portraits

Chimes began his celebrated series of panel paintings in the summer of 1973, appropriately enough, with a portrait of Alfred Jarry, whose unconventional life and radical nonconformism had interested him to the point of obsession since the early 1960s. He was conscious at the time of moving away from the metal boxes, with their references to Minimalism, McLuhan, and the Marquis de Sade, and building a new corpus based upon works of literature, rather than works of art, in line with Duchamp's famous comment to museum curator James Johnson Sweeney that "as a painter it was much better to be influenced by a writer than by another painter."[117] Duchamp had found inspiration in the writings of Raymond Roussel and Alfred Jarry, whose delirium of imagination informed his great allegory of frustrated desire, *The Large Glass* (see fig. 53), which Chimes visited repeatedly at the Philadelphia Museum of Art during the early 1970s. The artist wanted to continue Duchamp's legacy of putting "painting once again at the service of the mind" in the panel portraits, which required extensive research into the lives of his subjects, their writings, and their influence, before he could begin work on them.[118]

These intimate, sepia-toned panel paintings were inspired by the artist's profound interest in the writings of Jarry, who is best known for his anarchic play *Ubu Roi* (King Ubu; figs. 73, 74), which shocked audiences when it was first performed at Aurélien François Lugné-Poë's Théâtre de l'Oeuvre in Paris on December 10, 1896.[119] When Firmin Gémier, the well-known actor who played King Ubu on the first night, uttered the scatological opening word of the play, "Merdre!" (or "shite"—the additional "r" made the expletive even more subversive), several audience members erupted in hoots, jeers, and protests, while Jarry's friends and supporters cheered in delighted approval at this direct affront to the public, creating a cacophony that delayed the performance by fifteen minutes. The resulting uproar caused by this near-riot helped usher in the modern era of theater, and instantly brought Jarry scandalous fame. *Ubu Roi*'s frontal assault on naturalism helped to unleash the imagination of numerous twentieth-century artists and writers, especially those associated with Dada and Surrealism, who regarded Jarry as an important precursor to their own investigations of the irrational and the absurd.[120]

Ubu was Jarry's most famous literary creation, a mindless glutton whose rapacious greed for money and power prefigured the rise in the twentieth century of equally brutal and capricious dictators such as Adolf Hitler, Benito Mussolini, Francisco Franco, and Joseph Stalin. As Jarry announced in his introduction to the play, *Ubu Roi* "takes place in Poland, that is to say, Nowhere."[121] The plot is a thinly veiled pastiche of a number of William Shakespeare's plays, in which the grotesquely obese Père Ubu, encouraged by his scheming and ambitious wife, Mère Ubu, butchers the Polish royal family, usurps the throne, and proceeds to gorge himself on sausages and murder anyone with money in order to increase his own wealth.[122] However, Ubu's greed and stupidity mean that he also fatally abuses and betrays those who helped him seize power. His reign of tyranny comes to an end when his former coconspirators and henchmen, fed up with his treachery and antisocial behavior, escape to Russia and persuade the Tsar to declare war on King Ubu, who by now is slaughtering even the peasants and expropriating their meager funds. While Ubu marches off fearfully to meet the Russian invasion, his equally repulsive wife attempts to rob him of the accumulated treasure he has buried in the royal palace. Eventually, Mère Ubu is driven out by a popular revolt and flees to her husband, who

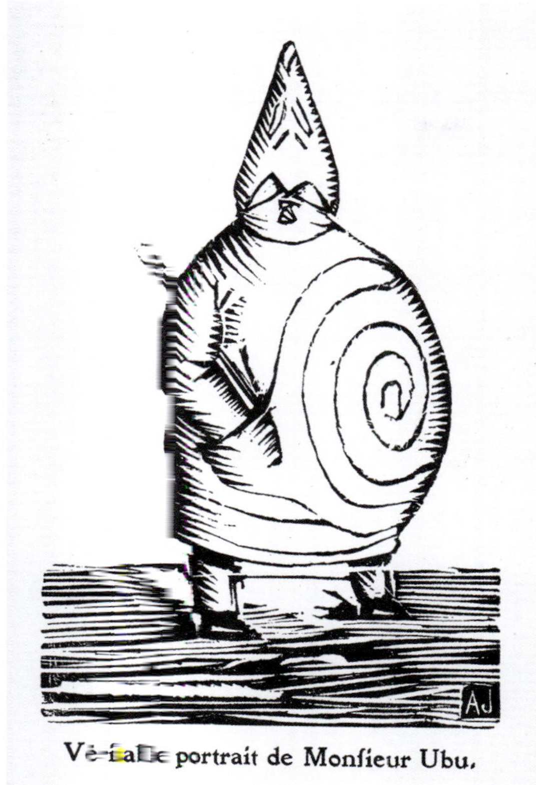

Véritable portrait de Monsieur Ubu.

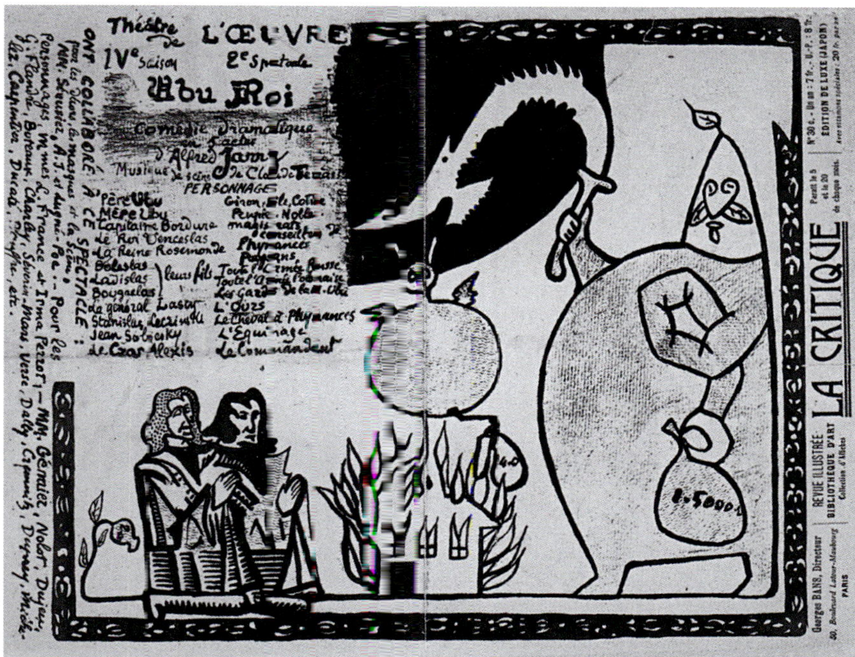

has been defeated, deposed, and, for good measure, attacked by a bear. In the end, Ubu and his wife manage to escape from their pursuers and set sail for France.

Full of slapstick humor, deliberately crude costumes and scenery, lewd obscenities, and untrained violence, *Ubu Roi* was intended to provoke, outrage, and appall its audience, and did just that, as William Butler Yeats, who attended the opening night, was quick to see. Yeats's eyewitness account highlights the shocking nature of the play, from the marionette-like performances by noted actors to King Ubu's outrageous toilet-brush scepter, while also lamenting the play's implications for the avant-garde, since he correctly interprets *Ubu Roi* as sounding the death knell of Symbolism:

> I go to the first performance of Alfred Jarry's *Ubu Roi* . . . and [my friend] explains to me what is happening on the stage. The players are supposed to be dolls, toys, marionettes, and now they are all hopping like wooden frogs, and I can see for myself that the chief personage, who is some kind of king, carries for a sceptre a brush of the kind that we use to clean a [water] closet. Feeling bound to support the most spirited party, we have shouted for the play, but that night at the Hotel Corneille I am very sad . . . I say "After Stéphane Mallarmé, after Paul Verlaine, after Gustave Moreau, after Puvis de Chavannes, after our own verse, after all our subtle colours and nervous rhythm, after the faint mixed tints of Conder, what more is possible? After us the Savage God."[123]

When Gémier unleashed his clarion call of "Merdre!" on Jarry's unsuspecting audience, he hysterical reaction confirmed that the play's satiric denigration of everything bourgeois had hit its mark. For Chimes, the figure of Ubu came to represent a sadistic instinctual being, an embodiment of the deeply ingrained primitive, unconscious, and libidinal forces that we all

Fig. 73
Alfred Jarry (French, 1873–1907), *True Portrait of Monsieur Ubu*, 1896. Woodcut and letterpress. Published in *Ubu Roi* (Paris: Editions du Mercure de France, 1896). Department of Special Collections, Kenneth Spencer Research Library, University of Kansas, Lawrence

Fig. 74
Alfred Jarry, *Program for Ubu Roi*, 1896. Special edition on salmon-colored paper inserted in the deluxe programs for the performance of the play at the Théâtre de l'Oeuvre, Paris. Lithograph, 9¾ x 12¾ inches (24.7 x 32.5 cm). Bibliothèque Nationale, Paris

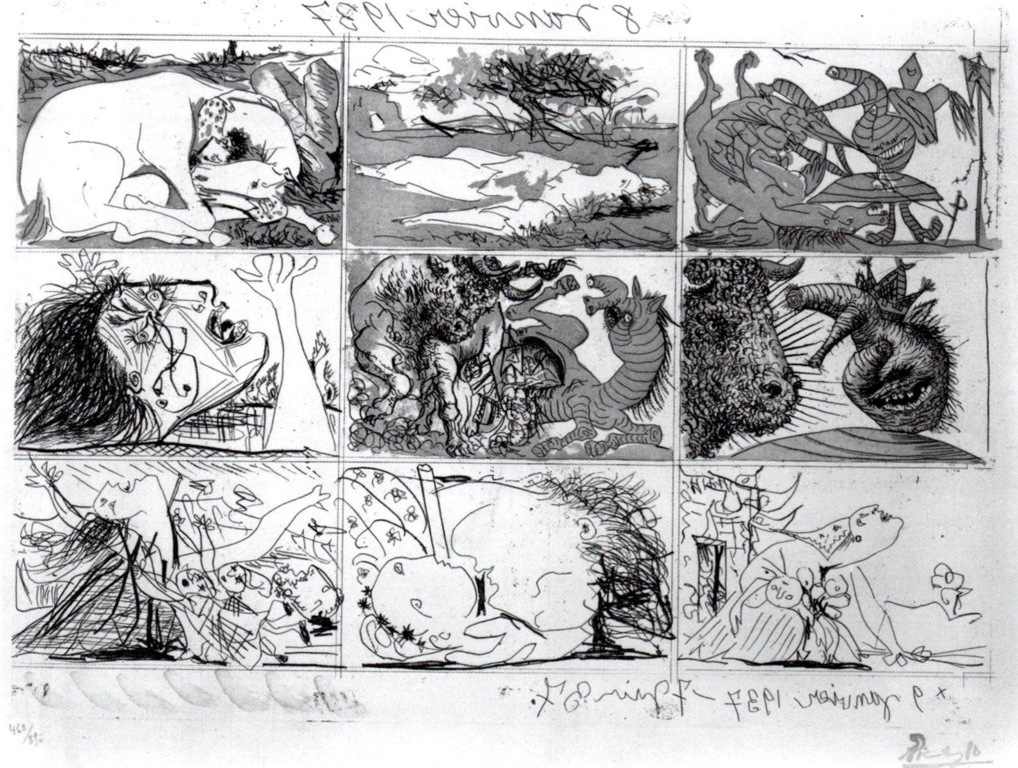

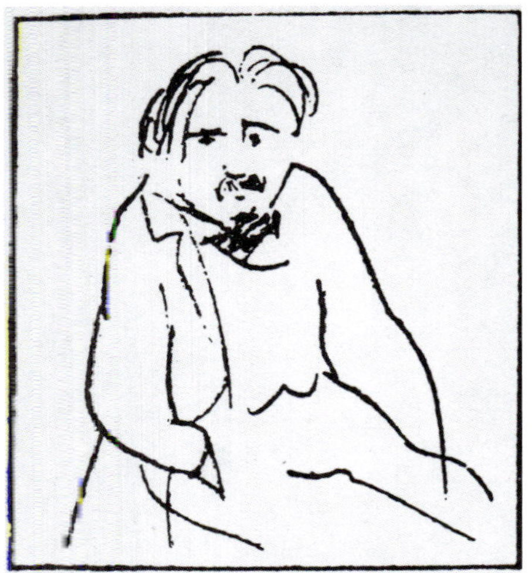

carry within us. He admired Jarry's ability to hold up a mirror to the polite, well-heeled members of middle-class Parisian society, who were clearly aghast at recognizing their own repressed feelings and brute instincts in this ignoble, archetypal *other*, whose rapacious greed and lust for power matched their own.

Chimes first came across Jarry's name through several fleeting yet provocative references to the iconoclastic writer in Alfred H. Barr, Jr.'s 1946 monograph *Picasso: Fifty Years of His Art*, which he had bought as a student at the Art Students League, shortly after it was published. It was the first art book he ever owned, and Chimes remembers buying it in order to read more about Picasso's *Guernica*, which he had recently seen at the Museum of Modern Art. The painting had disturbed the artist when he first saw it, but upon returning to the enormous canvas he began to appreciate the complexity and radical nature of Picasso's grisaille composition. Chimes reread Barr's critical study of Picasso's work in the early 1960s, after the legendary director of the Museum of Modern Art had shown interest in his own work, and was intrigued by his vivid description of the Spanish artist's bohemian life in the dilapidated tenement on the rue Ravignon in Montmartre—nicknamed the *bateau-lavoir*, or "floating laundry"—where Picasso lived and worked between 1904 and 1909. Among the poverty-stricken clerks, laundresses, actors, poets, and painters who lived or gathered on what Barr aptly describes as this "ark of talent"[124] were the French writers Max Jacob, Maurice Raynal, and Guillaume Apollinaire.[125] Barr also listed Jarry as among the visitors to Picasso's studio, since he was at that time thought to have been a close friend of the Spanish artist. The brief mention of Jarry's name in Barr's book was followed by an enigmatic reference in the footnotes to Picasso's "fairly realistic" portrait of the French playwright (fig. 75), which had been published in *Les soirées de Paris* in February 1914.[126] Two subsequent footnotes mention Jarry's "famous character, Ubu,"[127] from *Ubu Roi*, whose "shocking, slapstick tradition" had inspired Picasso to make his famous print *The Dream and Lie* of Franco (fig. 76) and to write a play entitled *Desire Caught by the Tail*.[128] What Chimes gleaned from Barr's passing remarks about Jarry, all of which were ticked in pencil by the artist for future reference, was that here was an important yet little-known figure in the fin-de-siècle Parisian avant-garde who was worthy of further research. It immediately occurred to Chimes that Jarry could be a missing link in the history of modernism, someone whose own radical engagement with avant-garde practice had encouraged Picasso to "break down the walls" and bring about the Cubist revolution in painting.[129]

In 1964, Herb Nelson, the artist's brother-in-law and a well-known film and television actor at that time, was clearing out his library and invited Tom to take any book or magazine that he wanted. Herb and his wife, Joan DeWeese, were moving out of their house in Fort Lee, New Jersey, and wanted to reduce the amount of clutter in their new home, as Herb prepared for his starring role in the daytime television soap opera *Days of Our Lives*. The artist's attention was quickly drawn to a set of magazines entitled *Evergreen Review*, which included the May–June 1960 issue devoted to Alfred Jarry, called "What is 'Pataphysics?" (fig. 77).[130] Chimes immediately seized the opportunity to own what has come to be viewed as the most important publication ever devoted to Jarry's life and work in the English language, and which has remained the artist's "bible" ever since.

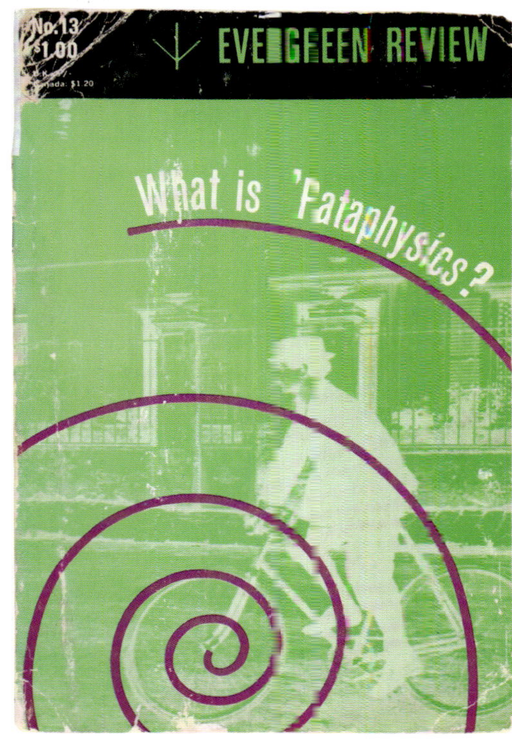

Fig. 77
Cover of the "What is 'Pataphysics?" special issue of the *Evergreen Review*, no. 13 (May–June 1960)

It was through this publication that Chimes became interested in Jarry's invented science of 'Pataphysics, which the author defined as "the science of imaginary solutions."[131] Like most modern artists who responded to Jarry's work, including Victor Brauner, Max Ernst, Matta, Dora Maar, Joan Miró, and Georges Rouault, Chimes initially found inspiration in the monstrous, dictatorial character of King Ubu, who inspired a number of nightmarish drawings that he made in the mid-1960s.[132] These drawings reveal Chimes's knowledge of Jarry's own graphic representations of King Ubu, as well as later manifestations such as Ernst's *Ubu Imperator*, of 1923 (fig. 78), in which the pompous dictator is shown as a hollow spinning top, perhaps in mocking reference to Benito Mussolini, who had recently usurped power in Italy in Ubu-like fashion.[133] In Chimes's caricatures, Ubu appears as a fish-eyed monster (fig. 79); a ghostly apparition in a hood (fig. 80), perhaps linking his vicious, threatening behavior with that of the Ku Klux Klan; and even in a self-portrait, where the artist, identifiable by the drooping fold of skin beside his eyes, wears Ubu's crown (fig. 81). But these initial efforts to translate King Ubu into Chimes's own visual language did not work to the artist's satisfaction, and he would not return to Jarry's work until the early 1970s.

Around 1973, Jarry's ideas again took hold of Chimes, this time through the realm of pure and boundless imagination presented in the dauntingly dense masterpiece *Gestes et opinions du Docteur Faustroll, 'Pataphysician* (Exploits and Opinions of Doctor Faustroll, 'Pataphysician).[134]

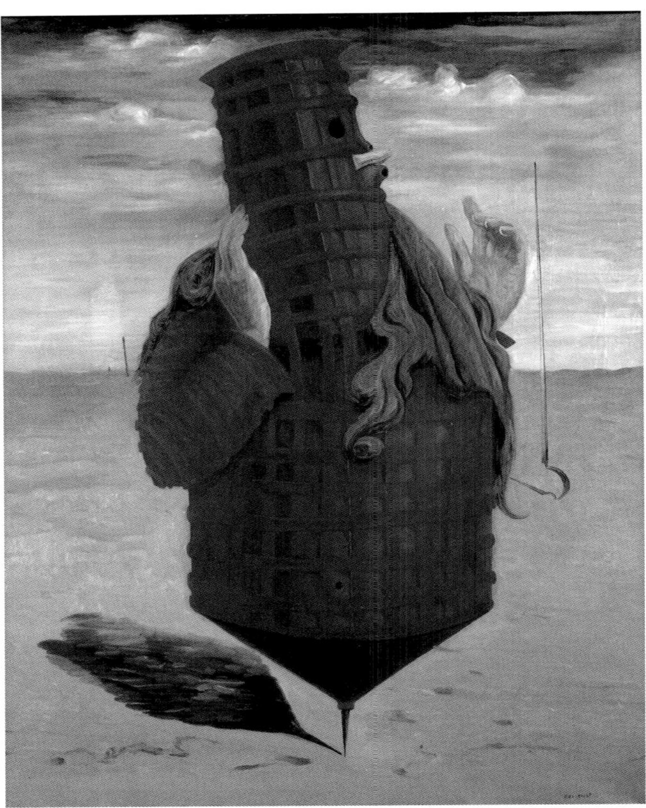

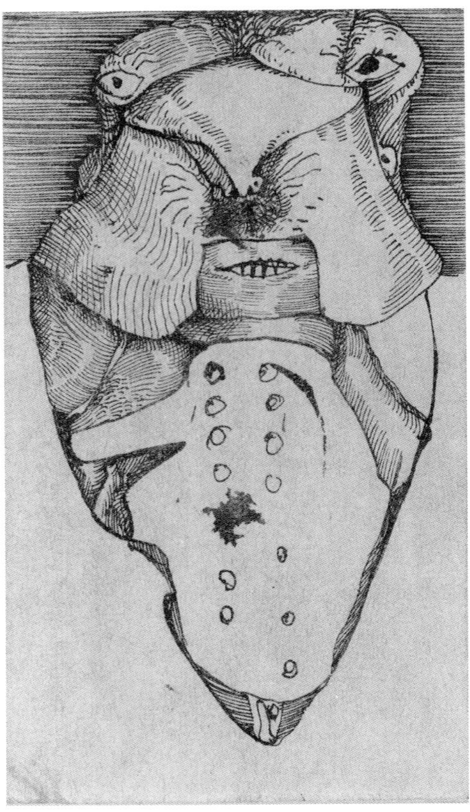

In this "neoscientific" novel, which was published posthumously in 1911 (although a few fragments of the book had appeared in the *Mercure de France* in 1895), Jarry presents a highly imaginative alternative universe where even the most absurd and contradictory propositions can make sense. In direct contrast to the adolescent nihilism, parody, and satire of the *Ubu* plays, *Faustroll* offers a positive vision of the future in which 'Pataphysics will harness the energy of the universe to extend the laws of science and physics and push the possible to the limits of the imaginable, thus anticipating to some extent quantum physics and other scientific developments of the twentieth century. Jarry's idea of extending frontiers clearly appealed to Chimes, who remains fascinated by the author's search for a new reality through humor and a heightened vision informed by science, poetry, classical learning, religion, and, above all, an unfettered imagination that allows his mind to conjure, for example, a supplementary universe made up entirely of exceptions.

The plot of this Rabelaisian, metatextual novel is worth recounting at length, given its central importance for Chimes's subsequent work. At the beginning of the book, the narrator, the bailiff Panmuphle (whose name translates roughly as "All-Snout" or "Everymug") arrives at the lodgings of the mysterious Doctor Faustroll to issue a summons to pay three hundred and seventy-two thousand francs and twenty-seven centimes, in respect of eleven quarters of unpaid rent. Unable to collect the money, the bailiff confiscates Faustroll's books and other worldly possessions.¹³⁵ Among these he finds a huge book entitled *Elements de 'Pataphysique*, which provides the following account of the basic premises of Jarry's science to end all sciences:

> 'Pataphysics will examine the laws governing exceptions, and will explain the universe supplementary to this one; or, less ambitiously, will describe a universe which can be—and perhaps should be—envisioned in the place of the traditional one, since the

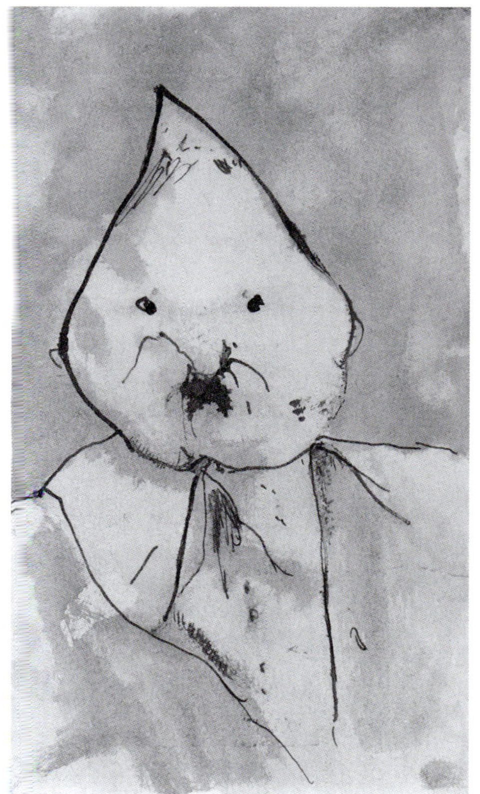

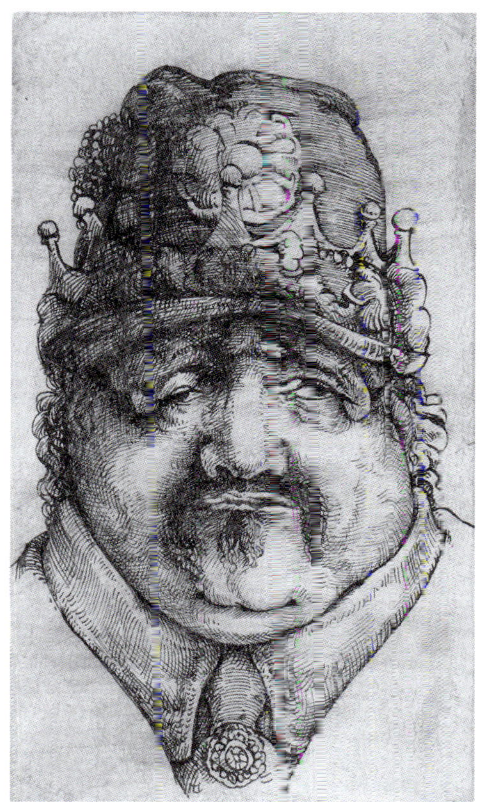

laws that are supposed to have been discovered in the traditional universe are also cor-relations of exceptions, albeit more frequent ones, but in any case accidental data which, reduced to the status of unexceptional exceptions, possess no longer even the virtue of originality.[136]

As his name suggests, the eponymous hero of the book is half Faust and half troll, no doubt referring to the fact that Jarry played the King of the Trolls in Lugné-Poë's 1896 production of Henrik Ibsen's *Peer Gynt* at the Théâtre de l'Oeuvre. As Jarry scholar Linda Klieger Stillman has pointed out, the French playwright was also inspired by Part II of Goethe's *Faust*, creating "his own rebel, an incarnation of man's quest to penetrate the paradoxes of life and his thirst for ultimate knowledge."[137] Faustroll has been described by Roger Shattuck as "the imp of sci-ence,"[138] a sort of man-god who, as Jarry writes, was "sixty-three years old when he was born in Circassia in 1898."[139] Faustroll embarks on a Homeric voyage "from Paris to Paris by sea,"[140] navigating across dry land in a sieve with his two companions, Panmuphle and Bosse-de-Nage (which translates loosely as "Bum-Face"), a baffled, dogfaced baboon with a callused, enlarged *derrière* whose vocabulary is limited to the repeated utterance of "Ha Ha!"[141] With Panmuphle as oarsman and Bosse-de-Nage as navigator, the trio's peregrinations carry them to exotic locales inhabited by Jarry's friends or enemies, where a variety of adventures, discussions, and a great banquet ensue.

Despite having dismissed death as "only for common people,"[142] Faustroll expires after sink-ing the skiff to avoid a collision. His death allows the secrets of his knowledge to be revealed to Panmuphle, as the roll of two-toned wallpaper designed by Maurice Denis in which his body has been draped unfurls to reveal, like a musical score, "all art and all science written between the lines of its spiral decorations.[143] Faustroll's death does not prevent him from continuing his scientific explorations, however, which now focus on the ethereal realms beyond the physical world, as in his "telepathic letters" to the Scottish mathematician and physicist Lord Kelvin regarding the latter's experiments in measurement, matter, and light. Finally, Faustroll undertakes the ultimate 'Pataphysical experiment: ascertaining the surface and nature of God, which he determines to be "the shortest distance between zero and infinity."[144]

Jarry's obsessively detailed and seemingly logical explanation of how the elongated sieve is not only seaworthy, but also unsinkable, typifies his synthesis of the absurd and the rational in *Exploits and Opinions of Doctor Faustroll, 'Pataphysician*, in which the author unrelentingly contorts external reality through a complete embracement of contradiction and paradox. Faustroll's ever-dry floating sieve, for example, should leak and sink, but due to Jarry's logical reversal can be used safely as a skiff.[145] Having established the magnificent seagoing properties of the sieve, which is propelled by oar blades and three steam rollers, Jarry informs the reader that "we shall not be navigating on water but on dry land."[146] There is, of course, no hint of irony or sarcasm in the novel's tone, which always remains clipped and pompous, like the "official" language of the military or government bureaucracy.

Chimes celebrated Faustroll's unique mode of transport in a 1977 painting (pl. 71) based upon an 1898 photograph (fig. 82) of Jarry looking on as his friend Alfred Vallette, editor of the *Mercure de France*, repaints his skiff. Vallette was not included in the finished work, which concentrates on the Doctor and the sieve in which he trundles through the streets and sidewalks of Paris. Faustroll and his companions visit fourteen islands or countries, each of which are subsumed by the world of a specific artist, writer, critic, composer, or scientist, among them Aubrey Beardsley, Emile Bernard, Pierre Bonnard, Félix Fénéon, Paul Gauguin, Stéphane Mallarmé, Rachilde, Marcel Schwob, and Paul Valéry. Each island is an imaginative synthesis of that figure's own writings, pictures, or ideas, often expressed by Jarry through affectionate parody.

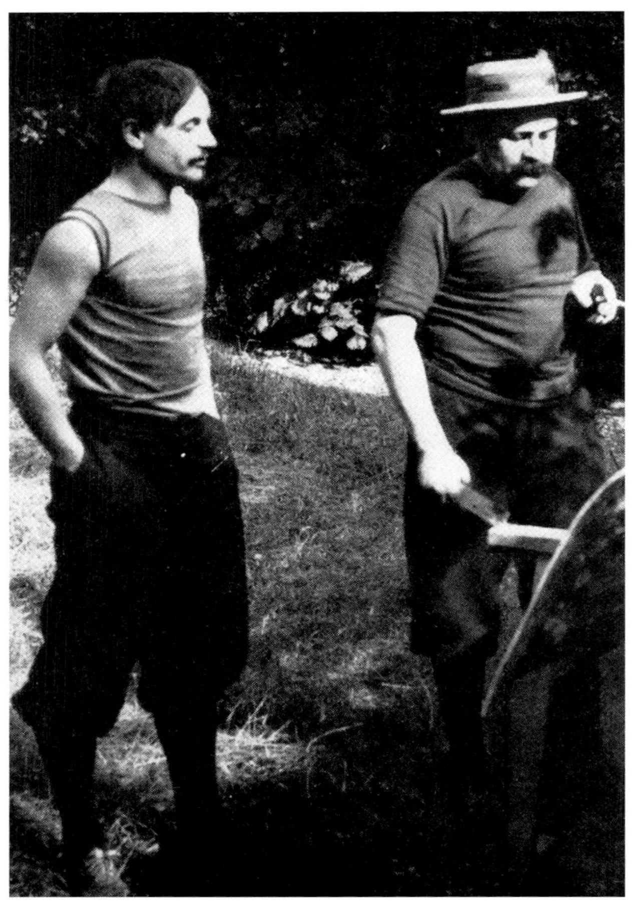

Fig. 82
Photograph of Alfred Jarry with Alfred Vallette repainting his skiff, 1898. Collection of Mme. G. Fort-Vallette, Paris. Reproduced in *The Selected Works of Alfred Jarry*, ed. Roger Shattuck and Simon Watson Taylor (New York: Grove Press, 1965), n.p.

Beardsley's kingdom, for example, is aptly titled the "Country of Lace," in reference to the English artist's dandy appearance, as well as his refined graphic technique. Jarry admired Beardsley's daring use of erotic imagery and sexual innuendo in his drawings, no doubt recognizing in him a kindred spirit who embraced scandal and refused to conform to the norms of respectable society during the early part of his career. The two men met in Paris in April 1897, and, although no details of their meeting have been recorded, it must have made a deep impression on both artist and writer. Beardsley even made a portrait of Jarry (now lost), which the French author describes in *Exploits and Opinions of Doctor Faustroll, 'Pataphysician* as a picture of the fictional Doctor Faustroll.[147] In the novel, Beardsley is portrayed as Ali Baba, following the English artist's magnificent cover design for *Ali Baba and the Forty Thieves*, which he completed shortly before he met Jarry. This drawing took advantage of the fact that the initia Letters of Ali Baba doubled as his own signature, which probably inspired Jarry to take his idea one step further and merge the artist with his subject. Our final glimpse of the "Country of Lace" is of Ali Baba howling in pain as he drowns in a jar of "pitiless oil." Jarry scholar Jill Fell has convincingly argued that this was the author's implicit condemnation of Beardsley, who had apparently succumbed to the very hypocrisy he had attacked in his earlier drawings, as seen in his behavior in the wake of the Oscar Wilde scandal, when he snubbed the Irish writer in Dieppe, as well as his decision at the end of his career to allow "shallow bourgeois standards and commercial arguments to direct which of his drawings should be published, repeatedly agreeing to more anodine alternatives."[148]

This idea of a hallucinatory voyage to the imaginative realms of a particular artist or writer would provide the impetus for Chimes's extraordinary series of panel paintings, which as Anne d'Harnoncourt first pointed out were similarly intended to refer less to the subject represented than to the ideas that person generated.[149] The panel portraits, as well as the more recent white paintings (see pp. 178–220 below), are all informed by Jarry's farcical, tongue-in-cheek philoso-phy of 'Pataphysics, which defies rational explanation. 'Pataphysics opened up for Chimes a new and exciting vocabulary of esoteric, quasiscientific imagery, along with a pantheon of like-minded "father figures" whose contributions to the world of ideas he continually pays homage to. Almost a decade went by between his first discovery of the "What is 'Pataphysics?" number of Evergreen Review and the artist's inaugural panel portrait of Alfred Jarry (Departure from the Desert) of 1973 (pl. 41), which portrays the writer above a mysterious, hovering cloud of "luminiferous ether."[150] During this time, Chimes was slowly but surely developing his artistic response to Jarry's ideas, which would supplant his interest in Artaud by the end of the 1960s, especially after he read Roger Shattuck's The Banquet Years. First published in 1955, Shattuck's classic biographical study of Jarry and his contemporaries helped to introduce a whole new generation of readers to the pint-sized French writer's extraordinary life and work, and it has become another "bible" to which Chimes has referred continually in his subsequent work.

In addition to the islands that Faustroll visited on his Gulliver-like travels with Bosse-de-Nage and Panmuphle, all of which represent an individual artist, writer, or critic who has inspired Jarry and to whom he pays heartfelt tribute, Chimes also made portraits of writers listed in the inventory of Faustroll's library, consisting of twenty-seven assorted volumes, including Charles Baudelaire's translations of Edgar Allan Poe, Arthur Rimbaud's Illuminations and Paul Verlaine's Wisdom, as well as a portrait of Doctor Faustroll by Aubrey Beardsley.[151] The portraits thus reveal Chimes's strong feelings of affinity and continuity with his iconoclastic avant-garde forebears, all of whom he regards as "possessed" characters whose work remains as relevant today as when it was first created. Chimes was especially fascinated with Poe, who had lived in Phila-delphia and whose romantic poetry influenced the artist's own poems of the early 1960s, written during the time of the crucifixion paintings. For his panel portraits of Poe (pl. 47; fig. 83), Chimes embarked on a voyage of discovery by immersing himself in the writer's macabre short stories and poems. He empathized with Poe's persistent theme of the alienated and tormented out-sider, often driven to the perilous brink of insanity. He also discovered a direct link with Jarry's work and ideas in the cosmological prose-poem "Eureka," Poe's most ambitious and elaborate work, which Chimes regards as an important precursor to 'Pataphysics, since it dissolves generic and disciplinary boundaries that had traditionally separated art and literature from science

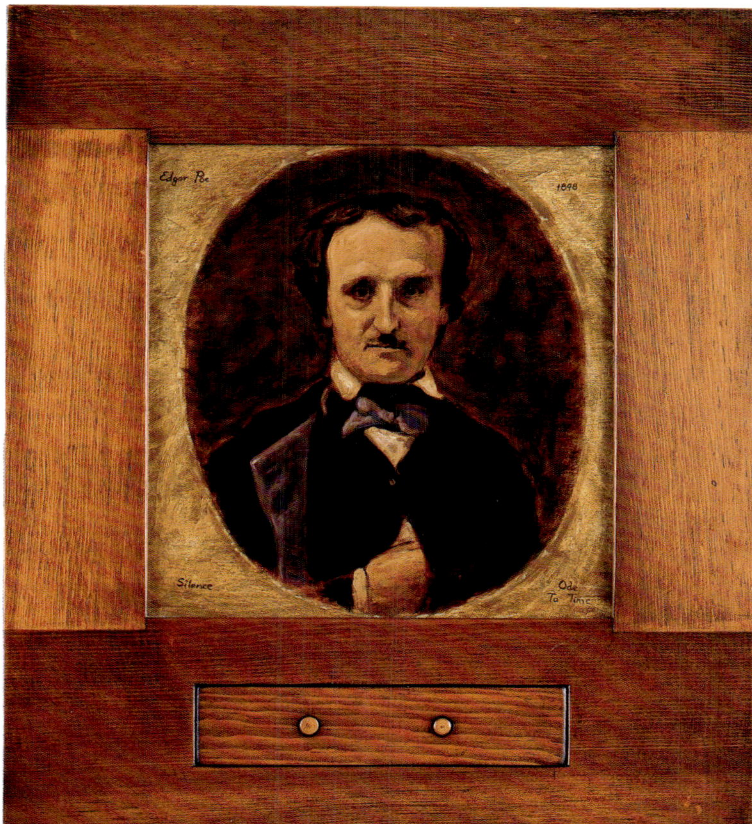

Fig. 83
Thomas Chimes, *Edgar Allan Poe*, 1974. Oil on panel, 20¾ x 18⅜ inches (52.7 x 46.7 cm). Private collection, courtesy of Locks Gallery, Philadelphia

Similarly, the English scientist Michael Faraday was included in the panel portrait series, since his fantastic intuition, independence, and originality of mind reminded Chimes of Doctor Faustroll and his invented science of exceptions. One of the great founders of modern physics, Faraday was a largely self-taught scientist who had no formal education beyond primary school and had only a rudimentary knowledge of mathematics. As in 'Pataphysics, Faraday's ignorance of accepted scientific theories inspired him to develop simple, nonmathematical concepts to explain electrical and magnetic phenomena. Chimes may also have been aware that Faraday consulted with William Thomson, later Lord Kelvin, whose ideas were central to Jarry's concept of 'Pataphysics. This conversation led Faraday to conduct a pioneering experiment in 1845, in which light was passed through heavy glass placed near a powerful magnet, leading to his discovery that an intense magnetic field can rotate the plane of polarized light, a phenomenon known today as the Faraday effect. Faraday's 1846 lecture "Thoughts on Ray-Vibrations," which laid the basis for the field theory of electromagnetism that the English scientist developed in the ensuing years, provided the inspiration for the following passage in Jarry's 1902 novel *The Supermale*:

> When a piece of copper is dropped between two poles of a powerful electromagnet, being of nonmagnetic metal it cannot be influenced; nevertheless it will not fall through. It will float down slowly as though a viscous liquid occupied the space between the magnetic poles. Now, if one is brave enough to place one's head in this spot—and Faraday, as we know, did carry out this experiment—absolutely nothing can be felt.[152]

In his portrait of the English scientist (pl. 43) inspired by this description, Chimes used a loosely brushed, copper-colored background, which gives the impression that Faraday is surrounded by waves of electricity and magnetic force lines.

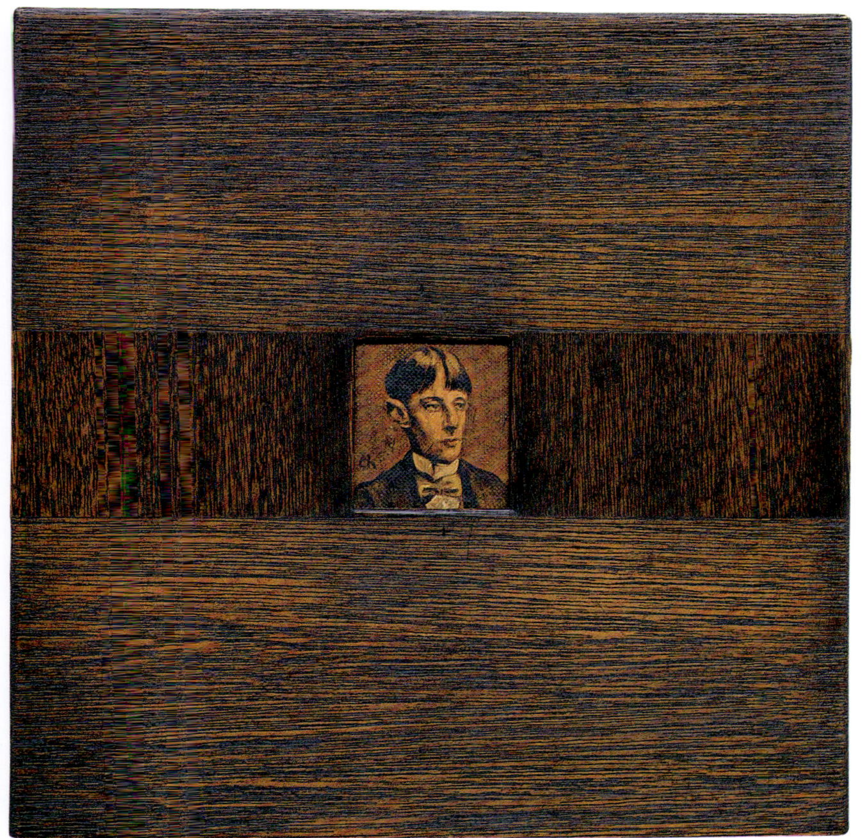

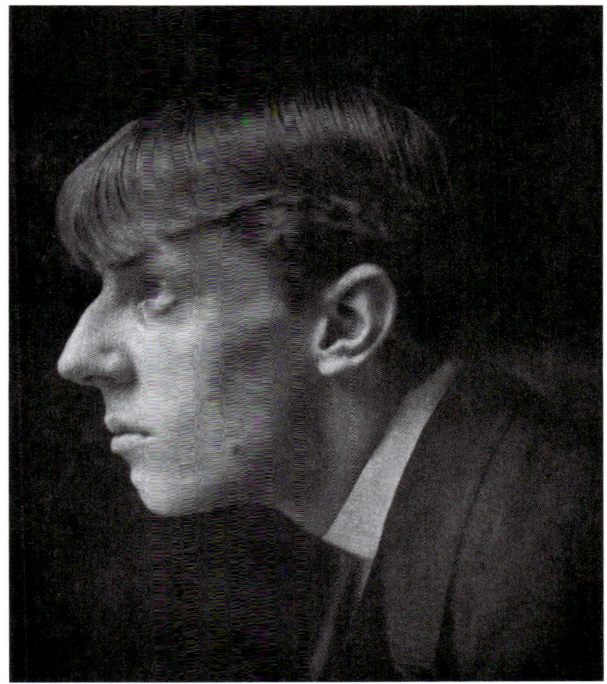

Several panel portraits depict Aubrey Beardsley (pls. 65, 66), reflecting the importance of the precocious English artist for Jarry as well as Chimes, whose own exquisite black-and-white drawings of the mid-1960s looked back to the sinuous line of Beardsley's erotic illustrations for Oscar Wilde's banned masterpiece *Salomé*. In Chimes's penetrating panel portraits which are after based upon Frederick Hollyer's photographs taken around the time of the publication of *Salomé*, Beardsley appears as the quintessence of fin-de-siècle sensibility. However, Beardsley's fashionable attire, replete with an elegant butterfly bowtie, fails to hide his gaunt features and sunken cheekbones, signs that he was slowly losing his battle with the tuberculosis that would eventually take his life (fig. 84). In a variant image, derived from Frederick Evans's celebrated 1893 photograph (fig. 85), Beardsley is shown in profile, affecting the pose of the Notre Dame gargoyle Le Stryge (pl. 66). Beardsley's distinctive features may have led his friend, a bookseller and photographer, to notice his resemblance to the famous gargoyle, although as Chris Snodgrass has pointed out, since the artist had made the grotesque the essence of his art, Beardsley himself may have assumed the pose of the stone sculpture.[153] For Chimes, Beardsley was yet another example of the artist as the misfit, the outsider, the alien, the monstrous, the Other—a lost soul who journeys toward physical, mental, and spiritual destruction. The English artist's depiction in the form of a gargoyle was thus the perfect embodiment of how so-called civilized society, through its courts, hospitals, asylums, and other repressive institutions of church and state, had demonized the artist in order to enforce a sense of rigid conformity and standardization.

Each panel portrait, reminiscent of a nineteenth-century daguerreotype, is enshrined within an oversized wooden frame resembling those found on the paintings of fellow Philadelphian Thomas Eakins, who often used flat boards of chestnut, sometimes almost a foot wide, to establish a great deal of space around his work (fig. 86). Chimes's frames situate his work somewhere

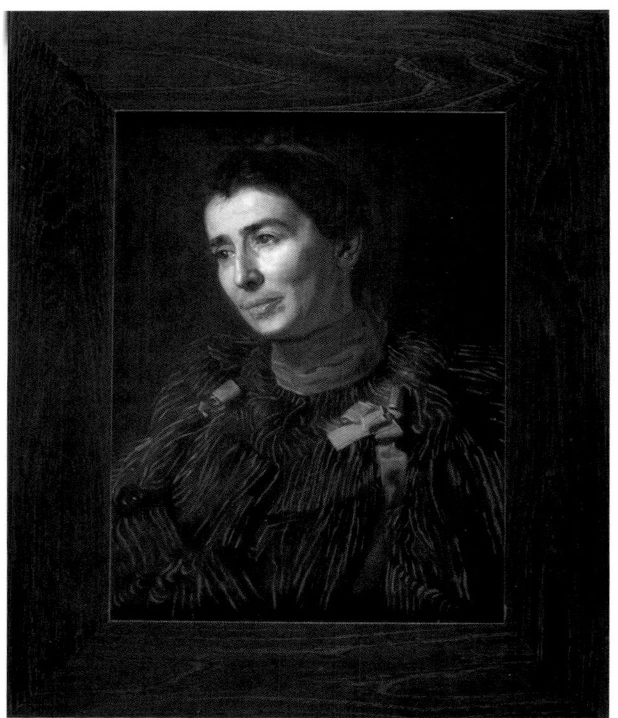

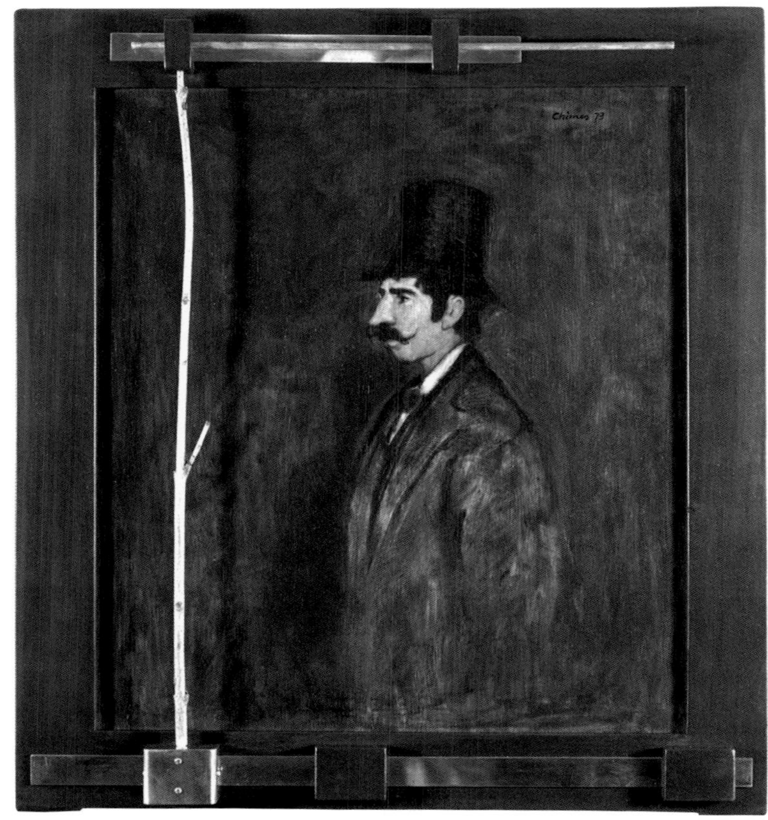

Fig. 86
Thomas Eakins, *Portrait of Mary Adeline Williams*, c. 1900. Oil on canvas, 30³⁄₁₆ x 24⅛ inches (76.6 x 61.3 cm) with frame, Philadelphia Museum of Art. Gift of Mrs. Thomas Eakins and Miss Mary Adeline Williams, 1929-184-10

Fig. 87
Thomas Chimes, *Jean Moréas* (in original frame with wooden branch), 1973. Oil on panel, 16¼ x 13⅛ inches (41.3 x 33.3 cm). Collection of the artist

between a family snapshot and a devotional icon, allowing him to isolate the particular person and hone in on his or her visage. These frames were specially constructed by the artist out of strips of oak, pine, mahogany, or ebony and were occasionally furnished with a small brass plaque denoting the subject's name. Several early works in the series, such as *Jean Moréas*, of 1973 (pl. 40), were housed in frames that incorporated extraneous details, such as a wooden branch (fig. 87), that Chimes later removed because he felt that the use of additional elements was related to the earlier metal box series and detracted from the emotional force of the individual portraits.[154] The artist often refers to these broad wooden structures as "frames of reference," a pun that also underlines their importance as a directional device to focus attention on the subject.[155] Chimes's reference to Eakins with these frames was a conscious one, since the latter lived in the same epoch as Jarry, and the brown hues of the portraits were also intended to evoke the palette of his nineteenth-century predecessor.

The genesis of each work began with the selection of the appropriate panel for the individual portrait, since the grain of the wood often played a decisive role in the finished painting. The panel was then coated with Elmer's glue and sanded smooth after the glue had dried. Once the wood support was prepared to his satisfaction, Chimes rubbed linseed oil onto the panel and painted directly into the slightly wet surface, using warm tones of raw umber to achieve the dark, varnished sheen he associated with Eakins's portraits, with occasional flashes of color to offset the otherwise monochrome surface. The portraits were painted with an intense, direct observation of the photographic source, which was often mounted on his easel for easy access during the slow process of recreating it on the panel.

Another important point of reference for the panel portraits was *Head of Christ* (fig. 88), a painting attributed to Rembrandt van Rijn in the John G. Johnson Collection at the

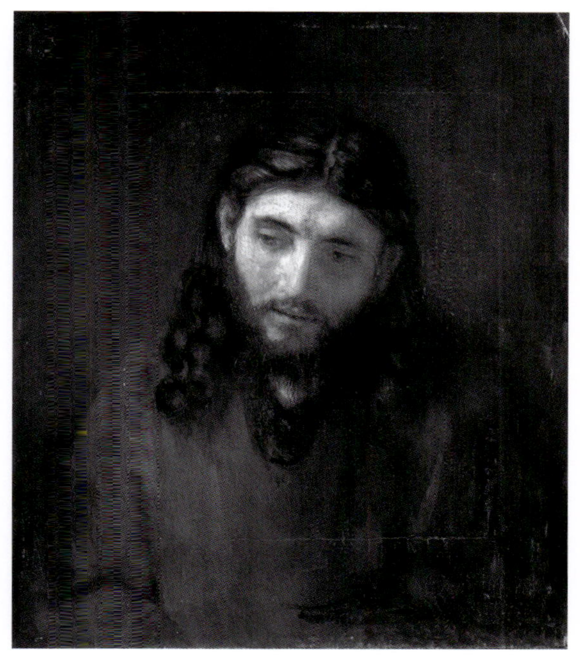

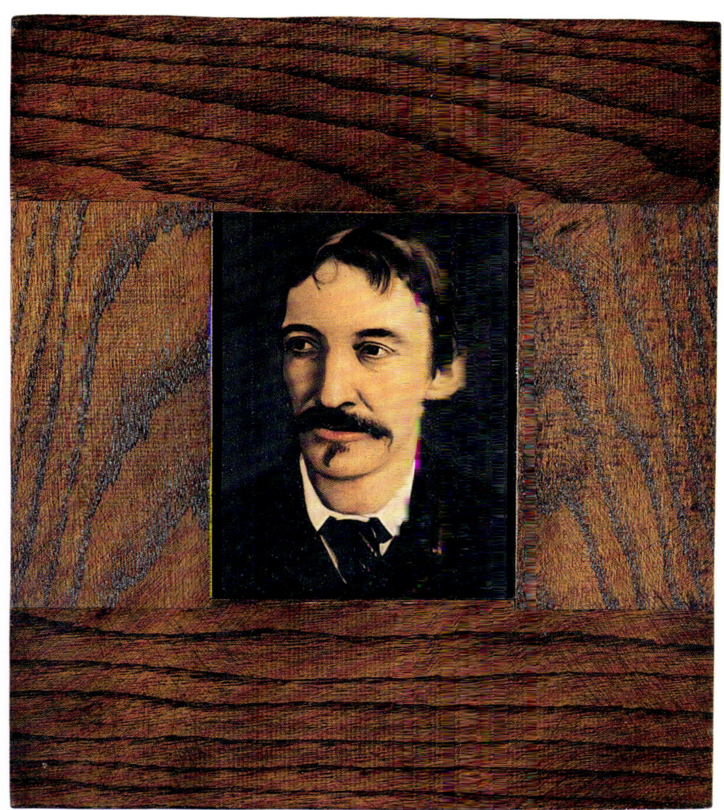

Philadelphia Museum of Art. This brooding image of the bearded Christ, shown in extreme chiaroscuro, hangs in a heavy wooden frame that anticipates those found on Chimes's paintings. The artist has admired the painting since he was a teenager, and associates it with one of his earliest and most powerful experiences with art: "I visited the Philadelphia Museum of Art and saw this *Head of Christ* by Rembrandt hanging there. A kind of hallucination took place. It was as if I saw myself in the studio where it was painted. I experienced the smells of that particular room, even the quality of moisture in the room. It was as if I were actually there, immersed in it as if a dream or a memory."[156]

Each subject in the panel portrait series relates in some way to Jarry, no matter how obliquely. Robert Louis Stevenson (pl. 68; fig. 89) is included because Jarry translated his 1885 short story "Olalla" into French, while Lord Kelvin (pl. 53) takes his place in the series because his scientific discoveries, calculations, and theorems, along with those of William Crookes and Charles Vernon Boys, profoundly informed Jarry's 'Pataphysical concepts, such as the idea of "luminiferous ether."[157] In the mid-1970s the panel portraits progressed from images of Jarry and his friends and colleagues, including Charles Baudelaire (pl. 46), Arthur Rimbaud (pl. 45), Paul Verlaine (pl. 52; fig. 90), and Oscar Wilde (pl. 58; fig. 103), to those featuring his heirs, such as Antonin Artaud (pl. 48) and Marcel Duchamp (pls. 59, 60, 74). In a 1986 letter to Chimes, Roger Shattuck described the panel portraits as "fetishes" whose curious power "lies in the fact that, through scale and technique, they face three ways at once: toward the historical reality of biography, toward the registered optical image of photography, and toward painting, whose infinite possibilities for modification and interpretation you hold in abeyance."[158]

Around 1976, the network of affinities between Jarry and his contemporaries began to extend and take on a life of its own. Chimes made a panel portrait of the flamboyant French

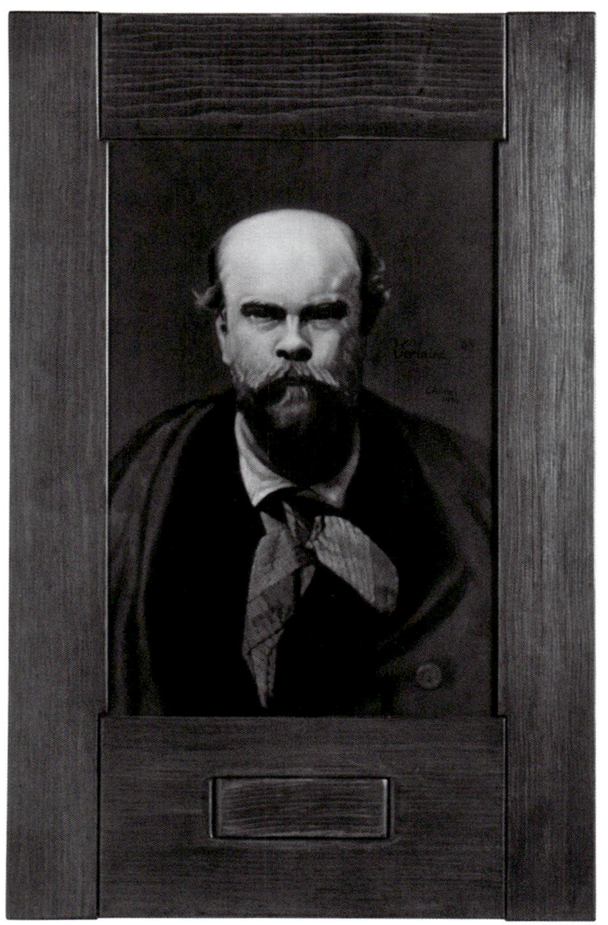

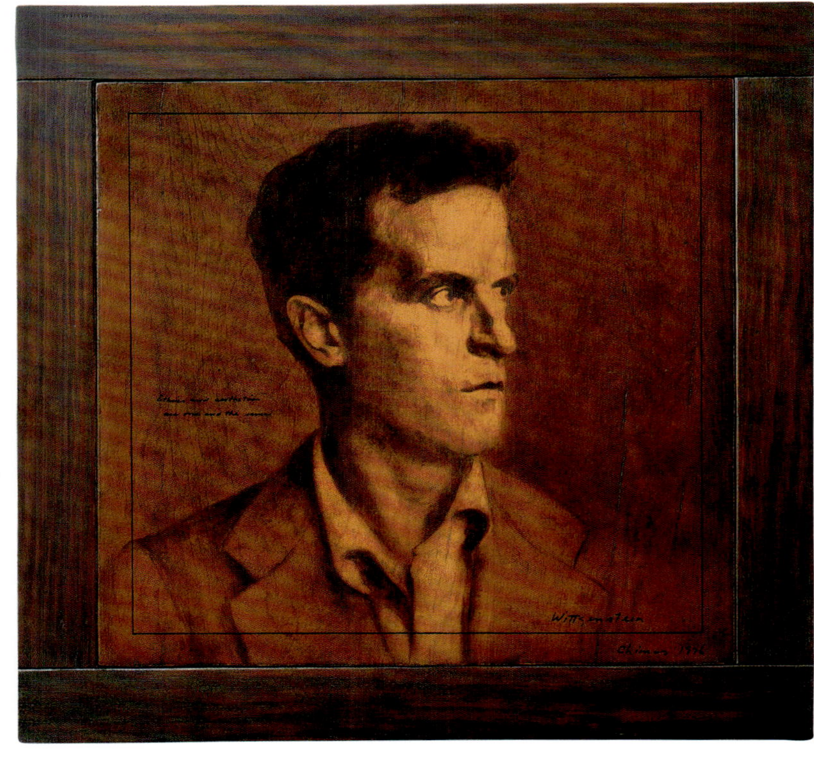

Fig. 90
Thomas Chimes, *Paul Verlaine*, 1974. Oil on wood, 24¼ x 15⅜ inches (61.6 x 39.1 cm). Collection of Mr. and Mrs. Si Newhouse, New York

Fig. 91
Thomas Chimes, *Ludwig Wittgenstein*, 1976. Oil on panel, 17¼ x 18 inches (43.8 x 45.7 cm). The Cartin Collection, Hartford, Connecticut

actress Sarah Bernhardt (pl. 61), who took her place in the artist's constellation of Jarry-related subjects due to her love of scandal and publicity, as well as her connections with Wilde and with Marcel Schwob, to whom Jarry had dedicated *Ubu Roi*.[159] Similarly, Chimes included Ludwig Wittgenstein in two paintings from 1976 (pl. 67; fig. 91), after reading the Viennese philosopher's famous statement that "ethics and aesthetics are one," which initially dumbfounded him, but in time began to resonate with his understanding of the panel portraits as a unified group expressing the continuity of Jarry's contradictory pseudoscience of 'Pataphysics.[160]

One panel portrait, *Doctor I. L. Sandomir*, of 1974 (pl. 54), even depicts a subject whose existence was, at best, 'Pataphysical. Sandomir was the fictitious vice-curator-founder of the Collège de 'Pataphysique, which was founded on May 11, 1948, in recognition of the fiftieth anniversary of the completion of *Exploits and Opinions of Doctor Faustroll, 'Pataphysician*.[161] According to Simon Watson Taylor, Sandomir "was for us not only the living presence of an incomparable past but the immensely erudite and brilliant inspirer of all our pataphysical endeavours, who guided us serenely through the shifting shadows of the real and unreal worlds."[162] Reputedly nine years older than Jarry, Sandomir was said to have passed away on April 10, 1956, after a long illness; a close friend reported that his last words were, "What is that making a noise?" When the Surrealist writer Jean Paulhan announced in the *Nouvelle Revue Française* that "his sorrow at the death was tempered by the suspicion that probably Dr. Sandomir had never existed," the Collège de 'Pataphysique took immediate action against this "provocative insinuation" by declaring publicly that Paulhan was considered henceforth to be "pataphysically non-existent" and issued printed postcards bearing the legend "Jean Paulhan n'existe pas" (Jean Paulhan does not exist).[163] Fully cognizant that Sandomir was the pictorial creation of the Collège, Chimes based his portrait on the dubious photograph of "His Late Magnificence" that was reproduced on page 178 of the Jarry issue of the *Evergreen Review*, which showed a bearded, white-haired old man with a button bearing the Ubu spiral on his lapel (fig. 92).

Once one finds the logic behind the series, it becomes a kind of game to deduce the referential and associative chain that links all the characters, and also work out why Chimes included certain people and excluded others. For instance, one of the artist's golden rules for the series was that all the people portrayed had to have "experienced something myste- rious, psychological and mythical. And were deeply affected by it."[164] This life-changing experience could range from Artaud's acute mental illness to Wilde's harsh prison sen- tence. In line with his own underground reputation, Chimes also tended to favor marginal artists and writers over famous ones. Thus Picasso was excluded, despite his early economic hardship and critical neglect, since his subsequent wealth and fame placed him outside the parameters of the series. Others, such as Friedrich Nietzsche and Honoré de Balzac, were con- sidered as subjects, often at the suggestion of friends who would send Chimes postcards and newspaper clippings in the hope that he would use them, yet ultimately rejected. In the end what mattered was that the artist felt a deep emotional attachment to the work and ideas of the person being portrayed.

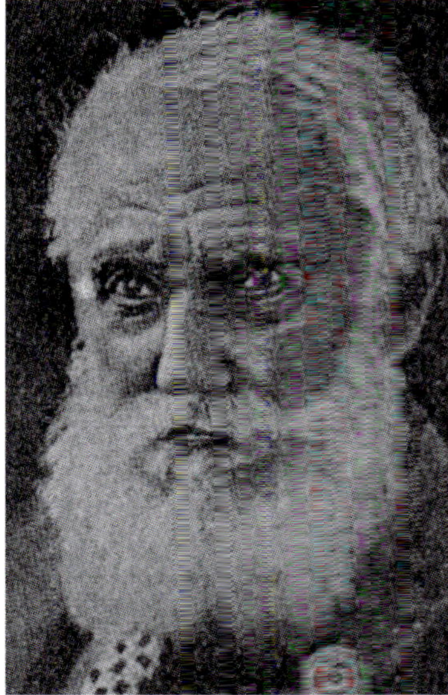

Fig. 92
Photograph of "Doctor I. L. Sandomir," repro- duced in the "What is 'Pataphysics" special issue of the *Evergreen Review*, May–June 1960, p. 178.

Another important factor was that each portrait would be made from a photograph. This idea came to Chimes in 1973 while reading chapter 12 of Joris-Karl Huysmans's decadent novel *À Rebours* (Against Nature), in which the depraved hero, Duc Jean Floressas des Esseintes, browses through the books in his library and comes across an intriguing volume entitled *L'Homme* by Ernest Hello. Chimes was especially struck by Huysmans's description of Hello's book, which "revealed the interesting comparisons that can be established between the processes of photography and memory."[165] This connection, within the context of a library of esoteric or forbidden literature that reminded him of Faustroll's inventory of books, made such a deep impression on the artist that he resolved to work from photographs in his panel portraits, drawn either from obscure sources or from sources that obscure the figure portrayed.

Chimes spoke of the importance of obscurity and obliqueness in the panel portrait series in an important, heretofore unpublished letter to Evan Turner, then director of the Philadelphia Museum of Art, dated September 15, 1975, in which he humorously recounted how he had just completed two preliminary studies "of modest dimensions" for the *Bicentennial Jarry* (pl. 63) "the intent being to reach his stature sometime in 1976; a midget with character and, I believe, an obscurity of compelling magnitude."[166] Chimes then went on to explain that two of his recently completed paintings of Duchamp, begun during the summer of 1975, were on view at Moore College of Art, and that he was at work on a third, titled *Rrose Sélavy*, "all of which are selectively oblique."[167] This statement is borne out by the fact that Duchamp, perhaps the most recognizable person in the series, is depicted in drag as his transgressive Rrose Sélavy alter ego (pl. 74); as *Mona* (pl. 60) in honor of his iconoclastic *L.H.O.O.Q.*, of 1919, in which he added a mustache and goatee to a postcard of Leonardo's *Mona Lisa*; and naked save for a well-placed rose over his genitals and a fake beard in a *tableau vivant* of Lucas Cranach's *Adam and Eve*

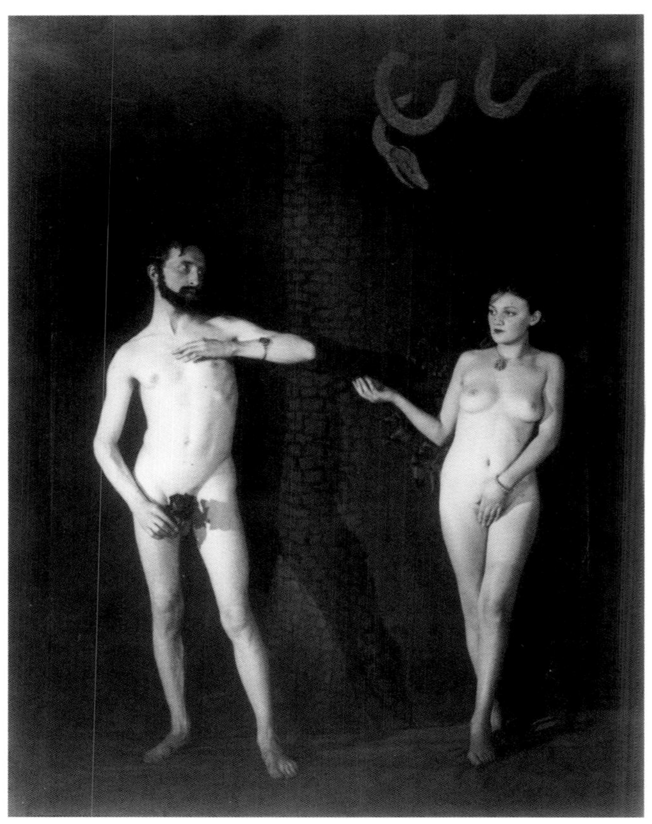

Fig. 93
Man Ray, *Ciné-Sketch: Adam and Eve (Marcel Duchamp and Bronia Perlmutter)*, 1924. Gelatin silver print, 11⅛ x 8⁹⁄₁₆ inches (28.2 x 21.7 cm). Philadelphia Museum of Art, The Lynne and Harold Honickman Gift of the Julien Levy Collection, 2001-62-784

(pl. 59). In the latter case, unless viewers are familiar with Man Ray's 1924 photograph *Ciné-Sketch* (fig. 93), which shows the French artist re-creating the famous painting with Bronia Perlmutter during the intermission of Francis Picabia's ballet *Relâche (No Performance)*, they are unlikely to recognize Duchamp as the naked man wearing the fake beard and the incongruous wristwatch.

The use of photographic source material also links the panel portrait series with Warhol's earlier silkscreen paintings and Gerhard Richter's photo-based paintings, as well as the portraits of Thomas Eakins, whose use of photography, while only recently emphasized in the literature on the artist, has long been observed by Chimes. Chimes's own approach to photographic source material can be understood through what Roland Barthes, in his beautiful essay on the dual nature of photography, published in English as *Camera Lucida*, identified as the *studium* and the *punctum*.[168] For Barthes, the Latin word *studium* implied an enthusiastic human interest in the subject portrayed, perhaps through study or general interest in a culture or time period, as opposed to the *punctum*, which seizes and irritates the viewer, like a pinprick or wasp's sting. The notion of the *punctum* conforms to Chimes's work, which pays personal homage to his artistic and literary precursors through powerful, highly emotional images, such as the poignant portrait of Marcel Proust of 1977 (fig. 94), derived from Man Ray's photograph of the bearded French novelist on his deathbed on November 20, 1922. According to Barthes's definition, the *studium* triggers a culturally mediated reaction, a universal effect, whereas the *punctum* moves the viewer, triggering a reaction that Barthes compares to a bruise.[169]

This emotional shudder can be felt in Chimes's *Guillaume Apollinaire*, of 1974 (pl. 49). In 1909, two years after Jarry's death, Guillaume Apollinaire wrote a long and insightful article praising his invention of Ubu. Apollinaire's tribute, in which he described Jarry as "the last sublime debauchee of the Renaissance," helped to introduce his provocative work and ideas to a new generation of artists and writers.[170] Two years later, Apollinaire was the only critic to review the posthumous publication by Eugène Fasquelle of Jarry's *Exploits and Opinions of Doctor Faustroll, 'Pataphysician*, which he described as "the most important publication of 1911."[171] Fully aware of the crucial role that Apollinaire played in the resuscitation of Jarry's reputation in the years leading up to World War I, Chimes chose to depict the avant-garde poet, critic, and playwright as he appeared shortly before attending the premiere of his best-known play, the farcical, Jarry-esque *Les mamelles de Tirésias* (The Breasts of Tiresias), at the Théâtre Maubel in 1917. In the portrait, Apollinaire wears the uniform of the French army, from which he had recently received a medical discharge after suffering a serious head wound when shrapnel from

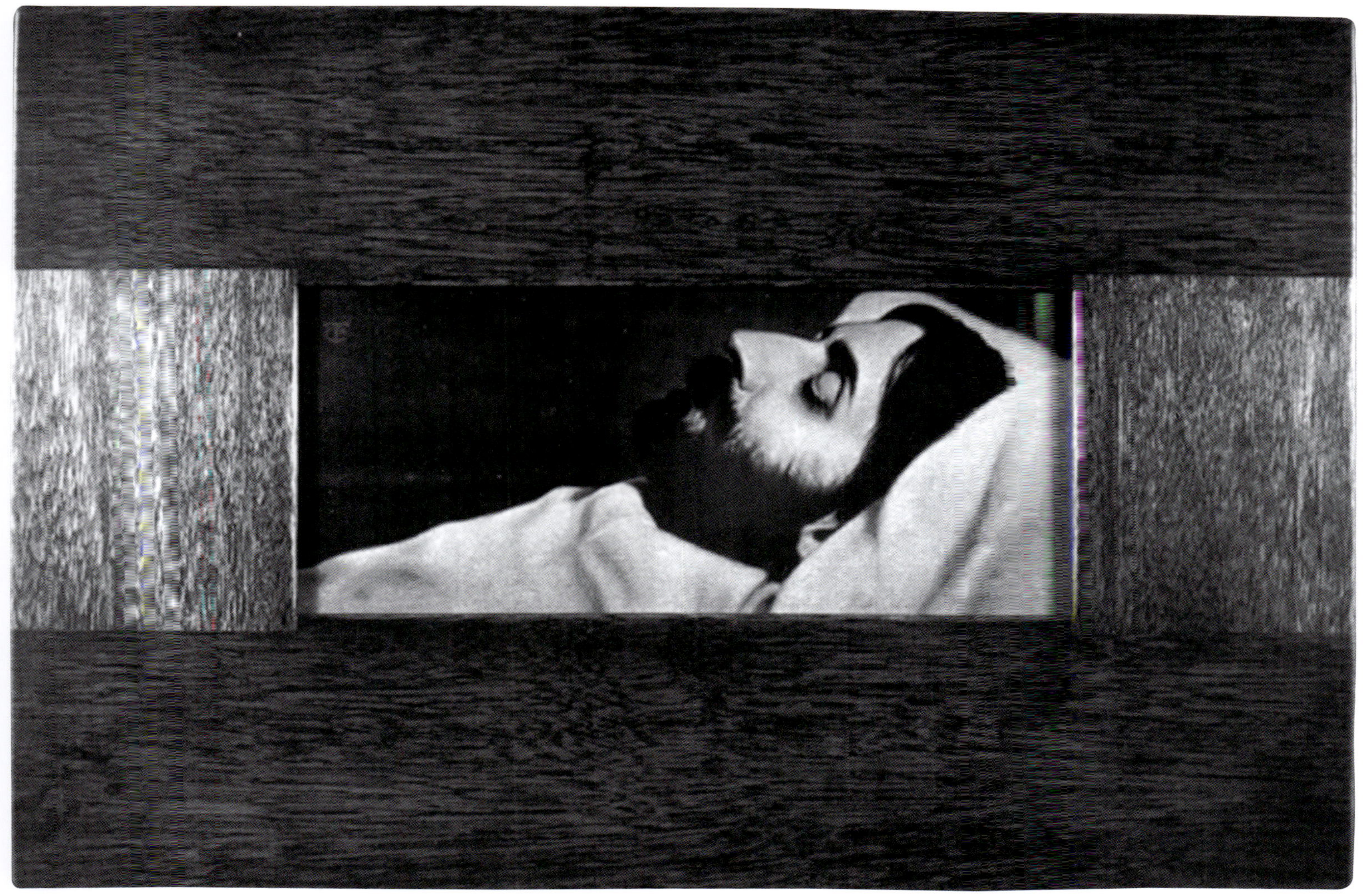

or exploding shell pierced his helmet. Chimes focuses our attention on the large collar, the stiffness of which contrasts with the soft vulnerability of the poet's chubby face, and the leather band around his forehead that protects his injury. This band, combined with the dark, deep-set eyes, adds a disquieting note to an otherwise jubilant image, thus reminding the viewer of Apollinaire's tragic early death the following year when his body, already severely weakened from the head wound, succumbed to the Spanish Influenza pandemic of 1918.[172]

Barthes's idea of the *punctum* helps to explain the methodology of Chimes's selection of photographs for the panel portraits, which were meant to encapsulate the world of the writer, artist, or scientist portrayed through a single moment of his or her life. Chimes thus employed an emotional objectivity when sifting through the range of photographs for, say, the 1974 portrait of Charles Baudelaire (pl. 46), and I believe that he eventually chose the 1862 *carte-de-visite* photograph by Gaspard-Félix Tournachon Nadar (fig. 95), rather than the slightly earlier and less aptly recognizable photograph taken by Etienne Carjat (fig. 96), because he wanted to highlight the romantic appearance and mesmerizing gaze of the influential French poet and art critic.

Chimes selected his source image from the 1969 anthology *Baudelaire: The Artist and His World*, which, along with biographical commentaries by Robert Kopp and a critical essay by Georges Poulet, was also generously illustrated with photographs, caricatures, and paintings.[17] Many of the other images reproduced in this anthology appear elsewhere in Chimes's work of

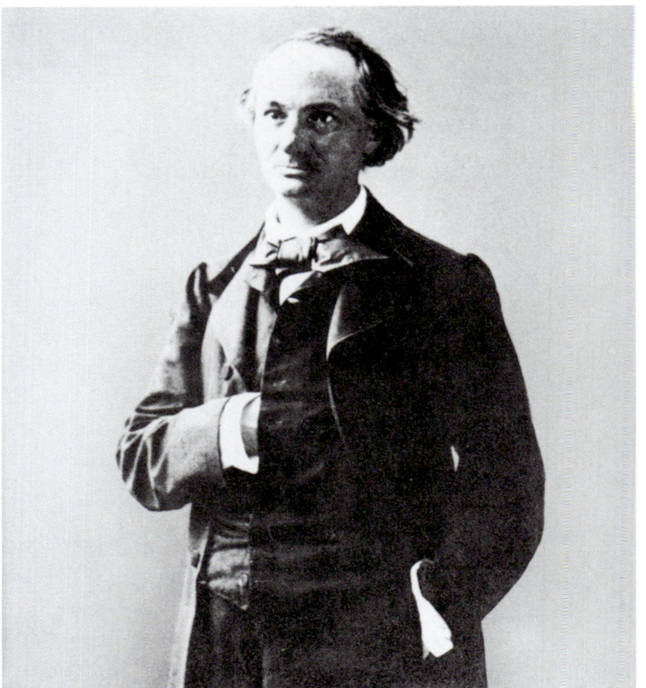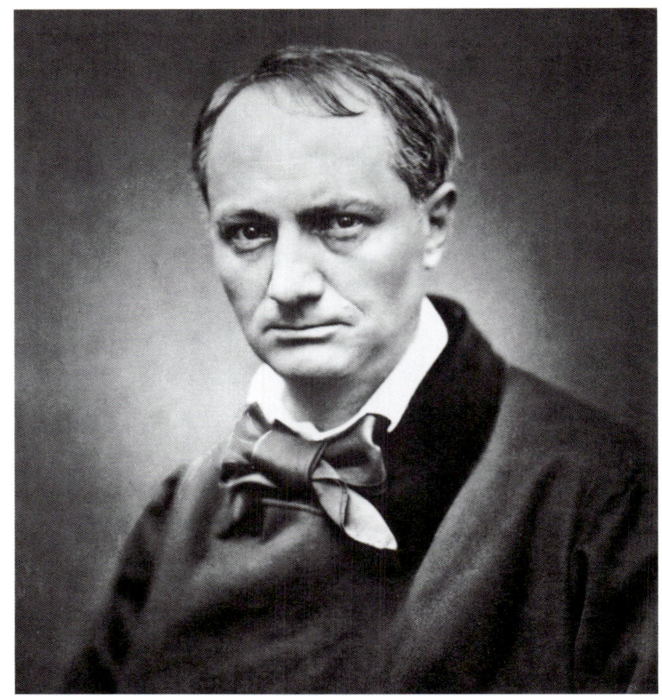

this time, including the panel portraits of Poe and an outstanding pencil drawing of Nadar wearing a top hat that Chimes made in 1975 (fig. 97). Although Nadar was too successful in his paid profession as a photographer to be included in the series himself, his photographs of his peers were used for several of Chimes's panel portraits, including the one of his close friend Baudelaire, standing with one arm in his trouser pocket and the other plunged into his vest like Napoleon. Nadar's smoldering image takes us into the realm of the *punctum* in that it awakens in the viewer a desire and curiosity to transcend what it permits us to see, to add to what is already there. The photograph captures the charisma and vitality of the poet-critic, but also hints at his life's struggle and exhaustion through the dark shadow that falls across Baudelaire's face like a curse. Chimes thus chose the photograph that best conveyed the French poet's life in its entirety, as a nineteenth-century man of letters, as well as the misunderstood, romantic bohemian who died of venereal disease five years later.

Once Chimes had chosen the photograph that would provide the point of departure for the portrait, the task of re-creating and translating the image in oil paint on a carefully prepared wood panel began. Working from the photographic reproduction in front of him, the artist would select the appropriate mode of representation to render the individual's likeness, believing that the technique itself would correspond to that particular person. As Chimes later recalled:

> In the case of someone like Baudelaire, having read his poetry, read the biographical
> material on him, I then started painting. I suddenly felt and thought I saw in the
> painting itself an almost ghostlike, moonlit face that I had used in some of the others.
> So I dropped this lunar quality in the work at that point and concentrated on the cut
> of his coat. And there's where the emphasis really is, which not only amused me, but
> I felt it was saying something significant about Baudelaire himself. So to sum it all up,
> my approach to these portraits was to use a technique and a way of working that would
> be appropriate to the individual that I was trying to represent.[174]

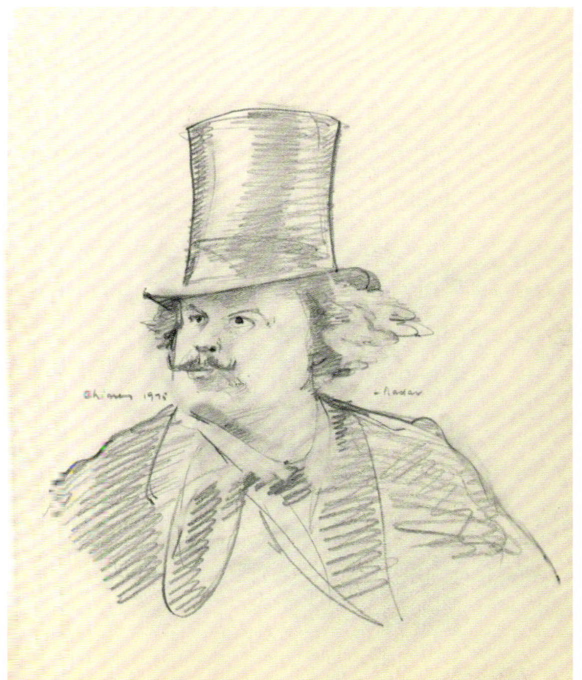

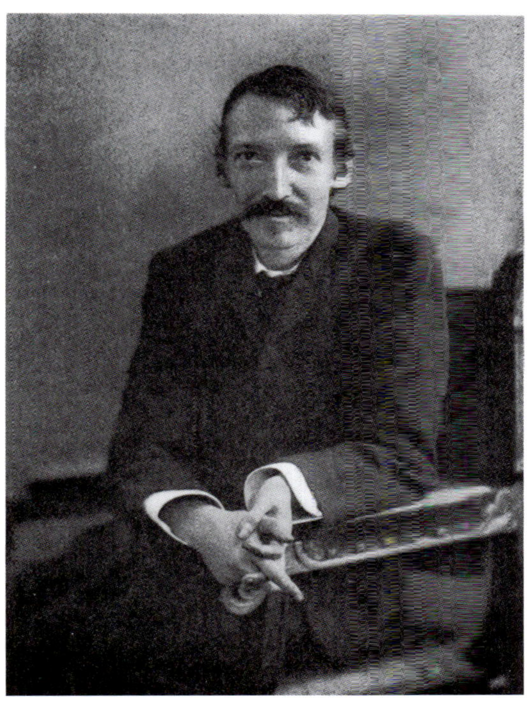

Fig. 97
Thomas Chimes, *Nadar*, 1975. Pencil on paper, 11⅞ x 8¹³⁄₁₆ inches (30.2 x 22.3 cm). Collection of the artist

Fig. 98
Robert Louis Stevenson, Sydney, Australia, c. 1893. Photographer and source unknown. Collection of the artist

Although the use of photographic source material linked Chimes's work to the Pop Art generation of painters, such as Warhol, Lichtenstein, James Rosenquist, and Richard Hamilton, the panel portraits do not share these artists' interest in consumer items, fast food, advertising comic strips, and the ephemeral nature of fame in celebrity culture. Chimes may have found inspiration in a more contemporary exponent of paintings derived from photographs, namely Gerhard Richter, whose work had achieved an international reputation by the early 1970s. Like Richter, Chimes often altered, edited, enlarged, blurred, or cropped his photographic sources to suit a particular composition. In *Michael Faraday*, of 1973 (pl. 43), for example, Chimes extended the composition beyond the source photograph, which showed the scientist from the waist up, even going so far as to incorporate an image of his own hand in the finished painting. The reverse was true of *Robert Louis Stevenson*, of 1976 (pl. 68), where Chimes cropped the source photograph of the Scottish writer seated in a chair (fig. 98). The original image had focused attention on his hands and graceful interlocking fingers, whereas Chimes honed in on Stevenson's quizzical expression and fragile countenance to reveal the tragic nature of this world-weary aesthete's life, which was far more fascinating to Chimes than any of his novels or adventure stories. As Chimes later wrote of Sir Arthur Conan Doyle, "In Sherlock Holmes, the mystery of the crime to be solved, is a reflection. And what it reflects is the other, the deeper mystery of what happened to Conan Doyle, story-teller."¹⁷⁵

Whereas Chimes's distortions and deformations are intended to increase the sense of mystery surrounding his subjects, Richter's deft manipulation of photographic sources has a political dimension. By challenging the widely accepted notion of the photograph as a lucid, mechanical, and thus truthful record, the German artist's photo-paintings question the veracity and objectivity of all reproductive images, from journalistic and advertisement photography to postcards and family albums. Chimes, conversely, sees photography as memory, rather than a faithful likeness that may or may not have been altered; in other words, a trace of a fleeting moment in the past that nonetheless survives in the continuous present of the photograph.

Chimes's use of photography in the panel portraits was linked to his concept of the present as an "arriving memory."[176] The artist has to somehow feel the past in these photographs as if he were actually there, in the room when the picture was taken, a state of mind that goes "beyond aesthetics."[177] His notion of an "arriving memory" was inspired by Jarry's 1899 essay "How to Construct a Time Machine," in which the French author imagined a contraption that could reverse the future, based upon H. G. Wells's celebrated novel *The Time Machine*, published four years earlier. Jarry's elaborate device was conceived with his customary blend of absurdity and precision, as when he described the specific details of the time machine's frame and mighty gyroscopes, which, as Roger Shattuck has pointed out, were based upon the bicycle on which he traveled every day![178] The machine's gyroscopes isolated the traveler from normal time and space, thus creating a present that was in effect the reverse of the future, leading Jarry to conclude: "Duration is the transformation of a succession into a reversion. In other words: 'THE BECOMING OF A MEMORY.'"[179]

Unlike Richter, for whom the world of mechanically reproduced images—especially ordinary, nonartistic images such as newspaper photographs, postcards, and family snapshots—presents a seemingly endless array of subjects to be painted, Chimes had a much smaller pool of

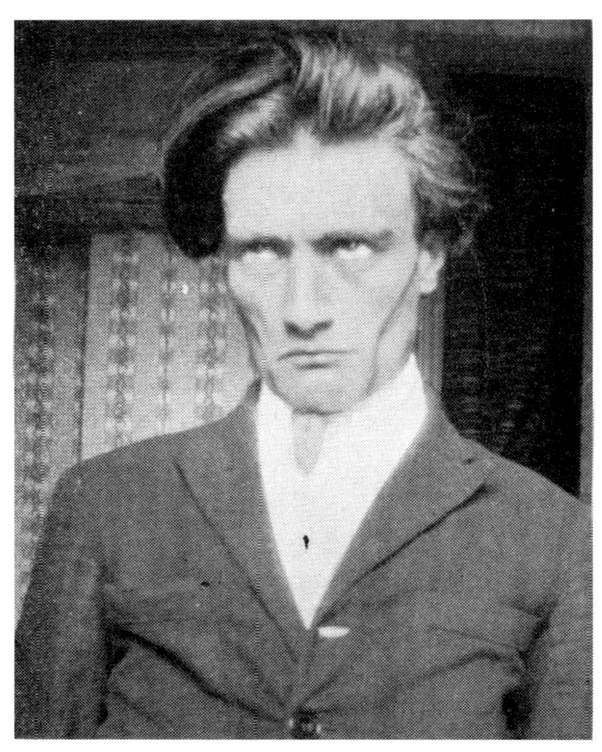

surviving images of Jarry, Artaud, and company, and his choice was always extremely subjective. For his *Antonin Artaud*, of 1974 (pl. 48), for example, Chimes selected as his source photograph an image, labeled "Artaud, the tragic poet, about 1920," that accompanied John Ashbery's impassioned essay on Artaud in the 1960 *Portfolio & Art News Annual* (fig. 99).[180] This photograph, in which all of the young writer's future psychological pain and traumatic suffering appears to be mapped out in his emaciated features and intense, upward-gazing eyes, was taken shortly before Artaud's departure to Paris at the age of twenty-three, after two years of treatment in a Swiss sanatorium specializing in nervous disorders. The image is a classic example of the *punctum* in Chimes's source material, since the photograph and the finished painting of Artaud *in extremis* cannot fail to move or even "bruise" the viewer, according to Barthes's definition. However, like all of the sources for the panel portraits, this photograph was selected for its ability to encapsulate Artaud's tragic life and work in a single image, rather than for its status as a document of the writer's psychological condition at that time, when an inner torment threatened to engulf his very existence.

Since nearly all of the images of his subjects were taken from black-and-white photographs, Chimes was immediately forced to "invent" the colors to be used in the portraits, and even when the source was a color photograph, the colors that the artist used do not necessarily relate to those found in the original image. In *James Joyce*, of 1974 (pl. 51), for example, Chimes used a rather unremarkable color photograph by Gisèle Freund that was taken for a photo-essay on the great modernist writer in *Time* magazine's issue for May 8, 1939, just four days after the publication of *Finnegan's Wake*.[181] However, the artist exacerbated the shadow that fell across one of

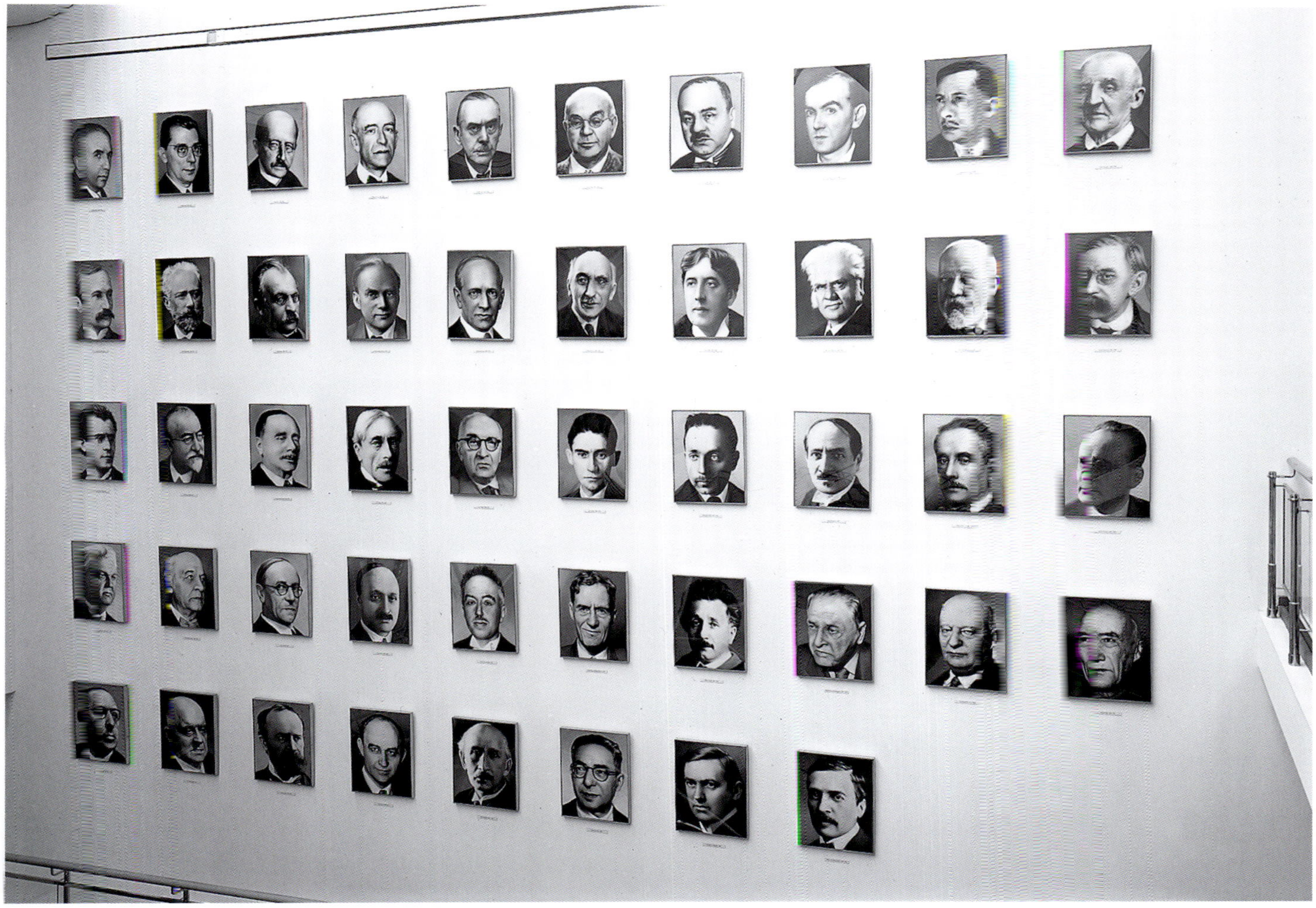

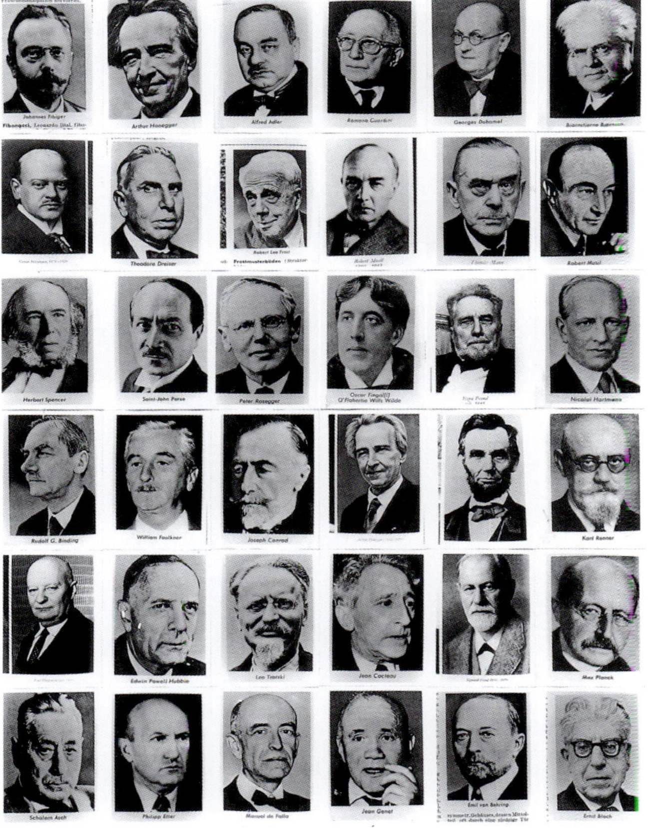

Fig. 100
Gerhard Richter
(German, born 1932)
48 Portraits, 1971–72. Oil
on canvas; 48 paintings,
each 27 9/16 x 21 5/8 inches
(70 x 55 cm). Museum
Ludwig, Cologne.
GR 324-1–48

Fig. 101
Gerhard Richter (born 1932),
*Panel 36: For 48
Portraits*, 1971. Thirty-six
black-and-white repro-
ductions from encyclope-
dia. Städtische Galerie im
Lenbachhaus, Munich

the writer's eyeglasses to allude to the Cyclops chapter of *Ulysses*, as well as Joyce's near-blindness in later life, an issue to which he would return in the white paintings of the 1980s. In doing so, Chimes transcended the original source material, turning the *studium* of Freund's *Time* magazine photo-essay, which emphasized "the paleness of his features and the fatigue in his voice" after finishing *Finnegan's Wake*, into the *punctum* of the panel portrait, which wounds the viewer with its image of a reflective and rather troubled-looking Joyce, who wears his darkened spectacles like an eye patch.[182]

Richter's and Chimes's differing approaches to photographic source material can be elucidated by an examination of the former's *48 Portraits*, a series Richter made in 1971–72 and exhibited in a large, high-ceilinged gallery in the West German Pavilion at the 1972 Venice Biennale, a year before Chimes began the panel portraits series. Unlike Chimes's series, in which each work stands on its own, Richter's series is intended to be seen as a painting in forty-eight parts (fig. 100), presenting the collective history of the twentieth century as it appeared in encyclopedias and history books. Upon closer inspection, however, this collection of influential individuals of the modern era, including writers, scientists, philosophers, psychologists, composers, and musicians, is revealed to be a highly selective choice of "father figures," since none of the portraits depicts a woman. Benjamin Buchloh has convincingly argued that the series represents the artist's compulsion to construct an imaginary congregation of acceptable paternal figures in the wake of the historical disaster of National Socialism.[183]

Richter took his source images for these impeccably rendered portraits from his *Atlas of Collected Photographs, Collages and Sketches* (fig. 101), a giant accumulation of photographs that he culled from newspapers, old encyclopedias, and other published sources that has supplied the subject matter for his photo-paintings since the early 1960s. The *Atlas* was also shown for the first time in December 1972, in an exhibition at the Museum voor Hedendaagse Kunst in Utrecht, Holland. This exhibition of Richter's massive repository of source material coincided with his presentation in the German Pavilion at the 1972 Venice Biennale, thus providing Chimes with ample opportunity to learn about *48 Portraits* and its sources through the numerous critical reviews and articles that accompanied the work.

Chimes does not recall hearing about Richter's series of portraits until after he had begun his own panel paintings in 1973. However, there are strong similarities in subject matter, size, and concept between their projects that reflect their shared identity as post–World War II artists whose work addresses the role of painting after photography. It is surely no coincidence that Chimes also limited his series to forty-eight portraits, suggesting that he unconsciously remembered this number from a review of Richter's Venice installation, but then forgot it once his own extended series found its momentum as a systematic investigation of the universe of Jarry and his followers. It is also interesting to note that Richter chose his forty-eight historically important modern figures from among 270 clipped images that covered eight pages of his *Atlas*. Among the possible candidates were Poe and Baudelaire, both of whom Richter rejected from his final constellation, but who appear in Chimes's own aesthetic genealogy based on Jarry's circle. The only historical figure to make it into both series was Oscar Wilde, whom Richter celebrates as a humanist writer repressed by an authoritarian regime, and whom Chimes connects to Jarry via Huysmans's *A Rebours*, the notorious "yellow book" that Wilde had under his arm at the time of his arrest for homosexual activities.[184]

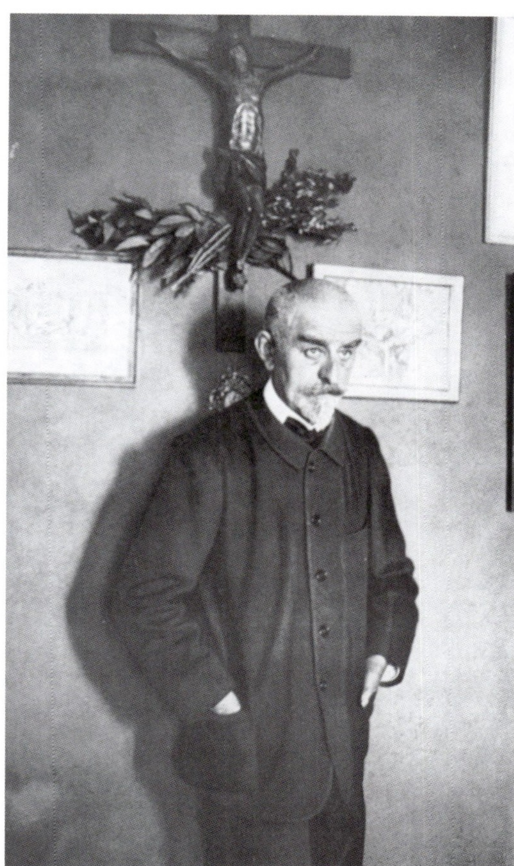

Fig. 102
Dornac et Cie (French, active 1900s), *Joris-Karl Huysmans*, c. 1907. Gelatin silver print. Published in *L'Illustration*, May 18, 1907

In Wilde's *Picture of Dorian Gray*, Huysmans's yellow-backed novel, lent to the eponymous hero by Lord Henry Wooton, is described as "the strangest book he had ever read. It seemed to him that in exquisite raiment and to the delicate sound of flutes, the sins of the world were passing in dumb show before him. Things that he had dimly dreamed of were suddenly made real to him. Things of which he had never dreamed were gradually revealed."[185] The novel recounts the exotic appearance and perverse sexual pleasures of the decadent main character, Duc Jean Floressas des Esseintes, whom Huysmans based upon the real-life figure of Robert de Montesquiou, a major publicist for the Art Nouveau movement. Chimes identified the character of Des Esseintes with Jarry due to their shared neurotic sensibility, eccentric behavior, loathing for mediocrity, passion for challenging preconceived ideas, and intense desire to extend the boundaries of physical and emotional experience. Chimes thus included Wilde in his panel portrait series, since like Des Esseintes and Jarry, the Irish writer was an openly homosexual dandy and aesthete who embraced scandal and reveled in subversive behavior and sensual pleasure. Huysmans also appears in Chimes's series, but in an image taken later in life, following his conversion to Catholicism, which the artist alludes to in the crucifix that hangs above his balding pate, and the candlestick on the table, which does not appear in the original photograph (fig. 102), but creates a marvelous visual rhyme with the writer's dark coat and white collar.[186]

A comparison between Chimes's portraits of Oscar Wilde (pl. 58; fig. 103) and Richter's (fig. 105) highlights the similarities, but more importantly the differences, between their artistic projects. Surprisingly, both Chimes and Richter chose to portray the Irish playwright as he appeared in the early 1890s (fig. 104). By this time, Wilde had abandoned the long hair and toned down the sartorial excesses of his Aesthetic phase in favor of a highly fashionable yet

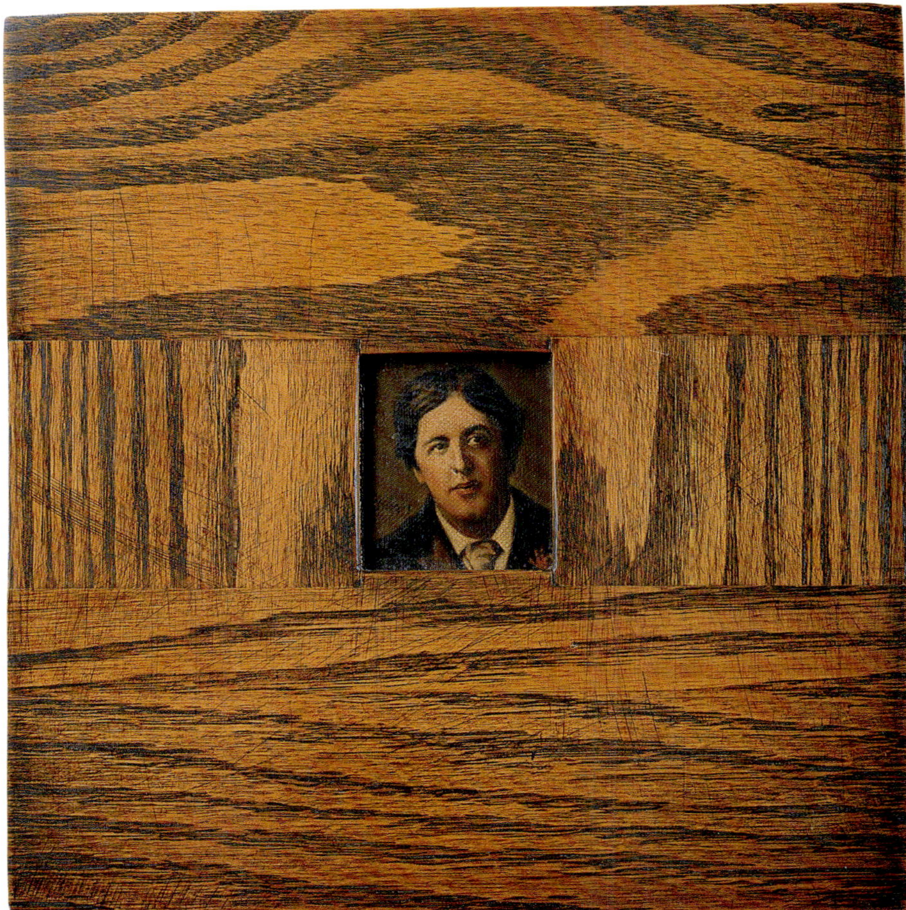

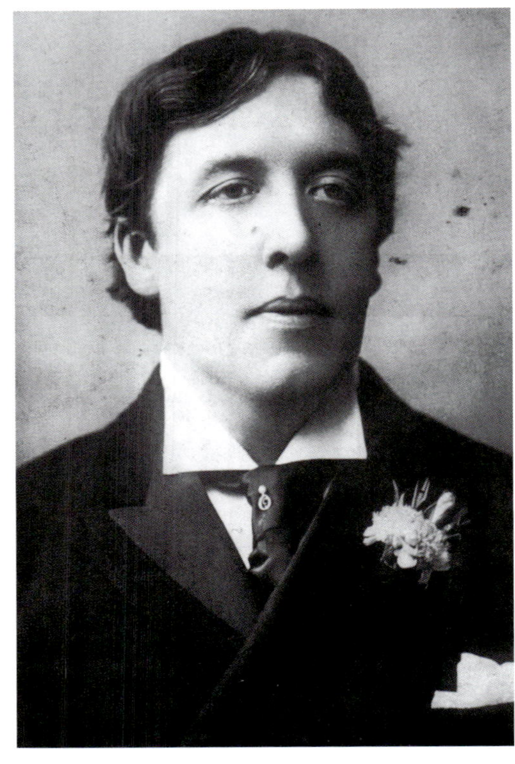

rather restrained dark suit with a white shirt and stiff collar, which allowed Richter to include him, in formal terms, as part of his series of important men in suits. Like all the figures in his series, Wilde is rendered in neutral, predominantly grayish tones that imbue the portrait with a morbid solemnity. Whereas the German painter cropped his image to exclude Wilde's elegant tiepin and ostentatiously well-made buttonhole, Chimes enhanced such details in the original black-and-white photograph through the use of symbolic color to denote the writer's heritage and sexual orientation. The flash of bright green foliage in his buttonhole underlines Wilde's identity as an Irish author, while his rouged lips speak to his courageous identity as an openly gay man in the repressed and virulently homophobic society of Victorian England.

In Richter's version, Wilde's slightly blurred visage appears to have been airbrushed, perhaps another reference to the artist's inherent distrust of those polished and idealized official portraits of political leaders that he remembered from his youth in East Germany, and that he himself had once created, having painted Stalin's likeness on banners as a young artist.[187] Reducing his palette to shades of gray, black, and white to imitate the source photograph of the Irish writer that he found in an old encyclopedia, Richter produced a smooth and fuzzy portrait of Wilde that remains as emotionally neutral and impersonal as the postage stamp–sized illustration on which it is based, which became blurred in the process of enlarging. Although Chimes's panel portraits are based on photographs, they never have the dispassionate, almost ghostly air of Richter's photo-paintings, whose slightly out-of-focus subjects are often reminiscent of police mug shots or morgue images. The death instinct so prevalent in Richter's work is far removed from that of Chimes, whose portraits celebrate, rather than mourn, the lives of his artistic pantheon.

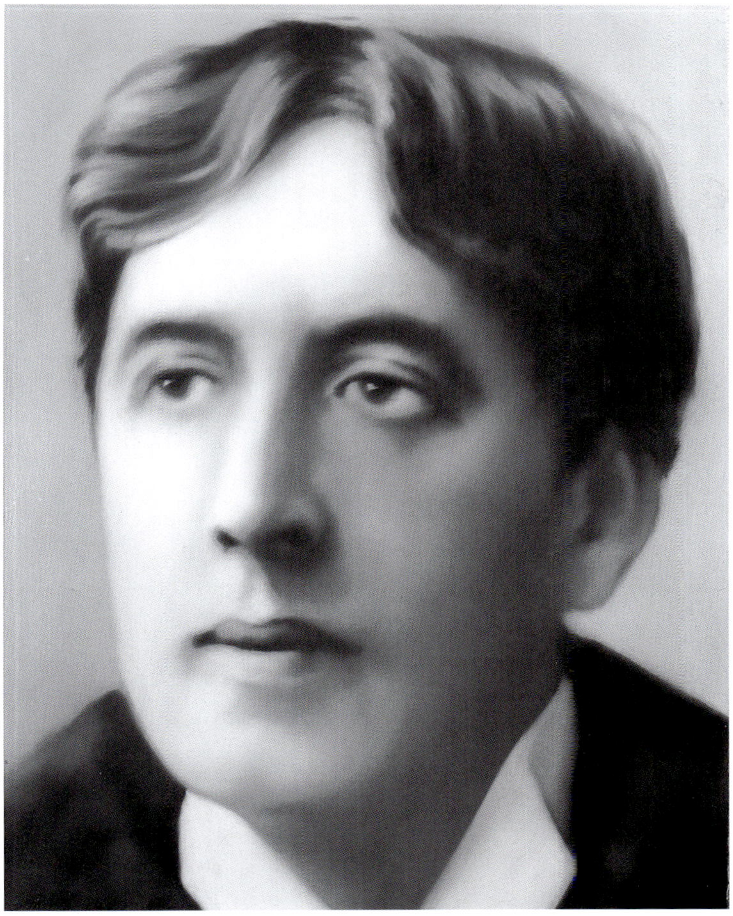

Fig. 105
Gerhard Richter, *Oscar Wilde*, from *48 Portraits*, 1971–72. Oil on canvas, 27 9/16 × 21[illegible] inches (70 × 55 cm). Museum Ludwig, Cologne

Given the formal structure of Richter's work as a compilation of historical figures that must be seen as a group, his image of Oscar Wilde also needs to be placed within the context of the row upon row of other monochromatic, identically sized paintings that comprise *48 Portraits*, since that it is how it was shown in the 1972 Venice Biennale. Situating Wilde alongside the other portraits showing the heads and shoulders of famous white men of the sciences, letters, and arts underlines the repetitive, serial nature of the German artist's project as a unified [illegible] whose power comes from its rigidly formal and restricted means. Despite the presence of a smattering of living luminaries, such as the English novelist Graham Greene, the vast majority of Richter's cultural icons were dead by 1972, their dark suits and predominantly gray tonalities reminiscent of the fading and soon-to-be-forgotten images of patriarchal figures found in libraries or boardrooms.

Enshrined on the curved walls of the West German Pavilion in Venice, *48 Portraits* transformed the fascist, neoclassical architecture of the building into a cultural mausoleum, which became, at least temporarily, a melancholic monument to the catastrophic destruction of humanist civilization by totalitarian regimes during the twentieth century. According to Richter, this lost cultural past could never be resuscitated, thus reinforcing the notion of *48 Portraits* as a mournful elegy: "It is not a restoration. It is a reference to this loss. It is a question of whether or not we do something. I don't believe it comes back."[188] But as Robert Storr has noted, Richter lived through National Socialism and Communism and emerged with a longing to fill the gap that totalitarianism created.[189] His *48 Portraits* is thus tinged with "regret at having been deprived of the chance of identifying with any part of the cultural legacy that fascism and

Communism suppressed or distorted," as well as pessimism over the prospects of reconnecting with and extending that legacy of Western humanism.[190]

The homogeneity of Richter's group of stereotypical intellectual forefathers, emphasized by the friezelike, symmetrical installation of *48 Portraits*, which were hung in a line centered on the curved alcove and apses opposite the main entrance to the Pavilion, recalls Warhol's tautological installation of *32 Campbell's Soup Cans* at the Ferus Gallery in Los Angeles in July 1962, where the evenly sized and almost identical paintings were displayed at eye level and evenly spaced on narrow shelves, thus bringing to mind the supermarket displays that inspired them. This is why Richter could not countenance the idea of including women in the series, as it would have detracted from the uniformity of poses and demeanors in these portraits. Chimes, however, depicted two women in his panel portrait series, namely the legendary actress Sarah Bernhardt (pl. 61) and the artist's wife, Dawn (pl. 62), whose inclusion was justified on the grounds that she represented the "Eternal Feminine."[191] At one stage Chimes considered painting Gertrude Stein, but later rejected her on the grounds that her links to Jarry were too tenuous, as opposed to those of other later figures like André Breton or Marcel Duchamp. Another difference can be seen in the hazy, manipulated appearance of Richter's portraits, which makes us immediately aware that we are looking at a series of paintings based upon retouched photographs.[192] The photographic source material is often much less evident in Chimes's panel paintings, which are more diverse than Richter's in size, color, and paint application, ranging from freely brushed, highly virtuosic "sketches" to highly detailed "realistic" portraits, often of the same person, as in the six versions of Beardsley (see pls. 65, 66).

The work of the late American artist Jess, who changed his name from Burgess Collins when he decided to become an artist, is much closer in spirit to Chimes's approach to painting from photographic source material than Richter's. In his "Translations" series, which he began in 1959, Jess created richly textured paintings, often derived from obscure sources culled from his own rich archive of old engravings, etchings, books, magazine illustrations, postcards, and photographs. This library was memorialized in *The Enamored Mage: Translation #6* of 1965 (fig. 106), in which Jess's partner, the poet Robert Duncan, is shown surrounded by a row of alchemical and kabbalistic texts.[193] Jess transformed his source material, which in this case consisted of his own 1958 snapshot of his partner, in oil paintings whose surfaces were painstakingly built up in heavy layers of pigment to a thickness resembling colored relief maps. Removing his source from its original context and transforming it through enlargement and a palette of bubblegum colors, Jess completed the work by wedding the image with a corresponding text, which he inscribed on the back of the canvas. Chimes would adopt a similar practice in the panel portraits, which frequently contain handwritten fragments of prose and poetry on both the recto and verso of the paintings.

Like Jess before him, Chimes can be seen as salvaging forgotten images that modern society has discarded, renewing their freshness and potency through the artist's visionary imagination and meticulous craftsmanship. Whereas Richter viewed his collective portrait as a closed system signifying, and commemorating, the humanist tradition of Western culture that was systematically destroyed by totalitarianism, Chimes's approach was more freewheeling, playful, and open to chance inspiration, random selection, and personal choice, at the risk of destroying the integrity of the entire series. The forty-eight panel portraits that Chimes created between 1973

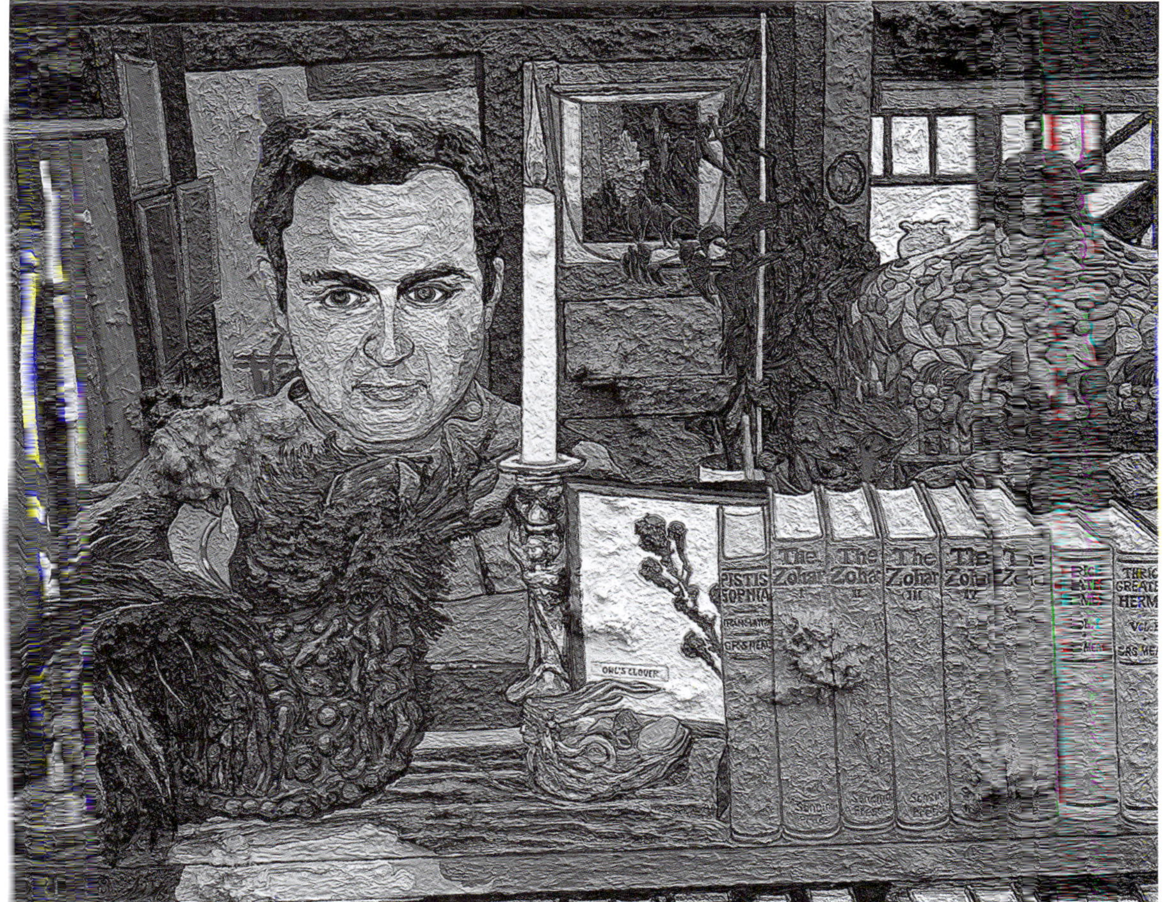

Fig. 106
Jess (Jess Collins; American, 1923–2004), *The Enamored Mage: Translation #6*, 1965. Oil on canvas on wood, 24½ x 30 inches (62.2 x 76.2 cm). Courtesy of Gallery Paule Anglim, San Francisco

and 1978 possess a clear and homogeneous pictorial identity of their own, an accomplishment that makes the series without doubt the most sustained, unified, and strongest body of work that Chimes has created.

Alfred Jarry, of 1974 (pl. 50), which Chimes based on a photograph taken by Nadar in 1896, at the height of the *Ubu Roi* scandal, is an excellent example of how the artist creates a memorable, deeply evocative portrait that transcends its source material. Nadar's famous photograph shows Jarry as a handsome young man with a distinctive mane of shoulder-length dark hair, oval face and piercing coal-black eyes (fig. 107). However, Chimes cropped the image to focus on the brooding visage of the twenty-three-year-old playwright, whom he had previously depicted only in half-length portraits, such as *Alfred Jarry (Departure from the Present)* (pl. 43) and *Alfred Jarry (Ethernity)* (pl. 44), both of 1973. Another important departure from the photographic source was Chimes's addition of a beard under the left-hand side of the French writer's chin. This subtle yet important change was made because the inky black shadow under Jarry's chin in the Nadar original, which Chimes knew through a reproduction in Roger Shattuck's *The Banquet Years*, reminded him of a self-portrait by Man Ray in which the American Surrealist appeared half-shaven.[194]

The addition of the half-beard underlines the role of chance and accident in Chimes's panel portrait series, while the use of cropping also brings to mind Henri Rousseau's 1894 *Portrait of Alfred Jarry*, which was exhibited at the Salon des Indépendents in Paris the following year, where it was mistakenly listed in a review as *Portrait de Madame A.J.*, a confusion apparently caused by Jarry's androgynous features and long black hair.[195] Like Rousseau, Jarry came

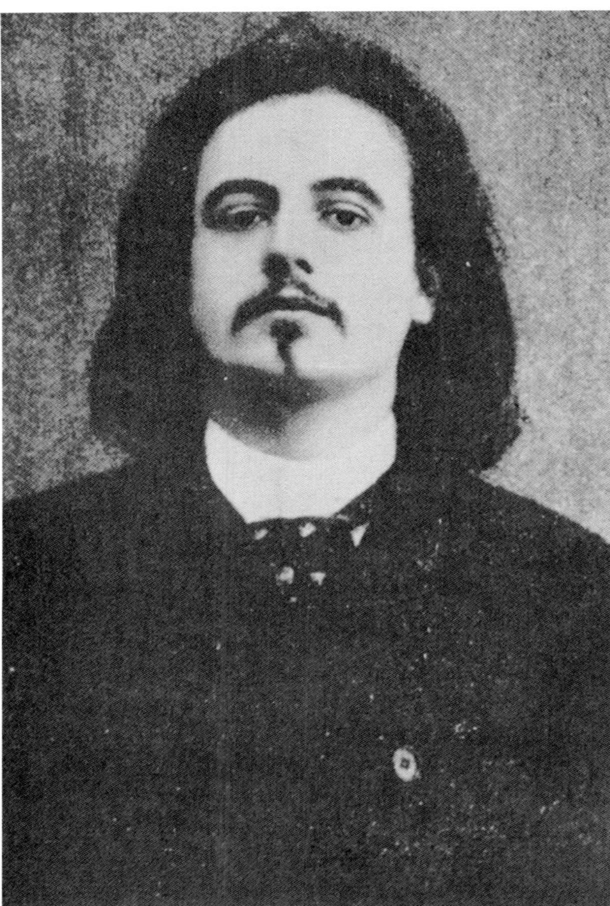

from Laval, a sleepy town on the border of Brittany, and he was one of the first writers to recognize the unique gifts of his fellow countryman, whose paintings were widely ridiculed at the time for their naiveté.[196] In *Faustroll*, Jarry nominated "M. Henri Rousseau, artist painter decorator, called the Customs-officer," to operate an anthropomorphic painting machine, which he dubbed the "mechanical monster" due to its lack of precision and control.[197] This futuristic device, which Jarry characterized as a half-machine, half-beast known as Clinamen, was intended to transform the holdings of the "national storehouse," a barely disguised reference to the Musée du Luxembourg, by ejaculating "onto the walls' canvas the succession of primary colors ranged according to the tubes of its stomach."[198] However, the act of putting his friend in charge of transforming the Musée du Luxembourg by spraying its hallowed walls with excrement also declared his confidence that the customs-officer-turned-painter would one day enliven the national museum through his use of flat colors and distorted perspectives, which he found to be far superior to the academic paintings that traditionally hung there.

Rousseau's portrait of his close friend and critical champion no longer survives. In later life, the bohemian author, no longer distinguishing Ubu from himself, apparently became disturbed by the image and used the portrait for target practice with his Browning pistol. By 1906, when Apollinaire saw the charred and fragmented portrait in Jarry's apartment at 7, rue Cassette, all that remained was the expressive head and shoulder-length hair. Shortly thereafter, the fragmented portrait is thought to have been destroyed, along with many of Jarry's papers, in a domestic fire in Laval. Chimes may have sought to re-create Rousseau's *Portrait of Alfred Jarry* in his haunting 1974 panel painting, which he regards today as a portrait of Jarry as a woman, or better still as a man in drag, in line with contemporary descriptions of Rousseau's entry to the Salon des Indépendants. This interest in portraying Jarry as a cross-dressed male may have prompted Chimes to paint Duchamp's lascivious alter ego Rrose Sélavy in 1976, based upon the original photograph by Man Ray (fig. 108).

Other panel portraits focus on Jarry's friends and contemporaries, such as Jean Moréas (pl. 40), Marcel Proust (pl. 57), Arthur Rimbaud (pl. 45), and Paul Verlaine (pl. 52). Always a voracious reader, Chimes immersed himself for weeks at a time in this world of nineteenth-century French literature and was rewarded with new ideas for paintings. Haunting second-hand bookstores in Philadelphia and New York, Chimes soon built a formidable library, finding even the rarest and most obscure books on Jarry and his fellow "journeyers" (to use his appellation) in places like Hacker Art Books at 57 West Fifty-fourth Street in Manhattan, which catered to his taste in Symbolist and

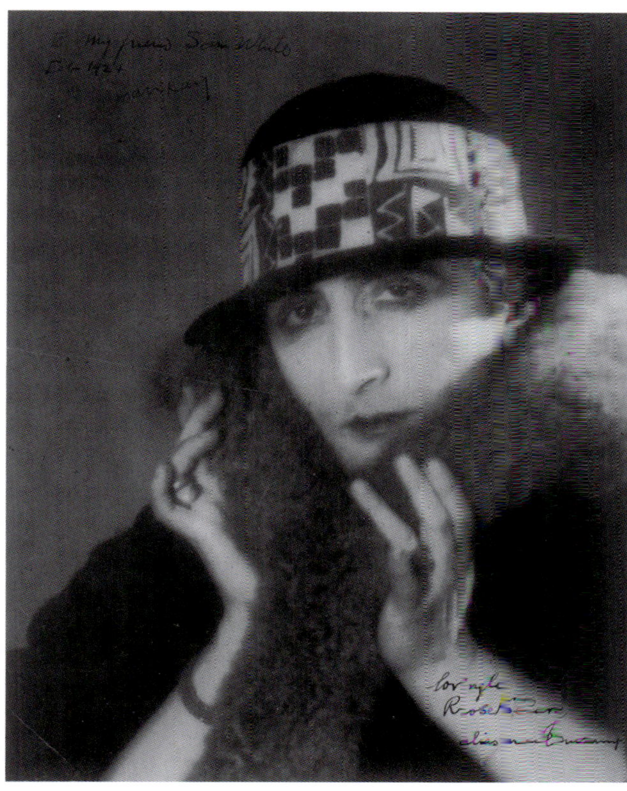

Fig. 108
Man Ray, *Marcel Duchamp as Rrose Sélavy*, c. 1920–21. Gelatin silver print; image and sheet 8½ x 6¹³⁄₁₆ inches (21.6 x 17.3 cm). Philadelphia Museum of Art. The Samuel S. White 3rd and Vera White Collection, 1957-49-1

Surrealist literature.[199] Even subjects that he had painted at the beginning of the series were rendered with a new intensity as the panel portrait series evolved in the mid-to-late 1970s.

At times, Chimes experimented with new forms of portraiture, as in the exquisitely rendered black glove that signifies André Breton. This 1977 portrait (pl. 69) was made at the request of the artist's friend Jerry Crimmins, a fellow painter and colleague at Moore College of Art, where Chimes was teaching at the time, who greatly admired Breton's writings. Rather than make a panel portrait from a photograph of Breton, whose authoritarian control of the Surrealist group Chimes despised, especially after he learned of Artaud's run-ins with the so-called Pope of Surrealism in the 1920s, the artist decided to use instead a photograph of a dropped glove that was reproduced in Breton's *Nadja*. This 1928 novel details the narrator's chance encounters and unpredictable wanderings through the streets of Paris, during the course of which he addresses an anemic girl with "fern-like eyes" named Nadja. At one point in the novel, Nadja, who is based on a woman that Breton met on the rue La Fayette on October 4, 1926,[200] is moved to tears by Jarry's poetry.[201] An uneducated, impoverished waif who suffered from severe emotional problems, the real-life Nadja soon became fascinated with the French writer to the point of obsession. Subverting realist fiction's conventional mimetic transposition of characters, places, and events through descriptive techniques, the narrative becomes the record of the author's search for these elements, detailing his aimless meanderings through the streets of Paris and his dreams and fantasies, which are interspersed with diary entries, found photographs, and fragments of Nadja's direct speech and her drawings.

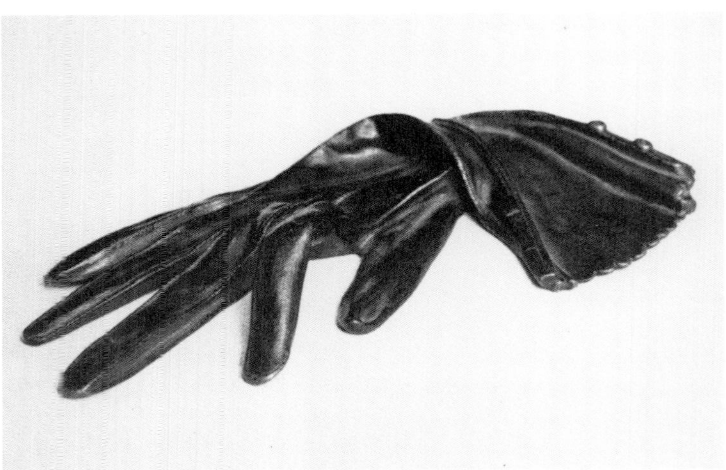

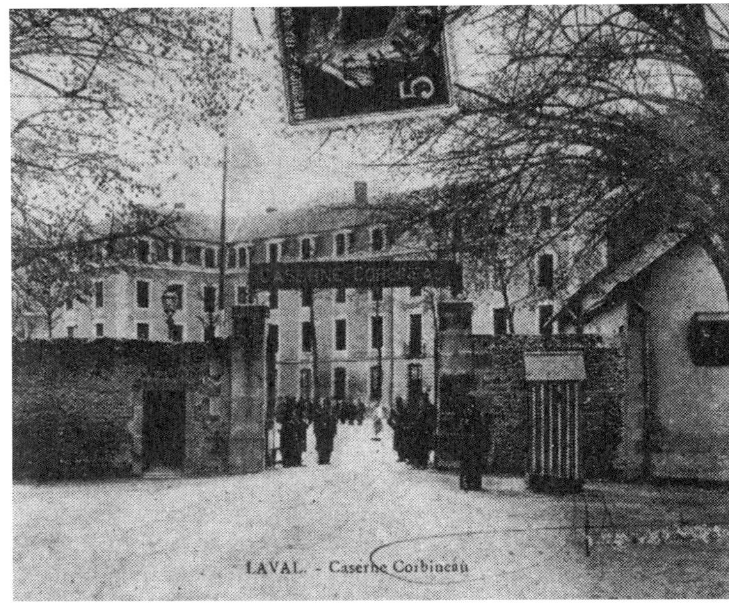

Chimes's portrait uses a similar pictorial strategy to represent Breton, who is portrayed through his displaced object of desire, namely the glove that is used as a surrogate for Nadja, of whom Breton writes, "When I am close to her, I am closer to the things which are close to her."[202] The black glove, which is reproduced in the novel with the caption "Gant de femme aussi" [Also a woman's glove] (fig. 109), thus symbolizes Breton's chance encounter with Nadja, but also functions as a fetish item through which his attraction to her is mediated.[203] By re-creating this photograph of a black glove, Chimes similarly underlines the ludic and fetishistic qualities of Breton's novel. His painting also conveys an implicit critique of the French writer, who became increasingly disturbed by Nadja's deranged state of mind and erratic behavior and eventually broke off the affair, cruelly discarding her like an unwanted yet hauntingly beautiful glove on the pavement. At the end of the novel, Nadja is committed to a psychiatric hospital, an incarceration that also took place in real life, where she remained until her death in 1941.

Chimes made a second oblique portrait of Breton (pl. 70) in the same year, this time using a photograph from *Nadja* of the Tuileries garden in Paris as a surrogate image of the Surrealist leader. In the novel, Breton and Nadja undertake a midnight ramble through the streets of the French capital, stopping to rest for a moment in the Tuileries, only for Nadja to become fascinated by the jet of a spurting fountain.[204] This use of a landscape or object instead of the subject's face continued in the 1978 cityscape entitled *Laval* (pl. 75), which can be seen as an oblique portrait of Jarry, or by extension Henri Rousseau, given their shared origins, although some viewers will recognize in this hazily rendered courtyard of the Caserne Corbineau in Laval (fig. 110) a suggestion of the artist's own birthplace in Elfreth's Alley, Philadelphia.

A later panel portrait of Jarry, appropriately called *Bicentennial Jarry* (pl. 63), since it was made during the two hundredth anniversary of American independence in 1976, depicts the French writer as an older, heavier man who has lost his charm and good looks. The source photograph for this work, as well as two earlier Jarry portraits (pls. 55, 56), was taken in 1906 at Maître Blaviel's fencing academy in Laval and shows the aging alcoholic writer in the stiff, upright pose of a fencer (fig. 111). The outmoded sword perhaps reminded Chimes of the arms used during the American Revolutionary War. In order to achieve the pared-down scale and composition he wanted for the painting, Chimes posed in the same stance as Jarry in a photograph that was taken outdoors and at a great distance (fig. 112). The painting of *Ubu*, also from 1976 (pl. 64), hones in on the tragic mask of Jarry's face in the same 1906 photograph. In a brilliant touch, Chimes let the heavy grain and natural lines of the wood show through the cropped portrait, which exacerbates the sinister side of the author's belligerent personality at the end of his life. In a bizarre act of self-destruction and literary mimesis, Jarry merged his own personality with that of Ubu, taking on his fictional alter ego's monotonous, evenly accented, staccato manner of speaking, as well as the aggressive mannerisms and boorish behavior that ultimately led to his tragic early death on November 1, 1907, of tuberculosis, to which he probably succumbed as a result of his prolonged addiction to ether as a cheaper alternative to the absinthe or wine in which he had previously drowned himself. As Chimes often relates, with pure delight, Jarry's last words were a request for a toothpick![205]

It is somewhat ironic that just as Jarry's tragic life ended in hallucinatory confusion with the Père Ubu character that he had created, so Chimes's series of panel portraits came to an end after he conflated the oppressive, frightening figure of Ubu with his own dreams and neuroses, as he later recounted:

> Later on somehow this impish little figure of Jarry as I observed it in the photographs and in the writings and the kind of things he had to say in his work, I connected with a dream I had when I was five years old that had really frightened me. Five years old, this was in South Georgia where we were living at the time. The dream is simply this—it's my earliest dream, but it terrified me. I see a desert. There is a mound, a dune in that desert, a single dune. And standing on that dune, there is this tiny little black figure with staring eyes looking directly at me and whose mouth is puckered in a shrill whistle, which just terrified me. I can still see the dream. Now, how I connected Jarry to that dream I don't know, except through my studies in psychology I had dreamed of an archetypal form and the connection was made.[206]

Hébert, of 1978 (pl. 76), the final work in the series, takes as its subject the monstrous character that Jarry based on one of his schoolteachers. The figure appears in black, just as Jarry had portrayed him in a painting he made as a schoolboy, but it also relates to Chimes's terrifying childhood nightmare of the wide-eyed, whistling demon on the sand dune. It is significant to note that this disturbing dream took place immediately after Chimes's first art class, in the first grade of his school in Ocilla, Georgia, in which the teacher unrolled a large sheet of craft paper, pinned it to the wall, and asked the children to get up and draw trees and houses in a long row, thus creating a cumulative landscape. Therefore, Chimes's genesis as an artist became associated with the bone-chilling dream that followed, whose whistling demon he later related to the grotesque black figure of Félix Hébert in Jarry's painting.

Hébert, nicknamed "le Père Heb" or "Le Père Ébé" by the irreverent schoolboys, was the unfortunate, bumbling physics teacher at the Lycée de Rennes, where Jarry completed his studies. Uninspiring and incompetent, Hébert became the butt of numerous schoolboy pranks and an object of derision to the entire school. Jarry and his fellow students staged a viciously satirical puppet show, under the title *Les Polonais* (The Poles), that detailed the imaginary exploits of

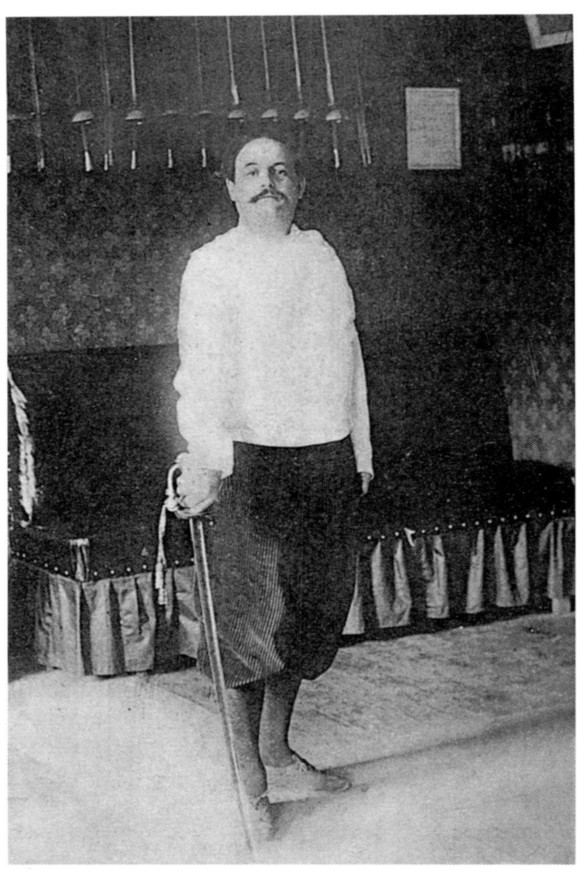

Fig. 111
Photograph of Jarry as a fencer, 1906. Reproduced in *Selected Works of Alfred Jarry*, n.p.

Fig. 112
Thomas Chimes posing for *Bicentennial Jarry* in a driveway in Villanova, Pennsylvania, 1976. Photograph by Laura Seniuk. Courtesy of the artist

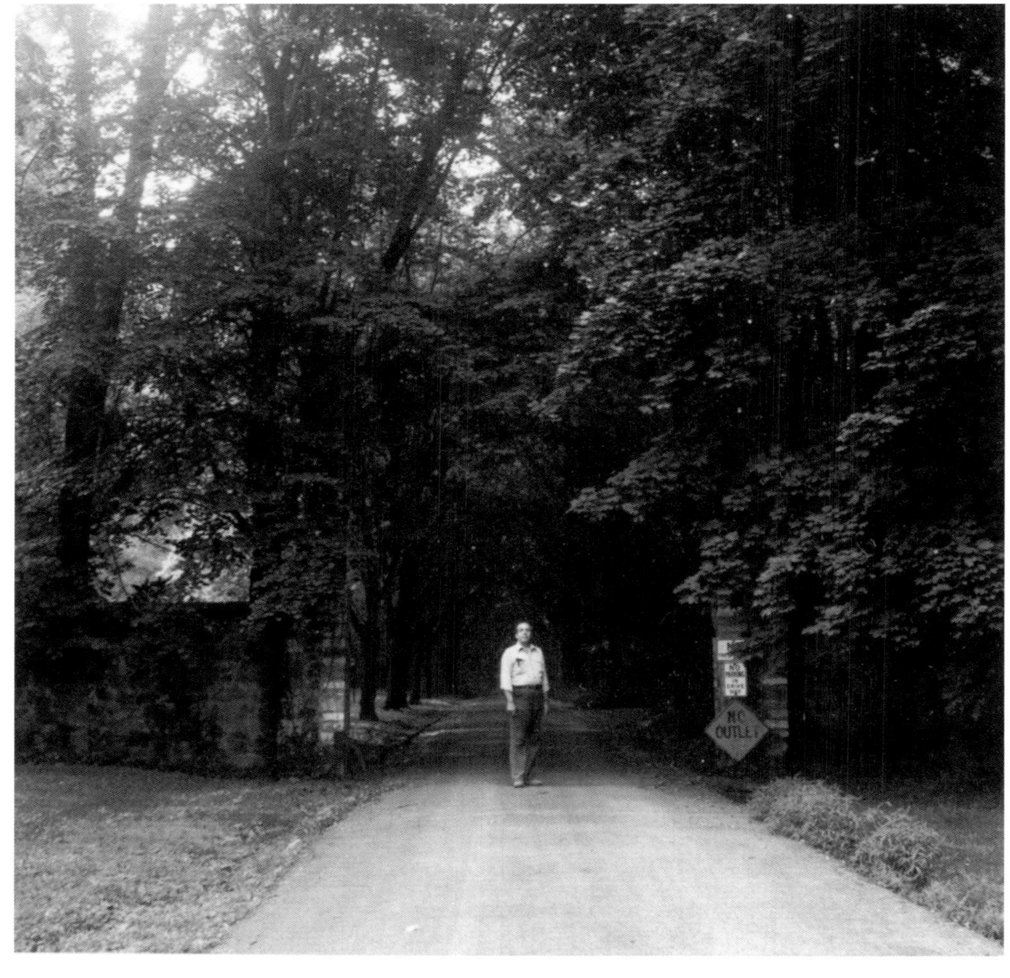

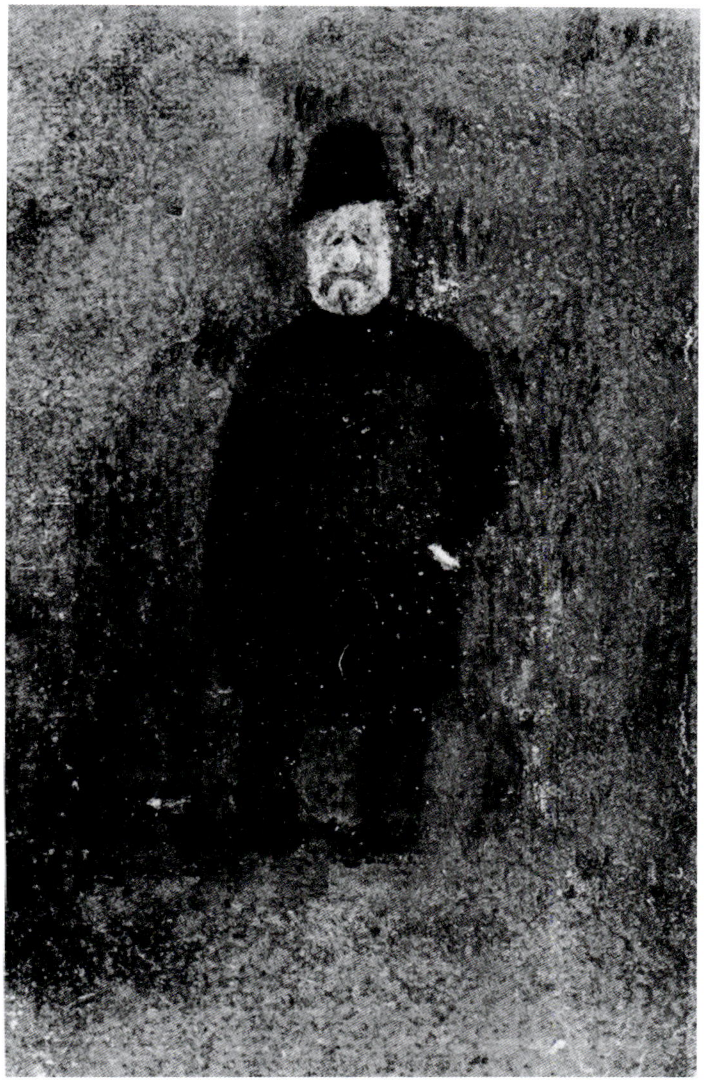

Fig. 113
Alfred Jarry, *M. Hébert, prophaiseur de physic*, painted while the artist was a pupil at the Rennes Lycée. Reproduced in *The Selected Works of Alfred Jarry*, n.p.

overleaf:
Figs. 114, 115
Opening and installation of *Thomas Chimes: Departure from the Present*, Peale House Galleries of the Pennsylvania Academy of the Fine Arts, Philadelphia, March 6, 1975. Courtesy of the Pennsylvania Academy of the Fine Arts, Philadelphia

their ill-fated physics master, whose botched experiments and idiotic statements fueled their drama. It was from this collective drama that the *Ubu* plays were born, as Jarry's agile mind transformed the luckless pedant into the archetypal tyrant Père Ubu, symbol of man's baser instincts, especially selfishness, avarice, cowardice, and greed.

Jarry's schoolboy obsession with "le Père Heb" as the embodiment of middle-class conformity and stupidity had clearly become fused in Chimes's mind with his own childhood memories and nightmares. It seems significant that this final painting in the panel portrait series was based, not on a photograph, but rather on Jarry's own portrait of his hapless former teacher, which was reproduced in the 1965 edition of the *Selected Works of Alfred Jarry* (fig. 113).[207] With the reckless insouciance of a schoolboy, Jarry transformed Hébert in his plays and works of art into a hideous, dehumanized creature that he compared to a walking bestiary. The author gave a revealing description of Ubu's appearance in "Les Paralipomènes d'Ubu," which was published in the *Revue Blanche* shortly before the first presentation of *Ubu Roi*: "If he resembles an animal he has especially a porcine face, a nose like the upper jaw of the crocodile, and the total effect of his cardboard carapace makes him the brother of the most aesthetically horrible sea-beast, the horseshoe crab."[208] Chimes remembers the feelings of dread that accompanied this painting and he never again finished a panel portrait, despite several attempts to do so.

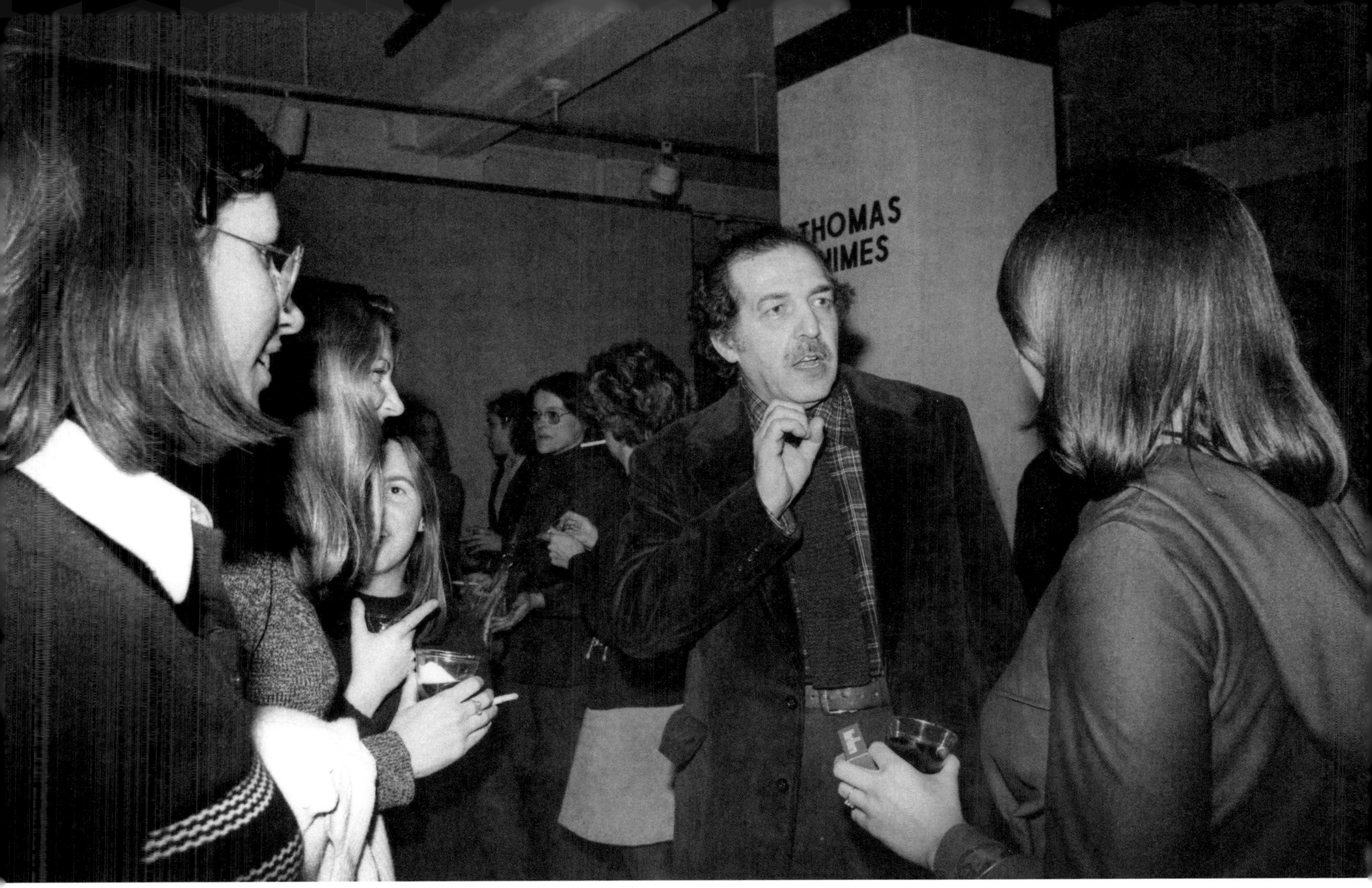

THOMAS
CHIMES

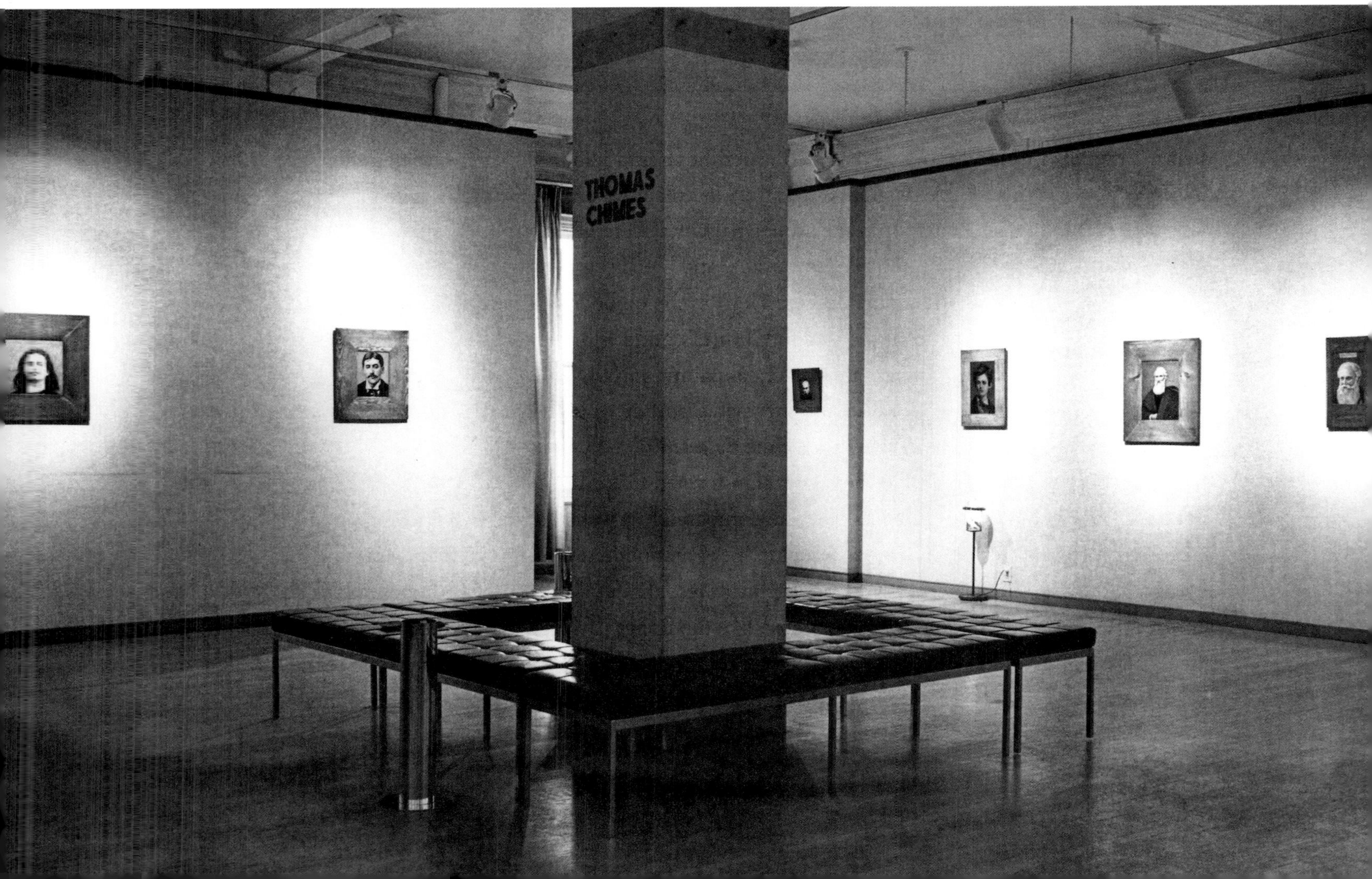

THOMAS
CHIMES

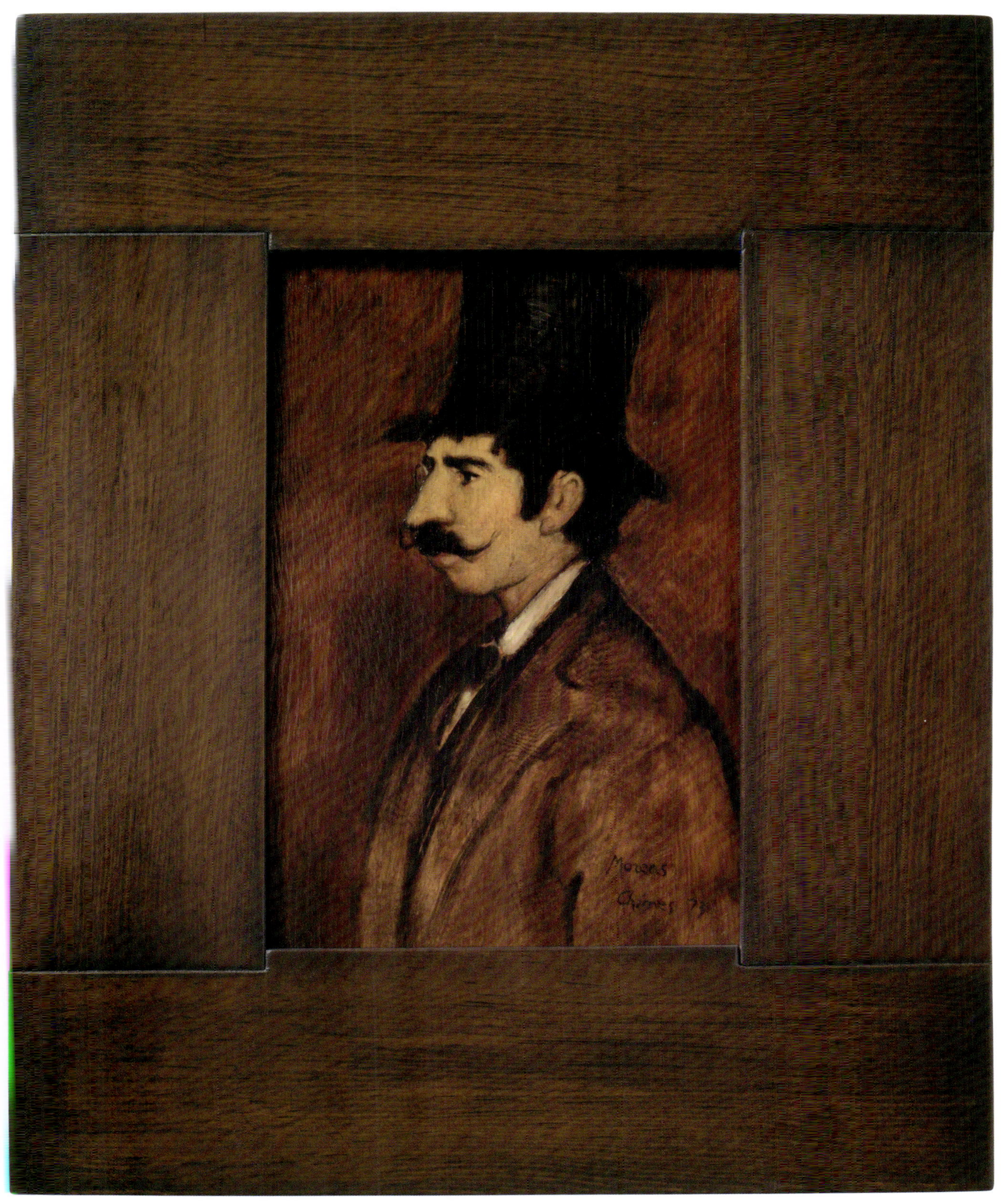

Jean Moréas, 1973

OIL ON PANEL

16¼ x 13⅛ INCHES (41.3 x 33.3 CM)

COLLECTION OF THE ARTIST

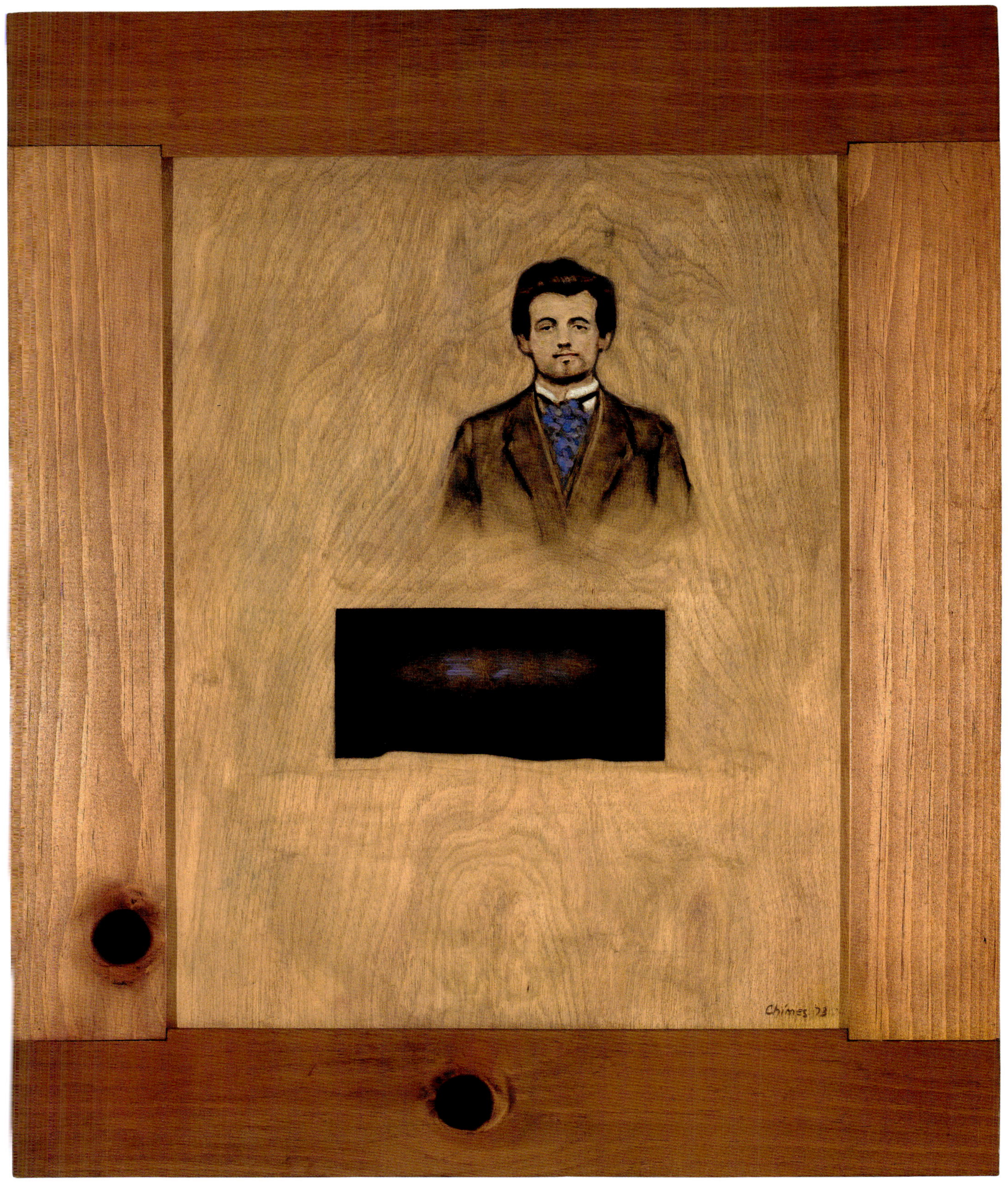

PLATE 41

Alfred Jarry (Departure from the Present), 1973

OIL ON PANEL

24¼ x 19⅞ INCHES (54 x 50.5 CM)

COURTESY OF LOCKS GALLERY, PHILADELPHIA

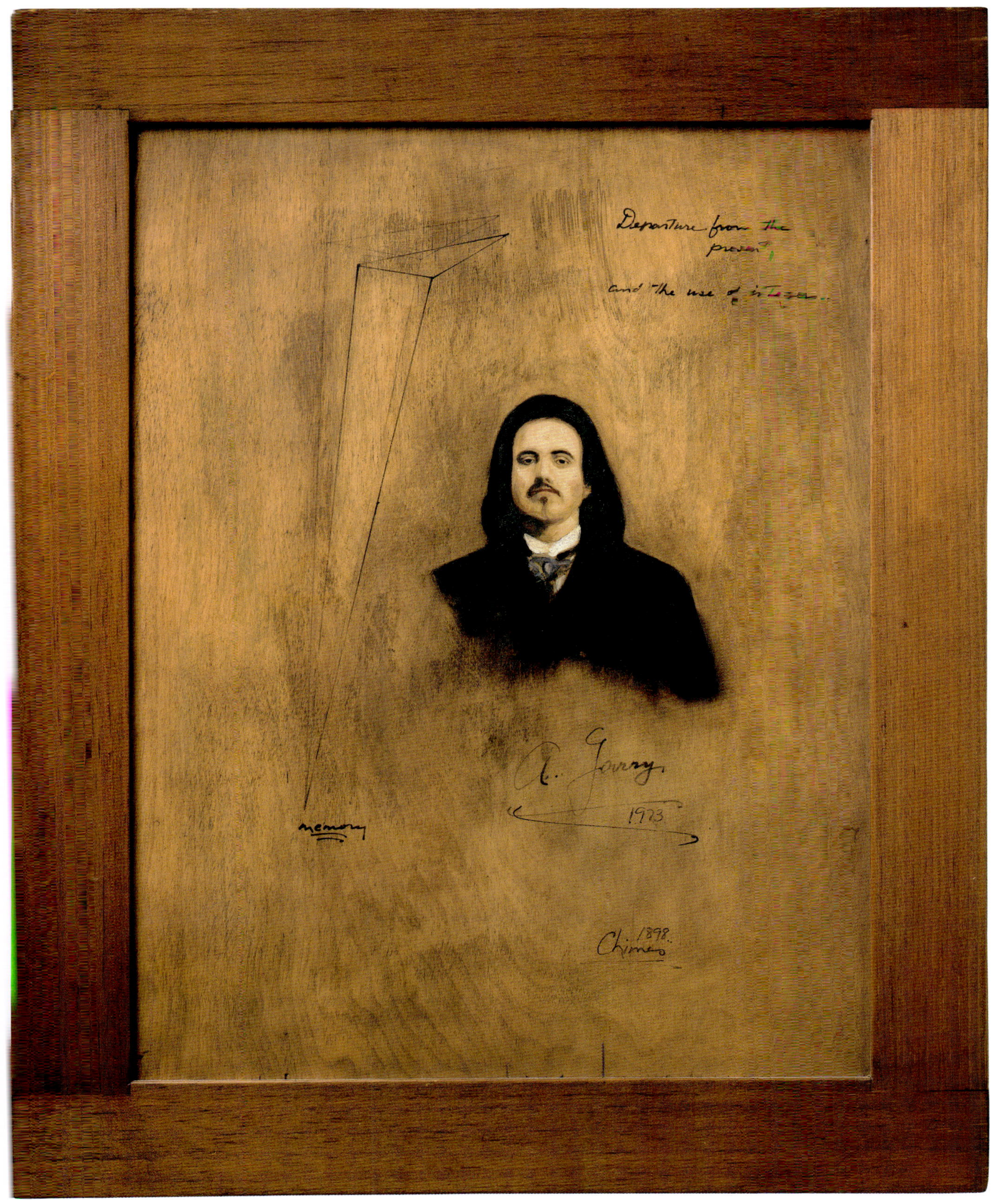

PLATE 42

Alfred Jarry (Memory), 1973

OIL ON PANEL

21¼ x 19⅜ INCHES (54 x 49.2 CM)

COLLECTION OF MR. J. FREDERICK CAIN AND MR. LARS CAIN, FORT MYERS, FLORIDA

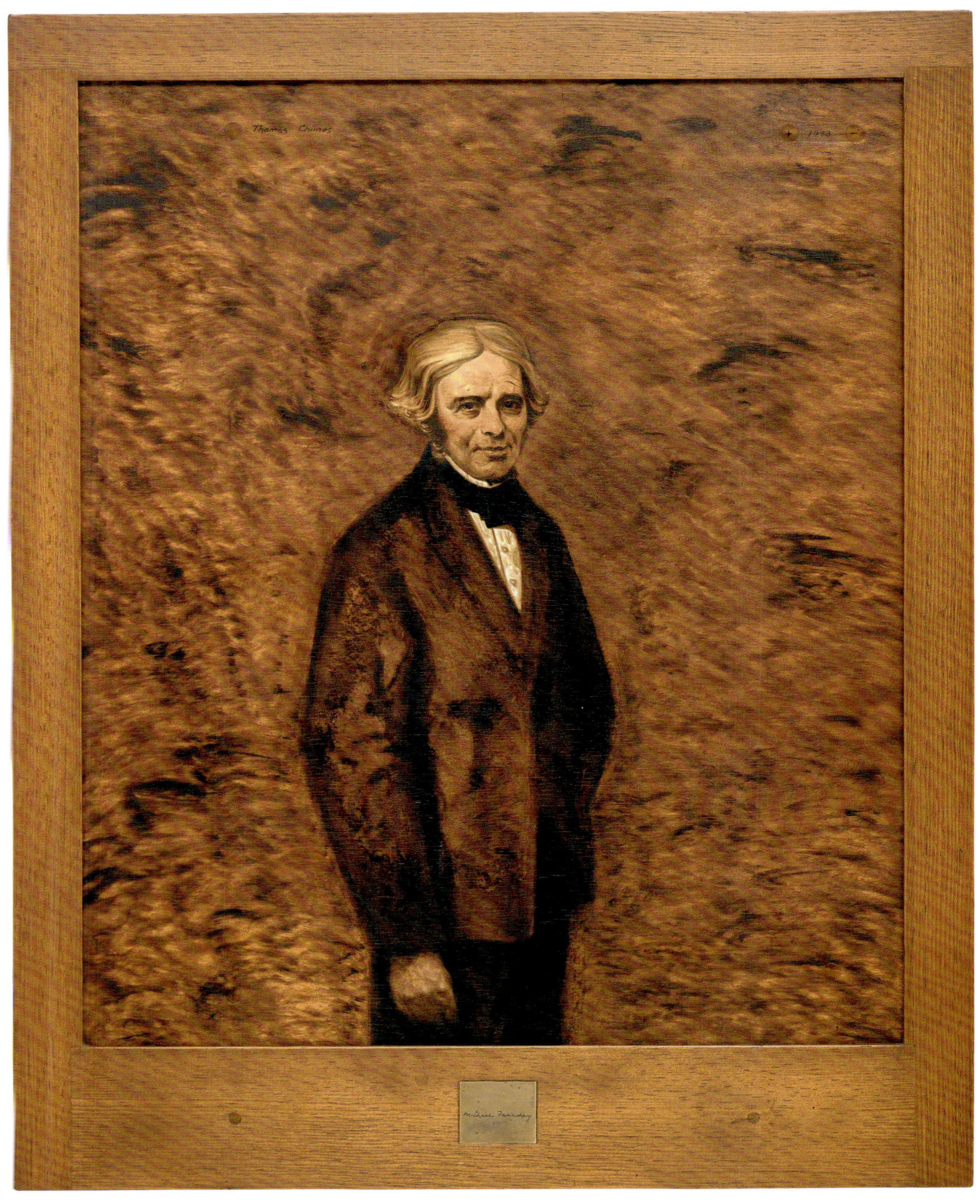

Michael Faraday, 1973

OIL ON PANEL

29 x 22⅞ INCHES (73.7 x 58.1 CM)

PRIVATE COLLECTION

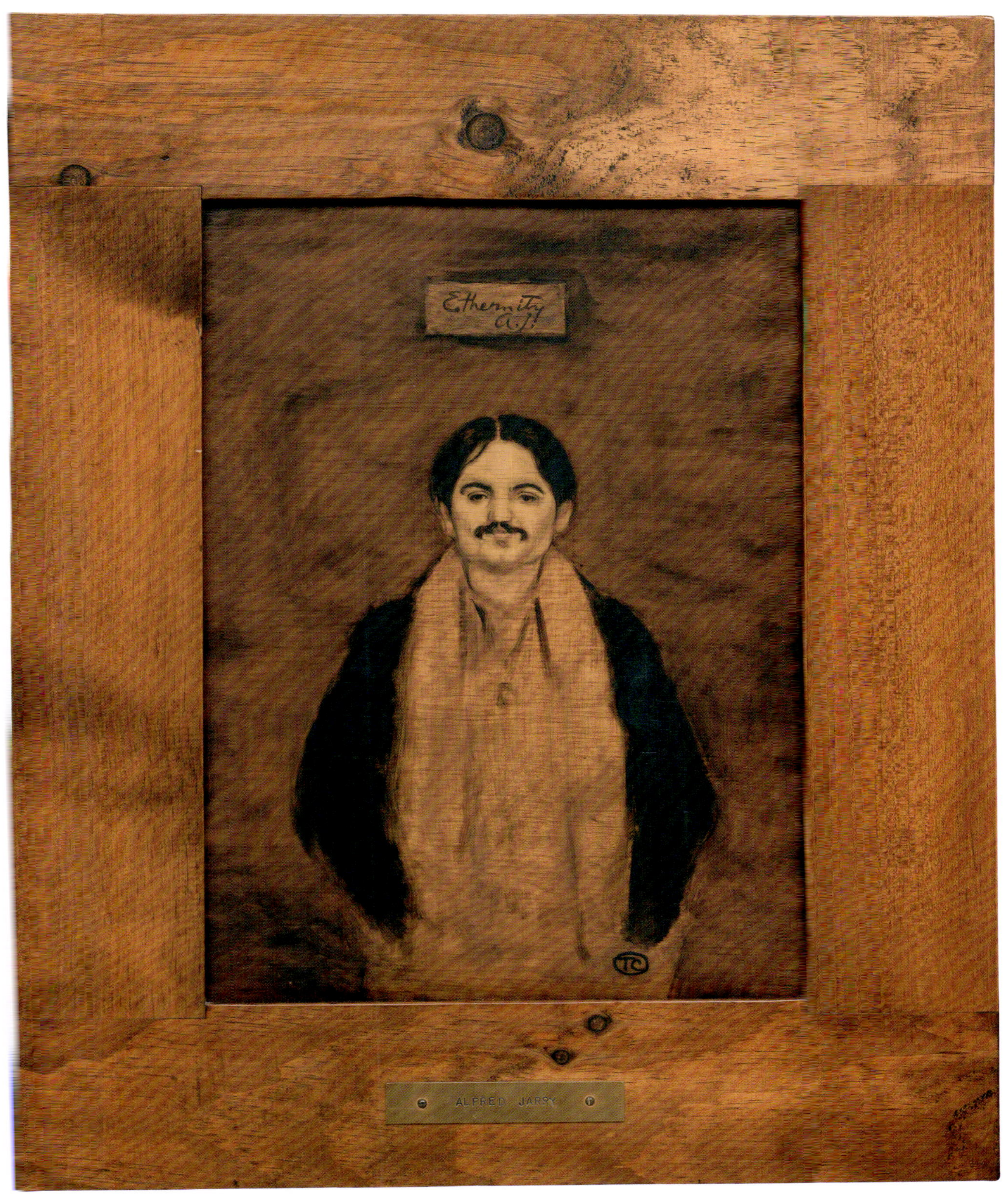

Plate 44

Alfred Jarry (Ethernity), 1973

Oil on panel

21¾ x 17¾ inches (55.2 x 45.1 cm)

Private collection

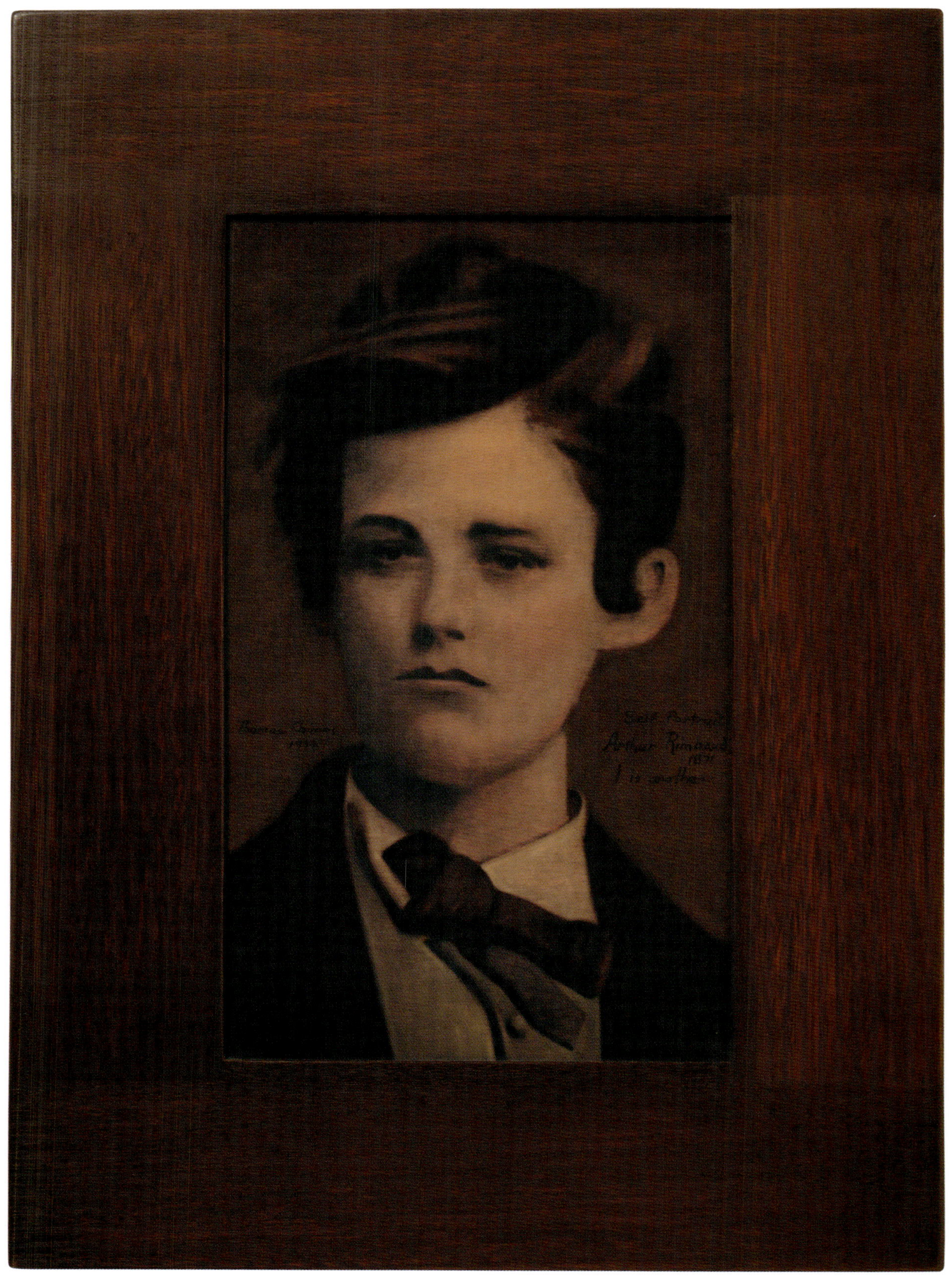

PLATE 45

Arthur Rimbaud, 1974

OIL ON PANEL

21¾ x 15¾ INCHES (55.2 x 40 CM)

COLLECTION OF DMITRI AND SHEILA CHIMES, PHILADELPHIA

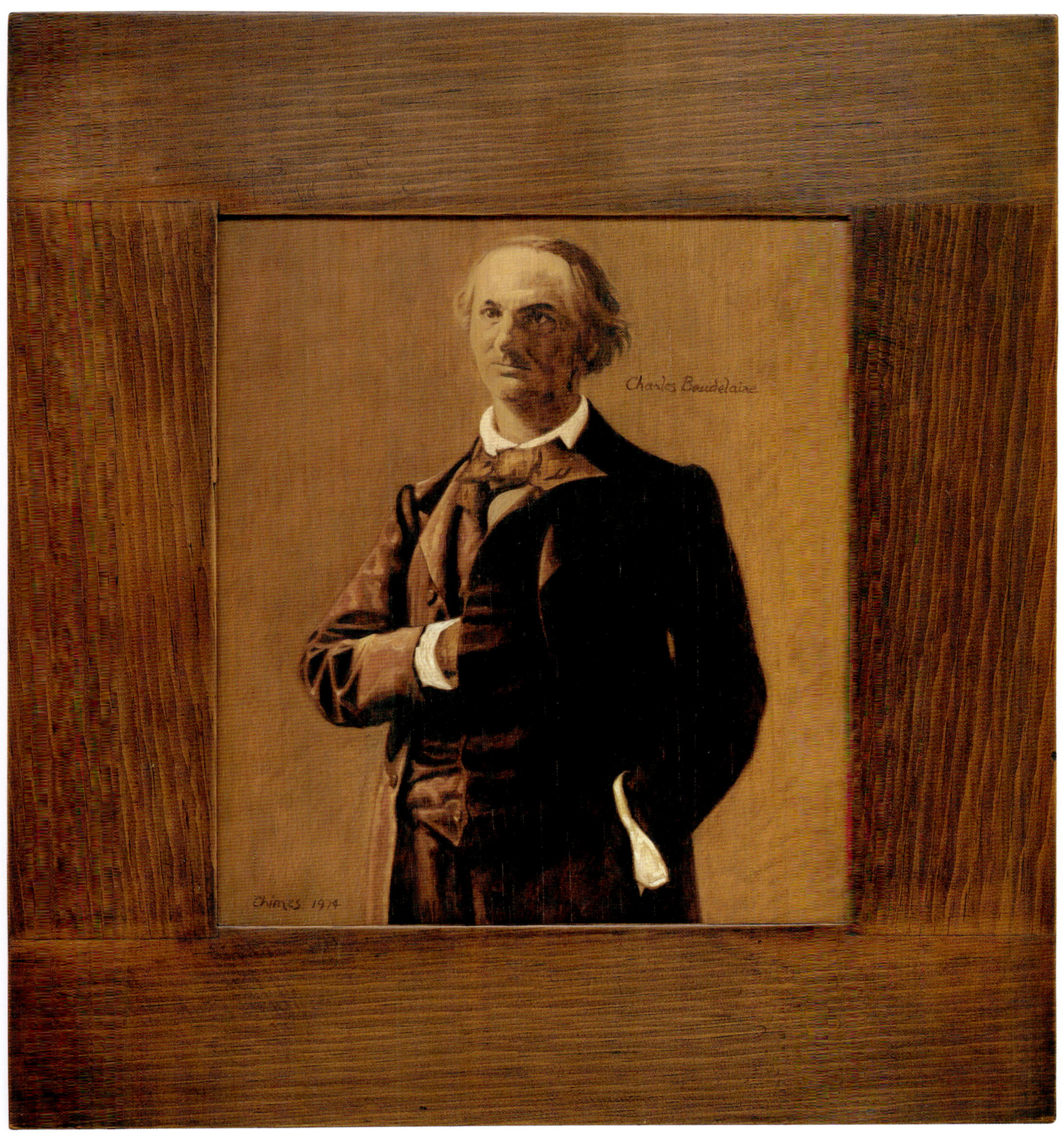

PLATE 46

Charles Baudelaire, 1974

OIL ON PANEL

19⅛ x 18⅜ INCHES (48.6 x 46.7 CM)

COLLECTION OF FRANCES AND BAYARD STOREY, PHILADELPHIA

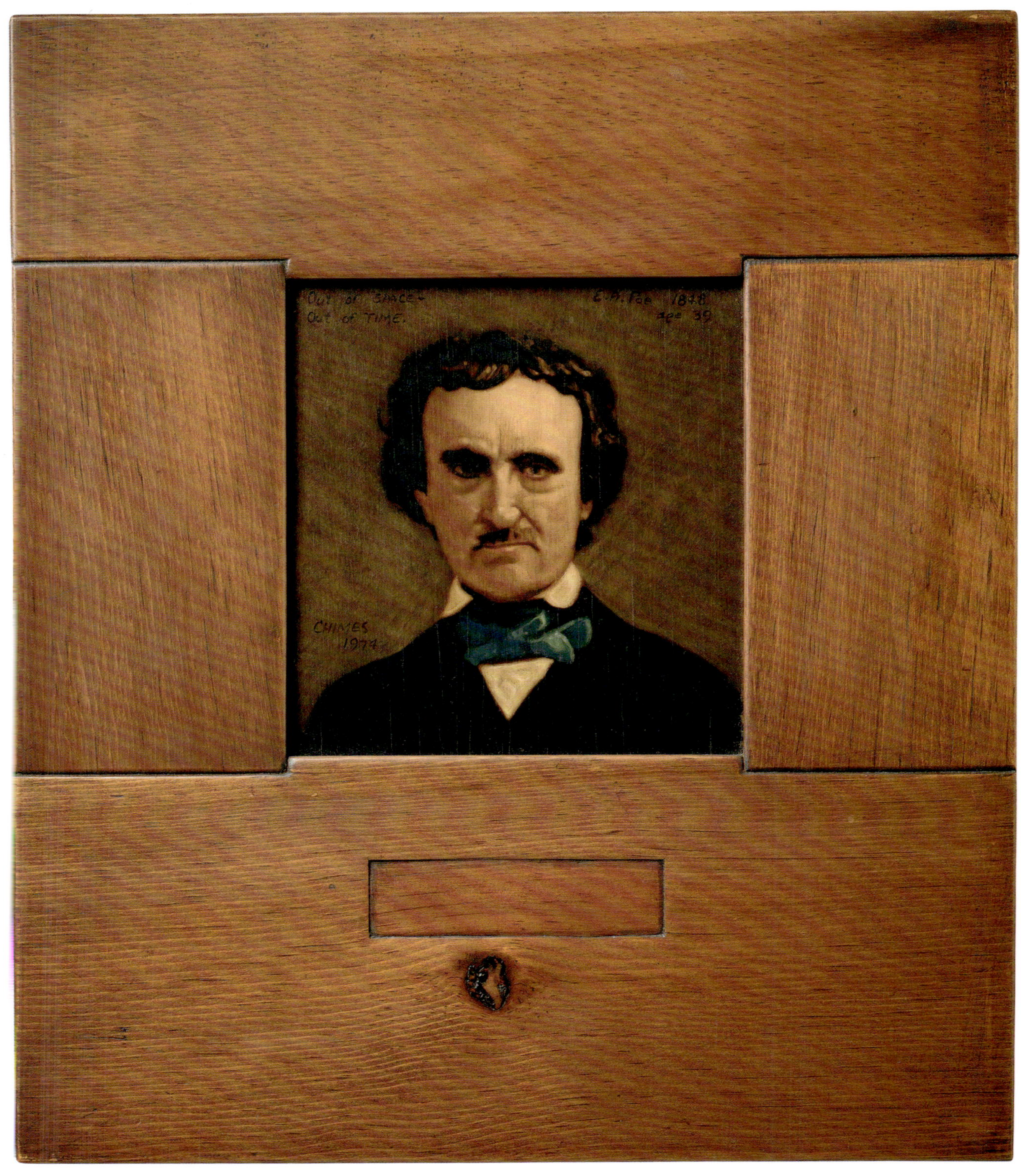

PLATE 47

Edgar Allan Poe, 1974

OIL ON PANEL

15¼ x 12⅞ INCHES (38.7 x 32.7 CM)

COLLECTION OF DANIEL W. DIETRICH II, CHESTER SPRINGS, PENNSYLVANIA

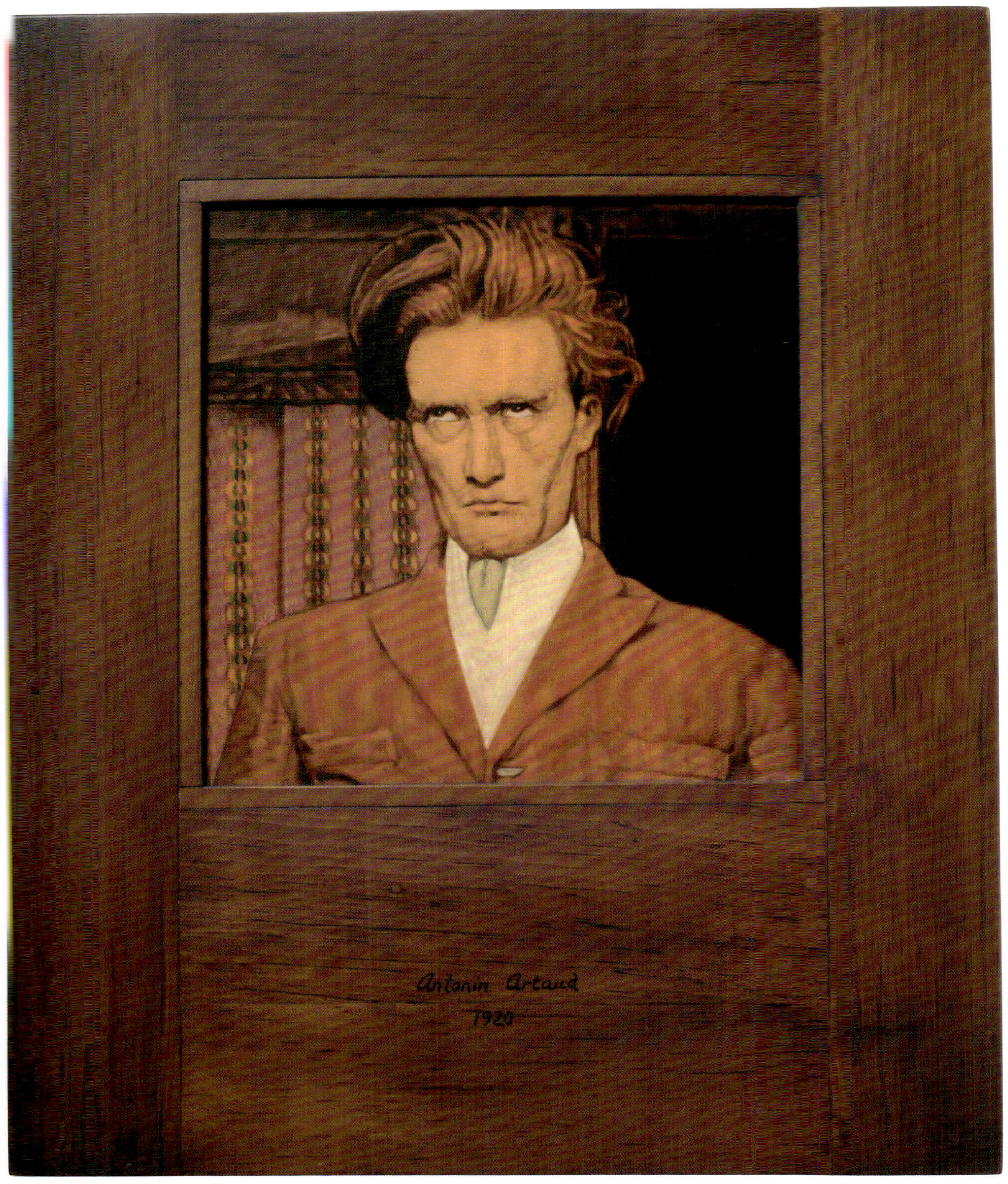

PLATE 48

Antonin Artaud, 1974

OIL ON PANEL

17¾ x 14¾ INCHES (45.1 x 37.5 CM)

PHILADELPHIA MUSEUM OF ART. GIFT OF THE ARTIST, 1975-78-1

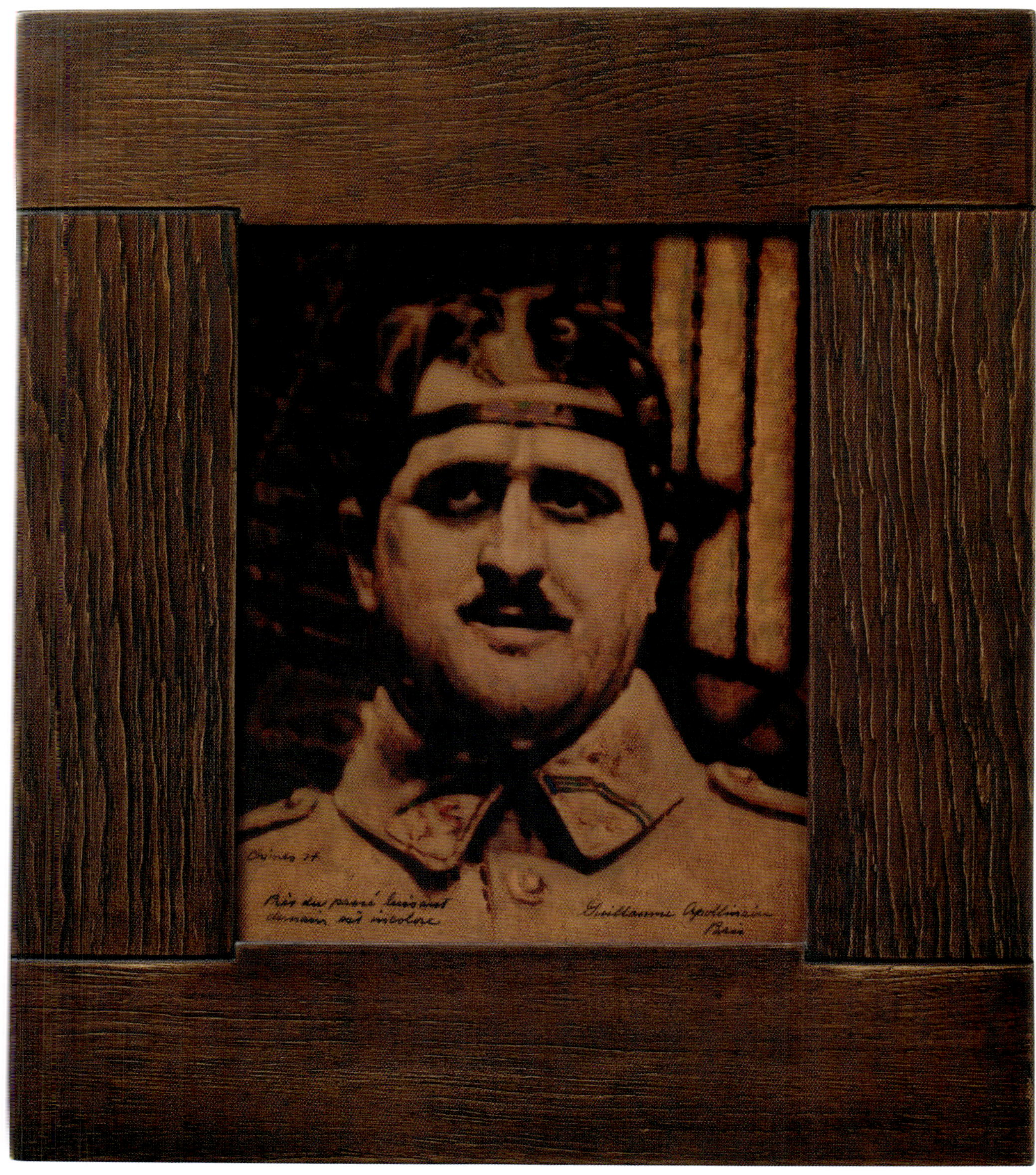

PLATE 49

Guillaume Apollinaire, 1974

OIL ON PANEL

18⅝ x 16 INCHES (47.3 x 40.1 CM)

PHILADELPHIA MUSEUM OF ART. PURCHASED WITH THE ADELE HAAS TURNER AND BEATRICE PASTORIUS TURNER MEMORIAL FUND, 1975-82-2

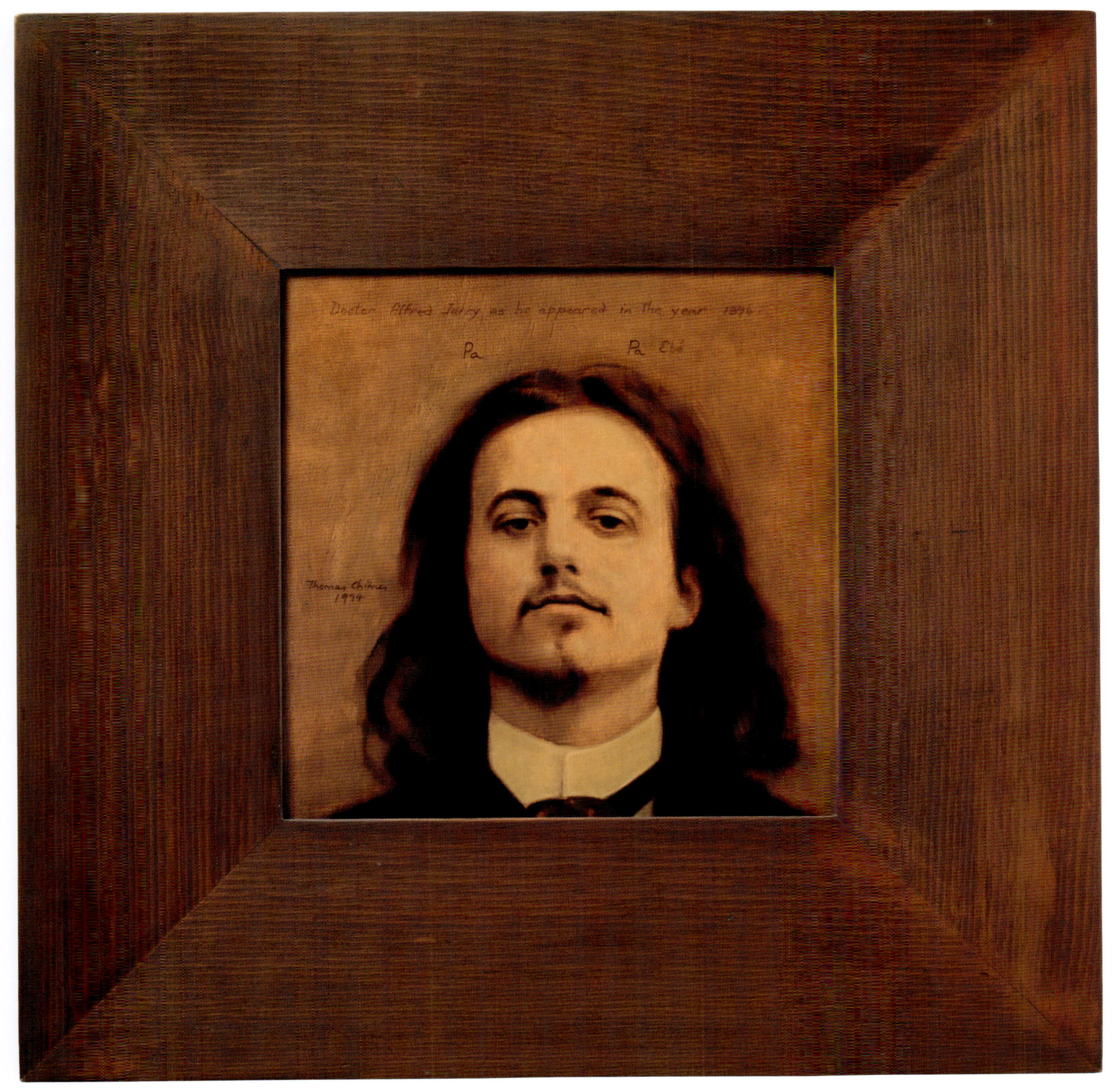

PLATE 50

Alfred Jarry, 1974

OIL ON PANEL

22½ x 22¼ INCHES (57.2 x 56.5 CM)

PHILADELPHIA MUSEUM OF ART. PURCHASED WITH THE ADELE HAAS TURNER AND BEATRICE PASTORIUS TURNER MEMORIAL FUND, 1975-82-1

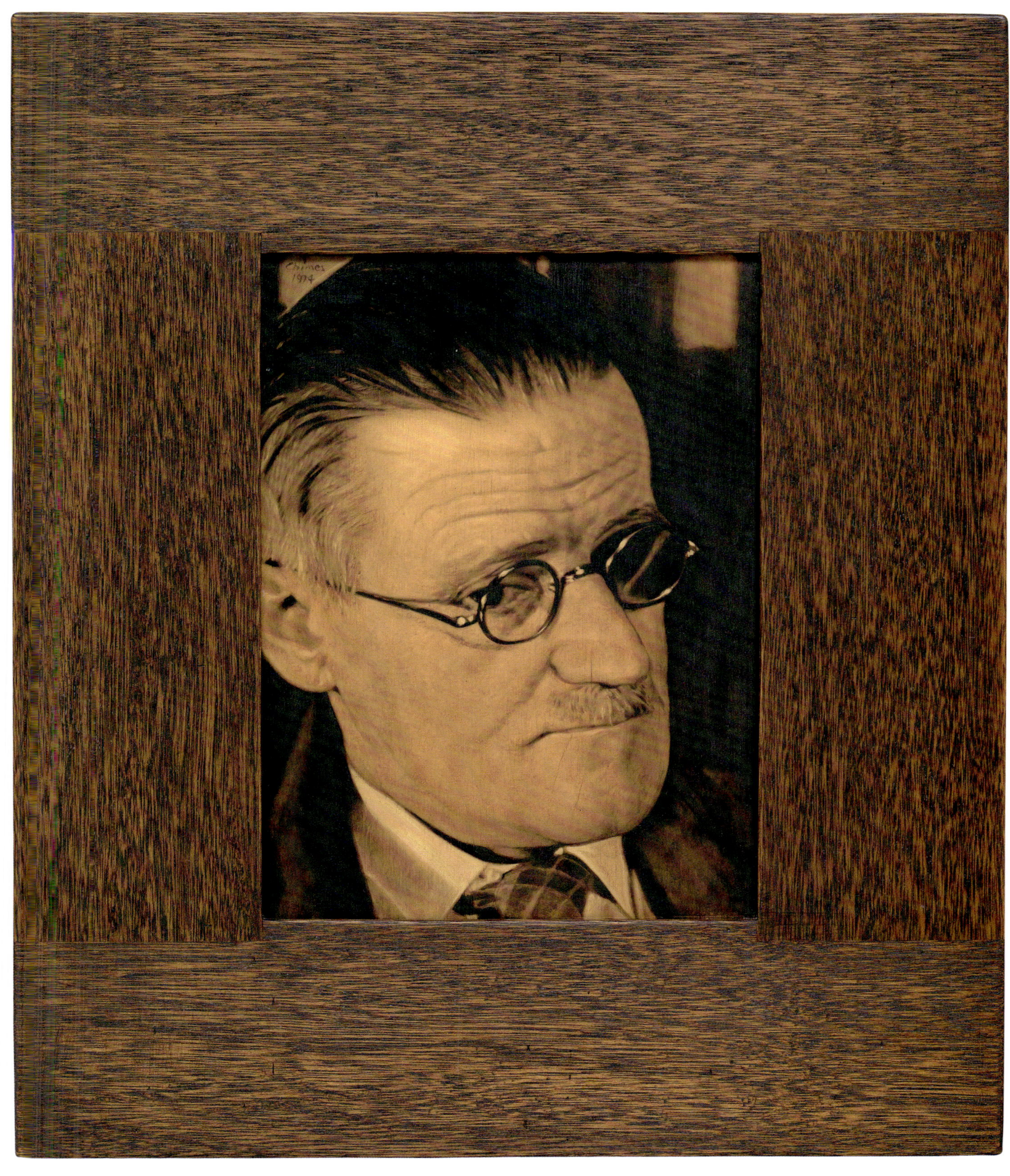

PLATE 51

James Joyce, 1974

OIL ON PANEL

17⅛ x 14⅜ INCHES (43.5 x 36.5 CM)

PRIVATE COLLECTION

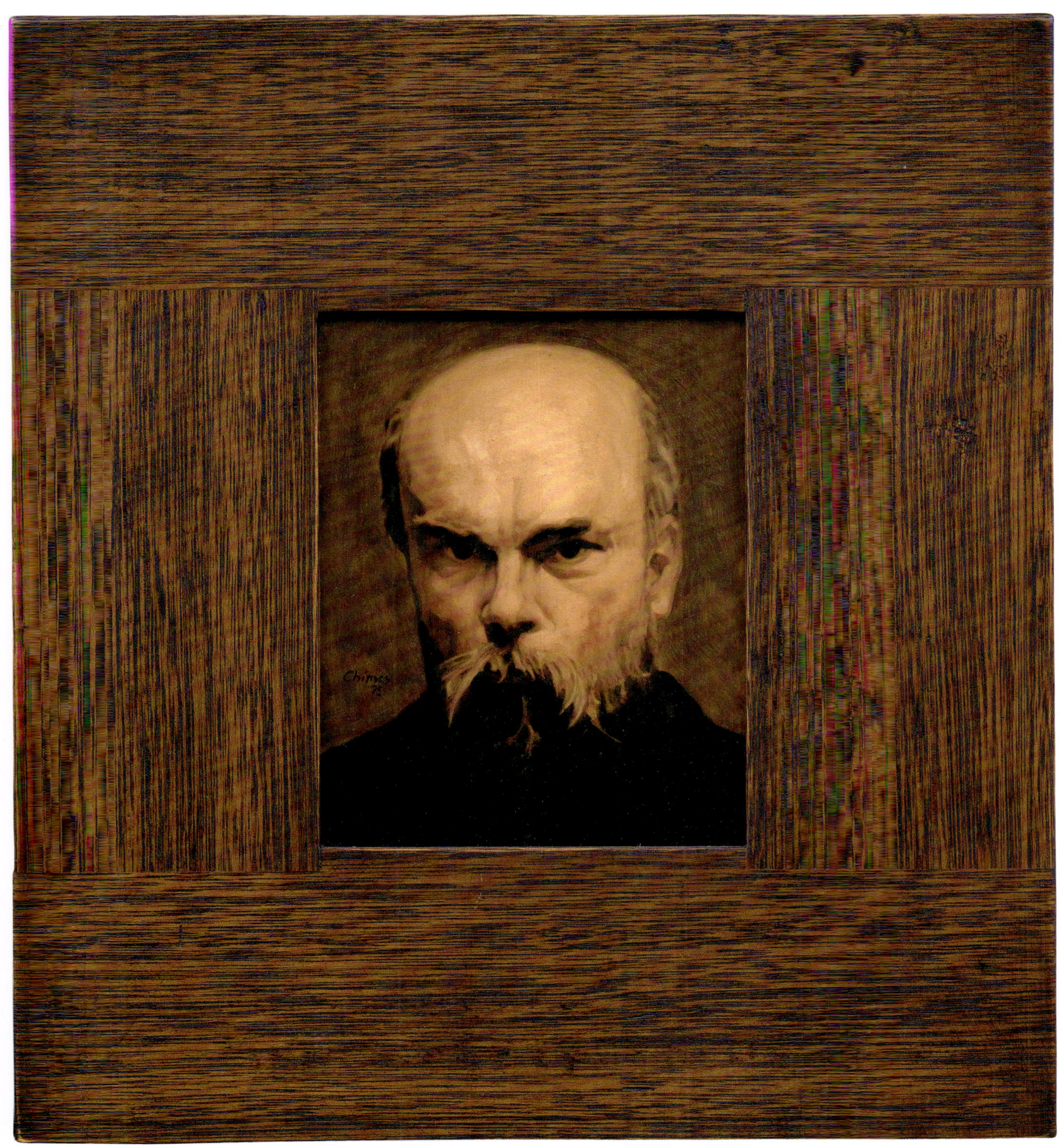

PLATE 52

Paul Verlaine, 1975

OIL ON PANEL

13⅜ x 12³⁄₁₆ INCHES (34.6 x 31 CM)

PRIVATE COLLECTION, COURTESY OF LOCKS GALLERY, PHILADELPHIA

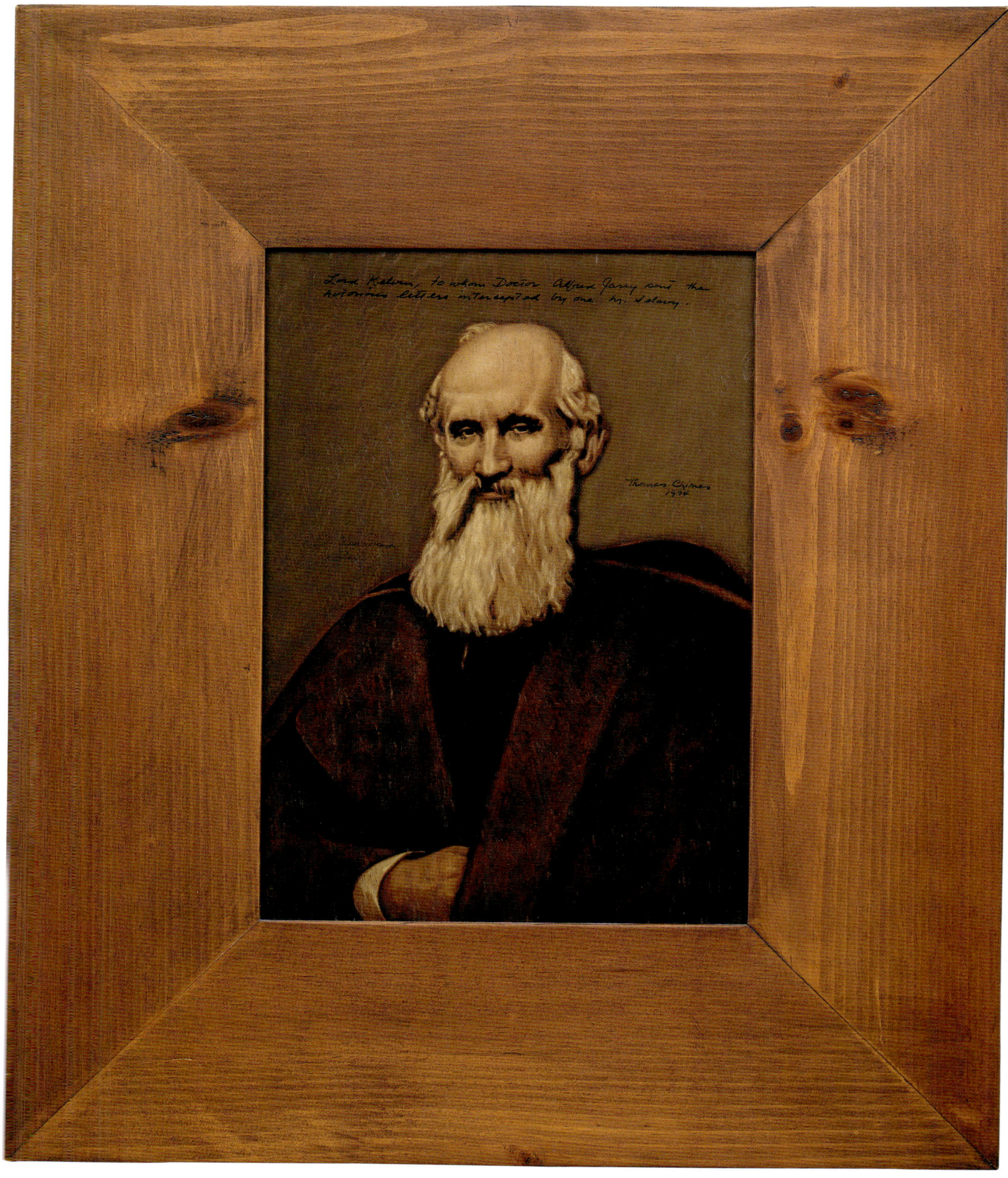

PLATE 53

Lord Kelvin, 1974

OIL ON PANEL

26 x 21½ INCHES (66 x 54.6 CM)

THE BUCKINGHAM FAMILY COLLECTION, LARCHMONT, NEW YORK

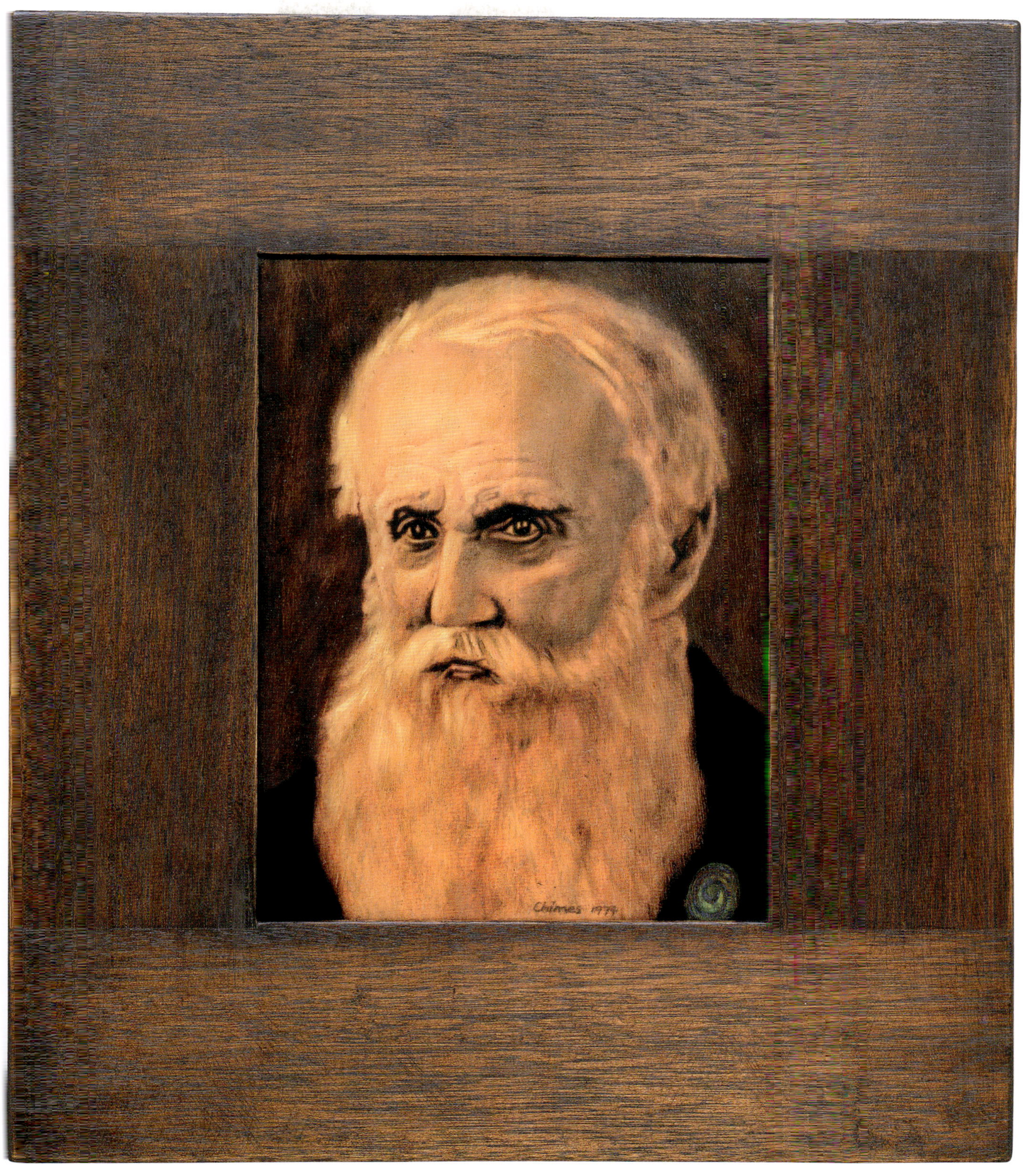

PLATE 54

Doctor I. L. Sandomir, 1974

OIL ON PANEL

17 1/16 x 14 1/2 INCHES (43.3 x 36.8 CM)

COLLECTION OF PHILLIP MITSIS AND SOPHIA KALANTZAKOS, NEW YORK

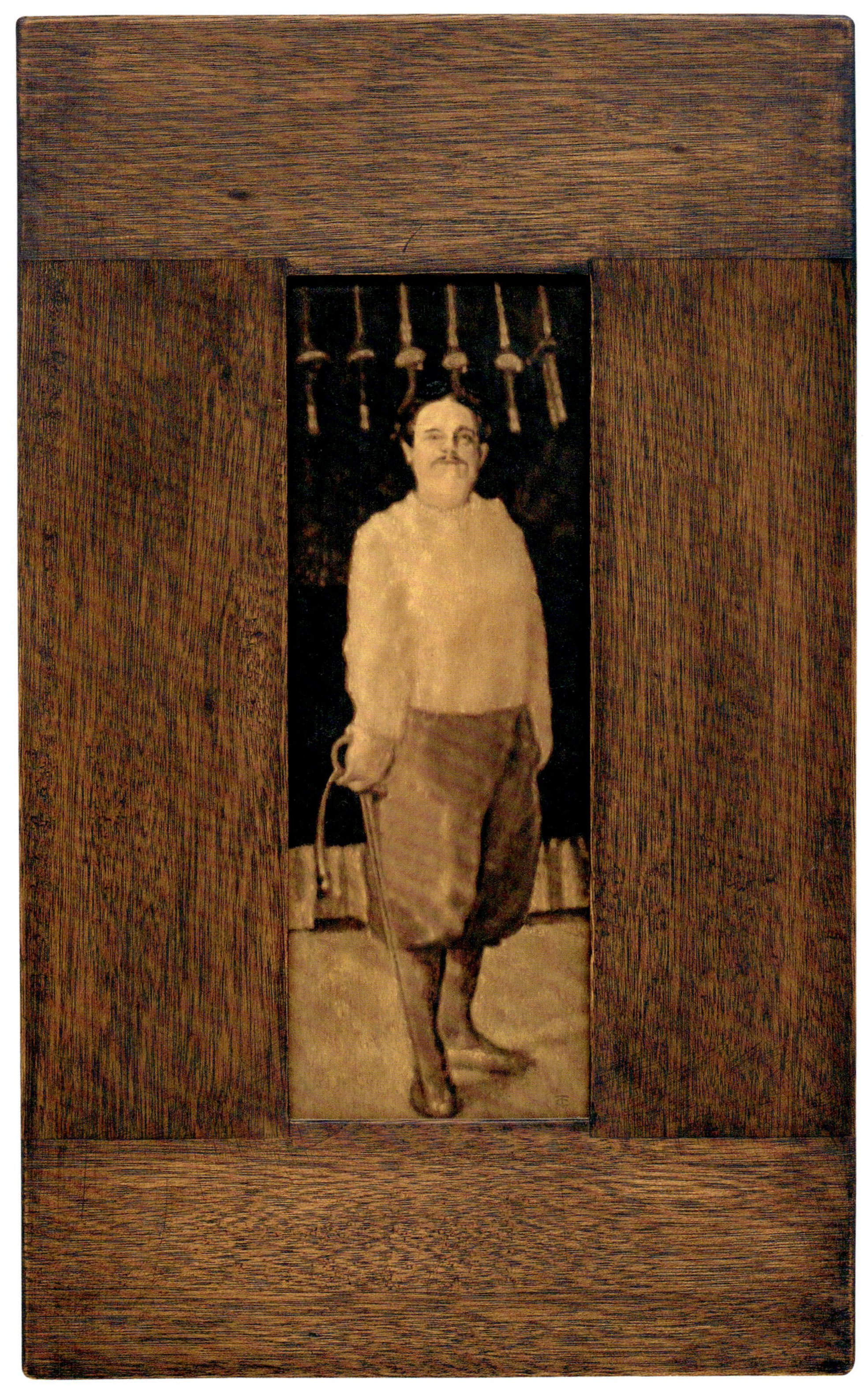

PLATE 55

Alfred Jarry (with Sword), 1975

OIL ON PANEL

19 x 11¼ INCHES (48.3 x 28.6 CM)

COLLECTION OF SMOKIE KITTNER AND HARRY ANDERSON, PHILADELPHIA

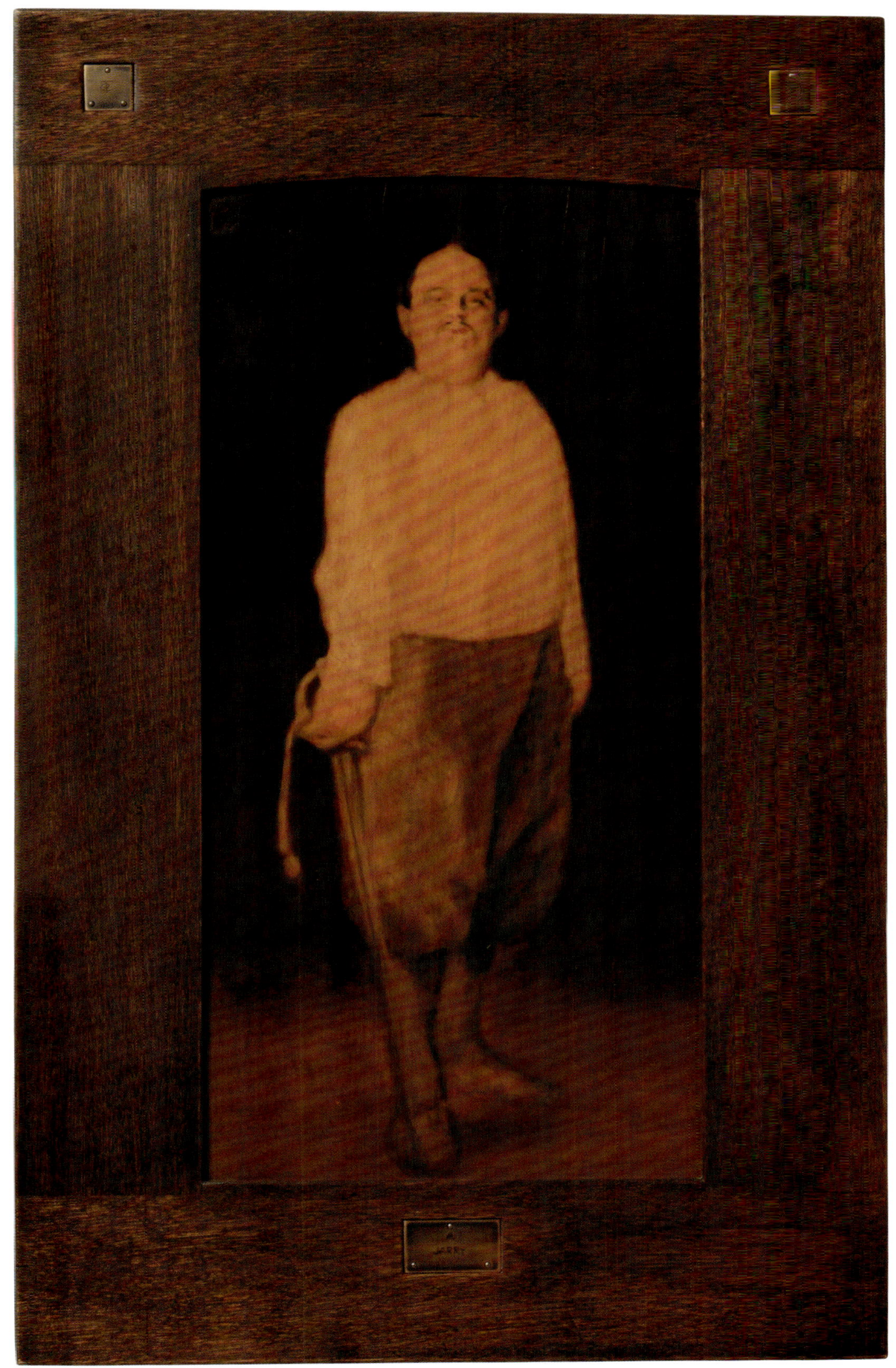

Alfred Jarry (with Sword), 1976

OIL ON PANEL

26¾ x 16¾ INCHES (67.9 x 42.5 CM)

COLLECTION OF MR. AND MRS. GEORGE AMROM, PHILADELPHIA

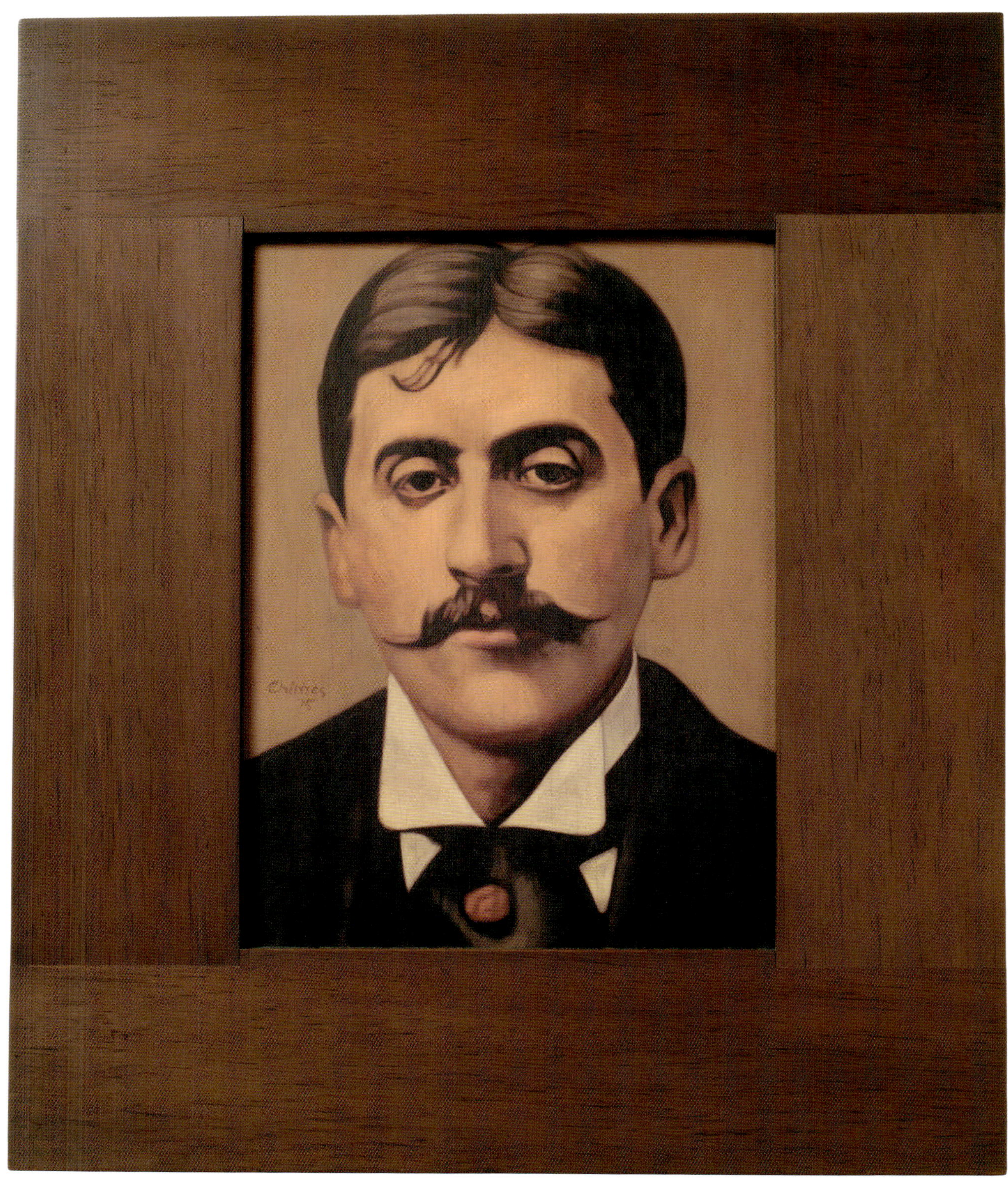

PLATE 57

Marcel Proust, 1975

OIL ON PANEL

17⅞ x 14¾ INCHES (45.4 x 37.5 CM)

COLLECTION OF ANNE D'HARNONCOURT AND JOSEPH J. RISHEL, PHILADELPHIA

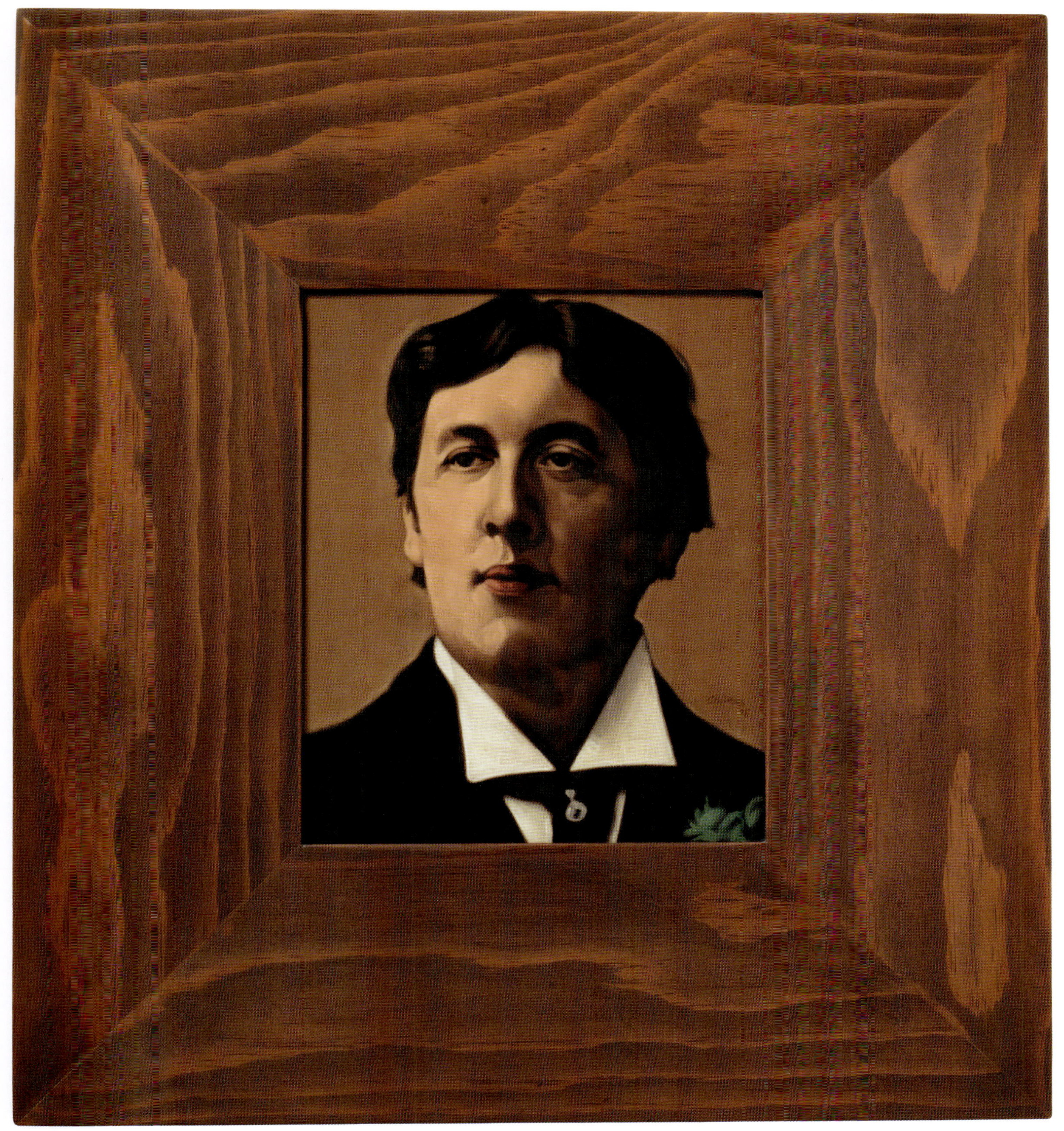

Plate 58

Oscar Wilde, 1975

Oil on panel

21¾ x 19¼ inches (55.2 x 48.9 cm)

Philadelphia Museum of Art. Gift of the artist, 1976-154-1

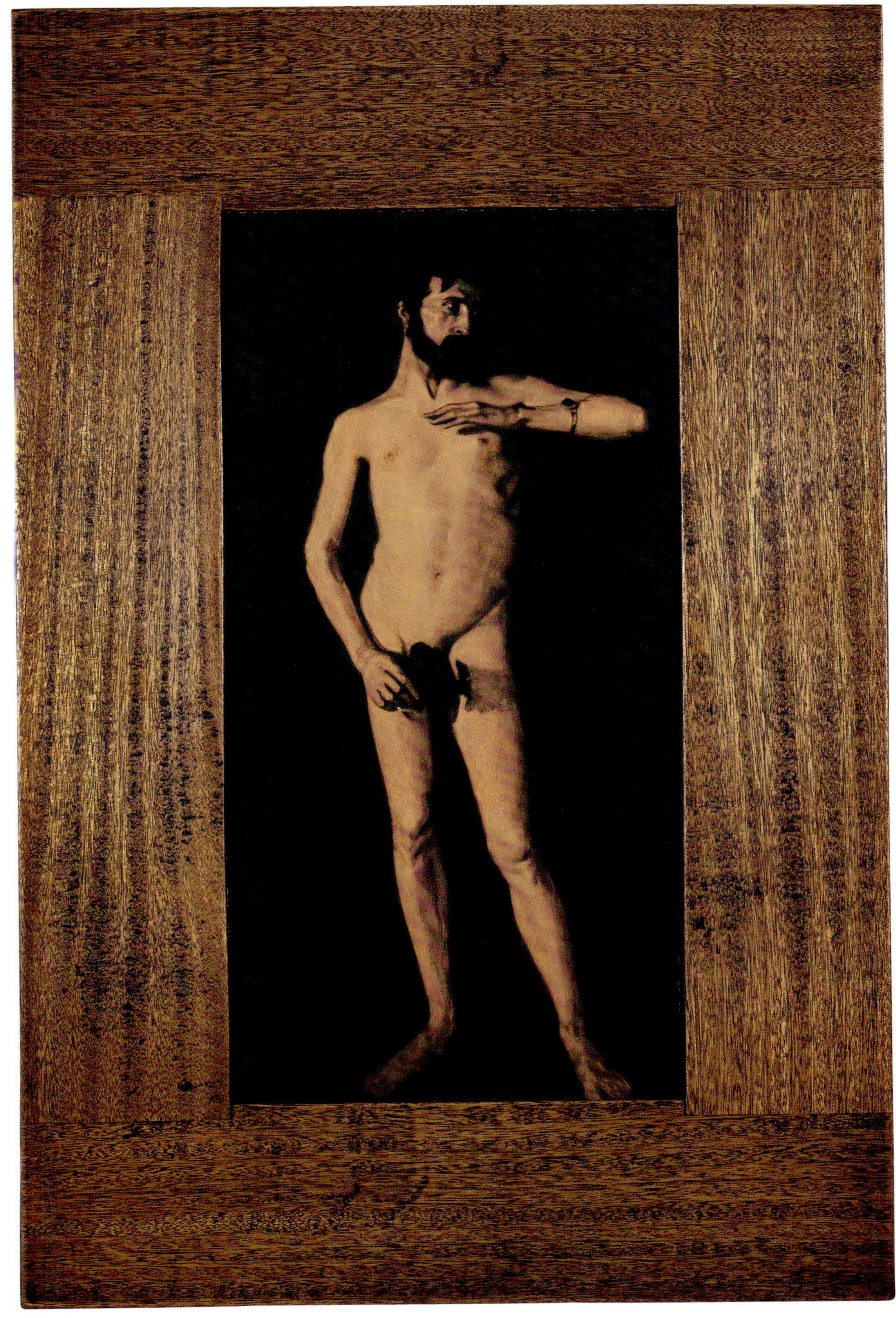

Adam (Duchamp), 1976

OIL ON PANEL

22¾ x 14¾ INCHES (57.8 x 37.5 CM)

PRIVATE COLLECTION, COURTESY OF LOCKS GALLERY, PHILADELPHIA

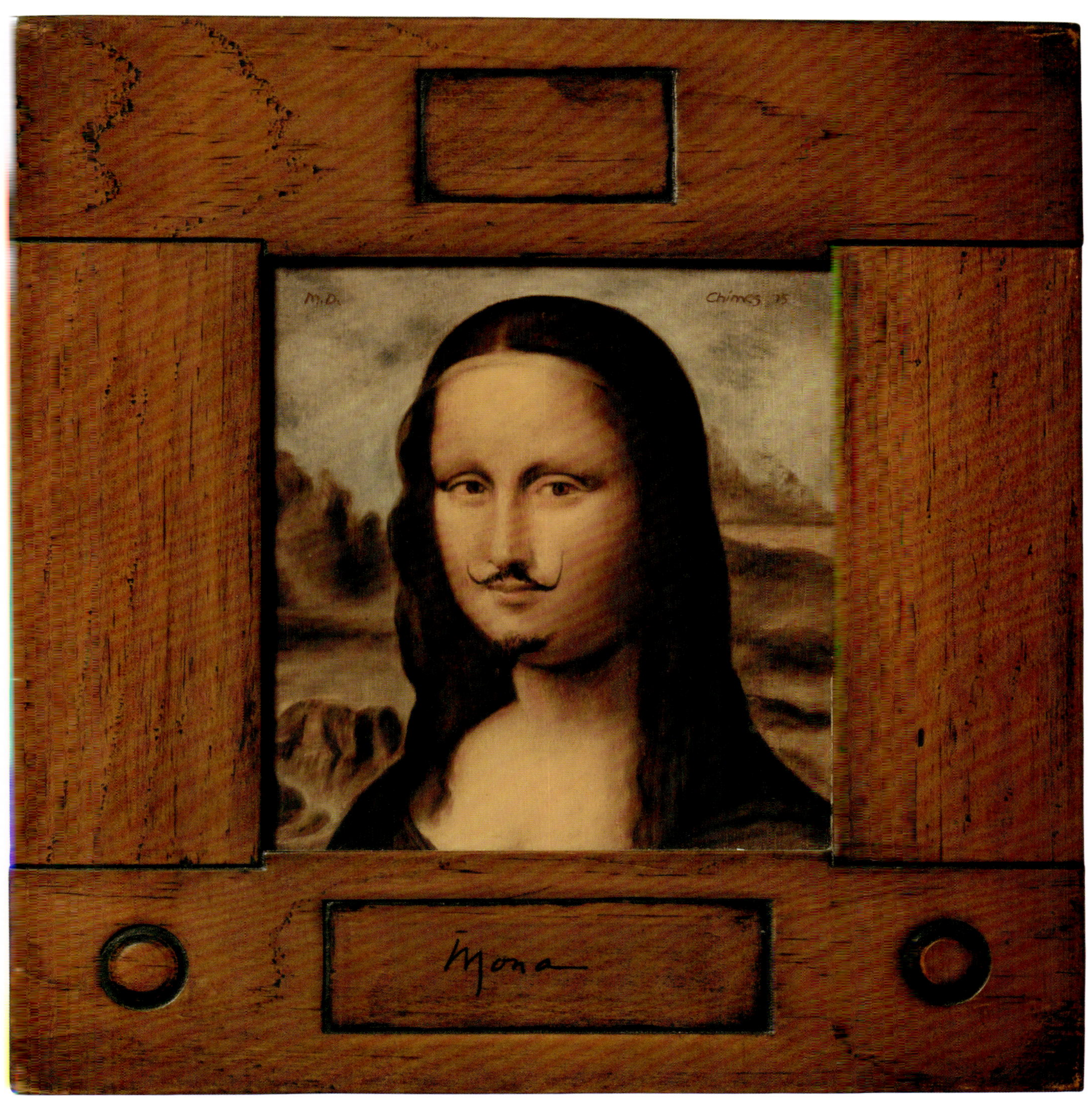

PLATE 60

Mona (Duchamp), 1976

OIL ON PANEL

11¾ x 11¼ INCHES (29.8 x 28.6 CM)

COLLECTION OF JANET FLEISHER, PHILADELPHIA

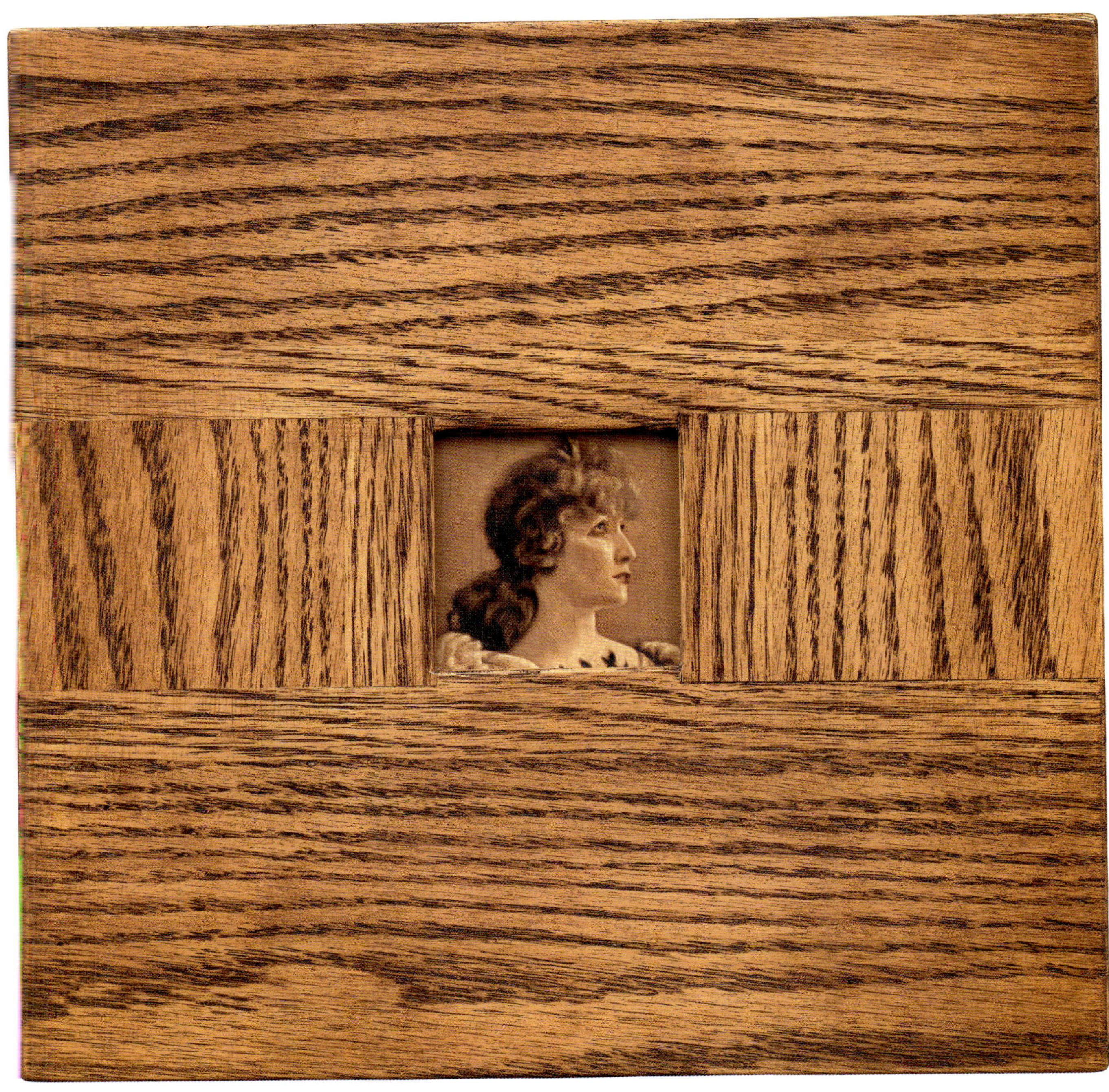

PLATE 61

Sarah, 1976

OIL ON PANEL

8½ x 8½ INCHES (21.6 X 21.6 CM)

COLLECTION OF MRS. BURTON S. SINGER, VILLANOVA, PENNSYLVANIA

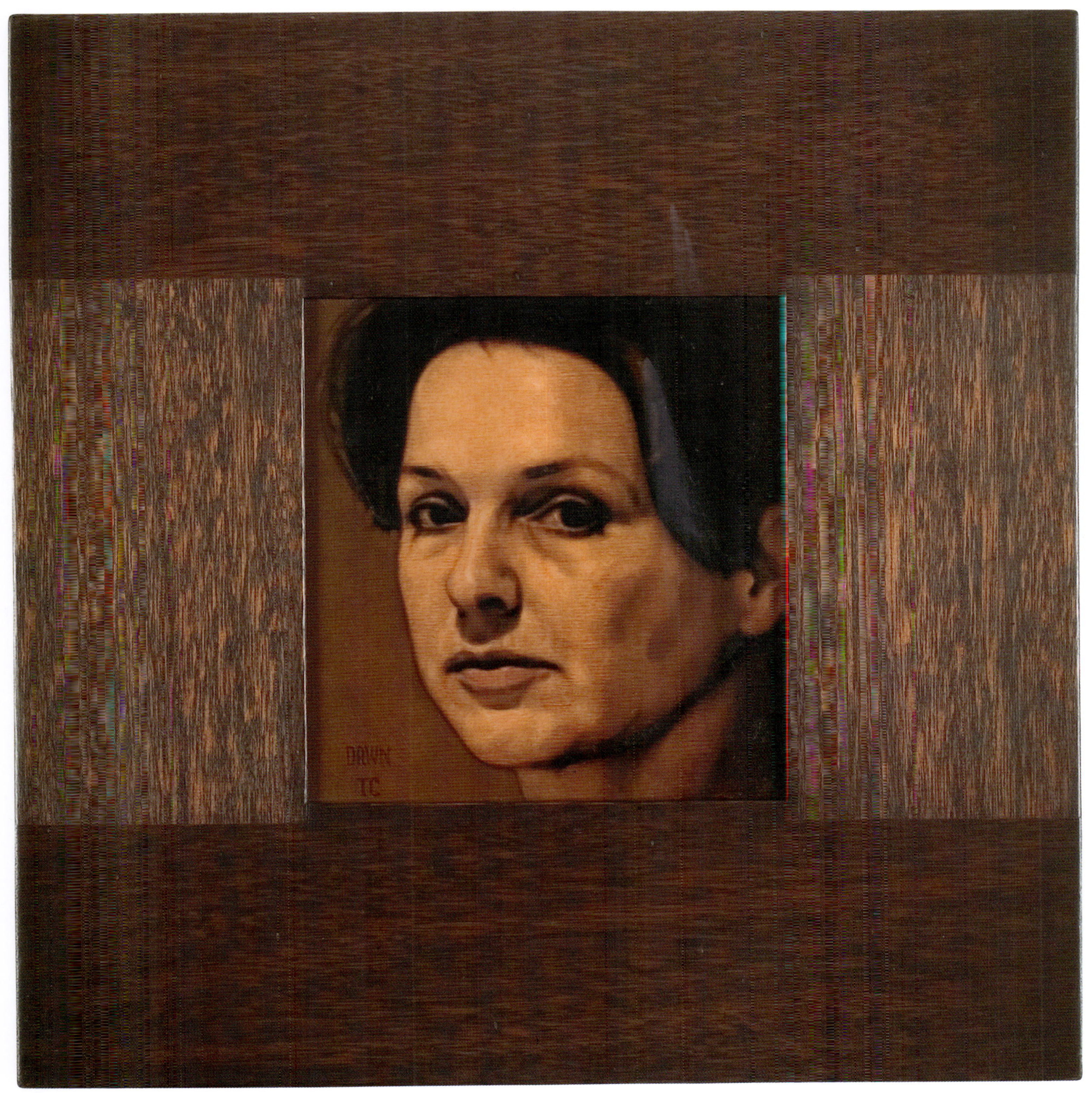

PLATE 62

Dawn, 1974

OIL ON PANEL

13½ x 13 INCHES (34.3 x 33 CM)

THE GÅRDER FAMILY COLLECTION, BANGOR, MAINE

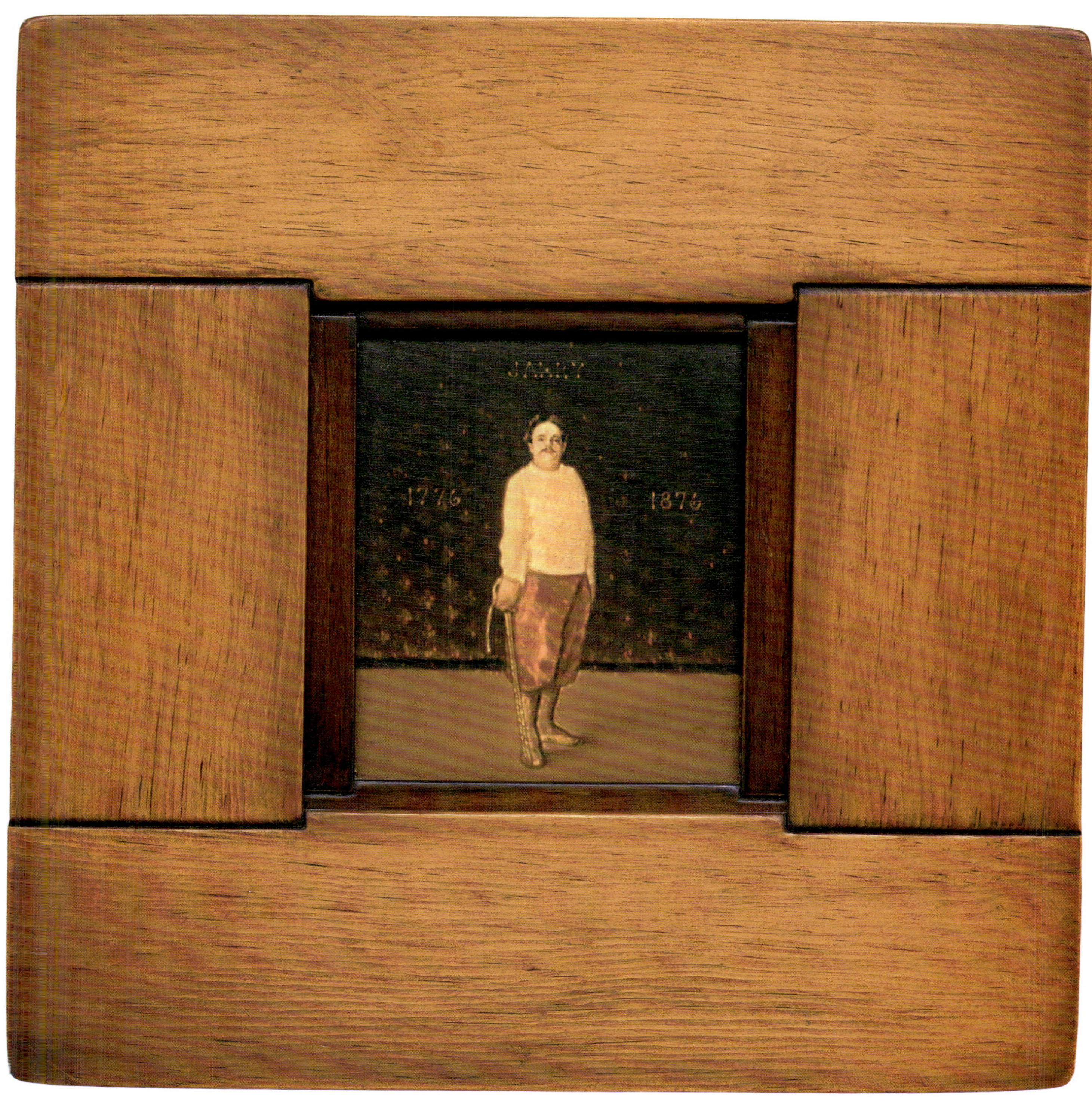

Bicentennial Jarry, 1976

OIL ON PANEL

13 x 13 INCHES (33 x 33 CM)

PRIVATE COLLECTION, COURTESY OF LOCKS GALLERY, PHILADELPHIA

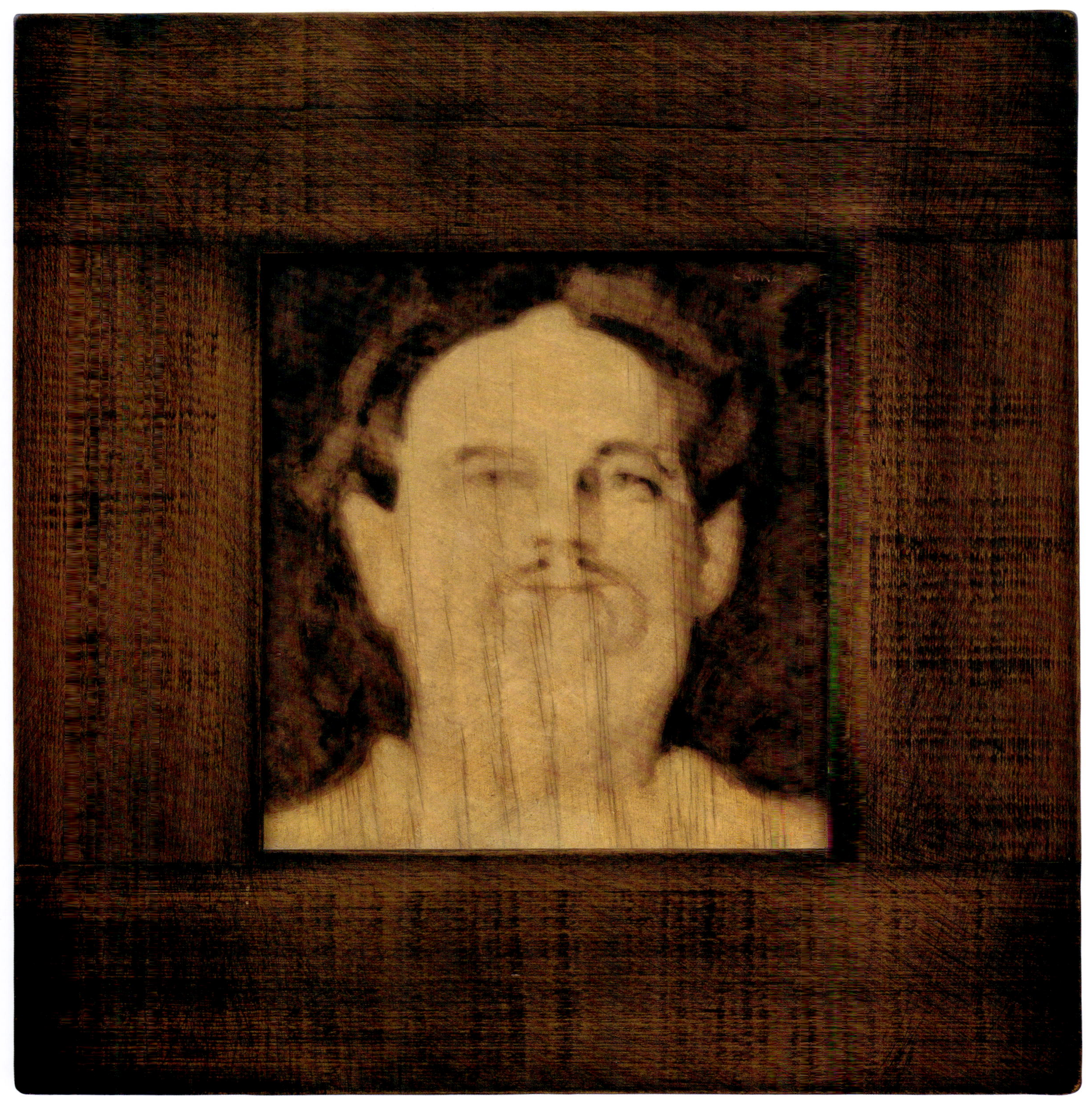

Ubu, 1976

OIL ON PANEL

15¼ x 14½ INCHES (38.7 x 36.8 CM)

PRIVATE COLLECTION, COURTESY OF LOCKS GALLERY, PHILADELPHIA

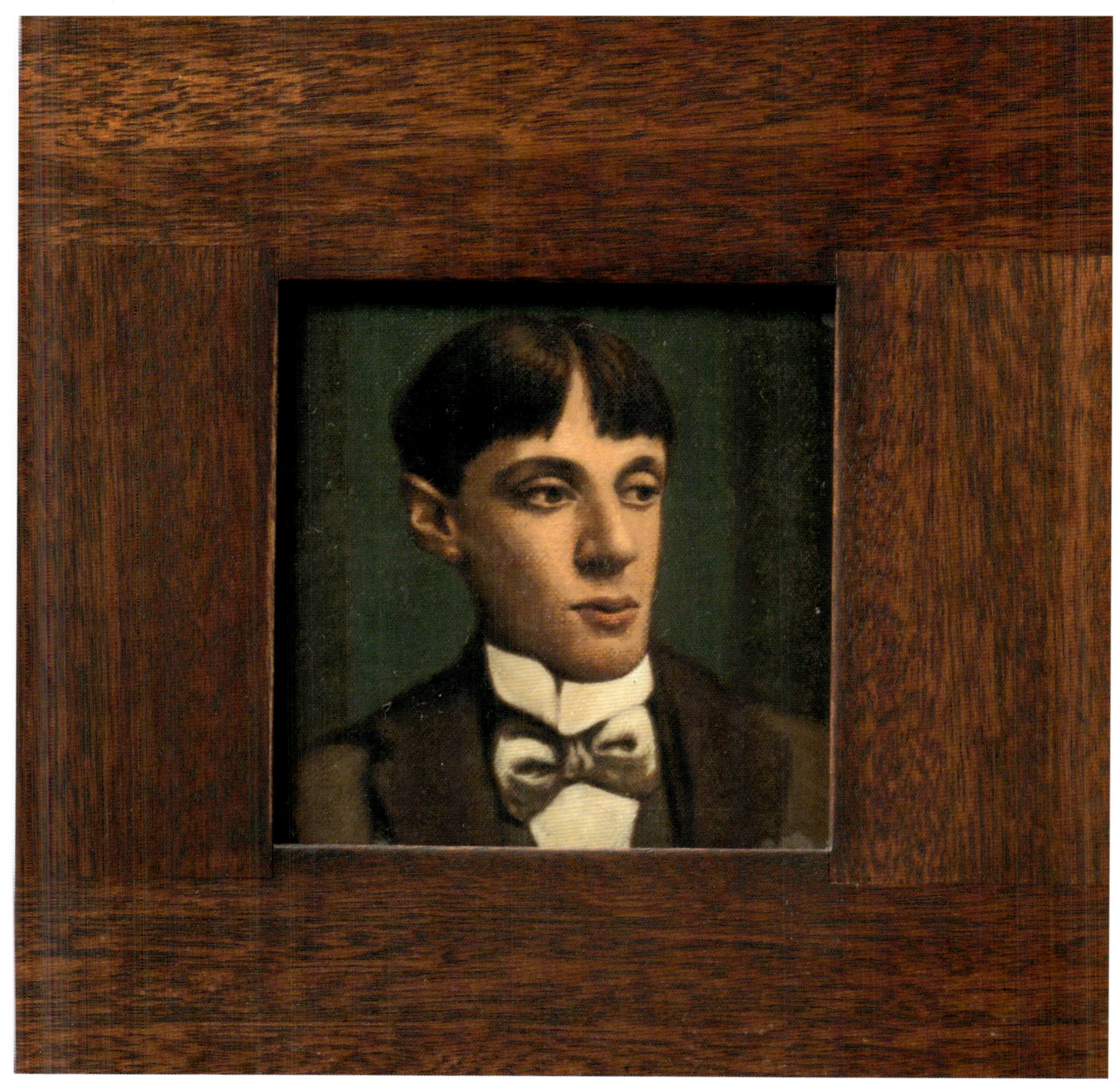

Aubrey Beardsley, 1976

OIL ON PANEL

11½ x 11⅜ INCHES (29.2 x 28.9 CM)

COLLECTION OF DAWN CHIMES, VENICE, FLORIDA

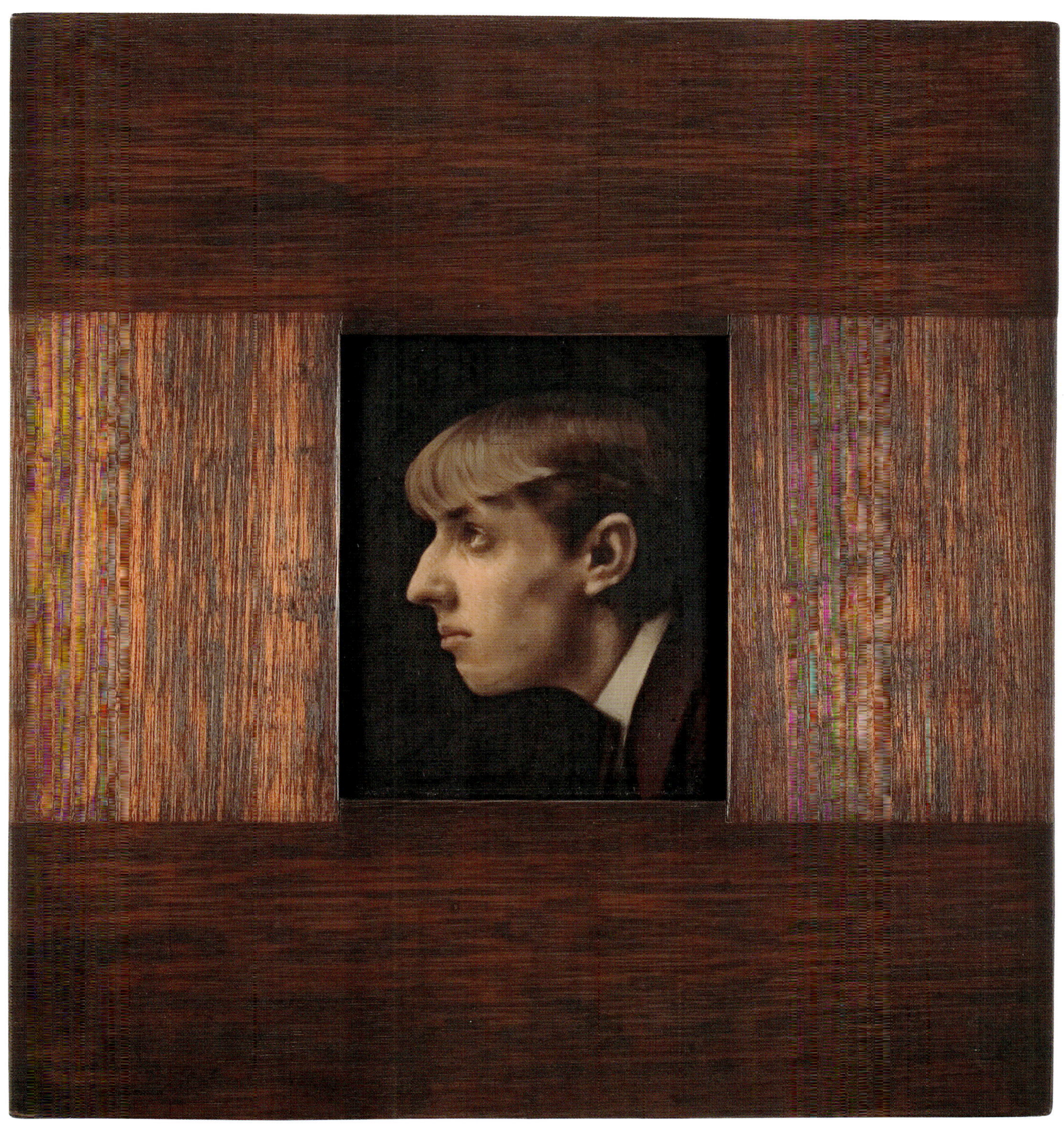

PLATE 66

Aubrey Beardsley, 1976

OIL ON PANEL

12⅜ x 11⅜ INCHES (31.4 x 28.9 CM)

THE GÅRDER FAMILY COLLECTION, BANGOR, MAINE

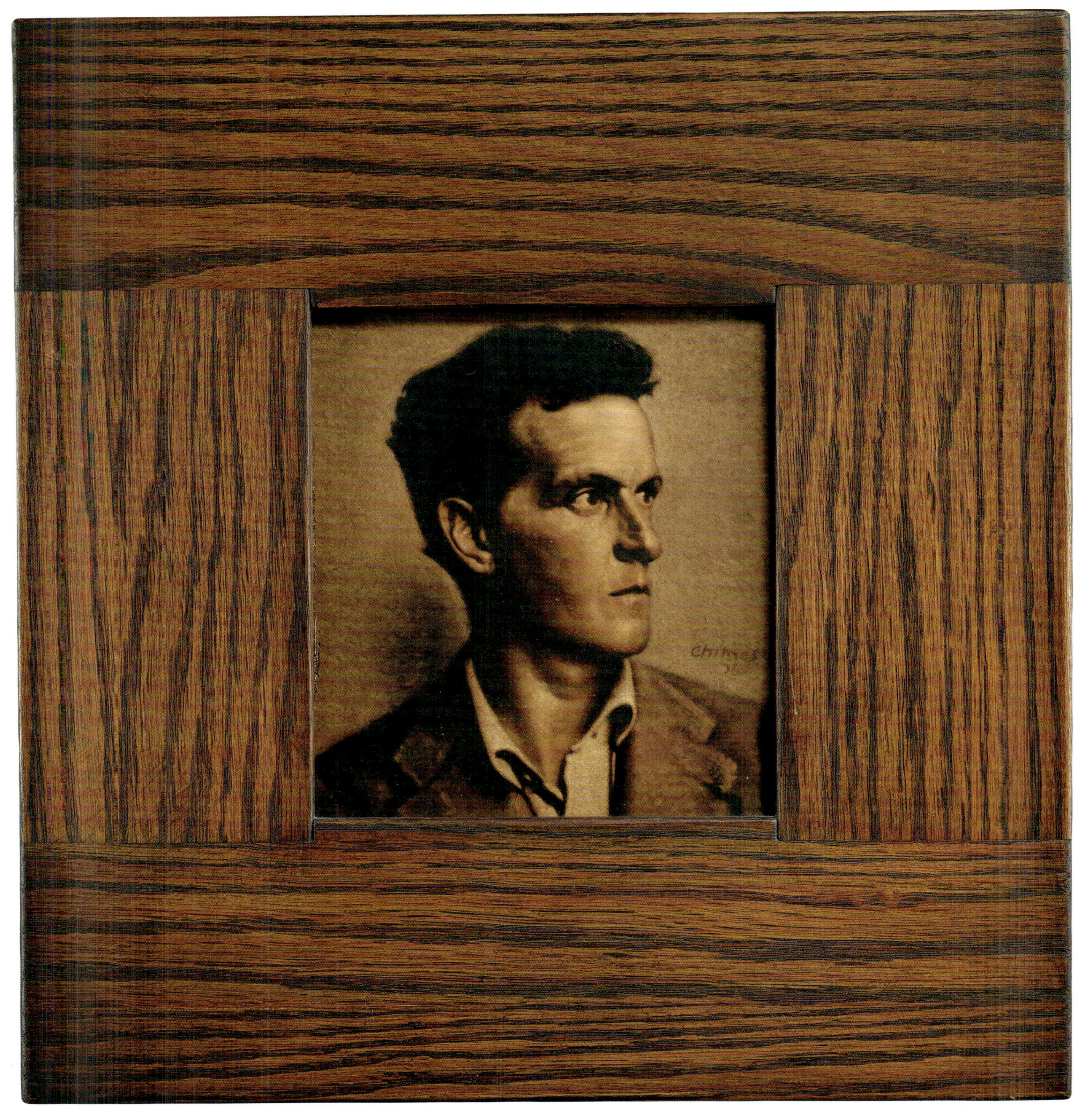

PLATE 67

Ludwig Wittgenstein, 1976

OIL ON PANEL

13¼ x 12⅜ INCHES (33.7 x 31.4 CM)

PRIVATE COLLECTION, COURTESY OF LOCKS GALLERY, PHILADELPHIA

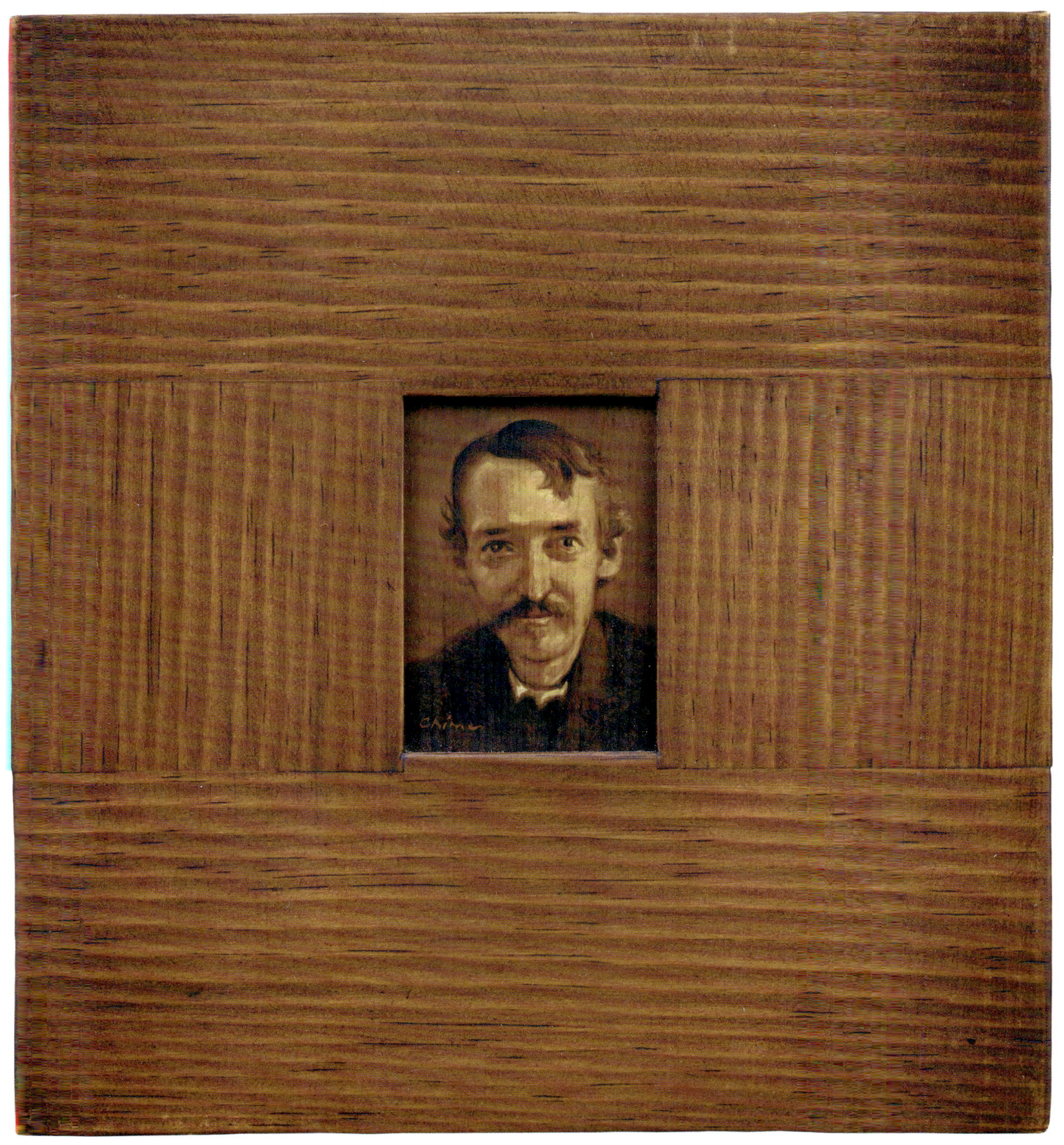

PLATE 68

Robert Louis Stevenson, 1976

OIL ON PANEL

10⅜ x 9¼ INCHES (26.4 x 23.5 CM)

COURTESY OF LOCKS GALLERY, PHILADELPHIA

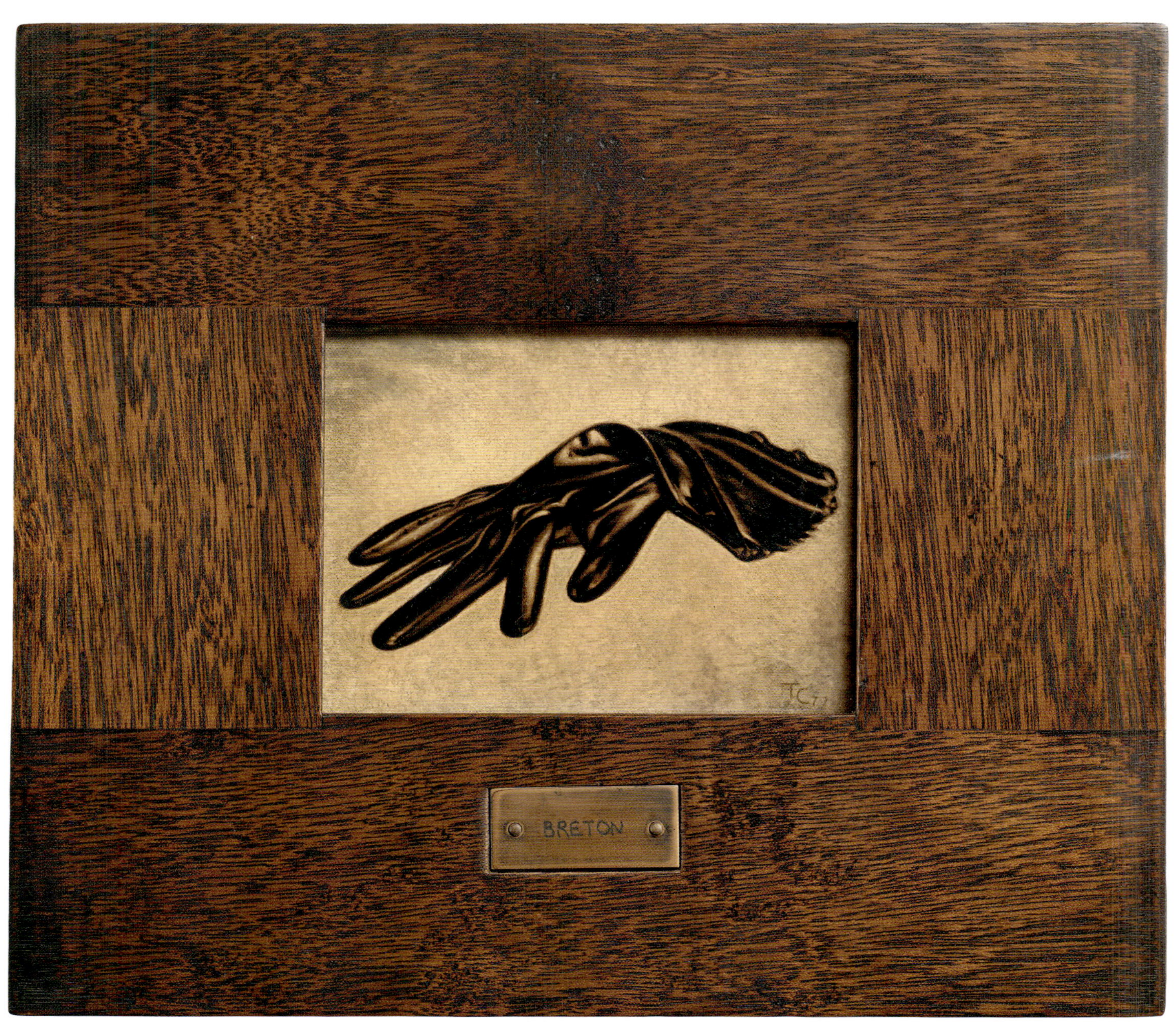

PLATE 69

André Breton (Glove), 1977

OIL ON PANEL

9¼ x 10⅜ INCHES (23.5 x 26.4 CM)

COLLECTION OF DR. AND MRS. PAUL RICHARDSON, PHILADELPHIA

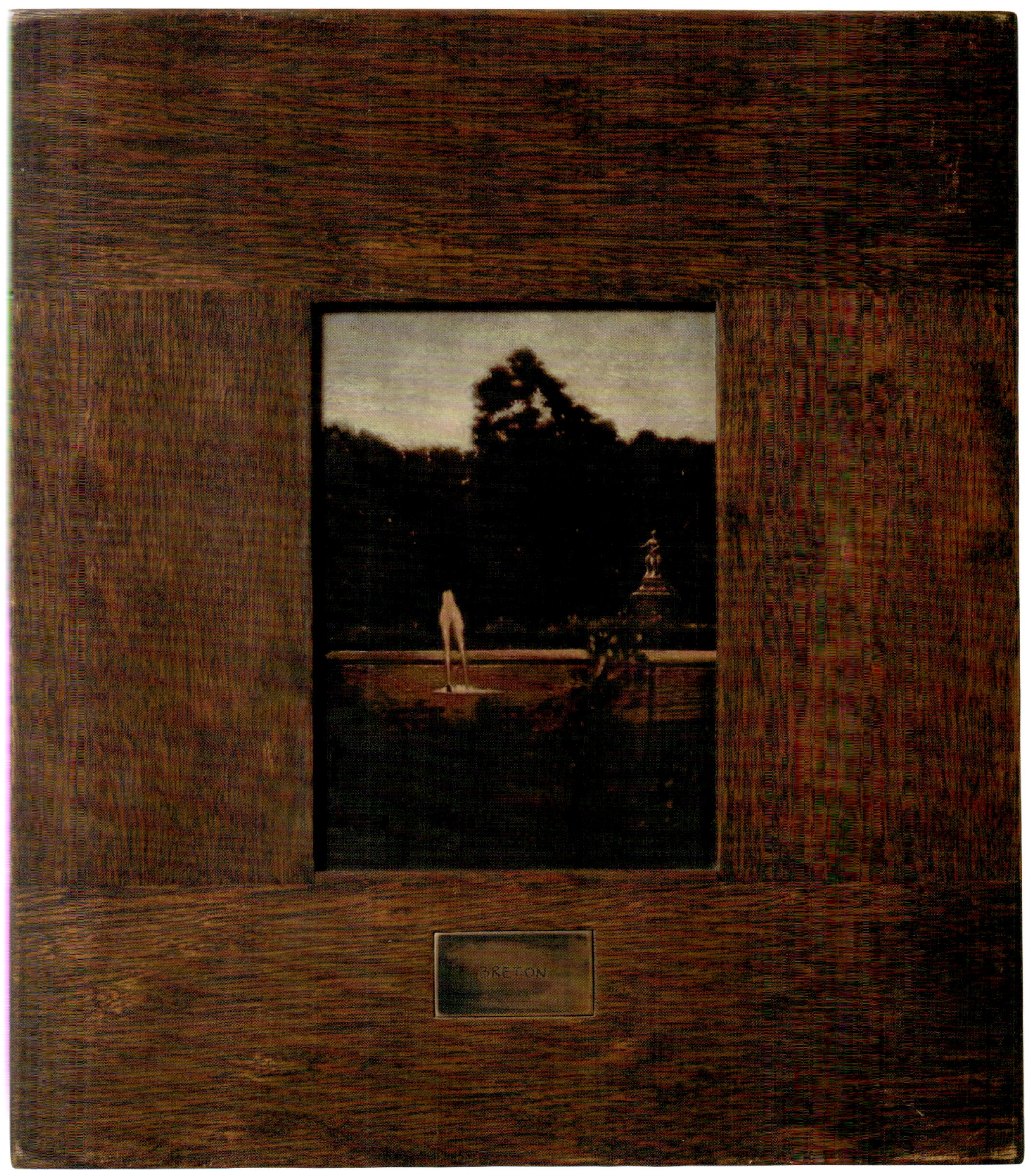

PLATE 70

André Breton (Landscape), 1977

OIL ON PANEL

14 x 12 INCHES (35.6 x 30.5 CM)

COLLECTION OF ROBERT EDWARDS, SWARTHMORE, PENNSYLVANIA

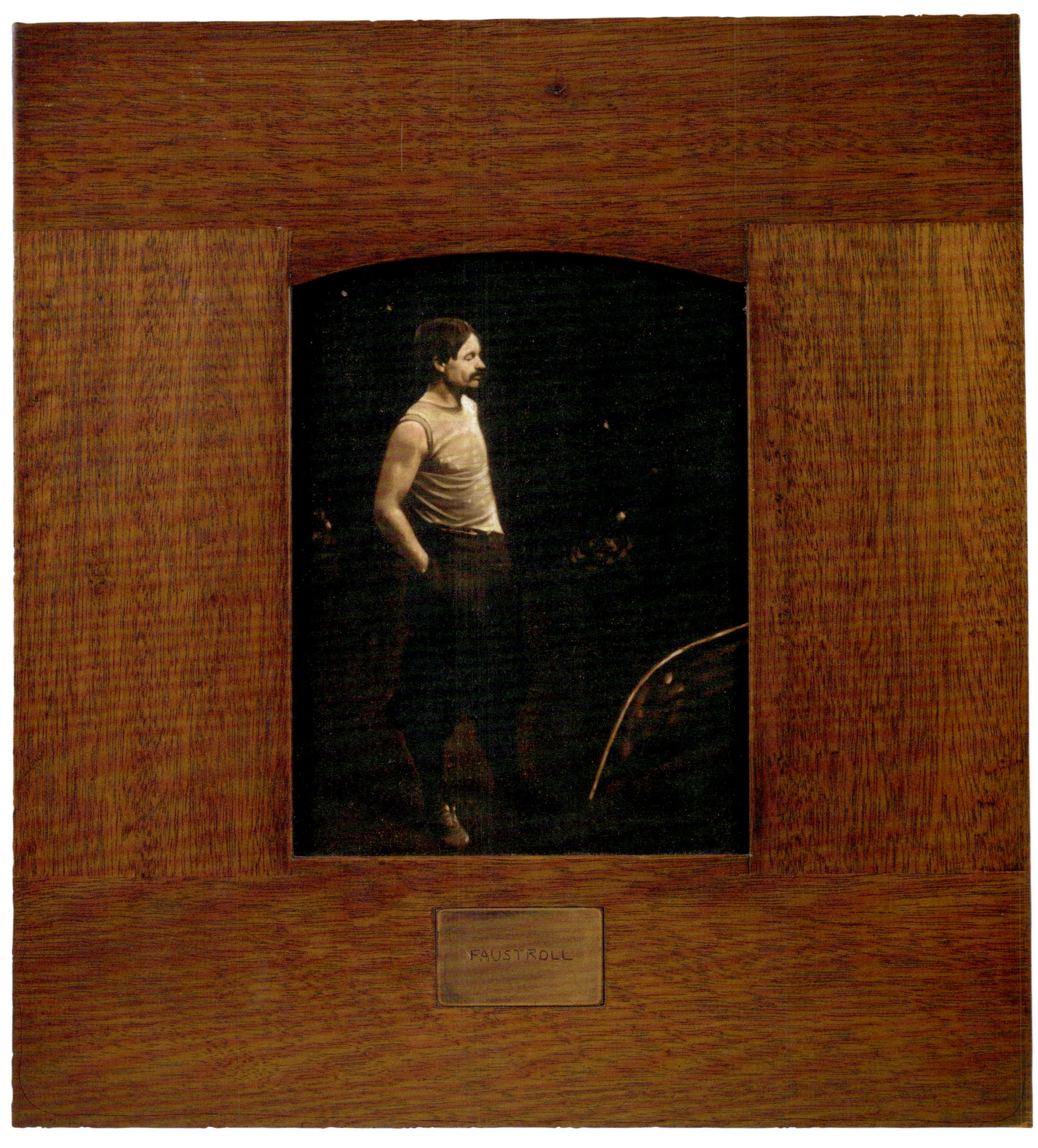

PLATE 71

Doctor Faustroll, 1977

OIL ON PANEL

14½ x 13 INCHES (36.8 x 33 CM)

THE FORBES COLLECTION, NEW YORK

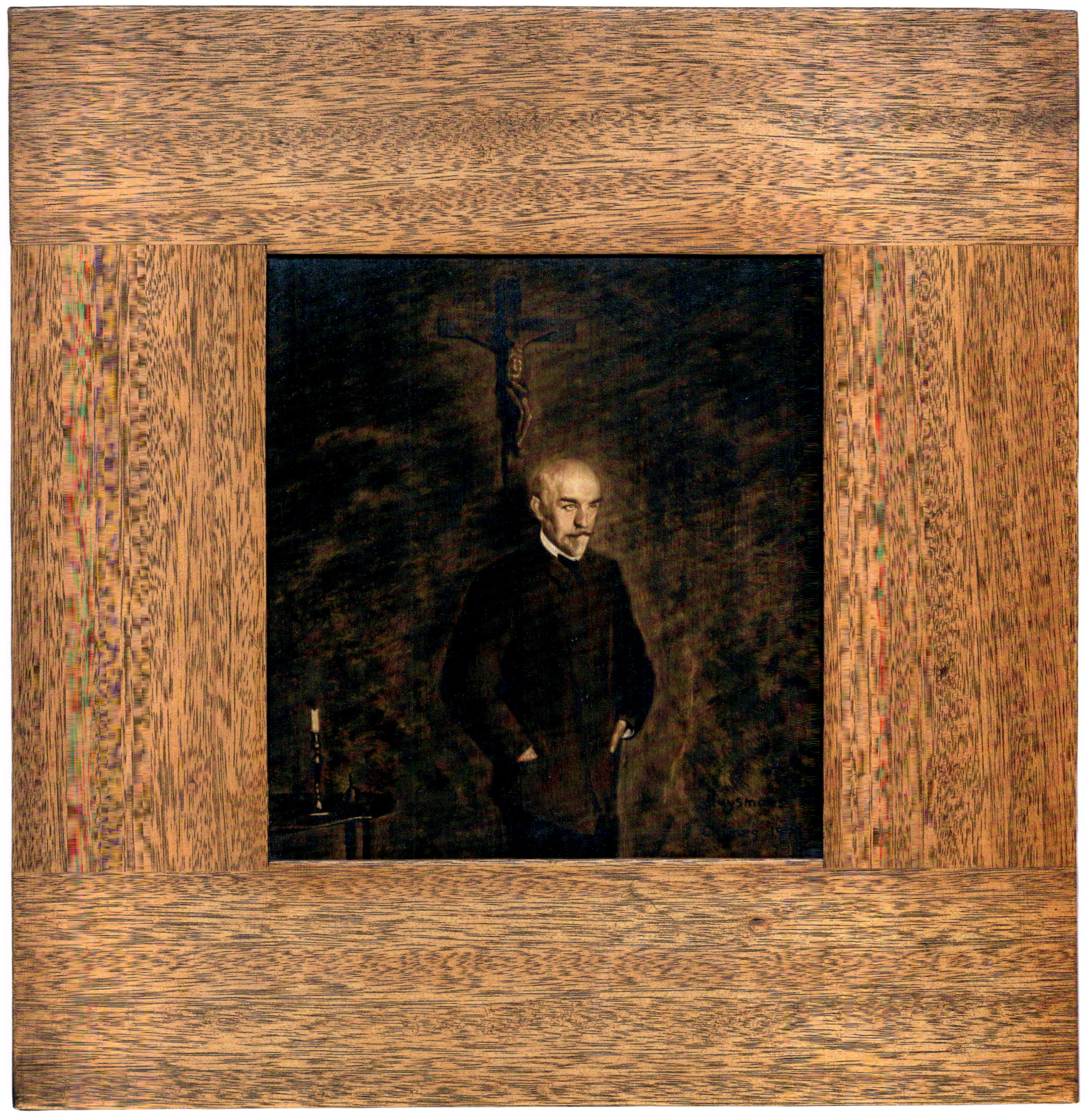

Plate 72

Joris-Karl Huysmans, 1978

Oil on panel

16 x 15⅟₁₆ inches (40.6 x 38.2 cm)

Private collection

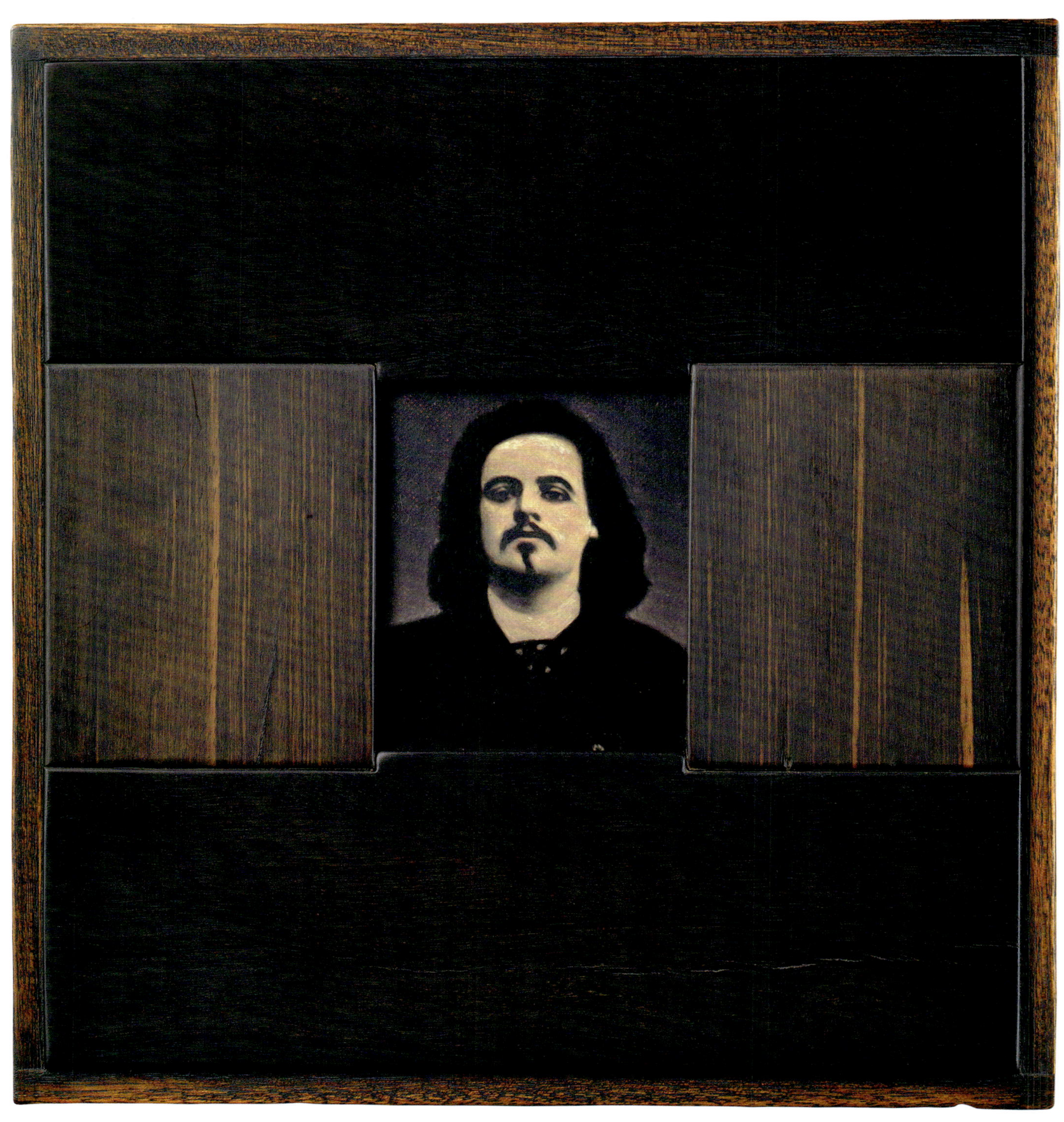

Alfred Jarry, 1978

OIL ON PANEL

9⅛ x 8½ INCHES (23.2 x 21.6 CM)

COLLECTION OF DR. AND MRS. ELLIOTT MANCALL, MIQUON, PENNSYLVANIA

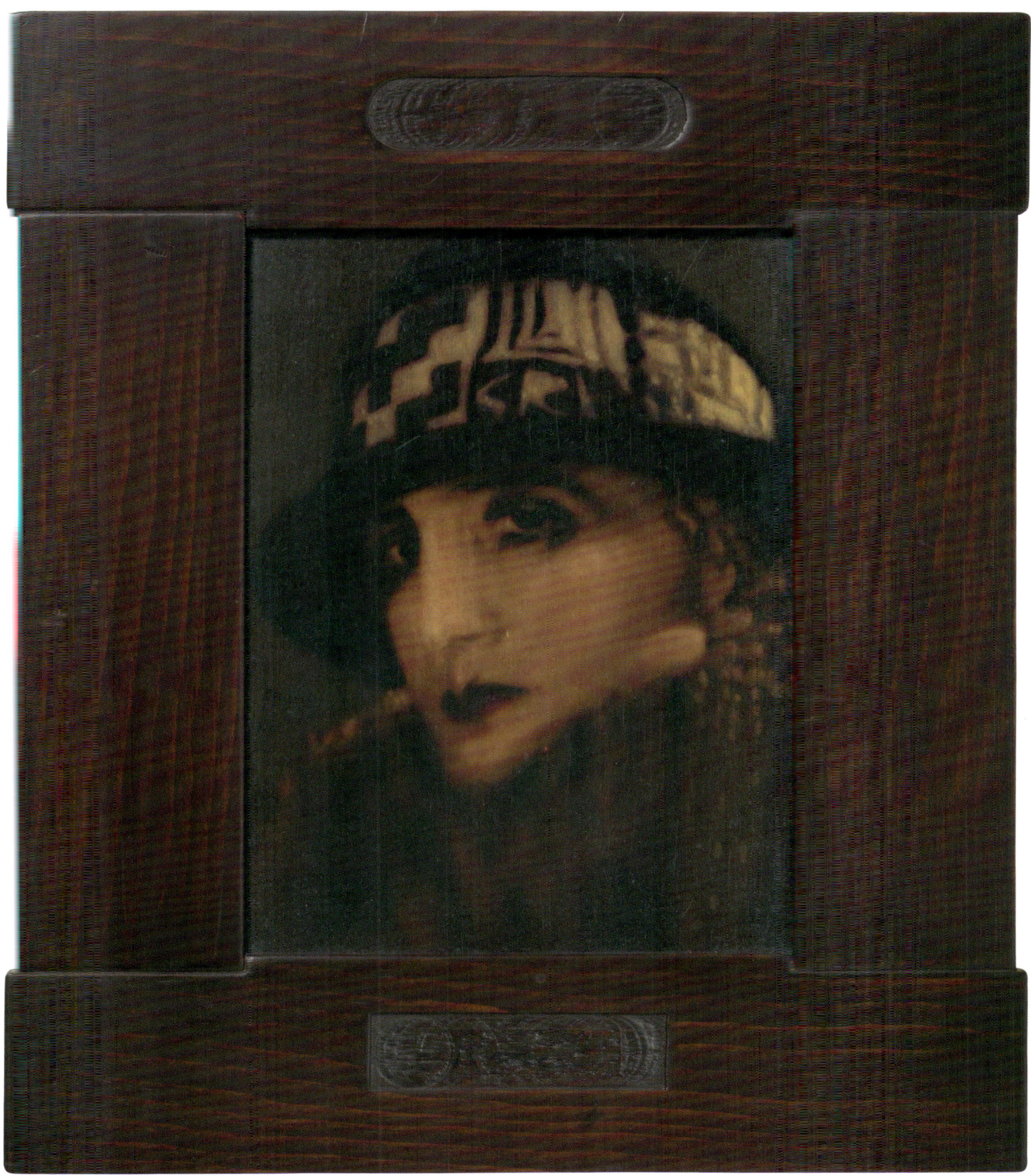

Rrose Sélavy, 1976

OIL ON PANEL

14⅝ x 12½ INCHES (37.1 X 31.8 CM)

PHILADELPHIA MUSEUM OF ART. GIFT OF DEBORAH J. ALLEN AND JUKKA HAMALAINEN 1991-97-1

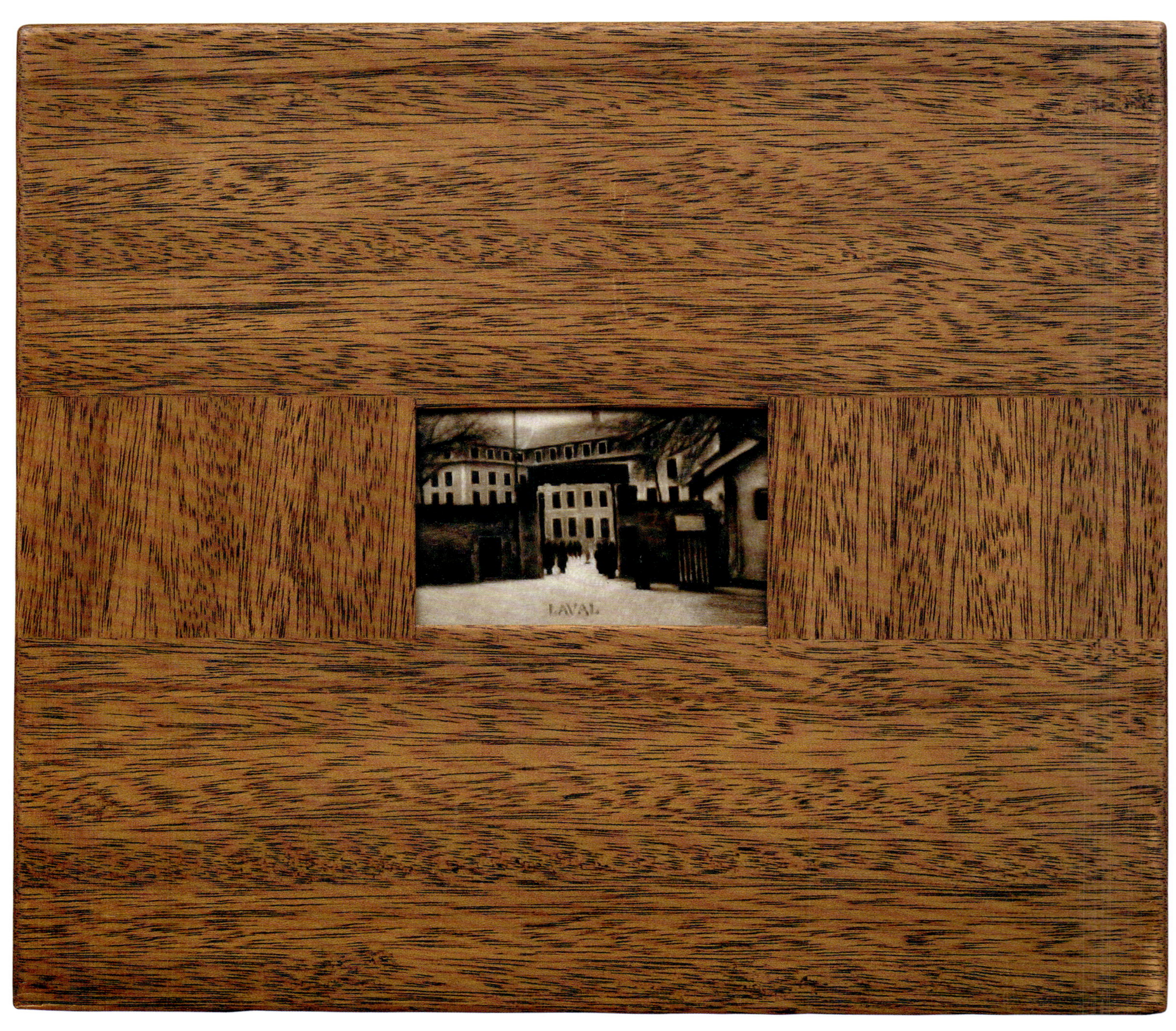

PLATE 75

Laval, 1978

OIL ON PANEL

9¼ x 10⅜ INCHES (23.5 x 26.4 CM)

PRIVATE COLLECTION, COURTESY OF LOCKS GALLERY, PHILADELPHIA

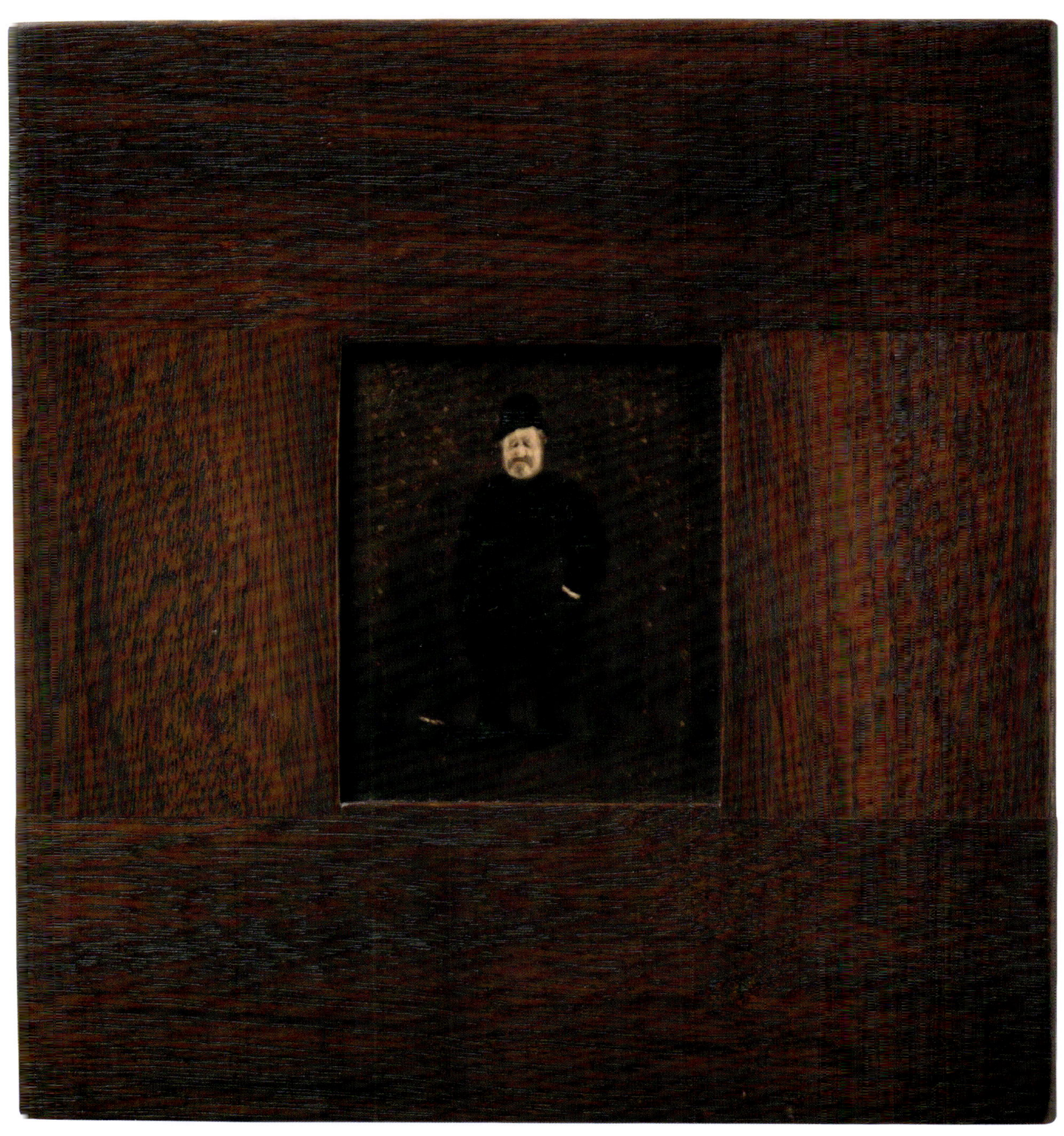

Hébert, 1978

OIL ON PANEL

9 x 8¼ INCHES (22.9 x 21 CM)

COLLECTION OF DMITRI AND SHEILA CHIMES, PHILADELPHIA

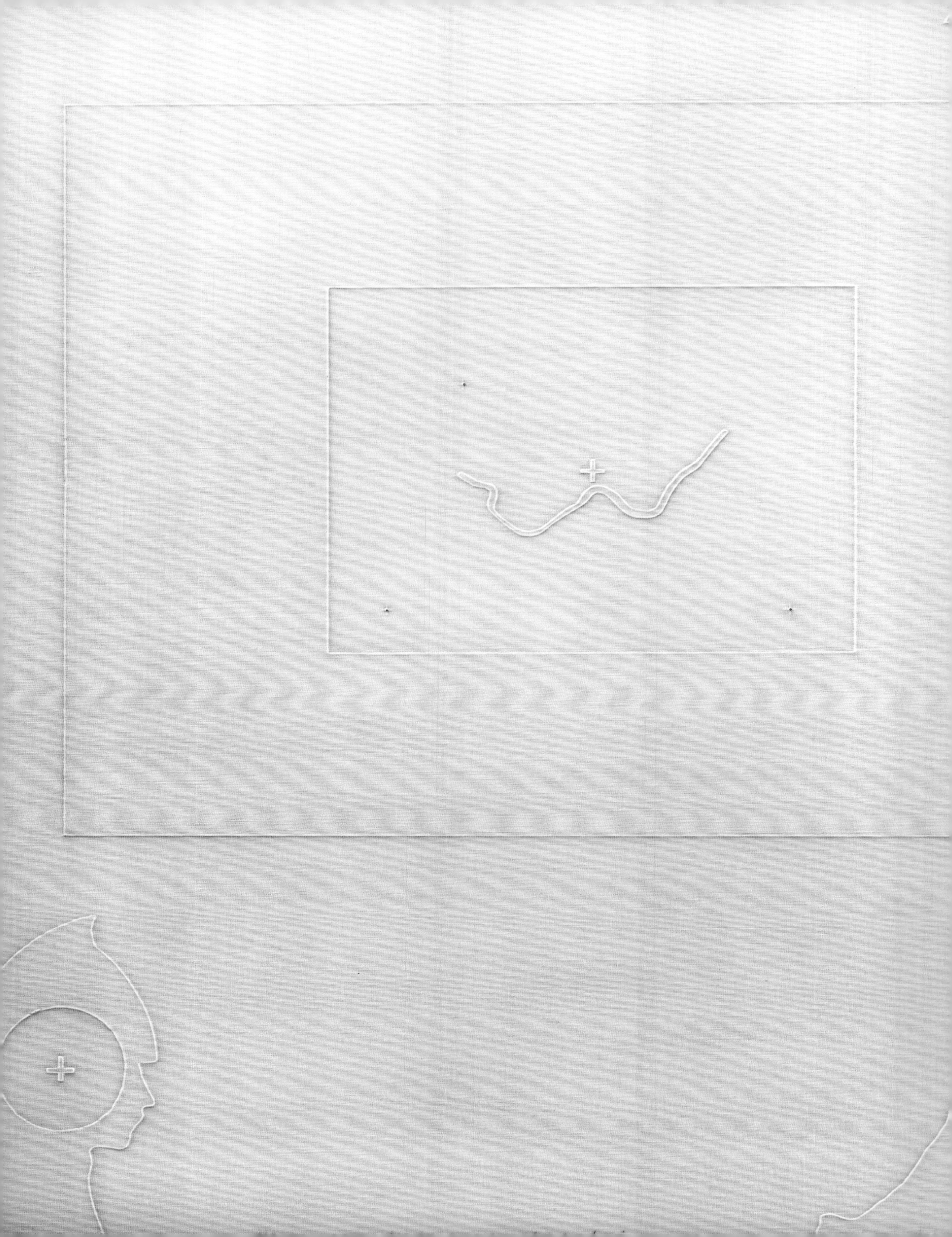

The termination of the panel portrait series coincided with painful events in the artist's life, specifically the decision by Dawn Chimes to move to Venice, Florida, in 1979. This separation from his wife of thirty-two years induced a crisis in both his work and his personal life, for which he received psychiatric counseling. In January 1980, Chimes moved from the space he had been renting on Church Street into a new, light-filled studio on the fifth floor of an apartment building on Spruce Street that had formerly been occupied by the artist Tommy Dale Palmore. Best known for his large, hyperrealistic paintings of gorillas, Palmore had left behind a huge stretched and primed canvas, measuring 90 by 114 inches, that had been taped to a pipe on the side of the studio facing the street, where it functioned as a screen to block the light from two side windows and prevent people across the street from looking in. Palmore had prepared this canvas with a mixture of gesso and Rhoplex, which gave it a malleable, textured ground that Chimes found so appealing that he purchased it from Palmore in March 1980 for $250. After having spent most of the previous decade working on the diminutive panel portraits, Chimes liked the challenge that this enormous canvas, with its beautiful, buttery surface, offered of working on such a formidable scale. He mounted the stretched canvas on the studio wall and began to examine its bare surface, in much the same way as he had done in 1953, when he returned to Philadelphia and scrutinized the surface and support of an empty canvas, only to discover the motif of the cross in the underlying stretcher bars. Although this period of study did not yield instant results, it did make Chimes determined to preserve in the finished painting the creamy texture of the priming he had inherited. He thought for a time of making a large painting based upon Monet's *Water Lilies*, but dropped this idea upon further reflection.

The solution to the problem of what to paint on this monumental canvas came one night when a high-spirited Chimes, having drunk a half-gallon of wine, climbed a ladder and began coating the pristine surface with a transparent ultramarine blue. He started painting with a regular artist's brush, but found it too intrusive and time consuming, since he wanted to capture the "to-hell-with-it" spontaneity of covering the entire surface in one evening. At one point, the artist even turned the brush on its side and used it to apply the paint liberally, although he disliked the marks left by the wooden handle and the metal clasp that holds the bristles in place, which scratched the otherwise immaculate surface of the canvas. Finally, the artist, now sober, went out to a kitchen supply store and bought a box of pastry brushes, which gave him the loose, impressionistic texture that he was after.

Having covered the canvas in ultramarine, Chimes then discerned a vague horizon line in the diluted washes of tingling blue that prompted him to turn the painting into a landscape with a waterfall. Once he knew his subject matter, the artist, trusting his intuition, transformed this timeless subject into a highly personal motif related to the collapse of his marriage. In 1950, the artist, his new wife, and his mother-in-law had driven from Chautauqua, New York, where Chimes had been teaching at the local art association during the summer, to Niagara Falls. Although not strictly speaking a honeymoon, this trip was filled with happy memories of their early marriage together, when they crossed from Buffalo into Ontario, Canada, to view the spectacular waterfall from the best vantage point.

The finished painting, entitled simply *Waterfall* (pl. 78), was completed during the summer

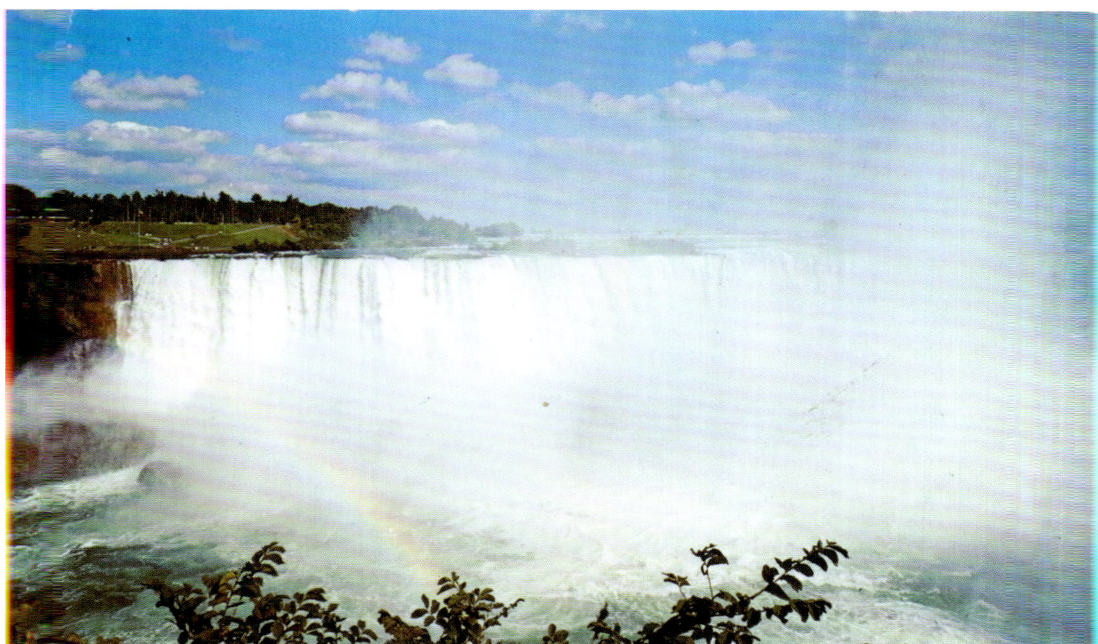

of 1980 with the aid of a color postcard of Niagara Falls (fig. 116) that Chimes purchased on that trip, thus infusing his majestic view of the cascading waterfall with personal associations, and continuing his reliance on photographic source materials, which had provided his imagery since the early 1970s. The vintage postcard offered a spectacular panorama of the vertiginous Horseshoe Falls from the Canadian side, where, as the caption described, "the churning waters of the great Niagara plunge gracefully to the churning, boiling turbulence of the 'Maid of the Mist pool.'" Chimes faithfully reproduced the wall of water falling over the precipice in the postcard, right down to the rainbow that spans the lower left-hand corner. This rainbow fascinated Chimes, and he even went so far as to study optics and color theory to obtain the vibratory effects of light and moisture in the work, which were achieved through calculated adjustments of color and tone from one brushstroke to the next, rather than through impressionist washes. The shimmering painting, which is bathed in a misty, vaporous atmosphere, deliberately evokes comparisons with nineteenth-century American painters such as Albert Bierstadt, Frederic Edwin Church, John Frederick Kensett, and Thomas Moran, all of whom painted Niagara Falls, often on a dramatic, monumental scale to convey the epic grandeur of the waterfall, which they believed to be a sublime wonder of the natural world and a source of national pride, even when viewed from the Canadian side.[209] Chimes was very much aware of these artistic precursors, especially Church's spectacular *Niagara* of 1857 (fig. 117), which he connects to the ideology of Manifest Destiny. However, the artist has also related the misty ineffability of his painting to the work of the American artist John Henry Twachtman (1853–1902), whose thinly painted snowy landscapes and evanescent scenes of sailboats in fog have been likened by the artist to the fleeting effect of moisture left by a breath on a windowpane.[210]

 Waterfall was also influenced by the virtuoso atmospheric effects of Joseph Mallord William Turner (fig. 118). The swirling, windblown clouds of mist and rain in Chimes's painting were clearly derived from Turner's technique of rendering mist, spray, and hazy distance. Indeed, such was Chimes's admiration for Turner at this time that he and Dawn, in an effort to rekindle their marriage, made a trip to Europe in October 1980, specifically to see the Turner paintings

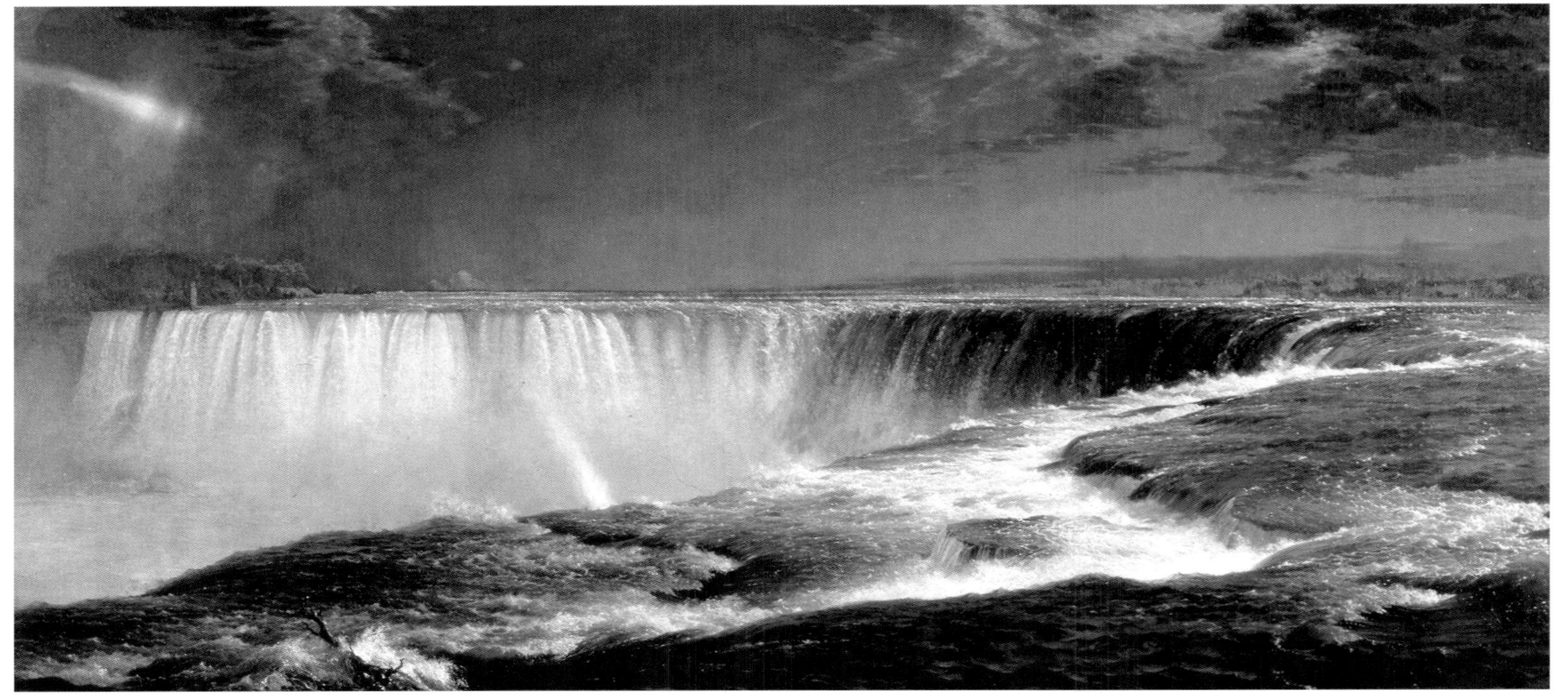

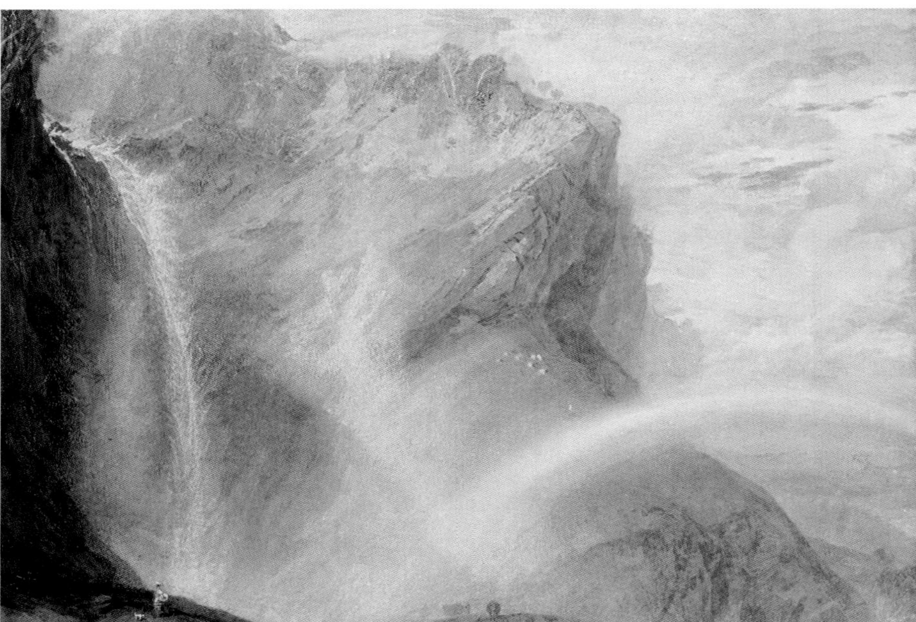

Fig. 117
Frederic Edwin Church
(American, 1826–1900),
Niagara, 1857. Oil on
canvas, 42½ x
90½ inches (108 x
229.9 cm). Corcoran
Gallery of Art,
Washington, DC,
Museum Purchase,
Gallery Fund, 76.15

Fig. 118
Joseph Mallord William
Turner (English, 1775–
1851), *Upper Falls of the
Reichenbach*, c. 1810.
Watercolor on paper,
10⅞ x 15½ inches
(27.6 x 39.4 cm).
Yale Center for British
Art, New Haven,
Connecticut. Paul
Mellon Collection

and watercolors at the Tate Gallery. This visit to England was followed by a trip to Switzerland, where Chimes viewed from a train window the famous Reichenbach Falls, near Meiringen in Haslital, which moved him to tears. The most famous literary association of this spot is with Arthur Conan Doyle's character Sherlock Holmes, who plunged to his apparent death over the falls in 1893 while struggling with his adversary, Professor Moriarty.[211] Chimes was fully aware of this fictional event when he glimpsed the waterfall from the train, connecting it to his own personal and artistic struggles of the time. Seeing this sublime phenomenon of nature, which Turner had painted in 1810, bolstered the artist's confidence and confirmed that he made the right decision to move away from the celebrated panel portrait series toward a new phase of his work characterized by luminous, ethereal landscapes.

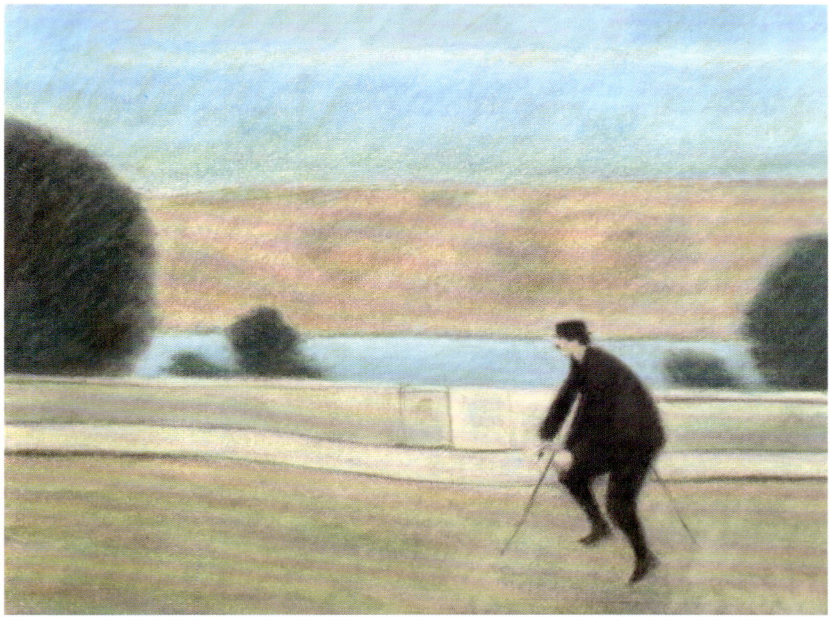

Fig. 119
Thomas Chimes, *Untitled (Faustroll on Bicycle)*, 1979. Pastel on paper, 19 x 25 inches (48.3 x 63.5 cm). Collection of Dawn Chimes, Venice, Florida

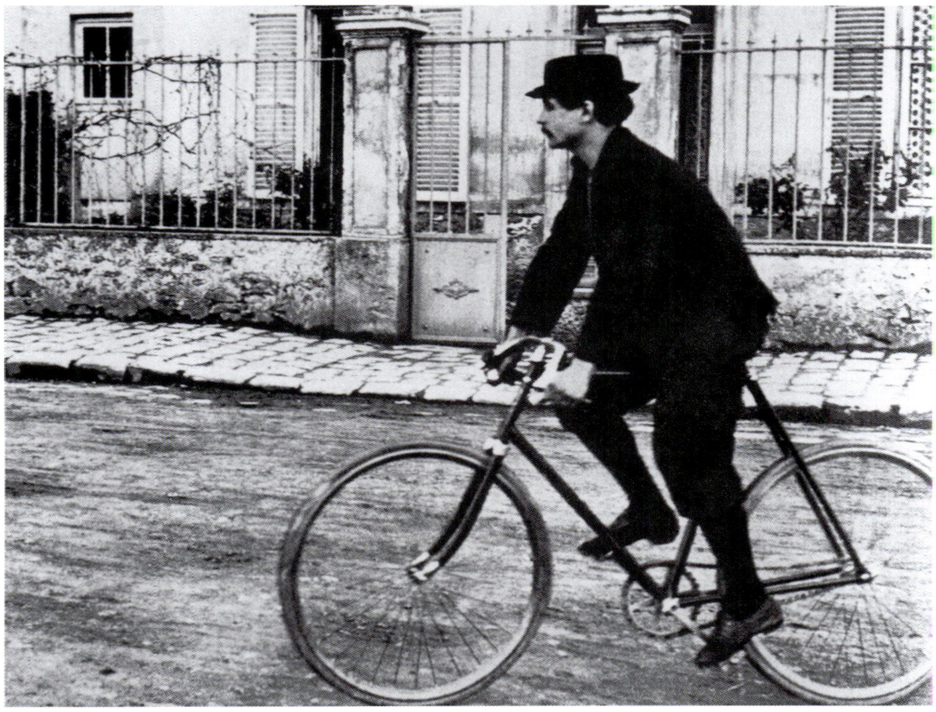

Fig. 120
Alfred Jarry on his Clément Luxe 96 bicycle, Corbeil, 1898. Photograph by Harlingue-Viollet, Paris. Reproduced in *Alfred Jarry: de los nabis a la patafísica* (Valencia: IVAM Centro Julio González, 2000), p. 10

Another key moment in the development of this new body of work was the artist's discovery of Jarry's bicycle in the arc of the rainbow that spans the lower left-hand corner of *Waterfall*, which Chimes read as the curved quadrant of a bicycle wheel. Once he was able to link the Niagara Falls painting with his earlier obsession with his literary hero, the artist began work on a number of landscapes populated by Jarry and his signature mode of transport. In *Morning*, of 1980 (pl. 77), and a related pastel study made the previous year (fig. 119), the artist took as his source material the striking photograph of Jarry, an avid bicyclist, riding his Clément Luxe through the streets of Corbeil in 1897 (fig. 120). Jarry had acquired the bicycle, the latest, fastest, and most elegant model on the market, in 1896 for the princely sum of 525 francs, of which he paid only a few derisory installments.[212] Chimes ingeniously removed the wheels of Jarry's bicycle, thus turning it into the skiff that Doctor Faustroll used to traverse Paris in *Exploits and Opinions of Doctor Faustroll, 'Pataphysician,* with the forks of the bicycle functioning as oars. The wheels are also alluded to in the shape of the two bushes that frame Faustroll in the landscape, which again refers to the view across the Schuylkill River that Chimes remembers from his youth, and which he had incorporated into his van Gogh–inspired landscape paintings of the late 1950s (see pl. 1; fig. 15).

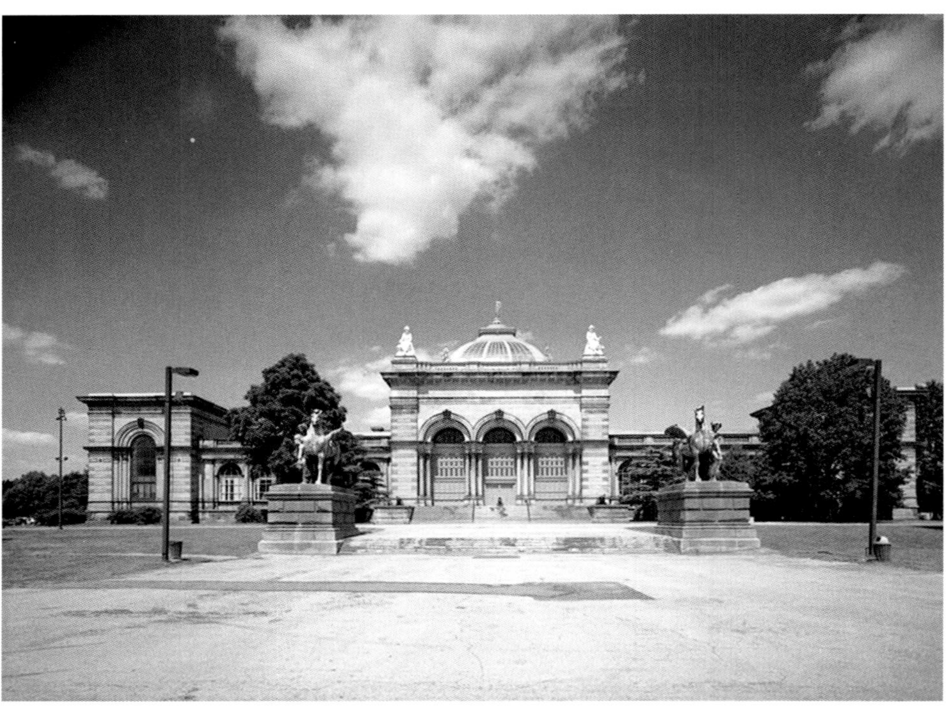

Fig. 121
Memorial Hall, Philadelphia, designed by Herman J. Schwarzmann and constructed for the International Exposition of 1876. Courtesy of the Library of Congress, Prints and Photographs Division, Washington, DC, HABS 114

Like *Waterfall, Morning* was painted in luminous colors applied with a pastry brush on a white ground, after Chimes read that Turner used a pure white ground for his paintings, whose colors have become increasingly brilliant with time.[213] However, the artist gradually drained all color from the landscapes that followed, many of them based on landmarks in Philadelphia such as Memorial Hall (fig. 121) and Belmont Plateau, as he sought to imbue his paintings with a glowing white light that eventually covered the entire canvas. First he jettisoned the secondary colors, then the primaries, and by 1985 Chimes's palette was reduced to titanium white and mars black in paintings such as *Rise Up, Man of the Hooths* (pl. 84), where an image of Memorial Hall is abstracted to the point of unrecognition.[214]

The purity associated with white made it an appropriate color for Chimes as he sought to re-create his childhood memories of Philadelphia. In 1981, Chimes began a series of paintings devoted to Memorial Hall, in which he distilled to its essence the image of this familiar public building in Fairmount Park, built for the nation's Centennial Exposition in 1876. Memorial Hall is situated across the Schuylkill River from his childhood home in the Brewerytown neighborhood of Philadelphia, near where his father ran a restaurant at Thirty-first Street and Girard Avenue. Memorial Hall takes on various forms in these paintings. At times the distant dome and flanking columns of the Smith Memorial Arch, of 1897–1912, combine to resemble the Taj Mahal, while in other works the Centennial structure is barely visible, shrouded in layer upon layer of white pigment as if a thick fog had descended on Fairmount Park (fig. 122). In these ethereal representations, Chimes presents us with the mere suggestion of Memorial Hall, recognizable only through its moundlike dome, which rises above the faint, blurry outline of the landscape. For art critic Barry Schwabsky, this image in the far distance of the breastlike protrusion of the Memorial Hall cupola, with the nipple formed by the standing statue of *Columbia* holding aloft a laurel wreath, represents "the euphoric resolution of a tension between the overwhelming nearness of the maternal breast and the elusiveness of a distant prospect, between origin and goal."[215]

In the years leading up to Chimes's divorce in April 1986, the white paintings hover on the edge of complete abstraction, thus reflecting the artist's sense of emptiness, pain, loneliness, and frustration during this difficult time. His feelings are perhaps best expressed in a poem he wrote at the time of his separation from Dawn in the early 1980s, which reads: "Winter is bitter / Everything is cold / Mutterings are distant now."[216] In the paintings that followed, Chimes takes on the role of the wandering Odysseus, missing his wife and trying to find his way home through a frigid wasteland that he connects with the final scene in James Joyce's melancholy short story "The Dead," which quotes a newspaper article announcing that "snow was general all over Ireland."[217] Joyce describes the accumulation of snow on the mountains, on the treeless hills, on the plains, and it "was falling, too, upon every part of the lonely churchyard on the hill where Michael Furey lay buried. It lay thickly drifted on the crooked crosses and headstones, on the spears of the little gate, on the barren thorns. His soul swooned slowly as he heard the snow falling faintly through the universe and faintly falling, like the descent of their last end upon all the living and the dead."[218]

In December 1982, Chimes had retired from his position as chairman of the sculpture department at Moore College of Art, which in 1986 honored him through a retrospective exhibition featuring twenty-seven paintings and five metal boxes. Early retirement allowed the artist to

Fig. 123.
Thomas Chimes,
Faustroll/Square, 1988.
Oil on canvas, 30 x
48 inches (76.2 x
121.9 cm). Pennsylvania
Academy of the Fine
Arts, Philadelphia.
Funds provided by the
Collector's Circle, 1992.5

devote more time to his work, since he had always found teaching to be a draining experience. The artist also devoted more time to reading and research, especially around the figure of Jarry, who reappears in the *Faustroll* paintings that the artist began making in 1984, such as *Faustroll (L'Infini)* (pl. 86) and *Faustroll/Square* (fig. 123), both of 1988, and *Watcher of the Night*, of 1989 (pl. 87). Using as his source the same 1897 photograph of Jarry on his bicycle, Chimes cropped the image so that only Jarry's hat, head, and shoulders are visible. In doing so, he drew attention to the fact that his own features had begun to resemble those of Jarry to the point where these works can be seen as self-portraits, especially after the artist took to wearing a soft porkpie hat that recalled the French author's headgear. As this imagery evolved, in works such as *Faustroll Helmet* (pl. 79), the head of Jarry/Chimes becomes streamlined and aerodynamic, thus recalling the earlier human-animal hybrid of the Mômo head (see pls. 19–22; fig. 49) and unifying the artist's themes and obsessions of the past twenty years in a single image, embedded in translucent layers of white paint that he began to associate with "emerging consciousness." As the artist explained to gallery owner Marian Locks in 1990, "What lays hidden and mysterious in the metal boxes and the panel portraits seems to show forth in the whiteness."[219] Also in 1984, which can in retrospect be seen as one of the key years in his career, Chimes returned to his pantheon of "possessed" poets, writers, and musicians, all of whom relate in some way to Jarry's life and work. Thus we have Jarry's one close female friend, Rachilde (the pseudonym of the novelist Marguerite Vallette-Eymery, wife of Alfred Vallette, who first published portions of *Faustroll* in his literary magazine, *Mercure de France*), whose canary-yellow high-heeled shoes Jarry wore to the funeral of the Symbolist poet and critic Stéphane Mallarmé in 1898.[220]

As Jarry's close friend and biographer, Rachilde (fig. 124) is often portrayed in Chimes's white paintings, beginning in a luminous work of 1986 in which her visage slowly emerges from underneath the flurry of white brushstrokes that covers it like a blanket of snow (pl. 80).[221] That year, Rachilde was joined in the white paintings by Poe and Joyce (pl. 82), both of whom had appeared in the panel portrait series (see pls. 47, 51; fig. 83), as well as the new figure of the avant-garde composer Erik Satie, whose musical compositions were just as revolutionary, humorous, and deeply personal as Jarry's writings. Chimes became interested in Satie through Shattuck's *The Banquet Years*,[222] and the composer would appear frequently in the white paintings—both as a young man, as in the 1987 painting *Sea-Bird Satie* (pl. 81), a reference to the fact that he had sailors in his family tree, and as the older, balding, and bespectacled *Satie Senex* (fig. 125), based upon a photograph taken by Constantin Brancusi in 1922.

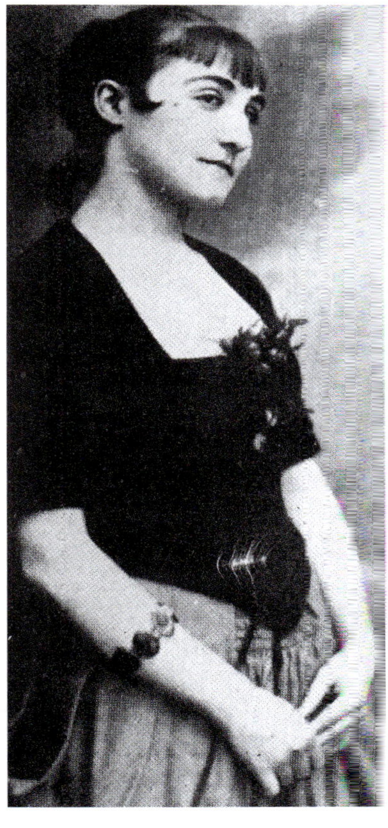

The longhaired figure of Jarry from the Nadar photograph also returns in *Alfred Jarry* (pl. 83), a large painting that Chimes completed in 1988, which reveals his utter veneration for the French writer. Jarry's head floats mysteriously in the center of the canvas, recalling the image of Christ impressed on the veil that Saint Veronica gave him to wipe his face with on the way to his crucifixion. Chimes also made a portrait of Doctor Faustroll's servant, the grotesque, dog-faced baboon named Bosse-de-Nage, who responded to any question or remark with a tautological "Ha-Ha." Jarry and his fictional character, as well as his former colleagues and followers, seem to emerge from within these paintings, as if seen under ice, suggesting that Chimes has summoned them from the spirit world and then allowed his imagination to project their visages through the many layers that make up the surfaces of the white paintings. The canvas thus becomes a membrane that is enlivened by the figures that appear like palimpsests on its surface, or pass through it to the other side, as in the impressively empty *Faustroll (L'Infini)*, of 1988 (pl. 86), in which Jarry is shown from the head up, endlessly traversing the unknown landscape of the imagination on his bicycle.

The writings of James Joyce had enthralled Chimes since the 1970s, especially after he learned that Jarry's work and ideas had informed the Irish author's literary technique.[223] By the mid-1980s, Chimes had digested *The Dead*, *Ulysses*, and *Finnegan's Wake* to the point where he identified with Joyce and his characters, such as Anna Livia Plurabelle from *Finnegan's Wake*, whose name appears on many paintings of that period (see fig. 122), perhaps as a surrogate for Dawn, whom he had finally divorced in 1986, as well as the Schuylkill River, since Joyce associated the River Liffey that runs through the heart of Dublin with Anna Livia's flowing tresses.[224] Like many visual artists, Chimes responded to Joyce's revolutionary use of language, word play, and stream of consciousness, which opened up new possibilities in his paintings.[225]

In his 1986 portrait of Joyce (pl. 82), Chimes took as his source material a 1915 photograph of the Irish writer in Zurich that was taken by Ottocaro Weiss (fig. 126). In the original photograph,

Joyce is shown strumming a guitar while seated on a stool. However, what drew Chimes to the image was the glare on Joyce's spectacles, which the artist exaggerated in his painting to the point where the glinting reflection on the eyeglasses appears to slice the writer's eyeball in two. Chimes painting thus brilliantly alludes to Joyce's poor eyesight, which had reduced him to near-blindness during his later years, through the chance discovery of the glinting eyeglasses in Weiss's 1915 photograph, which in turn reminded him of the opening sequence in *Un chien andalou* (An Andalusian Dog), the Surrealist film that Salvador Dalí and Luís Buñuel made in 1929, in which a passing cloud neatly bisects the moon only to dissolve into a horrifying image of an eyeball sliced open by a razorblade.

Like the recurrent motif of the moundlike dome of Memorial Hall, which Chimes painted throughout the 1980s, these works were created through the application of glaze upon glaze of blue, red, and green worked into a white ground and then wiped away to leave only a glowing suggestion of figures and faces, often floating in circles of pale light. The white paintings are thus imbued with a warm, atmospheric quality that separates them from the reductive purity and formal abstraction of work by the artist's American contemporaries, such as Agnes Martin, Robert Mangold, Robert Irwin, Robert Ryman, and Brice Marden. Although Chimes shares

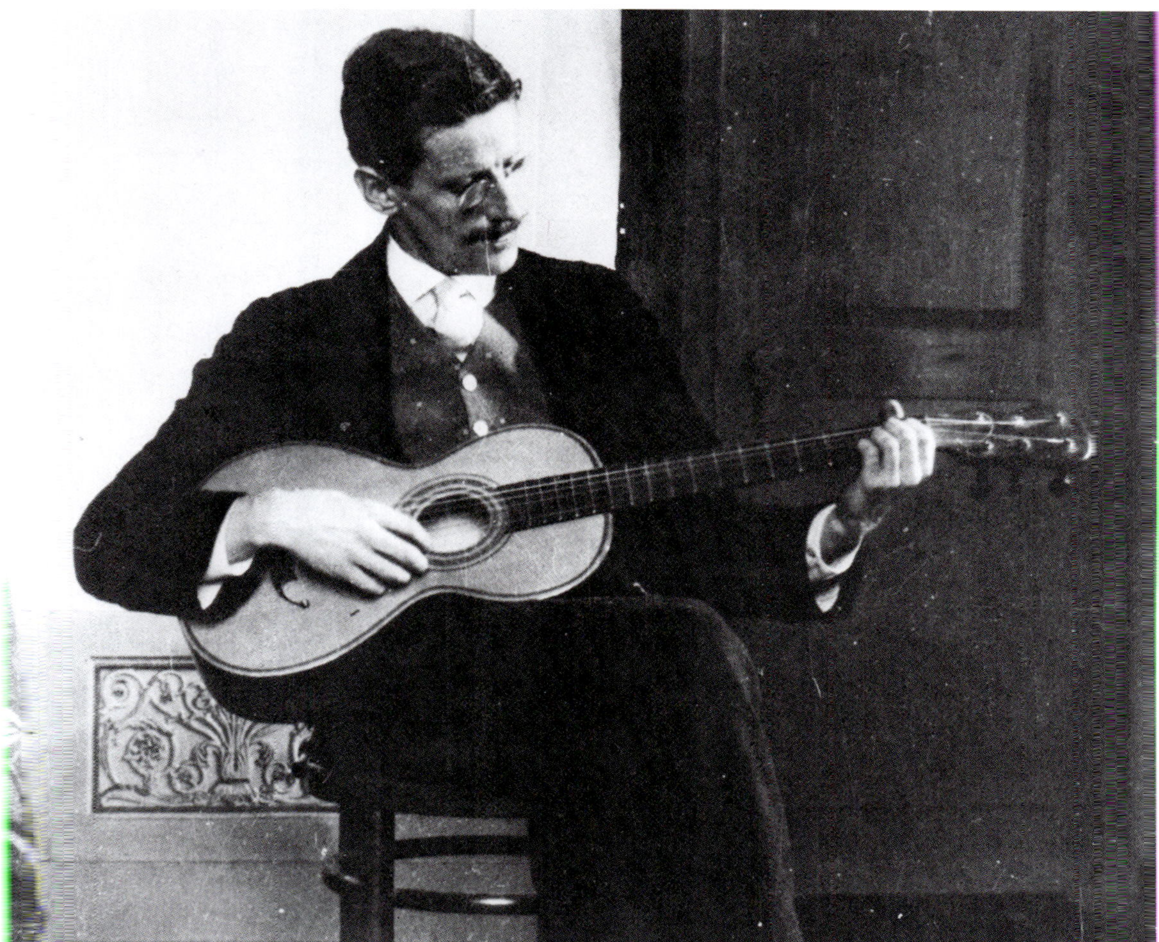

their interest in pristine, monochrome surfaces enlivened by exquisite mark-making, his interest in photography and memory separates his work from the pure opticality employed by the American painters of his generation. In a delightful pun on Jarry's use and abuse of ether, Chimes believes that his white paintings are truly ethereal in their translucent, many-layered surfaces, which is why his work contrasts so strongly with that of his peers.

These differences became apparent when Chimes's paintings were shown alongside those of the English artist Alan Charlton in an exhibition at the Institute of Contemporary Art in Philadelphia in 1994, entitled *Conversation Pieces* (fig. 127).[226] Although the works of these artists share a superficial resemblance in terms of restricted palettes and modular dimensions, Charlton's monotone gray paintings adhere to the rigorous formal program of Minimalism that Chimes had rejected in the mid-1960s due to its lack of humor and denial of sensuality. The cool, industrial aesthetic of Charlton's gray panels, whose flawless paint application and serial patterns of positive and negative space, especially when the deadpan surfaces of the evenly hung canvases play against the white walls of an art gallery, recalls the modular units of Donald Judd's Minimalist sculpture. In this respect they contrast starkly with Chimes's intimate white paintings, which upon closer inspection reveal a surprising level of detail, incident, and narrative content embedded in their sensuous surfaces. Unlike Charlton, whose work ends with the physical fact of the matte surface of his paintings, Chimes imagines a universe beyond the surface of his works, which he connects with Jarry's idea of luminiferous ether, the medium through which Doctor Faustroll travels after his death. The Philadelphia artist's divergent sources, which by the early 1990s included new interests such as the archetypal theories of Carl Gustav Jung, enhanced his preexisting fascination with the work and ideas of solitary sojourners like Jarry, Duchamp, and Joyce. This complex web of references was locked into place in his white paintings through a geometric organizational principle, often based on the Golden Section or the Fibonacci sequence of numbers, through which he calculated the exact placement of letters, circles, rectangles, stars, and other surface incidents.

At the end of the 1980s, Chimes began to enliven the surface of his large-scale Faustroll paintings with quotations from Jarry and other writers, from Homer to Joyce. According to the artist, as he "was painting one day, the landscapes were getting simpler and simpler, and a voice said, 'Write on the canvas,' so I did it. I wanted to do it."[227] This new development led the artist to dispense with the figure of Faustroll altogether in his paintings of the late 1980s and early 1990s, which consist of fields of

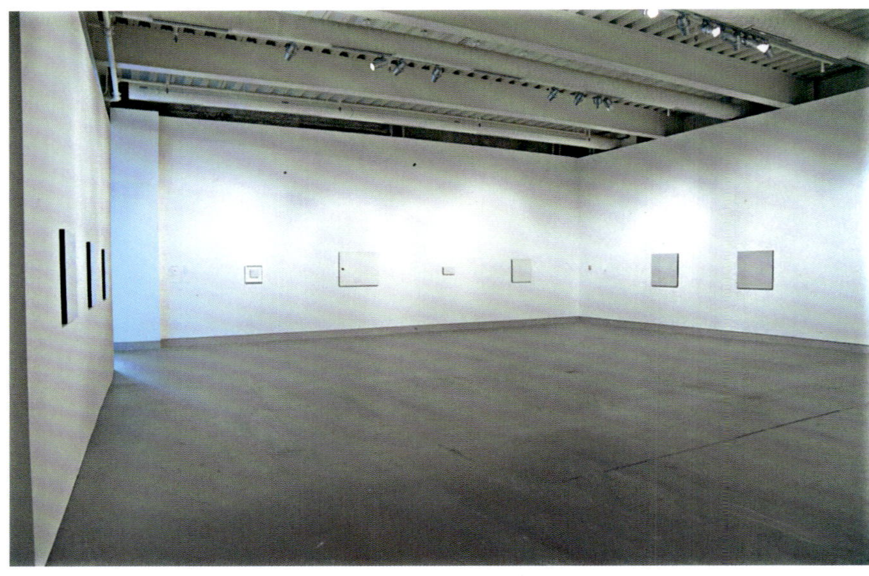

Fig. 127
Installation view of *Conversation Pieces*, Institute of Contemporary Art, University of Pennsylvania, Philadelphia, May 13–July 17, 1994. Courtesy of the Institute of Contemporary Art, Philadelphia

white paint containing written passages from Jarry's *Exploits and Opinions of Doctor Faustroll, 'Pataphysician* and Joyce's *Finnegan's Wake*, as well as Greek inscriptions. In works such as *Hermes*, of 1990 (pl. 88), Chimes was making paintings with the most minimal of means, having erased all letters from Jarry's writings except the Braille-like raised dots atop his "i"s. These points led Chimes to discover accidental constellations of his own making in this work and others that followed, which he related to actual configurations of stars in the night sky, such as Orion and Monoceros. This discovery would lead to a series of works in the 1990s in which Chimes developed complex geometric configurations reminiscent of the hermetic imagery of the metal boxes. These paintings often feature spirals, sickles, rotations, triangles, circles, charts, maps, and other arrangements derived from the books he was reading at the time, such as H. E. Huntley's *The Divine Proportion: A Study in Mathematical Beauty* and D'Arcy Wentworth Thompson's classic *On Growth and Form*. The mathematical precepts of these works, such as the Golden Section, provided the underlying structure of his hermetic imagery, which was increasingly based upon a complex intertwining of Jarry's writings and Greek mythology.

The figure of Hermes, the Greek god of commerce, eloquence, invention, travel, and theft, inspired an important series of paintings that Chimes made in the 1990s. Hermes fascinated the artist because ancient lore portrays him as a multivalent character capable of both good and evil: a cunning trickster and deceiver, as well as a healer and guide. According to Greek mythology, Hermes was the luck-bringing herald and messenger of the other gods, an intermediary who was also responsible for conveying souls to and from the underworld, thus connecting him with the artist's panel portraits of modernism's lost souls. As Chimes explained to his dealer and close friend, Marian Locks, Hermes was "the bearer of the golden wand, the caduceus, the symbol of the medical profession. Therefore, he is also the healer. He has a dark side in his connec-

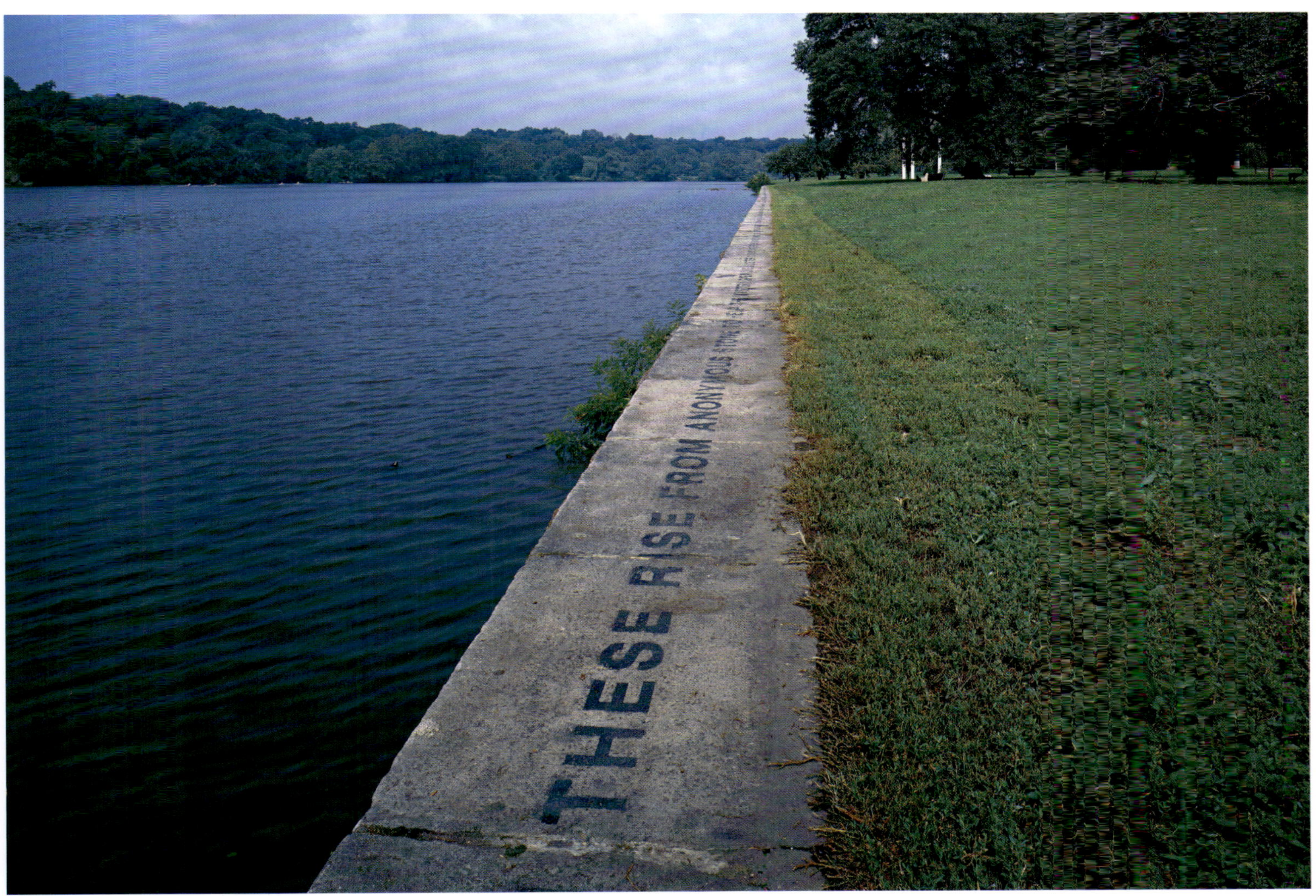

Fig. 128
Thomas Chimes and
Stephen Berg, *Sleeping
Woman*, Fairmount Park,
Philadelphia, 1991.
Photograph by Wayne
Cozzolino. Courtesy of
the Fairmount Park Art
Association, Philadelphia

tion with the night and the night is closely linked with Mnemosyne, the goddess of memory and the mother of the muses. When he whispers at night, we shudder. It is then that we must remember that he is also the healer and the bringer of light (the white shining)."[228] Chimes also conflated the figure of Hermes with that of Hermes Trismegistus, the legendary author of magical, astrological, and alchemical doctrines, whom Jung praised as "the patriarch of alchemy."[229] This would help to explain the deliberately veiled and indirect iconography of paintings such as *Hermes*, whose cryptic message remains mysterious.

SLEEPING WOMAN

Between 1986 and 1991 Chimes collaborated with Stephen Berg, the noted poet and founder of the *American Poetry Review* and the American Poetry Center, to create a 1,200-foot-long prose poem entitled *Sleeping Woman* (fig. 128) along the east bank of the Schuylkill River adjacent to Kelly Drive, in Fairmount Park. This collaborative project, commissioned by the Fairmount Park Art Association with generous financial support from the Pew Charitable Trusts, was created specifically for the retaining wall that runs along the grassy bank just past Boat House Row, and directly opposite Memorial Hall, which Chimes described as "this very special spot" where he and his friends had climbed cherry trees and played hide-and-seek when he was ten years old.[230]

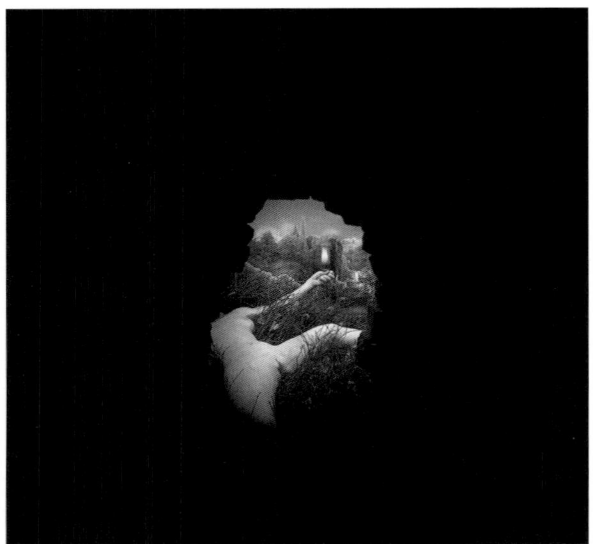

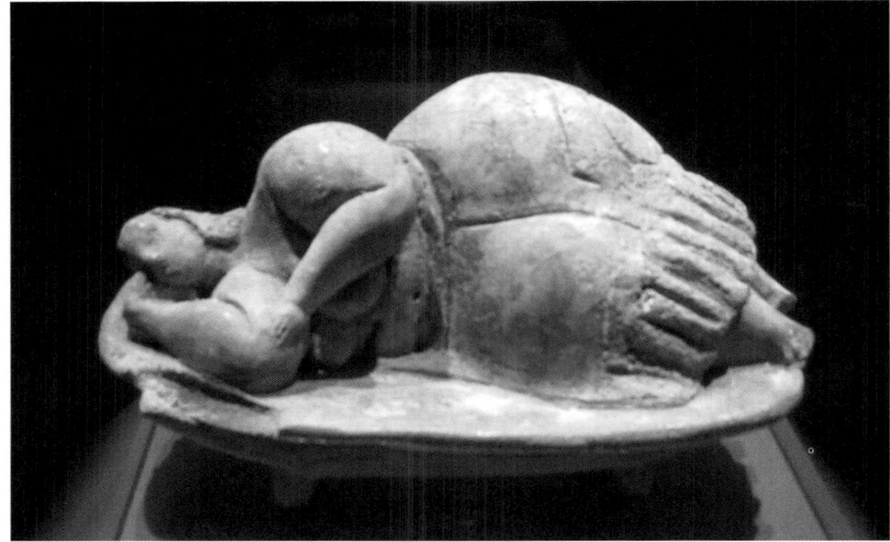

Berg also viewed the site as a sacred place imbued with personal memories, since it was where he came to mourn his father, Sidney Berg, who died of a heart attack in 1973, finding great solace in its natural beauty and consoling quietude.

Berg first submitted a proposal for the river-wall project to Penny Balkin Bach, executive director of the Fairmount Park Art Association, in a letter dated March 11, 1986, in which he outlined his plans for a "terrifically long" one-line poem that would be "imprinted" along the stone edge of the Schuylkill River.[231] Berg also suggested that the best artist for him to collaborate with on this project would be Chimes, "whose interest in literature is serious and whose ability to design a way of 'writing' the line I trust."[232] Berg and Chimes's initial proposal for a collaborative public art project was approved by the Fairmount Park Art Association in a letter dated November 6, 1986, and shortly thereafter they received a grant to further explore the possibility of "a literary and visual collaboration, accessible to the public, and responsive to the environment in which it is located."[233]

In a letter to Berg dated November 26, 1986, headed "Keep the River in Mind," Chimes described the "rush" of feelings and ideas that had come to him since accepting the commission.[234] At Chimes's suggestion, the two friends visited the Delaware Valley Regional Planning Office in the Bourse Building in Old City, where they researched the history of the site, and purchased aerial views of the Schuylkill River, seen from a height of 1,500 feet. These aerial maps, which showed the gentle curve of the river and the barely visible thread of the retaining wall, helped the two men conceptualize their project, while also reinforcing the connection in their minds between the Schuylkill and the curvaceous body of a reclining woman.

Chimes and Berg spent many hours walking along the stone wall at the river's edge, endlessly discussing the poem, whose dense, evocative, multilayered imagery comes out of these intense dialogues. Berg was initially inspired by Chimes's earlier paintings of Memorial Hall and the Belmont Plateau, which often contained sentences or titles written in India ink or pen along the bottom edge of the canvas, as in the Joyce-derived *O Tell Me All About Anna Livia Plurabelle* of 1981–88 (see fig. 122). These paintings were often filtered through the artist's deep appreciation for the writings of Joyce and Jarry, especially the passages of their work dealing with water and memory. However, Berg's first attempt to write the poem proved to be disastrous,

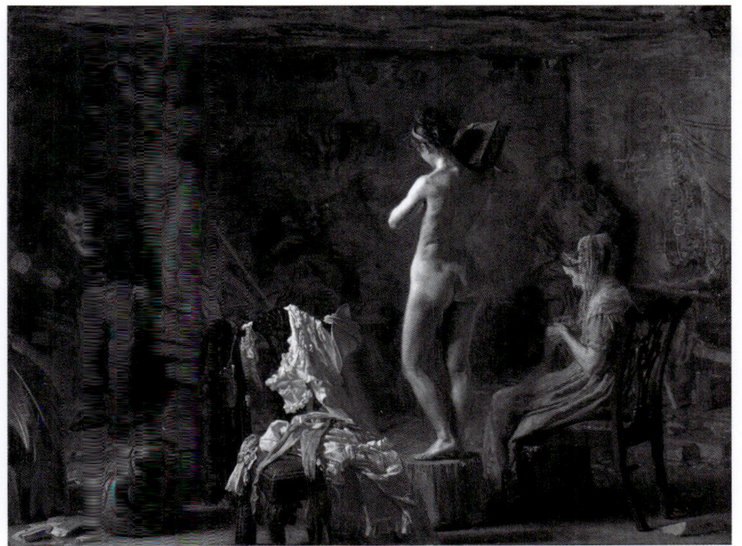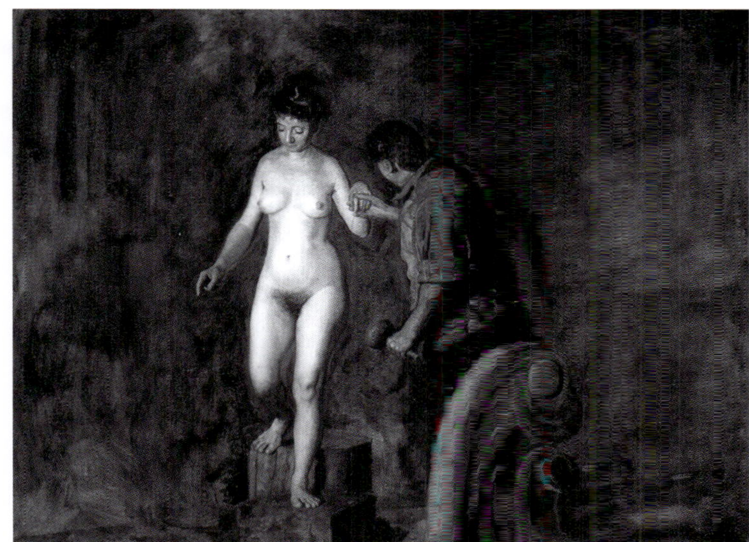

leading to a nine-month-long writer's block during which he produced a mere "three pages of very bad pseudopoetic prose," followed by a "string of little fake haikus."[235] Following the death of his mother, Hilda, in October 1987, Berg found his inspiration again, and the initial series of haikus metamorphosed into a single poem consisting of a long line of prose poetry with no sense breaks or punctuation, which Berg envisioned as "a long breath of speech."[236] The finished poem also gave voice to a wide range of earlier poets and writers, including fragments of haikus, and lines of verse and prose from Martin Buber, Yosa Buson, Emily Dickinson, Ezra Pound, Sappho, Sophocles, Wallace Stevens, Henry David Thoreau, and William Butler Yeats which give the sense of the work as a communal chorus.

Both men were conscious of associating the Schuylkill with the body of a woman, perhaps a mother or a goddess, or at the very least an androgynous figure tending toward the female to the point where they began reading a curve in the river as "the hip of a sleeping woman."[237] Once they had identified their subject, Chimes brought to the project a wide range of artistic sources, including Giacometti's hieratic sculptures and portraits of women, which he remembered seeing in the artist's dust-filled studio in Paris in 1952. Berg may have been inspired to write the line "a sleeping woman's luminous white face nameless breathing" after hearing his friend's recollections of this visit and looking at images of Giacometti's work, such as the extraordinary plaster busts of the early 1960s, which capture the gaunt features and hypnotic gaze of his wife, Annette.[238] The idea of the river as a primordial goddess or earth mother also brought to Chimes's mind the recumbent female figure in Duchamp's *Etant donnés: 1 la chute d'eau, 2 le gaz d'éclairage*, of 1946–66 (fig. 129), in the collection of the Philadelphia Museum of Art, as well as a Neolithic clay figurine of a recumbent woman (fig. 130), found in Malta that Berg discovered in the library of the University of Pennsylvania Museum of Archaeology and Anthropology. This figure was reproduced as *Sleeping Woman*, thus supplying the poet and artist with the title for their collaborative project.

Another important source was the work of Thomas Eakins, which became a constant reference point for both artist and poet during the project, due to the fact that the nineteenth-century artist had painted numerous rowing scenes on the banks of the Schuylkill, setting up his easel near and perhaps even on the site of their collaborative project. In his November 16

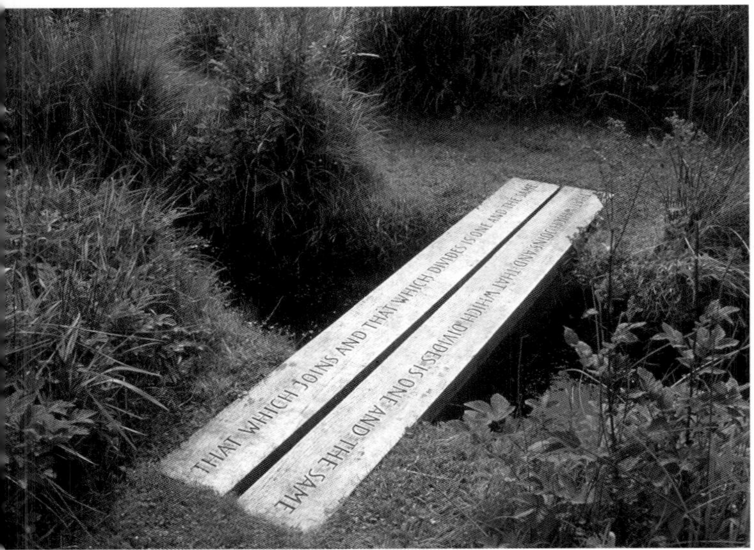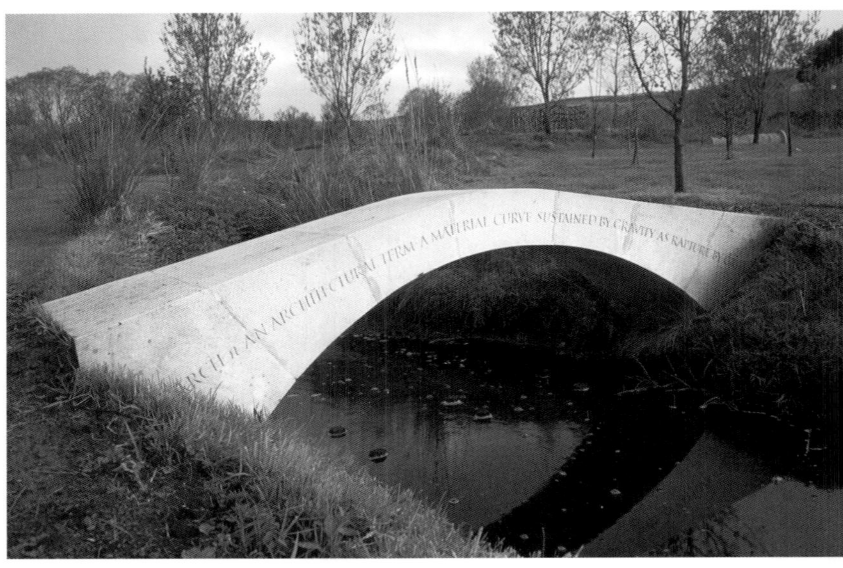

Fig. 133
Ian Hamilton Finlay
(Scottish, 1925–2006),
Little Sparta, Dunsyre,
Scotland, c. 2003. Bridge
(2 planks) with inscrip-
tions. Photograph by
Andrew Lawson

Fig. 134
Ian Hamilton Finlay,
Little Sparta. c. 2003.
Bridge with inscription.
Photograph by Andrew
Lawson

1986, letter to Berg, Chimes enclosed photocopies of two of Eakins's paintings depicting the Philadelphia-based sculptor and ship-carver William Rush working on an allegorical sculpture personifying the Schuylkill River for the Fairmount Waterworks, the neoclassical pavilions that still stand on the east bank of the river just west of the Philadelphia Museum of Art in Fairmount Park (fig. 131). For one of the paintings, *William Rush and His Model*, of about 1908 (fig. 132), Chimes added the subtitle "(The Schuylkill)" and speculated that the burly figure on the right leading the naked model down from her wooden plinth might have been Eakins himself. Chimes explained that he was sending Berg these photocopies "to show what I mean by personification. Note 'presence' of Rush (William) and river and . . . any presence can be personified."[239]

The use of language was a key component in contemporary artistic practice in the 1980s and 1990s, and Chimes and Berg were no doubt aware of the work of John Baldessari, Jenny Holzer, Barbara Kruger, Bruce Nauman, and Richard Prince, all of whom experimented with the written word as their primary visual medium during this period, through paintings, neon signs, installations, and carved inscriptions on stone benches. However, *Sleeping Woman* does not share the often humorous or polemical approach to language of these artists, which ranges from wordplay, puns, and jokes, in the case of Prince and Nauman, to the overtly political messages of Holzer and Kruger. In retrospect, Berg and Chimes's sensibility seems much closer to the work of the Scottish poet and artist Ian Hamilton Finlay, whose use of visual poetry within a landscape setting strongly resonates with *Sleeping Woman*.

Although his name has never been connected with the project, or even mentioned in passing by Berg and Chimes, Finlay's dramatic transformation of the upland landscape around the small farm where he has lived since 1966—*Stonypath*, or as it was rechristened in the 1970s, *Little Sparta*—similarly used the natural beauty of the Scottish countryside as the permanent site for one-word inscriptions and poems on stone plinths, paths, and bridges (figs. 133, 134), whose elegiac themes were often drawn from Greek mythology, philosophy, literature, and art history, such as the paintings of Claude Lorrain and Nicolas Poussin. Berg was aware of Finlay's concrete poetry and may have seen images of his *Little Sparta* and other, later public art projects that use text patterns to intervene within the institution of the sculpture park or public garden,

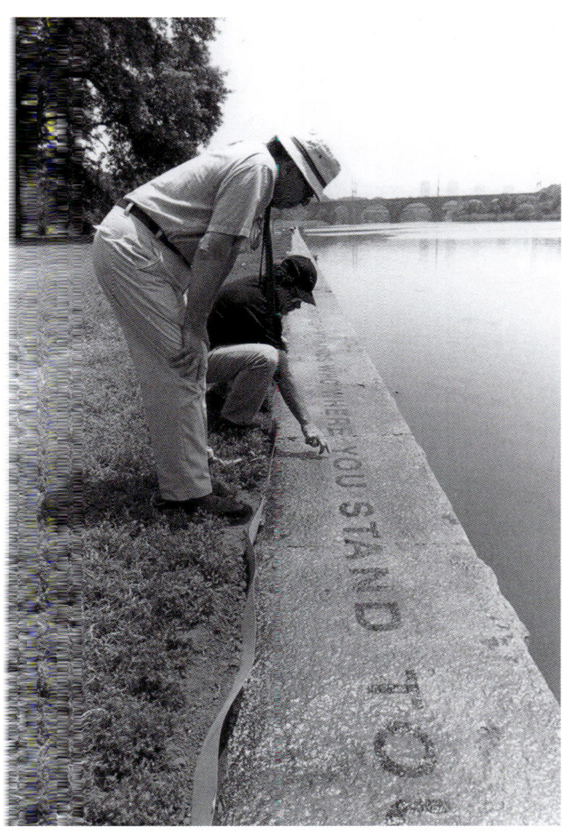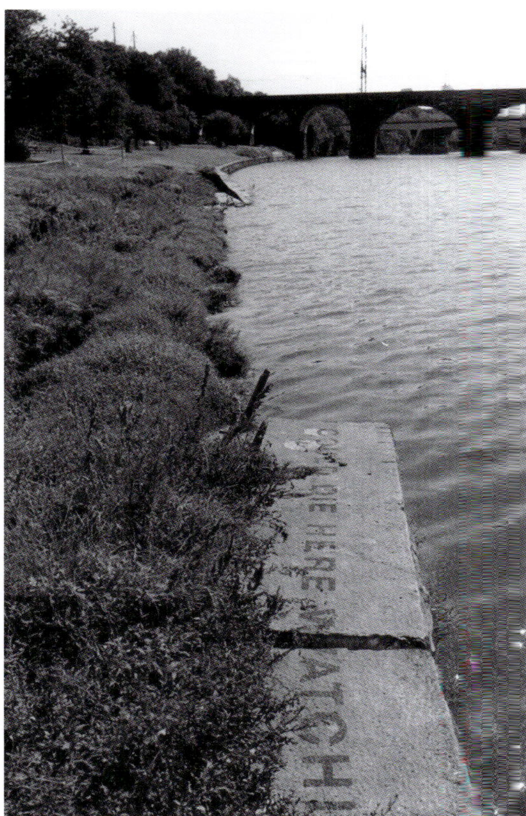

causing visitors to experience art and poetry in new and unexpected ways.[240] Like Finlay, Berg and Chimes augmented and transformed the public spaces along the Schuylkill River through a luminous, glassy ribbon of visual poetry that speaks to the reader from the ground, rather than the pages of a book, thus evoking the performative oral tradition of ancient Greek texts.

Over the next five years the two friends refined their ideas, rejecting an early suggestion to carve the letters directly into the stone slabs in favor of applying the words with several coats of clear acrylic polyurethane over a black-tinted acrylic polyurethane enamel paint, specially created by Tnemec Coatings Laboratory in Kansas City.[241] The final coat of the clear acrylic polyurethane contained a granular mix that enabled it to resist freezing, thawing, ultraviolet fading, goose droppings, graffiti, and skid marks from skateboards.[242] Drawing upon his extensive artistic training, Chimes designed the stenciled letters used in Berg's poem and dealt with the logistics of size and spacing. He also chose the special polyurethane paint used to adhere the text to the stone ledge. Once applied, the black-tinted letters created a sinuous, meandering line of poetry that separates the winding river from the grassy bank, thus allowing passersby to read and follow the text as it snakes its way upstream just beyond the Girard Avenue Bridge, like a "choral voice rising out of the site."[243]

The series of acrylic polyurethane coatings that formed the poem's 1,823 letters were applied between May and July 1991 by an outside contractor, Peter Freudenberg of Pine Street Studios (figs. 135, 136). Working with computer-generated stencils to Chimes and Berg's specifications, Freudenberg initially applied the letters by hand with a brush, often allowing the paint to trickle beyond the edge of the stencil. Although Berg and Chimes liked the accidental feeling that occurred with the brush, Freudenberg soon grew tired of this backbreaking application and finished the poem with a spray gun that gave the letters a clean outline.[244]

The words emerge from the stone retaining wall in much the same way that the visages of
Satie or Joyce shimmer and glow from within Chimes's white paintings, in which numerous
coats of thinly applied, translucent glazes accumulate to form a pristine surface like polished
glass. Chimes later described the text that meanders along the riverside as a "legible whisper,"
whose letterforms can appear and disappear according to the angle of view, changing weather
conditions, and variable light.[245] The entire poem was deliberately formatted without punctuation, using five-inch-high black capital letters, in a Helvetica typeface, that were carefully
spaced out so that the center of the text is marked by the word "RIVER."

An elaborate dedication ceremony was planned to commemorate the completion of the
work in July 1991, including a torchlight procession along the riverbank and Japanese Kodo
drummers and dancers. Unfortunately, just a month after the work was finished, and shortly
before the dedication ceremony was scheduled to take place, a 250-foot section of the Victorian-
era retaining wall containing the first sixty-one words of the poem collapsed into the muddy
waters of the Schuylkill River after a storm, thus permanently disrupting the flow of the text by
removing its opening section.[246] When Chimes first informed Berg, who was on vacation in
Vermont at the time, that a section of their work had sunk into the river, the poet was appalled,
viewing the collapse as a personal attack.[247] Citing Duchamp's acceptance of the cracks that
permeate *The Large Glass* (see fig. 53), after the two glass panes that make up the work were
accidentally shattered in transit in 1927, Chimes managed to convince Berg that the collapse in
August 1991 was an integral part of the project, which was intended to exist in cooperation with
the elements, and whose theme was the transformative power of nature. The two men always
knew that the letters would eventually fade and disappear, probably over the course of fifteen
to twenty years, at which time they would decide whether it should be restored. The collapse
of the retaining wall simply speeded up this decision-making process, while also adding new
meaning and complexity to the work, which they now viewed as having a will of its own, seemingly beyond their control.

When asked to comment publicly on the partial destruction of *Sleeping Woman*, Berg
replied: "I'm not depressed. I see it as something that extends meaning of the line." To his
mind, the collapse itself "embodies a major theme" of the poem, "which is that an awful lot of
what people are living through all the time has nothing to do with their will. . . . It was chosen
by a greater power."[248] After much debate, the poet and artist finally decided against replacing
the capstones bearing the lost lines when the wall was eventually repaired, requesting that blank
stone tablets be inserted in their place, thus acknowledging the assimilation of the missing
words into the natural environment.

The partial sinking of *Sleeping Woman* sparked the artist's interest in entropy, defined as
the quantitative measure of the degree of disorder in a system, which has continued to play an
important role in his work ever since. According to the Second Law of Thermodynamics, the
natural world, both organic and inorganic, moves from an orderly state to an ever-increasing
dissipation and degradation before arriving at a final state of maximum disorder.[249] The notion
of entropy and its implications have long fascinated artists and have been particularly associated
with the writings and artworks of Robert Smithson. In his 1966 article "Entropy and the New
Monuments," Smithson argued that recent large-scale Minimalist sculpture was "not built for
the ages but rather against the ages" and thus has "provided a visible analog for the Second

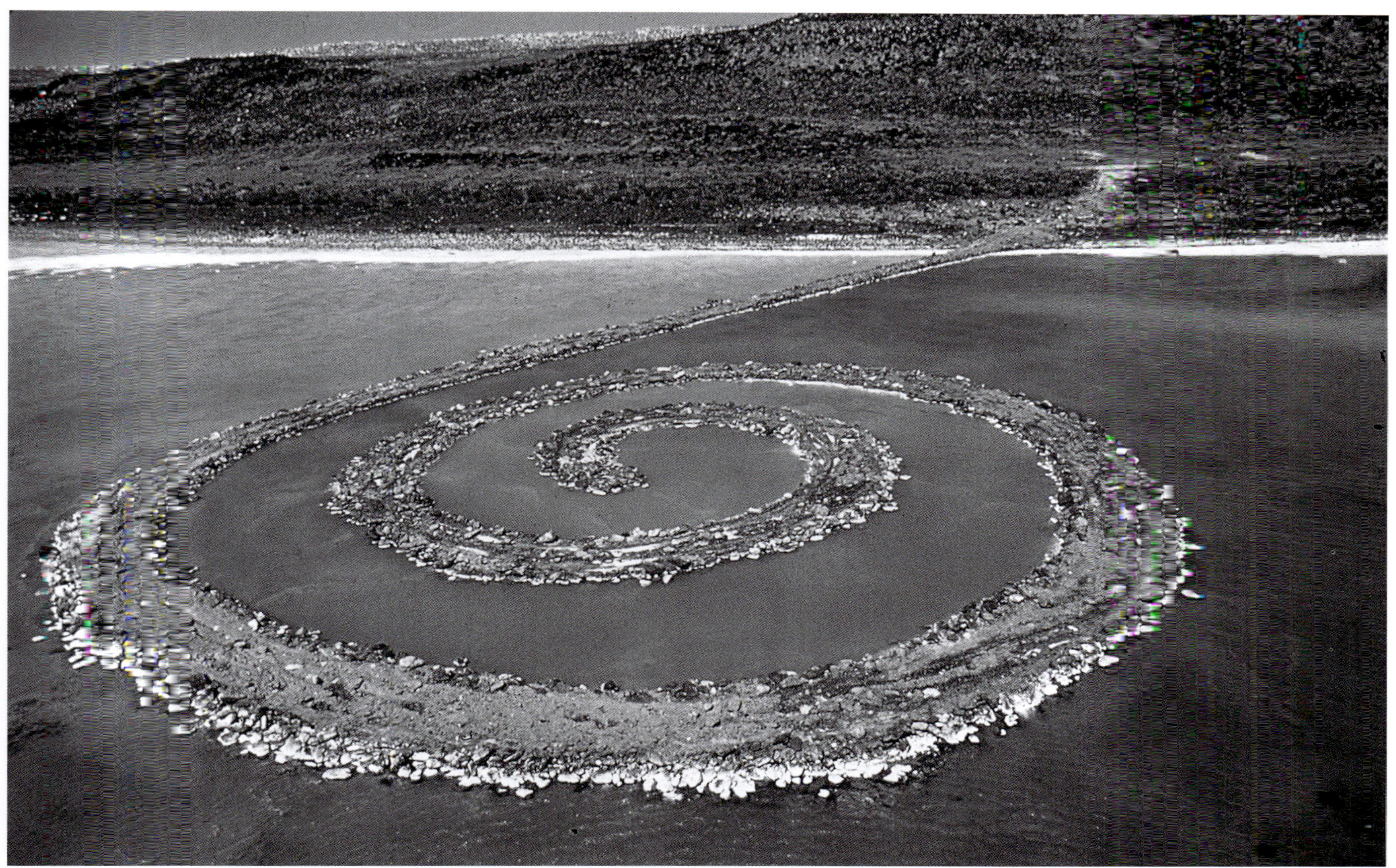

Fig. 137
Robert Smithson, *Spiral Jetty*, Great Salt Lake, Utah, April 1970. Black rock, salt crystals, earth, red water (algae); 3½ x 15 x 1,500 feet (1.07 x 4.57 x 457.2 meters). Courtesy of the James Cohan Gallery, New York

Law of Thermodynamics."[250] Smithson went on to describe this law, also referred to as Carnot's principle, after the pioneering French physicist Nicolas Sadi Carnot, as that "which extrapolates the range of entropy by telling us energy is more easily lost than obtained, and that in the ultimate future the whole universe will burn out and be transformed into an all-encompassing sameness."[251]

Smithson created a number of drawings of entropic landscapes, featuring backwaters or fringe areas, in the late 1960s and early 1970s, and also collaborated with the process of entropy in his epic "Earthworks" of the same period, which allowed for the imminent disappearance or destruction of the work through powerful acts of nature caused by climate change and harsh weather conditions. As Smithson explained in a 1971 interview with Gregoire Müller, "Wreckage is often more interesting than structure."[252] The artist favored chaos, degradation, and disorder over the utopian ideals of his contemporaries, who sought to tame nature rather than work with natural forces such as erosion and decay. In *Spiral Jetty* of 1970 (fig. 137), for example, Smithson anticipated and allowed for climate changes and natural disturbances in the Great Salt Lake in Utah, celebrating the magnitude of the untamable forces of wind and water by coexisting with them, rather than using modern technology to impose his will. *Spiral Jetty* was at one point completely submerged in the lake, but has recently reemerged coated in glistening white salt crystals, its form reminiscent of the famous spiral navel that adorns Ubu's belly.

Like Smithson, Chimes viewed the partial disintegration of *Sleeping Woman* as a natural occurrence that was bound to happen over time, as the river and grassy banks gradually

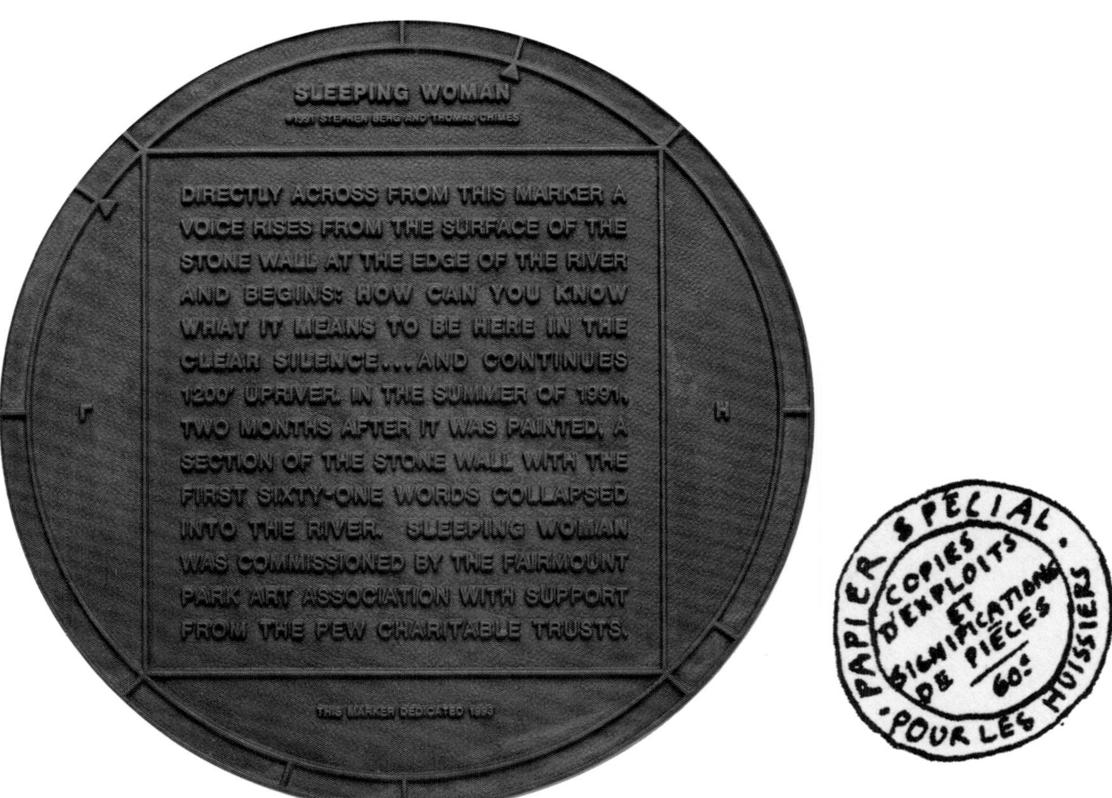

reclaimed the man-made barrier. Viewed in this way, the work becomes a part of this entropic process, rather than an attempt to stave off decay, floods, wind, and the ravages of time. Anticipating its own demise, the work "lives" all the more powerfully and poignantly while it is with us. Resisting all suggestions on how to restore the work, which ranged from placing facsimiles of the missing stones along the retaining wall to dredging the existing capstones from the bottom of the river, Chimes and Berg finally settled on a permanent bronze marker to commemorate the partial sinking of *Sleeping Woman*, which was placed near the site of the collapsed bulkhead on November 13, 1993 (fig. 138). This marker, which Chimes based on the "Official Paper for Bailiffs" stamp (fig. 139) used by Panmuphle in Jarry's *Exploits and Opinions of Doctor Faustroll, 'Pataphysician*, took the form of a bronze disk, thirty inches in diameter, with a twelve-inch border of exposed river stone aggregate. The marker is mounted on a three-inch raised-earth mound that gives it the appearance of a submerged sphere.

Like *Sleeping Woman*, the circular bronze plaque contains multiple meanings and personal associations for Berg and Chimes, who used the proportions of the Golden Section to determine its exact size and location. The disklike shape is intended to evoke associations with a shield, a clock, a mandala, a compass, a sundial, and the earth, a reading that is reinforced by the raised Greek letters *gamma* and *eta*, which signify "earth" while also reminding those reading the marker of Chimes's Greek heritage. Indeed, the artist no doubt intended these Greek letters to evoke the famous line from Xenophanes of Colophon, written in the sixth century B.C., "From Earth are all things, and to earth all things return," which is inscribed on an arched niche on the north side of the Philadelphia Museum of Art. Nature's reclamation of a portion of the retaining wall is also referenced in the triangular shapes inscribed on the disk's surface to indicate the axis lines that lead to the location of the collapsed sections of the curbstones.

A trip Chimes took to Greece with his son Dmitri in October 1995 led to a new body of work based upon maps, such as *Nous constaterons plus loins que de passé est par de la future vu de la machine*, of 1996 (pl. 90), which continues his references to the ancient world as well as his beloved Schuylkill River. This trip was prompted by the artist's strong resurgence of interest in the ancient history and mythology of the land of his heritage in the late 1980s and early 1990s, evidenced by the cycle of paintings devoted to Hermes (see pl. 88), the Greek messenger god who created music for mankind by a fashioning a lyre of tortoiseshell. Inspired by the Homeric Hymns of Hesiod, these paintings, including *Concerning the Tortoise*, of 1991, and *Concerning the Dimensions*, of 1992 (fig. 140), also refer to Jarry's *Exploits and Opinions of Doctor Faustroll Pataphysician*, which contains numerous chapter titles that similarly begin with the word "Concerning," as in "Concerning the Line" or "Concerning the Surface of God."

By 1990, the figure of Jarry had briefly disappeared from Chimes's paintings, only to be replaced by the abstract ideas that the author presents in his *Doctor Faustroll*. These concepts include Jarry's meticulous calculation for measuring the surface of God, which progresses, via an impeccable logic and mathematical notation, "from postulate to corollary to conclusion," in which he adduces proof that "God, being the shortest path from zero to infinity, is the point tangential to both."[253] Chimes began to write out this definition of God in India ink on the surfaces of his paintings of the early 1990s, thus precipitating a return to the figure of Jarry, now in incised relief, in the 1994 profile portrait *Concerning Roads* (pl. 89). The use of raised letters or lines in this work and others that followed connect them with the 1993 bronze marker commemorating the partial collapse of *Sleeping Woman*, as well as the tinted words of the outdoor poem itself, which like the words or letters found in his subsequent paintings emerge from and recede below the surface according to changing light conditions. The *Sleeping Woman* marker encouraged Chimes to take a more rigorously geometric approach to his work, in which the placement of words, figures, and shapes is determined by the Golden Section, as well as Jarry/Faustroll's own mathematical formulas and speculations.

For Chimes, the intellectual side of Jarry embodied in the character of Doctor Faustroll was much more interesting than the satirical schoolboy farces that make up the *Ubu* plays. Although he finds in Ubu, Jarry's grotesque personification of greed, ignorance, and cowardice, a hilarious and even profound condemnation of the base instincts of the human condition, it is the quasiscientific ideas of 'Pataphysics that have taken a remarkably tenacious hold on his imagination since the 1960s. Having said that, the figure of Ubu, identifiable from Jarry's famous woodcut (see fig. 73), and other images of Ubu with a walruslike mustache (fig. 141), began to reappear in Chimes's paintings in 1999 (pl. 92), based Jarry's own sketches of his protagonists. At times the artist conflated Ubu and Faustroll, as in *Portrait of Pa Ubu, Inventor of 'Pataphysics* (pl. 93).

Jarry's woodcut, which was reproduced in Paul Fort's monthly review *Le Livre d'art* on April 25, 1896, to accompany the first unabridged publication of *Ubu Roi*, created an easily identifiable, almost cartoonlike image of Ubu, with his strange pointed head and bulbous belly, for which Jarry invented the term *gidouille*.[254] This enormous gut bears the emblem of a nebular spiral, almost like a target or bull's-eye, which identifies the insatiable *gidouille* as the

Fig. 140
Thomas Chimes,
Concerning the Dimensions, 1992. Oil and india ink on wood, 12 x 12 inches (30.5 x 30.5 cm). The Buckingham Family Collection, Larchmont, New York

source of Ubu's unbridled greed and malice. In Chimes's most recent paintings, the embossed figure of Ubu appears alongside, or sometimes facing, Doctor Faustroll, their raised profiles immediately identifiable. Dispensing with the bloated, pear-shaped body with its spiral insignia, Chimes once again concentrates on the head as the locus of consciousness, often encircled by a nimbuslike arrangement of concentric circles.

Chimes has come to view the white paintings as the culmination of his career, which in retrospect he sees in terms of the four stages of alchemical transformation, leading through the *nigredo* of dissolution of the panel portraits toward the *albedo* of a new genesis in the white paintings. Indeed, as if to emphasize this point, in the past five years Chimes has allowed gold to enter his palette, creating ethereal white paintings with raised, gold-tinted lettering or imagery on carefully prepared, modular wood panels, all measuring approximately three by three inches (pl. 94). These paintings can be seen as a summation of his themes and obsessions, since the artist recapitulates earlier motifs such as the crucifixion and armor head imagery of the 1960s, and even variations on the classical head he produced at the Art Students League in 1946 (see

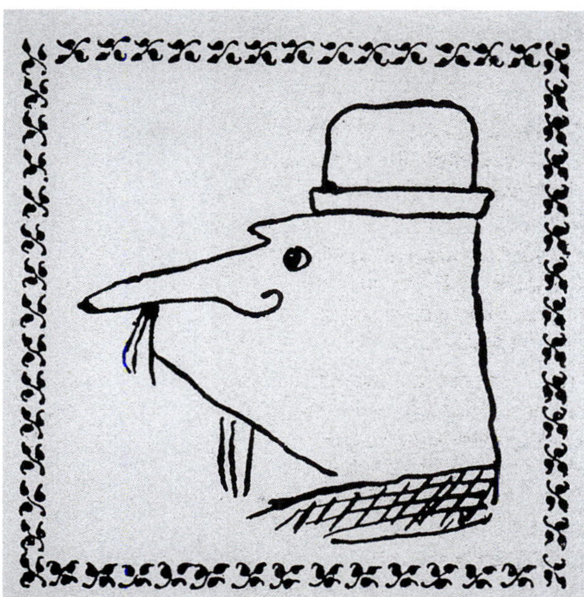

Fig. 141
Alfred Jarry, *Another Portrait of Monsieur Ubu*, drawing for *Ubu Roi*, 1896. Reproduced in *The Selected Works of Alfred Jarry*, n.p.

fig. 7). Preexisting imagery such as the hooded figure of Jarry and his trademark skiff is joined by new motifs, including a series of paintings devoted to the theme of entropy and numerous caricatures featuring Jean Moréas's stovepipe hat.

The artist installs these tiny works in gridlike patterns on the wall of his studio, high above Washington Square, where they receive daily coats of paint and glazes before being sanded down and returned to their resting place for the night, only for work on them to resume in the morning. When Chimes is satisfied with one of them as a finished work of art he packages it in a neat box and begins work on another carefully prepared wood panel, which replaces the completed work on the wall of his studio. The gridlike pattern he devised for hanging these works to dry inspired him to conceive of them as a visual poem, corresponding to the final line of *Finnegan's Wake*, which reads: "A way a lone a last a loved a long the."[255] The rhythm of Joyce's iambic pentameter corresponds with the five rows of five paintings, equally spaced, whose symmetry allows them to be seen as a single work of art, even though Chimes often titles the works individually. One such painting, *Keys to Given* of 2006 (fig. 142), references the end of *Finnegan's Wake*, although Joyce's original language has been slightly amended to allude to Duchamp's posthumously unveiled final masterpiece *Etant donnés*, which also translates as *Given*.[256]

Just as the final of line of *Finnegan's Wake* also suggests a new beginning, Chimes's latest paintings reveal new departures and interests. The works often take the form of coins or medallions that verge on caricature as the artist continues to mine the deeply provocative and absurd, contradictory ideas of Jarry and his successors.[257] For Chimes, caricature involves eliminating all inessential details and focusing intently on the essence of the subject. This is why the only round portrait that Chimes has kept for himself is *Jean Moréas* (pl. 40), since the painting verges on caricature in the way that the profile reduces the Greek poet to a distinctive mnemonic trait. Born Iannis Papadiamantopoulos, Jean Moréas is perhaps best known today as the author of the 1886 "Symbolist Manifesto" and went on to play an integral role in the "banquet years"

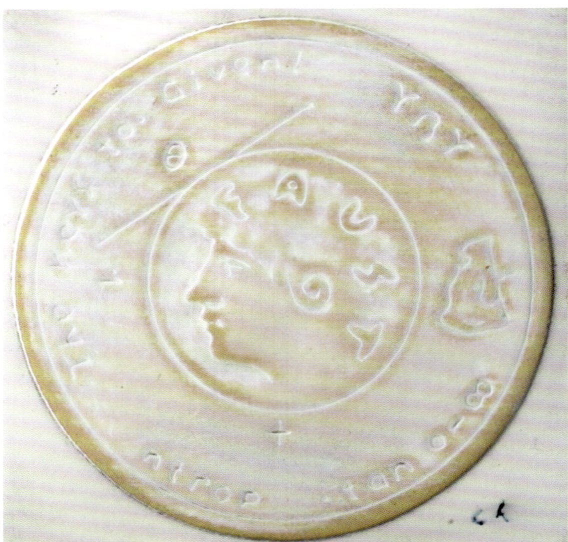

Fig. 142
Thomas Chimes, *Keys to Given*, 2006. Oil on pane , 2⅞ x 2⅞ inches (7.6 x 7.6 cm). Private collection

of the Parisian avant-garde at the turn of the twentieth century. A close friend of Gauguin, Picasso, Apollinaire, and Jarry, Moréas was a flamboyant dandy known for his acerbic wit and odes "To Immortal Greece," which took on a political dimension during the Balkan Wars.

In panel portraits such as this one, Chimes has attempted to encapsulate the writer's life and *oeuvre* in a single image, based upon a black-and-white photograph of the subject that he then transforms in the finished painting. Like an inspired spelunker, Chimes plumbs the depths of his subjects, such as Moréas, with whom he identified through their shared Greek roots and connection to Jarry, bringing back to the surface a resemblance that transcends literal description. This project continues in the artist's most recent paintings, only now he uses caricature and hermetic symbolism, the result of several decades of reflection upon the work and ideas of Jarry and his followers. For Chimes, the creative act often depends on a mirror effect in which he recognizes his own dreams, aspirations, fears, and neuroses in the imagination of another artist. This is why he continually reverts to Jarry's writings, regarding the French author as his artistic counterpart, a second self, whose work has enriched and sustained his own development as an artist for over forty years.

In a letter to Roger Shattuck, dated October 7, 1986, Chimes quotes from Georges Poulet's critical essay on Baudelaire in terms that reflect his own view of Jarry as a kindred spirit.[258] Poulet wrote of the French poet's need to combat the tragic isolation of his private life with a whole procession of like-minded writers and artists in his mental life:

> He surrounded himself with *kindred spirits*. It is these that he called his "*phares*," his beacons. Along a coast at night great beams of light can be seen flashing through the dark from a number of scattered points. Each stands alone, yet they are interrelated because each is like the other. For Baudelaire great artists and great poets are like beams of light set out at irregular intervals but visible to each other, and together constituting a chain over which the mind makes it way, link by link, noting how each resembles the other.[259]

Through his continuous evocation of Jarry's 'Pataphysical notion of a universe supplementary to this one, Chimes emerges from this account as the most radical heir to Alfred Jarry, whose work he has succeeded in extending, not through emulation, but rather through the reinterpretation of texts such as *Exploits and Opinions of Doctor Faustroll, 'Pataphysician,* which has provided the springboard for numerous paintings since the 1970s. Although sometime mistaken as the product of a nostalgic desire to re-create the past—in this case the decadent atmosphere of *belle-époque* Paris during the heyday of Symbolism—Chimes's pictorial vocabulary is in fact directly linked with events in his own life, such as his divorce or his prolonged battle with depression. Chimes restages these traumatic experiences through Jarry's creations, which become a cathartic force through which he can publicly confront his own demons and neuroses.

Seen in this light, the panel portraits and white paintings can no longer be viewed as "deliberately old fashioned," "anachronistic," or seduced by "the condition of nostalgia."[260] This fundamental misconception of Chimes's work pervades the critical discourse on his paintings, which are often seen as backward-looking despite Chimes's declaration in 1975 that "to get to the future you go to the past. To get to the past you go to the future."[261] This statement, inspired by Jarry's conception of the present as an "arriving memory,"[262] highlights Chimes's uniquely contemporary approach to the work of his intellectual and artistic forebears, using their exploits and achievements as the base for his own artistic journey, while in turn giving new power and energy to their revolutionary concepts and ideas by updating them through his current interests such as the psychology of Carl Gustav Jung, the philosophy of Ludwig Wittgenstein, or the scientific theories of Menas Kafatos.[263]

Chimes would never wish to emulate Jarry's dissolute lifestyle and antisocial behavior, since he finds the latter's abuse of drink and drugs, which led to his early death, to be an extraordinary waste of talent. Nor is he nostalgic for the decadent yet highly creative atmosphere of Paris in the late nineteenth and early twentieth centuries, since his early experience of making the neoclassical head at the Art Students League taught him that one can only make works of art in one's own time. This is why he constantly returns to Jarry's writings on 'Pataphysics, since these ideas often point the way forward for his work, pushing him into hitherto uncharted regions of time and space. The seemingly infinite number of meanings that Chimes finds in the figure of Doctor Faustroll underlines his consummate ability to reinterpret this fictional character freely in highly original paintings that, when seen together, comprise a potent visual testament to the enduring power of Jarry's literary creations and to Chimes's own deeply idiosyncratic art.

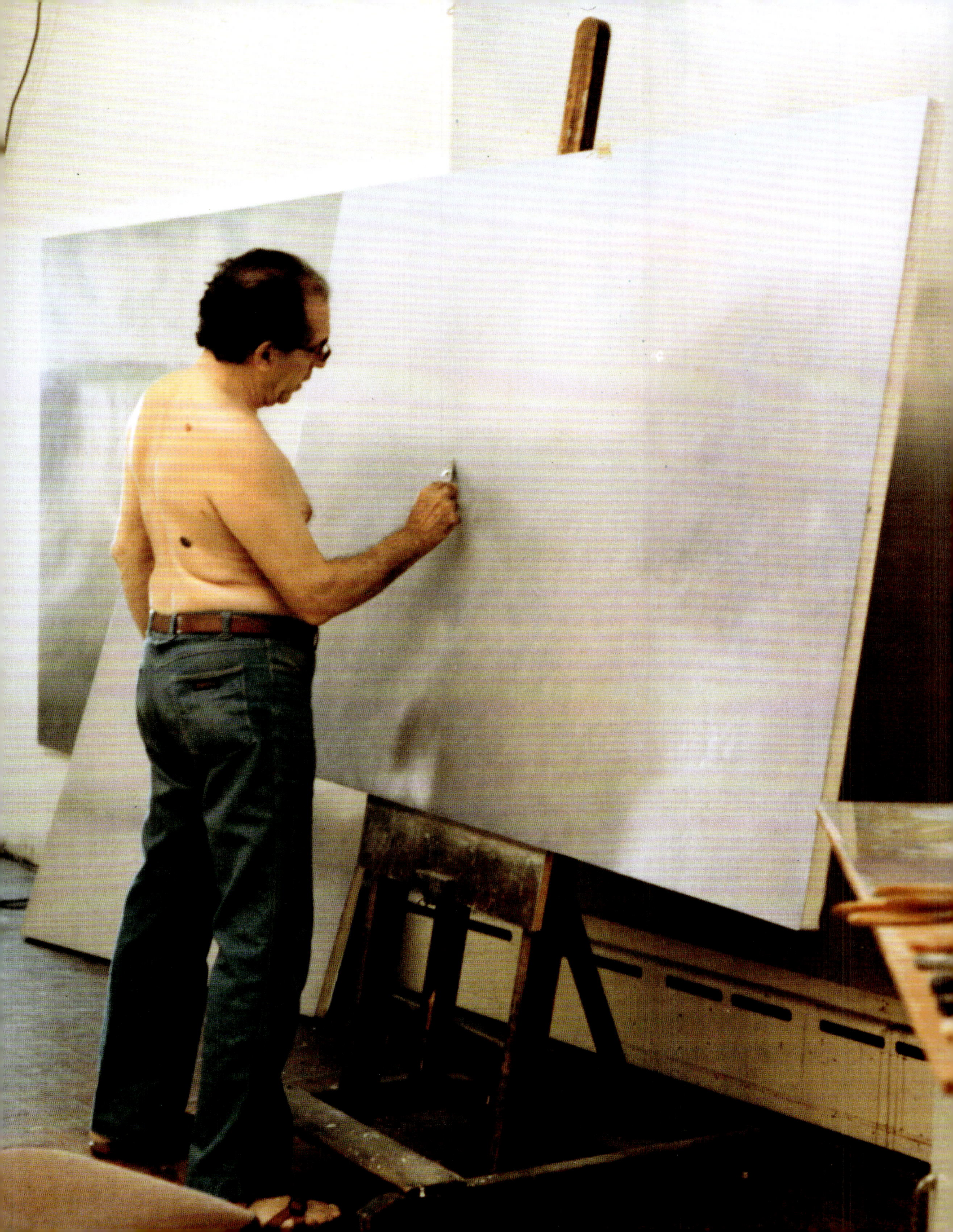

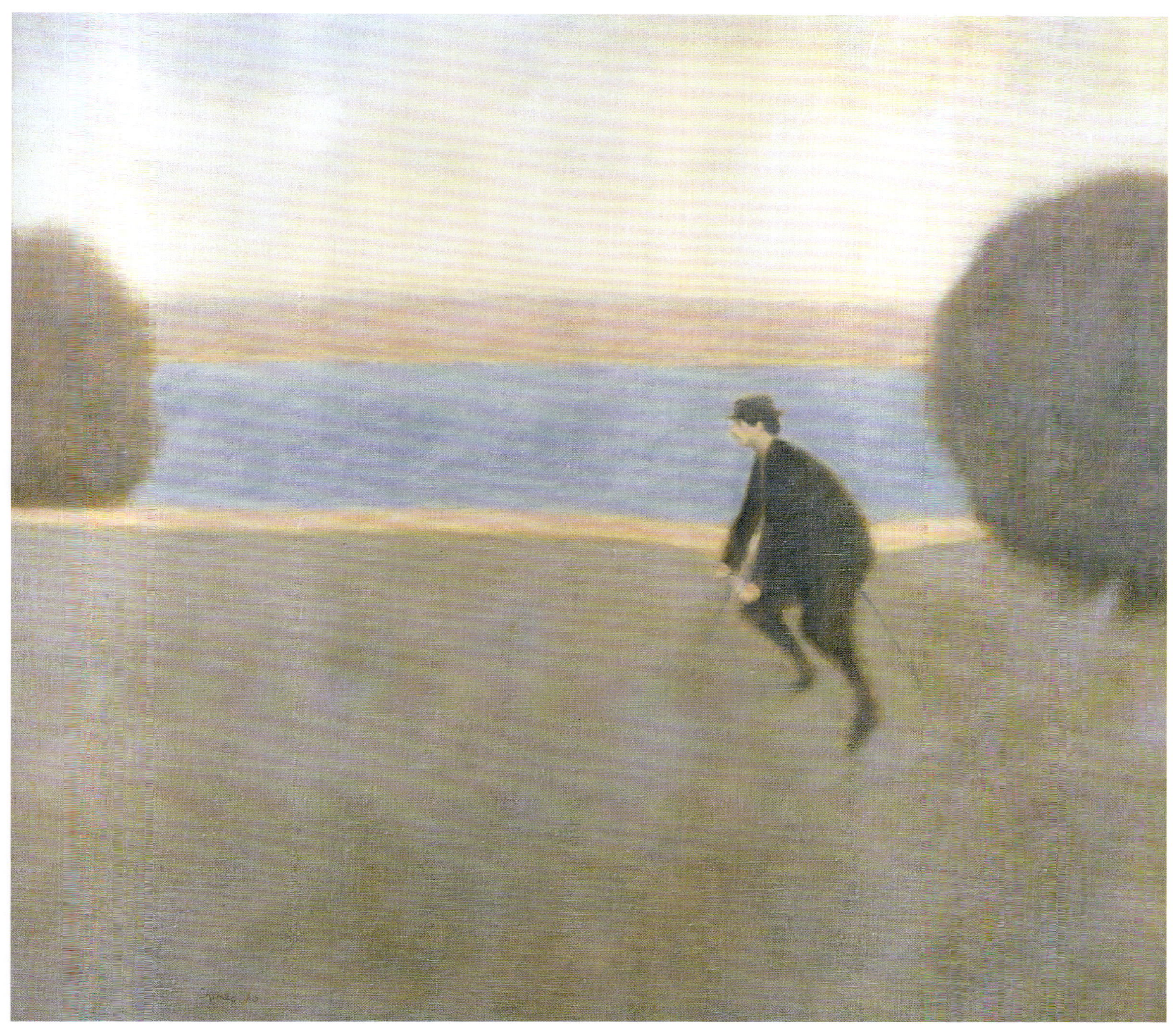

Morning, 1980

OIL ON CANVAS

36 x 40 INCHES (91.4 x 101.6 CM)

COLLECTION OF MR. AND MRS. ROBERT P. LEVY, BRYN MAWR, PENNSYLVANIA

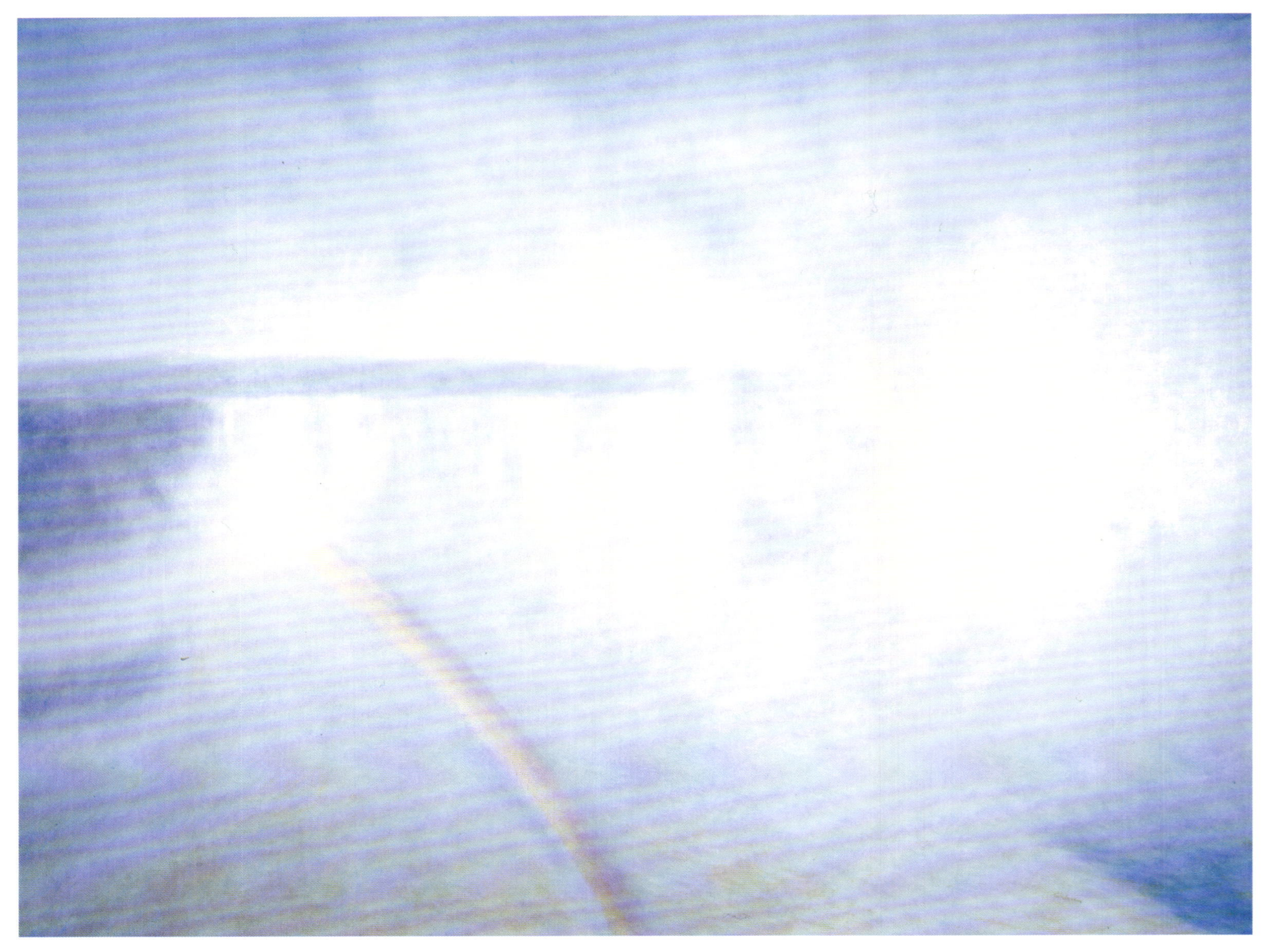

PLATE 78

Waterfall, 1980

OIL ON CANVAS

90 X 114 INCHES (228.6 X 289.6 CM)

CORCORAN GALLERY OF ART, WASHINGTON, DC. MUSEUM PURCHASE WITH FUNDS PROVIDED BY THE DIETRICH FOUNDATION,

WASHBURN AND SUSAN OBERWAGER, RICHARD A. MADLENER, AND MRS. R. F. LEVY, 2004.16

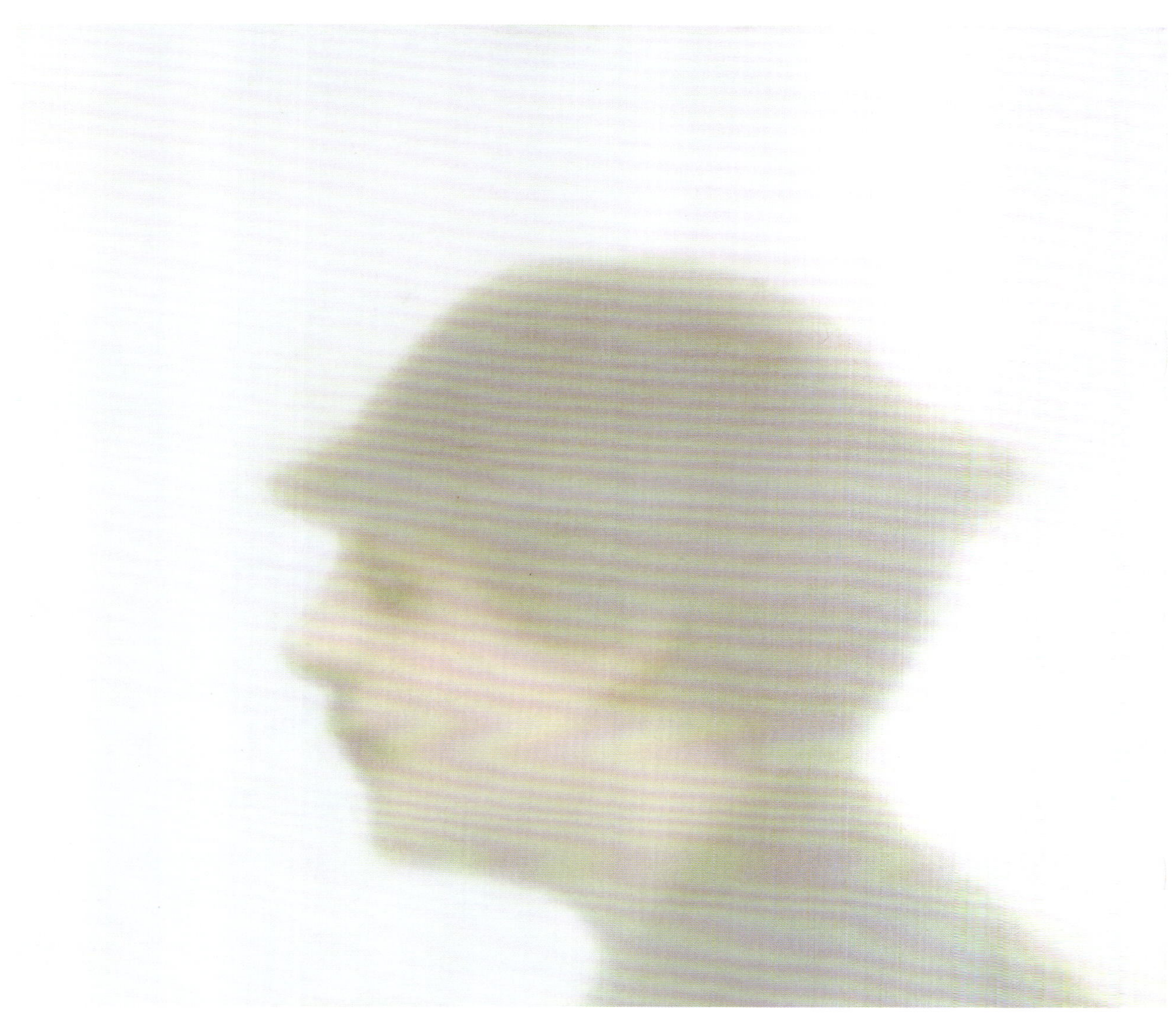

PLATE 79
Faustroll Helmet, 1984

OIL ON CANVAS

18½ x 22½ INCHES (47 x 57.2 CM)

PRIVATE COLLECTION, COURTESY OF LOCKS GALLERY, PHILADELPHIA

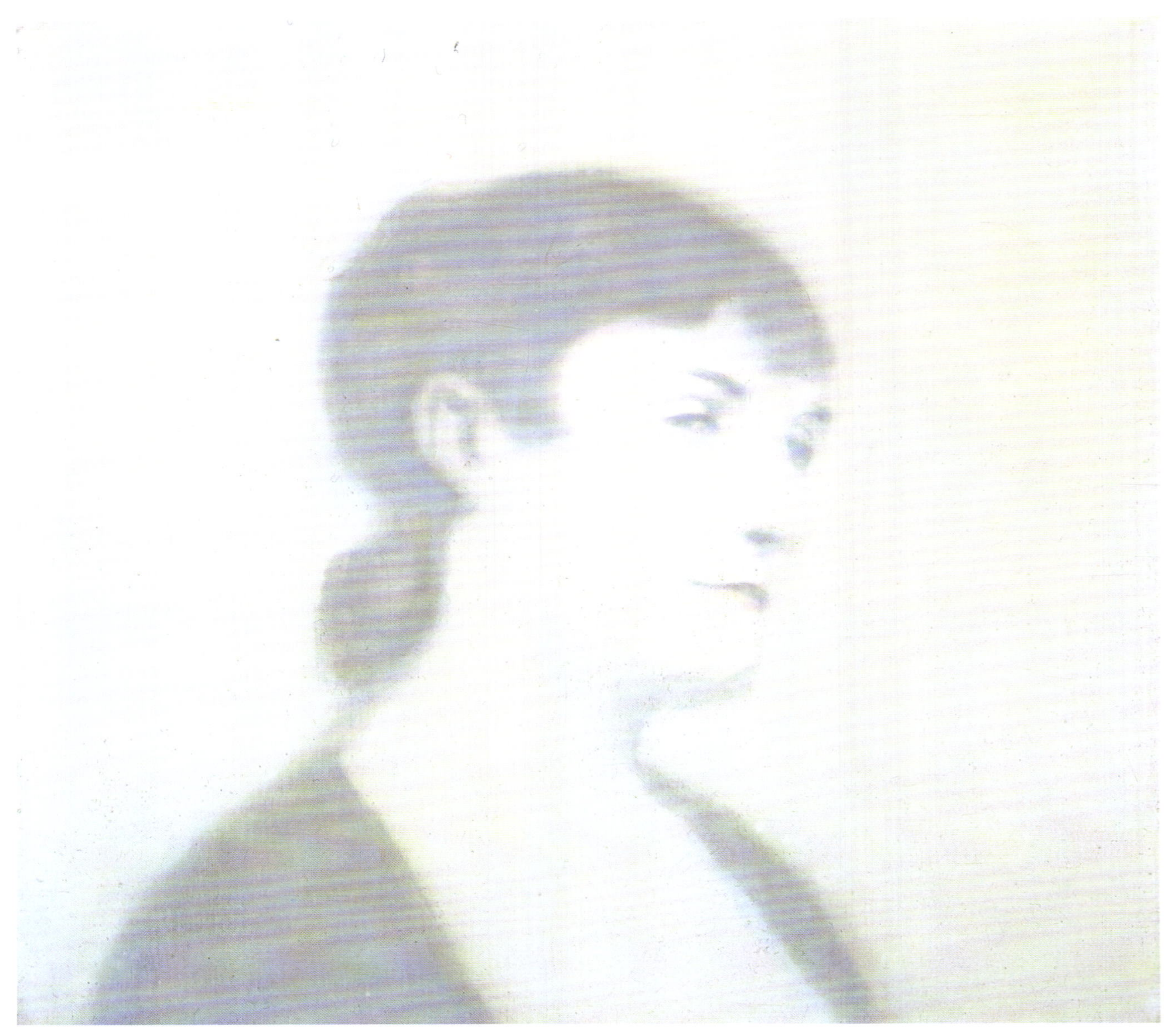

PLATE 80

Rachilde, 1986

OIL ON CANVAS

20¼ x 22¼ INCHES (51.4 x 56.5 CM)

PRIVATE COLLECTION, COURTESY OF LOCKS GALLERY, PHILADELPHIA

Sea-Bird Satie, 1987

OIL ON CANVAS, MOUNTED ON WOOD

48 X 48 INCHES (121.9 X 121.9 CM)

PRIVATE COLLECTION, COURTESY OF LOCKS GALLERY, PHILADELPHIA

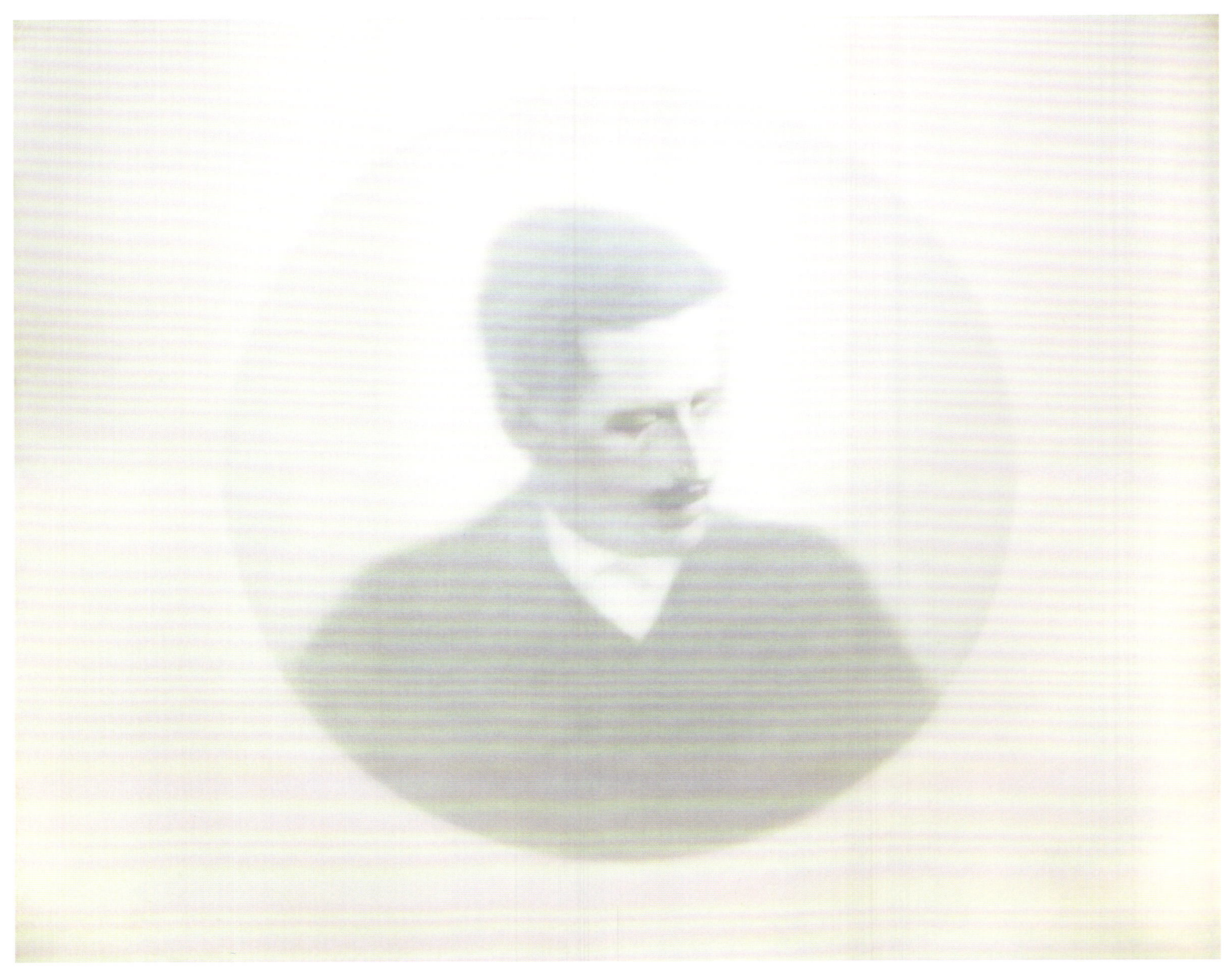

PLATE 82

James Joyce, 1986

OIL ON CANVAS

50 x 62 INCHES (127 x 157.5 CM)

PRIVATE COLLECTION, COURTESY OF LOCKS GALLERY, PHILADELPHIA

PLATE 83

Alfred Jarry, 1986–88

OIL ON CANVAS

52 x 60 INCHES (132.1 x 152.4 CM)

COLLECTION OF THE PENNSYLVANIA CONVENTION CENTER AUTHORITY, PHILADELPHIA

PLATE 84

Rise Up, Man of the Hooths, 1985

OIL ON CANVAS

18¼ x 22¼ INCHES (46.4 x 56.5 CM)

COURTESY OF LOCKS GALLERY, PHILADELPHIA

From Paris to Paris by Sea, 1988

OIL ON CANVAS

18½ x 22¼ INCHES (47 x 56.5 CM)

COURTESY OF LOCKS GALLERY, PHILADELPHIA

PLATE 86

Faustroll (L'Infini), 1988

OIL ON CANVAS

48 X 68 INCHES (121.9 X 172.7 CM)

PHILADELPHIA MUSEUM OF ART. JULIUS BLOCH MEMORIAL FUND PURCHASE, 1988-42-1

Watcher of the Night, 1989

OIL ON PANEL

27½ X 48 INCHES (69.9 X 121.9 CM)

COLLECTION OF MR. AND MRS. MARK E. RUBENSTEIN, PHILADELPHIA

PLATE 88

Hermes, 1990

OIL ON PANEL

6⅝ X 6¹³⁄₁₆ INCHES (16.8 X 17.3 CM)

COLLECTION OF DANIEL W. DIETRICH II, CHESTER SPRINGS, PENNSYLVANIA

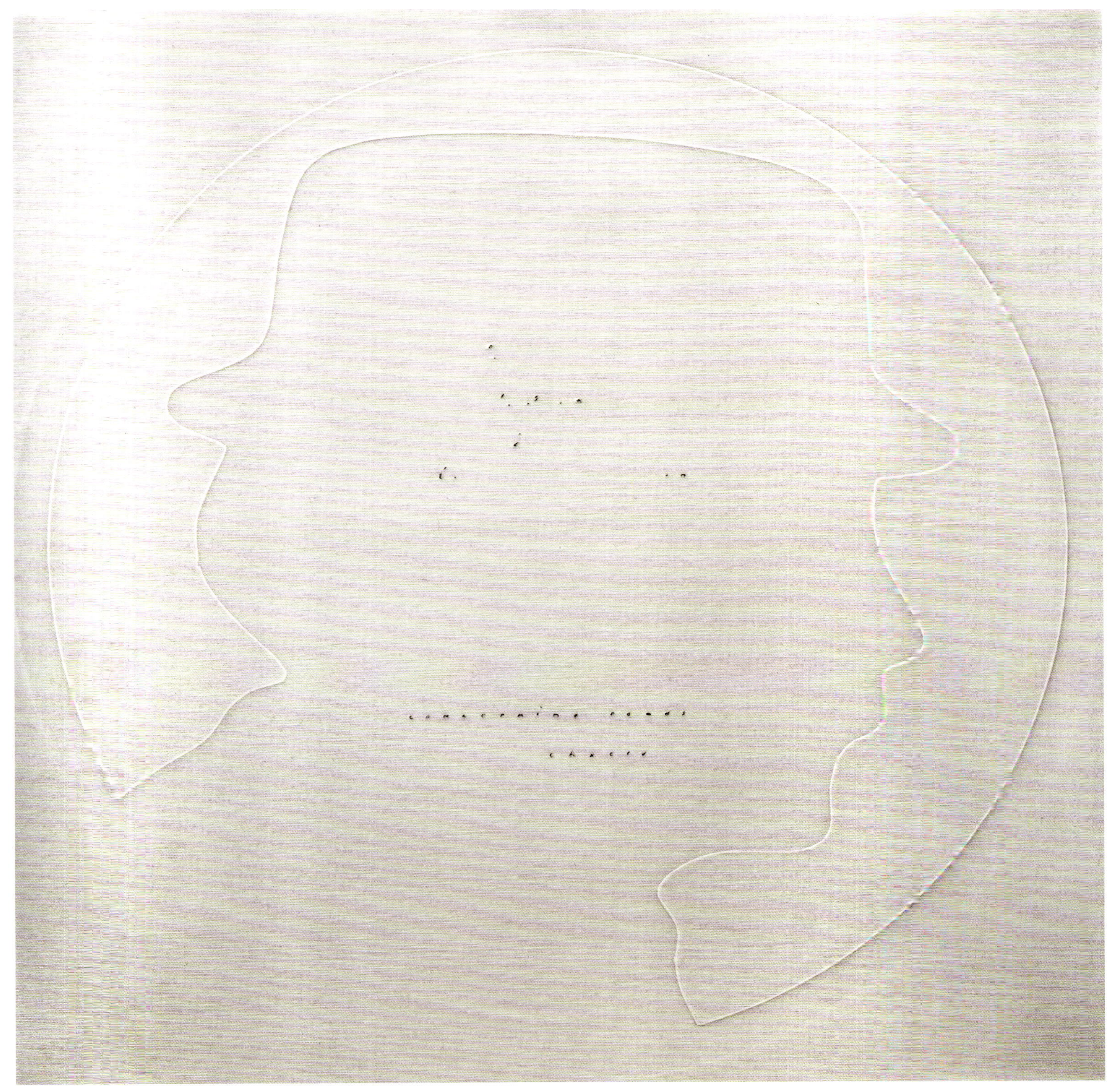

PLATE 89

Concerning Roads, 1994

OIL ON PANEL

11⅞ x 11⅞ INCHES (30.2 x 30.2 CM)

COURTESY OF LOCKS GALLERY, PHILADELPHIA

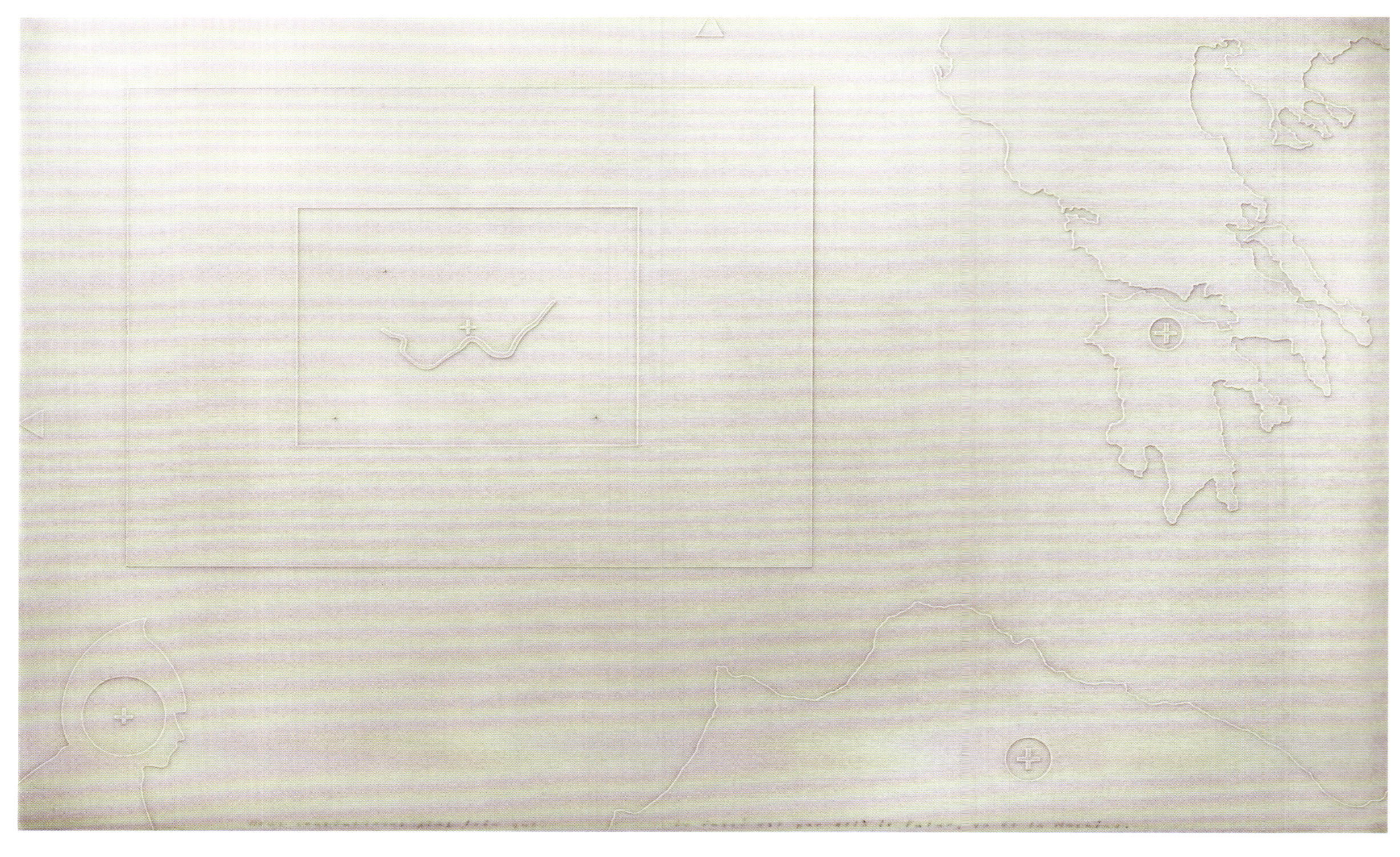

PLATE 90

Nous constaterons plus loins que de passé est par de la future vu de la machine, 1996

OIL ON PANEL

14⅝ x 23¾ INCHES (37.1 x 57.8 CM)

COURTESY OF LOCKS GALLERY, PHILADELPHIA

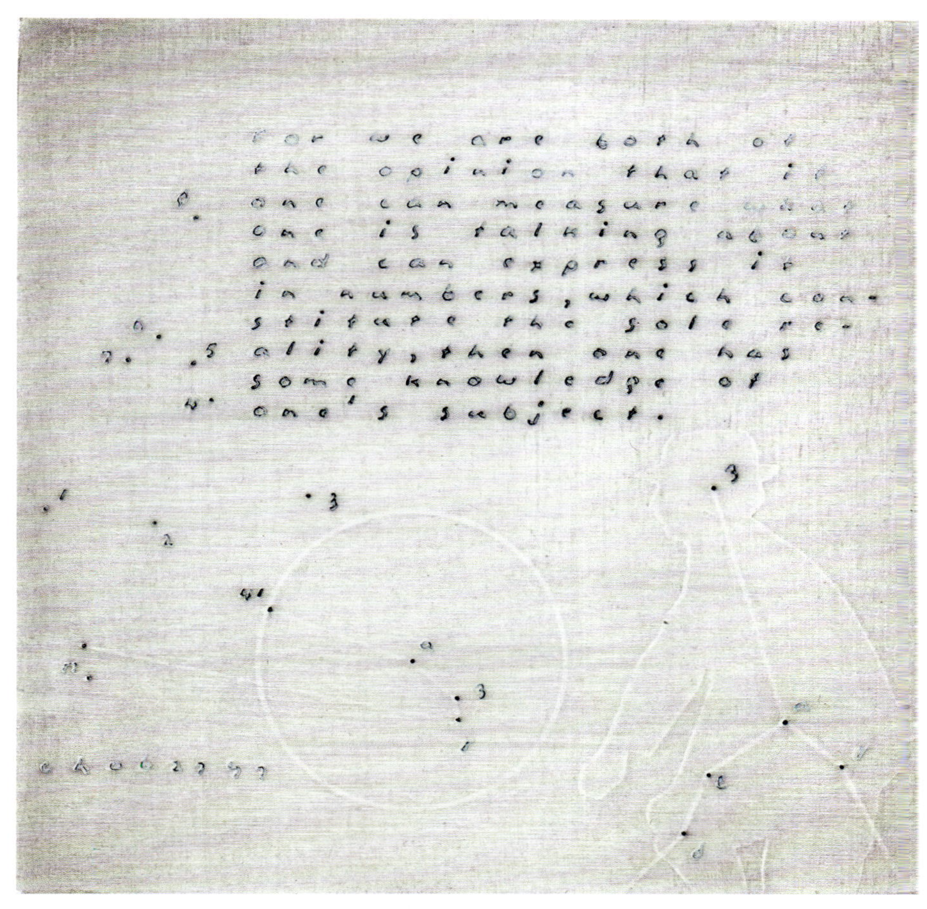

PLATE 91

For we are both of the opinion that if one can measure what one is talking about and can express it in numbers,
which constitute the sole reality, then one has some knowledge of one's subject (CH 06.27.97), 1997

OIL ON PANEL

5¾ x 5¾ INCHES (14.6 x 14.6 CM)

COLLECTION OF DR. AND MRS. PAUL RICHARDSON, PHILADELPHIA

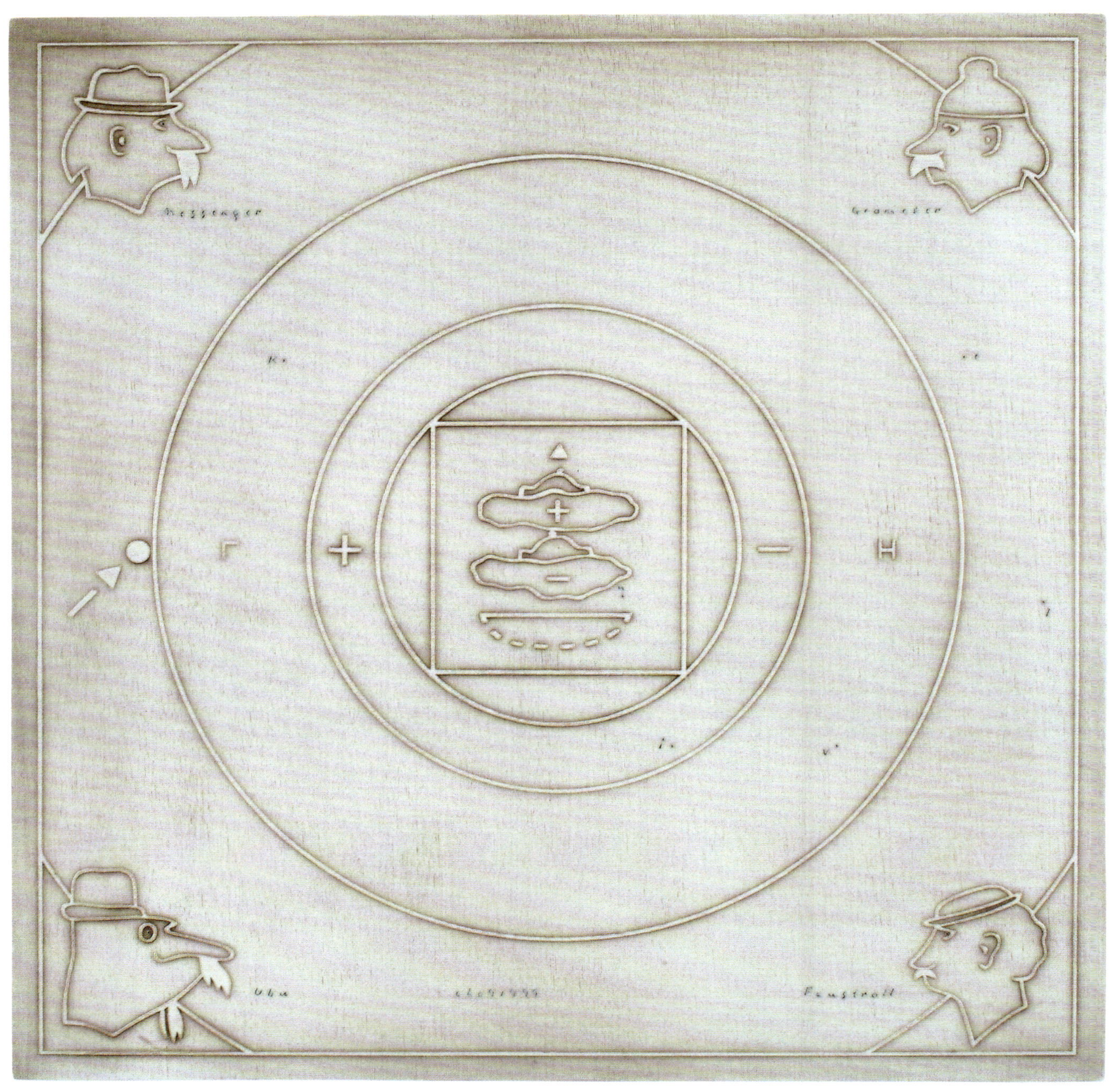

Portrait of All Four (CH 09.14.99), 1999

OIL ON PANEL

11⅞ x 11⅞ INCHES (30.2 x 30.2 CM)

DELAWARE ART MUSEUM, WILMINGTON. F. V. DU PONT ACQUISITION FUND, 2000

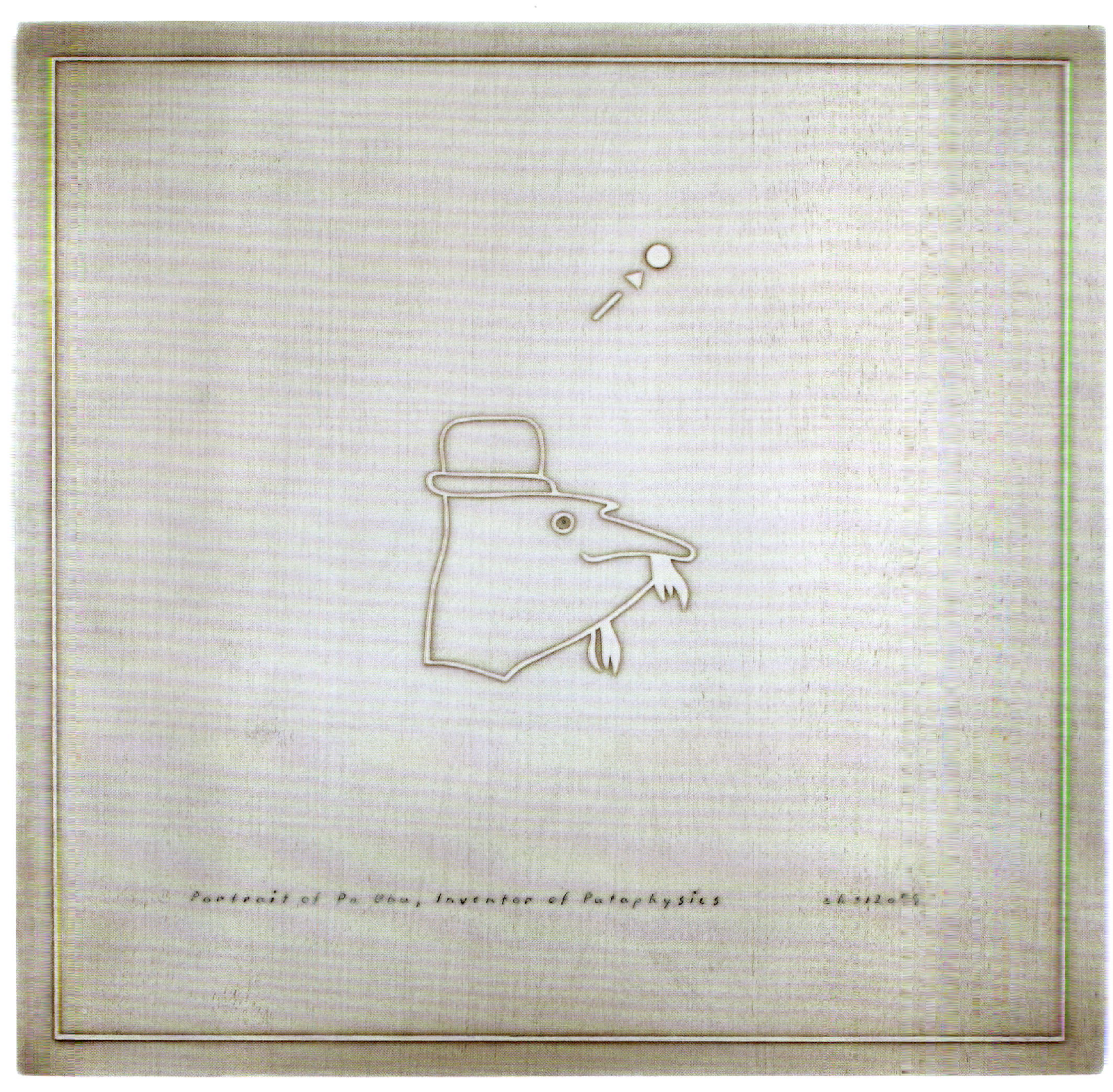

PLATE 93

Portrait of Pa Ubu, Inventor of Pataphysics (CH 11.20.99), 1999

OIL ON PANEL

11¹³⁄₁₆ x 11⅞ INCHES (30 x 30.2 CM)

DELAWARE ART MUSEUM, WILMINGTON. F. V. DU PONT ACQUISITION FUND, 2000

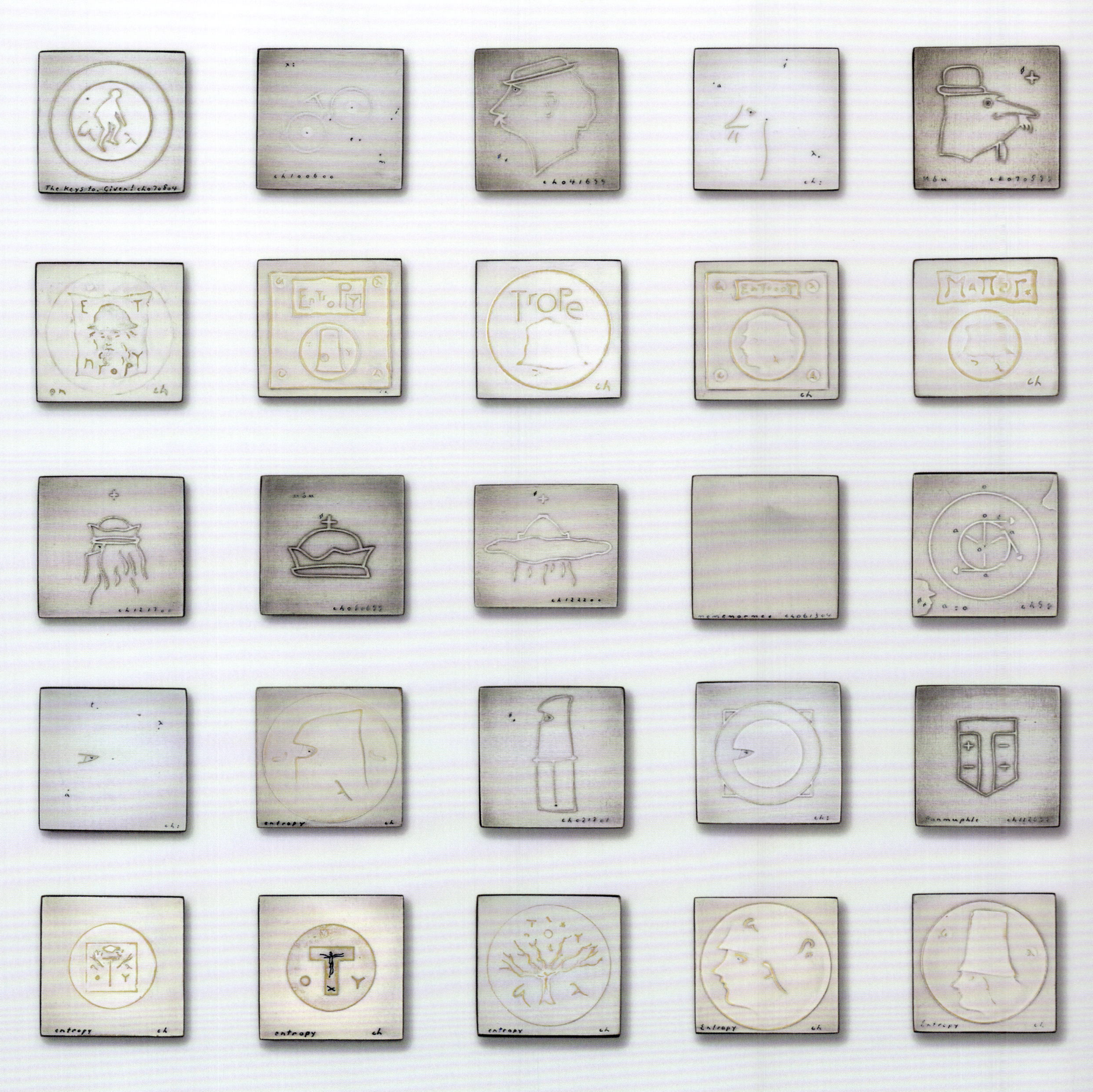

PLATE 94

Untitled (Finnegan's Wake), 2000–2006

OIL ON PANEL

TWENTY-FIVE WORKS, EACH APPROXIMATELY 3 X 3 INCHES (7.6 X 7.6 CM)

COURTESY OF LOCKS GALLERY, PHILADELPHIA

NOTES

1. John Canaday, "Whither Art?" *New York Times*, March 26, 1961, sec. X, p. 15.

2. Andy Warhol, Kasper König, Pontus Hultén, and Olle Granath, eds., *Andy Warhol*, exh. cat. (Stockholm: Moderna Museet, 1968), n.p.

3. Alfred H. Barr, Jr., letter to Thomas Chimes, November 14, 1961, Artists' Records, The Museum of Modern Art, New York.

4. Marcel Jean, statement in "A Collective Portrait of Marcel Duchamp," in Anne d'Harnoncourt and Kynaston McShine, eds., *Marcel Duchamp*, exh. cat. New York: The Museum of Modern Art; Philadelphia: Philadelphia Museum of Art, 1973), p. 203.

5. Miriam Seidel, "A Pop Star Is Born," *Applause* (Philadelphia) 18, no. 4 (April 1992), p. 26.

6. David Bourdon, "Help!" *Village Voice*, October 14, 1965, p. 13.

7. Duchamp's remarks were widely disseminated through John Canaday's coverage of the panel discussion; see Canaday, "Whither Art?"

8. Ibid.

9. Arthur Rimbaud, letter to Paul Demeny, May 15, 1871, in *Arthur Rimbaud: Oeuvres complètes*, ed. Antoine Adam (Paris: Gallimard, 1972), p. 251 (translation by the author).

10. Judith Wolfe, "Jungian Aspects of Jackson Pollock's Imagery," *Artforum* 11, no. 3 (November 1972), p. 71. Chimes read this essay in 1984, having originally been drawn to it through his interest at that time in the psychological theories of Carl Gustav Jung, especially those dealing with the collective unconscious, as well as Jackson Pollock's drip paintings, which he had greatly admired since his days at the Art Students League in New York in the late 1940s. Aware of Chimes's passion for Pollock, his wife, Dawn, gave him as a present a secondhand copy of the March 1979 issue of *Arts Magazine* that was devoted to the Abstract Expressionist painter's life and work. It was while reading this collection of essays, which he received in the summer of 1984, that Chimes came across a reference to Wolfe's essay, and thus discovered the alchemical connection to his own oeuvre; see Jonathan Welch, "Jackson Pollock's 'The White Angel' and the Origins of Alchemy," *Arts Magazine* 53, no. 7 (March 1979), pp. 138–41.

11. Carl Gustav Jung, "The Alchemical Process and Its Stages," in *Psychology and Alchemy*, trans. R. F. C. Hull (Princeton: Princeton University Press, 1968), pp. 228–32. While reading Jung's *Mysterium Coniunctionis*, the artist was astonished to find a quotation "from an old alchemical text in which the word for alchemist is C-H-I-M-E-S." Cynthia Veloric, interview with Thomas Chimes for the Archives of American Art, Philadelphia, July 2, 1990, p. 122.

12. R. D. Laing, "The Ten-Day Voyage," in *The Politics of Experience and the Bird of Paradise* (London: Routledge & Kegan Paul, 1967), p. 147. Laing's study was based upon a tape-recorded conversation in 1964 with Jesse Watkins, an English sculptor and painter who had studied at Goldsmiths College and Chelsea School of Art. Around 1940, Watkins went through a "psychotic episode" that lasted ten days. This voyage into inner space and time, which Laing documents through the transcript of their interview, constituted one of the most significant experiences of Watkins's life.

13. Pope, whom Chimes refers to as "Theo" (Greek for "uncle"), was actually his father's first cousin, who often talked about art with Chimes when he was a child: "I can remember one time we were sitting at the dinner table and he showed me, probably an illustration in a magazine that was simply a line drawing of a figure and he said, 'See, Tom, how with such simple means you can get results like that?'"; see Cynthia Veloric, interview with Thomas Chimes for the Archives of American Art, Philadelphia, June 14, 1990, p. 17.

14. Thomas Chimes, application to the Pennsylvania Academy of the Fine Arts, September 29, 1939, Archives of the Pennsylvania Academy of the Fine Arts, Philadelphia.

15. Thomas Chimes, interview with the author, October 15, 2002.

16. Patricia Stewart, "Poets, Pataphysics, and Painting," *Arts Exchange* (Philadelphia) 2, no. 2 (March–April 1978), p. 21.

17. In an interview with Elisabeth Stevens, Chimes recalled that when he informed his friends and colleagues in New York of his decision to return to Philadelphia, which they considered to be a cultural desert, "People said: Go to Philadelphia and die"; see Elisabeth Stevens, "Home Town Best Town for One Artist," *Trenton Times–Advertiser*, March 30, 1975, p. 1.

18. Georges Duthuit, "Maille à partir avec Bram van Velde," *Cahiers d'Art* (Paris) no. 1 (July 1952), pp. 77–81; René de Solier, "Hans Hartung," ibid., pp. 86–91.

19. Thomas Chimes, interview with the author, November 30, 2005.

20. Thomas Chimes, interview with the author, July 5, 2006.

21. Chimes worked for Ibarguen, whose office was at 312 South Sixteenth Street, from 1953 to 1962. The architect supported Chimes's efforts to become an artist by offering flexible hours, especially at the end of the 1950s and early 1960s when Chimes began exhibiting his work in New York.

22. Stephen Berg, " . . . Time and Space Made Perceptible to the Heart," in *Thomas Chimes: Portraying Ideas*, exh. cat. (Dublin: Royal Hibernian Academy 2001), p. 10.

23. Karl Nickel, "The Ringling Mural," in *Thomas Chimes: A Retrospective Exhibition*, exh. cat. (Sarasota, FL: John and Mable Ringling Museum of Art, 1968), n.p.

24. As Eliza E. Rathbone has argued, de Staël exerted a tremendous influence on American painters in the 1950s. His work was shown at numerous prominent commercial galleries in New York in the early 1950s, including Knoedler's, Sidney Janis, and Paul Rosenberg and Co., and was the subject of a retrospective, organized by the American Federation of Arts, that in 1956 traveled to seven venues throughout the United States, including New York and Washington, DC; see Rathbone, "Nicolas de Staël in America," in *Nicolas de Staël in America*, exh. cat. (Washington, DC: The Phillips Collection, 1990), pp. 11–39.

25. Dore Ashton, "Art: Arthur Kaufmann," *New York Times*, February 21, 1958, p. 21. The review of Chimes's exhibition at the Avant-Garde Gallery followed a lengthy review of the Arthur Kaufmann retrospective at the Jewish Museum, New York.

26. Thomas Chimes, interview with the author, September 14, 2005.

27. Antonin Artaud, "Van Gogh, the Man Suicided by Society," in *Antonin Artaud: Selected Writings*, ed. Susan Sontag, trans. Helen Weaver (New York: Farrar, Straus and Giroux, 1976), pp. 483–512.

28. John McGregor, *The Discovery of the Art of the Insane* (Princeton: Princeton University Press, 1989), p. 284.

29. Artaud, "Van Gogh," p. 484 (translation modified by the author).

30. Ibid., p. 485.

31. Henri Matisse, "La Chapelle du Rosaire," in *Chapelle du Rosaire des Dominicaines de Vence* (Vence, 1951); reprinted in *Matisse on Art*, ed. Jack D. Flam (Oxford: Phaidon, 1973), p. 128.

32. The Chapel of the Rosary of the Dominican Nuns was consecrated by the Archbishop of Nice, Monseigneur Rémond, on June 25, 1951.

33. See Alfred H. Barr, Jr., *Matisse: His Art and His Public* (New York: The Museum of Modern Art, 1952), p. 284.

34. John F. Morrison, "Museum of Modern Art Buys Painting of Phila. Artist 'With Places to Go,'" *Philadelphia Evening Bulletin*, January 14, 1962, sec. 1, p. 16.

35. Ibid.

36. Ibid.

37. Ibid.

38. Thomas Chimes, "Statement" (1961), Artists' Records, The Museum of Modern Art, New York.

39. Nikos Kazantzakis, *The Last Temptation of Christ*, trans. P. A. Bien (New York: Bantam, 1961).

40. Ibid., p. 487.

41. Darren J. N. Middleton, *Novel Theology: Nikos Kazantzakis's Encounter with Whiteheadian Process Theism* (Macon, GA: Mercer University Press, 2000), p. 147.

42. Chimes quoted in Stephen Martin, "Tom Chimes: A Personal Odyssey," in *Tom Chimes: A Compendium, 1961–1986*, exh. cat. (Philadelphia: Goldie Paley Gallery, Moore College of Art, 1986), p. 8.

43. Randolph Jordan, "The Dual Substance of Cinema: What Kazantzakis's Christ Can Teach Us about Sound/Image Relationships in Film," in Darren J. N. Middleton, ed., *Scandalizing Jesus: Kazantzakis's "The Last Temptation of Christ" Fifty Years On* (New York: Continuum, 2005), p. 206.

44. This interpretation of the Christ story can be understood only in light of the Greek author's own struggles as a writer who had to overcome severe obstacles, including the almost universal rejection of his novels by critics who distorted the meaning of his work, as well as the subsequent condemnation of his book by the Roman Catholic and Greek Orthodox churches as blasphemous and heretical. Pope Pius XII placed *The Last Temptation of Christ* on the Vatican's "Index of Forbidden Texts" in December 1953, which of course aided its sales around the world. The negative reactions of the Greek Orthodox and Roman Catholic churches to Kazantzakis's novel have been documented in Darren J. N. Middleton and Peter A. Bien, eds., *God's Struggler: Religion in the Writings of Nikos Kazantzakis* (Macon, GA: Mercer University Press, 1996).

45. Morrison, "Museum of Modern Art Buys Painting of Phila. Artist," p. 16.

46. Ibid.

47. Kazantzakis, *The Last Temptation of Christ*, p. 462.

48. Thomas Chimes, interview with the author, November 8, 2004.

49. Thomas Chimes, "Statement" (1963), Artists' Records, The Museum of Modern Art, New York.

50. Thomas Chimes, interview with the author, November 8, 2004.

51. Jennifer L. Roberts, *Mirror-Travels: Robert Smithson and History* (New Haven: Yale University Press, 2004), p. 16.

52. Douglas Hall, "Introducing Alan Davie," in Hall, ed., *Alan Davie* (London: Lund Humphries, 1992), pp. 18–20.

53. Thomas Chimes, interview with the author, April 18, 2006.

54. Thomas Chimes, "Here is the bread of my inner world," unpublished poem, c. 1961.

49. Michael Lekakis, "The Sphinx Garden," *Athene* (Chicago) 8, no. 3 (Autumn 1947), pp. 77–78. This quarterly magazine, which Chimes subscribed to as a student, was an important outlet for the promotion of Hellenic culture and thought after World War II and often featured articles on Greek-American artists such as William Baziotes, George Constant, Michael Lekakis, Theodoros Stamos, and Jean Xceron.

50. Alfred H. Barr, Jr., letter to Thomas Chimes, May 9, 1962, Artists' Records, The Museum of Modern Art, New York. In his response, dated May 14, Chimes wrote, "It is with great appreciation that I say you have my approval to do anything you wish with the drawing" (ibid.).

51. Charlotte Lichtblau, "Thomas Chimes," *Philadelphia Inquirer*, January 24, 1965, p. 6.

52. Alfred Scheinberg, "The Thomas Chimes Mural: A Modern Mystic's Search for the Self" (senior thesis, New College, Sarasota, FL, 1968), p. 5.

53. Vasoric, interview with Thomas Chimes, July 2, 1990, p. 65.

54. "'Mural 1963–1965' to Be Shown at Museum," *Herald Tribune* (Sarasota, FL), May 19, 1968, p. 1.

55. Charles Benbow, "Artist Turned Alchemist," *Saint Petersburg Times*, November 24, 1968, sec. G, p. 1.

56. Ibid.

57. Tony DeLap, "Statement," in *Twelfth Exhibition of Contemporary American Painting and Sculpture*, exh. cat. (Urbana: University of Illinois Press, 1965), p. 142.

58. Julien Levy, "Introduction," in *Surrealism: A State of Mind 1924–1965*, exh. cat. (New York: Arno Press; Santa Barbara: Art Gallery at the University of California at Santa Barbara, 1966), n.p. Levy had attended the opening of Chimes's solo show at the Bodley Gallery, New York, in 1965, which may explain the artist's inclusion in the Santa Barbara exhibition.

59. Bettina L. Knapp, *Antonin Artaud: Man of Vision* (New York: David Lewis, 1969), p. xiv.

60. Bonaventure des Périers, *Cymbalum Mundi*, trans. Bettina L. Knapp (New York: Bookman Associates, 1965).

61. Ibid., pp. 21–22.

62. Bonaventure, *Cymbalum Mundi*, p. 55. Animals and birds invested with magical powers are a recurrent motif in the *Cymbalum Mundi*. Chimes may also have been influenced in his jacket design by the reference to the fable of Sapho (p. 73), which as Knapp points out in an accompanying footnote refers to Psaphon, a Lydian god who "taught a few birds to repeat the following words: 'Psaphon is a great god,' and then let them go free in the woods. The people, hearing the birds repeat the words so frequently, thought they were inspired by the gods and began to worship him. It was in this dubious way that Psaphon was deified" (ibid., p. 60 n. 16).

69. Stephen Barber, *Antonin Artaud: Blows and Bombs* (London: Faber and Faber, 1993), p. 47.

70. For more on the short-lived Théâtre Alfred Jarry, which folded in 1929 after staging only four productions, and the impact of Jarry's writings on the development of Artaud's dramatic aesthetic, see Leonard R. Koos, "Comic Cruelty: Artaud and Jarry," in Gene A. Plunka, ed., *Antonin Artaud and the Modern Theater* (Rutherford, NJ: Fairleigh Dickinson University Press, 1994), pp. 37–50.

71. *Antonin Artaud Anthology*, ed. Jack Hirschman (San Francisco: City Lights Books, 1965).

72. For example, Georges Bataille observed that Artaud's emaciated features made him look "like a caged bird of prey with dusty plumage which had been apprehended at the very moment it was about to take flight, and had remained fixed in this posture"; see Bataille, "Antonin Artaud," in *The Absence of Myth: Writings on Surrealism*, trans. Michael Richardson (London: Verso, 1994), p. 43.

73. Dawn Chimes, interview with the author, March 11, 2006.

74. For more on Artaud's electroshock treatments at Rodez, see Barber, *Antonin Artaud*, pp. 106–12.

75. Antonin Artaud, *Watchfiends and Rack Screams: Works from the Final Period*, ed. and trans. Clayton Eshleman with Bernard Bador (Boston: Exact Change, 1995), p. 336.

76. Antonin Artaud, *Artaud le Mômo* (Paris: Bordas, 1947).

77. John Ashbery, "Antonin Artaud," *Portfolio & Art News Annual* (New York), no. 2 (1959), p. 115. Ashbery's critical assessment of Artaud the poet, actor, director, and playwright was another key source for Chimes during this period.

78. Antonin Artaud, "Artaud le Mômo," reprinted in *Watchfiends and Rack Screams*, p. 163.

79. John C. Stout, *Antonin Artaud's Alternate Genealogies: Self-Portraits and Family Romances* (Waterloo, ON: Wilfrid Laurier University Press, 1996), p. 115.

80. For an excellent account of Artaud's extraordinary performance on that fateful evening, see Roger Shattuck, "Artaud Possessed," in *The Innocent Eye: On Modern Literature and the Arts* (New York: Farrar, Straus and Giroux, 1984), pp. 169–86.

81. Maurice Saillet, "Close to Antonin Artaud," *Evergreen Review* 4, no. 13 (May–June 1960), p. 83. Artaud was so moved by Saillet's eloquent comments about his lecture, which were first published in the January 24, 1947, issue of *Combat*, that he wrote him a letter in which he lamented his own inability to express himself in words, and of his conviction that the world was nothing but a place where "all the rare lucid tortured souls have always been assassinated"; see Naomi

Greene, *Antonin Artaud: Poet Without Words* (New York: Simon and Schuster, 1970), p. 52.

82. Artaud's letter to André Breton was published in *Combat* (Paris) in March 1948 and is reprinted in Ronald Hayman, *Artaud and After* (Oxford: Oxford University Press, 1977), p. 135.

83. Saillet, "Close to Antonin Artaud," p. 81.

84. Antonin Artaud, letter to Pierre Bordas, February 6, 1947, cited in Stephen Barber, *Artaud: The Screaming Body* (New York: Creation Books, 1999), p. 92.

85. Stephen Barber, "Cruel Journey," *Art in America* 83, no. 2 (February 1995), p. 71.

86. For a detailed study of Artaud's drawings, see Paule Thévenin and Jacques Derrida, *Antonin Artaud: Dessins et portraits* (Paris: Gallimard, 1986).

87. Thomas Chimes, interview with the author, September 14, 2005.

88. Margit Rowell and Sylvère Lotringer, "A Conversation with Nancy Spero," in Rowell, ed., *Antonin Artaud: Works on Paper*, exh. cat. (New York: The Museum of Modern Art, 1996), p. 137.

89. For an insightful analysis of the *Codex Artaud*, see Benjamin H. D. Buchloh, "Spero's Other Traditions," in M. Catherine de Zegher, ed., *Inside the Visible: An Elliptical Traverse of Twentieth-Century Art*, exh. cat. (Cambridge, MA: MIT Press; Boston: The Institute of Contemporary Art, 1996), pp. 239–44.

90. Nancy Spero, "Creation and Pro-Creation," *M/E/A/N/I/N/G* (New York), no. 12 (November 1992), p. 39.

91. The eighth annual *Chautauqua Exhibition of American Art* was on view at the Chautauqua Art Association in Chautauqua, New York, July 4–25, 1965.

92. Peter Selz, *Prize Winning Art, Book 6* (Chautauqua, NY: Chautauqua Art Association, 1966), n.p.

93. Marcel Duchamp, *La Mariée mise à nu par ses Célibataires, même (The Green Box)* (Paris: Edition Rrose Sélavy, 1934), translated as *The Bride Stripped Bare by Her Bachelors, Even*, ed. Richard Hamilton, trans. George Heard Hamilton (London: Percy Lund, Humphries, 1960), n.p.

94. Paul Thek, "Beneath the Skin," *Art News* 65, no. 2 (April 1966), p. 67. As Scott Rothkopf has recently argued, "a group of New York artists and critics—Thek and Swenson among them—negotiated a qualified reemergence of Surrealism during the sixties"; see Rothkopf, "Returns of the Repressed: The Legacy of Surrealism in American Art," in Isabelle Dervaux, ed., *Surrealism U.S.A.*, exh. cat. (New York: National Academy Museum, 2005), pp. 66–75. I would add Chimes's name to the list of contemporary artists who embraced the psychosexual aspects of Surrealism in the age of Pop. Gene Swenson organized an important exhibition at the Institute of Contemporary Art in Phila-delphia in 1966, titled *The Other Tradition*, which cham-pioned non-formal art and criticism that investigated post-Freudian sexuality, advertising, and technology as an alternative to the formalist "mainstream" hypothesized by Clement Greenberg.

95. Caroline A. Jones, *Machine in the Studio: Construc-ting the Postwar American Artist* (Chicago: University of Chicago Press, 1996), p. 270.

96. Ibid., p. 302.

97. Gilles Deleuze and Félix Guattari, *Anti-Oedipus: Capitalism and Schizophrenia*, trans. Robert Hurley, Mark Seem, and Helen R. Lane (Minneapolis: Univer-sity of Minnesota Press, 1983), p. 18. Deleuze and Guattari made these remarks in relation to Michel Carrouges's descriptions of machines and their sexual content in the work of Jarry, Duchamp, and other mod-ern artists and writers in *Les machines célibataires* (Paris: Arcanes, 1954).

98. Kenneth Clark, *The Best of Aubrey Beardsley* (New York: Doubleday, 1978), p. 90.

99. Alyce Mahon, *Surrealism and the Politics of Eros, 1938–1968* (London: Thames and Hudson, 2005).

100. "Symposium Will Examine Culture, Art, and Batman," *Daily Pennsylvanian*, April 26, 1966, p. 2. The symposium was intended to discuss popular culture and the development of the visual and aural arts. Sponsored by the Annenberg School of Communication, the event began with McLuhan's keynote lecture, followed by a panel discussion featuring William Dozier, executive producer and developer of the *Batman* television series; William Jovanovich, author and president of Harcourt, Brace & World Publishers; and Dr. Dell Hymes, an associate professor of anthropology at the University of Pennsylvania.

101. "Among Other Things . . . ," *The Almanac* (Philadelphia), March 1966, p. 5. Marshall McLuhan, "From Gutenberg to Batman," the second annual A. V. B. Geoghegan Lecture at the Annenberg School of Communication, University of Pennsylvania, Philadel-phia, April 28, 1966; published as "Great Change-Overs for You," *Vogue* 148, no. 1 (July 1966), pp. 62–63, 114–17; reprinted in Harry J. Skornia and Jack William Kitson, eds., *Problems and Controversies in Television and Radio* (Palo Alto, CA: Pacific Books, 1968), pp. 26–36.

102. Marshall McLuhan, *The Mechanical Bride: Folklore of Industrial Man* (New York: Vanguard, 1951), p. v. Poe's "A Descent into the Maelstrom" was published in *Graham's Magazine* in 1841 and slightly revised for *Tales of the Grotesque and Arabesque* of 1845, which provided the final text that inspired McLuhan's working method.

103. Marshall McLuhan, *The Gutenberg Galaxy: The Making of Typographic Man* (Toronto: University of Toronto Press, 1962), p. 31.

104. Marshall McLuhan, *Understanding Media: The Extensions of Man* (New York: McGraw-Hill, 1964), p. 352.

105. McLuhan, "Great Change-Overs for You," in Stearn and Kitson, *Problems and Controversies*, p. 26.

106. Ibid.

107. Ibid., p. 35.

108. Ibid., p. 26.

109. Ibid., p. 36.

110. Chimes often wore metal boxes to openings in the 1960s. At a 1967 opening of a group exhibition organized by Jim McWilliams at the Socrates Perakis Art Gallery in Philadelphia, for example, a newspaper reporter recounted that "Tom Chimes, one of the artists, wore a work of art around his neck—flowers, metal, plastic . . . indescribable. He graciously let the art lovers try it on"; see Rose DeWolf, "Bouncing Jim Is Work of Art," *Philadelphia Inquirer*, May 16, 1967, sec. A, p. 29. Chimes also wore a medallion, measuring six and three-quarter inches in diameter, to the opening of the René Magritte retrospective at the Museum of Modern Art in 1965, where it was admired by Salvador Dalí, who considered it "très jolie."

111. Marshall McLuhan, "The Medium Is the Message," in *Understanding Media*, p. 20.

112. Marshall McLuhan, *Playboy* interview; reprinted in *Essential McLuhan*, ed. Eric McLuhan and Frank Zingrone (Concord, ON: House of Anansi Press, 1995), p. 253.

113. According to one version of the legend, Constable Alexander Fitzpatrick visited the Kelly home to arrest Ned's younger brother Dan, although the motive for the visit may also have been his interest in another sibling, Kate Kelly, whom he subsequently assaulted. After the family came to the aid of the young Kate, an indignant Fitzpatrick, slightly wounded by a gunshot to the wrist, swore an attempted murder charge against the Kelly family. It was this false report that led Kelly's mother to go to jail for three years and the brothers to go on the run, along with their friends Steve Hart and Joe Byrne. For an excellent biography of Kelly that separates fact from fiction, see Ian Jones, *Ned Kelly: A Short Life* (Port Melbourne, Australia: Lothian Books, 1995).

114. Winthrop Sargeant, "Dada's Daddy," *Life* 32, no. 17 (April 28, 1952), pp. 100–110.

115. Ibid., p. 108.

116. Jarry's apartment was on the "second and a half" floor of a building whose owner considered the ceilings too high and the rooms too wide, so he divided the space horizontally as well as vertically, thus creating a bizarre multi-storied building. While the diminutive French writer was just short enough to stand upright, few visitors were. This part of the building no longer exists, but photographs appear in Noël Arnaud, *Alfred Jarry, d'Ubu roi au docteur Faustroll* (Paris: La Table ronde, 1974), pls. 37–40.

117. James Johnson Sweeney, "Eleven Europeans in America," *The Museum of Modern Art Bulletin* 13, nos. 4–5 (1946), p. 21.

118. Ibid., p. 20.

119. The most engaging and useful general introduction to Jarry and his milieu remains Roger Shattuck, *The Banquet Years* (New York: Vintage, 1955). In recent years, a number of important critical studies have significantly enhanced our understanding of Jarry's life and work; see, for example, Keith Beaumont, *Alfred Jarry: A Critical and Biographical Study* (Leicester, UK: Leicester University Press, 1984); Henri Béhar, *Les Cultures de Jarry* (Paris: Presses Universitaires de France, 1988); and Jill Fell, *Alfred Jarry: An Imagination in Revolt* (Madison, NJ: Fairleigh Dickinson University Press, 2005). The vast majority of Jarry's writings are available in English translation in *The Selected Works of Alfred Jarry*, ed. Roger Shattuck and Simon Watson Taylor (New York: Grove Press, 1965), as well as individual editions of plays, novels, and other related publications. For the complete works of Jarry, see *Alfred Jarry: Oeuvres complètes*, 3 Vols., ed. Michel Arrivé, Henri Bordillon, Patrick Besnier, and Bernard Le Doze (Paris: Gallimard, Bibliothèque de la Pléiade, 1972–88).

120. For more on the influence of Jarry's *Ubu Roi* on the development of Dada, see Elizabeth K. Menon, "The Excrement of Power: Alfred Jarry, Ubu Roi, and Dada," in Elmer Peterson, ed., *Paris Dada: The Barbarians Storm the Gates* (Farmington Hills, MI: Gale Group, 2001), pp. 33–66.

121. Alfred Jarry, "Preliminary Address at the First Performance of *Ubu Roi*, December 10, 1896," trans. Simon Watson Taylor, in *Selected Works of Alfred Jarry*, p. 78. Poland, a country long condemned through wars and invasions to the nonexistence of partition, was an apt choice to represent "Nowhere."

122. As Christopher Innes has rightly pointed out, the action in *Ubu Roi* is "clearly a farrago of Shakespearean situations: the bloody murder of a good king, and the flight of his son from *Macbeth*; the father's ghost, and Fortinbras leading a revolt against the palace from *Hamlet*; Buckingham, whose reward for helping a usurper is refused, from *Richard III*; and the bear from *The Winter's Tale*"; see Innes, *Avant-Garde Theatre, 1892–1992* (London: Routledge, 1993), p. 24.

123. William Butler Yeats, *Autobiographies* (London: Macmillan, 1926), pp. 348–49.

124. Alfred H. Barr, Jr., *Picasso: Fifty Years of His Art* (New York: The Museum of Modern Art, 1946), p. 31.

125. According to John Richardson, the widely held belief that Jarry and Picasso were close friends is a collective fantasy, and it is quite possible that the two men never met; see Richardson, *A Life of Picasso*, vol. 1, *1881–1906* (New York: Random House, 1991), p. 360. It should be pointed out, however, that even if he never met the young Spanish artist, Jarry's influence at the *bateau-lavoir* was pervasive. Picasso would have heard tales of the legendary French writer through his friends Guillaume Apollinaire and Maurice Reynal, both of whom were fervent Jarry disciples; see Peter Read, "'A

Rendez-vous des poètes': Picasso, French Poetry, and Theater, 1900–1906," in Marilyn McCully, ed., *Picasso: The Early Years, 1892–1906*, exh. cat. (Washington, DC: National Gallery of Art, 1997), p. 215.

126. Barr, *Picasso: Fifty Years of His Art*, p. 261.

127. Ibid., p. 264.

128. Ibid., p. 266.

129. Thomas Chimes, interview with the author, November 8, 2004.

130. *Evergreen Review* 4, no. 13 (May–June 1960).

131. Alfred Jarry, *Exploits and Opinions of Doctor Faustroll, 'Pataphysician*, trans. Simon Watson Taylor (Boston: Exact Change, 1996), p. 22. Jarry proposed the word "'Pataphysics" to describe his science of imaginary solutions to avoid the simple pun of "patte à physique," which translates as, among other things, "to pat the belly."

132. For an excellent account of the enthusiastic response by modern artists, especially the Surrealists, to Jarry's immortal hero, see Renée Riese Hubert, "*Ubu Roi* and the Surrealist *livre de peintre*," *Word & Image* 3, no. 4 (October–December, 1987), pp. 259–78.

133. Ibid., p. 262.

134. For a good introduction to 'Pataphysics, see Roger Shattuck, "Superliminal Note," *Evergreen Review* 4, no. 13 (May–June 1960), pp. 24–33, later revised and updated as "What Is 'Pataphysics?" *The Innocent Eye: On Modern Literature and the Arts*, pp. 102–6.

135. The list of books and works of art in Faustroll's possession has been interpreted by Jarry scholars as a catalogue of Jarry's own library, perhaps drawn from the items seized by the bailiffs on the occasion of his eviction from the so-called Calvaire du Trucidé at 78, boulevard Port-Royal, or from the pictures that hung in his unusual apartment at 7, rue Cassette, the *Grande Chasublerie*; see Ben Fisher, *The Pataphysician's Library: An Exploration of Alfred Jarry's livres pairs* (Liverpool: Liverpool University Press, 2000).

136. Jarry, *Exploits and Opinions of Doctor Faustroll, 'Pataphysician*, pp. 21–22.

137. Linda Klieger Stillman, *Alfred Jarry* (Boston: Twayne Publishers, 1983), p. 27.

138. Shattuck, *The Banquet Years*, p. 241.

139. Jarry, *Exploits and Opinions of Doctor Faustroll, 'Pataphysician*, p. 7.

140. Ibid., p. 30.

141. Ibid., p. 27.

142. Ibid., p. 100.

143. Ibid., p. 99.

144. Ibid., p. 114.

145. A testimony to the validity of paradox, Faustroll's vessel also reveals Jarry's consummate skill in recasting scientific documents into literature. Linda Klieger Stillman has pointed out that the skiff is constructed from woven quartz fiber and coated with melted paraffin. When placed in water, the skiff would stay afloat according to the laws of surface tension, weightless membranes, surfaces without curvature, and the elastic skin of water demonstrated by the English physicist Charles Vernon Boys. All of these phenomena were central to Boys's experiments, the findings of which he published as *Soap Bubbles and the Forces Which Mould Them* (London: SPCK, 1890), which were appropriated and embellished by Jarry; see Klieger Stillman, *Alfred Jarry*, p. 21.

146. Alfred Jarry, *Exploits and Opinions of Doctor Faustroll, 'Pataphysician*, p. 17.

147. For more on Beardsley's portrait of Jarry, see Jill Fell, "The Deceptive Images of Alfred Jarry: Lost, Found and Invented Portraits by Beardsley, Rousseau and Rippl-Ronaï," *Word & Image* 15, no. 2 (April–June 1999), pp. 190–98.

148. By placing Beardsley/Ali Baba in the jar of burning oil, Jarry reversed the real ending of the Ali Baba story, in which Ali Baba himself pours the oil over the robbers hiding inside the jars. I agree with Jill Fell that this reversal of the original plot allows Jarry, an openly homosexual man who prided himself on his fearless artistic integrity, to attack Beardsley for his failure to offer any gesture of support when Wilde issued his great cry in favor of the silent multitude of homosexuals; see Fell, *Alfred Jarry*, pp. 133–34.

149. Anne d'Harnoncourt, "Thomas Chimes," in *Philadelphia: Three Centuries of American Art*, exh. cat. (Philadelphia: Philadelphia Museum of Art, 1976), p. 636.

150. Alfred Jarry, *Exploits and Opinions of Doctor Faustroll, 'Pataphysician*, p. 104.

151. Ibid., pp. 10–11.

152. Alfred Jarry, *The Supermale*, trans. Ralph Gladstone and Barbara Wright (New York: New Directions, 1977), p. 77.

153. Chris Snodgrass, *Aubrey Beardsley, Dandy of the Grotesque* (New York: Oxford University Press, 1995), p. 162. As Snodgrass relates, "Beardsley was fascinated and unusually preoccupied by the grotesque—not surprisingly, perhaps, for someone who as a child was nicknamed 'weasel' and whose physical appearance was generally mocked throughout his life" (ibid., p. 28).

154. Another example of Chimes's modifications of the panel portraits can be found in *Doctor I. L. Sandomir*, of 1974 (pl. 54), which was reduced from its original height of 20¼ inches to its current size of 17⁷⁄₁₆ inches.

155. Berg, " . . . Time and Space Made Perceptible to the Heart," p. 9.

156. Eileen Berger, "A Conversation with Tom Chimes," *Arts Exchange* (Philadelphia) 2, no. 2 (March–April 1978)

156. Chimes vehemently rejects the decision by some art historians to downgrade the painting to a pupil or follower of Rembrandt, believing that only the Dutch master could have painted such a powerful image of Christ.

157. As Linda Klieger Stillman has noted, Jarry pilfered entire sections of Lord Kelvin's *Popular Lectures and Addresses* (1855–1887) to describe Faustroll's sojourn away from earth, but by juxtaposing and melding these borrowed measurements and expressions "with others not closely associated in the original, he intensifies them, forging a new language more kelvinesque than Lord Kelvin's"; see Stillman, "Physics and Pataphysics: The Sources of Faustroll," *Kentucky Romance Quarterly* 36, no. 1 (1979), p. 86.

158. Roger Shattuck, letter to Thomas Chimes, September 23, 1986, collection of the artist.

159. Chimes had come across Sarah Bernhardt during his research for the Oscar Wilde panel portrait, noting that Jarry once praised a circus clown for looking like her; see John Stokes, *Oscar Wilde: Myths, Miracles, and Imitations* (Cambridge: Cambridge University Press, 1996), p. 115. Bernhardt's scandalous behavior was more than a match for Jarry's, and Chimes was also aware that the actress had played herself *en travesti* in Marcel Schwob's famous production of Shakespeare's *Hamlet* for the French stage; see Pascal Pia, "Marcel Schwob," *Evergreen Review* 4, no. 13 (May–June 1960), p. 111. Bernhardt's connections with Jarry, Wilde, and Schwob convinced Chimes to paint a portrait of the famous actress in the role of Tosca, in which her upturned eyes recall the artist's earlier representation of Artaud.

160. Ludwig Wittgenstein, *Tractatus Logico-Philosophicus*, trans. C. K. Ogden (London: Routledge and Kegan Paul, 1922), p. 183.

161. The Collège de 'Pataphysique was founded to preserve the memory of Jarry by publishing numerous *cahiers* and *dossiers* on his art and writings. For more on the history of the Collège, see Lewis Franklin Sutton, "An Evaluation of the Studies on Alfred Jarry from 1934 to 1963 (Ph.D. diss., University of North Carolina, 1966), pp. 139–55; and A *True History of the College of 'Pataphysics*, trans. Paul Edwards, ed. Alastair Brotchie (London: Atlas Press, 1995).

162. Simon Watson Taylor, "The College of 'Pataphysics: An Apodeictic Outline," *Evergreen Review* 4, no. 13 (May–June 1960), p. 154.

163. Ibid. Paulhan may have been suspicious of the fact that Ubu, as well as being former king of Aragon and captain of the Dragons, was also the Count of Sandomir.

164. Thomas Chimes, "Statement on Marcel Duchamp," Artists' Panel Discussion *Duchamp and Art Today: Where Do We Go from Here?* at the Philadelphia Museum College of Art, October 18, 1987.

165. Joris-Karl Huysmans, *Against Nature*, trans. Robert Baldick (London: Penguin, 1959), p. 158.

166. Thomas Chimes, letter to Evan Turner, September 15, 1975, Correspondence Series, Evan Turner Records, Philadelphia Museum of Art Archives.

167. Ibid. Chimes was fully aware that Jarry had exerted an enormous influence on Duchamp's work, especially *The Large Glass*, which the Philadelphia artist believes was made according to the principles of 'Pataphysics. For more on the role played by Jarry in the formation of Duchamp's art and ideas, see William Anastasi, "Duchamp on the Jarry Road," *Artforum* 30, no. 1 (September 1991), pp. 86–90.

168. Roland Barthes, *Camera Lucida: Reflections on Photography*, trans. Richard Howard (New York: Farrar, Straus and Giroux, 1981), pp. 25–28.

169. Ibid., p. 27.

170. Guillaume Apollinaire, "Souvenirs sur Alfred Jarry," *Les Marges* (Paris), November 1909, p. 28; reprinted in Nigey Lennon, *Alfred Jarry: The Man with the Axe* (San Francisco: Last Gasp, 1984), p. 91.

171. Roger Shattuck, "Introduction," in Alfred Jarry, *Exploits and Opinions of Doctor Faustroll, 'Pataphysician*, p. x.

172. For more on Apollinaire's final years, see Shattuck, *The Banquet Years*, pp. 291–97.

173. Georges Poulet and Robert Kopp, eds., *Baudelaire: The Artist and His World*, trans. Robert Allen and James Emmons (Geneva: Editions d'Art Albert Skira, 1969).

174. Thomas Chimes, interview with the author, September 20, 2000.

175. Chimes, "Statement on Marcel Duchamp."

176. Berger, "A Conversation with Tom Chimes," p. 24.

177. Ibid.

178. Roger Shattuck, *The Banquet Years*, p. 351.

179. Alfred Jarry, "How to Construct a Time Machine," in *Selected Works of Alfred Jarry*, p. 121.

180. Ashbery, "Antonin Artaud," p. 116. An inscription on the verso of Chimes's painting, which reads "I work / in infinity / itself / Antonin Artaud / 1925," was taken from Artaud's 1925 Surrealist poem "Fragments of a Journey in Hell," which had been reprinted, in a translation by Kenneth Koch, in the same issue as Ashbery's essay; ibid., pp. 117–18.

181. For a thought-provoking analysis of the 1939 *Time* photo-essay on Joyce, see Maurizia Boscagli and Enda Duffy, "Joyce's Face," in Kevin J. H. Dettmar and Stephan Watt, eds., *Marketing Modernisms: Self-Promotion, Canonization, Rereading* (Ann Arbor: University of Michigan Press, 1996), pp. 133–59. As Boscagli and Duffy argue, Freund's photograph of the restless, ill-at-ease writer and the accompanying *Time* article define Joyce "by his alienation; he allows himself to be presented to the public here as a modernist, 'obscure' author who can be recontained within popularly accepted categories

around the ideologeme of exile. As the modernist in exile, his is the stance of the restless artist who is always moving" (ibid., p. 145).

182. Gisèle Freund, *Three Days with Joyce* (New York: Persea Books, 1985), p. 43.

183. Benjamin H. D. Buchloh, "Divided Memory and Post-Traditional Identity: Gerhard Richter's Work of Mourning," *October* 75 (Winter 1996), pp. 61–82.

184. Although Wilde refused to divulge the identity of the author of this allegedly degenerate book during cross-examination at his 1895 Queensbury trial, it has subsequently been identified as *A Rebours*. The Irish writer admired Jarry and owned a complete collection of his works. In a letter to Reginald Turner, postmarked May 25, 1898, Wilde declared, "Jarry is now the rising light of the *Quartier Latin*. In person he is most attractive. He looks just like a very nice renter"; see *The Complete Letters of Oscar Wilde*, ed. Merlin Holland and Rupert Hart-Davis (London: Fourth Estate, 2000), p. 1075.

185. Oscar Wilde, *The Picture of Dorian Gray*, ed. Isobel Murray (London: Oxford University Press, 1974), p. 125.

186. The original photograph, taken around 1901, is reproduced in Pie Duployé, *Huysmans* (Brugge: Editions Desclée De Brouwer, 1968), p. 49, although Chimes probably knew the image through a cropped version that was used as the frontispiece to James Laver, *The First Decadent: Being the Strange Life of J. K. Huysmans* (New York: Citadel Press, 1955). Both reproductions reveal that Chimes removed a great deal of background detail in this austere panel portrait, such as the four works of art that originally hung on the wall behind Huysmans, as well as the bouquet of flowers that nestled between the bent legs of Christ on the cross, which were clearly superfluous to the artist's requirements and would have distracted from the triangular arrangement of the writer, the crucifix, and the candlestick. Stripped of his possessions, Huysmans has the appearance of a monk in a darkened cell, which perhaps conforms to Chimes's own image of the writer at the end of his life, when he devoted himself to the study of religious mysticism.

187. Robert Storr, "Gerhard Richter: Forty Years of Painting," in Storr, ed., *Gerhard Richter: Forty Years of Painting*, exh. cat. (New York: The Museum of Modern Art, 2002), p. 62.

188. Ibid., p. 64.

189. Ibid.

190. Ibid.

191. Thomas Chimes, interview with the author, October 15, 2002.

192. As Coosje van Bruggen has pointed out, "The absence of women enforces the impression of a male-dominated society; where are writers like Jane Austen, Emily Dickinson, Virginia Woolf; the composers Clara Schumann and Ethel Smyth; the astronomer Henrietta Leavitt or the scientist Marie Curie, to mention a few? But women are not allowed; according to Richter, because of their difference in features and clothing, the inclusion of one or two female portraits would disrupt the homogeneous, linear flow of the installation"; see Coosje van Bruggen, "Gerhard Richter: Painting as a Moral Act," *Artforum* 23, no. 9 (May 1985), p. 91.

193. Robert Duncan, "Iconographical Extensions," in *Translations by Jess*, exh. cat. (New York: Odyssia Gallery, 1971), n.p.

194. Shattuck, *The Banquet Years*, n.p.

195. *Selected Works of Alfred Jarry*, p. 272 n. 5.

196. For more on Jarry's friendship with and support for Rousseau, see Henri Béhar, "Jarry, Rousseau, and Popular Tradition," in *Henri Rousseau*, exh. cat. (New York: The Museum of Modern Art, 1984), pp. 23–27.

197. Alfred Jarry, *Exploits and Opinions of Doctor Faustroll, 'Pataphysician*, p. 86.

198. Ibid., p. 88.

199. Martin, "Tom Chimes: A Personal Odyssey," p. 10.

200. André Breton, *Nadja*, trans. Richard Howard (New York: Grove Press, 1960), p. 56. Breton recounted that the glove was "a bronze one she happened to possess and which I have subsequently seen at her home—also a woman's glove, the wrist folded over, the fingers flat—a glove I can never resist picking up, always astonished at its weight and interested, apparently, only in calculating its precise weight against what the other glove would not have weighed at all" (ibid).

201. Ibid., p. 72.

202. Ibid., p. 90 (translation slightly modified by the author).

203. Ibid., p. 57. The glove may also have been associated in Breton's mind with Max Klinger's famous suite of etchings, entitled *Paraphrase on the Finding of a Glove*, of 1881, which anticipates the role of chance and fetishistic desire in Surrealism.

204. Ibid., p. 86.

205. André Breton, "Alfred Jarry," in *Anthology of Black Humor*, trans. Mark Polizzotti (San Francisco: City Lights Books, 1997), p. 211.

206. Veloric, interview with Thomas Chimes, July 2, 1990, p. 79.

207. *Selected Works of Alfred Jarry*, n.p.

208. Alfred Jarry, "Les Paralipomènes d'Ubu," *La Revue Blanche* 11, no. 84 (December 1, 1896); reprinted in Stillman, *Alfred Jarry*, p. 44.

209. For more on the allure of Niagara Falls for nineteenth-century American artists, see Gail S. Davidson, "Landscape Icons, Tourism, and Land Development in the Northeast," in Davidson et al., eds., *Frederic Church,*

...low Homer, and Thomas Moran: Tourism and American Landscape*, exh. cat. (Boston: Bulfinch Press, in association with Cooper-Hewitt, National Design Museum, Smithsonian Institution, 2006), pp. 3–22.

210. Thomas Chimes, interview with the author, November 30, 2005.

211. Arthur Conan Doyle, "The Final Problem," in *The Memoirs of Sherlock Holmes*, Christopher Roden, ed. (Oxford: Oxford University Press, 1993), pp. 249–68.

212. Barbara Wright, "Introduction," in Alfred Jarry, *The Supermale*, trans. Ralph Gladstone and Barbara Wright (New York: New Directions, 1977), n.p.

213. Bernard Chaet, *An Artist's Notebook: Techniques and Materials* (New York: Holt, Rinehart and Winston, 1979), n.p.

214. *Rise Up, Man of the Hooths*, whose title comes from Joyce's *Finnegan's Wake*, is perhaps the most abstract painting that Chimes has ever made, a fact that was acknowledged by its inclusion in *The Big Nothing*, a city-wide exhibition organized by the Institute of Contemporary Art in Philadelphia in 2004, devoted to the concept of nothingness in contemporary art.

215. Barry Schwabsky, "Theater of Memory," *Art in America* 83, no. 1 (January 1995), p. 94.

216. Thomas Chimes, "Winter is white," c. 1980, unpublished poem, collection of the artist.

217. James Joyce, "The Dead," in *Dubliners* (New York: Penguin Books, 1993), p. 225.

218. Ibid.

219. Marian Locks, "A Conversation with Thomas Chimes and Marian Locks," in *Thomas Chimes*, exh. cat. (Philadelphia: Marian Locks Gallery, 1990), n.p.

220. For an excellent biography of Rachilde, see Diana Holmes, *Rachilde: Decadence, Gender, and the Woman Writer* (Oxford: Berg, 2001), especially pp. 52–53, which discusses her friendship with Jarry.

221. Rachilde, *Alfred Jarry ou le Surmâle de Lettres*, La Vie de Bohème (Paris: Bernard Grasset, 1928). Although the book consists of largely anecdotal reminiscences, Rachilde's biography, the first to be published on Jarry, contains invaluable material on his life and work.

222. See Shattuck, *The Banquet Years*, pp. 113–85. Chimes was particularly struck by a passage in Shattuck's book in which the author describes Satie's *Socrate* as a "pure phenomenon, utterly *white* music, which denies its own existence as it goes along by an absolute refusal of development" (ibid., p. 160). Chimes began his first painting of Satie after reading Shattuck's evocation of the avant-garde composer's masterpiece and then listening to his symphony on the death of Socrates, which he found deeply moving.

223. The art historian Carola Giedion-Welcker is to my knowledge the first person to find a link between the two writers, when she compared Jarry's multifaceted character Varia, in *L'Amour absolu*, with Joyce's Anna Livia Plurabelle; see Giedion-Welcker, *Alfred Jarry* (Zurich: Die Arche, 1960), p. 81. William Anastasi has also discovered many rich and fascinating, yet often serendipitous, correspondences between the writings of Joyce and Jarry; see Anastasi, "Joyce and Jarry," in Aaron Levy and Jean-Michel Rabaté, eds., *William Anastasi's Pataphysical Society* (Philadelphia: Slought Books, 2005), pp. 44–52.

224. In Irish, the River Liffey is known as *Eanach Life*, which led it to be anglicized on old maps of Dublin as Anna Liffey, thus leading Joyce to associate his Anna Livia Plurabelle character with the famous river; see Patrick A. McCarthy, *Joyce, Family, "Finnegan's Wake,"* National Library of Ireland Joyce Studies (Dublin: National Library of Ireland, 2005), p. 9.

225. In 2004 the Royal Hibernian Academy in Dublin mounted an important exhibition entitled *Joyce in Art: Visual Art Inspired by James Joyce*, which included Chimes's 1974 panel portrait of James Joyce, alongside the work of many other contemporary artists who have responded to Joyce's work, including Joseph Beuys, Richard Hamilton, William Anastasi, and John Latham; see Christa-Maria Lerm Hayes, *Joyce in Art: Visual Art Inspired by James Joyce*, exh. cat. (Dublin: Lilliput Press, 2004).

226. Patrick Murphy, ed., *Conversation Pieces: Alan Charlton, Thomas Chimes, Hamish Fulton, Bill Walton, Richard Torchia, Richard Wentworth*, exh. cat. (Philadelphia: Institute of Contemporary Art, University of Pennsylvania, 1994).

227. Thomas Chimes quoted in Stephen Berg, "Framed Faces, Infinite White," in *Tom Chimes: A Compendium 1961–1986*, p. 17.

228. Locks, "A Conversation with Thomas Chimes," n.p.

229. Carl Gustav Jung, *The Archetypes and the Collective Unconscious*, trans. R. F. C. Hull (New York: Pantheon, 1959), p. 311.

230. Joe Clark, "She'll Be Living on the Edge," *Philadelphia Daily News*, May 7, 1991, p. 6.

231. Stephen Berg, letter to Penny Balkin Bach, March 11, 1986, Fairmount Park Art Association Archives.

232. Ibid.

233. Charles E. Mather III, letter to Stephen Berg, November 6, 1986, Fairmount Park Art Association Archives.

234. Thomas Chimes, letter to Stephen Berg, November 26, 1986, Fairmount Park Art Association Archives. The word "rush" is a pun on nineteenth-century American sculptor William Rush, whose allegorical sculptures personifying the Schuylkill River were discussed by Chimes at the end of the letter.

235. Anndee Hochman, "A Man of His Word," *Philadelphia Inquirer Magazine*, July 16, 1995, p. 24.

236. Clark, "She'll Be Living on the Edge," p. 6.

237. Ibid.

238. Berg mentioned Giacometti in a letter to Penny Balkin Bach, in which he quoted the Swiss artist's description of his work as "conceptual confrontations with the unknown"; see Stephen Berg, letter to Penny Balkin Bach, March 27, 1987, Fairmount Park Art Association Archives.

239. Thomas Chimes, letter to Stephen Berg, November 26, 1986, Fairmount Park Art Association Archives.

240. For a general overview of the sources and symbolism of *Little Sparta* and other public art projects that Finlay has undertaken, see Yves Abrioux, ed., *Ian Hamilton Finlay: A Visual Primer* (Edinburgh: Reaktion Books, 1985), which was published the year before Berg submitted his application to the Fairmount Park Art Association.

241. Berg explained in 1986: "In my most recent talk with Tom, the idea of permanence came up, and we both agree that to carve the line of poetry into the stone might be a mistake. First of all it implies that the poem is already a classic, that time has had a chance to decide whether it should last. In response to that, we decided it would probably be best to print or paint the poem on the stone using a material that would last about twenty years, or a 'generation'"; see Stephen Berg, letter to Penny Balkin Bach, April 15, 1986, Fairmount Park Art Association Archives.

242. Evelyn Hess, "Disappearing Words Unveil the *Sleeping Woman*," *Welcomat* (Philadelphia), May 22, 1991, p. 32.

243. Penny Balkin Bach, *Public Art in Philadelphia* (Philadelphia: Temple University Press, 1992), p. 259.

244. Stephen Berg, interview with the author, July 26, 2006.

245. Clark, "She'll Be Living on the Edge," p. 6.

246. Edward Colimore, "Poem on Schuylkill Wall Has Gotten Even Deeper," *Philadelphia Inquirer*, August 22, 1991, sec. A, p. 1. According to the *Inquirer*, underground springs and recent heavy rains, combined with rotten wooden pilings beneath the turn-of-the-century retaining wall, caused it to collapse into the storm-churned river; ibid., p. 16.

247. Thomas Chimes, interview with the author, July 5, 2006.

248. Ibid.

249. Rudolf Arnheim, *Entropy and Art: An Essay on Disorder and Order* (Berkeley: University of California Press, 1971), p. 7.

250. Robert Smithson, "Entropy and the New Monuments," *Artforum* 4, no. 10 (June 1966), p. 26.

251. Ibid.

252. Robert Smithson, " . . . The Earth, Subject to Cataclysms, Is a Cruel Master" (1971), in *Robert Smithson: The Collected Writings*, ed. Jack Flam (Berkeley: University of California Press, 1996), p. 257.

253. Stillman, "Physics and Pataphysics," pp. 81–82.

254. According to Michel Arrivé, *gidouille* is a deformation of the Old French *guedoufle* or *guedouille*, a double vessel for oil and vinegar that Rabelais likened to a pair of testicles. Jarry's appropriation of this word for the potbelly of his middle-aged physics teacher, which thus becomes a gigantic pair of bollocks, seems entirely plausible. See Arrivé, *Les langages de Jarry: Essai de sémiotique littéraire* (Paris: Klincksieck, 1972), p. 211.

255. James Joyce, *Finnegan's Wake* (London: Penguin, 1976), p. 628.

256. The phrase in Joyce's *Finnegan's Wake* reads: "The keys to. Given!" (ibid.).

257. The artist's interest in the iconography of ancient coins and medallions was spurred by an exhibition of Roman coins organized by his daughter Eva at the University of Maine's Hudson Museum in Bangor, which opened in June 1993.

258. Thomas Chimes, letter to Roger Shattuck, October 7, 1986, pp. 1–2. Collection of the artist.

259. Georges Poulet, "Baudelaire and the Real World," in Poulet and Robert Kopp, eds., *Baudelaire: The Artist and His World*, pp. 165–66.

260. Patricia Stewart, "Tom Chimes" in *Tom Chimes: An Exhibition of Portraits, 1973–1978*, exh. cat. (Charleston, WV: The Museums at Sunrise, Department of Fine Arts, 1978), n.p.

261. Thomas Chimes, "Departure from the Present," in *Thomas Chimes*, exh. brochure (Philadelphia: The Peale House Galleries of the Pennsylvania Academy of the Fine Arts, 1975), n.p. Chimes's statement was directly inspired by Jarry's essay "How to Construct a Time Machine"; see p. 124 above.

262. Berger, "A Conversation with Tom Chimes," p. 24.

263. As this catalogue goes to press Chimes is reading Menas Kafatos and Robert Nadeau, *The Conscious Universe: Parts and Wholes in Physical Reality* (New York: Springer, 2000). Given his intellectual interests, it comes as no surprise to find that the artist is interested in the ideas of a Greek-American scientist, whose work on consciousness and quantum theory he relates to Jarry's concepts of 'Pataphysics.

Chronology

CLAIRE HOWARD

1921

April 20
Thomas James Chimes is born at the Jewish Maternity Hospital in Philadelphia. The eldest surviving son of James and Agnes Chimes, he is given the same name as his parents' first child, who died in infancy. At the time of his birth, the Chimes family lives at 114 Cherry Street, in Elfreth's Alley, the oldest continuously inhabited street in the United States.

Chimes's parents are both immigrants from Greece; his father, born Demetrius Tsamis in Kalávrita in 1883, came to the United States in 1911, returned to Greece briefly to fight in the Balkan Wars, and came back to the United States in 1913, when immigration authorities changed the family name to "Chimis." His mother, born Aglaia Colokythas in Sparta in 1892, came to America in 1900. At his parents' wedding in Philadelphia in 1918, the family was renamed "Chimes."

James Chimes runs a seafood restaurant in the Brewerytown section of Philadelphia. In a 2000 interview, the artist recalled the restaurant as "the most charming place. . . . It had a canopy out front, and long tables with tablecloths. And there was an oyster bar in the front where my mother would do the shucking."

1922

October 9
Thomas's brother George Chimes is born.

1924

April 1
Thomas's brother Nickon James Chimes is born.

1926

At the advice of his cousins, James Chimes moves his family to Ocilla, Georgia, and later to Fitzgerald, Georgia. In the South, he hopes to find the financial success that will allow the family to return to Greece.

1927

Chimes begins first grade at the age of six. He experiences his "awakening to art" when his teacher pins a piece of craft paper to the wall and asks the students to collaborate on a landscape image. He later recalls thinking how magical it was as these things began to "appear and emerge" across the paper's surface.

1929

Summer
The Chimes family moves back to Philadelphia. James reopens his Brewerytown restaurant.

October 24
The stock market crashes, marking the beginning of the Great Depression.

Financial difficulties will plague the Chimes family throughout the Depression. James's restaurant fails early on, and he works for other people until he is able to raise enough money to get back into business.

1931

Chimes attends Mastbaum School of Art, on Broad Street and Columbia Avenue, where he focuses mainly on sculpture in clay. He recalls making a relief of a fish and a three-dimensional lion's head.

1932

The Chimes family moves to 5944 Market Street in West Philadelphia. Thomas enrolls at the Hamilton School at 5700 Spruce Street. He also attends Greek school, where he learns Greek grammar as well as ancient Greek literature. He will develop a lifelong passion for the works of Homer.

1936

The Chimes family moves to 34 S. Redfield Street in West Philadelphia.

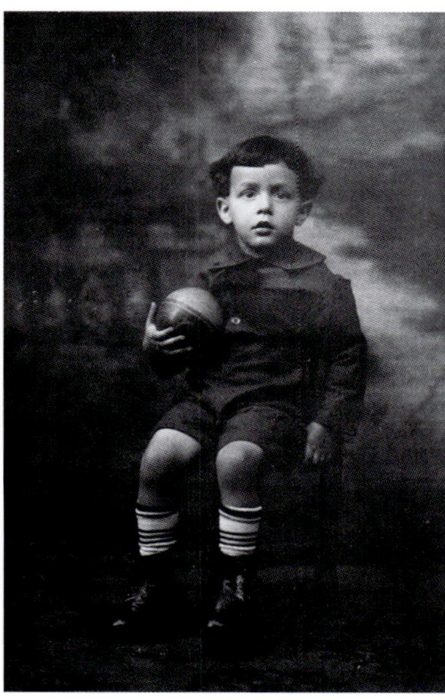

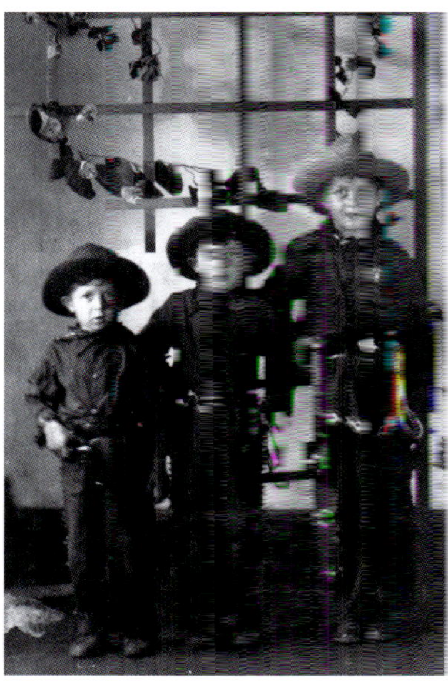

FIG. 14
Thomas Chimes, c. 1924.
Courtesy of the artist.

FIG. 15
Nick, George, and
Thomas Chimes, c. 1927.
Courtesy of the artist.

1938

The Chimes family moves to 5911 Market Street in West Philadelphia.

1939

Spring
Unable to establish a successful business in Philadelphia, James Chimes moves to Anniston, Alabama, to work at Fort McClellan's Post Exchange Restaurant as manager and chef. Agnes remains in West Philadelphia with the children for several months before joining her husband.

June
Chimes graduates from West Philadelphia High School (fig. 146). During his time there, he wins several prizes for his art, and his uncle, Thomas Pope, encourages him to pursue a career as an artist. Chimes later recalls that his parents' "desires for me were quite different. My father saw a career in the military. My mother saw business."

September 29
Chimes enrolls at the Pennsylvania Academy of Fine Arts (fig. 147). Francis Speight and Daniel Garber are among his instructors. He initially funds his education at the Academy with a $500 settlement he received after being assaulted while working for a subway newsstand company.

November 20
Following a disagreement with his instructor, Henry McCarter, and under mounting financial pressure, Chimes withdraws from the Academy and joins his family in Alabama, hoping to earn enough money to finish art school.

1940

James Chimes buys a dry cleaning business in Columbia, South Carolina, near the army base at Fort Jackson. It is the first time James is not involved in the restaurant business. Thomas works for his father.

1941

November
Chimes enrolls in the Art Students League on Fifty-seventh Street in New York, where he takes a class with Frank Vincent DuMond, who had taught John Marin and Georgia O'Keeffe. He lives with his aunt, Rose Coroneos, at 332 W. Forty-ninth Street, near Madison Square Garden.

December 7
The Imperial Japanese Navy attacks Pearl Harbor and the United States enters World War II. Chimes recalls hearing the news over the radio in his aunt's Hell's Kitchen apartment. He returns to Columbia, South Carolina.

1942

Spring
Chimes enrolls at the Palmeto School of Aeronautics in Columbia, South Carolina, where he obtains a license to become an aircraft mechanic.

1943

August 23
Chimes enlists in the U.S. Army Air Forces.

For basic training, he is posted in Greensboro, North Carolina, where Michael Lekakis teaches camouflage. Chimes and Lekakis will later study together at the Art Students League.

1944

While stationed in Sioux Falls, South Dakota, being trained as a radio operator, Chimes receives a telegram that his father has suffered a minor stroke and returns to South Carolina to visit him.

December
Chimes sees Van Gogh's landscapes in the exhibition *Art Treasures from Holland* at the Delgado Museum in New Orleans. He is in New Orleans on a stopover during a trip from Yuma, Arizona, where he had been taking target practice in the desert, to Columbia Air Base, South Carolina, where he was to train as a radio gunner on a B-25 bomber.

1945

April 17
Chimes's father dies of a heart attack in his son's arms in Columbia, South Carolina.

June 15
Chimes is released from service to help his now widowed mother run the family business.

Fig. 146
Chimes in his 1939 West Philadelphia High School yearbook. Collection of the artist

Fig. 147
Chimes's student identification card from the Pennsylvania Academy of the Fine Arts, 1939. Collection of the artist

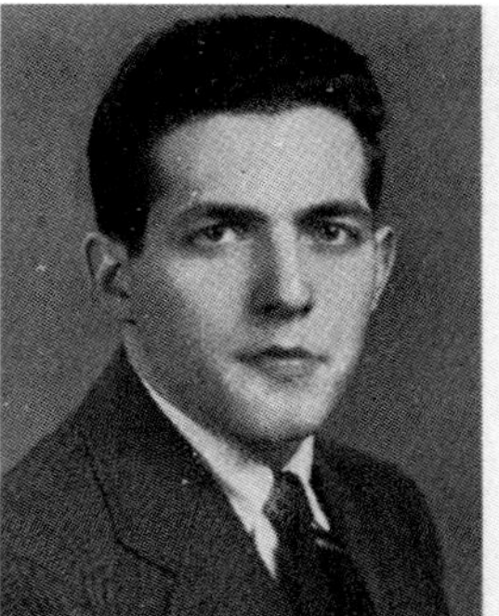

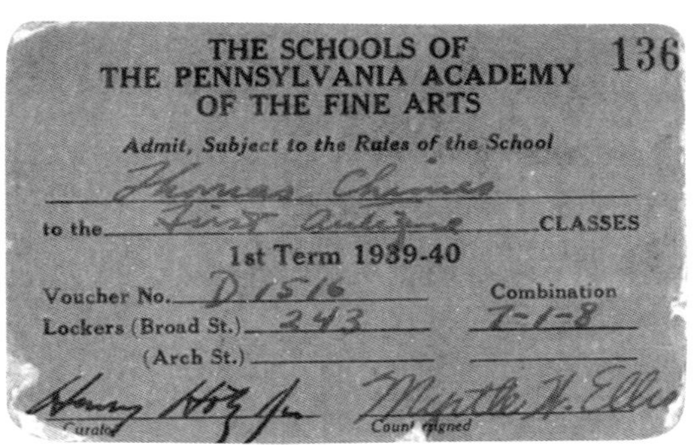

1946

January

Chimes tries to re-enroll at the Pennsylvania Academy of Fine Arts, but there are no openings due to the influx of students under the G.I. Bill. He returns to the Art Students League in New York and finds an opening in an evening class taught by Reginald Marsh, beginning February 1. He will continue to study at the Art Students League through February 1948, receiving most of his funding under the G.I. Bill. He again stays with his Aunt Rose, who has now remarried and lives in Washington Heights.

Spring

Chimes and Michael Lekakis are reunited in John Hovannes's sculpture class. Lekakis has lived in the city before and will introduce Chimes to many of the major avant-garde artists of the time. Chimes will come to consider Lekakis one of the closest friends he has in the city, and will fondly recall the dance parties that the latter hosted at his studio.

Chimes meets Dawn DeWeese in Reginald Marsh's evening class; Dawn is a fellow painting student who has family in Philadelphia, Mississippi.

Fall

Chimes and his brother George (fig. 148) move into the West Side YMCA at 5 West Sixty-third Street.

1947

June

Chimes and Dawn marry, just one year after meeting at the Art Students League, in the Broadway Tabernacle nondenominational church on Fifty-sixth Street and Broadway, between Seventh and Eighth avenues. Dawn's sister Joan and Thomas's brother George are witnesses.

Chimes enrolls at Columbia University, where he takes two philosophy courses and a medieval art class.

1948

February

Chimes completes his studies at the Art Students League but remains in contact with the individuals he met there; his mentors and friends include Michael Lekakis, Theodoros Stamos, and Tony Smith.

1949

Chimes leaves New York for Philadelphia, staying at his mother's house at 6158 Locust Street. Agnes would soon purchase the Victory Café at Thirtieth and Market streets, and Chimes would work mornings at the restaurant for seven months.

1950

May 29

Chimes's son Dmitri is born at Jefferson Hospital in Philadelphia.

Summer–Fall

Chimes leaves Philadelphia to teach a class in landscape painting at a community art center in Chautauqua, New York, where his wife's family has a house.

1951

Spring

The Chimes family leaves Chautauqua and lives temporarily with Dawn's sister Joan and her husband, Herb Nelson, in Fort Lee, New Jersey, while looking for an apartment in New York. The family finds an apartment on Ogden Avenue in the Bronx, where Chimes sets up a studio. He experiments with Abstract Expressionist paintings, including a dripped canvas resembling a work by Jackson Pollock, but is distracted by family life and money concerns.

1952

June–December

Chimes, Dawn, and two-year-old Dmitri embark on a seven-month trip through Europe, visiting Athens, Delphi, and Crete in Greece before traveling across Italy and southern France to Paris. Chimes tries to visit Kalávrita while in Greece, but is prevented from seeing his father's birthplace by a train derailment. In Vence, he is impressed by Matisse's Chapel of the Rosary of the Dominican Nuns, which he considers "the most powerful artistic statement of our time."

October–December

The Chimes family lives in a tiny second-floor apartment at 77, rue Taitbout, at the foot of Montmartre. Chimes shares a studio across from the Luxembourg Gardens with the painter Constantin Macris; André Derain had occupied the studio in the 1920s.

Lekakis and Chimes visit Alberto Giacometti's studio at 46, rue Hippolyte-Maindron in Montparnasse.

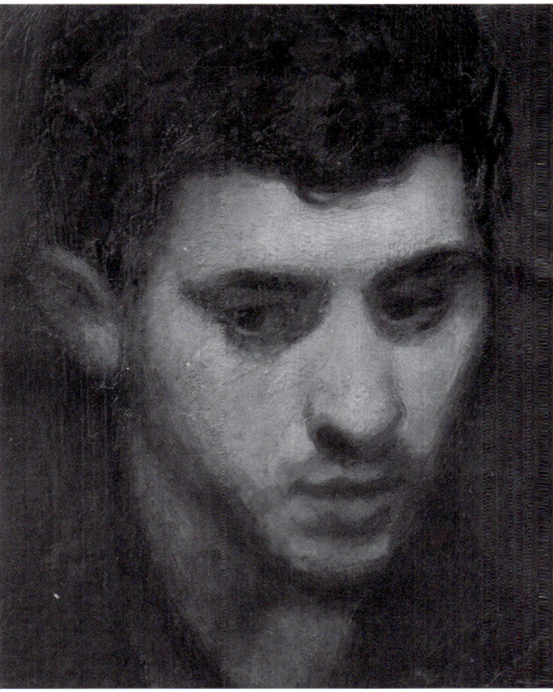

Fig. 148
Thomas Chimes, *Portrait of George Chimes*, 1948
Oil on canvas, 13⅜ × 11⅛
inches (34.1 × 28.4 cm)
Collection of the artist

1953

Chimes returns briefly to New York, living on West Thirteenth Street, before moving to Philadelphia in the summer. The Chimes family lives for a few months at George Chimes's former apartment at Woodland Terrace in West Philadelphia. Chimes and Dawn purchase a house at 315 South Forty-fourth Street, where Chimes sets up his studio. He works at Raoul A. Ibarguen's architectural and industrial design firm to support his family. Chimes has lived and worked in Philadelphia ever since.

1955

February 10
Chimes's daughter Eva is born.

1957

In the artist's first group exhibition, Chimes's early abstract landscapes are shown along with works by Reuben Nakian at the Avant-Garde Gallery in New York City, run by fellow Philadelphian Bernard Davis.

1958

February
Chimes's first one-man exhibition opens at the Avant-Garde Gallery. The artist shows a group of small oil paintings influenced by Nicolas de Staël.

1958–60

Chimes teaches evening drawing classes in the School of Architecture at the Drexel Institute (now Drexel University).

1959

In an attempt to find another gallery in New York, following the closure of the Avant-Garde Gallery, Chimes shows his paintings to curator Alicia Legg at the Museum of Modern Art. Legg suggests Alexander Iolas's gallery, which is at that time considered the city's most important venue for Surrealist art. After a series of discussions, Iolas decides not to exhibit Chimes's work, judging that the artist's inclusion of crucifixes in his canvases contra-

dicts Surrealism's anti-religious stance. Eventually Chimes exhibits at the Bodley Gallery run by David Mann, who once worked for Iolas, and Georgie Duffee, who would become an important advocate for Chimes's work.

1960

Chimes moves his workspace to a small studio in a downtown office building at 34 South Seventeenth Street. There he embarks upon a series of works combining landscape references with specific symbols from Matisse and from his Greek Orthodox upbringing, such as stars, ladders, X-shapes, and, most importantly, the crucifix.

1961

The Museum of Modern Art, New York, acquires *Study for "The Inner World"* (pl. 6) for $75. Alfred H. Barr, Jr., also purchases one smaller work for $50 for his own collection. Barr's actions startle the conservative Philadelphia art community, where Chimes's work is perceived as a challenge to the more traditional aesthetic associated with the city. *Study for "The Inner World"* is included in the museum's *Recent Acquisitions* exhibition, December 1961 to February 1962. In a January 14, 1962, article on the acquisition, Chimes tells the *Philadelphia Evening Bulletin*, "I've got places to go and things to do." Reporter John F. Morrison notes an eighteen-foot-wide canvas, which will eventually become *Mural* (pl. 15), in the corner of Chimes's Seventeenth Street studio.

Chimes's 1960 painting *Bazaar* is included in *Recent American Painting and Sculpture*, an exhibition coordinated by assistant curator of the Department of Painting and Sculpture Alicia Legg and circulated by the Museum of Modern Art in 1961–62. The exhibition travels to the Ringling Museum of Art in Sarasota, Florida, where the artist's first retrospective would later be held, and eventually to Helsinki, Finland.

1962

Chimes and his family move to 111 North Van Pelt Street, Philadelphia, where his neighbors include artist, print publisher, and eventual gallery owner Rodger LaPelle, as well as Pennsylvania Academy of the Fine Arts instructor Roswell Widener and his wife Marilyn.

Chimes's *Untitled* of 1961 (pl. 5), a study for *Mural*, is given anonymously (by Alfred H. Barr, Jr.) to the Museum of Modern Art. This work is part of a group of fifty-plus drawings executed as studies for his paintings of that time, his last intense period of drawing, after which he would draw less and try to invent his compositions directly on the canvas.

June 9–24
Chimes's canvas *Study #2 for "The Kingdom"* is included in the *Third Philadelphia Arts Festival*; it is his first work to be exhibited at the Philadelphia Museum of Art. The oil painting is priced at $2,200.

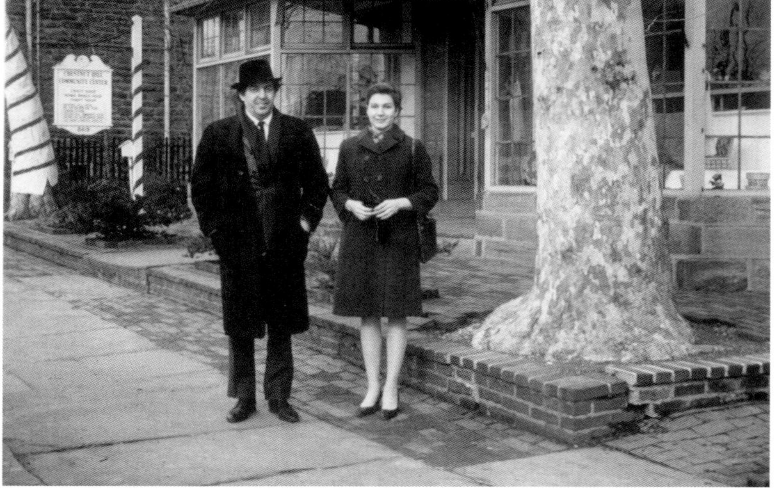
Fig. 149
Thomas and Dawn Chimes, Chestnut Hill, Philadelphia, mid-1960s. Courtesy of the artist

1963

Chimes begins work on *Man in Exile . . .* , later renamed *Mural*, an eighteen-foot-wide composition that he will complete in 1965.

Chimes's one-man exhibition at the Bodley Gallery is a huge success, attracting many prominent New York collectors. From this show, Alfred H. Barr, Jr., acquires *Crucifix* of 1961 (pl. 4) for the Museum of Modern Art.

1964

January 6–25

The Bodley Gallery includes Chimes in its *Six Surrealist Painters* exhibition, placing him in the company of Victor Brauner, Max Ernst, Eugenio Granell, René Magritte, and Matta.

Chimes's work is rented to members of the Museum of Modern Art through the museum's Junior Council Lending Service, a program to encourage the appreciation and purchase of contemporary art by new collectors who might otherwise be intimidated by the gallery system.

1965

Chimes completes *Mural*, the largest painting he has ever made.

January 18–30

Chimes has his second one-man show at the Bodley Gallery. The gallery's "Note to Collectors" declares Chimes a "New Name" poised to "attain stardom" and links him with other "great names of Surrealism," including Yves Tanguy, Arshile Gorky, and Joan Miró. In a review in the *Philadelphia Inquirer*, Charlotte Lichtblau echoes this sentiment, remarking that Chimes "may well emerge as one of the major new talents of contemporary painting."

March 7–April 11

Chimes's 1963–64 work *Baroque* (pl. 16) is included in the biennial survey *Contemporary American Painting and Sculpture* at the Krannert Art Museum, University of Illinois at Urbana-Champaign. The work is lent by the Bodley Gallery and is priced at $700. Chimes's response to a questionnaire sent by the museum to exhibiting artists lists his work in the collections of Larry Aldrich, Walter Bareiss, Alfred H. Barr, Jr., Armand Bartos, Mr. and Mrs. Raymond Braun, Arne Ekstrom, Betty Parsons, G. David Thompson, and several others. Chimes's work is shown alongside that of contemporaries including Roy Lichtenstein, Wayne Thiebaud, and Robert Indiana.

Chimes begins to create a series of metal box constructions that fuse the pristine, hard-edged quality of Minimalist art with the witty, sexy vitality of Pop Art. These mixed-media works incorporate small drawings of symbolic images within the austere confines of the metal casing. Chimes attends René Magritte's opening at the Museum of Modern Art wearing one of the earliest versions of these metal boxes, an aluminum medallion approximately 6¾ inches in diameter, which Salvador Dalí notices and calls "trés jolie." New York gallery owner Virginia Dwan would sell this medallion for $350 to the collector Frederic Ossorio the following year, an unauthorized sale that effectively ends Chimes's relationship with the Bodley Gallery.

July

Museum of Modern Art curator of painting and sculpture Peter Selz awards Chimes's aluminum construction *Momo Talk* (see fig. 49) the $500 Chautauqua Institution Award in the Chautauqua Exhibition of American Art Eighth National Jury Show in Chautauqua, New York. Chimes cannot attend the awards ceremony and sends his son Dmitri in his place (fig. 150). Chimes would destroy *Momo Talk* with a chainsaw in the early 1970s, a symbolic act intended to mark the end of his metal box phase as he begins work on the panel portraits.

1966

February–March

Chimes exhibits *Baroque* (1963–64) at The Art Gallery at the University of California, Santa Barbara, in a group exhibition entitled *Surrealism: A State of Mind, 1924–1965*. Selected by the legendary art dealer Julien Levy, this exhibition also includes major works by Salvador Dalí, Marcel Duchamp, Max Ernst, Man Ray, and André Masson.

1966–67

Chimes teaches painting at the Philadelphia College of Art (now the University of the Arts).

1967

March 17–April 16

Chimes is included in the Pennsylvania Academy of the Fine Arts Annual Exhibition of Painting and Sculpture, where his entry, *Untitled*, wins the Mary Butler Memorial Award for a work in any medium.

May 15

Chimes participates in an exhibition, organized by Jim McWilliams, at the Socrates Perakis Art Gallery along

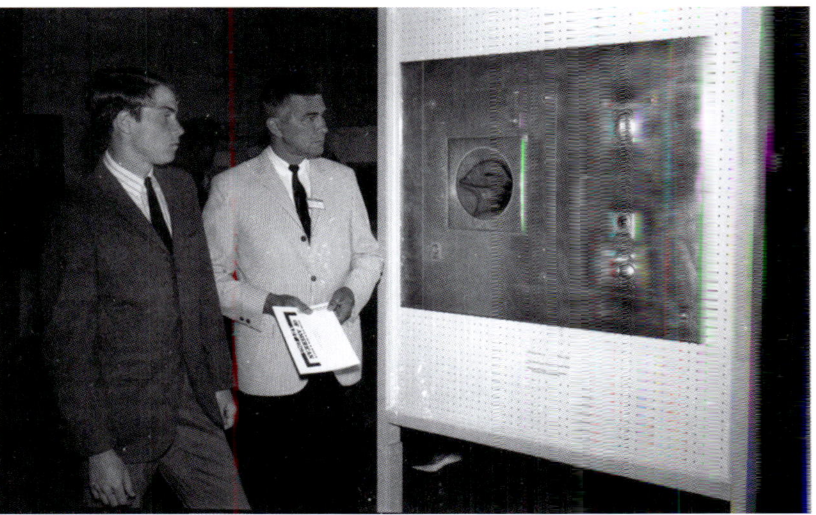
Fig. 150
Dmitri Chimes and Peter Selz with *Momo Talk* at the 1965 Chautauqua Exhibition of American Art, Chautauqua Art Association, Chautauqua, New York. Courtesy of the artist

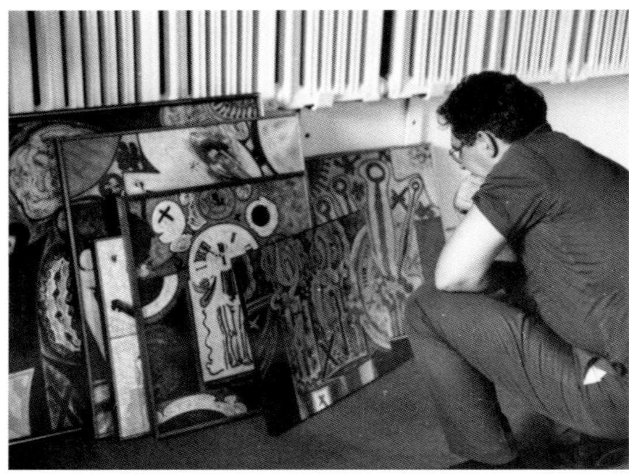
Fig. 151
James Harithas, then director of the Corcoran Gallery of Art in Washington, DC, in Chimes's studio in Merion, Pennsylvania, 1967. Courtesy of the artist

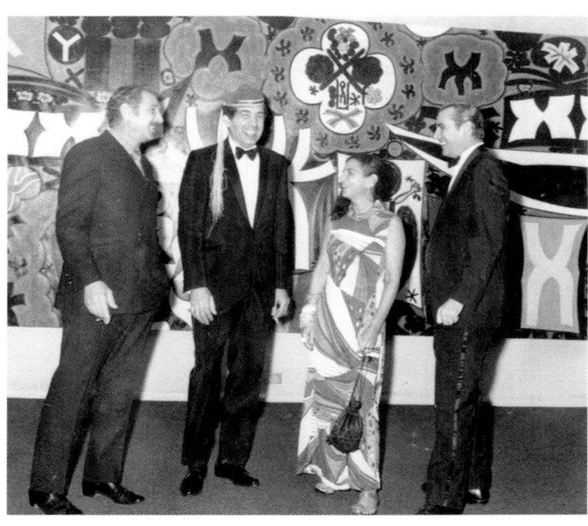
Fig. 152
Chimes (second from left) with artist Syd Solomon (left) and Curtis G. Coley (right), museum director, in front of Chimes's *Mural* of 1963–65 at the opening of his retrospective at the John and Mable Ringing Museum of Art in Sarasota, Florida, November 1968. Courtesy of the artist

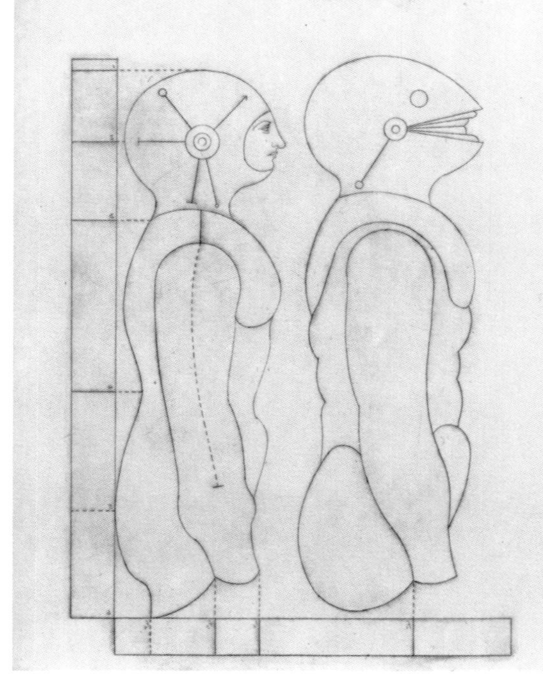
Fig. 153
Thomas Chimes, *Duo Neuter*, 1968. Dry point etching on Plexiglas (proof, not editioned), 10¾ x 8½ inches (27.3 x 21.6 cm). Collection of Rodger LaPelle, Philadelphia

with fellow instructors from the Philadelphia College of Art. Marking the unofficial start to the city's Philadelphia Arts Festival, the midnight opening attracts hundreds of people to Locust Street and a newspaper review describes the atmosphere as "pure party." Chimes wears a construction of flowers, metal, and plastic around his neck.

Summer
Chimes experiences a period of deep depression. He will intermittently seek treatment for his depression during the ensuing decade.

Fall
Chimes begins a job in the reproductions department at the University of Pennsylvania Museum of Archaeology and Anthropology, making casts of Egyptian statues.

1968

James Harithas (fig. 151), director of the Corcoran Gallery of Art, exhibits several of Chimes's works on loan, introduces Chimes to artist Sam Gilliam, and also helps Chimes get an exhibition of his metal boxes at the Henri Gallery in Washington, DC.

Chimes collaborates with Philadelphia print publisher Rodger LaPelle on *Duo Neuter* (fig. 153), a dry point etching on Plexiglas, but does not complete the edition.

Summer
Chimes and his family move to a carriage house at 331 Melrose Road in Merion, Pennsylvania.

November 18–December 22
The John and Mable Ringling Museum in Sarasota, Florida, holds the first large-scale retrospective exhibition of Chimes's work (fig. 152). The monumental *Mural*, valued at $5,000 and given to the museum by the Friends of the Ringling Museum of Art in May, is the centerpiece of the exhibition and the culmination of two decades of production. The Florida-based Abstract Expressionist painter Syd Solomon hosts a reception for Chimes at his home.

1969

January 4–March 2
The Chimes retrospective exhibition travels to the Jacksonville Museum of Art in Florida.

1970

January–February
Chimes's *Skyway*, a 1969 acrylic on Plexiglas and wood construction, is chosen for the exhibition *The Highway* at the Institute of Contemporary Art at the University of Pennsylvania, Philadelphia. According to the catalogue, the exhibition "seeks to survey, for the first time, the impact of the highway on the visual arts." Work by artists from Walker Evans and Edward Hopper to Robert Indiana and Christo are also included.

August
Chimes and painter/photographer William Crosby judge the painting entries for the Eighteenth Bestor Plaza Show in Chautauqua, New York.

Chimes exhibits his most recent work—small, purely abstract aluminum-framed constructions featuring grids of plastic and Plexiglas strips—in his one-man show *Plastic Art* at the Henri Gallery in Washington, DC. In a review for the *Washington Sunday Star*, Benjamin Forgey notes this break with the elegant, elusive imagery of the earlier metal boxes: "Many of the aluminum-framed plastic paintings on the walls at Henri's read like straightforward exercises in formalist painting—vertical or horizontal stripes of alternating colors or simple gray grids—and whatever else Chimes was in previous artistic incarnations, he was emphatically not a formalist."

Chimes participates in two group shows organized by the Mississippi Art Association, Jackson.

1971

March 5–April 4

Chimes's *Multiplex* of 1971 (fig. 154), a light-up metal box construction made of steel, Plexiglas, and paper in an edition of 100, is included in the Philadelphia Museum of Art's *Multiples, the First Decade*, an exhibition exploring the nature of multiplicity in art. Chimes is disappointed with the quality of the mass-produced work; it will be the only multiple he will ever make.

Fall

Chimes joins the faculty at Moore College of Art, where he will teach drawing, two- and three-dimensional design, and sculpture (but not painting) full-time until December 1982.

1972

Chimes creates two portraits that he houses in similar Art Nouveau–inspired frames, one of which (fig. 155) is modeled after Gustav Klimt's *Woman with Hat and Feather Boa* of 1898. He is also commissioned by entrepreneur Washburn Oberwager to paint a wedding portrait of his wife, Maria (fig. 156); along with *Set* (pl. 39), this work is one of the first portraits Chimes paints from a photograph. He affixes a Tiffany tile to its frame.

The artist's interest in decorative arts leads him to design an Art Deco sofa and coffee table for his home (fig. 157), as well as an upright piano, which eventually finds its way to the Khyber, a bar on Second Street in Philadelphia.

1973–78

Chimes works on a series of forty-eight sepia-toned panel portraits in oversized wooden frames. Painted from period photographs of artists, writers, philosophers, and scientists, these portraits are iconic representations of Chimes's influences, many drawn from his exploration of the works of Alfred Jarry.

1974

Chimes becomes chairman of the Sculpture Department at Moore College of Art.

1975

January 20–April 9

Chimes's 1974 panel portrait *Antonin Artaud* (pl. 48) is chosen for the 1975 *Biennial Exhibition* at the Whitney Museum of American Art in New York. This year's Biennial is unique, Whitney director Tom Armstrong writes in his foreword to the catalogue, in the curators' decision to present "a survey view of current work by artists from throughout the United States who have not become known through one-person shows in New York City or participation in previous Whitney Museum Biennials or Annuals."

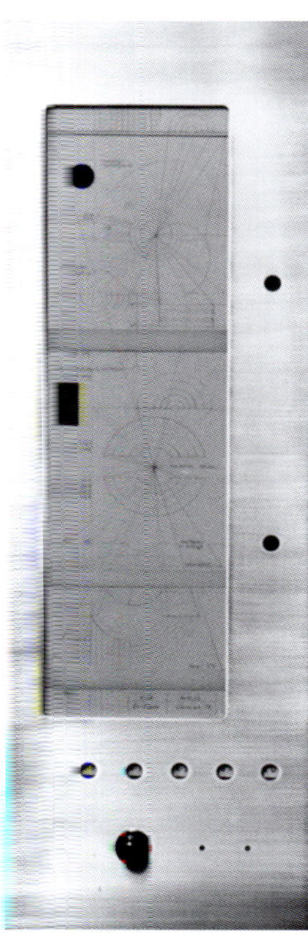

Fig. 154
Thomas Chimes, *Multiplex*, 1971. Steel, Plexiglas, and paper, 21 x 7 inches (53.3 x 17.8 cm). Edition of 100, signed and numbered, published by the Institute of Contemporary Art, University of Pennsylvania, Philadelphia

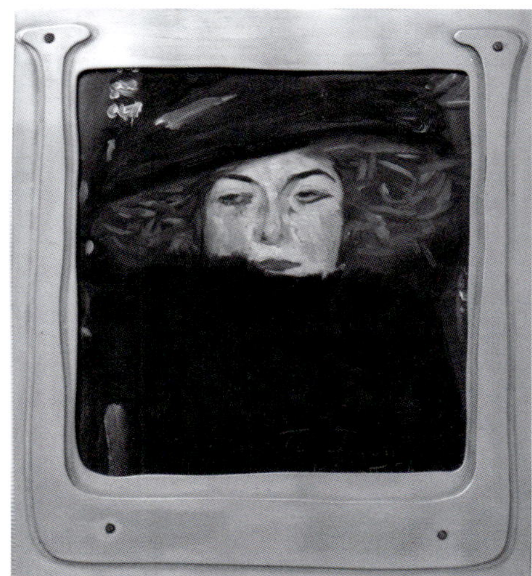

Fig. 155
Thomas Chimes, *Klimt Portrait*, 1972. Oil on panel with aluminum frame, 8⅛ x 7⅛ inches (20.6 x 18.1 cm). Collection of Dawn Chimes, Venice, Florida

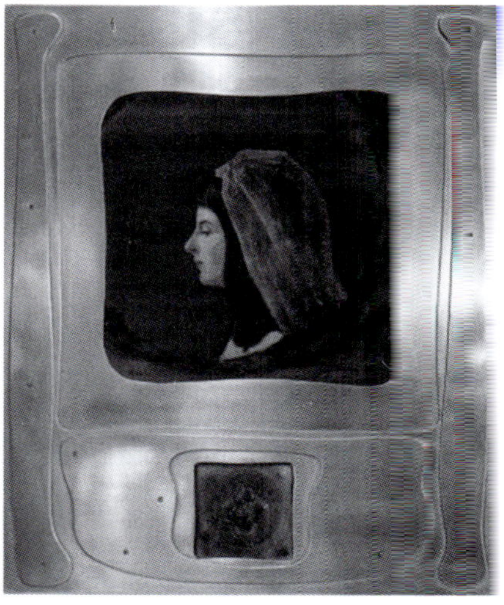

Fig. 156
Thomas Chimes, *Maria Oberwager*, 1972–73. Oil on canvas with aluminum frame, dimensions unknown. Private collection

March 6–April 13
Nineteen of Chimes's panel portraits are exhibited at the Peale House Galleries of the Pennsylvania Academy of Fine Arts, in a show titled *Departure from the Present* (fig. 158). The paintings are hung, the exhibition press release notes, "in the order in which they were painted, and the works were painted in the order of spiritual development. Jarry is the foundation, Wilde the culmination." In his accompanying artist's statement, Chimes reflects on his fascination with past writers and explains, "I'm not interested in the strictly literary aspects of their work but in the value issues enunciated though not necessarily explained, particularly in the writings of Alfred Jarry. . . . To get to the future you go to the past. To get to the past you go to the future."

The Philadelphia Museum of Art acquires Chimes's 1974 panel portraits of Guillaume Apollinaire (pl. 49) and Alfred Jarry (pl. 50), and Chimes donates his portrait of Antonin Artaud to the Museum. Anne d'Harnoncourt, then curator of twentieth-century painting, advocates for these first Museum acquisitions of Chimes's work.

October 16–November 21
The three works purchased by the Philadelphia Museum of Art are included in *PMA at MCA*, an exhibition of works by contemporary Philadelphia artists in the Museum's collection, at the Moore College of Art.

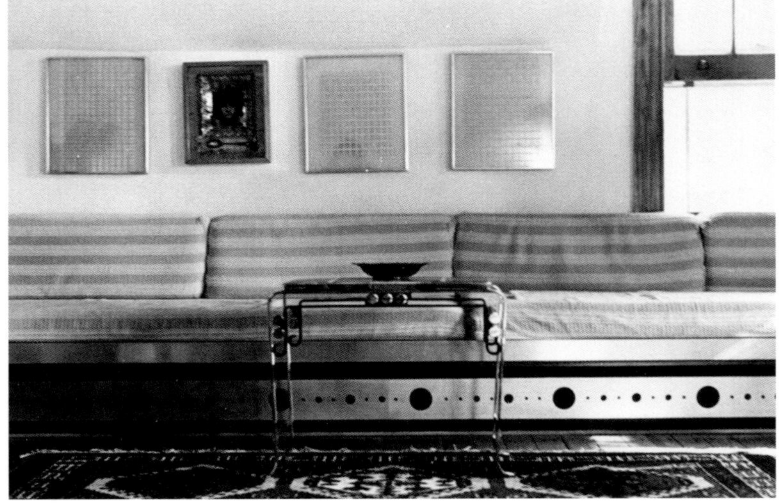

Fig. 157
The Chimes family's living room, c. 1970, with Art Deco-inspired sofa and coffee table designed by the artist. On the wall are *Untitled (Greta Garbo)*, c. 1967, and three untitled Plexiglas strip works from 1970. Courtesy of the artist

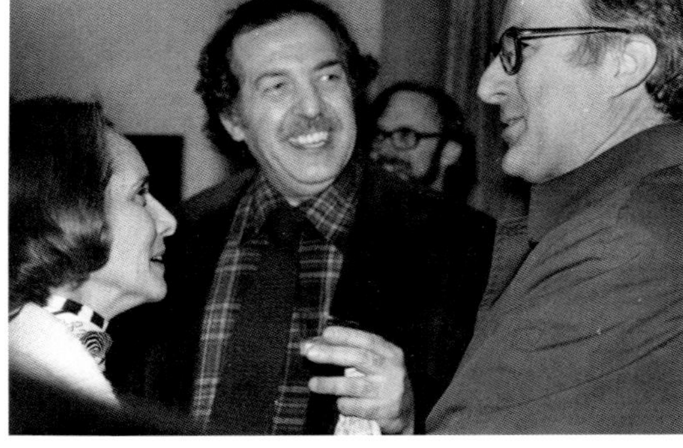

Fig. 158
Chimes (center) at the opening of his one-man show *Departure from the Present* at the Peale House Galleries, Pennsylvania Academy of the Fine Arts, Philadelphia, March 1975. Courtesy of the Pennsylvania Academy of the Fine Arts

1976

July 26
The artist's mother, Agnes, dies in Philadelphia.

Chimes and his family move to Villanova, Pennsylvania.

October 25
The artist's brother George dies of a heart attack in New York.

October 8–November 17
The Philadelphia Houston Exchange opens at the Institute of Contemporary Art in Philadelphia. The exhibition, a joint project between the ICA and the Contemporary Arts Museum in Houston (of which Chimes's old friend James Harithas is now the director), explores the concept of regional art in its comparisons of artists from both cities. Chimes's 1976 portrait *Bicentennial Jarry* (pl. 63) is exhibited with work by Charles Fahlen, Warren Rohrer, and Italo Scanga. The show will travel to Houston in the spring of the following year.

October 16–November 21
Chimes's *Antonin Artaud*, *Alfred Jarry*, and *Guillaume Apollinaire*, all of 1974, are included in the Philadelphia Museum of Art's landmark exhibition *Philadelphia: Three Centuries of American Art*. In her review of the exhibition for the *Philadelphia Inquirer*, Victoria Donohoe writes, "No invitation in recent memory was more coveted by local artists."

December 5–27
Chimes serves as juror for the exhibition *Square Is a Square* at the Cheltenham Art Center, Cheltenham, Pennsylvania.

Chimes donates his 1975 panel portrait *Oscar Wilde* (pl. 58) to the Philadelphia Museum of Art.

1977

January 18—February 19
In the exhibition *Spacescapes* at the Sid Deutsch Gallery in New York, guest curator Rita Simon includes Chimes among a diverse group of artists, among them Alexander Calder, Joseph Cornell, Marcel Duchamp, Max Ernst, Adolph Gottlieb, Man Ray, Joan Miró, Louise Nevelson, Georgia O'Keeffe, James Rosenquist, and Yves Tanguy.

September 16
Photographer Eileen Berger interviews Chimes at his home at 22 Villanova Road, Villanova, Pennsylvania, for the cover story of the March/April 1978 *Arts Exchange* magazine.

1978

Chimes participates in the group exhibition *Beyond the Canvas* at the Touchstone Gallery, New York.

Summer
The Chimes family moves to 4 Dawnwood Lane, Miquon, Pennsylvania.

Chimes's marriage with Dawn becomes troubled after he falls into a depression.

Fall

Chimes completes the panel portraits series with a painting of Jerry's bumbling physics teacher, M. Hébert (pl. 76).

October 13–November 26

Tom Chimes, an Exhibition of Portraits: 1973–1978 at the Museums at Sunrise in Charleston, West Virginia, includes thirty-nine of the forty-eight panel portraits the artist produced between 1973 and 1978.

November 8

Chimes participates with Emlen Etting, Marian Locks, and Mrs. H. Gates (Lally) Lloyd in a discussion entitled "State of the Arts in Philadelphia, Part II" at the Philadelphia Art Alliance.

1979

Chimes has a one-man exhibition at the Touchstone Gallery in New York, and is included in three of the gallery's group shows.

Chimes is awarded an Individual Fellowship in the Residency Program at the Pennsylvania Council of Arts.

Dawn Chimes moves to Venice, Florida.

1980

January

Chimes moves to a new studio on the fifth floor at 1722 Spruce Street (fig. 159), which he will occupy for more than twenty years. He paints *Waterfall* (pl. 78) on a large canvas left behind by the previous tenant, the artist Tommy Dale Palmore. In an interview with Cynthia Veloric for the Archives of American Art, Chimes deems his transition from the panel portraits to the white paintings the most drastic change in his work, which he sees as "a psychic compensation" for recent events in his life.

February 2–28

Chimes's 1977 panel portrait of Marcel Proust on his death bed (see fig. 94), based on a 1922 photograph by Man Ray, is judged by the *New York Times* to be "particularly well worth seeing" among the works by Hilla and Bernd Becher, Hamish Fulton, Lucas Samaras, William Wegman, and others included in the Touchstone Gallery's *The Photograph Transformed*.

October

In an attempt to save their marriage, Chimes and his wife travel together to London, where they see Joseph Mallord William Turner's paintings of waterfalls at the Tate Gallery, and to Switzerland, where they view the Reichenbach Falls. Upon his return to Philadelphia, however, Chimes focuses increasingly on the arc of Jerry's bicycle wheel that he sees emerging from his waterfall canvases, and will soon abandon waterfall imagery altogether.

1981

Chimes begins a series of paintings of Memorial Hall in Philadelphia's Fairmount Park. Drawing on a childhood memory of the far-off building seen from his family home, he increasingly dissolves the nineteenth-century structure's domed outline into the vaporous white background with each successive painting.

1982

April 17–May 30

Chimes exhibits a miniature portrait of Aubrey Beardsley in the juried exhibition *Small Paintings* at the New Britain Museum of Art in New Britain, Connecticut.

July 10–September 19

Chimes's 1981 painting *Crepuscule* is included in the *Philadelphia Invitational Painting Exhibition*, a show of seventy works by numerous Philadelphia artists at the Southern Alleghenies Museum of Art in Loretto, Pennsylvania.

1983

Chimes revisits the images of Memorial Hall that he had painted two years earlier, reducing its silhouette to no more than a suggestion of its dome rising above a horizon line across the white ground.

Troubled by the disappearance of image and color from his paintings, Chimes hears a voice telling him to "write on the canvas." "Write on the canvas?" Chimes questions aloud, "What the hell am I going to write?" As he stands in front of one of his large white paintings, lines from James Joyce's *Ulysses* and *Finnegan's Wake* and other works begin to surface in his mind. He writes the lines in India ink along the bottom of his canvases.

April

Chimes's first solo exhibition at the Marian Locks Gallery opens; it is the first show to include works from all four distinct periods of Chimes's artistic production. In the *Philadelphia Inquirer*, art critic Victoria Donohoe deems the panel portraits shown at Locks "the strongest things Chimes has done so far." Locks Gallery remains Chimes's dealer to the present day.

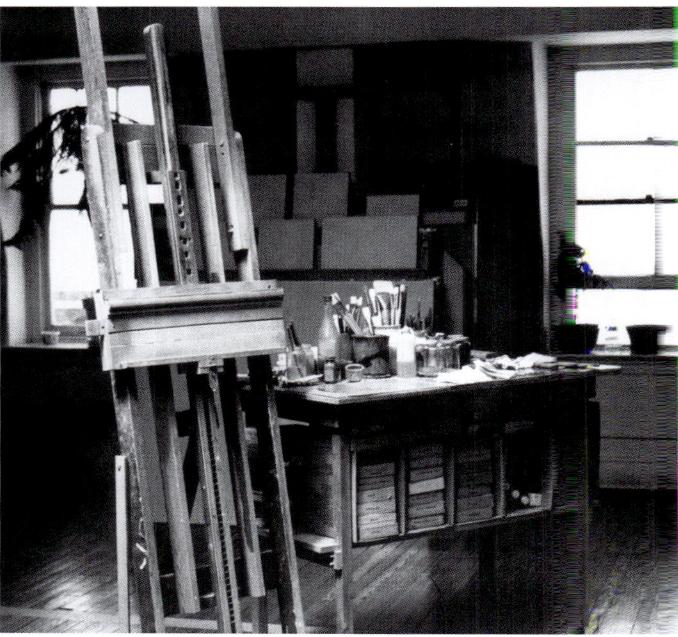

Fig. 159
Chimes's studio at 1722
Spruce Street. Courtesy
of the artist

1984

Chimes's work is included in *Contemporary Art* at One Penn Plaza in New York City and in a group show at the Matthews Hamilton Gallery, Philadelphia.

1985

Chimes begins to eliminate the horizon line entirely in his paintings of Memorial Hall, leaving only the white canvas with writing inscribed along the lower edge. He also decides to reduce his palette to titanium white and India ink. The resulting paintings, no larger than three feet by four feet, are built up layer by layer to create a surface that reveals no indication of mark-making. His enduring passion for Greek mythology, geometry, and Alfred Jarry become the subjects of these new works, as he begins to include writings and inscriptions across the canvas.

1986

The Philadelphia Museum of Art includes Chimes's *Rrose Sélavy* of 1976 (pl. 74) in the exhibition *Philadelphia Collects Art Since 1940*.

February 8–28
Chimes's *Bicentennial Jarry* of 1976 is included in *A Celebration of the Touchstone Gallery*. In an artist's statement, Chimes compares the panel portraits he had shown at Touchstone in the late 1970s to his recent works: "One of my portraits has been described this way—'In a sense, the portrait is not even figurative but rather metaphysical: a mysterious icon referring less to the man it represents than to the ideas he generated.' My current work is largely an effort to go beyond personification in order to get closer to certain ideas by using written quotations instead of images of a real person."

April 9
Chimes and Dawn's divorce is finalized.

September 5–October 18
The Goldie Paley Gallery at the Moore College of Art in Philadelphia hosts Chimes's second retrospective (fig. 160). *Tom Chimes, A Compendium: 1961–1986* includes work spanning from his crucifixions period to his more recent white portraits of James Joyce and Alfred Jarry. Chimes participates in a conversation with John McCoubrey, professor of art history at the University of Pennsylvania, and Stephen Martin, a Jungian analyst, titled "White Whiter Than White: The Unconscious and the Creative Act." Elsa Weiner Longhauser's catalogue essay explores the Jungian aspect of circularity and myth-making in Chimes's art: "Chimes explains the significance of the circle in a journal entry for 24 May 1986: 'The art of painting and sculpture is the showing of the *telling* of the myth. All art will recall mythical experience common to all mankind.' The circle, for him, is the symbol of the continuous cycle of life, of creativity, what Jung has called the collective unconscious." Chimes also relates this circularity to the last line of Joyce's *Finnegan's Wake*: "A way a lone a last a loved a long the," which feeds back into the book's opening line.

1987

Chimes is awarded a grant from the National Endowment for the Arts for work in visual arts.

September–October
Chimes participates in the Philadelphia Museum of Art's citywide centennial tribute to Marcel Duchamp, *Apropos of Marcel Duchamp*, showing in the exhibition *Duchamp: The Legacy Continues . . .* at the Fleisher Art Memorial. He joins artists Daniel Buren, William Copley, Hans Haacke, Jenny Holzer, and Nam June Paik in the Museum's panel discussion "Duchamp and Art Today: Where Do We Go from Here?" Comparing the experience of the unknown in Duchamp's *Etant Donnés* to the subjects of his panel portraits, Chimes says, "If an artist experiences something, unknown, the anaesthetic, his work reflects that experience. And we, the viewers, are confronted with the reflection."

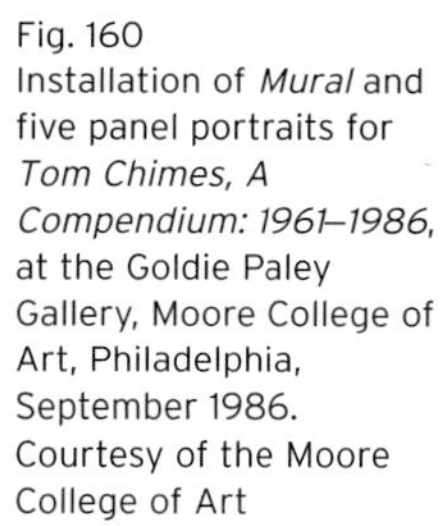

Fig. 160
Installation of *Mural* and five panel portraits for *Tom Chimes, A Compendium: 1961–1986*, at the Goldie Paley Gallery, Moore College of Art, Philadelphia, September 1986. Courtesy of the Moore College of Art

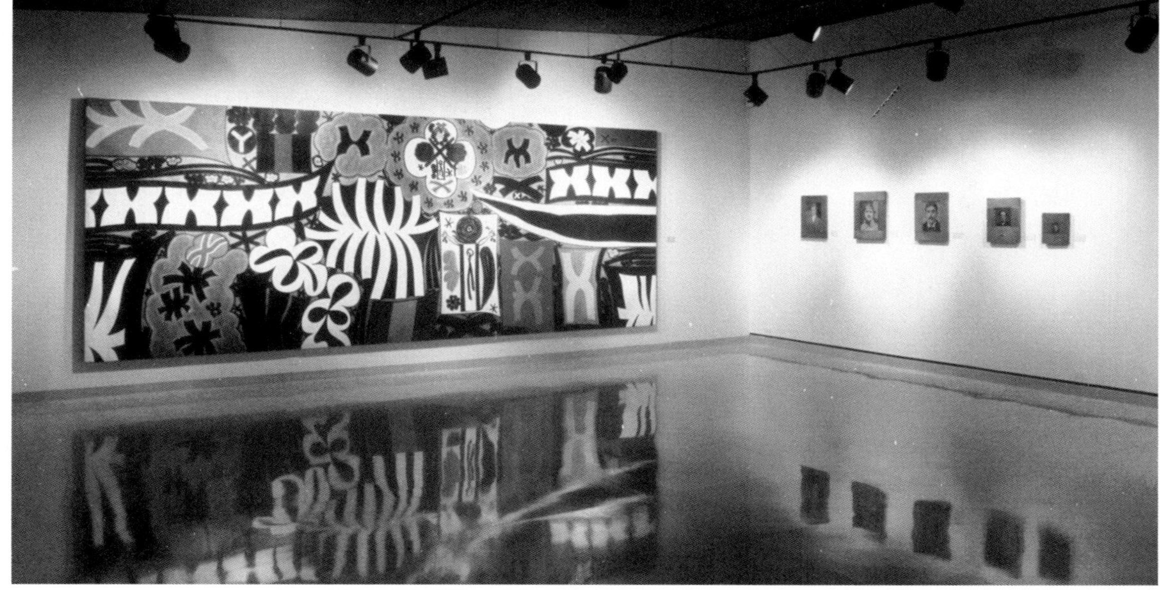

October 30

Chimes serves as a juror for the Ninetieth Annual Exhibition of the Fellowship of the Pennsylvania Academy of the Fine Arts.

1988

March 5–30

Chimes's solo show at the Marian Locks Gallery, *The White Portrait*, receives local acclaim from the *Philadelphia Inquirer*, where Victoria Donohoe writes, "Chimes stretches the definition of contemporary portraiture as he extends and enriches the content of his visual statements. Among living Pennsylvania artists, few have so consistently enriched our visual vocabulary." It also earns national praise from *Art in America*, where reviewer Patricia Stewart notes that Chimes has been able to "transform so many academic quotations into paintings with such simplicity and purity of address."

The Philadelphia Museum of Art acquires Chimes's *Faustroll (L'Infini)* of that year (pl. 86).

1989

Chimes shows in two group exhibitions, *Conspicuous Display* at Rutgers University in Camden, New Jersey, and *Landscapes of Thought* at the Momenta Gallery in Philadelphia. *Conspicuous Display* places Chimes's 1974 painting *Mona* in the company of works by Joseph Beuys, Christo, Joseph Cornell, Jasper Johns, Jeff Koons, Barbara Kruger, Robert Morris, Meret Oppenheim, Richard Prince, Andy Warhol, and other artists who exhibit a Duchampian interest in mass-produced objects and images and their presentation as art.

December

Chimes is included in a group exhibition at the Marian Locks Gallery entitled *Looking Back—The Seventies at Marian Locks*, which closes at the end of January. The exhibition includes five gallery artists: Edna Andrade, James Havard, Elizabeth Osborne, Warren Rohrer, and Chimes. *Philadelphia Inquirer* art critic Edward J. Sozanski deems Chimes the artist most "worth remembering . . . for his mysterious 'portraits' of other-era poets and writers, and for his exquisitely crafted and equally mysterious constructions of polished metal."

1991

Following Marian Locks's retirement, her son, Gene Locks, and his wife, Sueyun, manage the Locks Gallery.

The Philadelphia Museum of Art receives Chimes's *Erase Sélavy* of 1976 as a gift.

January 19–March 3

Chimes's work is included in *Philadelphia Art Now: Artists Choose Artists* at the Institute of Contemporary Art Philadelphia. Twenty-five well-known Philadelphia artists, including Chimes, are selected for the exhibition, and each in turn selects another artist to be included in the show.

May 13

Preliminary site work begins on *Sleeping Woman*, a collaborative art project by poet Stephen Berg and Chimes, and funded by the Fairmount Park Art Association and the Pew Charitable Trusts. Chimes designs the installation of Berg's poem, stenciled in five-inch-tall black capital letters along 1,125 feet of the Schuylkill River retaining wall beside Kelly Drive (fig. 161).

Sleeping Woman is completed in July; several months after the project is finished, a 200-foot section of the Victorian-era wall on which the poem is written collapses into the river. Engineers repair the wall, often using the letters of the verse to determine the stones' original locations. Although the restoration is largely successful, several of the stones are lost to the river. Chimes and Berg ask that blank stones be inserted in their place—sacrificing sixty-one words of the poem—as the installation is intended to coexist with nature.

1992

One of Chimes's portraits of Jarry is included in the *Transmodern* exhibition at the Baumgartner Galleries in Washington, DC, organized by artist and critic J. W. Mahoney. Chimes's *Faustroll (L'Infini)* is included in the Philadelphia Museum of Art's *Pertaining to Philadelphia: Contemporary Acquisitions from the Julius Bloch Memorial Fund*.

May 23

Stephen Berg and Chimes walk along and talk about *Sleeping Woman* as part of the Walt Whitman Centennial Celebration Poetry Series.

October 14–November 21

Chimes's fourth solo exhibition at the Locks Gallery opens, displaying his Hermes Cycle paintings. These works demonstrate his movement to an almost completely white canvas, which he relates to the unconscious. The cryptic inscriptions, often in Greek, are only noticeable when seen close up.

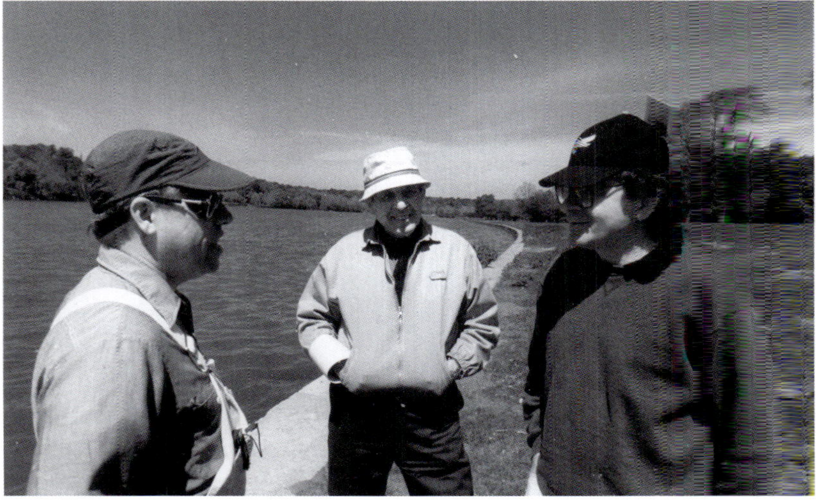

Fig. 161
Chimes (center) with Peter Freudenberg (left) and Stephen Berg (right) at the *Sleeping Woman* installation site along the Schuylkill River, Philadelphia, c. 1991. Courtesy of the Fairmount Park Art Association, Philadelphia

1993

Chimes shows work in three group exhibitions in the Spring and Summer: *Tom Chimes, Joel Fisher, and Bill Walton* at The Larry Becker Gallery in Philadelphia; *Cryptics* at the School 33 Art Center in Baltimore; and *Déjà Vu* at the Franklin Mint Museum in Franklin Center, Pennsylvania.

November 14
A bronze marker commemorating *Sleeping Woman* is dedicated. The marker, designed by Chimes, consists of a thirty-inch bronze disc with a twelve-inch stone aggregate border, embedded in the ground to create a slight earth mound. Across the monument are written the Greek letters *gamma* and *eta*, which signify "earth," as well as geometric designs derived from the Golden Section.

1994

May 14–July 17
Chimes's work is paired with that of the English artist Alan Charlton in the *Conversation Pieces* exhibition at the Institute of Contemporary Art, Philadelphia. In a conversation with Ivy Barsky, ICA Director Patrick Murphy compares the two artists' Minimalist aesthetics and emphasis on process, acknowledging that "to link Chimes with Alan Charlton is a superficial act, not in the derogatory association of that word but its strictest meaning—of or on the surface only," concluding that "they are complete opposites. Charlton is trying to be prosaic and make these things about banal modularity, while Tom is looking for the answers to life, death, and the cycle of existence."

November 10–January 27, 1995
New York University's Alexander S. Onassis Center for Hellenic Studies hosts a survey exhibition, charting Chimes's development from his metal boxes of the 1960s to the white paintings of the 1980s and 1990s. Organized by Dr. Phillip Mitsis, professor of Hellenic Culture and Civilization at NYU, this is Chimes's first solo show in New York in fifteen years.

1995

January
In an article in *Art in America*, Barry Schwabsky celebrates Chimes's treatment of Jarry in his panel portraits as distinctive from that of other artists: "Chimes is a soberly contemplative, reclusive painter who for once (and this is his virtue) purifies Jarry's heritage of everything puerilely transgressive, domesticating this tradition, as it were. In turning to Jarry, Chimes's portraits may represent a search for origins, an invention of artistic community, but they are hardly idealized and not really nostalgic."

May 16
Jean-Michel Rabaté, professor of English literature and a noted James Joyce scholar, moderates a conversation between Chimes and fellow visual artist William

Anastasi at the University of Pennsylvania, addressing the influence of Joyce's writings on their art.

1997

September 5–October 11
The Locks Gallery hosts Chimes's solo show *Jarry, Faustroll and the Cosmos*, exhibiting twenty of Chimes's recent paintings combining text from Jarry's writings with constellations and images of the author on his bicycle.

1998

December
Judy West's article about Chimes, "Character Studies," is published in *ARTnews*. Discussing his enduring interest in Jarry and the varied literary paths this passion has led him down over the past thirty years, Chimes says, "I'm not going to absorb all this stuff. What I'm looking for are the connections. Like Proust talks about when he takes the madeleine and dips it in his tea, and the childhood experiences come rushing right before his eyes. That connecting factor is absolutely important." The seventy-seven-year-old artist anticipates an active future, stating, "If I live to be a thousand years old, always there's a next step, and it's emotional, intriguing, fascinating. You don't know exactly how it's all going to wind up. That curiosity, and that impulse to keep moving as an artist, produces work."

1999

March 5–April 10
The Locks Gallery exhibition '*Pataphysician Redivivus, The Panel Portraits, 1973–78*, which includes a catalogue with an essay by Donald Kuspit, also features some of Chimes's more recent white paintings. Kuspit concludes that Chimes has become "an autonomous Pataphysician. . . . The transformations of the dark, brooding portraits into the abstract white paintings—the timely past into the timeless—is a major feat of self-understanding as well as transcendence." The show is favorably reviewed in *City Paper* as well *Art Forum* and is noted in the *Carnets Trimestriels du Collège de 'Pataphysique*, the quarterly journal of the Collège de 'Pataphysique dedicated to the study of Jarry and his intellectual heirs. *Philadelphia Inquirer* art critic Edward J. Sozanski writes, "Chimes may be the most challenging artist in Philadelphia."

2000

February 17–April 25
Chimes's 1989 works *Hermes II* and *The One Who Whispers* are chosen for *The Sea and the Sky* at Beaver College Art Gallery in Glenside, Pennsylvania, a traveling exhibition that focuses on the ocean, atmosphere, and cosmos as subjects for contemporary works by twenty-four American, Asian, and European artists; Chimes is included in the company of Felix Gonzalez-Torres, Eileen Neff, and Gerhard Richter. The show travels to the Royal Hibernian Academy in Dublin that summer.

November 3–December 2
Chimes's *André Breton (Glove)* (pl. 69), a 1977 painting of a glove from a photograph in Breton's *Nadja*, is included in the exhibition *Conceptual Realism* at the Rosenwald-Wolf Gallery at the University of the Arts in Philadelphia, along with works by artists including Chuck Close and Vija Celmins.

November 15
An article on Chimes's life and work in the *Philadelphia Inquirer* focuses on the artist's self-isolation and tireless work ethic. "To do your work," Chimes says, "you find yourself sort of outside everything. The attachment you have for your work is so deep and profound, it even challenges your feelings for your own children."

December 26
Chimes's daughter Eva passes away in Bangor, Maine.

2001

January 19–February 24
Chimes exhibits at the Locks Gallery, in a show entitled *Circle the Circle*, which draws a comparison between his metal boxes made between 1965 and 1973 and his newest series of white paintings created between 1997 and 2000. The show is favorably reviewed by a number of local and national publications, including *Art in America*, where Miriam Seidel concludes that the "fetishized, surrealistic Id gives way to enigmatic contemplations of an expanded, cosmic self."

February 3–March 16
Chimes's first international solo show, *Portraying Ideas*, at the Royal Hibernian Academy in Dublin, includes both his panel portraits and his white paintings.

October 15
Chimes participates in a public conversation and slide lecture with Michael Taylor at the University of Pennsylvania as part of the Graduate School of Fine Arts Visiting Artists Series. Taylor surprises the artist by showing slides of Chimes's early works, from the late 1950s and early 1960s, many of which Chimes had not seen in several decades.

The Philadelphia Museum of Art acquires four of Chimes's 1965 drawings of Mômo.

2002

The artist's brother Nick, an architect in Philadelphia, dies.

2003

February 28–April 5
Beginning with his waterfall painting completed in 1980, the exhibition *Faustroll: Landscape, 1980–1990*, at the Locks Gallery displays the progression of Chimes's work throughout the first stages of his white paintings, from his diminishing views of Memorial Hall to his hazy portraits of Jarry, Joyce, and Rachilde. Anne R. Fabbri, in *Art in America*, declares the show "an odyssey of myth and memory," and *City Paper* reviewer Robin Rice declares Chimes "local guardian of the Modernist avant-garde flame."

2004

May 1–August 1
Chimes's white paintings *Rise Up*, *Man of the Hooths* of 1985 (pl. 84) and *Messenger* of 1989 are included in *The Big Nothing* at the Institute of Contemporary Art, Philadelphia. The exhibition is part of a citywide initiative, also entitled *The Big Nothing*, involving thirty-six other institutions and exploring existence in the state of nothingness.

Chimes is also included in *Traces* at the Rosenwald-Wolf Gallery at the University of the Arts in Philadelphia, as well as in *Joyce in Art: Visual Art Inspired by James Joyce* at the Royal Hibernian Academy in Dublin.

The Corcoran Gallery of Art in Washington, DC, acquires Chimes's monumental 1980 painting *Waterfall* (pl. 78).

September
Chimes moves to a new, smaller studio in the St. James Building on Washington Square in Philadelphia.

2005

February 1–March 19
Chimes's latest solo exhibition at the Locks Gallery, *Confronting the Unconscious, 1958–1965*, shows the artist's early works, which he could no longer store in his new studio. *Philadelphia Inquirer* art critic Edward J. Sozanski identifies an intriguing, if mysterious, sort of "religiosity" in Chimes's brightly colored, symbol-laden early works, writing, "Looking at this show is like attending a religious service in a language you don't understand."

July 8–August 19
Chimes participates in the group exhibition *Summertime* at the Locks Gallery, along with Jennifer Bartlett, Diane Burko, Hans Hofmann, Alice Neel, and Warren Rohrer.

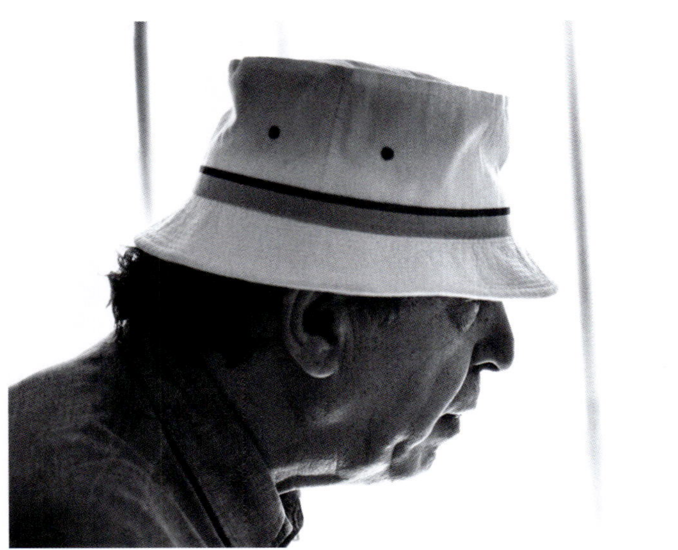
Fig. 162
Thomas Chimes c. 1998. Photographed by Ed Sachs. Courtesy of the artist

Exhibition History

Solo Exhibitions

2005
Locks Gallery, Philadelphia. *Thomas Chimes: Confronting the Unconscious: Early Works, 1958–1965.* February 1–March 19. Catalogue.

2003
Locks Gallery, Philadelphia. *Thomas Chimes: Faustroll: Landscape, 1980–1990.* February 28–April 5. Catalogue with essay by Faye Hirsch.

2001
Locks Gallery, Philadelphia. *Thomas Chimes: Complete Circle—Metal Boxes & Recent Paintings.* January 19–February 24. Catalogue with essay by David Cohen.

The Royal Hibernian Academy, Dublin. *Thomas Chimes: Portraying Ideas.* February 3–March 16. Catalogue with essay by Stephen Berg.

1999
Locks Gallery, Philadelphia. *Thomas Chimes: Pataphysician Redivivus, The Panel Portraits, 1973–78.* March 5–April 10. Catalogue with essay by Donald Kuspit.

1997
Locks Gallery, Philadelphia. *Jarry, Faustroll and the Cosmos.* September 5–October 11.

1995
Locks Gallery, Philadelphia. *Thomas Chimes: New Paintings.* April 19–May 27.

1994
Alexander S. Onassis Center for Hellenic Studies, New York University. *Thomas Chimes: Survey.* November 10–January 27, 1995.

1993
Locks Gallery, Philadelphia.

1992
Locks Gallery, Philadelphia. *Thomas Chimes: The Hermes Cycle Paintings.* October 14–November 21. Catalogue with essay by Jane Livingston.

1990
Marian Locks Gallery, Philadelphia. *Thomas Chimes.* May 1–May 31. Catalogue.

1988
Marian Locks Gallery, Philadelphia. *Thomas Chimes: The White Portraits.* March 1–March 30.

1986
Goldie Paley Gallery, Moore College of Art, Philadelphia. *Tom Chimes, A Compendium: 1961–1986.* September 5–October 18. Catalogue with essays by Stephen Martin and Stephen Berg.

1983
Marian Locks Gallery, Philadelphia. *T. Chimes: Time and Socrate.* March 28–April 23.

1979
Touchstone Gallery, New York. *Tom Chimes.* March 31–April 28.

Fig. 163
Installation view of *Thomas Chimes: A Retrospective Exhibition* at the John and Mable Ringling Museum of Art, Sarasota, Florida, 1968. Photograph by Joseph Janney Steinmetz; courtesy of Thomas Chimes

Fig. 164
Installation view of *Thomas Chimes: Departure from the Present* at the Peale House Galleries, Pennsylvania Academy of the Fine Arts, Philadelphia, 1975. Courtesy of the Pennsylvania Academy of the Fine Arts

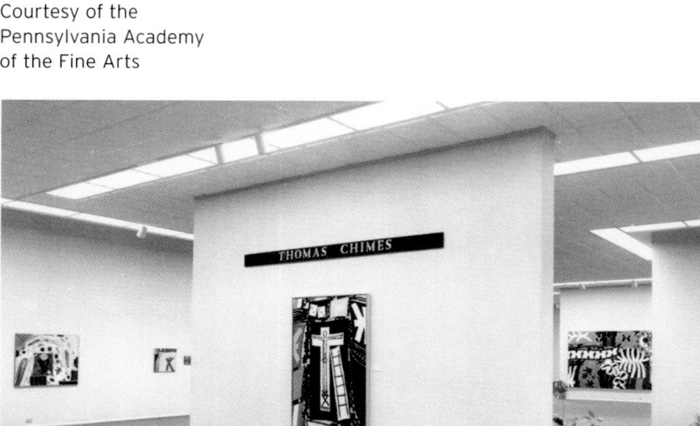

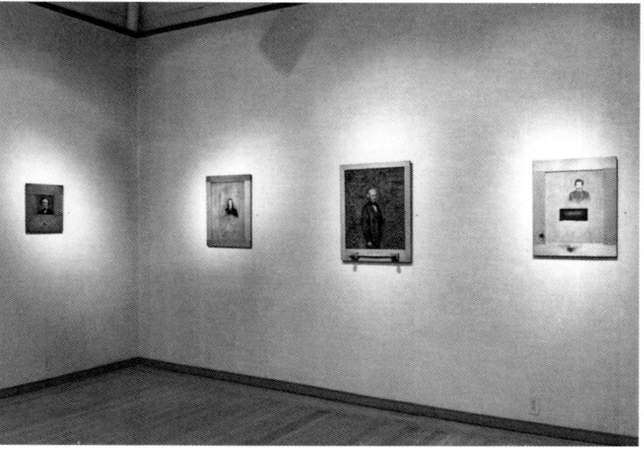

1978

Sunrise Museums at Sunrise, Charleston, West Virginia. *Thomas Chimes, An Exhibition of Portraits: 1973–1978.* October 15–November 26. Catalogue with essay by Patricia Stewart.

1975

Peale House Galleries, Pennsylvania Academy of the Fine Arts, Philadelphia. *Thomas Chimes: Departure from the Present.* March 6–April 13.

1970

Henri Gallery, Washington, DC. *Thomas Chimes: Plastic Art.* October 10–November 7.

1968

John and Mable Ringling Museum of Art, Sarasota, Florida. *Thomas Chimes: A Retrospective Exhibition.* November 18–December 22. Also shown at the Jacksonville Museum of Art, Jacksonville, Florida, January 4–March 2, 1969. Catalogue with essay by Karl Nickel.

1965

Bodley Gallery, New York. *Thomas Chimes.* January 18–January 30.

1963

Bodley Gallery, New York. *Thomas Chimes.* February 11–March 2.

1958

Avant-Garde Gallery, New York. February.

Selected Group Exhibitions

2005

Locks Gallery, Philadelphia. *Summertime.*

2004

The Royal Hibernian Academy, Dublin. *Joyce in Art: Visual Art Inspired by James Joyce.* June 10–August 28.

Rosenwald-Wolf Gallery, University of the Arts, Philadelphia. *Traces.* June 15–August 15.

Institute of Contemporary Art, University of Pennsylvania, Philadelphia. *The Big Nothing.* May 1–August 1. Catalogue.

2000

Beaver College Art Gallery, Glenside, Pennsylvania. *The Sea & The Sky.* February 17–April 25. Also shown at The Royal Hibernian Academy, Dublin, June 30–August 27. Catalogue.

Rosenwald-Wolf Gallery, University of the Arts, Philadelphia. *Conceptual Realism.* November 3–December 2.

1995

Nexus Foundation for Today's Art, Philadelphia. *The Realm of Morpheus: Dream Image in Art.* December 1–23.

Philadelphia Art Alliance, Philadelphia. *Fourscore and Forthcoming.* September 22–November 12. Catalogue.

1994

City Hall, Philadelphia. *Case Studies: An Exhibition Selected by the Art in City Hall Art Advisory Council.* February 16–April 29.

Institute of Contemporary Art, University of Pennsylvania, Philadelphia. *Conversation Pieces.* May 13–July 17. Catalogue.

1993

Larry Becker Gallery, Philadelphia. *Tom Chimes, Joel Fisher, and Bill Walton.* Early April–June 12.

School 33 Art Center, Baltimore. *Cryptics.* April 10–May 21.

The Franklin Mint Museum, Franklin Center, Pennsylvania. *Déjà Vu.* June 8–July 25. Catalogue.

1992

Philadelphia Museum of Art. *Pertaining to Philadelphia: Contemporary Acquisitions from the Julius Bloch Memorial Fund.* May 16–August 16.

Baumgartner Galleries, Washington, DC. *Transmodern.* June 10–July 11.

Moore College of Art, Philadelphia. *In the Realm of the Monochrome.* September 4–October 11.

1991

Institute of Contemporary Art, University of Pennsylvania, Philadelphia. *Philadelphia Art Now: Artists Choose Artists.* January 19–March 3. Catalogue with essay by Julie Courtney.

Marian Locks Gallery, Philadelphia. *Directions.* January 10–February 23.

1989

Stedman Art Gallery, Rutgers University, Camden, New Jersey. *Conspicuous Display.* January 23–February 25. Catalogue with essay by Sid Sachs.

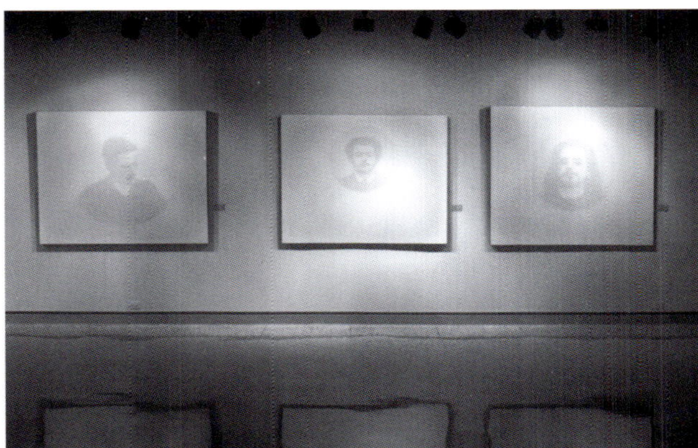

Fig. 165
Installation view of *Tom Chimes, A Compendium, 1961–1986* at the Goldie Paley Gallery, Moore College of Art, Philadelphia, 1986. Courtesy of Moore College of Art

Momenta Art Alternatives, Philadelphia. *Landscapes of Thought.* February 1–28.

Marian Locks Gallery, Philadelphia. *Looking Back: The Seventies at Marian Locks.* December 12–January 30, 1990.

1988
Carnegie Mellon University, Pittsburgh. *Perspectives from Pennsylvania.* Closed May 22.

1987
G. W. Einstein Gallery, New York. *Vistas: Approaches to the Panoramic Landscape, Part II.* March 28–April 25.

Fleisher Art Memorial, Philadelphia. *Duchamp: The Legacy Continues . . .* September 15–October 17.

1986
Touchstone Gallery, New York. *A Celebration of the Touchstone Gallery.* February 8–28. Catalogue.

Philadelphia Museum of Art. *Philadelphia Collects: Art Since 1940.* September 28–November 30. Catalogue with text by Mark Rosenthal.

1985
Marian Locks Gallery, Philadelphia. *Group Exhibition.* May 25–June 12.

1984
Contemporary Art at One Penn Plaza, New York. *Newscapes: Land and City/States of Mind.* January 23–May 4.

Matthews Hamilton Gallery, Philadelphia. *Landscape.* October 12–November 6.

1982
New Britain Museum of American Art, New Britain, Connecticut. *Small Paintings.* April 17–May 30. Catalogue.

Southern Alleghenies Museum, Loretto, Pennsylvania. *Philadelphia Invitational Painting Exhibition.* July 10–September 19. Catalogue.

1980
Touchstone Gallery, New York. *The Photograph Transformed.* February 2–28.

The Governor's Home, Harrisburg, Pennsylvania. *Made in Philadelphia III.* April 1–May 23. Organized by the Institute of Contemporary Art, University of Pennsylvania, Philadelphia.

Heritage Plantation of Sandwich, Sandwich, Massachusetts. *An American Flower Show.* May 9–October 13. Catalogue.

1979
Touchstone Gallery, New York. *New Work.* February 3–28.

Touchstone Gallery, New York. *Philadelphia Artists Today.* June 2–30.

Touchstone Gallery, New York. *Survey of the Season.* September 7–28.

1978
Touchstone Gallery, New York. *Beyond the Canvas.* November 4–November 30.

1977
Sid Deutsch Gallery, New York. *Spacescapes.* January 18–February 19.

Philadelphia Museum of Art. *Recent Acquisitions: Made in Philadelphia.* March 18–September 1.

Moore College of Art, Philadelphia. *Faculty Exhibition.* September 9–30.

1976
Philadelphia Museum of Art. *Philadelphia: Three Centuries of American Art.* April 11–October 10. Catalogue with text by Anne d'Harnoncourt.

Institute of Contemporary Art, University of Pennsylvania, Philadelphia. *The Philadelphia Houston Exchange.* October 8–November 17. Also shown at the Contemporary Arts Museum, Houston, Spring 1977. Catalogue.

1975
Whitney Museum of American Art, New York. *Biennial Exhibition.* January 20–April 9. Catalogue.

Moore College of Art, Philadelphia. *PMA at MCA: An Exhibition of Works by Contemporary Philadelphia Artists, Selected from the Collection of the Philadelphia Museum of Art.* October 16–November 21.

1971
Philadelphia Museum of Art. *Multiples: The First Decade.* March 5–April 4. Catalogue with text by John L. Tancock.

1970
Institute of Contemporary Art, University of Pennsylvania, Philadelphia. *The Highway.* January 14–February 25. Also shown at the Institute for the Arts, Rice University, Houston, March 12–May 18; The Akron Art Institute, Akron, Ohio, June 5–July 26. Catalogue with essays by Denise Scott Brown and Robert Venturi and John W. McCoubrey.

Mississippi Art Association, Jackson. *Mississippi Arts Festival.*

Mississippi Art Association, Jackson. *Five by Ten.*

1969
Socrates Perakis Gallery, Philadelphia. *An Opening Proposal.* January 23–February 14.

1968

John and Mable Ringling Museum of Art, Sarasota, Florida. *Recent Acquisitions in 20th Century American Art 1965–1968*. Opened May 19.

1967

Carnegie Institute Museum of Art, Pittsburgh. *Alcoa Collection of Contemporary Art: An Exhibition of Work Acquired from the G. David Thompson Collection*. January 12–February 5. Catalogue.

The Fellowship of the Pennsylvania Academy of the Fine Arts, Philadelphia. *Annual Exhibition of Painting and Sculpture*. March 17–April 16.

Van Trip Gallery, Philadelphia. Closed April 21.

Socrates Perakis Gallery, Philadelphia. Opened May 15.

Allan Stone Gallery, New York. *Four Object Makers*. May 31–June 17.

Philadelphia Art Alliance, Philadelphia. *Constructions*. September 22–November 8. Catalogue.

1966

The Art Gallery, University of California, Santa Barbara. *Surrealism: A State of Mind, 1924–1965*. February 28–March 27. Catalogue with introduction by Julien Levy.

1965

Museum of Modern Art, New York. Closed April 11.

Krannert Art Museum, College of Fine and Applied Arts, University of Illinois, Urbana-Champaign. *Twelfth Exhibition of Contemporary American Painting and Sculpture*, March 7–April 11. Catalogue with introduction by Allen S. Weller.

Chautauqua Gallery of Art, Chautauqua Art Association, Chautauqua, New York. *The Chautauqua Exhibition of American Art, Eighth National Jury Show*. July 4–25.

1964

Bodley Gallery, New York. *Six Surrealists Painters*. January 6–25.

YM/YWHA Gallery, Philadelphia. *A Tavoletta Show*. December 2–January 3, 1965.

1963

Museum of Modern Art, New York. *Recent Acquisitions*. January 1–December 31.

1962

Philadelphia Museum of Art. *Third Philadelphia Art Festival*. June 9–24. Catalogue.

1961–63

Museum of Modern Art, New York. *Recent American Painting and Sculpture*, traveling exhibition shown at the John and Mable Ringling Museum of Art, Sarasota, Florida, December 10–31, 1961; Weatherspoon Art Gallery, University of North Carolina, Greensboro,

January 16–February 6, 1962; J.B. Speed Art Museum, Louisville, May 4–25, 1962; Helsinki, Finland, July 20–August 7, 1962; Rochester Memorial Art Gallery, Rochester, New York, October 5–28, 1962; St. John's University, Collegeville, Minnesota, November 12–December 3, 1962; North Carolina State College Union, Raleigh, January 12–February 6, 1963; Wells College, Aurora, New York, February 28–March 21, 1963; Montgomery Museum of Fine Arts, Montgomery, Alabama, April 6–27, 1963.

1961–62

Museum of Modern Art, New York. *Recent Acquisitions*. December 18, 1961–February 25, 1962.

1961

David Herbert Gallery, New York.

1957

Avant-Garde Gallery, New York.

Selected Bibliography

Books and Exhibition Catalogues

Bach, Penny Balkin. *Public Art in Philadelphia.*
Philadelphia: Temple University Press, 1992.

Beaver College Art Gallery, Glenside, PA. *The Sea &
The Sky.* Glenside, PA: Beaver College Art Gallery, 2000.

Carnegie Institute Museum of Art, Pittsburgh. *An
Exhibition of Work Acquired from the G. David
Thompson Collection.* Pittsburgh: Aluminum Company
of America, 1967.

Courtney, Julie. *Philadelphia Art Now: Artists Choose
Artists.* Philadelphia: Institute of Contemporary Art, 1991.

d'Harnoncourt, Anne. "Thomas Chimes" and "Portrait
of Alfred Jarry." In Darrel Sewell et al., *Philadelphia:
Three Centuries of American Art.* Philadelphia:
Philadelphia Museum of Art, 1976.

Franklin Mint Museum, Franklin Center, PA. *Déjà Vu.*
Franklin Center, PA: Franklin Mint Museum, 1993.

Gould, Claudia, and Ingrid Shaffner. *The Big Nothing.*
Philadelphia: Institute of Contemporary Art, 2004.

Heritage Plantation of Sandwich, MA. *An American
Flower Show.* Sandwich, MA: Heritage Plantation of
Sandwich, 1980.

Institute of Contemporary Art, University of Pennsylvania, Philadelphia. *The Philadelphia Houston
Exchange.* Philadelphia: Institute of Contemporary Art,
1976.

Krannert Art Museum, College of Fine and Applied
Arts, University of Illinois, Urbana-Champaign. *Twelfth
Exhibition of Contemporary American Painting and
Sculpture.* Champaign, IL: Krannert Art Museum, 1965.

Lerm Hayes, Christa-Maria, et al. *Joyce in Art: Visual Art
Inspired by James Joyce.* Dublin: Lilliput Press, Dufour
Editions, 2004.

Locks Gallery, Philadelphia. *Thomas Chimes: Complete
Circle—Metal Boxes & Recent Paintings.* Essay by David
Cohen. Philadelphia: Locks Gallery, 2001.

———. *Thomas Chimes: Confronting the Unconscious:
Early Works, 1958–1965.* Philadelphia: Locks Gallery,
2005.

———. *Thomas Chimes: Faustroll: Landscape, 1980–1990.*
Essay by Faye Hirsch. Philadelphia: Locks Gallery, 2003.

———. *Thomas Chimes: Pataphysician Redivivus, The
Panel Portraits, 1973–78.* Essay by Donald Kuspit.
Philadelphia: Locks Gallery, 1999.

———. *Thomas Chimes: The Hermes Cycle Paintings.*
Essay by Jane Livingston. Philadelphia: Locks Gallery,
1992.

Marian Locks Gallery, Philadelphia. *Thomas Chimes.*
Philadelphia: Marian Locks Gallery, 1990.

Martin, Stephen, and Stephen Berg. *Tom Chimes: A
Compendium, 1961–1986.* Philadelphia: Moore College
of Art, 1986.

Murphy, Patrick, ed. *Conversation Pieces: Alan Charlton,
Thomas Chimes, Hamish Fulton, Bill Walton, Richard
Torchia, Richard Wentworth.* Philadelphia: Institute of
Contemporary Art, 1994.

The Museum of Modern Art, New York. *Painting and
Sculpture Acquisitions.* New York: The Museum of
Modern Art, 1961.

The Museums at Sunrise, Charleston, WV. *Tom Chimes:
An Exhibition of Portraits: 1973–1978.* Essay by Patricia
Stewart. Charleston, WV: The Museums at Sunrise,
1978.

New Britain Museum of American Art, New Britain,
CT. *Small Paintings.* New Britain, CT: New Britain
Museum of Art, 1982.

Peale House Galleries of The Pennsylvania Academy of
the Fine Arts, Philadelphia. *Thomas Chimes Exhibition.*
Philadelphia: Pennsylvania Academy of the Fine Arts,
1975.

Philadelphia Art Alliance. *Constructions.* Philadelphia:
Philadelphia Art Alliance, 1967.

———. *Fourscore and Forthcoming.* Philadelphia:
Philadelphia Art Alliance, 1995.

Philadelphia Museum of Art. *Third Philadelphia Art
Festival.* Philadelphia: Philadelphia Museum of Art, 1962.

Ringling Museum of Art, Sarasota, FL. *Thomas Chimes:
A Retrospective Exhibition.* Text by Karl Nickel. Sarasota,
FL: Ringling Museum of Art, 1968.

Rosenthal, Mark, with Ann Percy. *Philadelphia Collects Art Since 1940*. Philadelphia: Philadelphia Museum of Art, 1985.

Royal Hibernian Academy, Dublin. *Thomas Chimes: Portraying Ideas*. Essay by Stephen Berg. Dublin: Royal Hibernian Academy, 2001.

Schwabsky, Barry. "Thomas Chimes: Concerning the Surface." In *The Widening Circle, Consequences of Modernism in Contemporary Art*. Cambridge: Cambridge University Press, 1997.

Scott Brown, Denise, Robert Venturi, and John W. McCoubrey. *The Highway*. Philadelphia: Institute of Contemporary Art, 1970.

Selz, Peter. *Prize Winning Art, Book 6*. Chautauqua, NY: Chautauqua Art Association, 1966

Southern Alleghenies Museum, Loretto, PA. *Philadelphia Invitational Painting Exhibition*. Loretto, PA: Southern Alleghenies Museum, 1982.

Stedman Art Gallery, Rutgers University, Camden, NJ. *Conspicuous Display*. Essay by Sid Sachs. Camden, NJ: Stedman Art Gallery, 1989.

Tancock, John. *Multiples: The First Decade*. Philadelphia: Philadelphia Museum of Art, 1971.

Temkin, Ann, Susan Rosenberg, and Michael Taylor. *Twentieth Century Painting and Sculpture in the Philadelphia Museum of Art*. Philadelphia: Philadelphia Museum of Art, 2000.

Touchstone Gallery, New York. *A Celebration of the Touchstone Gallery*. New York: Touchstone Gallery, 1986

University of California, Santa Barbara, Art Gallery. *Surrealism: A State of Mind 1924–1965*. Introduction by Julien Levy. Santa Barbara: University of California, Santa Barbara, 1966.

Whitney Museum of American Art, New York. *Biennial Exhibition*. New York: Whitney Museum of American Art, 1975.

Articles

Allen, Nicholas. "A Glimpse of the Infinite." *Source* 24 (September 2000).

"Art Association Opens Show with Gala Party." *Clarion-Ledger Jackson (MS) Daily News*, April 19, 1970, p. D14.

Artner, Alan. "Art Lovers Get Double Helping of Expressions." *Chicago Tribune*, May 13, 1990.

Ashton, Dore. "Art: Arthur Kaufman." *New York Times*, February 21, 1958, p. 21.

Bannister, Charlie. "Around Our Town: Art a la Carte." *Philadelphia News*, March 5, 1965.

Benbow, Charles. "Artist Turned Alchemist." *Saint Petersburg (FL) Times*, November 24, 1968, sec. G, p. 1.

Berger, Eileen. "A Conversation with Tom Chimes." *Arts Exchange* (Philadelphia), March/April 1978, pp. 23–26.

Beyer, Rita. "Contemporary Artists View the 70's." *Chestnut Hill (PA) Local*, January 11, 1990, p. 32.

———. "Locks Celebrates with Exhibit of Own Artists." *Chestnut Hill (PA) Local*, January 31, 1991, p. 37.

"Beyond the Canvas . . . Artists' Books and Notations." *ARTnews* (January 1979).

Buonaguiro, Edgar. "Artists' Books and Notations." *Arts Magazine* (1978), p. 5.

Burnett, Clyde. "Ringling Museum's Board of Trustees Accepts $5,000 Painting as a Gift." *Sarasota (FL) Herald-Tribune*, May 17, 1968.

"CBS Foundation Brings Modern Art Exhibition." *Saint John's University Record* (Collegeville, MN), October 6, 1962.

"City Paper Summer Fun Map '91." *Philadelphia City Paper*, May 31–June 7, 1991.

Clark, Joe. "She'll Be Living on the Edge." *Philadelphia Daily News*, May 7, 1991, p. 6.

Colimore, Edward. "Poem on Schuylkill Wall Has Gotten Even Deeper." *Philadelphia Inquirer*, August 22, 1991, p. 1-A.

"Collegiate Art Shown at 'Fest'." *Clarion-Ledger Jackson (MS) Daily News*, April 12, 1970, p. C8.

Csaszar, Tom. "Thomas Chimes." *New Art Examiner* (February 1993), p. 32.

Dannatt, Adrian. "A Little Learning Is a Dangerous Thing." *Art Newspaper* (March 2005), p. 33.

"Departure from the Present." *News of Delaware County*, February 27, 1975.

DeWolf, Rose. "Bouncing Jim Is a Work of Art." *Philadelphia Inquirer*, May 16, 1967, p. A-29.

Donohoe, Victoria. "An Artist Working with a Single Vision." *Philadelphia Inquirer*, April 3, 1983, p. H-11.

———. "Chimes at Ringling Museum." *Philadelphia Inquirer*, June 16, 1968.

———. "Gallery at Jim Thorpe, Pa., Aims to Raise Town Spirit." *Philadelphia Inquirer*, July 23, 1971, p. 10.

———. "Moore Men Link Work with Photos." *Philadelphia Inquirer*, March 30, 1975.

———. "Past Cultural Lions in New Contexts." *Philadelphia Inquirer*, March 12, 1988, p. D-3.

———. "Pleasant Surprises in 'Three Centuries.'" *Philadelphia Inquirer*, August 15, 1976, p. D-11.

Dorsey, John. "Secrets Waiting to Be Discovered at School 33 Exhibit." *Baltimore Morning Sun*, April 14, 1993, p. 3C.

Dunne, Aidan. "Portraying Ideas." *Irish Times*, January 31, 2001.

———. "When the Sky's Not the Limit." *Irish Times*, August 12, 2000.

———. "Willfully Mysterious Chimes." *Irish Times*, February 7, 2001.

"Exhibition at Bodley Gallery." *ARTnews* (March 1963), p. 18.

Fabbri, Anne R. "Thomas Chimes at Locks." *Art in America* 91, no. 10 (October 2003), pp. 140–41.

Fallon, Roberta. "Of This Earth," *Philadelphia Weekly*, March 1, 2000, p. 51.

Forgey, Benjamin. "Art: Works of a Philadelphia Artist." *Washington (DC) Sunday Star*, October 18, 1970, p. H-3.

Forman, Nessa. "At the ICA: When Exchange Means Trade-Off." *Philadelphia Sunday Bulletin*, October 31, 1976.

———. "With Pride and Some Misgiving." *Philadelphia Sunday Bulletin.* April 24, 1977.

Frank, Peter. "Art: The Self and Others." *Village Voice*, November 27, 1978.

"Gallery and Museum Exhibitions." *New York Times*, January 17, 1965, p. 21.

Giuliano, Mike. "Cracking the Codes." *Baltimore City Paper*, May 14, 1993, p. 25.

Glueck, Grace. "Faces of the Centuries, Famous and Far from It." *New York Times*, September 17, 1999, p. E37.

Harrison, Jane. "Six Surrealist Painters." *Arts Magazine* (March 1964), p. 70.

Hartigan, Marianne. "Portraits of the Artists." *Dublin Sunday Tribune*, February 18, 2001.

———. "Where the Sea Meets the Sky in Breathtaking Art." *Dublin Sunday Tribune*, July 23, 2000.

Hess, Evelyn. "Disappearing Words Unveil the 'Sleeping Woman.'" *Philadelphia Welcomat*, May 22, 1991, p. 2.

Hochman, Anndee. "A Man of His Word." *Philadelphia Inquirer Magazine*, July 16, 1995, p. 24

Koroxenidis, Alexandra. "An Exhibition for Recognition." *Kathimerini* (English edition), August 30, 2006.

Lichtblau, Charlotte. "At New York Galleries: Thomas Chimes." *Philadelphia Inquirer*, January 24, 1965, p. 6.

"Locks Gallery." *Candela Viridis, Carnets Trimestriels du Collège de Pataphysique* 3 (March 2001), pp. 32–33.

Lotozo, Eils. "A Singular Voice, out of the Public Eye." *Philadelphia Inquirer*, November 15, 2000, p. D1.

Lowry, Patricia. "Pennsylvania Artists Draw You into Their World at CMU Show." *Pittsburgh Press*, May 13, 1988, p. C1.

Mahoney, J. W. "Thomas Chimes at Locks." *Art in America* 81, no. 6 (June 1993), pp. 108–9.

Mangravite, Andrew. "A Brave among Chiefs." *Philadelphia Forum*, October 9, 1997, p. 8.

Miller, Donald. "Alcoa's Thompson Collection Opening." *Pittsburgh Post-Gazette*, January 11, 1967.

Morrison, John F. "Museum of Modern Art Buys Painting of Philadelphia Artist with Places to Go." *Philadelphia Sunday Bulletin*, January 14, 1962, sec. 1, p. 16.

"Mural 1963–1965 to Be Shown at Museum." *Sarasota (FL) Herald-Tribune*, May 19, 1968.

Neff, Eileen. "Thomas Chimes." *Artforum International* (September 1999), p. 172.

Newhall, Edith. "Survey." *New York Magazine*, January 9, 1995, p. 75.

"Notable Artists Art Show Judges." *Uniontown (PA) Herald-Standard*, June 28, 1976.

Pacini, Marina. "Philadelphia Project." *Archives of American Art Journal* 30, nos. 1–4 (1990), p. 13.

"Past into Present." *Art in Focus* (Philadelphia), April 1975.

Rahaim, Liz. "The Charm of Chimes." *34th Street Magazine* (Philadelphia), February 15, 2001.

Raynor, Vivien. "Bodley Gallery, New York, NY." *Arts Magazine* (April 1963), p. 58.

———. "Bodley Gallery, New York, NY." *Arts Magazine* (March 1965), p. 61–62.

Rice, Robin. "Coming out of the Dark." *Philadelphia City Paper*, April 10, 2003, p. 24.

———. "Less Is Moore." *Philadelphia City Paper*, September 25, 1992, p. 10.

———. "Natural Wonders, Searching for Sublimity in Sea and Sky." *Philadelphia City Paper*, March 9–16, 2000, p. 38.

———. "On and Off the Grid." *Philadelphia City Paper*, March 10, 2005.

———. "Snapshots: Truth and Memory in the Photography-Based Paintings of Thomas Chimes and a Group of Contemporary Photorealists." *Philadelphia City Paper*, March 26, 1999.

"Ever Adds Voice to Stephen Berg's Poetic Line." *The Citizens* 7, no. 1 (March 1992).

Russell, John. "Art: At the Whitney, 28 Eric Fischl Paintings." *New York Times*, February 21, 1986, p. C25.

———. "Art: The Legacy of Ree Morton." *New York Times*, February 22, 1980.

———. "Pompeii Comes to Life Again." *New York Times*, April 22, 1979, pp. C1, C25.

Sappington, John. "Journeys through Darkness and Light." *Philadelphia City Paper*, April 1, 1988, p. 34.

Schoenberg, Alfred. "The Thomas Chimes Mural: A Modern Mystic's Search for the Self." Senior thesis, New College, Sarasota, FL, 1968

Schjeldahl, Peter. "Thomas Chimes: Paintings at Marian Locks." *Art Matters* (June 1990).

Schwabsky, Barry. "Theater of Memory." *Art in America* 83, no. 1 (January 1995), pp. 92–95.

Seidel, Miriam. "Conversation Pieces." *New Art Examiner* (December 1994), p. 46.

———. "Smart Money, Passion and Profit." *Applause Magazine* (Philadelphia), December 1992.

———. "Thomas Chimes at Locks." *Art in America* 89, no. 9 (September 2001), p. 158.

Sleeping Woman Commemorated." *Philadelphia Spot Lite*, November 6, 1993.

Sozanski, Edward J. "A Decorative Alternative Reality." *Philadelphia Inquirer*, February 11, 2005.

———. "A Stripped Down Take on Nature and the Sublime." *Philadelphia Inquirer*, March 5, 2000.

———. "At Levy, 24 Philadelphia Artists Explore Monochrome without Monotony." *Philadelphia Inquirer*, September 10, 1992.

———. "Chimes Alludes to Dark Beyond." *Philadelphia Inquirer*, March 21, 1999, p. F12.

———. "Chimes' 'White Paintings' Deepen His Ethereal Style." *Philadelphia Inquirer*, September 25, 1986, p. 6-C.

———. "*Directions* Launches a New Building." *Philadelphia Inquirer*, January 18, 1991, p. 34.

———. "Fading to White." *Philadelphia Inquirer*, March 28, 2003, p. W32.

———. "Galleries: Locks." *Philadelphia Inquirer*, October 30, 1992, p. 29.

———. "Metaphysical Boxes." *Philadelphia Inquirer*, February 2, 2001, p. 28.

———. "Nexus." *Philadelphia Inquirer*, December 15, 1995, p. W38.

———. "Painting in the New Year with Works from Old Ones." *Philadelphia Inquirer*, January 11, 1990.

———. "26 Works from Tom Chimes." *Philadelphia Inquirer*, May 17, 1990.

Stevens, Elisabeth. "Home Town Best Town for One Artist." *Trenton Evening Times*. March 30, 1975, p. 20.

Stewart, Patricia. "Philadelphia Artists at Moore." *The Drummer*, November 18, 1975, p. 16.

———. "Poets, Pataphysics, and Painting." *Arts Exchange* (Philadelphia), March/April 1978, pp. 18–22.

———. "Thomas Chimes at Marian Locks." *Art in America* 76, no. 9 (September 1988), p. 195.

"Thomas Chimes," *New York Magazine*, January 2, 1995.

"Thomas Chimes," *Philadelphia Inquirer*, January 24, 1965.

West, Judy. "Character Studies." *ARTnews* (December 1998), pp. 94–96.

Wilson, Janet. "*Transmodern* at Baumgartner." *Washington Post*, June 20, 1992.

Wilton, Kris. "Grapevine." *Philadelphia Weekly*, August 13, 2003, p. 15.

Windisch-Graetz, Caroline. "Modern Art Sold on Lend-Lease." *New York Herald Tribune*, March 4, 1964, p. 16.

Index of Names

Page numbers in italics refer to illustrations.

PHOTOGRAPHY CREDITS

Unless otherwise noted, works by Thomas Chimes were photographed by Graydon Wood and Andrea Simon at the Philadelphia Museum of Art.

In addition, we are grateful to the owners and/or the following institutions and individuals for supplying photography:

Art Resource, New York: fig. 56

Bildarchiv Preussischer Kulturbesitz / Art Resource, New York (photograph by Jens Ziehe): fig. 14

Bridgeman Art Library, New York: fig. 118

CBC Still Photo Collection, Toronto (photograph by Robert Ragsdale): fig. 61

CNAC/MNAM/Dist. Réunion des Musées Nationaux / Art Resource, New York: figs. 9, 67 (photograph by Christian Bahier and Philippe Migeat), 78 (photograph by Philippe Migeat)

James Cohan Gallery, New York: figs. 27, 55, 137 (photograph by Gianfranco Gorgoni)

Dreamworks: fig. 51

The Forbes Collection, New York (photograph by Ali Elai): plate 71

Gallery Paule Anglim, San Francisco: fig. 106

Solomon R. Guggenheim Museum, New York (photograph by David Heald): fig. 4

Michael Hallahan, Bangor, Maine: plates 62, 66

Rodger LaPelle: fig. 72

Mr. and Mrs. Robert P. Levy, Bryn Mawr, Pennsylvania: plates 13, 77

Library of Congress, Prints and Photographs Division, Washington, DC (photograph by Jack E. Boucher): fig. 12

Locks Gallery, Philadelphia: plates 13, 16, 17, 21, 29, 30, 35–39, 41–44, 46, 47, 51–55, 59, 61, 63, 64, 67–69, 72, 73, 78–80, 81; figs. 18, 33, 62, 83, 84, 89, 91, 103, 122, 140

Lowe Art Museum, University of Miami, Coral Gables, Florida: plate 14

The Menil Collection, Houston (photo by Janet Woodard): fig. 59

Motion Picture & Television Archive, Van Nuys, California: fig. 65

The Museum of Modern Art / Licensed by SCALA / Art Resource, New York: plates 4–6; fig. 36

Phoenix Art Museum (photograph by Ken Howie): plate 38

Photofest, New York: figs. 41, 68

Réunion des Musées Nationaux / Art Resource, New York (photographs by H. del Olmo): figs. 19, 20

Rheinisches Bildarchiv, Cologne: figs. 100, 105

The John and Mable Ringling Museum of Art, Sarasota, Florida: plates 8–11

Snark / Art Resource, New York: figs. 13, 15, 56

Tate Modern, London / Art Resource, New York: fig. 28

John Bigelow Taylor / Art Resource, New York: fig. 8

Time & Life Pictures / Getty Images, Los Angeles: fig. 70

Whitney Museum of American Art, New York (photograph by Robert E. Mates): fig. 35